Readings in Extraversion-Introversion
3

Bearings on Basic Psychological
Processes

Ex Umbris In Veritatem

THIS BOOK
WAS GIVEN TO

NEWMAN
COLLEGE

BY

Readings in Extraversion-Introversion

———

1. THEORETICAL AND METHODOLOGICAL ISSUES

2. FIELDS OF APPLICATION

3. BEARINGS ON BASIC PSYCHOLOGICAL
PROCESSES

Bearings on Basic Psychological Processes

———

Edited by

H. J. EYSENCK

PH.D., D.SC.

Professor of Psychology, University of London

Staples Press   London

Granada Publishing Limited
First published 1971 by Staples Press Ltd
3 Upper James Street, London W1R 4BP
Printed in Great Britain by
C. Tinling & Co Ltd, Prescot and London

ISBN 0 286 62739 6

ACKNOWLEDGEMENTS

Grateful acknowledgement for permission to reprint the articles in this volume is made to the following:

The editors of: *Acta Psychologica*, the *Australian Journal of Psychology*, the *British Journal of Psychiatry*, the *British Journal of Psychology*, the *British Journal of Social and Clinical Psychology*, the *Canadian Journal of Psychology*, the *Indian Journal of Psychology*, the *International Journal of Clinical and Experimental Hypnosis*, the *Japanese Journal of Psychological Research*, the *Journal of Abnormal and Social Psychology*, the *Journal of Applied Psychology*, the *Journal of Consultant Psychology*, the *Journal of Experimental Psychology*, the *Journal of Experimental Research in Personality*, the *Journal of Nervous and Mental Diseases*, the *Journal of Neurological and Neurosurgical Psychiatry*, the *Journal of Personality*, the *Journal of Personality and Social Psychology*, the *Journal of Psychiatric Research*, the *Journal of Social and Psychical Research*, *Language and Speech*, *Life Sciences*, *Nature*, *Perceptual and Motor Skills*, the *Proceedings of the 18th International Congress of Psychology*, *Psychological Reports*, *Psychophysiology*; and to J. A. Ardis, P. Bakan, M. J. F. Blake, H. Brierley, D. E. Broadbent, J. Butler, A. Cohen, W. P. Colquhoun, D. W. J. Corcoran, C. G. Costello, D. R. Davies, P. C. Dodwell, J. J. Dunstone, E. Dzendolet, F. J. Evans, S. B. G. Eysenck, F. H. Farley, B. J. Fine, D. W. Forrest, C. M. Franks, E. Fraser, C. D. Frith, W. D. Furneaux, R. C. Gahm, A. B. Gottlober, R. A. M. Gregson, R. H. Harrison, D. R. Haslam, O. Heuckeroth, G. R. J. Hockey, M. J. Hogan, D. S. Holmes, J. C. Kenna, A. B. Kerenyi, J. B. Knowles, L. Krasner, S. G. Laverty, P. J. Lang, A. Levey, P. Levy, L. E. H. Lindahl, R. Lynn, R. J. McLaughlin, M. Marton, E. Okamotu, C. R. Paramesh, R. W. Ramsay, G. F. Reed, R. D. Savage, G. Sedman, C. Shagass, S. L. Smith, S. H. Stein, R. Taft, N. Tranel, G. S. Tune, I. Urban, P. H. Venables, M. D. Vogel, M. A. Wallach, D. Watson, C. O. Weber, G. D. Wilson.

A*

CONTENTS

Contents

SECTION THREE: PERCEPTUAL

Contents

Contents

Contents

SECTION ONE

Physiological

Editor's Introduction

IN *The Biological Basis of Personality* (Ref. 1) the writer has put forward the view that extraverts may be characterised by low cortical arousal levels, introverts by high cortical arousal levels; he added that these differences might be caused in turn by differential threshold levels in the reticular formation (R.F.), whose main function is of course the control of arousal (and inhibition) levels in the cortex. He also made the assumption that individual differences in the threshold level of arousal of the visceral brain were responsible for phenotypic differences in neuroticism and dealt in some detail with the complications which arise from the known fact that stimulation of the visceral brain in turn produces cortical arousal, either directly or through collateral stimulation of the RF. This theory, which is presented in summary diagrammatic form on page 326, gives some physiological body to the writer's older view that excitation-inhibition differences were responsible for introversion and extraversion. These terms had been used purely in a psychological, intervening-variable sense; their translation into physiological terminology makes the theory susceptible to neurological, physiological and pharmacological study in a more direct way than was possible hitherto.

This section reprints some of the relevant articles in these areas. On the whole they support the theory, but in a field as complex and little understood as this it cannot of course be claimed that they do more than suggest that further experimental study of the theory is worth while. A critical review of the whole literature has been attempted in *The Biological Basis of Personality* (Ref. 1); it would obviously be impossible to attempt anything of the kind here. There are still many obscurities, puzzles and contradictions, but the general tenor of the findings seems to be one of cautious optimism; whenever significant results are achieved in reasonably well-controlled experiments, then the direction of the findings is practically always in the predicted direction, never in the opposite direction.

One word of explanation may be useful at this point. Terms like 'inhibition' are used in many different senses, and it is important not to mix up two contrary and contradictory meanings. Cortical inhibition refers to a lowering of arousal in the cortex; this reduces cortical control over lower centres and habit-structures, and consequently leads to less inhibited types of behaviour. Thus high cortical inhibition = uninhibi-

3

ted behaviour. The action of alcohol may make this point clearer. Alcohol is a depressant drug, i.e., it depresses cortical activity, thus disinhibiting lower centres and leading to uninhibited behaviour. This double usage of the term 'inhibition' has caused difficulties to many readers and might have been avoided by using other terms; unfortunately one cannot pick and choose in a field where certain terms have become accepted, and consequently a brief explanation seemed advisable.

H.J.E.

REFERENCE

1. EYSENCK, H. J., *The Biological Basis of Personality*. Springfield, Ill.: C. C. Thomas, 1967.

1

The Relationship between Brain Potentials and Personality[1]

ABRAHAM BER GOTTLOBER

First published in *Journal of Experimental Psychology*, **22**, 67–74, 1938

AFTER we had studied the electroencephalographic patterns of a group of individuals and found that each person possessed a pattern peculiar to himself (Refs. 4 & 5), the question arose as to whether these individuals, although having specific differences from one another, might not at the same time be classified into two or more large groups having some one or more brain wave characteristics in common.

Lemere (Ref. 3) has reported that in dealing with normal subjects alone he found no correlation between extraversion or introversion and the ability or inability to produce alpha waves. Although he used no special psychological or personality tests, he states that, 'most of them were questioned from a psychiatric point of view' and he 'gained the impression that "good" waves were produced in general by the cyclothymic type of individual while schizoid personalities gave "poor" waves as a rule'. The number of subjects studied was 26. The alpha rhythm was classified on the basis of its amplitude, regularity and constancy. No specific description of what 'regularity' and 'constancy' consisted is given. Apparently he differentiated between individuals with extraverted tendencies and those who were of the cyclothymic type and between those with introverted tendencies and those who were of the schizoid type. It would appear that he was studying two degrees of the same trait rather than two different traits.

The present study dealt only with extremely introverted and extraverted normal individuals and therefore concerned itself with cyclothymic and schizothymic personalities.

The problem was to find what relationships, if any, existed between the percentage of time alpha waves which are present in a given normal individual's record and (1) his degree of social introversion; (2) his degree

[1] A condensation of a part of a doctor's dissertation done under the direction of Professor Lee Edward Travis.

of emotionality; and (3) his degree of masculinity. These three factors were measured by the Nebraska Personality Inventory (Ref. 2).

In addition to gaining an estimate of an individual's degree of introversion or extraversion by the self-rating method through use of the inventory, 25 of the subjects were classified as belonging primarily to one group or the other by a psychiatrist, a clinical psychologist and the writer, while the remaining 42 were classified by only the psychologist and the writer.

SUBJECTS

In all, 67 subjects were studied, 18 women, 49 men, of which the diagnosticians classified 21 men as introverts and 28 as extraverts and 7 women as introverts and 11 as extraverts. This method of classification was used as a check against that of the inventory, which indicated that while 28 men rated themselves as extraverts and 21 as introverts, 10 women rated themselves as extraverts and 8 as introverts. Although the total number of introverts and extraverts as rated by self and by others agreed very closely, agreement on individual subjects amounted to 74·62 per cent of the cases or 50 of the 67 subjects.

APPARATUS AND PROCEDURE

As in the previous studies from this laboratory, recordings were made by means of standard amplifiers and a Westinghouse oscillograph. Experimental conditions from subject to subject were kept as constant as possible. The subject reclined on a bed in a dark room. He was instructed to keep his eyes closed and his mind as free from thought as was possible. A unipolar lead placed over the left occipital area was used. The ground lead was attached to the lobe of the left ear. An average of about 30 seconds of film was recorded from each subject.

DATA

The data were analysed as follows. All the waves of a record which would unequivocally fall into the classification of the alpha type (those waves with an average frequency of 10 per second) were marked off. The total number of such waves was counted. A time line having a frequency of 25 cycles per second plus the use of a constant speed motor for rolling the film during exposure assured an exact measurement of the duration of each wave. The duration of the total record in seconds was determined and the percentage of time occupied by alpha waves was calculated.

Finally, the average frequency of the alpha waves was obtained. This was an additional check for the purpose of determining whether the waves selected as being of the alpha type actually had an average frequency of 8 to 12 cycles per second. The length of the record in seconds was considered to consist of those portions in which alpha or beta waves were present. Those portions during which blocking of the amplifiers occurred due to movement, etc., of the subject were not considered as part of the total duration of the record. Using percentage of time alpha waves were present as the only criterion of judgment, correlations between percentage of alpha waves present and degrees of social introversion, emotionality and masculinity were calculated.

Using the same criterion, i.e., percentage of time alpha waves were present, each record was classified into one of four groups, dominant alpha, subdominant alpha, mixed alpha and rare alpha, in accordance with the Davis classification (Ref. 1).

Next it was determined what percentage of subjects diagnosed as introverts or extraverts fell into each of the four groups.

A second and grosser comparison was made. All records with alpha waves present from 0 to 50 per cent of the time were grouped together to make one classification, the mixed-rare, and all records with alpha waves present from 50 to 100 per cent of the time were grouped together to make another classification, the dominant-subdominant. Percentages of introverts and extraverts falling into each of these two classifications were obtained. This second category was made to determine whether tendencies for introverts and extraverts to fall into one or the other of the classifications more often might be revealed by using larger groupings if the smaller groupings failed to do so.

Finally, using only those subjects on which there was agreement of personality type between both the judges and the self-raters, calculations of percentages of extraverts and introverts falling into each of the two grosser classifications was made. The grosser method was felt to be sufficiently indicative here. Finer tendencies were already demonstrated when comparisons were made using only the judges' ratings.

RESULTS

An analysis of the data indicates that of the subjects classified by the judges as being predominantly introverted, 42·85 per cent (N = 12) fell into the dominant alpha group, 14·28 per cent (N = 4) into the subdominant alpha group, 10·71 per cent (N = 3) into the mixed alpha group and 32·14 per cent (N = 9) into the rare alpha group. Of those subjects classified as predominantly extraverted 51·28 per cent (N = 20) fell into the dominant alpha group, 30·76 per cent (N = 12) into the subdominant alpha group, 7·69 per cent (N = 3) into the mixed alpha group, and 10·25 per cent (N = 4) into the rare alpha group.

With the grosser classifications, 57·14 per cent (N = 16) of the introverts fell into the dominant-subdominant alpha group and 42·85 per cent (N = 12) into the mixed-rare group. Of the extraverts, 82·05 per cent (N = 32) fell into the dominant-subdominant alpha group and 17·95 per cent (N = 7) into the mixed-rare group.

TABLE 1

SIGNIFICANCE OF DIFFERENCES BETWEEN PERCENTAGES OF PERSONALITY TYPES
FALLING INTO VARIOUS BRAIN-POTENTIAL GROUPS (DAVIS CLASSIFICATION)
AS DETERMINED BY JUDGES' RATINGS

Type (Greater Percentage Given First)	Class	Difference in Percentage of Types in Class	δ diff.	$\frac{D}{\delta \text{ diff.}}$	Chances in 100 Diff. is True Diff. Greater than Zero
Extravert Dominant vs. Introvert Dominant		8·43	0·12	0·70	76
Extravert Subdominant vs. Introvert Subdominant		16·48	0·10	1·64	96
Introvert Mixed vs. Extravert Mixed		3·02	0·07	0·43	66
Introvert Rare vs. Extravert Rare		21·89	0·10	2·18	99
Introvert Dominant vs. Introvert Rare		10·71	0·12	0·89	82
Extravert Dominant vs. Extravert Rare		41·04	0·09	4·56	99·99

Both methods of classifying the data point to the same conclusions, although as was anticipated, the grosser method is the more indicative of definite tendencies. Both the introvertive and extravertive groups showed a greater percentage of the subjects with dominant or dominant-subdominant alpha rhythms than with rare or mixed-rare rhythms. The difference between the dominant and the rare alpha rhythms and the dominant-subdominant and mixed-rare alpha rhythms in the case of the extraverts is a statistically true one, but this is not the case for the introverts (Tables 1 and 2). Introverts show a greater percentage of cases with rare and

TABLE 2

SIGNIFICANCE OF DIFFERENCES BETWEEN PERCENTAGES OF PERSONALITY TYPES
(DETERMINED BY JUDGES) FALLING INTO THE DOMINANT-SUBDOMINANT AND
MIXED-RARE ALPHA CLASSES (DAVIS CLASSIFICATION MODIFIED)

Type (Greater Percentage Given First)	Class	Difference in Percentage of Types in Class	δ diff.	$\dfrac{D}{\delta \text{ diff.}}$	Chances in 100 Diff. is True Diff. Greater than Zero
Extravert Dom.-Subdom. vs. Introvert Dom.-Subdom.		24·91	0·11	2·3	99
Introvert Mixed-Rare vs. Extravert Mixed-Rare		24·20	0·11	2·2	99
Introvert Dom.-Subdom. vs. Extravert Mixed-Rare		39·19	0·11	3·6	99·99
Extravert Dom.-Subdom. vs. Introvert Mixed-Rare		39·90	0·11	3·6	99·99
Introvert Dom.-Subdom. vs. Introvert Mixed-Rare		14·99	0·132	1·14	87
Extravert Dom.-Subdom. vs. Extravert Mixed-Rare		64·10	0·087	7·5	99·99

mixed-rare alpha rhythms than do extraverts, with a statistically true difference. In the grosser method of classification it was found that the extraverts showed greater percentage of cases with the dominant-subdominant alpha rhythm than did the introverts and that the difference also was statistically a true one.

Considering the results obtained from the self-rating Nebraska Personality Inventory, it was found that the correlations of social-introversion (S score), emotionality (E score) and masculinity (M score) with percentage of time alpha waves are present are -0.2262 ± 0.0781, -0.0482 ± 0.0822, and -0.2102 ± 0.0787 respectively (Table 3). These low order correlations indicate that there is no relationship between self-ratings and percentage of time alpha waves are present.

TABLE 3

CORRELATIONS BETWEEN NEBRASKA INVENTORY RATINGS AND
PERCENTAGE OF TIME ALPHA WAVES ARE PRESENT

r alpha waves · S score -0.2262 ± 0.0781 N = 67
r alpha waves · E score -0.0483 ± 0.0822 N = 67
r alpha waves · M score -0.2102 ± 0.0787 N = 67

TABLE 4

PERCENTAGES OF INTROVERTS AND EXTRAVERTS, DETERMINED BY JUDGES,
FALLING INTO THE TWO CATEGORIES OF THE MODIFIED DAVIS CLASSIFICATION

Type	Class	N	Percentage of Type in Class
Introvert	Dom.-Subdom.	16	65·00
Introvert	Mixed-Rare	12	35·00
Extravert	Dom.-Subdom.	32	83·33
Extravert	Mixed-Rare	7	16·66

When the cases on which both the judges and self-raters agreed are considered, the following is found to be true. As in the calculations based on the judges' ratings alone, extraverts showed the dominant-subdominant alpha rhythm more often than the mixed-rare and this difference was statistically significant (Table 5). All other differences found were not statistically true ones.

It is to be observed that these results do not agree with Lemere's findings either with his introverts and extraverts or cyclothymes and schizothymes. The explanation for this may rest in the fact that his cases

TABLE 5

SIGNIFICANCE OF DIFFERENCES BETWEEN PERCENTAGES OF PERSONALITY TYPES
FALLING INTO THE DOMINANT-SUBDOMINANT AND MIXED-RARE ALPHA CLASSES
(DAVIS CLASSIFICATION MODIFIED) OF CASES WHERE RATINGS BY JUDGES AND
SELF-RATERS AGREED (BASED ON TABLE 4)

Type (Greater Percentage Given First)	Class	Difference in Percentage of Types in Class	δ diff.	$\frac{D}{δ \, diff.}$	Chances in 100 Diff. is True Diff. Greater than Zero
Extravert vs. Dom.-Subdom. Introvert		18·33	0·12	1·52	93
Introvert Mixed-Rare vs. Extravert Mixed-Rare		18·34	0·12	1·52	93
Introvert Dom.-Subdom. vs. Extravert Mixed-Rare		48·34	0·12	4·02	99·99
Extravert Dom.-Subdom. vs. Introvert Mixed-Rare		48·33	0·12	4·02	99·99
Introvert Dom.-Subdom. vs. Introvert Mixed-Rare		30·00	0·15	2·00	98
Extravert Dom.-Subdom. vs. Extravert Mixed-Rare		66·67	0·09	7·63	99·99

were fewer in number and his methods of classification of types different.
In addition, his criteria for designating alpha waves as 'good' or 'poor'
and the criteria used in this study for classifying records into dominant-
subdominant or mixed-rare groups are not exactly comparable.

CONCLUSIONS

From these findings it may be concluded that a majority of the normal
individuals exhibiting a high degree of extraversion will show a

12   *Bearings on Basic Psychological Processes*

dominant-subdominant alpha rhythm. It cannot yet be stated that introverts will show a predominantly mixed-rare rhythm.

Remembering always that the electroencephalogram is a manifestation of a fundamentally neurophysiological phenomenon, it seems not unreasonable to believe that its characteristic nature is neither a cause nor a result of the subject's degree of extraversion or introversion but rather that both are concomitants in an organismic whole. It is suggested only that an organismic pattern in which a dominant-subdominant rhythm appears accompanied by an extraverted personality as determined by our methods of rating will be more common than one in which it appears accompanied by an introverted personality. In the light of the present evidence, no other definite statement can be made.

REFERENCES

1. DAVIS, H. & DAVIS, P. A., Action potentials of the brain in normal persons and in normal states. *Arch. Neurol. Psychiat.*, **36**, 1214–1224, 1936.
2. GUILFORD, J. P. & GUILFORD, R. B., Personality factors S, E and M, and their measurements. *J. Psychol.*, **2**, 109–127, 1936.
3. LEMERE, F., The significance of individual differences in the Berger rhythm. *Brain*, **59**, 366–375, 1936.
4. TRAVIS, L. E. & GOTTLOBER, A. B., Do brain waves have individuality? *Science*, **84**, 532–832, 1936.
5. —— & ——, How consistent are an individual's brain potentials from day to day? *Science*, **85**, 223–224, 1937.

2

Electro-Cerebral Activity, Extraversion and Neuroticism

R. D. SAVAGE

First published in *British Journal of Psychiatry*, **110**, 98–100, 1964

INTRODUCTION

SEVERAL investigators have attempted to relate cerebral activity to extraversion and neuroticism. These include Berger (Ref. 1), Jasper (Ref. 9), Gottlober (Ref. 7), Henry & Knott (Ref. 8), Knott (Ref. 10), Darrow (Ref. 3), Lindsley (Ref. 11), McAdam & Orme (Ref. 12), Gastaut (Ref. 6) and Brazier (Ref. 2). The results, however, have been inconclusive.

The specific problem investigated by the present experiment is the relationship between extraversion, neuroticism and the amplitude of alpha rhythm recorded by the EEG. According to Eysenck, extraverts and hysterics (neurotic extraverts) would be considered to have high cortical inhibition, whilst introverts and dysthymics (neurotic introverts) would be characterized by having low cortical inhibition (Ref. 4). Indeed, Eysenck has shown that the build up of reactive and conditioned inhibition over a constant period is faster and greater in extraverts than in introverts (Ref. 4).

It is suggested by the present author that extraversion resulting from high cortical inhibition will result in significantly higher alpha rhythm amplitude than that recorded from introverts whose cortical inhibition is low. In addition, neuroticism should generally depress the alpha amplitude: (1) hysterics (neurotic extraverts) should show lower alpha amplitude than extraverts and (2) dysthymics (neurotic introverts) should show lower amplitude than introverts.

SUBJECTS, APPARATUS AND PROCEDURE

The subjects were 20 female students, average age 18 years 8 months, S.D. 4 months, from the University of New England. They were divided

13

into four equal groups according to extraversion and neuroticism scores. Using the notation that E stands for high extraversion, e for low extraversion, N for high neuroticism and n for low neuroticism, the groups were (1) EN, (2) eN, (3) En, (4) en. Subjects with extraversion scores above 30 were rated as E, and those with scores below 30, as e. High neuroticism N had a cut-off point of 28, those below being in the n category. The correlation between extraversion and neuroticism in this sample was 0·24.

Each subject was tested in a screened EEG room adjacent to the recording apparatus. The resting alpha rhythms were recorded by a bipolar technique with a Standard Ediswan Four-Channel Electro-encephalographic machine and analysed by an Ediswan Mk IIA Low Frequency Analyser. The Maudsley Personality Inventory (Ref. 5) was used to obtain measures of extraversion and neuroticism.

The subject was given the Maudsley Personality Inventory prior to the EEG examination, but extraversion and neuroticism scores were recorded after EEG scores had been calculated. Electroencephalogram data were taken whilst the subject lay on a couch with her eyes closed. The four electrodes, treated with E.K.G. paste to minimize resistance, were attached in pairs to the skull corresponding to EEG placements 8 and 10 on the parietal and 18 and 20 on the occipital cortex. The data analysed were collected over 24 ten-second artefact-free epochs 10 seconds after eyes closed. They were taken from the two electrodes on the occipital areas placements 18 and 20. These data were analysed by the Ediswan Mk IIA Low Frequency Analyser. The amplitude of alpha between 8–13 cps was given. The average amplitude above a base line of all alpha frequencies between 8–13 cps recorded over the 240 seconds was calculated for each subject. This score was taken as an index of cortical activity. The amplitude of alpha was preferred to the alpha index or alpha frequency, since previous investigations using the latter scores have been inconclusive.

RESULTS

The alpha amplitude scores were treated by analysis of variance (Table 1), as the Pearson-Hartley test showed the data to be homogeneous. The variance between the extraversion groups was significant at the 0·01 level. The mean score for high extraversion (EN, En) was 81, S.D. 14·9. The low extraversion groups (eN, en) had a mean of 28·7 and a standard deviation of 8·55. The high neuroticism group (EN, eN) had a mean

Electro-Cerebral Activity

15

TABLE 1

ANALYSIS OF VARIANCE OF ALPHA AMPLITUDE SCORES

Source of Variance	Sum of Squares	d.f.	M.S.V.	F.
Total variance	31,842	19		
Variation between extraversion groups	16,302	1	16,302	23 8*
Variance between neuroticism groups	994	1	994	1 45
Interaction between E and N groups	3,611	1	3,611	5 28†
Residual	10,935	16	683·4	

* Significant at 0·01 level † Significant at 0·05 level

alpha amplitude of 61·5, S.D. 16·9, whilst the low neuroticism group (En, en) had a mean 50·2, S.D. 11·08. These groups were not significantly different.

The interaction between extraversion and neuroticism was significant at the 0·05 level.

An alternative orthogonal analysis demonstrated that EN and En, E (N+n) and e (N+n) were significantly different, whereas eN and en were not significantly different (Table 2).

The extraversion scores on the Maudsley Personality Inventory showed a mean score of 28·87, S.D. 7·01; the neuroticism mean was 28·4, S.D. 7·99.

TABLE 2

ALTERNATIVE ORTHOGONAL ANALYSIS OF ALPHA AMPLITUDE SCORES

Source of Variance	Sum of Squares	d.f.	M.S.V.	F.
Total variance	31,842	19		
Variance between EN, En	4,202	1	4,202	6·15*
Variance between eN, en	409 6	1	409·6	0·59
Variance between E, e	16,302	1	16,302	23·8†
Residual	10,935	16	683·4	

* Significant at 0·01 level † Significant at 0·05 level

DISCUSSION

The sample of students used in this investigation did not differ significantly from a normal population in the distribution of their extraversion and neuroticism scores. However, the correlation between extraversion and neuroticism for this group was 0·24, which is not significant; this differs from that for the general population, which shows a slightly negative relationship at the high N low e end of the scales.

The four groups of subjects, divided in accordance with their extraversion and neuroticism scores, gave data which supported the main hypothesis derived from the theory of Eysenck (Ref. 4). The higher alpha amplitude of extraverts was significantly different from that of the introvert group. These data relate to the view that extraverts have greater cortical inhibition, be it 'basal', reactive or conditioned, than introverts, as previous investigations have shown that alpha synchronization corresponds to cortical inhibition (Ref. 14).

The amplitude measure of alpha activity taken in this investigation may well account for the highly significant results obtained compared with the indecisive data of Gottlober (Ref. 7), Henry & Knott (Ref. 8), Knott (Ref. 10) and McAdam & Orme (Ref. 12). The former investigators used the alpha index or percentage alpha as their measures of cortical activity. The present results would seem to relate positively to the investigations of Mundy-Castle who reported that there is a high negative correlation between alpha frequency and secondary function (Ref. 13).

The insignificant differences between the high neurotic and low neurotic groups indicate that overall, neuroticism does not significantly depress alpha amplitude. It is of interest to note, however, that the effect of neuroticism in reducing alpha amplitude is dependent on the degree of extraversion. This is seen in the significant interaction between neuroticism and extraversion. The alternative orthogonal breakdown (Table 2) showed that the variances between groups eN and en were not, whilst those between the EN and En groups were significantly different. These data possibly cast light on the previous contradictory evidence of the investigations of Berger (Ref. 1) and many other writers on the one hand, and of Darrow (Ref. 3) and Gastaut (Ref. 6) on the other. Perhaps the Darrow and Gastaut subjects had a low extraversion factor. It would seem that neuroticism will reduce alpha amplitude, given the sufficiently high alpha amplitude which relates to the high level of cortical inhibition as in extraverts.

The present results relating alpha rhythm to extraversion and neuroticism have important theoretical implications towards Eysenck's theory of personality classification. The results also allow further testable hypotheses to be made—for example, it can be predicted that extraverts will show greater reduction in alpha rhythm when subject to external stimulation than will introverts. This hypothesis is being tested.

SUMMARY

This study investigated the relationship between alpha rhythm amplitude, inhibition, extraversion and neuroticism. Twenty subjects were divided into four groups according to their extraversion and neuroticism scores. It was found that extraversion was significantly related to high alpha amplitude, whilst neuroticism as such did not relate to this measure. An alternative orthogonal breakdown showed that EN was significantly different from En, but the differences between eN and en were not greater than expected by chance.

ACKNOWLEDGEMENTS

This work was carried out whilst the author was at the University of New England, Australia. He is indebted to Mr P. E. H. Barratt and Miss H. Beh for EEG facilities and assistance.

REFERENCES

1. BERGER, H., Uber das Elektrenkephalogramm des Menschen (Fünfte Mitteilung). *Arch. f. Psychiat.*, **98**, 231–254, 1933.
2. BRAZIER, M. A. B., *The Electrical Activity of the Nervous System.* 2nd edition. London: Pitman Medical Publishing Co. Ltd.
3. DARROW, C. W., Psychological and psychophysiological significance of the electroencephalogram. *Psych. Rev.*, **54**, 157–168, 1947.
4. EYSENCK, H. J., *The Dynamics of Anxiety and Hysteria.* London: Routledge & Kegan Paul, 1957.
5. ——, *Maudsley Personality Inventory.* London: London University Press, 1959.
6. GASTAUT, H., In *Conditionnement et Réactivité en Encéphalographie.* H. Fischgold & H. Gastaut (eds.). Paris: Masson et Cie, 1957.
7. GOTTLOBER, A. B., The relationship between brain potentials and personality. *J. exp. Psychol.*, **22**, 67–74, 1938.
8. HENRY, C. E. & KNOTT, J. R., A note on the relationship between 'personality' and alpha rhythm of the electroencephalogram. *J. exp. Psychol.*, **28**, 363–366, 1941.
9. JASPER, H. H., Electrical signs of cortical activity. *Psychol. Bull.*, **34**, 411–481, 1937.

B

10. KNOTT, J. R., Electroencephalography and physiological psychology: evaluation and statement of problem. *Psychol. Bull.*, **38**, 144–175, 1941.

11. LINDSLEY, D., Emotion and the electroencephalogram. In *Feelings and Emotions* (Reymert, N. L., ed.). New York: McGraw-Hill, 1950.

12. McADAM, W. & ORME, J. E., Personality traits and the normal electroencephalogram. *J. ment. Sci.*, **100**, 913, 1954.

13. MUNDY-CASTLE, A. C., The relationship between primary-secondary function and the alpha rhythm of the electroencephalogram. *J. Nat. Inst. Pers. Res.*, **6**, 95–102, 1955.

14 WERRE, P. F., *The Relationship between Electroencephalographic and Psychological Data in Normal Adults*. Leiden: Leiden University Press, 1957.

An Electroencephalographic Investigation of Individual Differences in the Processes of Conditioning

M. MARTON & I. URBAN

First published in

Proceedings of the 18th International Congress of Psychology, **9,** 106–9,
1966

THE purpose of our work was to obtain characteristics of typical patterns of the central dynamics of conditioning in the course of a study of elementary processes of conditioning in extravertal and introvertal types of personality.

The subjects were two groups of students, aged 17–26 years, who were homogeneous in typical personality traits and selected through complex personality tests. One group consisted of 20 subjects with extraversive traits (E), the other—20 subjects with intraversive traits (I).

At first all subjects took part in experiments in which the process of habituation of electroencephalographic (EEG) responses to a weak sound stimulus (400 cps, presented for 2 sec. with 10–30 sec. intervals), as well as the process of habituation to skin galvanic responses (GSR), was studied. Then 10 subjects from each group were employed in a test in which a 'neutralized' sound stimulus was combined with a light stimulus presented for 1·5 sec. The sound stimulus was presented 500 m/sec. before the light flash.

The other subjects (10 in each group) were instructed to press a rubber balloon upon the presentation of light. Trials were repeated until the conditioned link was consolidated. Afterwards, the conditioned reactions were extinguished in both groups through the presentation of the sound stimulus without reinforcements. The process of conditioning and extinction of EEG, GSR and motor reactions (in the form of action potentials) was registered. EEG-tracings at rest were also analysed.

The identification of the stages of the processes of habituation, conditioning and extinction was brought about on the basis of a complex criterion with a glance at desynchronization-synchronization phenomena, non-specific evoked potentials and GSR. In these cases,

19

even when the alpha-rhythm is poorly expressed, the identification of the indicated stages does not present any difficulty and does not lead to controversy.

Parameters of EEG at rest were also measured for the comparison with the results obtained in the study of the nervous system (Ref. 3). The alpha-index and the frequency of the alpha-rhythm were determined. The magnitude of the absolute resistance of the skin served as an indicator of the activation level.

RESULTS

In the subjects with traits of extraversion the EEG-background is characterized by the spindle alpha-activity. In most cases (80 per cent) the habituation, acquisition and extinction of the conditioned link are reflected both in the change in non-specific evoked responses and in the dynamics of desynchronization. In the introvertal group in 11 subjects (9 of them were without alpha-rhythm), the process of conditioning may be traced with certainty by the dynamics of the non-specific evoked responses. In other members of this group the elaboration of the conditioned link manifests itself also in the dynamics of desynchronization.

The groups E and I significantly differ in the process of conditioning. In the members of group E the habituation occurs after 12–15 presentations. Soon after the non-specific response to the stimulus decreases, or after the stimulus begins to evoke synchronization, there occurs the change of the background activity which is characteristic of sleepiness and then of sleep.

In the subjects with traits of introversion the habituation occurs after 28–45 presentations.

In case of further stimulation the background activity characteristic of sleep was not observed at all in them.

When combining conditioned and unconditioned stimuli in group E, the conditioned link is consolidated after 15–28 trials. In the subjects of I the acquisition and consolidation of the conditioned link proceeds more slowly, and occurs only after 30–40 trials.

The extinction of the conditioned link in both groups as a whole proceeds as in the case of the habituation, except in that the extinction of motor responses in the subjects of group E required 30–45 trials, i.e., significantly more than in the subjects of group I.

As for the characteristics of the EEGs when at rest, the values of alpha-index calculated for the first two tracings show statistically significant differences; then, however, these discrepancies disappear. The average frequency of alpha-rhythm in the subjects of the group E amounts to 9·15 c/sec., and in the subjects of group I—11·1 c/sec.; the differences between mean values are statistically significant (at the 1 per cent level).

No differences in values of the absolute resistance of skin were found between the two groups of subjects.

Assessing data obtained overall one notes the following: In the subjects of group E the discrimination of the neutral meaning of stimuli proves to be more effective; in the estimation of the probability of the combined occurrence of stimuli, they require less information in order to identify combinations as 'real'. The motor conditioned link, which is quickly coupled and consolidated in them, undergoes changes with difficulty, however. The inhibition of reactions is difficult and may lead to micropathological experiences.

In the subjects of group I the assessment of characteristics of environmental stimuli and the analysis of their relationship takes a longer time. But the duration of the flexible phase in the course of conditioning enables them to conceive a more exact conception of the conditions of reality, and thus contributes to an adequate planning of behaviour with a glance at many circumstances.

Such an interpretation of the psychophysiological content of the processes of conditioning in extraverts and introverts is consistent with our accumulated psychological knowledge of their behavioural manifestations. This consistency contributes to the comprehension of the processes underlying the formation of complex behavioural models and to the development of the experimental procedures of individual diagnoses.

Our data confirmed the thesis according to which the 'inhibitory potential' develops faster in persons with traits of extraversion although our comparison covered the indicators of the development of internal inhibition during habituation rather than the indicators of accumulation of reactive inhibition according to Hall. Of the typological characteristics of the nervous system, the indicators of EEG at rest (alpha-index, the average frequency of alpha-rhythm) and the rate of habituation define the parameters of the equilibrium of nervous processes. The higher value of the alpha-index, the lower frequency of the alpha-rhythm, and the faster development of habituation in extraverts shows the predominance of the processes of inhibition in them.

Thus, our thesis put forward earlier according to which the formation of extraversive patterns of behaviour is related to the predominance of inhibitory tendencies in the nervous system, is also confirmed by the EEG data.

4

Neurophysiological Studies of Personality[1]

CHARLES SHAGASS & ALBERT B. KERENYI

First published in
Journal of Nervous and Mental Diseases, **126**, 141–147, 1958

IN the field of personality, the identification and measurement of pertinent dimensions are one of the major problems. MacKinnon has listed a number of dichotomous typologies, or bipolar factors, which have been proposed as fundamental dimensions of personality (Ref. 10). Examples are the hysterical and obsessional types of Janet, the cycloid and schizoid types of Kretschmer, and the extraverted and introverted types of Jung. Although the typologies have been subject to a great deal of criticism, many of the terms engendered by them, such as 'extravert', have found wide acceptance, suggesting a basis in everyday clinical observation. Over the past decade, the investigations of Eysenck and his group have indicated that some dichotomous typologies may represent the extremes of valid and measurable dimensions of personality. By applying factorial analysis to data obtained with a variety of test procedures, Eysenck isolated three personality factors, which he called: neuroticism, introversion-extraversion and psychoticism (Refs. 3 and 4). The investigations to be reported in this paper bear on a possible neurophysiologic basis for the introversion-extraversion dimension.

The present research arose from a previous study of the sedation threshold in psychoneurosis (Ref. 16). The sedation threshold, which is an objective neurophysiologic determination of the amount of sodium amytal required to produce certain EEG changes, was found to differentiate between various types of neurosis. Thresholds were low in patients with hysteria, intermediate in patients with mixed neurosis, and high in patients with anxiety states and neurotic depressions. These findings supported the hypothesis that the threshold was correlated with degree

[1] Read before the Annual Meeting of the Society of Biological Psychiatry, Atlantic City, June, 1957. This study was assisted by grants from the Department of National Health and Welfare and the Defense Research Board (Grant No. DRB 9345–04, Project No. D50–45–04) of Canada.

of manifest anxiety. However, they could also be taken to indicate a relationship between the threshold and the position of the patient on a personality continuum ranging from hysterical to obsessional. It was then noted that the order in which the sedation threshold arranged the psychoneuroses corresponded closely to the order in which Hildebrand (Ref. 8) found them to be arranged by a battery of Eysenck's tests of introversion-extraversion. Furthermore, as Eysenck has recently pointed out (Ref. 5), the sedation threshold results in psychoneurosis appeared to confirm, in every detail, predictions made from his theory that reactive inhibition is greater in hysterics than in dysthymics (obsessive-compulsives, neurotic depressions, anxiety states) (Ref. 2).

From the parallels between Eysenck's results on introversion-extraversion and those obtained with the sedation threshold, it seemed reasonable to suggest that the sedation threshold might reflect the state of neural mechanisms involved in this dimension of personality. However, more direct studies of these relationships seemed desirable, as they had so far been inferred mainly from differences between diagnostic groups. Two investigative approaches were employed for this purpose in the present study. In the first, clinical ratings of hysterical-obsessional trend were compared with the sedation threshold. In the second, introversion-extraversion was measured by questionnaires and by determining the ease of formation of the conditioned eyeblink response; these measures were then compared with the sedation threshold. The questionnaires used had contributed the greatest weight to Hildebrand's battery (Ref. 8). The eyeblink conditioning measure was based on the work of Franks (Ref. 6), who found that conditionability was correlated with questionnaire measures of introversion-extraversion, and differed in hysterics and dysthymics in the direction expected from Eysenck's reactive inhibition theory.

MATERIALS AND METHODS

Rating Study

Subjects were 308 patients, including all those classified as psychoneurotic in a consecutive series of 750; diagnoses and other details have been described elsewhere (Ref. 14). There were 104 men and 204 women, aged from 16 to 71.

Questionnaire Study

Data-taking for this study had not been completed at time of writing.

Results for the first 36 patients will be presented. The only factors influencing selection of these patients were availability for testing and absence of any clinical evidence to suggest the possibility of psychosis. There were 13 men and 23 women, ranging in age from 15 to 57, with a mean of 35 years. The group contained most types of psychoneurosis.

Sedation Threshold Procedure

The procedure has been described in detail in previous publications (Refs. 13 & 16). Sodium amytal is injected intravenously at the rate of 0·5 mg. per kg. every 40 seconds until well after slurred speech is noted, while the frontal EEG is continuously recorded. The amplitude of the fast (15 to 30 cps) waves elicited by the drug is measured. Measurements in the earlier cases were done by a hand method (Ref. 13); an electronic integrator (Ref. 1) was used in about the last one-third of the 'rating' series and in all of the 'questionnaire' cases. The amplitude measurements are plotted against the amount of drug to yield a curve, which is usually of sigmoid shape and contains an inflexion point, preceding which the amplitude rises sharply and following which it tends to plateau. This point corresponds roughly to the onset of slurred speech. The sedation threshold is the amount of sodium amytal, in mg. per kg., required to produce this inflexion point.

Ratings of Hysterical-Obsessional Trend

Ratings were based on case records, which usually consisted of assistant resident's admission note, intern's case history, and attending psychiatrist's discharge summary. As none of the histories was taken specifically for the purpose of assessing hysterical-obsessional trend, it was anticipated that some cases could not be rated. Two psychiatrists, who had not seen any of the patients, independently rated the case records without knowledge of the sedation threshold. The rating scale consisted of the following points: H3, H2, H1, M1, M2, O1, O2, O3. 'H' referred to hysterical, 'M' to mixed and 'O' to obsessional personality traits. Patients with clear hysterical conversion symptoms were to be rated H3 and patients with clear obsessive-compulsive symptoms were to be rated O3. The intermediate categories were intended to reflect varying degrees of intensity of one or other personality trend. Following are some illustrative descriptive phrases from the case records, which were used as a basis for rating: under *hysterical*, histrionic, manipulative, usually outgoing, immature, eager to communicate, exhibitionistic; under *obsessional*, meticulous, perfectionistic, conscientious,

B*

rigid, hard driving with guilt over failure, preoccupied with detail, afraid of losing control.

Introversion-Extraversion

The Rhathymia (R) and Social-Introversion (S) scales of the Guilford Inventory of factors S, T, D, C and R (Ref. 7) were used to measure introversion-extraversion. Individual questions were typed on cards; the subject answered them as yes, no or uncertain, by sorting them into three appropriately labelled compartments of a box. The cards were presented in a random order. A French translation was used for French-speaking patients; the French version seemed to give approximately the same results as the English one when both were given to a few bilingual persons. For convenience in presenting the statistics, the raw scores for each of the scales were converted into standard C scores, according to tables supplied in the test manual. The C score statistics did not differ to any extent from those based on the individual raw scores, which were also worked out. As the C scores in the manual were arranged in such a way that they increased with increasing extraversion, they were reversed in order to avoid negative correlations. Also the C scores for R and S were added to provide a combined C score with a possible range from 0 to 20; the higher the combined C score, the greater the degree of introversion.

Conditioning Procedure

In the main, Franks' procedure (Ref. 6) was followed. The conditioned stimulus was a tone of 1100 cycles, produced by an Ediswan oscillator, Type R666, at an output of 22·5 volts, and delivered through S.C. Brown Type K moving-coil headphones. The unconditioned stimulus was an air puff to the cornea. The air source was a compressed air supply, with the valve at the main outlet set so that the pressure was $2 \pm 0 \cdot 5$ lb. Overall timing was controlled by a R.W. Cramer switch, Type M8 120S with a 0·5 r.p.m. motor, which was set so that 8 interstimulus intervals varying from 11 to 19 seconds would be repeated serially. The tone lasted 650 milliseconds, and, in reinforced trials, it was followed immediately by an air puff, lasting 275 milliseconds. Release of the air was effected by means of an Asco air valve, with relay activated by an electronic timing circuit. The air tube was held in place by a plastic frame attached to the headphones. There were 48 stimuli in the conditioning series; 30 included both tone and air puff and 18 consisted of tone alone. Before the first stimulus of the conditioning series, there was a preliminary series of stimuli; the first 3 were tone alone, then there were 3 air puffs alone, and finally 3 tones alone. Following the conditioning series, there was an extinction series consisting of 10 reinforced tones.

The retinocorneal potential from two electrodes near the eye provided a recording of eyeblink on one channel of a Grass EEG. The subject was seated during the conditioning procedure; some degree of eye fixation was obtained by having the subject look at a coat hook on the wall in front of him. The experimenter could observe the subject through a window. The subject's room was in semi-darkness. In evaluating the conditioning records, all eyeblink deflections of at least 3 mm. amplitude, beginning from 500 to 1000 μseconds after the onset of the tone, were scored as a response. Subjects with 3 or more out of a possible 6 responses to the tones preceding the conditioning series were rejected.

RESULTS

Hysterical-Obsessional Rating

One or the other psychiatrist was unable to rate 84 of the 308 cases. To obtain some estimate of the degree of agreement between raters in the remaining 224 cases, the H3 and O3 scale was treated as an eight point rating scale and the product-moment correlation between the two ratings was determined. The correlation coefficient was 0·78, indicating reasonably good agreement.

Again with the ratings determined as an eight-point scale, the correlation between the mean of the two ratings and the sedation threshold was determined. The correlation coefficient was 0·53, which is highly significant statistically and indicates that the sedation threshold was positively correlated with hysterical-obsessional trend. Fig. 1 shows the mean hysterical-obsessional rating for each sedation threshold. The graph shows that thresholds of 3·0 or less were obtained in patients generally rated as hysterical, and thresholds of 4·5 or more were obtained in patients generally rated obsessional. Fig. 1 also suggests that the sedation threshold discriminates only three, or at the most four, points on a hysterical-obsessional continuum.

It was of some interest to determine whether the correlation between hysterical-obsessional trend and the sedation threshold was based more upon symptoms or upon assessments of behaviour characteristics. One of the raters was asked to indicate the basis for his ratings in these terms. The reasons could be classified into five categories: conversion symptoms, obsessive-compulsive symptoms, and either hysterical, mixed, or obses-

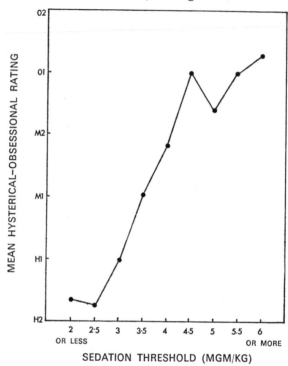

Figure 1. Mean hysterical-obsessional rating by sedation threshold, 224 patients. Rating for each patient
was the mean of two psychiatrist's ratings.

sional personality characteristics. Fig. 2 shows the proportion of above
and below average sedation thresholds for each of these categories in the
254 patients assigned ratings by this psychiatrist. Sedation threshold
differences were greatest between patients with frank conversion and
obsessive-compulsive symptoms. The differences were less marked
between the groups classified on personality characteristics alone but the
trend was statistically significant at better than the 1 per cent level of
confidence. Thus, although it appeared that symptoms provided a
firmer basis for discrimination with respect to the sedation threshold,
there was also a definite relationship between the threshold and personality evaluations based on behavioural characteristics.

As the ratings were based on heterogeneous case materials gathered in
a non-standard fashion, it seemed reasonable to assume that those subjects to whom both psychiatrists assigned the same ratings might offer

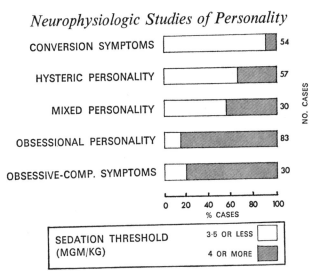

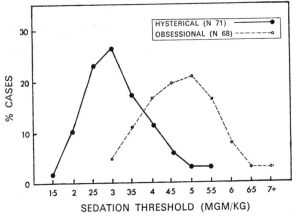

Figure 2. Relationship between sedation threshold and main reason for hysterical-obsessional ratings made by one psychiatrist. Note that differences between ratings made because of symptoms are greater than differences between ratings based on personality characteristics.

some approximation of the true relationship between the sedation threshold and hysterical-obsessional trend. Fig. 3 shows the distributions of sedation thresholds for all those cases assigned either an H or O

Figure 3. Percentage distributions of sedation thresholds in patients classed as hysterical or obsessional by both raters.

rating by both psychiatrists. There was relatively little overlapping between these groups with concordant ratings. The biserial correlation coefficient for the data in Fig. 3 was 0·84; this coefficient is spuriously high because the mixed group was omitted, but it gives some indication of the possible relationship.

Guilford Introversion Score

The 36 patients for whom questionnaire scores and sedation thresholds were available contained a somewhat greater than usual number of patients with high thresholds, thus restricting the possible range of variation. Even with a restricted range, the coefficient for the correlation between the threshold and the introversion C score, which was 0·60, was highly significant statistically. The S scale contributed more to the correlation than the R scale. Fig. 4 illustrates the relationship between

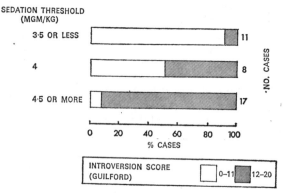

Figure 4. Relationship between sedation threshold and introversion (Guilford combined C score for R and S scales).

the sedation threshold and the introversion score. These data confirm the hypothesis that the sedation threshold is positively correlated with degree of introversion.

Conditioning

Acceptable conditioning results were available for only 22 of the 36 patients. It was necessary to reject 7 patients because of apparatus breakdown during the conditioning experiments, and 7 more because they gave three or more blink responses during the six preconditioning presentations of the tone alone. Taking the total number of conditioned responses during the unreinforced trials of the conditioning and extinction series as a total conditioning score, the correlations between this score and the introversion C score and sedation threshold were determined. The coefficient for conditioning score *versus* introversion was 0·45, and for conditioning *versus* sedation threshold was 0·23. The former was significant at the 5 per cent level of confidence, while the latter was not significant.

The absence of a significant correlation between conditioning and sedation threshold suggests that these two procedures measure factors which are not similar. If one takes conditioning as another measure of central nervous system function, it is a matter of interest to determine how well introversion-extraversion could be predicted by a combination of the sedation threshold and the conditioning tests. In the 22 subjects for whom all three sets of data were available, the coefficient of multiple correlation between the introversion score and a combination of the sedation threshold and the conditioning score was 0·67. This was significant at the 1 per cent level of confidence.

DISCUSSION

Present data support the conclusion that the sedation threshold is correlated with degree of hysterical-obsessional trend or introversion-extraversion. The results are in agreement with Jung's view that the characteristic neurosis of the extrovert is hysteria, whereas that of the introvert is psychasthenia (Ref. 9), and they confirm Hildebrand's results showing that hysterics and dysthymics differ on measures of introversion-extraversion (Ref. 8). Franks' findings with respect to conditionability and introversion-extraversion (Ref. 6) are also confirmed, although the hypothesis that the sedation threshold would be correlated with conditionability was not supported by the data.

It is possible that our failure to demonstrate a relationship between conditionability and the sedation threshold may be due to undiscovered technical faults in the conditioning procedure, or that a larger series will yield more positive results. However, these possibilities seem dubious in view of the fact that the present correlation of 0·45 between the conditioning and introversion scores was almost identical with the correlation which Franks found. The present negative conditioning data are not critical for the theory that the dimension of introversion-extraversion is associated with a dimension of central nervous excitation-inhibition, in so far as the sedation threshold, which is a more direct measure of central excitability, was definitely correlated with introversion-extra-version.

In previous studies of the sedation threshold in nonpsychotic subjects, it seemed appropriate to stress the positive correlation between the threshold and degree of manifest anxiety (Refs. 16 & 17). The relation-ship between the threshold and hysterical-obsessional trend, which present results confirmed, was also noted. As it would be desirable to avoid the problems raised by multiple concepts, one might attempt to bring these two correlates of the sedation threshold together, if it could be demonstrated that manifest anxiety is really dependent upon introversive tendencies. This is a possibility which agrees with much clinical experi-ence, but one cannot ignore the fact that hysterics manifesting apparent anxiety reactions are by no means uncommon. Another reason for retaining the anxiety correlate comes from data showing that, when patients with anxiety states and high sedation thresholds responded to therapy with reduction of anxiety, the sedation threshold decreased (Ref. 15). To account for these facts, it was suggested that there are several neurophysiologic mechanisms of anxiety, that the 'choice' of mechanism is linked with personality structure, and that the sedation threshold reflects the activity of that anxiety mechanism predominating in obsessional or introverted persons (Ref. 15). However, if retest studies were to show that a decrease in sedation threshold is accompanied by a corresponding decrease in both anxiety and introversion, it would be possible to regard the personality factor as the primary correlate of the threshold. It should be possible to carry out the research necessary to clarify this issue.

Eysenck has drawn attention to a pharmacologic implication of the sedation threshold (Ref. 5); it suggests that the position of a person on the introversion-extraversion continuum may be perhaps the most important factor influencing his therapeutic dosage requirements for a stimulant or depressant drug. Impressions gained by one of us from clini-cal experience with sedatives seem to substantiate this view. In hysterical patients, small doses of sedatives are often adequate, whereas the larger doses, which are required by dysthymics, tend to produce disturbing side effects. These side effects are often reported in the form of exagger-ated complaints, which may sometimes be interpreted by the physician as a need for more sedation; if more is given, this may lead to further side effects, and so on. This differential effect of sedatives in hysterics and dysthymics is allied to Pavlov's observations on the quantitative therapeutic requirements of bromides in dogs with experimental neuroses (Ref. 11, p. 92). A practical clinical application would be to use personality assessment as a guide to sedative dosage.

Although the exact neurophysiologic function reflected by the sedation threshold is not certain, it most probably measures a time characteristic of neuronal excitability (Ref. 12). In demonstrating that introversion-extraversion is correlated with a neurophysiologic factor of this order, the present study provides strong support for a theoretical approach to personality which is orientated along neurophysiologic lines.

SUMMARY

The purpose of this study was to test the hypothesis that the sedation threshold is correlated with a personality factor, similar to Eysenck's introversion-extraversion dimension or, in neurotics, a hysterical-obsessional continuum. In one part of the study, two psychiatrists independently rated 308 case records for hysterical-obsessional tendency. Their ratings were significantly correlated with the sedation threshold, a high threshold being associated with obsessional tendencies and a low one with hysterical tendencies. Another investigative method used was to correlate the sedation threshold with questionnaire scores of introversion-extraversion (Guilford R and S scales) in 36 neurotic patients and with ease of conditioned eyeblink formation. The threshold was significantly correlated with the questionnaire scores in the predicted direction, high thresholds being associated with introversion. The threshold was not significantly correlated with conditionability, although high introversion on the questionnaire was associated with greater conditionability. The main conclusion reached from the findings was that there is an objectively demonstrable neurophysiologic basis for the introversion-extraversion dimension.

Acknowledgements

Thanks are due to Dr J. F. Davis for designing the apparatus used in this study, to Dr A. L. Jones for rating the case records, to Dr J. L. Lapointe for translating the Guilford scales into French, and to Herbert Lorenz and Genevieve Servin for technical assistance.

REFERENCES

1. DAVIS, J. F., Low Frequency Analysers in Electroencephalography. Paper (No. 56–24–1) presented at the Instrument Society of America Meeting, September, 1956.

2. EYSENCK, H. J., A dynamic theory of anxiety and hysteria. *J. ment. Sci.*, **101**, 28, 1955.

3. ——, *Dimensions of Personality*. London: Routledge & Kegan Paul, 1947.

4. ——, *The Scientific Study of Personality*. London: Routledge & Kegan Paul, 1952.

5. ——, Drugs and personality. 1. Theory and methodology. *J. ment. Sci.*, **103**, 119, 1957.

6. FRANKS, C. M., Conditioning and personality. A study of normal and neurotic subjects. *J. abnorm. soc. Psychol.*, **52**, 143, 1956.

7. GUILFORD, J. P., *An inventory of factors S, T, D, C, R. Manual of Directions and Norms*, California: Sheridan Supply Co., 1940.

8. HILDEBRAND, H. P., A Factorial Study of Introversion-Extraversion by Means of Objective Tests. Unpublished Ph.D. thesis, University of London Library, 1953.

9. JUNG, C. G., *Psychological Types*. London: Routledge & Kegan Paul, 1924.

10. MACKINNON, D. W., Personality and the behaviour disorders. In *The Structure of Personality* (J. McV. Hunt, ed.). New York: Ronald Press Co., 1944.

11. PAVLOV, I. P., *Conditioned Reflexes and Psychiatry* (Trans. W. H. Gantt). New York: International Publishers, 1941.

12. SHAGASS, C., The sedation threshold. A method for estimating tension in psychiatric patients. *Electroenceph. clin. Neurophysiol.*, **6**, 211, 1954.

13. ——, A measurable neurophysiological factor of psychiatric significance. *Electroenceph. clin. Neurophysiol.*, **9**, 101, 1957.

14. —— & JONES, A. L., A neurophysiological test for psychiatric diagnosis. Results in 750 patients. *Amer. J. Psychiat.*, **114**, 1002–1010, 1958.

15. ——, MIHALIK, J. & JONES, A. L., Clinical psychiatric studies using the sedation threshold. *J. psychosom. Res.*, **2**, 45, 1957.

16. —— & NAIMAN, J., The sedation threshold as an objective index of manifest anxiety in psychoneurosis. *J. psychosom. Res.*, **1**, 49, 1956.

17. —— & ——, The sedation threshold, manifest anxiety and some aspects of ego function. *A. M. A. Arch. Neurol. and Psychiat.*, **74**, 379, 1955.

5

Sodium Amytal and Extraversion

S. G. LAVERTY

First published in

Journal of Neurology and Neurosurgery and Psychiatry, **21**, 50–54, 1958

INTRODUCTION

'EXTRAVERSION' and 'introversion' are descriptive terms denoting two types of behavioural reaction and personality organization widely recognized and described in psychological literature (Refs. 3 & 5). 'Extraverted behaviour' is characterized clinically by the outward expression of feelings and attitudes, in words, gestures, and acts, in a spontaneous and direct manner, little impeded by reflection, indecision or reserve. The contrary, 'introverted behaviour', comprises a tendency to limit or moderate spontaneous outward expression, reflection, preoccupation and rumination rather predominating. A reserved or even withdrawn attitude may be maintained. While individual people may be predominantly introverted or extraverted in their behaviour, fluctuation normally occurs from one form to the other. Introducing these types Jung writes:

'But every individual possesses both mechanisms—extraversion as well as introversion—and only the relative predominance of the one or the other determines the type' (Ref. 7, p. 10).

And again:

'A rhythmical alternation of both forms of psychic activity may correspond with the normal course of life. . . .

'Outer circumstances and inner disposition frequently favour the one mechanism or hinder the other; whereby a predominance of one mechanism naturally arises. If this condition becomes in any way chronic a type is produced, namely an habitual attitude, in which the one mechanism permanently dominates; not of course that the other can ever be completely suppressed in as much as it also is an integral factor in psychic activity' (p. 13).

35

Persistently introverted or extraverted attitudes and behaviour patterns are frequently seen in neurotic subjects; marked fluctuations occur here also.

In the course of intoxication with alcohol or a sedative drug, such as barbiturate, a shift is often seen from introverted towards extraverted behaviour. Verbal and motor expression, both spontaneous and responsive, become conspicuous in behaviour, reflection and passive experiencing minimal. A particular pattern of 'uninhibited' behaviour, often at variance with the normal and conventional practice of the subject, may be a constant or recurrent response to alcohol or sedation. Attitudes may appear which are never or seldom expressed in the normal state. Strong affective expression may appear ('be released') such as euphoria, expansiveness, resentment, anger or depression.

During the initial stages of anaesthesia, with say ether or 'pentothal', patterns of motor activity or excitement may appear, similar to those extraverted patterns described, but usually short-lived and associated with a more definite clouding of consciousness. This activity is not constant; the majority of subjects become progressively sedated and do not show it. My own observation of many patients receiving pentothal before E.C.T. showed such initial excitement regularly in the same subjects, suggesting that it may be a constant response for certain individuals.

Introverted behaviour may lessen and extraverted behaviour emerge under the influence of many other factors; each is appropriate to certain situations. However, a shift towards extraversion appears to be facilitated in certain people by drugs with a particular type of depressant action on the central nervous system.

An objective measure of extraversion (the 'Rhathymia' or R scale; Ref. 6) was given to a group of introverted neurotic (dysthymic) subjects after injections of placebo and sodium amytal (Ref. 8). The R score was significantly higher after sodium amytal, confirming the extraverting effects of the drug. These subjects also answered the questionnaire more often in the affirmative after injections of 'amytal'.

Shagass (Ref. 10) and Shagass & Naiman (Refs. 11 & 12) used sodium amytal to establish an objective measurement of sedation, 'the sedation threshold'. This measure, the quantity of drug (mg./kg. body weight) required to produce inflection in the amplitude of the 'barbiturate-fast' activity of the electroencephalogram (a point usually concurrent with the onset of slurred speech), was found to be high for introverted neurotics, low for extraverted and normal subjects, and intermediate for 'mixed neurotics'.

'A high sedation threshold seems to be associated with obsessional personality traits, introversion, and a predisposition to anxiety, tension, and depressive symptoms; a low threshold . . . with hysterical personality traits, extraversion, and a predisposition to conversion symptoms' (Ref. 13).

It may be argued from this that introversion depends on a cerebral activity which is opposed by sodium amytal (before full sedation), in the course of which opposition a shift from introversion towards extraversion takes place; the overcoming of this activity may be presumed to require a certain quantity of the drug and this could account for the higher doses necessary to produce the sedation threshold in introverted subjects. If introversion is the factor in question both neurotic and normal introverted subjects should behave in the same way, becoming more extraverted after amytal and showing a high sedation threshold. Extraverted subjects, on the other hand, should show little or no increase in extraversion and have a low threshold.

The present investigation was carried out to test these expectations.

METHOD

Forty subjects were tested as to their degree of 'extraversion' using Guilford's R scale. Each subject was tested on two occasions, once after amytal and once after injection of placebo. Four groups of 10 subjects tested in this way were made up as follows:

Group 1. Introverted neurotic subjects
Group 2. Introverted normal subjects
Group 3. Extraverted neurotic subjects
Group 4. Extraverted normal subjects

The neurotic subjects were in-patients or out-patients of the Maudsley Hospital and were all complaining of current neurotic symptoms or showed neurotic disturbances of behaviour. They were selected as 'introverted' or 'extraverted' on the basis of their behaviour and history taken during a preliminary interview. The normal subjects were psychiatrically unsophisticated acquaintances of my own, selected as being 'extraverts' or 'introverts' according to their known personalities and free from a history of mental illness or neurotic symptoms. The proportion of men to women in each group (1 to 4) was 6:4, 6:4, 5:5, 6:4. Ages were between 18 and 37.

The subjects were asked to participate in an experiment in which their experience of the passage of time would be tested after the injection of a drug: such a test was given after each injection but does not form a part of the investigation reported here.

Amytal injections were given in the manner described by Shagass *et al.* (Ref. 13). Sodium amytal solution, freshly prepared, in a dose of 0·5 mg./kg. body weight/ml. sterile water, was injected at a rate of 1 ml. in 40 sec. At 40 sec. intervals the subject was requested to read a sentence on a card held before him and from this response the onset of slurring of speech was assessed. At this point the injection was stopped.

Placebo injections of sterile water were given in the same way.

After the patient was able to sit up and walk about comfortably, and did not appear to be drowsy, the Guilford R scale was presented in the form of cards. The subject was requested to sort the questionnaire cards into boxes labelled 'Yes', '?' and 'No', answering them according to the way he felt at the time.[1]

A random order for the administration of placebo or amytal at the first or second session was prepared and followed for each group. The subject's behaviour and mental state before and after injection was assessed and recorded. No positive suggestions with regard to symptoms were given. All the verbal comments made by the subject during the card-sorting tests were recorded as giving an indication of the presence and quantity of spontaneous talk.

RESULTS

These are reported as follows: (a) questionnaire scores; (b) spontaneous talk; (c) symptoms reported; (d) behaviour observed; (e) sedation threshold.

(a) Questionnaire Scores (R Score, 'Yes' Score, '?' Score): The mean scores for each group after injection of a placebo may be assumed to be little different from what they would be without injection since placebo injection and 'no treatment' scores were not significantly different in the former investigations (Ref. 8).

Mean R scores for the introverted groups (1 and 2) were: after placebo 22·8 (S.D. 3·3)[2] and 24·8 (S.D. 4·5); after amytal these groups showed

[1] In the former investigation (Ref. 8) the number of 'Yes' answers was significantly increased after amytal. In the present investigation questions 8, 16, 18, 19, 57, 106, 110, 118 and 119 were put in their negative form, bringing the possible number of 'Yes' responses to 43 and the 'No' responses to 42.

[2] Standard deviations for means given in brackets.

higher R scores than after placebo, the means being 29·6 (S.D. 3·4) and 26·3 (S.D. 7·9). The extraverted groups (3 and 4) showed higher R score means than the introverted groups as follows: after placebo 46·1 (S.D. 5·3) and 46 (S.D. 8·3); after amytal 48·9 (S.D. 5·8) and 48·1 (S.D. 4·5).

There is a consistent increase in the R score after amytal, being for each group (1 to 4) 6·8 (S.D. 3·3), 1·5 (S.D. 3·4), 2·8 (S.D. 4·8), and 2·1 (S.D. 4·5). The difference is highly significant for the introverted neurotic group (1) at the 0·1 level of confidence. For the other groups (2 to 4) the differences are not significant, but if the scores are combined, significance at the 2·5 per cent level is obtained.

'Yes' scores (the number of cards placed in the 'Yes' box) after placebo showed lower means for introverted subjects: group 1, 44·2 (S.D. 13·4), group 2, 47·9 (S.D. 10·9) than for extraverted subjects, group 3, 57·0 (S.D. 12·5), group 4, 54·0 (S.D. 7·7). An increase in the 'Yes' score after amytal occurred in each group, being for group 1, 7·1 (S.D. 9·4), group 2, 3·6 (S.D. 10·0), group 3, 4·0 (S.D. 3·0) and group 4, 2·4 (S.D. 3·3). The difference is significant for the introverted neurotic group at 2·5 per cent level, but not for the other groups. Similarly '?' scores (number of cards placed in the '?' box) showed a tendency to decrease after amytal as compared with placebo, but the scores being small and frequently zero the differences are insignificant. However, the number of subjects in each group showing a decrease is high for the introverted groups (10 in group 1, 8 in group 2), and lower for the extraverted groups (5 in group 3, 5 in group 4).

(b) Spontaneous Talk: Spontaneous talk during the card-sorting test was greater (number of words recorded) for extraverted groups both after a placebo and amytal. After amytal an increase in spontaneous talk was recorded for all groups, particularly for groups 1 and 3, the mean increase being for each group 1 to 4 65·5 (S.D. 56), 14·9 (S.D. 126), 46·0 (S.D. 115), 17 (S.D. 47). Introverted subjects showing a restriction in speech became noticeably more talkative after amytal, often showing a sudden flow of spontaneous talk during injection.

During the card sorting subjects who had received amytal tended to read the questions aloud or to themselves, moving their lips. After a placebo this was noted only in 4 subjects, 2 in each extraverted group. After amytal it was more common for subjects to break off from the card sorting to speak directly to the investigator.

(c) Current Symptoms Reported: Symptoms were reported spontaneously or elicited by questioning at each interview. 13 of the neurotic subjects (8 in the introverted group, 5 in the extraverted group) described symptoms as troublesome most or all of the time; the other 7 described definite fluctuations in degree and persistence. 2 subjects in the introverted normal groups and one in the extraverted normal group described feelings of anxiety.

Relief from symptoms was frequently reported after amytal. This was most evident in the introverted neurotic group; placebo injection seldom afforded relief. Seven of the neurotic introverted group reported relief after amytal from pain and somatic discomfort, 4, anxiety or depression, 4, recurrent or obsessional thoughts, 1, depersonalization and 3, other symptoms. 4 of the neurotic extraverted group reported relief from pain and somatic discomfort, 3, anxiety and 3, other symptoms. Introverted subjects described relief more often than extraverted subjects; extraverted subjects described exacerbation more often than introverts. Exacerbation of previously reported symptoms was more common after placebo than after amytal; after amytal drowsiness and dizziness were more commonly complained of, but this was transient except in two subjects who both belonged to the extraverted neurotic group.

The only introverted neurotic subject who failed to report relief from at least one symptom experienced a compulsive fear that he would commit some indiscretion under the influence of the drug. He remained anxious about this after both injections.

Attitudes: Besides differences in reported symptoms certain alterations in attitudes were observed after amytal. These were not consistently enquired for but in 5 subjects were sufficiently striking to record. A dysthymic patient who had consistently expressed anxious solicitude for a married woman with whom he was involved, after amytal abused her for compromising him. A second dysthymic subject went to a dance on the evening after injection of amytal and surprised those who knew him by his sociable attitude; formerly in hospital he had been persistently shy. A third dysthymic patient went out with her friends the day after injection of amytal; one reported 'she was brighter than she ever was before, she read our fortunes out of cups—I never knew her to do that before'. A fourth dysthymic subject after injection of amytal displayed for the first time in hospital a markedly paranoid attitude. A tense, extraverted patient with an hysterical weakness of the arm became excited and aggressive towards the doctor after amytal and the weakness was no longer apparent; he was previously overtalkative but polite.

(d) Behaviour Observed: Abnormal behaviour patterns were noted for each interview.

Repetitive tension movements (tapping, fidgeting, etc.), restlessness or restricted movements with the appearance of tension, were noted, particularly in the introverted neurotic group; these signs were associated with complaints of tension or anxiety, and appeared relieved after injection of amytal in all the dysthymic subjects except one. Anxious behaviour of this type was seen to a lesser extent in the extraverted group of neurotics and was rather less consistently relieved after amytal. Other individual items of symptomatic behaviour in the extraverted group were unrelieved after amytal in 5 cases (abnormal gait, aphonia, facial tic, weakness of leg, anaesthesia), but relieved in two (retching, weakness of arm). Both these latter patients appeared relieved of anxiety, one after abreaction.

Overtalkativeness after amytal was frequently noted, often with euphoria or other affective display and in one case with motor excitement and aggressiveness. This latter patient had shown similar behaviour after alcohol on at least three occasions.

A tendency to fall asleep after the injection was observed in 2 subjects in the extraverted neurotic group; in other subjects drowsiness was frequently reported at an early stage in the injection but passed off to reappear transiently at about the onset of slurred speech but not lasting more than a few minutes after the injection and not reappearing after testing had begun. 3 subjects felt 'more alert', 'more wide awake' after amytal (2 in group 1, 1 in group 2).

Three other minor observations on behaviour in the introverted neurotic group may be mentioned. Three of these subjects showed an incapacity to carry out different actions simultaneously; movements of the hands, breathing, speaking, shifting, and so on were performed separately while other actions were temporarily suspended. This breaking up of the normal rhythm of movements was associated with a general restriction of movements, with feelings of anxiety or tension and was never seen after amytal, when these subjects became relaxed. Subsequent questioning showed these subjects to be very conscious of movements normally carried out unattended.

The same subjects and one other in the introverted neurotic group and one in the introverted normal group were observed to cease breathing during the time that they were reading and considering the questions on the cards; respiration was resumed with a deep inspiration as they placed the card into the appropriate box. This, and other examples of intermittent hyperpnea were not seen after amytal; even yawning was rarely observed in this group.

Restricted and hesitant talk in 3 subjects of the introverted neurotic group was associated with prefatory inarticulate sounds ('Er-er') and then failure to talk. It was noted that a remark or even a slight movement on the doctor's part immediately caused the patient to make another verbal response, often with a movement of the subject's hands or body. Following this response the patient became stuck again, unable to utter and restricted in movement. This did not occur after amytal.

No consistent relief from abnormal behaviour was noted after a placebo.

(e) Sedation Threshold: The 'sedation threshold', as assessed by the point of onset of slurring of speech, was in some cases difficult to ascertain. Other changes in speech, such as slowing, drawing out of vowels, alteration in pitch, and mumbling, were noted, sometimes preceding definite slurring. Speech which was not quite clear at one point was sometimes distinct at the next. Certain subjects spoke slowly, carefully endeavouring not to slur when aware of the tendency to do so. However, a decision as to the point at which slurring occurred was made in each case.

Mean sedation thresholds (mg./kg.) for each of the four groups were: Group 1, 6·4 mg./kg. (S.D. 4·0), group 2, 6·1 (S.D. 3·7), group 3, 4·15 (S.D. 3·5), group 4, 5·25 (S.D. 5·1). Differences between means for all groups of 10 (1 to 4) are not significant. The combined means for the introverted groups 1 and 2 (20 subjects) are 12·5 (S.D. 3·9) and for the extraverted groups 3 and 4 (20 subjects) 9·4 (S.D. 4·4). The standard error of difference for these means, 1·33, is less than half the difference between means (3·1), indicating a significant difference at the 5 per cent level. Combining the means for the neurotic groups (1 and 3) and the normal groups (2 and 4) does not show a significant difference between means, the difference being only 0·8.

CONCLUSIONS

Administration of sodium amytal intravenously to the point at which speech becomes slurred was associated with consistent differences in responses to questionnaires and behaviour as compared with the same observations following injection of a placebo. After amytal 'R' scores, 'Yes' scores (Ref. 6) and 'number of words spoken' were higher than after the placebo; '?' scores were less. These differences were most significant in the introverted neurotic (dysthymic) group of subjects. This group also showed a consistent relief from symptoms and from 'introverted behaviour patterns'. The neurotic introverted group and the normal introverted group required a larger mean dose of amytal to produce slurred speech (sedation threshold) than the extraverted groups.

DISCUSSION

Brazier has presented a hypothesis for the mode of action of barbiturates on the central nervous system based on electroencephalographic evidence in animals and human subjects. Brazier describes three phases of barbiturate action: (i) an initial action is exerted on neurones in the cerebral cortex (based on findings with depth electrodes in human subjects). (ii) At a slightly deeper level of narcosis

'barbiturates appear to have a differential depressant action on a subcortical inhibitory system, the result being an augmentation of response in the non-specific sensory system that carries "Forbes secondary responses" '.

Brazier continues:

'The phenomenon suggests a release effect, as though at *this stage* of barbiturate anaesthesia some inhibitory system, possibly in the diffuse ascending system (of the reticular substance) had been put out of action by the drug, thereby releasing from control the responses carried rostrally from this system. Such a concept envisages that there would be in normal circumstances a condition of balance between inhibition and activitation and that by increasing very gradually the depth of anaesthesia the action of the one (inhibition) can be depressed before the other' (Ref. 1).

The augmentation of this cortical response to sensory stimulus is maximal in the pre-motor area. The suggestion that it is analogous to the K-complex (Refs. 2 & 4) is contested (Ref. 9). (iii) At a deeper level still the differential action on inhibitory and activating systems is lost and the sole remaining activity is the 'barbiturate burst'. At this stage the subject is drowsy or asleep.

It is tempting to relate the first two of these three phases to the initial stages of early barbiturate anaesthesia observed here. The first subjective report during amytal injection is usually of dizziness, warmth, or other slight sensation and occurs after 50 to 150 mg. The group of changes that follows appear related to the shift towards extraversion; relief from anxiety experiences and preoccupation, increased talkativeness and readiness of affective motor expression. The change of attitude that occurs at this point appears to be the same as underlies the differences to questionnaire responses; the subject feels less inhibited, more spontaneous, says 'Yes' more often and is less indecisive (low '?' score); the observed behaviour gives a similar impression. The terms used by Brazier to describe the altered EEG in the second phase serve to describe the form of altered behaviour response also: 'inhibition' is reduced, 'activation' is unimpeded. The alteration is smooth in most cases, but when abreaction and abrupt excitement occur the impression of a 'release effect' is obtained.

The larger sedation threshold shown by the introverted subjects confirms the findings of Shagass & Naiman (Ref. 12). Possibly the extra quantity of the drug is used in overcoming greater inhibitory activity of the kind referred to above. That the neurotic introverted subjects showed more shift towards extraversion in response to the questionnaires and in behaviour may suggest that in this group the inhibitory mechanism is more labile and associated with and sustained by anxiety.

As portrayed by Jung (Ref. 7), introversion and extraversion are two forms of personality organization and expression between which a fluctuating balance or equilibrium is maintained. At a certain stage of amytal sedation shift of this equilibrium appears, in the direction of extraversion. As described by Brazier, barbiturate anaesthesia at a certain point causes a shift in the equilibrium normally maintained between two discharging ascending neuronal systems in the central nervous system. Further study is required to discern how closely these two effects of barbiturate are linked and how far their similarities can be pursued.

SUMMARY

Injections of sodium amytal and placebo were given to 40 subjects divided into 4 groups of 10 (neurotics, normals, introverts, extraverts): scores on Guilford's R scale (extraversion) were higher after amytal than after the placebo. Changes in reported symptomatology and behaviour were noted. The sedation threshold, as measured by the onset of slurred speech, was highest for neurotic introverts and this group showed the most marked changes towards extraversion. A possible physiological basis for the shift towards extraversion after amytal is proposed.

REFERENCES

1. BRAZIER, M. A. B., In *Brain Mechanisms and Consciousness*. A Symposium organized by the Council for International Organizations of Medical Sciences. Oxford: Blackwell, 1954.
2. DAVIS, H., DAVIS, P. A., LOOMIS, A. L., HARVEY, E. N. & HOBART, G., Electrical reactions of the human brain to auditory stimulation during sleep. *J. Neurophysiol.*, **2**, 500–514, 1939.
3. EYSENCK, H. J., *The Structure of Human Personality*. London: Methuen, 1953.
4. GASTAUT, H., Etude électrographique chez l'homme et chez l'animal des décharges éliptiques dites 'psychomotrices'. *Rev. neurol.*, **88**, 310–354, 1953.
5. GUILFORD, J. P., Introversion-extraversion. *Psychol. Bull.*, **31**, 331–354, 1934.
6. ——, *An Inventory of Factors STDCR*. Beverly Hills, California: Sheridan Supply Co., 1940.
7. JUNG, C. G., *Psychological Types*. London: Kegan Paul, 1923.
8. LAVERTY, S. G & FRANKS, C. M., Sodium amytal and behaviour in neurotic subjects. *J. Neurol. Neurosurg. Psychiat.*, **19**, 137–143, 1956.
9. ROTH, M., SHAW, J. & GREEN, J., The form, voltage distribution and physiological significance of the K-complex. *EEG clin. Neurophysiol.*, **8**, 385, 1956.
10. SHAGASS, C., The sedation threshold: a method for estimating tension in psychiatric patients. *EEG clin. Neurophysiol.*, **6**, 221, 1954.
11. —— & NAIMAN, J., The sedation threshold, manifest anxiety and some aspects of ego function. *A.M.A. Arch. Neurol. Psychiat.*, **74**, 397, 1955.
12. —— & ——, The sedation threshold as an objective index of manifest anxiety in psychoneurosis. *J. Psychosomatic Res.*, **1**, 49–57, 1956.
13. ——, —— & MIHALIK, J., An objective test which differentiates between neurotic and psychotic depression. *A.M.A. Arch. Neurol. Psychiat.*, **75**, 461–471, 1956.

The Effects of Time of Day and Social Isolation on the Relationship between Temperament and Performance

W. P. COLQUHOUN & D. W. J. CORCORAN

First published in
British Journal of Social and Clinical Psychology, **3**, 226–231, 1964

In an experiment on cancelling letters in English prose the relationship between output and degree of introversion was found to depend both on the time of day at which the task was performed and on the social situation in which subjects were tested. Performance correlated positively with introversion in morning test sessions when subjects were isolated from each other, but when testing was in the afternoon, or when subjects worked together in a group, this relationship was destroyed. The results are discussed in relation to an arousal theory of introversion-extraversion.

INTRODUCTION

It has been reported by Colquhoun (Ref. 1) that the efficiency with which a subject detects brief, rarely appearing signals when working alone at a paced inspection task is related to his score on the 'unsociability' scale of the Heron Personality Inventory (Ref. 4). In tests conducted during the morning good performance was associated with a high unsociability score, i.e., with a high score of introversion; in tests carried out in the afternoon the relationship was reversed. In the experiment to be described this 'time of day' effect was investigated using an unpaced task—letter cancellation—in order to test the generality of the earlier finding. In addition, the effect of social isolation on the relationship was determined by having subjects work either alone, as in the previous study, or, alternatively, when seated together in a single room.

METHOD

122 ratings of the Royal Navy served as subjects. They became available for testing in batches of 4, 5 or 6 over a period of about a year. Each

46

batch of subjects (the members of which were previously unknown to each other) was assigned to one of the following four testing conditions:

1. Morning, isolated (working alone at 8.30 a.m.)
2. Afternoon, isolated (working alone at 1.30 p.m.)
3. Morning, group (working together at 8.30 a.m.)
4. Afternoon, group (working together at 1.30 p.m.)

In the 'isolated' conditions each subject occupied a separate room opening off a corridor from which the experimenter observed their work. In the 'group' conditions the subjects were seated all together around a circular table, while the experimenter remained in the same room.

Each subject was given a pencil and a booklet consisting of several pages of printed English prose. He was asked to check this material line by line for 15 minutes, crossing out each letter 'e' as he did so. The instructions given emphasized both speed and accuracy.

The Heron Personality Inventory was administered as normal laboratory routine within a few days of the test session.

RESULTS

Differences Between Experimental Conditions

Two scores were obtained: (1) *output*—the number of lines of text checked in 15 minutes; (2) *error*—the percentage of letters 'e' remaining uncancelled. Means and S.D.s of these performance scores and those obtained from the Heron Inventory are shown in Table 1.

Although differences in performance between conditions were slight, mean output was consistently greater in the isolated conditions than in

TABLE 1

SCORES OBTAINED FROM A TEST OF CANCELLING 'ES' IN ENGLISH PROSE, AND FROM THE HERON PERSONALITY INVENTORY

Condition	N.	No. of lines checked		Per cent omissions		'Unsociability' score	
		Mean	S.D.	Mean	S.D.	Mean	S.D.
1. Morning, isolated	29	85·6	14·3	8·8	6·9	4·7	2·7
2. Afternoon, isolated	33	84·0	12·8	7·3	5·0	3·4	2·2
3. Morning, group	30	80·8	10·0	9·7	6·3	4·5	2·4
4. Afternoon, group	30	80·3	11·8	8·0	4·4	4·6	2·9

the group conditions. The difference of 4·4 lines checked between the overall means in the two situations is just statistically significant at the 5 per cent level of confidence.

Due to chance errors of sampling the mean unsociability score in Condition 2 was significantly lower than the scores in the remaining conditions ($p < 0.05$). However, this is not considered to have affected the conclusions drawn from the main analysis (see below), since when the groups were equated by matching subjects in terms of their unsociability score very similar results were obtained.

Output × Introversion

The relationship between output score and unsociability score in each condition was assessed by product-moment correlation; the coefficients obtained are shown in Table 2.

TABLE 2

PRODUCT-MOMENT CORRELATIONS OF NUMBER OF LINES CHECKED AND INTROVERSION SCORE IN FOUR TESTING CONDITIONS

	Morning (M)	Afternoon (A)	Difference (M)−(A)
Isolated (I)	Condition 1 (N 29) +0·443*	Condition 2 (N 33) −0·056	+0·499†
Group (G)	Condition 3 (N 30) −0·164	Condition 4 (N 30) +0·066	−0·230
Difference (I)−(G)	+0·607†	−0·122	

* P(r) <0·05 (two-tailed test)
† P(Diff.) <0·05 (two-tailed test)

There was a statistically significant positive correlation between unsociability score and output in Condition 1 (the morning, isolated situation). Table 2 shows that this correlation was destroyed either by altering the time of administration of the test from morning to afternoon, or by testing in a group rather than in isolation. The difference between the correlation coefficients for Condition 1 and Condition 2, and that between Condition 1 and Condition 3 are both statistically significant at the 5 per cent level of confidence.

Table 3 shows the mean output scores of 'extraverted' subjects (those

TABLE 3

MEAN OUTPUT SCORES OF 'EXTRAVERTED' AND 'INTROVERTED' SUBJECTS
IN DIFFERENT TESTING CONDITIONS

	Extraverted subjects			Introverted subjects		
Condition	N.	Mean unsociability score	No. of lines checked	N.	Mean unsociability score	No. of lines checked
1. Morning, isolated	14	2·4	78·6	15	6·9	92·9
2. Afternoon, isolated	25	2·4	84·4	8	6·4	82·8
3. Morning, group	15	2·4	82·8	15	6·3	78·7
4. Afternoon, group	13	2·0	79·2	17	6·5	81·1

Difference (2)−(1) : +5·8   Difference (2)−(1) : −10·1
Difference (3)−(1) : +4·2   Difference (3)−(1) : −14·2*

* t = 2·92, p<0·01

with an unsociability score of 4 or less) and 'introverted' subjects (those with a score of 5 or more) in each condition. Also shown are the alterations that occurred in the output of extraverts and introverts when the testing conditions of Condition 1 were changed from morning to afternoon, or from the isolated to the group situation.

Fewer lines of text were checked by introverted subjects when tested in a group. The difference is statistically significant (p<0·01). Extraverted subjects tended to increase their output when tested in a group or in the afternoon, but neither of these changes is statistically significant. Finally, introverted subjects tended to reduce their output in the afternoon, but not to a significant extent (Figs. 5 and 6).

Error

The pattern of relationships between unsociability score and percentage of letters 'e' remaining uncancelled in the four conditions was similar to that for output, but in this case no individual correlation coefficient, nor any of the differences between pairs of coefficients, were statistically significant (Condition 1, r = +0·350; Condition 2, r = +0·063; Condition 3, r = −0·004; Condition 4, r = −0·023).

DISCUSSION

The positive correlation between output and introversion in the morning, isolated testing condition corroborates the finding of Colquhoun (Ref.

C

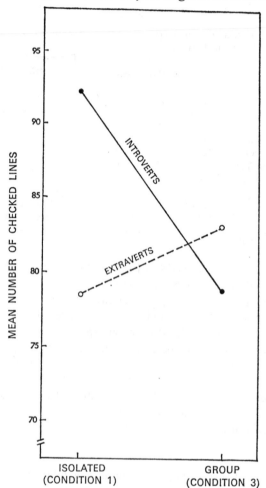

Figure 5. Mean output scores of 'extraverted' and 'introverted' subjects in different social situations when tested in the morning.

1), and demonstrates that this relationship is not specific to the form of inspection task employed. The present results further suggest that the change in the relationship with time of day reported by Colquhoun was due to a differential effect on introverts and extraverts; in the cancellation tasks the performance of introverts would seem to deteriorate and, to a lesser extent, that of extraverts to improve when testing takes place in

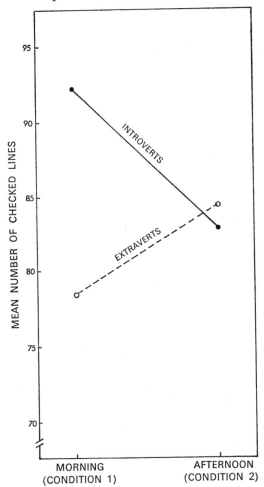

Figure 6. Mean output scores of 'extraverted' and 'introverted' subjects at different times of day in isolated testing conditions.

the afternoon rather than in the morning. Similar effects were observed on changing from isolated to group testing conditions.

Although these results are difficult to explain in terms of existing ·theories (e.g., Refs. 3 & 6), it is possible to account for the findings in terms of a model for the effects of incentives and hyper-arousing situations suggested by Corcoran (Ref. 2). This assumes that (*a*) intro-

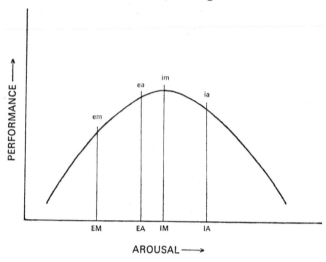

Figure 7. The 'inverted-U' relationship between performance
and arousal used as a possible explanation of the results.

verts are characteristically higher in arousal than extraverts, (*b*) that the
relationship between level of performance and degree of arousal is
inverted-U shaped, and (*c*) that certain environmental and task conditions affect level of arousal. The inverted-U relationship is shown
diagrammatically in Fig. 7.

Since such measures as body temperature and heart rate indicate that
level of arousal is low in the morning (Ref. 5), the first assumption of the
model (*a*) would place introverts in a more favourable (optimal) position
at this time, say IM in Fig. 7. Extraverts, on the other hand, would be at
some position to the left of IM, say EM. A general rise in arousal in the
afternoon would shift EM to EA and IM to IA, which would result in
poorer performance by introverts and better performance by extraverts.
The same kind of model can be applied to the change from isolated to
group testing conditions, provided it is assumed that the incentive
provided by group testing raises level of arousal.

Finally, it should be emphasized that separate groups of subjects
were used under the different conditions, and that although a definite
alteration in the relationship between introversion-extraversion and
performance has been shown, the precise effect of the changes in testing
conditions on individual subjects of a particular temperamental type
requires further investigation.

Acknowledgements
Thanks are due to the Royal Navy for supplying the subjects for these experiments, and to Mr P. Freeman for statistical advice.

REFERENCES

1. COLQUHOUN, W. P., Temperament, inspection efficiency and time of day. *Ergonomics*, **3**, 377–378, 1960.
2. CORCORAN, D. W. J., Individual Differences in Performance After Loss of Sleep. Unpublished Ph.D. thesis, University of Cambridge Library, 1962.
3. EYSENCK, H. J., *The Dynamics of Anxiety and Hysteria*. London: Routledge & Kegan Paul, 1957.
4. HERON, A., A two-part personality inventory for use as a research criterion. *Brit. J. Psychol.*, **47**, 243–251, 1956.
5. KLEITMAN, N., *Sleep and Wakefulness*. Chicago: University Press, 1939.
6. SPENCE, K. W., *Behaviour Theory and Conditioning*. Yale: University Press, 1957.

7

Relationship between Circadian Rhythm of Body Temperature and Introversion-Extraversion

M. J. F. BLAKE[1]

First published in *Nature*, **215**, 896–897, 1967

IT has frequently been alleged that people can be divided into 'morning' or 'evening' types (Ref. 4). Supporting evidence for this view has been obtained by Colquhoun (Ref. 1) and Colquhoun & Corcoran (Ref. 2), who found that the sign of the correlation of a personality measure—degree of introversion—and performance efficiency was dependent on the time of day at which testing was done. At two visual inspection tasks, introverted subjects performed better than extraverts in the early morning; the position was reversed in afternoon tests. The aim of the investigation reported here was to determine whether these differences were associated with underlying differences in circadian physiological rhythm as indicated by body temperature.

Using standard clinical thermometers the sub-lingual body temperatures of 74 young men were recorded twenty times during a single 24 hr. period, on two occasions separated by approximately 1 week. Readings were taken hourly between 0700 and 2300 hrs., and twice hourly between 2300 and 0700 hrs. during the sleep period of the subject. From 0800 to 1630 hrs. the men were intermittently employed on light duties (mainly short psychological tests); meals were taken at 0700, 1200 and 1700 hrs. The evening was devoted to light indoor recreation. All subjects were given the Heron Personality Inventory (Ref. 3) to determine their placing on the personality dimension of introversion-extraversion as measured by their score on the 'unsociability' scale. Body temperature at each of the 20 times of day was taken as the mean of the two readings obtained. Although the grand average of these 20 means was not significantly correlated with introversion-extraversion ($r = -0.044$) some significant correlations were observed when individual times of day were considered separately (see Table 1).

[1] This chapter was prepared by his colleagues from data collected by Mr Blake before his accidental death in October 1965.

Table 1

Correlation Coefficients (r) of Body Temperature and Introversion Rating at Twenty Times of Day (N = 74)

Time	0500	0700	0800	0900	1000	1100	1200	1300	1400	1500	1600
r	−0·053	0·133	0·435*	0·163	0·043	−0·013	−0·106	−0·054	−0·075	0·006	−0·057

Time	1700	1800	1900	2000	2100	2200	2300	0100	0300
r	−0·042	0·060	−0·016	−0·114	−0·239†	−0·167	−0·229‡	−0·207‡	−0·025

* p (one-tailed) <0·001
† p (one-tailed) <0·025
‡ p (one-tailed) <0·05

Not only the magnitude of the correlation but also its sign appeared to vary in a systematic manner depending on the time of day. Thus the correlation changed from significantly positive (introverts with higher temperatures) to significantly negative over the period from 0800 to 2100 hrs., that is, over the 'active' part of the waking day. During sleep this trend was reversed.

39 of the subjects had a score of three or less on the Heron Inventory; the remaining 35 subjects had a score of 4 or more (a high score indicates a relatively high degree of introversion). Average temperatures for these two groups were computed separately at each time of day. Two-point rolling means of the resulting values are shown in Fig. 8.

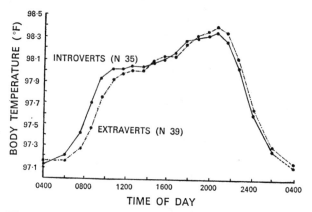

Figure 8. Mean circadian rhythm of body temperature in introvert and extravert groups.

The curve of body temperature through the 24 hr. period was in both groups characterized by a division into three distinct phases: (i) a rapid rise between 0500 and 1000 hrs.; (ii) a further, considerably slower rise between 1000 and about 2000 hrs.; (iii) a rapid fall between about 2000 and 0500 hrs. Thus the curve is not, as is sometimes suggested, a simple sinusoid.

There was no significant difference in the mean maximal range of temperatures recorded from the two personality groups ($t = 0.178$, $p = 0.22$); the peak-trough change was about $1.2°F$ in both groups. Inspection of the curves in Fig. 8 suggests that the temperature of the more introverted subjects rose more rapidly in the early morning and (possibly) started to fall at an earlier point in the late evening. This is brought out more clearly in Fig. 9, in which average temperatures are shown for only those subjects having Heron Inventory scores of either 2 or less (22 cases) or 5 or more (25 cases); again, there was no significant difference in mean temperature range for these more extreme personality groups ($t = 0.186$, $p = 0.21$). Analysis of variance of the temperatures of the extreme groups revealed a statistically significant interaction between Inventory score and time of day ($F_{19,855} = 1.85$, $p < 0.025$). It can therefore be concluded that the differences in the circadian rhythms shown in Fig. 9 are reliable.

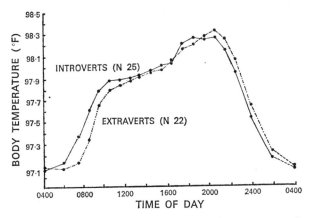

Figure 9. Mean circadian rhythm of body temperature in relatively extreme introvert and extravert groups.

Although relatively small, this relationship between personality, body temperature and time of day may help to explain the performance differences in introverts and extraverts, referred to previously, if it is assumed that temperature reflects the level of arousal of the nervous system, and that performance efficiency is related to this level. Comparative measurements with a variety of different groups would be necessary to determine whether the relationship (and also the form of the body temperature curve observed) is characteristic of the particular type of subject used, or whether it is typical of the population at large.

C*

REFERENCES

1. COLQUHOUN, W. P., Temperament, inspection efficiency and time of day. *Ergonomics*, **3**, 377–378, 1960.
2. —— & CORCORAN, D. W. J., The effects of time and day and social isolation on the relationship between temperament and performance. *Brit. J. Soc. Clin. Psychol.*, **3**, 226–231, 1964.
3. HERON, A., A two-part personality inventory for use as a research criterion. *Brit. J. Psychol.*, **47**, 243–251, 1956.
4. KLEITMAN, N., *Sleep and Wakefulness*. Chicago: University Press, 1963.

8

On the Unitary Nature of Extraversion

H. J. EYSENCK & SYBIL B. G. EYSENCK[1]

First published in *Acta Psychologica*, **26**, 383–390, 1967

STUDIES of extraversion-introversion as a dimension of personality have raised two difficult problems (Ref. 6): is extraversion a *unitary* dimension of personality, and are extraversion and neuroticism *independent* dimensions of personality? Carrigan reviewed the evidence and concluded (a) that 'unidimensionality of extraversion-introversion has not been conclusively demonstrated', and (b) that 'a clear-cut answer cannot be given' with respect to the independence of these two dimensions of personality (Ref. 1). In an earlier paper Eysenck & Eysenck have shown that one objection to the unitary nature of extraversion is not in fact tenable; sociability and impulsivity are not independent varieties of extraversion, but are significantly correlated with each other to form one supraordinate concept of extraversion (Ref. 10). This finding has since been duplicated by Sparrow & Ross (Ref. 12). The independence of E and N has been investigated in several large-scale factorial analyses, in which over 100 items previously found relevant to these two factors were intercorrelated and factor-analysed, for 600 men and 600 women separately; the method of rotation used was developed in our laboratory to permit analytic oblique rotation and extraction of higher-order factors (Ref. 11). Two higher orders factors, corresponding to E and N were found, and the angle between them did not deviate significantly from 90°, although the method of rotation did not prescribe independence of factors, but was determined entirely by the actual relationships obtaining within the data (Ref. 9). There is thus some evidence of both the unitary nature of extraversion, as well as of the independence of E and N. In this paper both problems will be taken up from a rather different point of view, which may throw some new light on this controversy.

Consider the conception of a factor as in some sense an underlying cause of the observed correlations (Ref. 5). The correlation of any given

[1] We are indebted to the Research Fund of the Maudsley and Bethlem Royal Hospitals for the support of this investigation.

test with that factor would then be an index of the degree to which that test measured that factor, i.e., its validity. If a criterion test could be found which correlated sufficiently highly with a given factor, i.e., which had sufficiently high validity as a measure of that factor, then it would be possible to use this test in a search for an answer to the two questions posed above. If the factor was unitary in nature, then the tests (or test items) constituting it should have correlations with the criterion which were *proportional* to their factor loadings, and if the factor was independent of another factor, then the criterion should not correlate significantly with any test (item) constituting this other factor.

The choice of the criterion test would of course be crucial in this argument. In the first place, the criterion should be chosen from a domain different from that from which the tests making up the factor were chosen. If the factor were determined by the intercorrelations between inventory items, then the criterion should not be an inventory item or a compound of inventory items. It could be a psychiatric diagnosis, as for instance in the studies using criterion analysis (Refs. 3 & 4), or it could be some objective behavioural test, or even some physiological reaction measure. Even more important is a second desideratum. The criterion should be chosen in such a way that it embodied a theory which predicted that it would be a good measure of one factor, but not of the other. Only by relating the criterion in some such way to explicit psychological (or physiological) theories about the nature of the factor in question can we hope to escape from the tautological arguments implicit in factor analysis.

The theory here chosen asserts that introversion is a product of cortical arousal, mediated by the reticular formation; introverts are habitually in a state of greater arousal than extraverts, and consequently they show lower sensory thresholds, and greater reactions to sensory stimulation. The theory in question has been discussed in great detail elsewhere (Ref. 7), as has the evidence regarding these and other deductions from it; on the whole the evidence, both physiological and psychological, appears to be in line with predictions made from the theory. The test used in the present investigation is the lemon test, so called because it measures the salivary reaction of subjects to the stimulus of having four drops of lemon juice placed upon the tongue for twenty seconds. The test was originally suggested by Corcoran, who has furnished data regarding its reliability and validity as a measure of extraversion (Ref. 2). The score on the test is the amount of salivation produced under lemon juice stimulating conditions, as compared with the amount of salivation produced under neutral conditions, i.e., when no lemon juice is present. Extreme extraverts show little or no increment in salivation, while extreme introverts show an increment of almost 1 gram; intermediate groups show intermediate amounts of increment. Eysenck & Eysenck have found a correlation of 0·71 on 50 male and 50 female Ss between increment scores and introversion, as measured by the EPI (Ref. 8); the correlation with N was effectively zero. No sex differences were observed.

The present analysis is concerned with results on the lemon test obtained from 45 men and 48 women, i.e. a total sample of 93 Ss; all these subjects formed part of the population of the above-mentioned study; 7 subjects were dropped because of failure to complete one question in the inventory. This inventory (the EPI Form A) contains 57 questions, of which 24 measure E, 24 measure N and the remainder constitute a Lie scale. The scores of the 93 Ss on the lemon test and the 57 questions of the EPI were intercorrelated, and the resulting 58×58 matrix of product-moment correlations factor-analysed by means of the principal components method, and rotated by means of the Promax Programme (Ref. 11). The first factor to emerge was clearly identified as extraversion, the second as neuroticism. Table 1 gives the items used, the scoring key (E, N, and L; when a minus sign follows the letter then the 'no' answer is scored positively), and the factor loadings for the first two factors. Item 58 is the increment score on the lemon test. It will be seen that the lemon test score has a loading of $-0·74$ on extraversion, and a completely insignificant one of 0·01 on neuroticism. The analysis was repeated for men and women separately; the factor loadings were $-0·70$ and $-0·60$ respectively on the E factor, and 0·02 and $-0·06$ on the N factor. Factor-analytically, then, the lemon test seems to be a pure (univocal) measure of introversion.

TABLE 1

1. Do you often long for excitement?	E	−0·48	0·33
2. Do you often need understanding friends to cheer you up?	N	−0·25	0·39
3. Are you usually carefree?	E	−0·36	−0·22
4. Do you find it very hard to take no for an answer?	N	−0·11	0·03
5. Do you stop and think things over before doing anything?	E−	0·40	−0·07
6. If you say you will do something do you always keep your promise, no matter how inconvenient it might be to do so?	L	0·07	−0·09

7. Does your mood often go up and down?	N	0·01	0·56
8. Do you generally do and say things quickly without stopping to think?	E	−0·57	0·12
9. Do you ever feel 'just miserable' for no good reason?	N	−0·02	0·49
10. Would you do almost anything for a dare?	E	−0·32	−0·05
11. Do you suddenly feel shy when you want to talk to an attractive stranger?	N	0·29	0·46
12. Once in a while do you lose your temper and get angry?	L−	0·22	0·19
13. Do you often do things on the spur of the moment?	E	−0·53	0·13
14. Do you often worry about things you should not have done or said?	N	0·17	0·61
15. Generally, do you prefer reading to meeting people?	E−	0·71	−0·02
16. Are your feelings rather easily hurt?	N	0·26	0·46
17. Do you like going out a lot?	E	−0·63	0·07
18. Do you occasionally have thoughts and ideas that you would not like other people to know about?	L−	0·09	0·28
19. Are you sometimes bubbling over with energy and sometimes very sluggish?	N	−0·17	0·57
20. Do you prefer to have few but special friends?	E−	0·40	0·06
21. Do you daydream a lot?	N	−0·05	0·66
22. When people shout at you, do you shout back?	E	−0·29	0·05
23. Are you often troubled about feelings of guilt?	N	−0·02	0·57
24. Are *all* your habits good and desirable ones?	L	−0·16	−0·00
25. Can you usually let yourself go and enjoy yourself a lot at a gay party?	E	−0·74	−0·00
26. Would you call yourself tense or 'highly-strung'?	N	0·08	0·07
27. Do other people think of you as being very lively?	E	−0·53	−0·27
28. After you have done something important, do you often come away feeling you could have done better?	N	0·20	0·50
29. Are you mostly quiet when you are with other people?	E−	0·62	0·21
30. Do you sometimes gossip?	L−	−0·07	0·07
31. Do ideas run through your head so that you cannot sleep?	N	−0·25	0·35
32. If there is something you want to know about, would you rather look it up in a book than talk to someone about it?	E−	0·54	−0·13
33. Do you get palpitations or thumping in your heart?	N	−0·20	0·35
34. Do you like the kind of work that you need to pay close attention to?	E−	0·22	0·01
35. Do you get attacks of shaking or trembling?	N	−0·25	0·50
36. Would you always declare everything at the Customs, even if you knew that you could never be found out?	L	0·12	0·13
37. Do you hate being with a crowd who play jokes on one another?	E−	0·49	−0·22
38. Are you an irritable person?	N	0·07	0·26

39. Do you like doing things in which you have to act quickly?	E	−0·39	−0·27
40. Do you worry about awful things that might happen?	N	−0·16	0·31
41. Are you slow and unhurried in the way you move?	E−	0·25	0·11
42. Have you ever been late for an appointment or work?	L−	−0·02	0·06
43. Do you have many nightmares?	N	−0·18	0·38
44. Do you like talking to people so much that you never miss a chance of talking to a stranger?	E	−0·25	0·02
45. Are you troubled by aches and pains?	N	−0·23	0·08
46. Would you be very unhappy if you could not see lots of people most of the time?	E	−0·40	−0·11
47. Would you call yourself a nervous person?	N	0·06	0·24
48. Of all the people you know, are there some whom you definitely do not like?	L−	0·07	0·04
49. Would you say that you were fairly self-confident?	E	−0·27	−0·51
50. Are you easily hurt when people find fault with you or your work?	N	0·35	0·36
51. Do you find it hard to really enjoy yourself at a lively party?	E−	0·65	−0·05
52. Are you troubled with feelings of inferiority?	N	0·01	0·73
53. Can you easily get some life into a rather dull party?	E	−0·48	−0·36
54. Do you sometimes talk about things you know nothing about?	L−	−0·08	0·20
55. Do you worry about your health?	N	0·04	−0·18
56. Do you like playing pranks on others?	E	−0·32	0·06
57. Do you suffer from sleeplessness?	N	−0·21	0·17
58. Lemon Test		−0·74	0·02

If, as pointed out above, the lemon test may be regarded as a relatively pure criterion test of E, then (1) its correlations with the individual items of the E scale should be proportional to the factor loadings of that scale, and (2) its correlations with the individual items of the N scale should be effectively zero. Such a test might have been carried out on the factor loadings obtained in this study, and given in Table 1; however, it might have been objected that such a comparison capitalizes on whatever non-relevant factors were present on the occasion of this experiment and might have influenced both the EPI responses of the Ss and their lemon test scores. Consequently we have chosen to use factor loadings obtained in a different and much larger study, using 500 Ss, half men, half women, who had been given the same items printed in Table 1, together with another 50 items (Ref. 9). This whole matrix of 107 × 107 items had been factor analysed in the same manner as the matrix discussed above, i.e., by means of the principal components method, followed by Promax rotation. In this manner the scales are weighted against our hypothesis;

not only are the factor loadings derived from a different population from that from which the item correlations with the lemon test are obtained, but in addition the factor analysis was carried out on a sample of items different from, and larger than, that used in our present experiment and factor analysis.

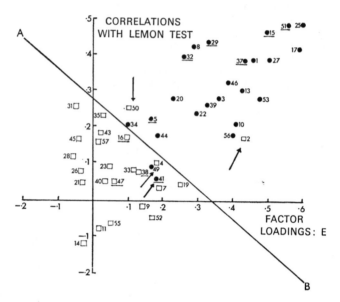

Figure 10. Factor loadings on extraversion (abscissa) and correlations with lemon test (ordinate) of neuroticism items (squares) and extraversion items (circles).

Results are shown in Fig. 10, where factor loadings have been plotted along the abscissa, the item correlations with the lemon test along the ordinate. Items constituting the E scale have been printed as dots, items constituting the N scale, as squares. L scale items, being irrelevant to this comparison, have been omitted in order not to confuse the picture. Items with negative loadings larger than 0·10 have been reversed in sign (multiplied by −1); these items have been indicated by underlining. It will be seen that practically all the E items have both high factor loadings on the extraversion factor and reasonable correlations with the lemon test, whereas N items have low loadings and low correlations. The line A-B has been drawn at the (arbitrary) level approximating a correlation value of 0·3, to divide the diagram into two parts; to the right (i.e., in quadrant 1) are the high loading—high correlation values; to the left are the low loading—low correlation values.[1] The former should be E items, the latter N items; it will be clear that in fact this is so. There are only two N items to the right of the line, and two E items to the left; arrows have been inserted to point to these four values. It will be seen that for all items (both E and N) having loadings of 0·20 or above, correlation with the lemon test are 0·15 or higher; at loadings below 0·15, only three are above 0·20. There is thus a remarkable correspondence between the two sets of values.

It is obvious to the eye that the correlation values are roughly proportional to the factor loadings for the E items; a correlation was made both with and without regard for signs. Both correlations are positive, with the former of course much larger; the actual values are 0·97 and 0·71. Both are sufficiently larger to allow us to say that the view that the items of the EPI extraversion scale measure a factor which is, as far as this experiment is concerned, unitary. This outcome is particularly reassuring in view of the fact that the criterion test used was chosen on the basis of quite specific theories regarding the psychological and physiological nature of extraversion and introversion; only by thus extending the circular arguments of broader coverage can we bring together the psychometric and experimental approaches.

SUMMARY

Scores of salivary reactivity to lemon juice were intercorrelated with 57 personality questionnaire items for 45 men and 48 women, and the matrix of correlations factor analysed. Two factors corresponding to extraversion and neuroticism were extracted; the lemon test score had a loading of −0·74 on the former, and of 0·02 on the latter, confirming theoretical predictions. It was also shown that questionnaire items having high loadings on E were also highly correlated with the lemon test score, while items having low loadings had low correlations. The implications of these findings were discussed for the unidimensional nature of extraversion, and for the independence of extraversion and neuroticism.

[1] The line is actually slanted towards the right because the average size of the factor loadings is greater than the average size of the correlations in the ratio of 6/5; in order to compensate for this, the intercepts of the line on abscissa and ordinate have been changed from 0·3 to be in roughly the same proportion.

REFERENCES

1. CARRIGAN, P. M., Extraversion-introversion as a dimension of personality: a reappraisal. *Psychol. Bull.*, **57**, 329–360, 1960.
2. CORCORAN, D. W. J., The relation between introversion and salivation. *Amer. J. Psychol.*, **77**, 298–300, 1964.
3. EYSENCK, H. J., Criterion analysis—an application of the hypothetico-deductive method to factor analysis. *Psychol. Rev.*, **57**, 38–53, 1950.
4. ——, Schizothymia-cyclothymia as a dimension of personality. *J. Pers.*, **20**, 345–384, 1952.
5. ——, The logical basis of factor analysis. *Amer. Psychologist*, **8**, 105–114, 1953.
6. ——, *The Structure of Human Personality*. London: Methuen, 1960.
7. ——, *The Biological Basis of Personality*. Springfield, Ill.: C. C. Thomas, 1967.
8. —— & EYSENCK, S. B. G., *The Eysenck Personality Inventory*. London: Univ. of London Press, 1965.
9. —— & ——, *Personality Structure and Measurement*. London: Routledge & Kegan Paul, 1967.
10. EYSENCK, S. B. G. & EYSENCK, H. J., On the dual nature of extraversion. *Brit. J. soc. clin. Psychol.*, **2**, 46–55, 1963.
11. HENDRICKSON, A. & WHITE, P. O., Promax: a quick method for rotation to oblique simple structure. *Brit. J. Stat. Psychol.*, **17**, 65–70, 1964.
12. SPARROW, N. H. & ROSS, J., The dual nature of extraversion: a replication. *Austral. J. Psychol.*, **16**, 214–218, 1964.

Sensory Stimulation and Deprivation

Editor's Introduction

IT is possible to make direct and verifiable deductions from the theory briefly outlined in the last section to the field of sensory stimulation and deprivation. High cortical arousal (introversion) can be seen to act as an amplifying valve for incoming sensory stimulation, while low cortical arousal (extraversion) can be seen to act as an inhibitor for incoming sensory stimulation, compared with the average degree of arousal (ambiversion). Thus sensory thresholds would be expected to be lower in introverts, higher in extraverts; as we shall see, this prediction is indeed borne out in several studies. However, it is possible to make other deductions by linking the views so far expressed with a general law in psychology relating in a curvilinear fashion level of stimulation with hedonic tone (adience and abience). This law, and the predictions to be made, are illustrated in Fig. 11, which is taken from the writer's *Experiments with Drugs* (Ref. 1).

The thickly drawn line shows that mean levels of sensory stimulation are in general preferred; high levels (pain) and low levels (sensory deprivation) are both known to be avoided. For reasons discussed in the

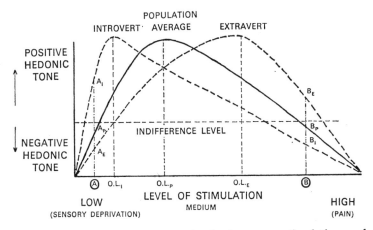

Figure 11. Relationship between level of sensory stimulation and hedonic tone, showing expected shift of introverted subjects to the left and extraverted subjects to the right. From H. J. Eysenck, *Experiments with Drugs*. Oxford: Pergamon Press, 1963.

previous paragraph, the curve for introverts is shifted towards the left, that for extraverts towards the right; in other words, introverts should tolerate sensory deprivation better than extraverts, and pain less well. The letters O.L. refer to optimum level of preference; E, P and I to extravert, population average, and introvert. A and B are two arbitrarily chosen points on the stimulation continuum at which marked differences in predicted hedonic tone are found between extraverts and introverts.

Yet another set of results can be predicted when it is realized that vigilance tests depend for their successful performance on high levels of cortical arousal; extraverts would be expected to perform poorly, introverts relatively well. Possibly inhibition plays a part here too but since such differences would lead to identical predictions, it is difficult to differentiate between the two alternative theories. Not many studies have been done in this field, but those which are available suggest that the theory is along the right lines.

H.J.E.

REFERENCE

1. EYSENCK, H. J. (ed.), *Experiments with Drugs*. Oxford: Pergamon Press, 1963.

9

Extraversion and Sensory Threshold[1]

STUART L. SMITH[2]

First published in *Psychophysiology*, **5**, 293–299, 1968

IT was predicted that introverts would have lower auditory thresholds than extraverts, in line with other physiological differences between these groups. Using an ear-choice technique and controlling the factor of guessing, the prediction was verified, using non-patients who score at the two ends of the Eysenck Personality Inventory. The extraverted behaviour of hysterics and psychopaths has been thought to have partly a constitutional or physiological basis and this experiment points in that direction.

Physiological differences in the nervous systems of patients with hysterical traits or psychopathic personality have been suggested on the basis of the ease with which such patients tire and become bored, and the difficulty they have in controlling impulses and acquiring conditioned responses.

Hysterics and psychopaths are marked by a high degree of extraversion (Ref. 4). This and other facts have given rise to the postulation of differences in the nervous systems of introverts and extraverts.

Eysenck following Pavlov, has argued that extraverts are marked by an excess of 'inhibition' in the cortex and he has postulated that they are relatively insensitive to sensory stimuli (Ref. 4). Teplov (quoted in Ref. 5) feels that the 'strong' nervous system, in some ways very similar to Eysenck's 'extravert', is less sensitive to stimuli, and Witkin, speaking of field dependence, points to differences between extraverted hysterical people and others, in perceptual studies (Ref. 10).

This study is an effort to test the hypothesis that extraverts have higher sensory, in this case, auditory, thresholds than introverts. To avoid any

[1] Grateful acknowledgement is made to Professor H. J. Eysenck for advice and criticism; also to the Tobacco Research Foundation whose funds were used to pay the subjects.

[2] Work done while holder of a travelling fellowship from the R. Samuel McLaughlin Foundation, Canada. The author is now Clinical Associate, Department of Psychiatry, McMaster University, Hamilton, Ontario, Canada.

post-experimental criticism that differences found might be due to possible difference in reporting or guessing patterns which may vary systematically between subject groups, the threshold was obtained by the standard technique but with the use of a simple guessing correction and also under conditions of forced choice.

The thresholds were also retested under forced choice conditions for all subjects after small doses of drugs (seconal 90 m.gms., nicotine 0·2 m.gms. and placebo). This was done to see whether any differences found between groups would hold up under various conditions, and also to see whether, unlikely as it seemed, even small doses of drugs would affect threshold. Small doses had to be used since subjects had to receive both drugs in one day and drive home by themselves.

Blackwell has shown that forced-choice techniques give stable and useful threshold measures (Ref. 1) and Swets (Ref. 9) and others (Ref. 11) have used such methods in the study of the decision-making process and signal detection. The forced choice technique used by these authors for measuring auditory threshold has been one in which tones are presented singly or in pairs or in one of two or more time intervals. Because this could be claimed to require an additional skill such as a memory geared to compared recent events with past ones, an ear choice method was adopted in this experiment. It is a method similar to that used in some screening tests (Refs. 2 & 8), although it has not been used on a forced-choice basis heretofore, as far as one can determine.

Forced-choice thresholds were said to be insensitive to certain drugs but no details of the testing have been provided (Ref. 7).

It was decided to test normals (i.e., non-patients) who lie near the ends of the extraversion and neuroticism scales of the Eysenck Personality Inventory.

METHOD

Apparatus: Peters clinic Audiometer; Model—SPD5, Alfred Peters & Son Ltd., England; a timer in circuit to cut off tones automatically at 135 m/sec. Morse signal key with flash-light bulbs. 6v. battery.

Method: Single tones were presented to one ear at a time. The choice of ear was random but equal numbers of presentations were made to the right and left sides. No masking was used.

Duration of tone: 135 m/sec.
Frequency: 500 cps.

Subjects: Ss were 12 male volunteers, paid for their services. All were office workers at various establishments. They were chosen in four groups of three people each. Each group was selected on the basis of E.P.I. scores so that it consisted of individuals with E scores and N scores which were high or low (more than one S.D. from the mean) in the four possible combinations. Between the two groups who differed significantly on E score, there was no significant difference in N score; similarly between people high and low on N score, there was no significant difference in E score. The mean age of the subjects was 35·8 years and the personality sub-group means did not differ significantly with respect to this variable (Table 1). They were also given the Taylor Manifest Anxiety Scale. Table 1 gives the means of these measurements.

Subject and experimenter were alone in a dark sound-proofed room. S was seated in a chair facing away from E. Tones were played through earphones.

The onset of each tone was announced one second earlier by a flash of light. S responded by pressing a Morse key either on the right or on the left, thus flashing the appropriate one of two lights in front of E and avoiding the necessity to speak.

All Ss were tested without E knowing their personality category.

An initial estimate of S's threshold was made using one ear at a time and it was ascertained whether the two ears were equal in acuity. This took about five minutes to perform. A tone well above threshold was chosen to begin the testing proper.

S was told that a tone would be played after each light flash but that many would be beyond his range of hearing. He was instructed to signal to the E according to whether he heard the tone in the R or L ear.

Yes-No Technique: S was instructed to 'listen for each tone' and to 'signal appropriately whenever able to tell on which side the tone was played'.

Forced-Choice Technique: S was instructed to 'listen for each tone' and then to 'signal appropriately on *every* presentation irrespective of whether confident' the tone had been heard. He was told: 'Please make a genuine guess at each tone; please do not guess according to some fixed pattern'.

Tones at any one loudness level were played in groups of five. A test session consisted of playing such groups of tones, starting with a loudness level where all five tones were identified correctly until a 'low point' was reached; then ascending similarly to a 'high point', then descending and ascending again.

TABLE 1

SUBJECTS: MEAN AGE AND TEST SCORES

	Mean Age	Mean E score	Mean N score	Mean MAS[1] score
High extraversion	35·33 ($\sigma = 10·5$)	17·67 ($\sigma = 1·6$)	10·67 ($\sigma = 6·9$)	13·17 ($\sigma = 8·5$)
Low extraversion	38·17 ($\sigma = 8·4$)	5·50 ($\sigma = 2·7$)	9·33 ($\sigma = 6·9$)	14·33 ($\sigma = 10·3$)
High neuroticism	38·00 ($\sigma = 8·7$)	11·17 ($\sigma = 6·9$)	16·67 ($\sigma = 2·1$)	21·17 ($\sigma = 7·4$)
Low neuroticism	35·50 ($\sigma = 10·5$)	12·00 ($\sigma = 6·0$)	3·33 ($\sigma = 1·4$)	6·33 ($\sigma = 6·6$)

There were no heavy smokers but there were three light smokers whose scores did not differ from those in their personality groups at any time.

[1] The MAS scores were taken merely to confirm the neuroticism classification in this experiment.

Results were recorded by the experimenter who noted the number of correct responses at each loudness level during 'ascent' and 'descent'. There was a maximum of twenty presentations at each loudness level.

Scoring

The score for any one loudness level was registered as the number correct out of the total presentations at that level during the session. This 'raw score' was suitable for forced-choice experiments. A 'guessing correction' was made however, to the yes-no scores to make them comparable to the forced-choice scores, and to control for possible differences in risk-taking. Since it is to be assumed that if guessing took place on a random basis, 50 per cent of those tones not guessed at in the testing would in fact have been guessed correctly, the scores during the yes-no technique were augmented by a number equal to half the number of presentations at which there was no guess attempted by the subject. Only in this way could the results by forced-choice and yes-no techniques be comparable. Failure to make this 'guessing correction', gives spuriously large differences between the techniques.

Threshold Determination

The threshold for any one test was determined by choosing the loudness level at which the score correct was such that it was probable beyond the 5 per cent level of significance (one-tailed test) that it was better than chance. The significant values were as follows: 8 correct out of 10 presentations; 11 out of 15; 14 out of 20; 17 out of 25; 20 out of 30; 23 out of 35; 26 out of 40; 28 out of 45; 31 out of 50; 34 out of 55; 37 out of 60.

All decisions about threshold were made without knowledge of the personality of the subject or of the drug condition.

Two Ss showed a slight difference in acuity between the Right and Left ear. For them, tones in the weaker ear were always played at a slightly higher loudness level. Their thresholds were determined in the usual way and the mean of the two threshold loudness levels was taken as S's threshold.

Balanced Order

All Ss had a forced-choice and yes-no threshold test for the first 40 minutes of testing; half the Ss within each personality group had the yes-no condition first and half had forced-choice testing first.

Next, all Ss had the 3 drugs, seconal, nicotine and placebo in varying

TABLE 2

Experimental Design and Individual Results

Subject	EPI score Rating	Order of Basic Testing (YN vs FC)	Drug Order Sec.	Drug Order Nic.	Drug Order Plac.	Results: Thresholds under each condition YN	FC	Placebo	Seconal	Nicotine
1	EN	YN. FC	P	S	N	+7	+4	+3	+2	+3
2	EN	YN. FC	N	S	P	−1	−6	−4	0	−3
3	EN	FC. YN	S	N	P	−1	+1	+1	0	+1
4	En	YN. FC	S	P	N	+10	+3	0	+1	+1
5	En	FC. YN	N	P	S	+2	+3	−7	−5	−4
6	En	FC. YN	P	N	S	+3	+2	0	+6	+1
7	eN	YN. FC	N	P	S	0	+1	−1	−4	−6
8	eN	FC. YN	P	N	S	0	−5	−8	−4	−6
9	eN	FC. YN	S	P	N	−7	−10	−8	−10	−7
10	en	YN. FC	N	S	P	+3	+5	−4	−5	+3
11	en	YN. FC	P	S	N	−4·5	−3·5	−5·5	−5·5	−5·5
12	en	FC. YN	S	N	P	−2	−2	−3	−2	0

Legend: E = High Extraversion score
e = Low Extraversion score
N = High Neuroticism score
n = Low Neuroticism score
YN = 'Yes-No' technique
FC = Forced Choice technique
P = Placebo p.o.
S = Seconal 90 mg p.o.
N = Nicotine 0·2 mg s.l.

TABLE 3

MEAN THRESHOLD[1]: EXTRAVERTS VS INTROVERTS

Condition	Extravert	Introvert	Difference (E–I)	t (one-tailed)[2]	p
Yes-No Technique (Adjusted)	+3·33	−1·75	5·08	2·21	<0·05
Forced Choice Technique	+1·17	−2·42	3·59	1·42	>0·05 <0·10
After Seconal	+0·67	−5·08	5·75	3·16	<0·01
After Nicotine	−0·17	−3·58	3·41	1·71	>0·05 <0·10
After Placebo	−1·17	−4·92	3·75	1·97	<0·05
Overall Mean	+0·77	−3·55	4·32	2·54	<0·05

[1] Thresholds are expressed in terms of Hearing Loss Units (db). Zero indicates average normal threshold; positive values mean a raised threshold and negative values, a lower one.

[2] df =10

sequence so that the main personality groups were balanced evenly with regard to order of drug administration.

Drug Administration

Doses were as follows: Nicotine (sub-lingually) 0·2 mg.; Seconal (orally) 90·0 mg.; Placebo—one white tablet orally—*No Drug.* Subjects were tested (15 minute testing session) after allowing time for absorption. Before administration of the next drug, time was allowed for effects to wear off as follows: For nicotine—1 hour and 40 minutes; for Seconal —3 hours; for placebo—5 minutes. The Experimental Design and Individual Results are given in Table 2.

RESULTS

The outstanding result (Table 3) shows that thresholds for the introverted group were considerably lower than those for the extraverted subjects under all conditions. Despite the small number of subjects, these results were significant for most individual conditions, dipping just slightly below significant levels ($p < 10$) for nicotine and initial forced-choice conditions. The difference between the means of the two groups was significant.

All other differences were insignificant. The pre-drug and post-drug means for the High Neuroticism group were $-1·42$ and $-2·83$; for the Low Ns. $+1·59$ and $-1·92$. The mean using the forced-choice technique ($-0·63$) was lower than that with the corrected yes-no technique ($+0·79$), but not significantly so. Had the uncorrected scores been used the difference would certainly have been significant, though spurious.

Neither seconal (mean $-2·21$) nor nicotine (mean $-1·88$) caused

TABLE 4

ANALYSIS OF VARIANCE: DRUG CONDITIONS

	df	ss	ms	F	P
Between E	1	166·8403	166·8403	6·84	0·05
Between N	1	7·5625	7·5625	—	N.S.
Between Drugs	2	8·6667	4·3333	1·00	N.S.
E × N	1	37·0069	37·0069	1·52	N.S.
Between people within groups	8	195·2778	24·4097		
Residual	22	95·3333	4·3333		
Total	35	510·6875			

thresholds to differ significantly from placebo levels (mean $-3 \cdot 04$); this, despite the reporting of numerous subjective effects from the 90 mg. dose of seconal. An analysis of the variance during the drug experiments is in Table 4.

There was an improvement in threshold between the pre-drug and the drug sessions, irrespective of which drugs were used. Although this might be regarded as a placebo effect, the results from pilot studies make it far more likely that this is in fact a practice effect.

DISCUSSION

This is thought to be the first report linking personality with sensory threshold.

The main result is the finding that introverts have significantly lower auditory thresholds than extraverts as measured by an ear-choice method. This difference, in line with the predictions, appears to hold whether testing is done under yes-no or forced-choice conditions and also whether or not small doses of drugs are used.

Although the forced-choice technique gave lower threshold values than corrected yes-no techniques, suggesting a sub-threshold 'awareness', the difference was not significant. The $0 \cdot 2$ mg. of nicotine failed to cause thresholds to differ from placebo values and, although the 90 mg. seconal was followed by raised thresholds, mainly in the extraverts, this change was far from significant. It may be that higher doses of drugs are necessary to produce an effect; it may be that this particular experimental technique is such that the seconal causes artificially low thresholds by causing subjects to keep still; it may be that such drugs simply do not affect sensory threshold, at least when a forced-choice technique is used; or it may be that CNS drugs have atypical effects on subjects who are at the extreme ends of various personality dimensions.

Gray, in discussing the work at Teplov's laboratory in U.S.S.R., has taken some steps toward identifying the Russian concept of 'strength' of the nervous system with that of 'arousal' (Ref. 5). Eysenck has argued that his measure of introversion is related to 'cortical excitation', and extraversion to 'excessive inhibition'. The 'inhibition' theory has been supported by Eysenck for some time (Ref. 3) but he has recently suggested the physiological basis of the hypothesized 'excitation' to be higher arousal levels, presumably due to a relatively excitatory reticular activating system (Ref. 4). Since 'inhibition' in Eysenckian terms, is unlikely to play a part in auditory threshold determination, the results of this experiment may be thought to give some support to the idea that *introverts* are marked by higher levels of excitation or *arousal* than are extraverts. As mentioned earlier, he has considered that introverts would be more easily aroused by stimulation than extraverts would be and he used this postulated relative lack of sensitivity in extraverts to account, in part, for the preferences shown by extraverts for strong sensations. Whether, at the other end of the scale, extraverts are better able to tolerate very high levels of sensation has not been proved, although the greater pain tolerance of extraverts is suggestive of such a state of affairs (Ref. 6).

The results of this experiment would appear to point in the direction of physiological differences in the nervous systems of extraverts and introverts and, by inference, lend further support to the concept of a physiological difference between hysterics (and psychopaths) and others.

REFERENCES

1. BLACKWELL, H. R., Psychophysical thresholds—experimental studies of measurement. *Engineering Res. Bull.*, No.36. Engineering Research Institute, University of Michigan, Ann Arbor, 1953.
2. CURRY, E. T. & KURTZROCK, G. H., A preliminary investigation of the ear-choice technique in threshold audiometry. *J. Speech & Hearing Disorders*, **16**, 340–345, 1951.
3. EYSENCK, H. J., *Dynamics of Anxiety and Hysteria*. London: Routledge & Kegan Paul, 1957.
4. ——, Personality and drug effects. In: *Experiments with Drugs* (ed. H. J. Eysenck). Oxford: Pergamon Press, 1963.
5. GRAY, J. A., *Pavlov's Typology: Recent Theoretical and Experimental Developments from the Laboratory of B.M. Teplov*. Oxford: Pergamon Press, 1964.
6. LYNN, R. & EYSENCK, H. J., Tolerance for pain, extraversion and neuroticism. *Percept. mot. Skills*, **12**, 161–162, 1961.
7. MILLER, J. G., Drugs and human information processing: perception, cognition and response. In: *Drugs and Behaviour* (ed. L. Uhr and J. G. Miller). New York: John Wiley & Sons, 1960.
8. NAGEL, R. F., Evaluation of ear-choice technique. *Dissertation Abstract*, **17**, 435, 1957.

9. SWETS, J. A., Indices of signal detectability obtained with various psychophysical procedures. *J. Acoust. Soc. Amer.*, **31,** 511–513, 1959.
10. WITKIN, H. A., *Psychological Differentiation.* New York: Wiley & Sons, 1962.
11. ZWISLOCKI, J., MARIE, F., FELDMAN, A. S. & RUBIN, H., On the effects of practice and motivation on threshold of audibility. *J. Acoust. Soc. Amer.*, **30,** 254–262, 1958.

D

Effect of Some Personality Variables on Electrical Vestibular Stimulation[1]

JOHN J. DUNSTONE, ERNEST DZENDOLET &
OTTO HEUCKEROTH

First published in
Perceptual and Motor Skills, **18**, 689–695, 1964

SEVENTEEN graduate student Ss were divided into higher and lower scoring groups on 13 scales of the MMPI. Their objective and subjective absolute thresholds (RLs) to sinusoidal electrical stimulation at 1·0 and 0·20 cps, applied by electrodes on the mastoid processes, were determined, and a mean difference score between these RLs was calculated. Analyses of variance showed that significant differences were present at 0·20 cps in the objective RLs for the Depression, Social Introversion-Extraversion, and Manifest Anxiety scales, in the subjective RL for Paranoia, and in the difference score for Paranoia. At 1·0 cps, significant differences occurred in the subjective RLs for the Hysteria, Psychopathic Deviate, and Paranoia scales, and in the difference score for Paranoia. The results with the Manifest Anxiety scale were discussed in terms of a Hull-Spence framework. The lowering of the objective RLs at 0·20 cps was discussed as a possible mechanism for facilitating the appearance of motion sickness symptoms.

INTRODUCTION

In an earlier study (Ref. 1), the development of criteria for objectively determining the absolute threshold (RL) for a lateral sway response to low-frequency sinusoidal electrical stimulation of the human vestibular apparatus was reported. The objective RL can be contrasted with the subjective RL which is based on the verbal report of a human S. A plot of either of these RLs expressed in milliamperes (ma) against the stimu-

[1] This investigation was supported in part by Public Health Service Research Grant NB–03675–02 from the National Institute of Neurological Diseases and Blindness.

lating frequencies in cycles per second (cps) has been termed the electrical vestibulogram. In that paper, it was noted that some Ss did not report a sensation of swaying although they could be seen by E to be swaying, in addition to which the objective criterion mentioned above showed that the stimulus was above the RL. Other Ss did, however, report that they were swaying, very close to the time when they reached the objective criteria for the RL. It was originally hoped that this objective technique would avoid the possible interference of subjective or personality factors in obtaining an electrical vestibulogram, such as might enter when a vestibulogram based on subjective report was determined. The present study was undertaken to test directly whether or not there were personality variables involved which would be related to the difference between objective and subjective RLs. That personality might be a factor was indicated in a review by Meehl in which it was pointed out that a number of quantitative studies had indicated that schizophrenics showed a marked dysfunction of the vestibular system (Ref. 11). It was of interest, therefore, to see whether or not other personality variables would also show some effect upon RLs for electrical vestibular stimulation.

METHOD

Apparatus

The apparatus was the same as that used earlier (Ref. 1), except that only two stimulus frequencies were employed in the present experiment. These were 0·20 and 1·0 cps, and were chosen because they appeared to represent different types of responses in Ss. This assumption was based on data from an earlier experiment in which quality reports to stimuli of 1·0 and 2·0 cps were predominantly of oscillation of the head and torso, whereas they were of swaying sideways to stimuli from 0·05 to 0·5 cps. In addition, both subjective and objective vestibulograms showed separate minima within these ranges (Ref. 1, Figs. 3 and 4).

Subjects

There were 16 males and 3 females originally, all graduate students in the Department of Psychology at the University of Massachusetts. Two males were eliminated because they showed rhythmical lateral swaying in the absence of the stimulus. Participation in this and a number of other experiments, was required in a graduate course entitled 'Theories of Personality'.[1]

[1] The authors wish to thank Dr R. H. Harrison, the instructor, for his valuable advice and comments.

Procedure

Personality Tests: The MMPI was administered to all Ss early in the semester during two laboratory sessions, with half of the Ss in each session. The raw scores were obtained by means of hand-scoring stencils for the following scales: Hypochondriasis (Hs), Depression (D), Hysteria (Hy), Psychopathic Deviate (Pd), Interest (Mf), Paranoia (Pa), Psychasthenia (Pt), Schizophrenia (Sc), Hypomania (Ma). Social Introversion-Extraversion (Si), Neuroticism, Manifest Anxiety (MAS), and Ego-Strength. The raw scores on all scales except Ego-Strength, MAS, and Neuroticism were converted to T-scores according to norms in the revised MMPI Manual (Ref. 5). In addition, the norms adjusted by Hathaway & Briggs (Ref. 4) for Hs, Pd, Pt, Sc, and Ma were used.

The final scores on each scale were ranked, and Ss were assigned to either a high or a low category with respect to the particular scale on the basis of two considerations: (1) it was desired to have approximately one-half of the Ss in each category, (2) it was desired to maximize the differences between the two categories so that there would be a maximum spread between the highest score on a scale obtained by the low category and the lowest score obtained by Ss classified in the high category. When the second consideration could not be applied because of the homogeneity of scores, the first consideration alone was used to determine the basis of sorting. Anonymity of Ss was maintained by the assignment of code numbers and the utilization of other masking procedures with regard to the personality tests and the vestibular thresholds to be discussed below.

Absolute Thresholds: In the latter part of the semester, each S had his subjectively and objectively based RLs determined. The same psychophysical method and scoring criteria were used as reported earlier (Ref. 10), except that each of the two frequencies used was presented five times in random order to each S in one session. Ss were not required to describe their sensations, but merely to indicate by pressing a switch if they swayed. Authors J.J.D. and O.H. each served as E for one-half of Ss. A third measure, the difference score, was also used. This was computed by subtracting the objective from the subjective RL for each S at each frequency at each session. The mean of these differences for each S was then calculated and used in the analysis.

RESULTS

The data were analysed by simple randomized, or single factor, analyses of variance[1] with adjustment for unequal cell frequencies (Ref. 15, p. 96). Since such an analysis showed no significant difference between males and females for the two RLs and for the difference scores on each of the scales, the data were pooled. Of the 13 scales used in this study, six gave significant results which were divided in different ways among the various stimuli and measures employed. Because of the relative homogeneity of scores on these tests, significance levels of up to 0·1 are reported.

TABLE 1

ABSOLUTE THRESHOLDS (RL) IN MILLIAMPERES FOR ELECTRICAL VESTIBULAR STIMULATION AT 1·0 CPS, AND THE DIFFERENCE SCORE BETWEEN OBJECTIVE AND SUBJECTIVE RLs AS A FUNCTION OF SCORES ON PERSONALITY SCALES: HYSTERIA (HY), PSYCHOPATHIC DEVIATE (PD) AND PARANOIA (PA)

Scale	Score	Subjective RL	Diff. score
Hy	High	1·19	
	Low	0·53 ($p<0·1$)	
Pd	High	1·00	
	Low	0·31 ($p<0·1$)	
Pa	High	1·15	0·78
	Low	0·35 ($p<0·025$)	0·18 ($p<0·1$)

1·0 cps

Objective RL: There were no significant effects with this stimulus frequency.

Subjective RL: The higher scoring groups on the Hy, Pd, and Pa scales gave higher thresholds. These were significant at the 0·1, 0·025, and 0·1 levels, respectively.

Difference Score: A significant difference occurred only with the Pa scale, and at the 0·1 level.

0·2 cps

Objective RL: Significant differences occurred with the D, Si, and MAS scales, at the 0·1, 0·05, and 0·1 levels, respectively. The differences were all in the same direction, in that higher scorers on these scales had lower RLs.

[1] Print-outs for the analyses of variance have been filed with the American Documentation Institute, Auxiliary Publications Projects, Photoduplication Service, Library of Congress, Washington 25, D.C. Order Document No. 7888, remitting $6·25 for photocopies or $2·50 for 35 mm. microfilm.

TABLE 2

ABSOLUTE THRESHOLDS (RL) IN MILLIAMPERES FOR ELECTRICAL VESTIBULAR STIMULATION AT 0·20 CPS AND THE DIFFERENCE SCORE BETWEEN OBJECTIVE AND SUBJECTIVE RLS AS A FUNCTION OF SCORES ON PERSONALITY SCALES: DEPRESSION (D), PARANOIA (PA), SOCIAL INTROVERSION-EXTRAVERSION (SI) AND MANIFEST ANXIETY (MAS)

Scale	Score	Objective RL	Subjective RL	Diff. score
D	High	0·07		
	Low	0·17 (p<0·1)		
Pa	High		1·70	0·98
	Low		0·55 (p<0·1)	0·36 (p<0·1)
Si	High	0·05		
	Low	0·17 (p<0·05)		
MAS	High	0·07		
	Low	0·18 (p<0·1)		

Subjective RL: Only the Pa scale showed significance at the 0·1 level, with the direction of the difference being the same as with the 1·0-cps stimulus. Higher scores gave higher RLs.

Difference Score: The Pa scale was also significant here at the 0·1 level, again just as with the 1·0-cps stimulus.

DISCUSSION

One of the primary questions of this study, whether or not Ss scoring higher on the Sc scale would have significantly higher objective RLs, was not positively answered. The tendency, however, was in the hypothesized direction.

On the other hand, Ss scoring higher on the D, Si, and MAS scales did have significantly lower absolute RLs. Because these RLs all varied in the same direction, rank-difference correlations (Ref. 8, pp. 158–159) were computed for the MAS and D scores, and the MAS and Si scores. Coefficients of 0·45 (p<0·05) and 0·72 (p<0·01), respectively, were obtained, indicating overlap of these scales. It is apparent that another primary question of the study was also answered negatively, in that some personality variables or variable are related to differences in the objective electrical vestibulogram, apparently only at 0·20 cps.

The above finding is of interest in two ways. The first concerns motion sickness because it has been shown (Ref. 2) that Dramamine, a drug used to prevent motion sickness symptoms, acts in a very specific manner, raising the objective RL only at 0·20 cps, the same frequency which seems to be important for producing motion sickness. It is also known that various psychological factors such as anxiety operate to facilitate the occurrence of motion sickness (Ref. 14, p. 1207). These relationships suggest that a low RL at 0·20 cps may be a necessary condition for the occurrence of motion sickness regardless of how the low RL may be produced.

The second way that these findings are of interest is that the variation of objective RL with score on the MAS can be fitted into the Hull-Spence theoretical framework. This system assumes the existence of a supra-threshold excitatory potential, $_s\dot{E}_r$, which is defined by

$$_s\dot{E}_r = {_sE_r} - {_sL_r}$$

in which $_sE_r$ is the reaction potential and $_sL_r$, the reaction threshold (Ref. 7, p. 77). Other factors being equal, $_sE_r$ is defined by

$$_sE_r = D \times {_sH_r}$$

in which D is drive and $_sH_r$, the habit strength, a learned response depending only on the number of trials. If the second equation is substituted in the first, the result is

$$_s\dot{E}_r = D \times {_sH_r} - {_sL_r}$$

This equation is useful to explain the finding (Ref. 13) that classical eyelid conditioning proceeded faster with Ss who scored higher on the MAS. Both Malmo (Ref. 10, p. 243) and Spence (Ref. 12) have suggested that difference scores on the MAS scale can be considered as indicating differences in amount of drive. If $_sL_r$ is assumed to be constant for any group of organisms, and the number of trials, hence $_sH_r$ is kept constant, then $_s\dot{E}_r$ will vary as drive is varied. Greater $_s\dot{E}_r$ is presumed to lead to greater intensity of the conditioned response.

A similar analysis can be made for the variation in objective RL with MAS score. It is necessary first to substitute $_sU_r$, a concept concerning receptor-effector connections of an unlearned response, for $_sH_r$ in the last equation. Since Ss used in this experiment did not report any abnormal vestibular history, it can be assumed that $_sL_r$ is essentially constant for the group. As pointed out by Hull (Ref. 6, p. 59), a particular response to a stimulus is graded as a function of the intensity of the stimulus, hence, $_sU_r$ is a variable in this question. However, the stimulus was given to all Ss in exactly the same manner so that $_sU_r$ can be considered a constant for all Ss at any given time. Drive, on the other hand, is a variable because of the assumption of different drive levels as indicated by different MAS scores. Thus, with a given subthreshold stimulation and a constant $_sL_r$ for all Ss, whether or not an objective RL occurs is determined by the amount of drive present. If drive is sufficiently high, an RL will be reached with a lower stimulus value.

A third interest concerned Ss who had reached an RL as determined by objective sway criteria but who did not report any swaying. The size of this discrepancy was indicated by the difference score which was shown to be significantly different at both stimulus frequencies for Ss scoring higher on the Pa scale. This behaviour appears consistent with one aspect of the paranoid disposition, the exaggeration of well-being and denial of weakness (Ref. 3, p. 483; Ref. 9, p. 237) which the presence of this novel type of stimulation could evoke.

A discussion of the findings concerning the subjective RLs, namely, the occurrence of a higher RL with higher score on the Hy, Pd, and Pa scales at 1·0 cps, and the Pa scale at 0·20 cps, is beyond the scope of interest of this paper. The data have been included here only for the sake of completeness, although they were primarily used to obtain the difference scores already discussed.

The fact that significant findings did not overlap between the two stimulus frequencies, except for the Pa scale, gives further support to the idea that there may be separate processes acting in the vicinity of these frequencies. What these processes might be is not at all clear, and neither is their possible manner of interaction with personality variables.

REFERENCES

1. DZENDOLET, E., Sinusoidal electrical stimulation of the human vestibular apparatus. *Percept. mot. Skills*, **17**, 171–185, 1963.
2. ——, Effect of Dramamine on the objective electrical vestibulogram. *Percept. mot. Skills*, **18**, 465–468, 1964.
3. GUILFORD, J. P., *Personality*. New York: McGraw-Hill, 1959.
4. HATHAWAY, S. R. & BRIGGS, P. F., Some normative data on new MMPI scales. *J. clin. Psychol.*, **13**, 364–368, 1957.
5. —— & MCKINLEY, J. C., *The Minnesota Multiphasic Personality Inventory*. New York: Psychological Corp., 1943.
6. HULL, C. L., *Principles of Behaviour*. New York: Appleton-Century, 1943.
7. ——, *Essentials of Behaviour*. New Haven: Yale Univer. Press, 1951.

8. LACEY, O. T., *Statistical Methods in Experimentation.* New York: Macmillan, 1953.

9. LEARY, T. *Interpersonal Diagnosis of Personality.* New York: Ronald, 1957.

10. MALMO, R. B., Measurement of drive: an unsolved problem in psychology. *Nebraska Symposium on Motivation* (ed. M. R. Jones), Lincoln, Neb.: Univer. of Nebraska, 1958.

11. MEEHL, P. E., Schizotaxia, schizotypy, schizophrenia. *Amer. Psychologist,* **17,** 827–838, 1962.

12. SPENCE, K. W., A theory of emotionally based drive (D) and its relation to performance in simple learning situations. *Amer. Psychologist,* **13,** 131–141, 1958.

13. TAYLOR, J. A., The relation of anxiety to the conditioned eyelid response. *J. exp. Psychol.,* **41,** 81–92, 1951.

14. WENDT, G. R., Vestibular functions. In *Handbook of Experimental Psychology* (ed. S. S. Stevens). New York: Wiley, 1951.

15. WINER, B. J., *Statistical Principles in Experimental Design.* New York: McGraw-Hill, 1962.

D*

11

Individual Differences in Pain Threshold and Level of Arousal

DIANA R. HASLAM

First published in *British Journal of Psychology*, **58,** 139–142, 1967

THE pain thresholds of a group of introverts and extraverts were assessed. It was found that the mean pain threshold of the introverts was significantly lower than that of the extraverts. In a further experiment it was found that caffeine, a stimulant drug, lowered the mean pain threshold significantly. The relation between the perception of pain and level of arousal is discussed, and it is argued that the difference in mean pain threshold values as between introverts and extraverts is attributable to a difference in level of arousal.

INTRODUCTION

Hardy, Wolff & Goodell suggested that when the pain threshold is measured in 'instructed' subjects there is little variation between individuals in threshold values (Refs. 6 and 7). (Subjects are termed 'instructed' when a description is given to them of the sensations they are likely to experience.) Other experimenters, however, using the radiant heat technique, have failed to confirm this uniformity (e.g. Refs. 10 and 18).

Since there is evidence of individual differences in pain threshold, it would seem that the relation between pain threshold and personality might be a fruitful area of enquiry. It is one, however, which has received little attention so far, and the results of experiments designed to assess the relation between constitutional-temperamental types and pain threshold in a normal population are inconclusive (Refs. 1 & 9). The present investigation has been concerned, therefore, with the relation of individual differences in pain thresholds to introversion/extraversion rather than to the 'body types and emotional patterns' that have been studied previously.

EXPERIMENT 1

METHOD

Subjects

Subjects were selected on the basis of scores obtained on the extra-version scale of the Maudsley Personality Inventory (Ref. 2). 35 students served as subjects, of whom 20 were extraverts (11 male and 9 female) and 15 were introverts (8 male and 7 female).

Apparatus and Procedure

A modified Hardy-Wolff radiant-heat apparatus (Ref. 5) was used, in which the heat from a 500 w bulb was concentrated by a lens through an aperture 2 cm. in diameter. Mains power was supplied to the lamp through a 'Variac' transformer and monitored by means of a voltmeter. The apparatus was calibrated by means of a 'Moll' thermopile and millivoltmeter in terms of mc/sec/cm², and the calibration was checked before each experimental session.

For the reasons mentioned by Chapman & Jones (Ref. 1, p. 82), a small area of skin in the centre of each subject's forehead was blackened with indian ink. This area was exposed to the radiant heat source for 3 sec at 1 minute intervals. (Repeated stimulation of the same area of skin if done in rapid succession will cause lowering of the pain threshold and local hyperalgesia. However, Hardy, Wolff & Goodell have shown that with a 1 minute interval between successive stimulation of the same skin area there is no lowering of the pain threshold (Ref. 7).) Each subject was told that the procedure was not an endurance test and was not intended to discover how much pain he could stand, but was an experiment to find out at what stage the stimulus was first felt as painful; that is, when he felt a small stab of pain at the end of the 3 sec exposure.

The energy level of the first stimulus was 98 mc/sec/cm², which the majority of subjects described as warm. The intensity of each successive stimulus was increased by approximately 16 mc/sec/cm² since Haslam & Thomas have found this interval to be optimal for the assessment of pain thresholds (Ref. 8), in the sense of giving the most reliable threshold values. The stimulus intensity was increased in this way until the subject reported a small stab of pain at the end of the 3 sec exposure. In assessing pain thresholds it is not possible to carry out the corresponding descending series because of the danger of blistering the skin at high intensities of stimulation.

Before stimulation began, subjects were given a description of the sensations they were likely to experience, and therefore are termed 'instructed subjects'.

Hardy, Goodell & Wolff reported that skin temperature has a modifying influence on pain threshold in the sense that the higher the skin temperature the lower the pain threshold (Ref. 4). Forehead skin temperature was therefore measured at the beginning of the experiment. Room temperature was always between 20·5°C and 22·0°C.

RESULTS

The main results are shown in Table 1.

Introversion-Extraversion

A Mann-Whitney U test (Ref. 17) showed that the introverts had a significantly lower forehead pain threshold than the extraverts ($p < 0.002$, two-tailed); but differences between the pain thresholds of male and female subjects were not significant for either introverts or extraverts.

Skin Temperature

No significant correlation was found between forehead pain threshold and skin temperature for either introverts or extraverts ($p = +0.47$ and $+0.07$ respectively). Unlike the results of Hardy, Goodell & Wolfe (Ref. 4), however, the trend was for a high skin temperature to be accompanied by a high pain threshold.

EXPERIMENT 2

Experiments have been carried out in the Soviet Union in which assessment was made of the effect of caffeine upon visual and auditory thresholds (Refs. 14 & 15). An experiment is reported here in which the effect of caffeine upon pain threshold was assessed.

METHOD

Subjects

22 students served as subjects: 14 male and 8 female.

Apparatus and Procedure

The apparatus and procedure for the assessment of pain threshold were the same as those described above.

TABLE 1

MEAN VALUES OF SUBJECTS' AGES, INTROVERSION/EXTRAVERSION SCORES, SKIN TEMPERATURES AND PAIN THRESHOLDS

	n	Mean age of subjects in years	Mean introversion/ extraversion score	Mean forehead skin temperature (°C)	Mean forehead pain threshold (mc/sec/cm²)	Range of forehead pain thresholds (mc/sec/cm²)
Introverts	15	24	16	33·8	218	176–264
Extraverts	20	21	33	33·95	249	212–302

Each subject took part in one experimental session and one control session. In each session pain threshold was assessed twice, with a 30 minutes interval between the two assessments, during which subjects sat and read. In the experimental session the assessment of pain threshold was followed by the immediate administration of 6 grains of caffeine citrate; in the control experiment no caffeine citrate was administered. Half the subjects underwent the experimental session first and the other half underwent the control session first. The experimental and control sessions were on different days.

In all sessions care was taken to see that subjects had neither just eaten nor been long without food; also that they had not recently had any alcohol, coffee, tea or drugs. They were not allowed to smoke in the 30 minutes interval.

Caffeine citrate was used in the present experiment as it is absorbed two to three times more quickly than caffeine. The amount of citric acid present is so small that its effect is thought to be negligible (personal communication from M. E. Jarvik, 1964).

RESULTS

The effect of caffeine on the mean pain threshold of the total group was to lower it by 14 mc/sec/cm^2 from 223 mc/sec/cm^2 to 209 mc/sec/cm^2. A Wilcoxon matched-pairs signed-ranks test (Ref. 17) showed this change to be significant ($p < 0.01$). After the administration of caffeine, pain threshold went down in thirteen subjects, up in three subjects and remained unchanged in six subjects. In the control sessions no subject showed any threshold change after the 30 minutes interval.

DISCUSSION

Arousal is defined by Malmo as 'the continuum extending from deep sleep at the low activation end to "excited states" at the high activation end' (Ref. 12). In defining arousal in this way, Malmo is following Lindsley, whose activation theory of emotion (Ref. 11) was based largely on findings made with EEG recordings in various states of alertness, and on the discovery of the activating functions of the reticular formation of the brain stem (Ref. 13). The reticular formation not only activates the cortex; it also increases somatic and autonomic activity.

The continuum of arousal suggested by Malmo (Ref. 12) might well be extended to include drug-induced anaesthesia at the low activation end, and it seems evident from everyday experience that the relation between arousal and pain perception is of an inverted-U form as follows. Pain is least likely in profound anaesthesia, more likely in superficial anaesthesia and in natural sleep, most likely in a normal waking state, and unlikely in an extremely excited state, as, for instance, in combat and on the playing-field, where it is well-known that wounds and injuries go unnoticed. Hence, pain is likely to be perceived when the level of arousal is neither very low nor very high, but when it is somewhere between these two extremes.

Further evidence that pain perception is related to level of arousal comes from the finding of Experiment 2 that caffeine lowers the pain threshold significantly. Caffeine gives rise to an increased level of arousal of the organism as it is a stimulant drug which excites all portions of the central nervous system, in particular the cortex, medulla and spinal cord (Refs. 3 & 19).

The work of Shagass & Kerenyi on the sedation threshold indicates that introverts are more aroused than extraverts (Ref. 16). It therefore seems possible to explain the finding that introverts have a lower pain threshold than extraverts on the ground that they function at characteristically different levels of arousal.

REFERENCES

1. CHAPMAN, W. P. & JONES, C. M., Variations in cutaneous and visceral pain sensitivity in normal subjects. *J. clin. Invest.*, **23,** 81–91, 1944.

2. EYSENCK, H. J., *Manual of the Maudsley Personality Inventory.* London: University of London Press, 1959.

3. GOODMAN, L. S. & GILMAN, A., *The Pharmacological Basis of Therapeutics.* New York: Macmillan, 1955.

4. HARDY, J. D., GOODELL, H. & WOLFF, H. G., The influence of skin temperature upon the pain threshold as evoked by thermal radiation. *Science.* **114,** 149–150, 1951.

5. ——, WOLFF, H. G. & GOODELL, H., Studies on pain: A new method for measuring pain threshold: observations of spatial summation of pain. *J. clin. Invest.*, **19,** 649–657, 1940.

6. ——, —— & ——, The pain threshold in man. *Proc. Ass. Res. nerv. Dis.*, **23,** 1–15, 1943.

7. ——, —— & ——, *Pain Sensations and Reactions*. Baltimore: Williams and Wilkins, 1952.

8. HASLAM, D. R. & THOMAS, E. A. C., An optimum interval in the assessment of pain threshold. *Quart. J. exp. Psychol.*, **19**, 54–58, 1967.

9. JANOFF, I. Z., BECK, L. H. & CHILD, I. L., The relation of somatotype to reaction time, resistance to pain and expressive movement. *J. Pers.*, **18**, 454–460, 1950.

10. LEDUC, E. H. & SLAUGHTER, D., The effects of a combination of cetanilid, caffeine and sodium bromide on the pain threshold in man. *Anesth. Analg.*, **24**, 147–154, 1945.

11. LINDSLEY, D. B., Emotion. In *Handbook of Experimental Psychology* (ed. S. S. Stevens). New York: Wiley & Sons, 1951.

12. MALMO, R. B., Activation: a neuropsychological dimension. *Psychol. Rev.*, **66**, 367–386, 1959.

13. MORUZZI, G. & MAGOUN, H. W., Brain stem reticular formation and activation of the EEG. *Electroenceph. clin. Neurophysiol.*, **1**, 455–473, 1949.

14. NEBYLITSYN, V. D., The relationship between sensitivity and strength of the nervous system. In *Typological Features of Higher Nervous Activity of Man*. Moscow: Akad. pedagog. Nauk RSFSR, 1956.

15. ——, Individual differences in the strength and sensitivity of both visual and auditory analysers. In *Recent Soviet Psychology* (ed. N. O'Connor). Oxford: Pergamon Press, 1961.

16. SHAGASS, C. & KERENYI, A. B., Neurophysiologic studies of personality. *J. nerv. ment. Dis.*, **126**, 141–147, 1958.

17. SIEGEL, S., *Nonparametric Statistics for the Behavioural Sciences*. New York: McGraw-Hill, 1956.

18. SLAUGHTER, D. & WRIGHT, T., A modification of the Hardy-Wolff-Goodell pain-threshold apparatus. *Anesth. Analg.*, **23**, 115–119, 1944.

19. SOLLMANN, T., *A Manual of Pharmacology and Its Applications to Therapeutics and Toxicology*. Philadelphia: Saunders, 1948.

12

Tolerance for Pain, Extraversion and Neuroticism[1]

R. LYNN & H. J. EYSENCK

First published in *Perceptual and Motor Skills*, **12**, 161–162, 1961

It may be deduced from Eysenck's theory of personality (Refs. 2 & 4) that pain tolerance should be *positively* related to extraversion (E) and *negatively* to neuroticism (N). Extraverted Ss are postulated to develop inhibition/satiation more quickly, and dissipate it more slowly; prolonged pain sensations should thus be inhibited more quickly and strongly in extraverts, leading to diminished pain sensations. Furthermore, as Beecher has pointed out, physiological pain sensations are always accompanied by the *apprehension of future pain*, which may be conceived as a conditioned fear (anxiety) response which summates with the physiological pain (Ref. 1). Extraverts are posited to condition less well, and would therefore not develop this component of the total pain to the same extent as introverts. The prediction relating to N is perhaps less secure; it rests on the assumption that the strength of the autonomic reaction to pain stimulation would be likely to be related directly to N, which is conceived of in terms of autonomic lability (Ref. 5). This autonomic reaction would be expected to summate with the physiological pain due to the stimulus.

30 volunteer university students, the experimental group, were given the Maudsley Personality Inventory as a measure of E and N (Ref. 3), as well as the Rotating Spiral After-effect test which is an objective measure of E (Ref. 4). Ss' foreheads were blackened with indian ink, and they were then subjected to heat stimulation by a thermostimulator modelled after the description given by Hardy, Wolff & Goodell (Ref. 7). The radiation intensity was set at 166 w, and Ss were instructed to report the onset of pain, which is usually characterized by a sharp prick following a sensation of warmth. They were then to try to tolerate the pain for as long as they could. Pain tolerance was the number of seconds from the first report of pain to the final withdrawal. All Ss reported pain

[1] We are indebted to the Society for Research in Human Ecology for a grant which made this study possible.

within 3 to 5 sec after exposure. There appears to be a habituation effect after about 12 sec of pain, such that, if pain could be tolerated for this long, Ss reported that they felt it could be endured indefinitely. Five Ss tolerated the pain for 60 sec, after which the trial was terminated. A time limit of 20 sec was finally set because of blisters which began to develop after about 8 sec exposure.

When Ss are divided into three groups of 10 according to their E scores, their pain tolerance decreases from 17·2 (high E) through 9·3 to 5·6 (low E); in the most extraverted group 8 out of 10 reach the 20 sec limit, while in the most introverted group none do. Mean score for the whole group is 10·9 sec. The product-moment correlation of E with pain tolerance is 0·69 ($p = 0·01$). The correlation of N with pain tolerance is $-0·36$ ($p = 0·05$). The Spiral After-effect correlates $-0·30$ with E, $-0·02$ with N, and $-0·08$ with pain tolerance. None of these correlations is significant, although the first approaches significance.

The very positive findings regarding E duplicate those of Petrie (Ref. 8), Petrie, Collins & Solomon (Ref. 9) and Poser (Ref. 10). The latter used 18 female students, subjected to ischemic pain, and found a correlation of 0·53 with E, as measured on the M.P.I.; the former has also used the M.P.I. on 55 Ss subjected to surgical or experimental pain and has reported significant differences between extraverts and introverts. (She also verified a complementary prediction deriving from the hypothesis, to wit that *stimulus deprivation* would be better tolerated by introverts.) The extensive data of Hall & Stride (Ref. 6) on some 400 psychiatric patients may also be quoted in support; they found least pain tolerance in dysthymics, i.e., introverted neurotics. They also report an increase in tolerance after pre-frontal leucotomy, which is an *extraverting* operation (Ref. 11).

SUMMARY

Significant correlations were found between pain tolerance on the one hand, and extraversion and (low) neuroticism on the other. These results are in line with deductions from Eysenck's theory of personality and are supported by other studies reported in the literature.

REFERENCES

1. BEECHER, H. K., *Measurement of Subjective Responses: Quantitative Effects of Drugs.* New York: Oxford Univ. Press, 1959.
2. EYSENCK, H. J., *Dynamics of Anxiety and Hysteria.* New York: Praeger, 1957.
3. ——, *Manual of the Maudsley Personality Inventory.* London: Univ. of London Press, 1959.
4. —— (ed.), *Experiments in Personality.* (2 vols.) London: Routledge & Kegan Paul, 1960.
5. ——, *The Structure of Human Personality.* New York: Wiley & Sons, 1960.
6. HALL, K. R. L & STRIDE, E., The varying response to pain in psychiatric disorders: a study in abnormal psychology. *Brit. J. med. Psychol.*, **27**, 48–60, 1954.
7. HARDY, J. D., WOLFF, H. G. & GOODELL, H., *Pain Sensations and Reactions.* Baltimore: Williams & Wilkins, 1952.
8. PETRIE, A., Some psychological aspects of pain and the relief of suffering. *Ann. N.Y. Acad. Sci.*, **86**, 13–27, 1960.
9. ——, COLLINS, W. & SOLOMON, P., The tolerance for pain and for sensory deprivation. *Amer. J. Psychol.*, **73**, 80–90, 1960.
10. POSER, E., Der Figurale After-effect als Persoenlichkeitsmerkmal: Theorie und Methodik. Paper read at the XVIth Int. Congr. of Exp. Psychol., Bonn, 1960.
11. WILLETT, R. A., The effects of psychosurgical procedures on behaviour. In *Handbook of Abnormal Psychology* (ed. H. J. Eysenck). New York: Basic Books, 1960.

13

Effects of Illumination on Perceived Intensity of Acid Tastes

G. D. WILSON & R. A. M. GREGSON

First published in *Australian Journal of Psychology*, **19**, 69–73, 1967

CHANGES in ambient light have been reported to affect taste intensity perception. In an experiment designed to clarify the nature of this effect 48 Ss each tasted 27 pairs of citric acid samples, judging the intensity of the second sample relative to the first. Four sets of acid stimuli varying in discriminability were used, and three conditions of ambient illumination change. Half the Ss received systematic reinforcement of their responses, the others did not. Results suggest that Ss use heteromodal cues as an alternative response basis when the primary discrimination task is relatively difficult.

INTRODUCTION

Gregson reported a small intersensory effect of ambient light on perceived relative intensity of acid tastes, facilitatory for most Ss but with marked individual differences (Ref. 5). The effect of light was apparently multiplicative on perceived intensity and therefore not consistent with the simple threshold shift mechanism more usually invoked in studies of sensory interaction (e.g., Ref. 10). This observation was confirmed by a subsequent experiment using a signal-detectability paradigm, which suggested that the light changes probably influence S's response strategy, rather than shift his taste sensitivity at the receptor-system level (Ref. 6).

From these considerations it was hypothesized that the apparent intersensory effect of light on taste arises as a result of the process that Garner has described as a 'search for structure' (Ref. 4): the utilization of cues irrelevant to a defined judgment task, when that task is comparatively ambiguous or difficult. More specifically, the experiment reported here was designed to test the following hypotheses:

1. The smaller the taste stimulus differences which are required to be judged, the more readily will S relate his responses to the light changes.

2. The light changes will have a greater effect when knowledge of results (or systematic reinforcement) of taste judgments is withheld.

3. Individual differences in the intersensory effect will be related to personality variables which have been shown in other contexts to correlate with performance on cognitive tasks (e.g., Ref. 1).

METHOD

Ss were 24 male and 24 female undergraduates, aged 17–24. They were tested in the taste laboratory described previously (Ref. 5) and also given the MPI (Ref. 3).

Four sets of taste stimuli, each of three citric acid concentrations, were used (see Table 1). The three stimuli in Set 1 were physically identical, though apparent discrimination may have resulted from time-order effects if not intersensory phenomena. At the other extreme, stimuli in Set 4 were fairly consistently though not perfectly discriminable.

TABLE 1

INTENSITIES[1] OF EXPERIMENTAL TASTE STIMULI

Acid set	Stimulus reference		
	A	B	C
1	0·0006	0·0006	0·0006
2	0·0007	0·0006	0·0005
3	0·0008	0·0006	0·0004
4	0·0009	0·0006	0·0003

[1] In gms. citric acid/ml. deionised water

Directed by signals from a buzzer, Ss judged pairs of samples, rating the second sample in each pair relative to the first according to the following scale (numbers not shown to Ss but used in analysis of results):

1. Certainly less intense
2. Very probably less intense
3. Probably less intense
4. Possibly less intense
5. Equally intense
6. Possibly more intense
7. Probably more intense
8. Very probably more intense
9. Certainly more intense

Ss were divided into two groups of 24: (a) non-reinforced (b) rewarded threepence for each 'correct' response, indicated to S immediately it was made by three short buzzes. Responses treated as correct were Likert values 1, 2 or 3 (to acid pairs CA, CB or BA); Likert values 4, 5 or 6 (to pairs AA, BB or CC); and Likert values 7, 8 or 9 (to pairs AC, BC or AB). For acid set 1, where A = B = C, this was equivalent to giving random 1 in 3 reinforcement.

Three lighting conditions were used: M, constant illumination (140V through an overhead 150w bulb); L, change from 140V to 230V immediately before S ingested the second sample in a pair, and return to 140V immediately after his response; D, a period of dim light (80V) extended through the same interval as in L between ingesting and judging. Brightness changes were gradual over a 1 sec period. Since each trial began in 140V illumination and conditions M, L and D were randomly ordered, Ss were not able to anticipate which light shift, if any, would occur on a given trial. A hue factor was introduced by using a yellow filter for half the Ss and a red filter for the rest.

Each of the 48 Ss judged 27 pairs of taste stimuli on one session. The 27 pairs comprised a random sequence of all combinations of L, M and D with the 9 permutations of pairs from A, B and C. The 48 Ss were allocated 12 to each acid set; Ss 1–6 were not reinforced, Ss 7–12 were reinforced, Ss 1–3 and Ss 10–12 tasted in yellow light, Ss 4–9 tasted in red light, even were male, odd were female.

RESULTS

Taking algebraic differences between mean ratings under L and D conditions for each individual S as an index of light effect, a $4 \times 2 \times 2$ analysis of variance with 3 observations per cell was conducted (Table 2). Preliminary examination suggested that all interactions with hue (considered as a random factor) could be dropped to give 39 df in the error variance and greater F-test sensitivity. Reinforcement was found to be a significant main effect ($p < 0.05$). Plotting mean light effect against acid sets for both reinforcement conditions (Fig. 12) showed that light was facilitating in its effect for the non-reinforcement group, and negative for the reinforcement group. In both cases the light effect dropped off at acid set 4, in which real stimulus differences were readily perceived.

The mean modular deviation (from Likert value 5) of the ratings of each S was also calculated as a measure of S's tendency to give extreme scale responses. This effect increased significantly with real stimulus differences, giving F (3, 39) = 4·55, p <0·01, but also showed some inter-subject variability.

TABLE 2

ANALYSIS OF VARIANCE OF DIFFERENCES BETWEEN LIGHT AND DARK CONDITIONS IN TOTAL RELATIVE INTENSITY RATINGS FOR EACH S

Source	df	MS
Acid sets	3	36·03
Reinforcement	1	363·00*
Hue	1	14·08
Acids × Reinforcement	3	85·17
(a) Acids × Hue	3	24·70
(b) Hue × Reinforcement	1	108·00
(c) Acids × Reinforcement × Hue	3	30·39
(d) Within cell	32	89·98
Pooled error (a+b+c+d)	39	80·81

* F(1,39) = 4·49 p <0·05.

Some variables which correlated with light effect are shown in Table 3. As extraversion and use of extreme ratings did not correlate significantly (r = 0·10, df = 46), it may be asserted that those two variables together accounted for up to 19·3 per cent of the response variance which was associated with lighting condition differences (0·33², 0·29² = 0·193).

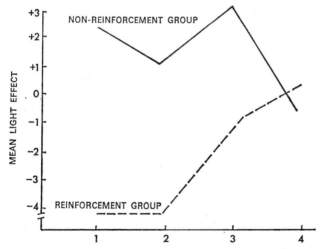

Figure 12. The effect of light changes on perceived taste intensity as a function of taste stimulus differences and re-inforcement.

TABLE 3

CORRELATIONS BETWEEN INDIVIDUAL DIFFERENCES AND EFFECT OF LIGHT

	Non-reinforcement group (df = 22)	Reinforcement group (df = 22)	Both groups (df = 46)
MPI Extraversion × Light Effect	−0·32	−0·37	−0·33*
MPI Neuroticism × Light Effect	0·03	−0·41*	−0·19
Use of Extreme Ratings × Light Effect	−0·35	−0·16	−0·29*
No. Correct Responses × Light Effect	−0·42*	0·16	−0·14

* $p = <0·05$

DISCUSSION

Writers who have committed themselves to an account of possible mechanisms producing intersensory effects have often espoused a general arousal theory. Such a theory translates readily into physiological terms. The central process causing arousal has been variously identified as: cortical irradiation (Ref. 8), the 'hell' hormone (Ref. 2), the sympathetic nervous system (Ref. 9) and, more recently, the reticular activating system (Ref. 10). As Halpern observes, well-established neurophysiological information is too frequently correlated with inadequately measured behavioural data of questionable generality and reliability (Ref. 7). It is felt that the neurological mechanisms cited have been invoked prematurely, without first clarifying whether a shift in sensitivity or a change in response strategy occurs.

In this experiment, if results are treated so as to bring out the differences between Ss in their responses under the D and L conditions, and these differences pooled, then evidence of an intersensory effect does emerge. However, the presence or absence of reinforcement is a crucial variable in determining the direction of that effect, and it does not appear when the taste stimuli are relatively discriminable.

The number of correct responses for a given S is an *a posteriori* measure of his response difficulty, and in the non-reinforcement group it is negatively correlated with the differential (D compared with L) light effect. That is, in the absence of reinforcement, the effect of light tended to be more facilitatory when S was less able (or less motivated) to discriminate real differences in the taste stimuli. This relationship failed to appear when reinforcement was provided. Tendency to use extreme ratings may be taken as another indirect measure of response difficulty, and this was inversely related to light effect for the total group.

A negative correlation between light effect and extraversion implies that extraverts tend to be negatively influenced by the light, while introverts tend to be positively influenced. The correlation between neuroticism and light effect in the reinforced group only also suggests that personality variables are involved. Evidence hardly justifies an excursion into personality dynamics to explain these correlations, but it should be noted that extraverts and introverts here use information differently, and that such individual differences cannot be neglected in studying intersensory phenomena.

It is concluded that heteromodal stimuli may produce an apparent sensory interaction by providing an alternative, and more readily utilizable, source of cues to which Ss can relate their responses. The magnitude and direction of the effect so produced depends upon (a) difficulty of the primary task, (b) the presence or absence of systematic reinforcement, and (c) S's personality characteristics.

REFERENCES

1. BAKAN, P., BELTON, J. A. & TOTH, J. C., Extraversion-introversion and decrement in an auditory vigilance task. In *Vigilance: a Symposium* (ed. D. N. Buckner & J. J. McGrath). New York: McGraw-Hill, 1963.

2. BORNSTEIN, W., On the functional relations of the sense organs to one another, and to the organism as a whole. *J. Gen. Psychol.*, **15**, 117–131, 1936.

3. EYSENCK, H. J., *The Maudsley Personality Inventory*. London: University of London Press, 1959.

4. GARNER, W. R., *Uncertainty and Structure as Psychological Concepts*. New York: Wiley & Sons, 1962.

5. GREGSON, R. A. M., Modification of perceived relative intensities of acid tastes by ambient illumination changes. *Aust. J. Psychol.*, **16**, 190–199, 1964.

6. —— & WILSON, G. D., *Effects of Illumination on the Detection and Perceived Relative Intensity of Acid Tastes*. Canterbury: University of Canterbury, Dept. Psychol. and Sociol., Res. Rep. 10, 1966.

7. HALPERN, B. P., Neural-behavioural interrelationships in taste. In *Biological Prototypes and Synthetic Systems* (ed. E. E. Bernard & M. R. Kare). Vol. 1. New York: Plenum, 1962.

8. KRAVKOV, S. V., Changes in visual acuity in one eye under the influence of the illumination of the other, or acoustic stimuli. *J. exp. Psychol.*, **17,** 805–812, 1934.

9. LONDON, I. D., Research in sensory interaction in the Soviet Union. *Psychol. Bull.*, **51,** 531–568, 1954.

10. SYMONS, J. R., The effect of various heteromodal stimuli on visual sensitivity. *Quart. J. exp. Psychol.*, **15,** 243–251, 1963.

14

Personality and Time Estimation in Sensory Deprivation

G. F. REED & J. C. KENNA

First published in *Perceptual and Motor Skills*, **18**, 182, 1964

INTRODUCTION

DESPITE interest in 'biological clocks' there is abundant evidence that our estimation of time may profitably be viewed as cue-learned behaviour. Sturt (Ref. 5) argued against William James' view that the estimation of a period of time is determined by affective tone as well as the number of occurrences within the period (Ref. 3). Sturt found that the duration of an interval was judged according to the number of 'mental events' it contained, by which she meant all experiences, whether due to external or internal stimuli.

Under sensory deprivation (S.D.) conditions, where external stimuli are reduced, the number of mental events experienced will be directly related to personality. By definition the introvert's psychic energy is normally directed toward himself, whereas the extravert is more attentive to external cues. It may be predicted, therefore, that under S.D. the extravert will suffer a relatively greater diminution of mental events. Thus, according to Sturt's theory, both introvert and extravert will tend to judge the duration of a given interval of S.D. as being shorter than it is by clock time but the extravert's error in estimation will be greater than the introvert's.

METHOD

Ten normal Ss with scores on the Maudsley Personality Inventory Extraversion scale of 30 and above and 10 normal Ss with scores of 20 or less were asked to judge when 15 minutes had elapsed (method of production) under normal and under S.D. conditions (described in Ref. 4). In every case both estimates were made on the same day; the order of conditions was reversed for half of each personality group. No significant difference was found between the group estimates under normal conditions ($M_{EXT} = 13 \cdot 3$; $M_{INT} = 15 \cdot 0$).

Under S.D. conditions errors in estimation were significantly greater;

furthermore, all but one S made positive errors. In other words, clock time of 15 minutes would be judged by 19 Ss to be shorter than this. This offers support for the experimental prediction and is in line with previous findings over short intervals (e.g., Refs. 1 & 2). Although all errors were in the same direction, there was a pronounced difference between groups in size of error ($M_{EXT} \pm$ S.D. = 29·8 minutes $\pm$ 11·92; $M_{INT} \pm$ S.D. = 19·9 $\pm$ 6·95, p = 0·025, 1-tail Mann Whitney U).

SUMMARY

The larger errors made by the extraverts also accord with the experimental prediction, suggesting that the extravert, because of his higher dependence on external cues, is more affected in his time estimates under S.D. than is the introvert.

REFERENCES

1. BANKS, R. & CAPPON, D., Effect of reduced sensory input on time perception. *Percept. mot. Skills*, **14,** 74, 1962.
2. COHEN, S. I., SILVERMAN, A. J., BRESSLER, B. & SHMAVONIAN, B., Problems in isolation studies. In *Sensory Deprivation* (ed. P. Solomon, *et al.*). Cambridge, Mass.: Harvard Univ. Press, 1961.
3. JAMES, W., *Principles of Psychology*. Vol. 1. London: Macmillan, 1901.
4. REED, G. F. & KEENA, J. C., Sex differences in body imagery and orientation under sensory deprivation conditions of brief duration. *Percept. mot. Skills*, **18,** 117–118, 1962.
5. STURT, M., *The Psychology of Time*. London: Routledge & Kegan Paul, 1925.

15

Personality and Depersonalization under Sensory Deprivation Conditions

G. F. REED & G. SEDMAN

First published in *Perceptual and Motor Skills*, **18**, 659–660, 1964

OF 28 normal Ss undergoing brief sessions of S.D., 8 reported depersonalization experiences. They were found to be significantly more introverted than the rest of the group.

INTRODUCTION

Depersonalization and derealization are terms used in psychopathology to refer to a range of experiences connected with the sense of apparent loss of reality either of S, his body or the environment. Such experiences may be reported by normal Ss under certain conditions. Thus Federn (Ref. 2) refers to the association between shock and depersonalization, while the latter has been noted in 'Model Psychosis' studies of the effects of mescaline and LSD (Ref. 4), sleep deprivation and sensory isolation (Ref. 3). However, little is known about individual differences among normal Ss reporting the experience.

By definition the introvert is one whose psychic energy is directed toward himself and his experiences, as compared with the extravert who is more attentive to his environment and thus may be regarded as more stimulus bound. Under conditions of diminished sensory input, therefore, the introvert should experience less 'stimulus hunger' than the extravert, and his tendency toward divorce from his environment should be facilitated. It may thus be predicted that under S.D. conditions feelings of depersonalization will be reported more readily by introverts than by extraverts.

METHOD

28 normal Ss between the ages of 19 and 42 were subjected to periods of S.D. of 20 to 60 minutes. They were required to lie as still as possible on a couch in a sound-attenuated laboratory. Non-patterned visual and auditory input was provided by translucent goggles and white noise fed

through padded earphones. Ss were requested to report any experiences or changes in sensation, and told that verbalizations would be recorded. They were observed through a one-way vision screen. No changes whatsoever in the experimental conditions were made during sessions. Measures of extraversion/introversion had previously been obtained from the E scale of the M.P.I. (Ref. 1).

During subsequent intensive phenomenological interviewing precise descriptions were obtained of reported ego changes. An experience was only classified as depersonalization if S definitely reported feelings of unreality about himself or his surrounds. (Several Ss reported apparent movement and/or disturbed body imagery without experiencing an actual lack of reality.) 8 Ss reported depersonalization in this strict sense. In 5 cases this was accompanied by disturbed body imagery and in the other 3 cases by 'disembodiment'. The remaining 20 Ss reported no depersonalization.

6 of the 8 Ss in the depersonalization group had the lowest E scores (highest introversion) of the total group. The Mann-Whitney test showed a statistically significant difference between the E scores of the depersonalized and non-depersonalized groups (U = 23, p = 0·01, one-tail rest) thus offering clear support for the experimental prediction.

SUMMARY

Previous studies of personality factors in depersonalization have been largely concerned with psychiatric patients. Shorvon (Ref. 8) and Roth (Ref. 5) have stressed the association between depersonalization and obsessionalism, while Sedman & Reed (Ref. 7) have reported a high incidence of the experience in cases of what Schneider (Ref. 6) called 'insecure personality' (Ref. 6) or in another terminology anxious introverts. These psychiatric studies are in line with the present finding that under S.D. conditions depersonalization is associated with introversion in normal Ss.

REFERENCES

1. EYSENCK, H. J., *Maudsley Personality Inventory*. London: University of London Press, 1959.
2. FEDERN, P., Narcissism in the structure of the ego. *Int. J. Psychoanal.*, **9**, 401–419, 1928.

3. LUBY, E. D., GOTTLIEB J., COHEN, B. D., ROSENBAUM, G. & DOMINO, E. F., Model psychoses and schizophrenia. *Amer. J Psychiat.*, **119**, 61–65, 1962.

4. MCKELLAR, P., Scientific theory and psychosis: the 'Model Psychosis' experiment and its significance. *Int. J. soc. Psychiat.*, **3**, 170–182, 1957.

5. ROTH, M., The phobic anxiety-depersonalization syndrome and some general aetiological problems in psychiatry. *J. Neuropsychiat.*, **1**, 293–306, 1960.

6. SCHNEIDER, K., *Psychopathic Personalities*. (9th ed.) London: Cassell, 1958.

7. SEDMAN, G. & REED, G. F., Depersonalization phenomena in obsessional personalities and in depression. *Brit. J. Psychiat.*, **109**, 376–379, 1963.

8. SHORVON, H. J., The depersonalization syndrome. *Proc. R. Soc. Med.*, **39**, 779–785, 1946.

Psychogenic Deafness, Perceptual Defence, and Personality Variables in Children

G. F. REED

First published in
Journal of Abnormal and Social Psychology, **63**, 663–665, 1961

INTRODUCTION

In a recent discussion, Kodman & Blanton have suggested examination of the perceptual defence hypothesis, using as subjects children who manifest psychogenic auditory behaviour (Ref. 6). Indicating the theoretical difficulties involved, they observe that a preponderance of the cases encountered by them were children whose normal thresholds for speech contrasted with losses on the pure tone audiogram, i.e., in response to *meaningless* stimuli.

It may be postulated that conventional pure-tone audiometry pre-supposes conditions of set and attention different in quality from those obtaining in normal speech communication. If this is so, then personality may well be an important variable in the determination of responses in the two situations. The present study reports a preliminary check on this prediction, with some observations on the applicability of perceptual defense theories to psychogenic deafness.

METHOD

The files (totaling over 3,000) of a large city child guidance clinic and school psychological service were searched for cases presenting psychogenic or functional deafness for speech where responses to pure-tone audiometric testing had been judged to be normal. A further group of children was found whose thresholds for pure tones had been relatively high but whose responses to speech had been within normal limits. In both groups the age range was restricted to 8–14, and cases of below 75 IQ, those where there was any evidence of brain injury, and those where the psychiatric diagnosis was in doubt were excluded. All cases were psychiatrically diagnosed, independently of this investigation, as being predominantly 'hysteric' or 'anxiety state'. The children in the first group presented outgoing behaviour problems, whilst those in the second were characterized by timidity, withdrawal, or mild phobic symptoms.

Both groups were roughly equal in distributions of age, sex, and IQ.

RESULTS AND DISCUSSION

Findings are summarized in Table 1. Despite the statistically high significance (p = 0·005), confidence in generalization is, of course, diminished by considerations of the small numbers involved and the unreliability of psychiatric diagnosis. But there seems to be a clear tendency in this sample for those children whose auditory threshold for pure tones is high to be categorized as hysteric (as opposed to anxious) and some tendency towards the reverse among those who display a lack of response to speech.

Kleinman, in a careful experimental comparison of subjects with psychogenic hearing loss and a control group with organic hearing loss, found a decreased practice effect rather than heightened auditory thresholds in the experimental group (Ref. 5). However, Kleinman pointed out that 'individuals whose auditory thresholds are characteristically raised as a defence against anxiety-provoking stimuli can be identified on the basis of their perceptual behaviour', and interpreted his results as being generally consistent with perceptual defence theory. Other workers have concurred with this view and it may well be presumed that some relationship does exist between psychogenic deafness and perceptual defence. Indeed, investigations into the latter have, to some extent, been stimulated by clinical findings. But theoretical difficulties at once become apparent, as Kodman & Blanton have pointed out (Ref. 6).

Most relevant experimental studies have been designed to show whether there are differences between subjects' responses to 'threatening', as opposed to neutral, *words or sentences*. In practice, our cases reacted abnormally to *situations*. Group A showed high or inconsistent thresholds for pure tones during audiometric testing, but not for speech, Group B members were hard of hearing among strangers or in class, but responded normally to pure-tone testing. Thus it is difficult to explain the behaviour of Group A in terms of perceptual defence as presented in Eriksen's review (Ref. 3) or in Blum's more specifically psychoanalytic

E

account (Ref. 1) unless it is postulated that pure-tone audiometry constitutes a threatening stimulus.

On the other hand, Solomon & Howes' argument regarding the relative lowness of appropriate responses in the subjects' response hierarchies (Ref. 12) might well explain the high thresholds of Group A, but not those of Group B. In what to them are presumably anxiety provoking situations, these children show a relative lack of response, not only to unfamiliar or 'tabu' words, but to the bulk of verbal stimuli.

TABLE 1

DISTRIBUTION OF CHILDREN WITH PSYCHOGENIC DEAFNESS BY PERSONALITY TYPE

	Anxiety state	Hysteric	Totals
Elevated thresholds for:			
Pure Tones (Group A)	1	13	14
Speech (Group B)	9	3	12
	10	16	26

χ^2 (after Yates' Correction) $= 9.86$

In short, the concept of perceptual defence in its original forms is not directly applicable to the behaviour of children in Group A. Their type of response is more readily studied in terms of laboratory and industrial studies of 'vigilance' as defined by Mackworth (Ref. 9). Furthermore the early experiments on perceptual defence do not seem to have a direct bearing upon the behaviour of children in Group B unless wide generalizations from the early theory are to be permitted. If the behaviour of both groups is in fact explicable in terms of perceptual defence, then we would suggest, as did Singer in a lucid review and experimental study (Ref. 11), that the most rewarding type of approach is one using 'hypothesis' concepts as presented, for instance, by Postman (Ref. 10). Crudely put, it may be argued that some children adopt a generalized anxious set for certain social situations and thus show elevated thresholds for all verbal stimuli in those situations. Other children adopt faulty expectations in perceptual tasks demanding heightened attention and thus produce insensitive or inconsistent responses. It remains now to attempt to account for the individual differences in response to these two types of situation, which are highlighted by the distributions of clinical categories in the present data.

Where personality variables are concerned, the present findings, for reasons given above, cannot be directly compared with those of Lazarus, Eriksen & Fonda, who set out to study personality mechanisms as reflected in the 'auditory recognition of sexual and aggressive material' (Ref. 8). It is of interest to note, however, that they found that their freely verbalizing or 'intellectualizer' group, which included obsessive-compulsives, showed greater accuracy in the perception of threatening material than did their 'repressor' group, which included conversion hysterics. Objection may be made to the clinical aptness of these workers' classificatory procedure. But their empirical results are clear and seem to point in the opposite direction to that indicated by the present data. Kurland, on the other hand, found no difference between obsessional-compulsives and hysterics in their recognition threshold of emotional words (Ref. 7). Again these results are not directly comparable with the present ones, but would appear to be different in implication.

The different distributions of clinical classifications in our two groups are predictable, however, from Eysenck's formulations (Ref. 4). Pure-tone audiometry is a task which might be expected to discriminate between dysthymic individuals, with their relatively high levels of drive, aspiration, and persistence, and hysterics, who have been found to build up reactive inhibition more rapidly and to be behaviourally more distractible. In this connection, Kodman & Blanton point out the importance for accurate signal detection of freedom from competing response tendencies (Ref. 6) and a most stimulating account of the differential performance of introverts and extraverts in relevant experimental tasks is given by Broadbent (Ref. 2).

A similar explanation, coupled with considerations of attention gaining behaviour, might be given for the existence of a proportion of hysterics in Group B. As far as the majority of children in this group is concerned, however, a different set of mechanisms must be postulated; but, again, a plausible explanation is readily derived from Eysenckian theory. Dysthymic children are highly reactive and readily conditionable. They tend to demonstrate strong fear reactions, which, linked with oversocialization, may be triggered off by apparently neutral stimuli in social situations. Heightened thresholds for speech may thus be acquired as an anxiety reducing avoidance mechanism by these children more readily than by hysterics.

SUMMARY

Survey of a child guidance population showed that of 26 functionally hard-of-hearing cases, 14 presented elevated thresholds for pure tones but were within normal limits for speech. The other group, though normal on pure-tone testing, presented elevated thresholds for *all* speech, rather than for relatively threatening stimuli. It would appear that both groups were reactive to situations, as opposed to specific auditory stimuli within those situations. Furthermore, the majority of the pure-tone group were clinically classified as 'hysteric', whereas the majority of the speech group was classed as 'anxiety state'.

The applicability of 'defence' theories to such cases is discussed, and it is suggested that the behaviour of both groups may best be studied in the light of a 'hypothesis' approach.

It is pointed out that the pure-tone testing situation demands 'vigilance' in the experimental sense, and it is then shown that the differing distributions of clinical categories in the two groups is predictable from Eysenck's formulations.

REFERENCES

1. BLUM, G. S., Perceptual defence revisited. *J. abnorm. soc. Psychol.*, **51**, 24–29, 1955.
2. BROADBENT, D. E., *Perception and Communication.* Oxford: Pergamon Press, 1958.
3. ERIKSEN, C. W., The case for perceptual defence. *Psychol. Rev.*, **61**, 175–182, 1954.
4. EYSENCK, H. J., *The Dynamics of Anxiety and Hysteria.* London: Routledge & Kegan Paul, 1957.
5. KLEINMAN, M. L., Psychogenic deafness and perceptual defense. *J. abnorm. soc. Psychol.*, **54**, 335–338, 1957.
6. KODMAN, F. & BLANTON, R. L., Perceptual defence mechanisms and psychogenic deafness in children. *Percept. mot. Skills*, **10**, 211–214, 1960.
7. KURLAND, S. H., The lack of generality in defence mechanisms as indicated in auditory perception. *J. abnorm. soc. Psychol.*, **49**, 173–177, 1954.

8. LAZARUS, R. S., ERIKSEN, C. W. & FONDA, C. P., Personality dynamics and auditory perceptual recognition. *J. Pers.*, **19**, 471–482, 1951.

9. MACKWORTH, N. H., Some factors affecting vigilance. *The Advancement of Science*, **53**, 389–393, 1957.

10. POSTMAN, L., On the problem of perceptual defence. *Psychol. Rev.*, **60**, 298–306, 1953.

11. SINGER, B. R., An experimental inquiry into the concept of perceptual defence. *Brit. J. Psychol.*, **47**, 298–311, 1956.

12. SOLOMON, R. L. & HOWES, D. H. Word frequency, personal values and visual duration thresholds. *Psychol. Rev.*, **58**, 256–270, 1951.

Effects of Perceptual Isolation on
Introverts and Extraverts[1]

NED TRANEL

First published in *Journal of Psychiatric Research*, **1,** 185–192, 1962

INTRODUCTION

RECENTLY there has been increasing attention directed to 'perceptual isolation' or 'sensory deprivation' as a stressful condition. Extensive reviews of this literature are available in other sources (Ref. 4) and will not be repeated here.

Within the framework of Jungian theory, sensory deprivation phenomena such as hallucinations and daydreams can be interpreted as concomitant features of the process of introversion. When the environment becomes very stressful by virtue of its ambiguity, there is a turning away from reality to fantasy. If there is no meaningful information in the environment there is no way for the ego to mediate between unconscious forces and external reality. Action and judgment are no longer possibilities, consequently there must be some substitute for action. This substitute is provided by the introverted type of thinking with the ascendance of the 'archaic forces of the unconscious' in the form of hallucination, fantasy, changes in effect, daydreams.

Out of this formulation arises a question regarding the reactions of the individual whose usual attitude is introversive, in the Jungian sense, to the conditions of perceptual isolation. If introversion refers to a progressive withdrawal from reality, it should be expected that individuals on the extreme end of this dimension would be little affected by sensory alterations and perceptual changes in the environment. It is the purpose of this study to investigate the following hypotheses:

1. Introverts are able to tolerate perceptual isolation better than extraverts.

[1] Data of this chapter were used as part of the author's Ph.D. thesis. The project was supported in part by a research grant from Washington State University.

2. Introverts show smaller changes in emotional experiences as a function of perceptual isolation than do extraverts. For the purposes of this study, a change in emotional experience is defined as a change in ratings of words on the Semantic Differential.

METHOD

SUBJECTS

Subjects used in the study were selected on the basis of their scores on the Myers-Briggs Type Indicator (Ref. 2). This is a group administrable paper-pencil personality test designed within the framework of Jungian theory. It was administered to a group of 318 male undergraduate students at the University of South Dakota. Their scores on the intro-version-extraversion scale ranged from -27 to $+27$. The mean was -0.303 and the standard deviation was 12.5. For the purposes of this study, introverts and extraverts were defined as those subjects who had scored 1.5 standard deviations or more beyond the mean on the Myers-Briggs Type Indicator. A total of 40 Ss, 20 introverts and 20 extraverts, were available for the entire experimental procedure. In order to provide two scores on the Semantic Differential, 10 Ss of each group were randomly assigned to a control group. The Ss ranged in age from 18 to 29 with a mean age of 20.

APPARATUS

The Semantic Differential

The semantic differential used for the study followed the form developed by Osgood, *et al.* (Ref. 1). The form used in this study was composed of 16 concepts and each was to be assigned a rating on 16 scales. The concepts included two groups of words: One group consisting of eight emotionally descriptive abstract nouns, the other of eight abstract nouns not emotionally descriptive. The two lists were equated for familiarity by checking them against the Thorndike-Lorge Frequency Count (Ref. 5). The list of emotional words consisted of boredom, fear, worry, anger, grief, loneliness, anxiety, frustration. The nonemotional words were sample, survey, system, situation, formation, structure, metal, frequency.

Description of the Room

The room used for the 20 experimental Ss was an $8 \times 7 \times 9$ft sound-treated room used for conducting hearing tests. Illumination was provided by a 60-watt bulb placed 5ft from Ss eyes. This light was diffused by a piece of heavy asbestos 12×24in. in size suspended 3in. from the light.

White noise was administered through a set of headphones by a Grason-Stadler, 950-C Twin Oscillator. This noise was compared with a 70 dB complex noise generated by Maico H-I audiometer in order to obtain the level of loudness at which the white noise was to be presented. The white noise and the sound-treated room excluded all ambient noise from the subjects.

Halved pingpong balls were affixed to Ss eyes. A pair of perforated rubber gloves was placed on his hands and his arms were placed in cardboard cuffs extending from the elbow to beyond the finger-tips. A recording was made for each S of all vocal sounds and audible movements produced while he was in the room. This was accomplished through a microphone placed in the room and connected to a tape recorder through a noise relay. In this way a comparable, quantifiable record of audible events was obtained for each S.

PROCEDURE

All 40 Ss reported two weeks before the experiment for the first administration of the Semantic Differential and for scheduling an appointment for the experiment. When each experimental subject reported for his appointment he was taken to the experimental room and given the following instructions:

'Lie here as motionless as you can. Keep your eyes open and don't go to sleep. Every time you think a half hour has passed, say "half an hour is up". The microphone which you may have noticed here on the wall is connected to a tape recorder outside the room and your half-hour estimates will be recorded. Feel free to express any other thoughts or feelings whenever you like. The experiment will last all afternoon, but you can terminate it any time you feel you really must'.

S was observed at all times while in the room. He was awakened by a sudden, brief increase in the intensity of the white noise if: (1) he overestimated a half-hour period by more than 20 minutes and there was no movement in the room, or (2) he was obviously sleeping as judged by his constant, heavy breathing.

The subject remained in the room for 4 hrs or until he voluntarily terminated the experiment, whichever occurred first. After leaving the room he was immediately given the second administration of the semantic differential. He was then interviewed by the experimenter using a standard form for all Ss.

When control subjects reported for their appointments they were not placed in the isolation room but were again given the semantic differential and after completing this, they were given the MMPI. The control group was needed only to provide a basis of comparison of scores on the Semantic Differential. This group was not put in the isolation room. The comparison on all sources of data except the Semantic Differential was made by comparing extraverts and introverts who were in the isolation room. All subjects were paid at the rate of $1.15 per hour for all time spent in the experiment.

Data were provided by the following five sources:

(a) Length of time spent in the isolation room.
(b) The post-isolation interview.
(c) Observations and recordings of audible events during S's stay in isolation.
(d) Change scores on the semantic differential.
(e) The Minnesota Multiphasic Personality Inventory. The MMPI was administered to provide a clinical description of the two groups of subjects.

RESULTS

1. *Time in the Room:* As a group, extraverts tolerated the isolation conditions significantly better than introverts in terms of time spent in the room. Eight of the extraverts, but only one of the introverts remained the entire 4 hrs. Comparison of the 'stay' and 'quit' groups is shown in Table 1.

TABLE 1

NUMBER OF SUBJECTS REMAINING THROUGH OR
QUITTING THE 4 HOUR STAY IN ISOLATION

Group	Extraverts	Introverts
Stay	8	1
Quit	2	9

Applying Fisher's exact probability test (Ref. 3), the probability of this outcome and of all more deviant outcomes in either direction is

E*

0·014. This finding did not support Hypothesis One—introverts are able to tolerate perceptual isolation better than are extraverts.

2. *The Post-Isolation Interview:* Data obtained from the interview were analysed most appropriately in a qualitative way. These data consisted of the following statements made by the two groups.

EXTRAVERTS

R.B.: 'I thought I was in there for experimental purposes; I could have stayed longer but I have exams coming up; it didn't bother me too much'.

T.D.: 'I guess I could have stayed all night. Seemed like I was only in there about 2 hrs. I don't think I slept but I was relaxed'.

L.L.: 'At first it felt calm, like when I went up in a decompression chamber in the Air Force. I felt like sleeping. The pay made no difference, I wouldn't do it just for the money'.

M.M.: 'I thought it was kind of a challenge. I figured you wanted to see how long I could stay'.

R.M.: 'It was very relaxing, almost too relaxing. I was able to relax and forget my troubles'.

L.S.: 'It reminded me of something in the movies like a Korean Prisoner of War or something. I've been through rough things before so I didn't leave'.

C.T.: 'Seemed like a test of endurance, seemed like a test of resistance against boredom. Wanted to see how close I could estimate the time'.

P.H.: 'I knew I gave too many estimates but thought I could maybe make the time go by if I threw in a few extra half-hours'.

At 1 hr: complained about need for cigarette; at 2 hrs 10 min.: raised arms and waved them about in a fanning motion; at 2 hrs 25 min.: buried head in pillow; at 2 hrs 30 min.: felt glasses, 'These damn things'; at 2 hrs 55 min.: tried to reach for the light; at 3 hrs 15 min.: moved the microphone up and down in its stand.

J.G.: 'Thought I was in a space ship. It felt like I was movin' real fast, like maybe in a rocket ship'.

F.S.: 'This is the biggest waste of time I've ever seen'.

INTROVERTS

S.B.: 'I found it difficult to breathe towards the end. Thought I was in there to see how the noise would affect a person'.

G.D.: 'I didn't know what was on my hands. I didn't know what to do, whether you wanted me to talk or not'. (After 1 hr 45 min.: 'I think I've made my contribution for tonight'.)

T.I.: 'I was most uncomfortable, my hands felt boxed up. I didn't think I'd last the full half hour'.

D.L.: 'Didn't like laying still; kept getting more restless. I thought maybe you were cutting people off from the world to see what happens to them'.

C.L.: 'I thought the whole situation was kinda ridiculous'.

B.S.: 'I was nervous due to all the equipment and I wondered what kind of approach I'd use'.

K.S.: 'I was a little shaky at the end and had a slight headache. I thought maybe you expected me to panic; maybe you wanted to see how stable a person is'.

S.W.: 'You asked me not to move so I didn't. I could have stayed longer if I could have moved'.

T.L.: 'I thought about getting mad but knew I couldn't get too mad because I could leave anytime'.

T.V.: 'I laid for a long time not thinking about anything; I couldn't think of anything'.

These data, in general, suggest that the extraverts tended to regard the situation as a challenge, while introverts regarded it as a stressful condition. Most Ss reported difficulty in concentrating or in maintaining consistent thought patterns. Ss in both groups reported pleasant as well as unpleasant thoughts.

Their comments also indicate that those Ss who remained in the room longest were able to engage in some form of pleasant reverie. None of the introverts mentioned remote past experiences as part of their thought patterns. This group concentrated on what might be called 'stimulus bound' thought. Attention was devoted to the room, the equipment, the purpose of the experiment. Extraverts, on the other hand, mentioned experiences more removed from the present situation, e.g., 'my girl', 'my buddies', 'getting drunk', 'high-school days'. There was no mention of hallucinations or dreams made by any member of either group.

3. *Observations and Recordings of Audible Events:* In general, the extraverts reacted by ignoring the instructions to 'lie quietly and estimate the time each half-hour', while the introverts reacted by attempting to adhere rigidly to instruction. This result is indicated by the fact that 10 of the extraverts who spoke during isolation mentioned

difficulty in staying awake. None of the introverts mentioned such a difficulty.

In addition, extraverts made more movements per minute than did the introverts. While this difference was not statistically significant, the tendency of the extraverts to sleep would decrease the number of movements for this group even if sleep did not actually occur. Comparison of the number of movements per minute made by the two groups is shown in Table 2.

TABLE 2

COMPARISON OF NUMBER OF MOVEMENTS MADE BY EXTRAVERTS AND INTROVERTS

Group	Mean movements per minute	Mean difference	Standard error of mean difference	t[1]
Extravert	0·3834			
Introvert	0·2315	0·152	0·11	1·39

[1] For 18 degrees of freedom, t = 1·73 is significant at the 0·05 level of confidence for a one-tail test.

Introverts also spoke of a greater degree of discomfort during isolation than did extraverts. Eight members of this group complained about discomfort caused by lack of movement and four of them spoke about quitting before putting their desires into action. None of the extraverts spoke of quitting, and this latter group also moved about sufficiently to alleviate discomfort caused by lying in one position even though this was in violation of instructions.

This finding, of difficulty in staying awake and violation of instructions among the extraverts, and greater discomfort and tendency to quit among the introverts, did not support Hypothesis One.

4. *The Semantic Differential:* Data on the semantic differential were analysed by calculating 'factor change scores' for each subject. That is, changes in ratings from pre- to post-testing were obtained by algebraically summing change scores on each of four factors for emotional and non-emotional words separately. The four factors included were those previously identified by Osgood *et al.* (Ref. 1) as activity, potency, evaluative and stability.

As shown in Table 3, an analysis of variance of these data indicated that there was no significant between-groups difference in ratings of

TABLE 3

ANALYSIS OF VARIANCE OF FACTOR CHANGE SCORES FROM
PRE- TO POST-ISOLATION TESTING ON THE SEMANTIC DIFFERENTIAL

Source of variation	Sum of Squares	df	Mean Square	F[1]
Experimental-Control	708·06	1	708·06	2·079
Extraversion-Introversion	1193·52	1	1193·52	3·504
Experimental-Control by Extraversion-Introversion	288·80	1	288·80	<1
Subjects within Groups	12260·34	36	340·57	
Emotional-Nonemotional	12·80	1	12·80	<1
Between Factors	1085·11	3	361·70	2·71
Emotional-Nonemotional by Factors	730·64	3	243·55	1·900
Subjects by Emotional-Nonemotional	10378·07	39	266·10	2·076
Subjects by Factors	15625·76	117	133·55	1·042
Residual	14997·49	117	128·18	
Total		319		

[1] For 1 and 36 degrees of freedom, F = 4·11 is significant at the 0·05 level of confidence. For 3 and 117 degrees of freedom, F = 2·69 is significant at the 0·05 level of confidence. For 39 and 117 degrees of freedom, F = 1·87 is significant at the 0·01 level of confidence.

words on the semantic differential. This result was interpreted to mean that the words were not rated differently by the two groups from the pre- to post-isolation testing. This result did not confirm Hypothesis Two: introverts show smaller changes in emotional experiences as a function of perceptual isolation than do extraverts.

5. *The MMPI:* The MMPI resulted in a code of 96–345 78 1/20: for the extraverts. In general, the shape of this profile indicated that members of this group presented themselves in a somewhat guarded fashion as very active, trouble-free, poised, socially adept, optimistic individuals who are unusually suspicious and mildly disdainful of customary social standards. The most striking feature of their profile was that scale 5 (Paranoia) was relatively and absolutely a high point in the code. This, plus a very low score on scale 0 (Social Introversion) suggested an unusual degree of interpersonal sensitivity among these subjects.

For the introverts the mean MMPI profile was 507–28 46 19/3. The shape of this profile indicated that this group presented themselves candidly as experiencing an unusual degree of discomfort in social situations. They have a more feminine interest pattern and are more passive and dependent than the extraverts. They are prone to ruminate and reflect on their own problems and generally experience an unusual amount of anxiety and discomfort.

DISCUSSION

The results of the study indicated that there were striking contrasts between the two groups in their reactions to the experimental condition. In general, the introverts reacted to the condition by leaving it, whereas the extraverts reacted by restructuring it. The introverts perceived the experimental condition as uncomfortable, but they followed the instructions to 'lie quietly and don't go to sleep' more closely than did the extraverts. The introverts were more preoccupied with 'stimulus bound' thought, that is, they attended more closely to the immediate experimental situation. As a result they reported greater discomfort while in the room than did the extraverts. They did not become as sleepy and at the same time, they did not move about as much while awake. In other words, the introverts responded to the situation by accepting the specified condition but they left it after it became too difficult to tolerate.

The extraverts perceived the experimental condition as a challenge and in general they remained in it for the specified period of time. In contrast to the introverts they responded to the situation by rejecting the specified conditions. They tended to go to sleep, to move about while awake, to engage in some form of pleasant reverie and to whistle or hum tunes. As a result, they reported less discomfort while in the room than did the introverts.

Since the introverts left the situation and the extraverts modified it by disobeying instructions, it is difficult to draw definitive conclusions about the actual effects of perceptual isolation on these groups. The evidence does suggest, however, that personality factors measured by the Myers-Briggs Type Indicator are predictive of response to conditions of perceptual isolation. This is a finding which remains to be validated by future work.

The results of this study also emphasize the severe methodological problems involved in research on perceptual isolation. Investigators have tended to use time spent in isolation as a criterion of tolerance. The present data suggest that this criterion may not be the most appropriate measure of tolerance. If some subjects are able to remain in isolation for a long period of time they may do so partly because they do not actually experience isolation conditions. Response measures indicating what the subject does while in isolation may be more appropriate to index tolerance limits.

The results also indicated that the Semantic Differential was not appropriate as a measure of the kinds of changes that occurred under these conditions.

SUMMARY

This study utilized 40 Ss, 20 extraverts and 20 introverts, in an investigation of the reactions of extraverts and introverts to perceptual isolation. Ten subjects of each group were subjected to perceptual isolation by being placed in a sound-treated room with white noise fed into their ears, halved ping-pong balls affixed to their eyes and rubber gloves and cardboard cuffs on their hands. They remained in the room for 4 hrs or until they voluntarily terminated the experiment, whichever occurred first.

Reactions of the two groups to perceptual isolation were measured by (1) changes in ratings of words on the semantic differential, (2) length of time spent in the isolation room, (3) tape recordings of audible events during S's stay in isolation, and (4) a post-isolation interview. The following two hypotheses were tested:

1. Introverts are able to tolerate perceptual isolation better than are extraverts.
2. Introverts show smaller changes in emotional experiences as a function of perceptual isolation than do extraverts.

The findings of this study were as follows:

1. In general, introverts and extraverts showed markedly different reactions to perceptual isolation.
2. Reactions of introverts were characterized by leaving the isolation room, but while in the room, this group adhered closely to instructions, tended to engage in 'stimulus-bound' thought, remained awake and did not move about.
3. Reactions of extraverts were characterized by remaining in the room for the specified period of time, but while in the room, this group tended to violate instructions, to engage in some form of pleasant reverie, to go to sleep, and to move about while awake.

4. As measured by the semantic differential, changes in emotional experiences as a function of perceptual isolation were not significantly different for the two groups.
5. Characteristic phenomena—hallucinations, delusions, fantasy—usually reported in isolation studies, failed to occur.

It was concluded that criteria of tolerance for perceptual isolation are generally so ambiguous that Hypothesis One was not clearly confirmed. Hypothesis Two was not confirmed by results of the semantic differential. The two groups of subjects showed markedly different reactions to the experimental condition and these reactions were not inconsistent with Jungian theory, on which the hypotheses were based.

REFERENCES

1. Osgood, C. E., Suci, G. J. & Tannenbaum, P. H., *The Measurement of Meaning*. Urbana, Ill.: University of Illinois Press, 1957.
2. Saunders, D. R., Preliminary Discussion of the Myers-Briggs Type Indicator. Unpublished report, Educational Testing Service, Princeton, New Jersey, 1958.
3. Siegel, Sidney, *Nonparametric Statistics for the Behavioural Sciences*. New York: McGraw-Hill, 1956.
4. Solomon, P., Kubzansky, P. E., Leiderman, P. H., Mendelson, J. H., Trumbell, R. & Wexler, D., (eds.), *Sensory Deprivation*. Cambridge, Mass.: Harvard University Press, 1961.
5. Thorndike, E. L. & Lorge, I., *The Teacher's Word Book of 30,000 Words*. New York: Columbia University Press, 1944.

18

Extraversion-Introversion and Improvement in an Auditory Vigilance Task[1]

PAUL BAKAN[2]

First published in *British Journal of Psychology*, **50**, 325–332, 1959

THE study deals with the effect of a secondary signal-detection task on performance in a primary signal-detection task in an auditory vigilance situation. 40 subjects were tested under two conditions. In one condition they listened to an 80 minute recording of a sequence of digits in order to detect the occurrence of primary signals defined as *three successive odd digits which are all different*. In another condition they listened for primary signals as described above, but in addition they also had to detect secondary signals defined as the occurrence of *the digit 6*. The primary signals occurred 10 times every 16 minutes; there were about 10 times as many secondary signals (digit 6) as there were primary signals (odd-odd-odd).

The over-all detection of primary signals was better when subjects were listening for both primary and secondary signals than when they listened for primary signals alone. Extraverts benefited more by the secondary task than introverts. No significant relationship was found between either neuroticism or intelligence and vigilance performance. A theoretical account of the events in a vigil is proposed and the difference between introverts and extraverts is considered in terms of this account.

[1] An earlier draft of this paper has appeared in unpublished form as M.R.C. Applied Psychology Unit Report No. 311. The author wishes to express his thanks to the members of the Applied Psychology Research Unit for their critical interest in the research and especially to Sir Frederic Bartlett, Donald Broadbent and Dr N. H. Mackworth.

[2] The research reported in this paper was carried out in 1956–57 while the author was a post-doctoral Fellow of the National Science Foundation at the M.R.C. Applied Psychology Research Unit, Cambridge. The work was done under the general direction of Dr N. H. Mackworth.

INTRODUCTION

Vigilance has been defined by Mackworth as a state of readiness to detect and respond to certain specified small charges, occurring at random time intervals in the external environment (Ref. 17). Experimentally the level of vigilance is inferred from the performance of the subject by considering the number of signals which are not responded to (Ref. 16) or the intensity to which signals have to be raised in order to be responded to (Refs. 3 & 8).

Much of the experimental work with vigilance tasks has been concerned with environmental variables, either in the work situation, or in the general surroundings. Experiments have been designed to evaluate the effects of task duration (Refs. 2, 16 & 19), signal frequency (Ref. 7), signal intensity (Refs. 1 & 16), signal duration (Ref. 1), inter-signal interval (Ref. 3), noise (Refs. 5, 13, 14 & 15), temperature (Ref. 18) and isolation (Ref. 11). In some instances the state of the subject has been varied, as in studies on the effect of drugs (Ref. 16), sleep deprivation (Ref. 20), rest periods (Ref. 16), and knowledge of results (Ref. 16).

Large individual differences in both over-all performance and in the course of performance over time are characteristic of performance in vigilance tasks. Though most investigators have reported wide individual differences in performance on vigilance tasks, there has been very little research on the correlates of these differences, though some workers have suggested the possible importance of personality factors in accounting for them (Refs. 7 & 11).

The present study is concerned with the evaluation of the effect of an environmental task variable on performance in an auditory vigilance task and the relationship between personality variables and vigilance performance. The task variable consists of the addition of a secondary task to a primary vigilance task resulting in a large increase in the total number of relevant stimuli to be responded to. The problem is to determine whether the introduction of a secondary task results in an increase in signals detected on the primary task. It has been shown that vigilance performance improves as the number of relevant signals increases where all of the signals are of the same kind (Ref. 7). In most practical situations, however, it is not feasible to increase artificially the number of signals when 'real' and 'artificial' signals are of the same kind and when responses to both are identical. Therefore, in the present experiment a secondary task was added to a primary vigilance task, resulting in an increase in the *total* number of relevant signals coming from an auditory display. However, the primary and secondary signals, though coming from the same display, were different and required different responses to be made. The hypothesis under consideration was that subjects would detect more primary task signals when listening for both primary and secondary task signals than when listening for primary task signals alone.

In addition to measures of performance on the vigilance task, information was available for each subject on two personality variables, neuroticism and extraversion-introversion. Analyses were carried out to test the hypothesis that personality variables are related to individual differences found in performance on vigilance tasks.

METHOD

Stimulus Material

The stimulus material consisted of a tape-recording consisting of digits presented at the rate of one per second. The randomness of these digits was somewhat restricted but they gave the general impression of a random series. Subjects were required to listen for a signal which was defined as *three successive odd digits which are all different*. The frequency of occurrence of such signals was every 16 minutes. The entire tape consisted of 5 10-minute periods with no break between periods. The 16-minute subperiods were equivalent with respect to number of signals and their distribution in time. Within each subperiod the time in seconds between successive signals was as follows: 71, 154, 25, 185, 110, 104, 46, 15, 143. The time between the last signals of one subperiod and the first signal of the next subperiod was 146 sec.

Primary and Secondary Task

The primary task consisted of listening for signals (primary) as described above (odd-odd-odd) and writing down the actual digits constituting the signal whenever it was detected. The secondary task consisted of listening for the digit 6, the secondary signal, and pressing a button whenever a 6 was detected. The secondary signal also appeared irregularly but with a far greater frequency than the primary signal. The digit 6 appeared on the average of once every 10 sec, as contrasted with an average of about once every 1·6 minutes for primary signals. Subjects were told that of the two tasks the primary one was the more important in contributing to their score, but that they should get as many of both kinds as possible. The analyses in the present paper are based on detection of primary signals.

Subjects

Subjects were Royal Naval ratings. There were 40 subjects in this experiment and each subject served in two conditions. On one day a subject would listen for primary signals alone (0—0—0) and on another day he would listen for primary and secondary signals (0—0—0+6). Half the subjects did the primary task on day 1 and the primary plus secondary task on day 2 and the other half did the tasks in the reverse conditions. Experimental sessions were usually about a week apart.

Practice

After it was clear that the subject understood the instructions he listened to a practice tape of 10·5 minutes which contained 6 primary signals (0—0—0) and 97 secondary signals. The practice tape was used both days for each subject and the practice corresponded to the experimental condition for that day. During practice there was knowledge of results in the form of the experimenter calling out signals about 3 sec after their passage. Immediately after the practice period there was a 10 minute break during which the subject left the testing room.

Test Conditions

During the 80 minute test period which followed the break, subjects were left alone in a cubicle in the room with the tape-recorder going. They were instructed not to leave until they were told the experiment was over. Wrist-watches were taken away for the duration of the test session. Subjects were not permitted to smoke during the test period.

Other Available Data

Measures of intelligence, neuroticism and introversion-extraversion were available for each subject. The intelligence measure available was the A.H.4 Intelligence Test and the personality measures came from the Heron Personality Inventory.

RESULTS

Over-all Effect of Secondary Task on Primary Task Performance

The effect of the secondary task was to improve the over-all performance on the primary task. Of the 40 subjects there were 39 who did not get perfect scores with the primary task alone and thus could show improvement. Of these 39 there were 23 who improved with the addition of the secondary task, 11 who did worse with the secondary task and five whose performance was the same under both conditions. The improvement with the secondary task is significant by a sign-test at better than the 5 per cent (1-tail) level. Over the 80 minute test-period the mean number of failures in detecting a primary signal when subjects were listening for primary signals alone was 9·95; when listening for both primary and secondary signals together the mean number of detection failures was 7·90. This improvement was independent of the order of administration of experimental conditions.

Subject Stability between Conditions

In order to determine whether over-all performance under one condition was related to over-all performance on the other condition, a correlation was computed between signal omissions on the primary task alone (0—0—0) and omissions on the primary and secondary tasks (0—0—0+6). The correlation coefficient (Pearson) between omission scores on these two tasks was 0·71, which is significant at the 1 per cent level. This means that despite the improvement taking place with the secondary task, the relative standing of subjects was not changing very much. This tends to suggest that the performance of subjects on vigilance tasks may be relatively stable.

Introversion-Extraversion and Vigilance

Measures of introversion ranging from 0–9 were available for all subjects. A split was made as close to the median as possible to divide the subjects into two subgroups, extraverts (N = 19) and introverts (N = 21). All subjects with scores of three or less were classed as extraverts and all subjects with scores of four or more were classed as introverts. There was no significant difference either in neuroticism or intelligence between these groups. It was found that the extraverts were more likely to improve with the secondary task than the introverts. Of the 19 extraverts there were 14 who improved with the secondary task, whereas only 9 of the 21 introverts improved with the secondary task. This relationship between introversion-extraversion and over-all improvement with the secondary task was significant ($X^2 = 3·97$; p = 0·05).

Analysis of the data by 16-minute sub-periods results in further infor-

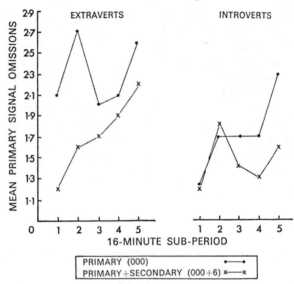

Figure 13. Relationship between mean number of primary signals omitted and time in the experimental situation under primary signal condition and primary plus secondary signal condition for subjects classified as extravert and introvert.

mation on the nature of this relationship (see Fig. 13). The improvement of the extraverts with the secondary signal seems to be related to the fact that in the first two subperiods (32 minutes) their performance in detecting primary signals (with no secondary signals) is worse than that of the introverts (1-tail, U-test; $p = 0.03$). With the introduction of the secondary task there is no significant difference between introverts and extraverts in the first two subperiods. The main effect of the secondary task is to improve performance of the extraverts in the first two subperiods. The result is that the extraverts with the secondary task behave like the introverts without it with respect to the detection of primary signals. For periods 1 and 2 the extraverts do significantly better with the secondary task than without it (sign-test, 1-tail; $p = 0.001$ for period 1 and $p = 0.029$ for period 2). The difference is not significant for the remaining periods (3, 4 and 5), though there are small differences in the direction of better performance with the secondary task.

The effect of the secondary task on the performance of introverts is different. In the first two periods there is no appreciable difference in primary signal detection as a function of the secondary task. But for periods 3, 4 and 5 there are differences in the direction of improved performance with the secondary task, with the difference between conditions reaching significance in the fifth period (sign-test, 1-tail; $p = 0.006$).

The evidence presented so far indicates that there is a relationship between introversion-extraversion and improvement with a secondary task which serves to increase considerably the total number of signals to be detected. Extraverts benefit from this secondary task during the first 32 minutes of the session, whereas introverts do not. This difference seems to be due to the fact that without the extra task the extraverts do significantly worse than the introverts in the first two periods, but with the extra task they improve significantly. A correlational analysis of this relationship would indicate whether the effect of the extra task is related to the *degree* of introversion-extraversion. The correlation between score on introversion-extraversion and algebraic differences between primary signal omissions in the two experimental conditions for the first two periods is -0.38 (significant at 0.05 level).

Neuroticism, Intelligence and Vigilance

A number of analyses were carried out to determine the nature of the relationship between neuroticism scores from the Heron Inventory and the scores on the vigilance tasks. No significant relationships were found in the sample studied. Relationships between intelligence as measured by the A.H.4 test and vigilance scores were also insignificant in the sample studied.

DISCUSSION

The main findings of this experiment were (a) that the addition of a secondary task, which markedly increases the number of signals to be responded to, results in improved signal detection performance in a primary task, and (b) that extraverts, who do not do as well with the primary task alone, show greater improvement than introverts with the addition of the secondary task. These results need to be considered in the context of the particular experimental arrangements used.

In considering the effect of the secondary task on primary task performance it should be noted that the secondary task used in this experiment was easy, was compatible with the primary task, required detection of signals from the same display as the primary task and was presented to the subjects as the less important of the two tasks. It is likely that there are many possible relationships between primary and secondary tasks which would result in findings quite different from those of this experiment.

The relationship found between introversion-extraversion and performance in the vigilance task should also be considered in the context of the details of the experiment. It should be noted that subjects were tested individually under conditions of isolation. It is difficult, therefore, to make a generalization about the relationships between introversion-extraversion and vigilance performance because of the possibility that social isolation may have enhanced the differences between introverts and extraverts. Further studies need to be carried out to analyse the interaction between personality variables and situational variables in vigilance situations.

One of the main features of a vigilance task is the freedom of the subject in determining the extent and distribution of his attentive activity with respect to the relevant stimulus material. At the beginning the subject may be instructed to pay attention and to detect as many signals as he can, but once the vigil begins he is usually free to make his own decisions about how much to listen to, or look at, the relevant stimulus display for the appropriate signals. He is also free to attend to irrelevant stimuli, either external or internal (e.g., day-dreams) and this may be incompatible with efficient detection of relevant signals. In the present experiment the freedom of the subject was probably enhanced by the absence of both the experimenter and knowledge of results during the test session.

In a situation where the subject has so much freedom, we may expect to find rather wide variation among individuals, and such variation has certainly been characteristic of data from vigilance experiments. The discovery of a relationship between a personality variable, introversion-extraversion and performance in a vigilance task helps to account for some of this variation between subjects.

It seems that extraverts are more likely to listen when there are more signals to listen for, whereas the listening behaviour of introverts is less influenced by frequency, at least in the early part of the vigil. The data also suggest that the higher signal rate maintains the level of performance of the introverts for a longer time and reduces their tendency to show a decrement.

Before considering the reasons for the difference between introvert and extravert performance in the vigilance task it would be helpful to try to construct a general account of what may happen in a vigilance situation. It is assumed that when subjects are instructed to listen for certain types of signals, the occurrence of these signals in the stimulus display serves to reinforce the attentive behaviour which makes the detection of signals possible. Holland has shown the reinforcing effect of signals in a visual task (Ref. 12). If the attentive behaviour is not sufficiently reinforced by the appearance of signals, then it is possible for the behaviour to undergo extinction. To put it in other words, when a subject listens and he frequently hears what he is listening for, he is more likely to continue listening than when he listens and only rarely hears what he is listening for. The same thing would be true for a visual task if we substitute 'looks' in place of 'listens'. In a vigilance task with a low signal frequency the lack of reinforcement in the form of signals may induce the subject to stop listening.

Several consequences may follow when a subject stops listening. Though he may stop listening for signals he doesn't necessarily stop hearing the stimulus material. (Likewise he may stop looking for signals, but may still see the display where the signals may appear.) When a subject is hearing the display but not actively listening for signals, the display becomes dedifferentiated as far as the subject is concerned since he is not making discriminations within the display. To be specific, in the vigilance task used in the present experiment, when a subject stops listening for signals he stops making the discriminations required by the task of listening for sequences of three successive odd digits, which are all different. These discriminations involve successiveness of digits, oddness-evenness of digits, identity of digits and memory for previous digits while listening for current digits. Making these discriminations in the stimulus material has the effect of differentiating the material. When the discriminations are not made, i.e., when the subject stops listening for signals, he hears instead undifferentiated sound, or a sequence of undifferentiated numbers. The effect of this dedifferentiation of the sound is to produce monotony in the afferent stimulation, which is conducive to drowsiness or sleep. In fact, reports of drowsiness are very common from subjects in vigilance tasks (Refs. 2 & 3). The consequence of this state of drowsiness may be sleep itself, or an attempt on the part of the subject to redifferentiate his stimulus world by means other than listening for signals. The latter course is usually chosen by human subjects.

The means used by subjects to redifferentiate their environment may include attending to irrelevant (from the point of view of the experi-menter) stimuli in the external environment, or attending to internal stimulation in the form of daydreams or irrelevant mind-wandering. These irrelevant activities are usually incompatible with efficient detection of signals. The point is that when a subject stops doing what he should be doing he may initiate a chain of events which further decreases the probability that he will again do what he should be doing. The sequence consists of the following steps:

1. Initial inattentiveness due to low signal frequency, or low reinforcement frequency;
2. Dedifferentiation of stimulus material in the relevant display;
3. Drowsiness due to undifferentiated stimulation;
4. Redifferentiation of stimulus environment by attention to irrelevant stimuli and mind-wandering;
5. Inefficient signal-detection behaviour.

With this general construction of the events in a vigilance task we may now turn to the observed difference between extraverts and introverts in the early part of a vigil and the improvement of performance of extraverts with the introduction of the secondary task.

It appears that the difference between extraverts and introverts is in the first step of the sequence of events listed above. It seems that in the early part of the vigil the listening behaviour of the extravert is influenced more by the frequency of occurrence of signals. When the extravert listens for signals and doesn't hear any he tends to stop listening (step 1). The introvert persists in listening for signals even though they occur infrequently. This difference between introvert behaviour and extravert behaviour can be thought of in terms of the *extinction* of the responses involved in listening for signals. If the occurrence of signals reinforces these listening responses and if signals occur infrequently, then there is not much reinforcement of the listening response and the result is a tendency for these responses to be extinguished. This means that when signals are infrequent the subject is less likely to listen for them. It may be that extinction of listening responses takes place earlier for extraverts than for introverts. A relationship between extinction and introversion-extraversion has been suggested by Eysenck (Ref. 9) and Franks (Ref. 10).

The addition of the secondary task, which involves about a tenfold increase in signals to be detected, should serve to increase the reinforcement of listening responses and prevent the early extinction of these responses. This would explain the early improvement of the extraverts with the secondary task.

The secondary task also seems to produce some improvement in the introverts, but in this case the improvement comes in the latter part of the vigil. It can be assumed that eventually there is extinction of listening responses for the introverts, but this tends to occur later in the vigil and produces a decrement in performance. The secondary task seems to help prevent this decrement.

REFERENCES

1. ADAMS, J. A., Vigilance in the detection of low-intensity signals. *J. exp. Psychol.*, **52**, 204–208, 1956.
2. BAKAN, P., Discrimination decrement as a function of time in a prolonged vigil. *J. exp. Psychol.*, **50**, 387–390, 1955.
3. ——, Vigilance: Discussion 3. *The Advancement of Science*, **53**, 410, 1957.
4. BAKER, C. H., *Biasing Attention to Visual Displays During a Vigilance Task*. App. Psych. Res. Unit 227/56, RNP 58/876. Cambridge: Medical Research Council, 1956.
5. BROADBENT, D. E., Classical conditioning and human watchkeeping. *Psychol. Rev.*, **60**, 331–339, 1953.
6. ——, Noise, paced performance and vigilance tasks. *Brit. J. Psychol.*, **44**, 295–303, 1953.
7. DEESE, J., Some problems in the theory of vigilance. *Psychol. Rev.*, **62**, 359–368, 1955.
8. ELLIOTT, E., Auditory vigilance tasks. *The Advancement of Science*, **53**, 393–399, 1957.
9. EYSENCK, H. J., A dynamic theory of anxiety and hysteria. *J. ment. Sci.*, **101**, 28–51, 1955.
10. FRANKS, C. M., Personality factors and the rate of conditioning. *Brit. J. Psychol.*, **48**, 119–126, 1957.
11. FRASER, D. C., The relation of an environmental variable to performance in a prolonged visual task. *Quart. J. exp. Psychol.*, **5**, 31–32, 1953.
12. HOLLAND, J. G., Technique for behavioural analysis of human observing. *Science*, **125**, 348–350, 1957.
13. JERISON, H. J. & WING, S., Effects of noise and fatigue on a complex vigilance task. *Technical Report* 57–14, WADC, U.S.A.F., 1957.
14. —— & WALLIS, R. A., Experiments on vigilance: Performance on a simple vigilance task in noise and quiet. *Technical Report 57–318*, WADC, U.S.A.F., 1957.

15. LOEB, M. & JEANTHEAU, G., The influence of noxious environmental stimuli on vigilance. *J. appl. Psychol.*, **42**, 47–49, 1958.

16. MACKWORTH, N. H., *Researches on the Measurement of Human Performance*. London: H.M.S.O. Medical Res. Council Spec. Rep. Ser. No. 268, 1950.

17. ——, Some factors affecting vigilance. *The Advancement of Science*, **53**, 389–393, 1957.

18. PEPLER, R. D., *The Effect of Climatic Factors on the Performance of Skilled Tasks by Young European Men Living in the Tropics. 4. A Task of Prolonged Visual Vigilance*. App. Psych. Res. Unit Rep. No. 156, Cambridge: Medical Research Council, 1953.

19. WHITTENBURG, J. A., ROSS, S. & ANDREWS, T. G., Sustained perceptual efficiency as measured by the Mackworth 'clock' test. *Percept. mot. Skills*, **6**, 109–116, 1956.

20. WILKINSON, R. T., *Effects of lack of sleep*. Interim Report (OES 287, FPRC 961·3) App. Psych. Res. Unit, Cambridge: Medical Research Council.

19

The Effects of Noise and Doubling the Signal Frequency on Individual Differences in Visual Vigilance Performance

D. R. DAVIES & G. R. J. HOCKEY

First published in *British Journal of Psychology*, **57**, 381–389, 1966

4 GROUPS of 6 extraverts and 4 groups of 6 introverts, selected by the Maudsley Personality Inventory, performed a 32 minute visual cancellation task under one of two conditions of signal frequency, high and low and in either noise (95 db) or quiet (70 db). In quiet, at both levels of signal frequency, extraverts showed a steady decline in the number of signals detected correctly but introverts did not. Neither group showed a decrement under noise conditions. Noise, compared with quiet, significantly increased the number of correct detections made by extraverts under low signal frequency conditions but a similar increase under high signal frequency conditions was not significant. The addition of noise had no significant effect on the number of correct detections made by introverts. Doubling the signal frequency had no significant effect on the performance of introverts or extraverts in either noise or quiet. Introverts made significantly more errors of commission in quiet than in noise while extraverts made significantly more in noise than in quiet. Possible reasons for the findings are discussed.

INTRODUCTION

Many experiments have demonstrated that, with increasing arousal, performance at several different tasks improves up to an optimal point and thereafter declines (Refs. 10, 14 & 16). The relation between arousal level and performance is thus considered to take the form of an inverted U-shaped curve. A subject's arousal level is sometimes regarded as lying on a continuum bounded at one end by deep sleep and by extreme excitement at the other. Various physiological measures, such as EEG frequency and amplitude, heart rate and skin conductance have been thought to provide an indication of a subject's arousal level (Ref. 11) but some investigators have preferred to rely on operational defini-

141

tions of arousal, such as 'the inverse probability of falling asleep' (Ref. 7). Corcoran considered sleep-deprived subjects to be at a lower level of arousal than subjects who have slept normally; quite apart from the fact that this accords well with common sense, there is some physiological evidence to support the assumption (Ref. 8). Intense stimulation, in the form of white noise for example, is generally held to raise the arousal level. Given the assumption of an inverted U-relation between arousal and performance, the effect on performance of adding noise to a task situation should depend upon the initial arousal level of the subject. A greater improvement in performance would be expected from subjects who are initially at a low level of arousal, for example, sleep-deprived subjects, than from subjects who have had their normal night's sleep, who are more highly aroused and thus nearer the optimal arousal point to begin with. This expectation has been confirmed by Corcoran (Ref. 5).

The amount of sensory input can also be increased by increasing the quantity of relevant information fed to the subject in a given interval of time, for example, increasing the signal frequency in a vigilance task. Thus the effects of increasing the signal frequency on the performance of sleep-deprived and 'normal' subjects should parallel the effects of added noise. This has also been confirmed by Corcoran (Ref. 6). Both noise and signal frequency seem to be arousing in their effects, therefore, given that sleep-deprived subjects are less aroused than subjects who have slept normally.

The performance of extraverts and introverts, whether selected by the Heron Sociability Scale (Ref. 15) or by the Maudsley Personality Inventory (Ref. 13) would appear to be analogous to that of sleep-deprived and 'normal' subjects and it is possible to think of introverts as being more aroused than extraverts (Refs. 4 & 9). Bakan found that the addition of a secondary task, which had the effect of increasing signal frequency, resulted in a significantly greater improvement in the vigilance performance of extraverts as compared to introverts (Ref. 1).

Two assumptions underlay the present experiment. They are: (a) that noise and increasing the signal frequency are arousing in their effects and (b) that introverts are more aroused than extraverts. The purpose of the experiment was to observe the effects of adding noise and doubling the signal frequency on the vigilance performance of introverts and extraverts. Expectations were: (i) that in quiet the vigilance performance of introverts will be superior to that of extraverts, (ii) that extraverts will show a greater improvement when noise is added and that this improvement will be greater under conditions of low signal frequency and (iii) that compared to quiet conditions the performance of introverts will either show no change or be impaired under conditions of noise, the probability of impairment being greater under conditions of high signal frequency.

METHOD

Subjects, divided into groups of introverts and extraverts, performed a visual cancellation task lasting for 32 minutes in which they were instructed to detect discrepancies between two sources of information, each discrepancy constituting a signal. Each subject performed the task under one of two conditions of signal frequency, high (HSF) and low (LSF). In the HSF condition there was a total of 48 signals to be detected during the task and in the LSF condition a total of 24. Each subject performed the task in either noise (95 db) or quiet, in which extraneous noise was masked by a noise level of 70 db.

Subjects

The Maudsley Personality Inventory was administered to 86 women undergraduates. From this group 24 introverts (mean E scale score 14·37, S.D. 3·73, mean N scale score 28·80, S.D. 10·91) and 24 extraverts (mean E scale score 33·50, S.D. 4·11, mean N scale score 22·00, S.D. 11·01) were selected. Each group was further subdivided into 4 groups of 6 subjects, making 8 experimental groups in all. The 8 groups were matched as closely as possible on N scale scores. Subjects were tested between 10 a.m. and noon in groups of 12.

Apparatus

The task used was a visual cancellation task, consisting of a series of 1800 digits, from 1 to 9 inclusive, selected from a table of random numbers. Consecutive divisions of 360 digits were drawn on five recording traces and fitted on the drum of a spiral kymograph in turn. The guide-line for the digits was obtained by attaching the pen of the kymograph to a 1 sec timer with the drum revolving at a speed of 12 mm/sec. One number was hand drawn in the first half of each 1 sec space by means of a template with a window of dimension 10×6 mm. The five traces were used consecutively in the experiment by the alternate use of two drums on which the traces were mounted. A short break of 6–7 sec occurred each time the drums were changed over. The display was situated in a small room adjoining the subjects' room and relayed to it by means of closed-circuit television. The camera was focused on a window 10×6 mm cut in a piece of white cardboard and attached to the kymograph by means of a clamp. During the experiment the kymograph drum revolved at a speed of 9 mm/sec and each digit was visible on the screen for $\frac{2}{3}$ sec. The digits on the traces were magnified $\times 9$ on the 30 inch screen. The task lasted for 32 minutes and was continuously watched on a television monitor in the experimental room. In the noise condition white noise was relayed from the television set in the subjects' room into the open field at a level of 95 db. In the quiet condition the level was 70 db.

Procedure

Subjects were instructed to check the order of the digits, as they appeared on the screen, against a typescript of digits and to note any discrepancy between the digits on the screen and those on the script by cancelling the digit on the script and replacing it by the appropriate digit on the screen. Each discrepancy constituted a signal. In the LSF condition there were six signals in each 8 minute subperiod of the task and in the HSF condition there were 12. Alternate HSF signals were omitted in the LSF condition. The temporal arrangement of signals in each subperiod of the task was the same. The total of 1800 digits on the typescript was divided into eight sheets of 225 digits arranged in 25 rows of 9. Two 'dummy' sheets were added to these 8, to minimize the occurrence of the 'end-spurt' effect observed when the length and present point in the vigil are known (Ref. 3). Subjects were also asked to remove their watches. Two practice periods were given after the task had been explained to subjects. In the first, which lasted for 2 minutes, the occurrences of signals were pointed out to subjects. They were then invited to ask questions. The second practice period lasted for 8 minutes and the task followed after a short break. In this second period knowledge of results was not given. Two response measures were taken; correct detections and errors of commission, i.e., when a subject reported the detection of a signal when one had not in fact been presented.

RESULTS

Each of the three variables of the experiment, extraversion or introversion, noise or quiet, high or low signal frequency, was examined in a $2 \times 2 \times 2$ factorial design. The four time-periods of the task were also taken into consideration. The data were treated by means of a trend analysis (Ref. 12). The detection scores from the LSF conditions were doubled to facilitate comparison with those from the HSF conditions. The analysis for correct detections is shown in Table 1 and for errors of commission in Table 2. In both analyses, mean squares were tested against the corresponding between-subjects or within-subjects residuals. In the analysis of correct detections the within-subjects residual includes the $E \times N \times S \times P$ interaction which was not calculated since it was clear that most of the variance was accounted for by the other interactions. The residual is therefore larger than the usual subjects pooled $\times$ periods error term and the F test more stringent. It is most unlikely that the two non-significant F ratios would have been affected by this. Fig. 14 shows the mean correct detection and commissive error scores of introverts and extraverts plotted against time for the four conditions of the experiment.

TABLE 1

TREND ANALYSIS OF CORRECT DETECTION SCORES FOR INTROVERTS
AND EXTRAVERTS OVER THE FOUR CONDITIONS OF THE EXPERIMENT

Source of variation	S.S.	D.F.	M.S.	F
	Between subjects			
Extraversion (E)	23·37	1	23·37	3·22
Noise levels (N)	18·13	1	18·13	2·50
Signal frequency (S)	2·75	1	2·75	0·38
$E \times N$	17·75	1	17·75	2·45
$E \times S$	0·89	1	0·89	0·12
$N \times S$	24·63	1	24·63	3·40
$E \times N \times S$	10·18	1	10·18	1·40
Residual (subjects pooled)	290·04	40	7·25	—
Total	387·74	47	—	—
	Within subjects			
Periods (P)	19·05	3	6·35	3·29*
$E \times P$	54·78	3	18·26	9·46†
$N \times P$	63·86	3	21·29	11·03†
$S \times P$	16·31	3	5·44	2·81*
$E \times N \times P$	43·48	3	14·46	7·49†
$E \times S \times P$	5·84	3	1·95	1·01
$N \times S \times P$	3·62	3	1·21	0·63
Residual (including $E \times N \times S \times P$)	237·91	123	1·93	—
Total	444·75	144	—	—

* $p < 0.05$
† $p < 0.001$

F

TABLE 2

TREND ANALYSIS OF ERRORS OF COMMISSION FOR INTROVERTS AND
EXTRAVERTS OVER THE FOUR CONDITIONS OF THE EXPERIMENT

Source of variation	S.S.	D.F.	M.S.	F
	Between subjects			
Extraversion (E)	0·02	1	0·02	0·005
Noise levels (N)	1·01	1	1·01	0·28
Signal frequency (S)	6·01	1	6·01	1·67
E×N	15·19	1	15·19	4·23*
E×S	1·04	1	1·04	0·28
N×S	11·04	1	11·04	3·21
E×N×S	37·42	1	37·42	10·42‡
Residual (subjects pooled)	143·50	40	3·59	—
Total	215·23	47	—	—
	Within subjects			
Periods (P)	70·85	3	23·62	16·75‡
E×P	3·75	3	1·25	0·88
N×P	1·80	3	0·60	0·42
S×P	4·75	3	1·58	1·12
E×N×P	7·74	3	2·58	1·82
E×S×P	26·72	3	8·91	6·24†
N×S×P	22·87	3	7·62	5·40†
E×N×S×P	35·57	3	11·86	8·41‡
Residual	169·70	120	1·41	—
Total	343·75	144	—	—

* $p < 0.05$
† $p < 0.01$
‡ $p < 0.001$

Table 1 and Fig. 14 suggest four principal findings for correct detections. (a) Significant effects appear only when time at work is taken into account. The significant periods effect indicates that the shape of the overall performance curve changed significantly with time at work. Performance, averaged over the eight experimental conditions, declined with time on task and the linear component of the performance curve is significant ($F = 7.76$; D.F. 1, 123; $p < 0.025$). The significant extraversion × periods interaction indicates that the effect of time at work on the shape of the performance curve is significantly different for introverts and extraverts, the latter showing a greater tendency to defect fewer signals as the task progresses. (b) The significant noise ×

periods interaction would appear to indicate that noise improves performance to a greater extent towards the end of the task. (c) The signal frequency × periods interaction would appear to indicate that in the first, third and fourth periods of the task, HSF groups are superior to LSF groups, whereas in the second period, LSF groups are superior to HSF groups. (d) The significant extraversion × noise × periods interaction indicates that the differential shift in efficiency of introverts and extraverts with time at work depends on the noise level. The decrement found in the performance of extraverts at both levels of signal frequency in quiet disappeared in noise, although the performance curves for introverts remained very much the same under both conditions. In other words, extraverts are more likely than introverts to show decrement in quiet, a finding which is similar to that of Bakan, Belton & Toth (Ref. 2). This difference is not apparent in noise.

Chi-square analyses of decrement were made, following a procedure

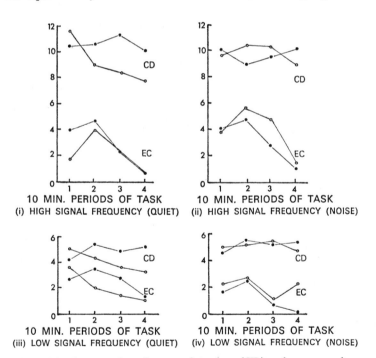

Figure 14. Mean number of correct detections (CD) and mean number of errors of commission (EC) made by introverts (filled circles) and extraverts (open circles) in the four conditions of the experiment.

adopted by Bakan, Belton & Toth (Ref. 2): decrement was indicated by a subject detecting fewer signals in periods 3 and 4 than in periods 1 and 2. Since no differences were found between comparable high and low signal frequency groups with respect to this measure, the results were pooled and the analyses carried out between the variables of extraversion and noise level only. Only one significant result was obtained: the comparison between introverts (quiet) and extraverts (quiet) yielded a χ^2 value of 8·17 (p<0·005) indicating that in quiet more extraverts (10/12) than introverts (2/12) show decrement. This finding is in agreement with that reported by Bakan, Belton & Toth (Ref. 2) and supports the significant extraversion × noise × periods interaction noted in the trend analysis.

When the mean level of performance of introverts and extraverts was considered in each of the four task conditions, introverts were found to detect significantly more signals than extraverts in quiet at both low and high signal frequencies (Mann-Whitney U tests, p<0·05 and p<0·03 respectively). Extraverts improved significantly with noise under LSF conditions (Mann-Whitney U test, p<0·008) but their improvement with noise under HSF conditions failed to reach significance. Noise had little or no effect on the performance of introverts at either level of signal frequency and doubling the signal frequency did not significantly alter the performance level of either group in noise or quiet.

For errors of commission, it can be seen from Table 2 that there are two significant main effects, the extraversion × noise and the extraversion × noise × signal frequency interactions. Introverts made more errors of commission in quiet than in noise, while extraverts made more in noise than in quiet. Under LSF conditions extraverts made the same number of errors of commission in noise as in quiet, while introverts made twice as many in quiet as in noise. Under HSF conditions introverts made about the same number of errors in quiet as in noise while extraverts made nearly twice as many in noise as in quiet.

When time at work is taken into account there is a significant effect of periods, as with correct detections. The number of errors of commission increased from the first period to the second and declined sharply from the second period to the fourth. The linear component of the trend is significant (F = 35·75; D.F. 1, 120; p<0·001). This decline in commissive errors with time on task can perhaps be interpreted as the result of practice (Ref. 17); subjects gradually learn what constitutes a signal and what does not and their criterion for responding becomes more cautious.

The other three significant interactions appear to have the following implications. (a) Under quiet conditions more errors were made under LSF conditions than under HSF conditions, in each period of the task. This difference was most marked in the first period and gradually diminished during the succeeding three periods. Under noise conditions, the HSF and LSF trend lines fall between the two trend lines for quiet conditions. The difference between the two trend lines in noise is much less than the difference in quiet. (b) Extraversion also interacted with signal frequency and time at work. The trend lines for introverts in both signal frequency conditions lie between those for extraverts. Extraverts made more errors under HSF conditions and these were substantially reduced under LSF conditions. Introverts made slightly more errors under LSF conditions than under HSF conditions. Noise also affected this relation, as might be expected from the significant $E \times N \times S$ interaction.

Summarizing these results, correct detections decreased over time, but this finding can be attributed entirely to the results for extraverts working under quiet conditions. They showed a considerable decline in performance, while extraverts under noise, and introverts under noise or quiet, showed essentially no change with time at work.

As far as total scores for errors of commission are concerned, extraverts made most errors under the condition characterized by noise and HSF, while introverts made most errors under the condition of quiet and LSF. Thus the number of errors of commission was greatest for extraverts in the most 'stimulating' condition and for introverts in the least 'stimulating' condition. When changes over time are taken into account, it is apparent that the number of errors decreased over time but the extent of the decrement varied with different experimental conditions. Signal frequency affected the steepness of the decline in that the decrement was greater for LSF than for HSF groups, but only under quiet conditions or when extraverts alone are considered.

Finally, the total number of responses (correct detections+errors of commission) and correct detections expressed as a percentage of all responses for introverts and extraverts under the 4 task conditions are shown in Table 3. The percentage of all responses that were correct detections made by extraverts in quiet at both levels of signal frequency was about the same as that for introverts. The difference between the number of correct detections made by introverts and extraverts in quiet can be accounted for by the fact that introverts in quiet made more responses; it is not necessary to suppose that they are more likely to be

TABLE 3

MEAN NUMBER OF RESPONSES
(CORRECT DETECTIONS + ERRORS OF COMMISSION) FOR EACH SUBJECT

	Low signal frequency		High signal frequency	
	Quiet	Noise	Quiet	Noise
Introverts	29·33	25·50	49·16	45·16
Extraverts	22·66	29·33	41·50	48·33
	Correct detections as a percentage of all responses			
Introverts	67%	80%	86%	86%
Extraverts	65%	73%	90%	84%

correct when they do respond. In noise the rate of responding increased for extraverts and decreased for introverts by about the same amount at both signal frequency levels. In HSF conditions, although the percentage of responses that were correct detections increased, compared with LSF conditions, there is again very little difference between introverts and extraverts. In noise introverts respond less but are more correct when they do, while extraverts simply respond more.

DISCUSSION

The hypotheses put forward in the introduction to this paper are in the main confirmed and the results would seem best suited to an interpretation in terms of arousal. However, some qualifications are indicated. The effects of noise, signal frequency, extraversion and time at work interact in a complex manner. It is therefore unrealistic to specify what effect each of the variables is exerting upon performance, since any such effect will be highly dependent upon other experimental variables. This finding underlines the difficulty of comparing results from different studies unless they are obtained under identical conditions.

Three assumptions were stated in the introduction: that introverts are more aroused than extraverts, that noise is more arousing than quiet and that a high signal frequency is more arousing than a low one. The relation between arousal and performance was considered to take the form of an inverted U-shaped curve. Given these assumptions and the further assumption that adding noise is more arousing than increasing the signal frequency, the 8 groups can be ordered in terms of arousal as shown from left to right on the abscissa in Fig. 15. When the total number of correct detections is plotted on the ordinate the result can be

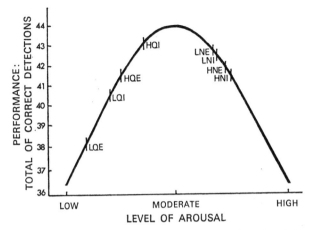

Figure 15. Total correct detection scores for the eight experimental groups plotted against the hypothesized level of arousal. L, low signal frequency; H, high signal frequency; Q, quiet; N, noise; I, introverts; E, extraverts.

seen to fit an inverted U. However, no such relation applies to errors of commission or to the total number of responses. Arousal must therefore be envisaged as affecting correct detections in a predictable manner but the way in which it affects the other two response measures, if at all, remains unclear. In any case there is no independent measure of arousal in Fig. 15.

Moreover, it is difficult to explain extraversion-introversion differences in terms of arousal, if this is taken to imply an underlying physiological variable. Reason & Benson (personal communication), using 48 subjects, have found no correlation between Maudsley Personality Inventory scores and either (a) the resting level of heart rate, muscle tension or skin resistance, or (b) the difference between the resting level and the working level during performance of a tracking task. The former variables could be regarded as measures of arousal and the latter as measures of arousability. Thus extraverts and introverts could be held to differ in arousal only if by arousal is meant a cognitive state not directly related to activation as measured physiologically.

In the case of the individual variables in this experiment there are at least equally efficient alternatives to the arousal explanation. However, since the significant effects to be explained are predominantly interactional, an arousal theory has the advantage of accounting for the complex effects of different factors in terms of variation along a single hypothetical continuum. Thus, in spite of some difficulties of interpretation, an arousal theory of vigilance performance provides a reasonably parsimonious account of the present findings, although a conclusive test of its adequacy remains to be made.

ACKNOWLEDGEMENTS

The authors are grateful to members of the Department of Psychology, University of Leicester and to Dr D. W. J. Corcoran, for their comments on earlier drafts of this paper. This research was supported in part by a grant from the Medical Research Council.

REFERENCES

1. BAKAN, P., Extraversion-introversion and improvement in an auditory vigilance task. *Brit. J. Psychol.*, **50**, 325–332, 1959.
2. ——, BELTON, J. A. & TOTH, J. C., Extraversion-introversion and decrement in an auditory vigilance task. In *Vigilance: a Symposium* (eds. D. N. Buckner & J. J. McGrath). New York: McGraw-Hill, 1963.
3. BERGUM, B. O. & LEHR, D. J., End spurt in vigilance. *J. exp. Psychol.*, **66**, 383–385, 1963.
4. BROADBENT, D. E., Possibilities and difficulties in the concept of arousal. In *Vigilance: a Symposium* (eds. D. N. Buckner & J. J. McGrath). New York: McGraw-Hill, 1963.
5. CORCORAN, D. W. J., Noise and loss of sleep. *Quart. J. exp. Psychol.*, **14**, 178–182, 1962.
6. ——, Doubling the rate of signal presentation in a vigilance task during sleep deprivation. *J. appl. Psychol.*, **47**, 412–415, 1962.
7. ——, Individual Differences in Performance After Loss of Sleep. Unpublished Ph.D. thesis, University of Cambridge Library, 1963.
8. ——, Changes in heart rate and performance as a result of loss of sleep. *Brit. J. Psychol.*, **55**, 307–314, 1964.
9. ——, Personality and the inverted-U relation. *Brit. J. Psychol.*, **56**, 267–274, 1965.
10. DUFFY, E., The psychological significance of the concept of arousal or 'activation'. *Psychol. Rev.*, **64**, 265–275, 1957.

11. ——, *Activation and Behaviour*. New York: Wiley & Sons, 1962.
12. EDWARDS, A. L., *Experimental Design in Psychological Research*. New York: Holt, Rineheart and Winston, 1960.
13. EYSENCK, H. J., *The Manual of the Maudsley Personality Inventory*. London: University of London Press, 1959.
14. HEBB, D. O., Drives and the C.N.S. (conceptual nervous system). *Psychol. Rev.*, **62**, 243–254, 1955.
15. HERON, A., A two-part personality inventory for use as a research criterion. *Brit. J. Psychol.*, **47**, 243–251, 1956.
16. MALMO, R. B., Activation: a neuro-psychological dimension. *Psychol. Rev.*, **66**, 367–386, 1959.
17. MCGRATH, J. J., Some problems of definition and criteria in the study of vigilance performance. In *Vigilance: a Symposium* (ed. D. N. Buckner & J. J. McGrath). New York: McGraw-Hill, 1963.

F*

20

Influence of Motivation on Reactive Inhibition
in Extraversion-Introversion

MARTIN J. HOGAN

First published in *Perceptual and Motor Skills*, **22**, 187–192, 1966

THE present study was designed to examine the influence of reactive inhibition (defined as involuntary rest pauses) on the performance of a vigilance task by extraverts and introverts. It was hypothesized that extraverts would perform more poorly than introverts when level of motivation was held constant. A personality inventory, a motivation questionnaire and a psychomotor (vigilance) task were administrated to 50 female Ss, who were grouped as extraverts or introverts on the basis of their personality test scores. Level of motivation for the two groups was equated. Mean performance scores on the vigilance task for the two groups were compared. The results suggest that the concept of reactive inhibition as applied by Eysenck may be used to explain the vigilance performance of extraverts and introverts. There was some support for Eysenck's finding that high levels of drive tend to obscure the performance difference between introverts and extraverts.

INTRODUCTION

Eysenck suggests that extraverted and introverted behaviours are a function of certain properties of the central nervous system, especially those of the cortex (Ref. 3). He has published two studies which support the concept of reactive inhibition (I_R) as he applied it from the work of C. L. Hull (Ref. 11) to explain individual differences between extraverts and introverts (Refs. 3 & 4). In these two studies, he used the concept of reactive inhibition to explain the individual differences within different types of populations and across different tasks.

Studies by others tend to support Eysenck's hypothesis. Franks found that dysthymics are conditioned more rapidly than hysterics (Ref. 10). He used the eyeblink reflex simultaneously with the GSR and attributed his results to the presence of greater reactive inhibition in the extravert.

However, Rechtschaffen points out that it is difficult to defend the reactive inhibition hypothesis with eyelid conditioning data (Ref. 13). He feels that the interval between trials is not favourable to account for the cumulative effect of reactive inhibition. Rechtschaffen reported that this result neither supported the relationship between the amount of aftereffect and extraversion, nor the accumulation of I_R and extraversion. Eysenck seems to have reconciled these apparently negative results in his Satiation/Inhibition theory (Ref. 5). Furthermore, Becker states that Rechschaffen's results could be attributed to chance since no correction for multiple comparisons of data was employed (Ref. 1).

Becker used modifications of several of Eysenck's tests for reactive inhibition, cortical inhibition (basal), and satiation (Ref. 1). He found that the concept of basal cortical inhibition seemed to be a unitary factor, unrelated, however, to extraversion-introversion. Eysenck's assumption that satiation and reactive inhibition compose a unitary trait was thus not supported. There was no evidence that satiation co-varied with extraversion, but there was minimal support for covariation of reactive inhibition and extraversion.

Eysenck suggested that reactive inhibition may be inversely related to level of motivation (Ref. 7) and cited his finding that a high level of motivation tends to neutralize higher degrees of reactive inhibition as support (Ref. 15). In this case, then, Eysenck believes that level of motivation is a crucial variable in extraversion-introversion comparisons. There are at least two possible explanations of the influence of motivation on the psychomotor performance of these two groups. On the one hand, motivation might obscure the differential effects of reactive inhibition of introverts and extraverts. And on the other hand, different levels of motivation may account for performance differences observed between extraverts and introverts. The latter alternative would certainly be a more parsimonious explanation, if true. Either explanation may account for the contradictory findings of various researchers.

Since Becker (Ref. 1), whose negative findings have been discussed previously, did not attempt to control for level of motivation even by matching his introvertive and extravertive Ss, his results are difficult to interpret.

Eysenck assessed level of drive from an external criterion; Ss were candidates for selection to an industrial training school. Since the level of drive was not quantified, one can only assume that all were motivated to the same degree. An attempt was made in the present research to assess level of motivation by means of a self-report questionnaire given at the time of administration of the task. In a recent study (Ref. 8), Eysenck reported extraverts produced more frequent involuntary rest pauses (as measured by number of gaps within a tapping series) than introverts during massed practice. However, according to Kimble involuntary rest pauses must be distinguished from the cessation of activity which results from neuromuscular impairment (Ref. 12). In the present experiment a psychomotor task was employed which would minimize the cessation of activity resulting from neuromuscular fatigue. The task required that S respond to the correct stimulus by pressing a button over a 10 minute period of 20 massed trials. Occurrence of involuntary rest pauses or I_R is defined here as the number of correct responses over the 20 trials. It was predicted that there would be a difference between extraverts and introverts in performance on this psychomotor task after both groups were equated for level of motivation.

Eysenck claims that level of motivation tends to obscure the effects from the degree of inhibition which the extravert and introvert are said to possess. If, therefore, both groups are equated for level of motivation, statistically significant differences in performance can be more readily attributed to the differential degrees of reactive inhibition which introverts and extraverts are said to possess.

METHOD

Subjects

The sample was composed of 90 nursing students in the Washington D.C. area. All Ss were female, full-time students in a university and between the ages of 17 and 23. Ss were equated on the verbal scores of the College Entrance Examination Board (CEEB). The means, standard deviations and results of tests of significance, for age and the CEEB verbal scores of the extraverts and introverts are given in Table 1.

TABLE 1

MEANS AND STANDARD DEVIATIONS OF AGE AND CEEB-VERBAL SCORES

		Extravert	Introvert	t	p
Age	M	18·88	20·12	3·456	0·01
	SD	0·82	1·56		
	N	25	25		
CEEB-Verbal	M	545·12	531·40	0·616	
	SD	62·12	77·13		
	N	25	25		

Apparatus

The Motivation Scale (MS),[1] a self-report inventory, was constructed by the investigator to measure S's motivation to perform a continuous performance task. Each of 50 items, given to six psychologists, all of whom had a minimum of 2 year graduate training, was rated on a 5-point scale as to whether the item assessed level of motivation.

The average interrater reliability (Ref. 2) was 0·94. In order to minimize the sources of error in the inventory, those items on which two or more raters disagree were eliminated. For the 34 items retained, the average rater inter-correlation was 0·97. The split-half reliability coefficient for the MS scores of all 50 Ss, computed by the Spearman-Brown Formula, was 0·97.

The Continuous Performance Test (CPT) is an instrument which Rosvold, *et al.* constructed for the study of brain damage in humans (Ref. 14). It consists of a revolving drum on which are 31 letters, coming into view at approximately 0·92 sec intervals. The drum revolves approximately twice a minute in a boxlike case equipped with a visor through which S is required to look. The letters are briefly illuminated by five 0·5w neon bulbs inside the case, fired by the discharge of an 8-microfarad condenser. A response was correct if S pressed the response key for every X followed by an A within 0·69 sec after its illumination. Following this interval there was a period of 0·23 sec before the illumination of the next letter. Correct and incorrect responses were automatically recorded on a set of counters facing the back of the machine where E sat.

The test-retest reliability coefficient for the number of correct responses by normal Ss is 0·74 (Ref. 14).

Procedure

Ss were separated into two groups according to their scores on the MPI. The 25 Ss who scored lowest on the E scale of the Maudsley Personality Inventory (Ref. 6) constituted the introverts and the 25 Ss who scored highest on the E scale of the MPI comprised the extraverts. The means, standard deviations and tests of significance for E scale scores and Neuroticism scale scores are given in Table 2.

The responses on the CPT for the first two trials were for practice

---

[1] Copies of the MS are available from the author upon request or from the ADI Auxiliary Publications Project, Photoduplication Service, Library of Congress, Washington, D.C. 20540. Remit $1.25 for photocopies or 35-mm. microfilm of Document No. 8636.

TABLE 2

MEANS AND STANDARD DEVIATIONS OF NEUROTICISM AND EXTRAVERSION
SCALE SCORES AND MOTIVATION SCALE SCORES (N = 25)

Score		Extravert	Introvert	t	p
Neuroticism	M	22·72	20·40	0·95	
	SD	6·86	9·77		
Extraversion	M	39·94	19·94	15·97	0·001
	SD	2·94	5·45		
Motivation	M	27·96	26·28	1·74	NS
	SD	2·71	3·87		

and were not counted in Ss' scores. Following a 2 minute rest period,
Ss were given a 10 minute test (20 trials) in which there were 120 possible
correct responses.

Immediately following this, S was asked to fill out the MS by encircling
'yes' or 'no', to each item, choosing the alternative which best described
her attitude while taking the CPT.

Reference to Table 2 shows that there was no significant difference
between the means of the two groups on level of motivation and so it
can be concluded that the groups were equated.

RESULTS

Since the two groups differed significantly with respect to age, the results
of the study could be attributable to the age variable, but when a
Pearson product-moment correlation was computed between age and
CPT scores, the value was 0·02. In view of this zero order correlation, it
can be safely concluded that the age variable is not related to performance on the CPT.

Extraverts produced significantly fewer responses than introverts
(t = 3·98; p = <0·01). In order to determine whether or not the
difference between the introverts' and extraverts' performance could
have been due to an initial over-all performance difference, analysis of
variance and the Newman-Keuls method of testing all possible means
were employed (Ref. 16). The latter analysis showed that the mean of
Trials 5, 6, 7, 8, 9, 10, 11, 14, 15, 16, 17 and 20 is significantly different
from the mean of Trials 1, 2, 3, 4 (p<0·05). Trial means of 2 and 3 are
different from those of 8 and 10 (p<0·05). All other possible combinations are not significant. It seems safe to infer from this analysis that the

overall difference observed between the two groups was not due to an initial performance differential.

The results of the analysis of variance for repeated measures of correct responses of the two groups are summarized in Table 3. As predicted, the main effect of trials is significant, that is, extraverts produced significantly more involuntary rest pauses than did the introverts.

TABLE 3

ANALYSIS OF VARIANCE OF CORRECT RESPONSES
FOR EXTRAVERTS AND INTROVERTS (N = 50)

Source	df	F	p
Between Ss	49		
Extraversion	1	13·48	0·01
Ss within groups	48		
Within Ss	950		
Trials	19	3·73	0·01
Trials × Extraversion	19	0·75	
Trials × Ss within groups	912		

In an attempt to try to find the relationship of motivation to the dimension of introversion-extraversion, another analysis of variance was computed. The two groups of Ss were split at the median on the Motivation test. The main effect of motivation was not significant but trials again were. However, there was a significant interaction of trials and motivation (F = 1·87; df = 19/912). Although the effects of motivation and extraversion are confounded, these results would not be inconsistent with Kimble's prediction (Ref. 12) and Eysenck's finding that high drive prevents the occurrence of frequent involuntary rest pauses (Ref. 8).

The evidence of the present study indicates that, although both groups were equated on level of motivation, the extraverts did significantly worse on the performance task. Consequently, the expectation that the extraverts' decrement in performance would be due to the lack of control for motivation for both groups is not supported. However, level of motivation is a crucial variable in this type of study. Whether or not higher levels of motivation will tend to obscure the differential degrees of reactive inhibition (defined as involuntary rest pauses) of the extraverts and introverts is not clear.

Since Becker's experimental procedure consumed approximately 8 hours of testing time, it is quite possible that the level of motivation could have influenced his results. At least, it can be said that he had little or no control for this variable.

The level of motivation in the present study was assessed by Ss' self reports. While this method is more readily quantifiable and more relevant to the task at hand, there are problems. It is possible that the extravert is able to present himself as socially desirable and yet not be highly motivated. The motivation scale is transparent and the extravert has social acumen. Consequently, the higher scores obtained by the extraverts may not reflect a high level of motivation at all, but rather their desire to appear in a socially desirable light.

The present study suggests that the construct of reactive inhibition is useful in explaining the differences between the extraverts and introverts to the extent that the MS is an adequate measure of motivation. The MS should be further refined and be used in conjunction with more objective tests of motivation, such as those suggested by Eysenck & Willett (Ref. 9).

REFERENCES

1. BECKER, W. C., Cortical inhibition and introversion-extraversion. *J. abnorm. soc. Psychol.*, **61**, 52–66, 1960.
2. EBEL, R. L., Estimation of reliability of ratings. *Psychometrika*, **16**, 407–424, 1951.
3. EYSENCK, H. J., Cortical inhibition, figural aftereffect and the theory of personality. *J. abnorm. soc. Psychol.*, **51**, 94–106, 1955.
4. ——, Reminiscence, drive and personality theory. *J. abnorm. soc. Psychol.*, **53**, 328–333, 1956.
5. ——, Comments on a test of the personality-satiation theory. *Psychol. Rep.*, **5**, 395–296, 1959.
6. ——, *Manual of the Maudsley Personality Inventory*. London: University of London Press, 1959.
7. ——, *Experiments in Motivation*. New York: Macmillan, 1964.
8. ——, Involuntary rest pauses in tapping as a function of drive and personality. *Percept. mot. Skills*, **18**, 173–174, 1964.
9. —— & WILLETT, R. A., The measurement of motivation through the use of objective indices. *J. ment. Sci.*, **107**, 961–968, 1961.
10. FRANKS, C. M., Conditioning and personality: a study of normal and neurotic subjects. *J. abnorm. soc. Psychol.*, **52**, 143–149, 1956.

11. HULL, C. L., *Principles of Behaviour*. New York: Appleton-Century, 1943.
12. KIMBLE, G. A., An experimental test of a two-factor theory of inhibition. *J. exp. Psychol.*, **39**, 15–23, 1949.
13. RECHTSCHAFFEN, A., Neural satiation, reactive inhibition and introversion-extraversion. *J. abnorm. soc. Psychol.*, **57**, 283–291, 1958.
14. ROSVOLD, H. R., MIRSKY, A. F., SARASON, I., BRANSOME JR., R. D. & BECK, L. H. A continuous performance test of brain damage. *J. consult. Psychol.*, **20**, 343–350, 1956.
15. WILLETT, R. A. & EYSENCK, H. J., Experimentally induced drive and difficulty level in serial rote learning. *Brit. J. Psychol.*, **53**, 35–39, 1962.
16. WINER, B. J., *Statistical Principles in Experimental Design*. New York: McGraw-Hill, 1962.

21

Physiological Reactivity to Sensory Stimulation as a Measure of Personality

S. B. G. EYSENCK & H. J. EYSENCK[1]

First published in *Psychological Reports*, **20**, 45–46, 1967

6 INTROVERTS and 6 extraverts were tested with respect to the increment of salivary activity as a consequence of (a) putting 4 drops of lemon juice on their tongues and (b) having them swallow 4 drops of lemon juice. Under condition (a) introverts salivated significantly more than extraverts; under condition (b) extraverts salivated significantly more than introverts. Pavlov's theory of transmarginal inhibition was suggested as a possible explanation of this reversal.

INTRODUCTION

It has been shown that introverts react more strongly with salivation to the placing of 4 drops of lemon juice on the tongue than do extraverts (Refs. 1 & 4). Correlations between the increment in salivation so produced and E.P.I. scores are in the neighbourhood of 0·7 and these findings are in good accord with theoretical prediction (Ref. 2). The present paper is concerned with the effects of increasing the strength of the stimulus by asking Ss to swallow the lemon juice rather than to keep it on the tongue; subjectively at least this produces a much stronger sensation and the greater number of taste buds stimulated gives reasonable physiological grounds for accepting this introspective comment universally made by Ss. What kind of prediction would one make for the increased stimulation, as far as the salivary reaction of extraverts and introverts is concerned? At first sight it seems likely that increasing the strength of stimulation would increase the differentiation between introverts and extraverts, with introverts even more responsive than extraverts. However, Pavlov's law of transmarginal inhibition suggests that

[1] We are indebted to the Research Fund of the Maudsley and Bethlem Royal Hospitals for the support of this investigation, and to Mrs N. Humphery for the carrying out of testing.

when intensity of stimulation goes beyond a certain point reactions become inhibited and Teplov and his school have demonstrated that individuals with 'weak nervous systems' show transmarginal inhibition earlier than do individuals with 'strong nervous systems' (Ref. 5). If we may identify the concept of 'weak nervous system' with introversion (Ref. 2), then it is possible to argue that strong stimulation might have the paradoxical result of producing greater reactivity in extraverts. The present experiment may throw some light on this point.

METHOD

Six extreme introverts and 6 extreme extraverts were chosen to take part in the experiment; their scores on the E.P.I. (Ref. 3) ranged from 1 to 6 for the introverts and from 12 to 21 for the extraverts (M, 4·2 and 15·7, respectively). No mean differences were found with respect to neuroticism. Each S was tested twice, once under ordinary conditions, i.e., with 4 drops of lemon on the tongue for 30 sec and once with instructions to swallow the drops immediately. In each case the test was preceded by establishing the salivation rate (first trial) without any stimulation, by positioning a standardized dental cotton-wool swab on S's sublingual salivary gland for 30 sec and weighing it. The same procedure was followed during the second trial; in addition, the lemon juice was introduced. Our previous work has shown that Trial 2 scores and difference scores (Trial 2 minus Trial 1) give equally good correlations with personality scores; first trial scores do not correlate with personality to any appreciable extent.

RESULTS

Results under lemon-on-the-tongue conditions show that the introverts increased their salivation by 0·58 gr. on the average, extraverts by 0·15 gr. The difference is significant at the 5 per cent level by t test and in the same direction as previous studies. Results under lemon-swallowed-immediately conditions, however, are very different. Introverts show an increment of 0·83 gr., extraverts one of 1·25 gr. (t test, $p<0·01$). Thus an incremental difference of 0·43 gr. of introverts relative to extraverts under lemon-on-the-tongue conditions turns into a relative decrement of 0·42 gr. under lemon-swallowed-immediately conditions ($p<0·01$). It is interesting that only one S (of the 6), with an E score of 15, had a low difference score under 'swallowing' conditions and a high difference score under 'on tongue' conditions, i.e., contrary to the average results; this S also had a lie scale score of 4, as compared with a mean of less than 1 for the rest of the girls. It is thus possible that in her case the phsyiological test may have given a truer result than the inventory, which of course can be easily faked.

DISCUSSION

These results suggest that possibly transmarginal inhibition may have been active in producing the reversal in salivary reactivity of introverts and extraverts under conditions of slight and strong stimulation of the taste buds. Alternative possibilities exist, of course, and must be ruled out before such a conclusion can be firm. Thus it is possible that the first touch of the lemon juice on the tongue produces a burst of salivation in introverts; all this saliva would then be swallowed with the lemon juice, so that introverts would start out with a deficit. Only direct recording from the salivary glands, both sublingual and parotid, will permit a decision between such widely different theories.

REFERENCES

1. CORCORAN, D. W. J., The relation between introversion and salivation. *Amer. J. Psychol.*, **77**, 298–300, 1964.
2. EYSENCK, H. J., *The Biological Basis of Personality*. Springfield, Ill.: Thomas, 1967.
3. —— & EYSENCK, S. B. G., *Manual of the Eysenck Personality Inventory*. San Diego: Educ. and Indust. Testing Service, 1964.
4. EYSENCK, S. B. G. & EYSENCK, H. J., Salivary response to lemon juice as a measure of introversion. *Percept. mot. Skills*, **24**, 1047–1053, 1967.
5. GRAY, J., *Pavlov's Typology*. Oxford: Pergamon Press, 1964.

22

The Interaction of Noise and Personality with Critical Flicker Fusion Performance

C. D. FRITH

First published in *British Journal of Psychology*, **58**, 127–131, 1967

A THEORY of the interaction of arousal, performance and personality is outlined. On the basis of this theory it is predicted that an increase in noise will improve the performance of extraverts in a CFF task more than that of introverts. An experiment confirming this prediction is described.

INTRODUCTION

In an investigation of the effects of drugs and their interactions with personality it was intended to use critical flicker fusion (CFF) threshold as an indication of the initial level of cortical arousal in a subject and as a measure of the effect of the drug.

As an essential preliminary to this investigation the relation between CFF performance and personality was studied in relation to an arousing agent (auditory noise) whose mode of operation is, theoretically at least, more readily apparent. Arousal is defined in terms of Hebb's theory (Ref. 9). Hebb proposed that afferent impulses serve two quite different functions as a result of the two different pathways to the cortex. One of these is an indirect route through the ascending reticular formation, the non-specific, or diffuse projection system which bombards large areas of the cortex with afferent impulses. This bombardment serves an arousal function, 'toning up' the cortex with a background of supporting activity. Lindsley has shown that the discrimination of two flashes in the visual cortex of cats can be enhanced by stimulating the reticular formation electrically (Ref. 10). This result suggests that CFF thresholds should reflect activity in the reticular formation and thus level of arousal. In line with this hypothesis it is well established that stimulant drugs raise c.f.f. while depressant drugs lower it (Ref. 7).

Less well established are the relations between CFF and personality.

165

Some studies have shown that extraverts have lower CFF than introverts (e.g., Ref. 13). Eysenck has put forward a model to explain such individual differences in terms of cortical arousal (Ref. 5). He suggests that introverts are characterized by dominance of 'excitatory' processes and extraverts by 'inhibitory' ones, the terms 'excitation' and 'inhibition' being defined by means of clearly demarcated experiments. These concepts are also used in Pavlov's Typology and his weak and strong nervous systems are roughly equivalent to introversion and extraversion respectively. Yerkes & Dodson (Ref. 15) and many others (e.g., Refs. 12 & 14) have found a curvilinear relation between arousal and performance. A similar curvilinear relation between performance and stimulus intensity (the law of strength and transmarginal inhibition) is an important feature of Pavlov's system and has been interpreted by Gray in terms of arousal (Ref. 8). There is also evidence that the optimum level of arousal is lower for 'difficult' than for 'easy' tasks (Ref. 1).

Introverts, because of the dominance of excitatory processes and their greater sensitivity to incoming stimulation, will, under the same conditions, be more aroused than extraverts. If the curvilinear relation between arousal and performance is also taken into account the relation between personality, arousal and performance will be as shown in Fig. 16. It should be noted that the abscissa in this figure is not the level of arousal, but the extent of arousing factors, i.e., the intensity of

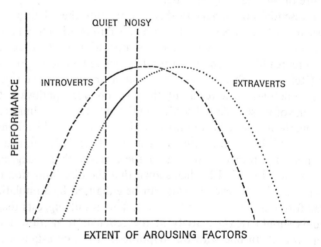

Figure 16. Hypothesized relationship between the extent of
arousing factors, personality and performance.

external or internal stimulation. This formulation has the advantage that the units on both axes are measured rather than inferred. Such a relation between weak and strong nervous systems has been shown in Teplov's laboratory for reaction time and the critical frequency of flashing phosphene, with stimulus intensity as the arousing factor (Ref. 8) and also between introverts and extraverts for more complex tasks by Corcoran (Ref. 4), arousal being manipulated by incentives and sleep deprivation.

In line with this model of arousal, personality and performance is a finding of Yermolayeva-Tomina that with irrelevant distraction (the sound of a metronome) the absolute visual sensitivity of subjects with weak nervous systems decreased while that of those with strong nervous systems increased (Ref. 16). These changes tended to reduce the differences between the groups. Claridge found similar effects with a vigilance task (Ref. 2). When a second vigilance task was introduced as distraction, performance on the main task improved in hysterics (neurotic extraverts) and got worse in dysthymics (neurotic introverts).

It seems likely that this model should also apply to CFF performance. Some studies have shown a facilitating effect of auditory noise on CFF, others have not (e.g. Ref. 11). These contradictions might be resolved by taking into account initial levels of arousal and personality variables. If CFF performance were to be used as an indication of the effects of drugs it was essential that there should be some prior knowledge of the relationship between arousal, performance and personality for this task. It might be assumed that the task is a relatively easy one and the situation a relatively unarousing one for the subjects. Thus they would be operating below the optimum level of arousal. Fig. 16 shows that in these conditions an increase in the external arousing factors would produce a greater improvement in the performance of extraverts than in that of introverts. The investigation reported here tested this hypothesis using auditory noise as the arousing factor.

METHOD

A forced choice technique for measuring CFF threshold was used. Such a technique has been found to be more reliable than the classical psychophysical methods (Ref. 3) and it also cuts out the effects of differing strategies used by subjects which might well be related to personality The subjects were required to say which of four lights was flickering. At the threshold area errors rose from zero to 75 per cent. This threshold area was first found approximately for each subject. Five frequencies, whole numbers of c/s differing by 1 c/s, were then chosen to span the threshold area. Changes in the subject's performance could be measured more sensitively in terms of changes in numbers of errors, rather than in terms of changes in some threshold point measured in c/s. Each testing session lasted 8 minutes and is described in detail below. Subjects were tested under two noise levels, corresponding to 'quiet' and 'noisy' experimental conditions.

Subjects

There were 40 subjects, 29 male, 11 female. All were normal adult volunteers aged between 18 and 50. The subjects were split into four groups, first, by procedure, half the subjects having the noisy condition and the other half the quiet condition first, and secondly, by personality, subjects being divided into introverts and extraverts on the basis of their EPI scores (Ref. 6). Details of the four groups are shown in Table 1. Within personality groups the order of presentation of conditions was assigned randomly.

TABLE 1

MEANS AND RANGES OF EPI SCORES FOR THE FOUR EXPERIMENTAL GROUPS

		Noise-Quiet		Quiet-Noise	
		Mean	Range	Mean	Range
Extraverts	E	15·3	12–18	16·4	12–22
	N	9·9	4–14	7·6	0–21
Introverts	E	7·2	0–11	6·9	3–11
	N	7·4	0–14	9·0	1–16

Apparatus

The flicker was generated electronically. A blocking oscillator provided pulses to an Eccles-Jordan bi-stable multivibrator, which was connected to a Ferranti CL 40 glow modulator tube, which emitted a blue light. The light-dark ratio was 1:1 over the range of frequencies used (33–51 c/s). A control panel with four switches produced, for 2 sec, one flickering and three stable lights, each switch producing the flickering light in a different position. The lights were displayed in a square array on a white background, with a central orange fixation point. The white background was a square of side 39 cm, the four lights being centred in it at the corners of a square of side 7 cm. The lights, which were 8 mm in diameter, were numbered anticlockwise, starting at the top left-hand corner. The display was illuminated by a slide projector 100 cm away, illumination of the face and lights being 101·9 ft/Lamberts. The subjects viewed the display at a distance of 160 cm through an artificial pupil 2 mm in diameter, movement of the head being reduced by a chin rest and the necessity to keep all four lights in view. The test field was thus 2 degrees in angular diameter. Noise for the noisy condition was produced by apparatus (power packs, oscillators and electric fans) which gave an average noise level of 50 db. The quiet condition was obtained by the subject wearing a pair of ear guards giving a noise level of 20 db.

Procedure

The approximate threshold was found for each subject under noisy conditions. Five frequencies differing by 1 c/s were then chosen to fall within the threshold area. In the testing session that followed these frequencies were given to the subject 5 times each in a latin square design. Thus there were five *occasions* on which all frequencies were presented. Within each occasion each frequency was presented five times in quick succession. Thus there were five *presentations* containing all frequencies and all occasions. The exact timing of the session was as follows: five presentations of frequency 1, lights being on for 2 sec and off for 1 sec; 4 sec gap during which frequency was changed; 5 presentations of frequency 2; and so on. Thus the whole session lasted just under 8 minutes. Subjects were tested thus under both experimental conditions, there being a 5 minute rest between sessions. The subject was instructed to call out the number of the flickering light. He was told that if no light appeared to be flickering then he must guess. The position of the flickering light was randomized.

RESULTS

The number of correct responses in each session (125 presentations) was found for each subject. An analysis of variance for these scores is shown in Table 2. From the analysis it can be seen that there was a significant order effect, subjects tending to do better on the second testing session and a significant interaction between conditions and personality. Table 3 shows that this interaction was due to improved performance in noisy conditions of the extravert group only. The data were also subdivided in terms of conditions, presentations and frequencies but little further information was gained from this. There was a significant difference between frequencies, in that subjects performed better at low frequencies.

TABLE 2

ANALYSIS OF VARIANCE; TOTAL NUMBER OF CORRECT RESPONSES IN EACH SESSION

Source	Sums of squares	D.F.	Mean squares	F	P
Between subjects	26,076	39	—	—	—
Personality (P)	189	1	189·0	—	—
Groups within P	2,773	2	1,386·5	2·16	—
Subjects within G	23,114	36	641·0	12·44	0·001
Within subjects	3,643	40	—	—	—
Order (O)	1,178	1	1,178·0	22·90	0·001
Conditions (C)	278	1	278·0	4·40	0·05
O×P	63	1	63·0	1·22	—
C×P	270	1	270·0	5·25	0·05
Error within	1,854	36	51·5	—	—
Total	29,719	79			

TABLE 3

PERCENTAGE OF CORRECT RESPONSES FOR EACH PERSONALITY GROUP UNDER EACH CONDITION

	Noisy	Quiet
Extraverts	58·56	52·64
Introverts	53·16	53·12

DISCUSSION

The results confirm the prediction made from the theory relating arousal, performance and personality outlined in the introduction, in that extraverts showed a greater improvement in CFF performance with an increase in auditory noise than did introverts. Table 3 indicates that the introverts showed no change in performance suggesting that they were already at their optimum level of arousal for this task. Such an interpretation could account for the equivocal results of previous experiments which have investigated individual differences or the effects of auditory noise on CFF. Clear differences between personality groups would only appear if the groups were operating well below or above their optimum levels of arousal. The same would apply to the effects of arousing factors. If the arousal of a group of subjects already in the region of the optimum level of arousal were increased then about half would show improved performances and the rest depressed performances. However, the clear increase in performance produced by stimulant drugs is not consistent with this hypothesis. A further complication is the marked order effect found in the present study. This suggests that a learning effect operates to produce changes in performance quite independently of changes in arousal. Quite apart from these complications, if it is correct that in normal conditions subjects are close to their optimum level of arousal for CFF performance, then CFF performance should not be a good measure of changes in arousal, since points from the top of the inverted-U must give the least sensitive and the least reliable reflections of changes in arousal.

ACKNOWLEDGEMENTS

The author is indebted to Prof. H. J. Eysenck and Dr G. W. Granger for their help and encouragement and to the Maudsley and Bethlem Royal Research Fund for financial assistance.

REFERENCES

1. BROADHURST, P. L., The interaction of task difficulty and motivation: The Yerkes-Dodson Law revived. *Acta Psychol.*, **16**, 32–38, 1959.
2. CLARIDGE, G. S., The excitation-inhibition balance in neurotics. In *Experiments in Personality*, vol. II (ed. H. J. Eysenck). London: Routledge & Kegan Paul, 1960.
3. CLARK, W. C., RUTSEMANN, J., LINK, R. & BROWN, J. C., Comparison of flicker fusion thresholds obtained by the methods of forced choice and limits on psychiatric patients. *Percept. mot. Skills*, **16**, 19–30, 1963.
4. CORCORAN, D. W. J., Personality and the inverted-U relation. *Brit. J. Psychol.*, **56**, 267–273, 1965.
5. EYSENCK, H. J., *Experiments with Drugs*. Oxford: Pergamon Press, 1963.
6. —— & EYSENCK, S. B. G., *Manual of the Eysenck Personality Inventory*. London: University of London Press, 1964.

7. GRANGER, G. W., Abnormalities of sensory perception. In *Handbook of Abnormal Psychology* (ed. H. J. Eysenck). London: Pitman, 1960.

8. GRAY, J. A., *Pavlov's Typology*. Oxford: Pergamon Press, 1964.

9. HEBB, D. O., Drives and the C.N.S. (conceptual nervous system). *Psychol. Rev.*, **62**, 243–253, 1955.

10. LINDSLEY, D. B., The reticular system and perceptual discrimination. In *Reticular Formation of the Brain* (ed. H. H. Jasper). London: Churchill, 1957.

11. MAIER, B., BEVAN, W. & BEHAR, I., The effect of auditory stimulation upon the critical flicker frequency for different regions of the visual spectrum. *Amer. J. Psychol.*, **74**, 67–73, 1961.

12. SCHLOSBERG, H. S., Three dimensions of emotion. *Psychol. Rev.*, **61**, 81–85, 1954.

13. SIMONSON, R. & BROZEK, J., Flicker fusion frequency: background and applications. *Physiol. Rev.*, **32**, 134–178, 1952.

14. STENNETT, R. G., Performance level and level of arousal. *J. exp. Psychol.*, **54**, 54–61, 1957.

15. YERKES, R. M. & DODSON, J. D., The relation of strength of stimulus to rapidity of habit formation. *J. comp. Neurol. Psychol.*, **18**, 458–482, 1908.

16. YERMOLAYEVA-TOMINA, L. B., Concentration of attention and strength of the nervous system. In *Pavlov's Typology* (ed. J. A. Gray). Oxford: Pergamon Press, 1964.

23

The Influence of Age and Temperament on the Adult Human Sleep-Wakefulness Pattern

G. S. TUNE

First published in *British Journal of Psychology*, **4,** 431–441, 1968

OVER 600 adult subjects (aged 20–79) were asked to keep a day by day record of their hours of sleep on sleep-charts, for a period of 56 days. When completed the charts gave details of the duration of sleep, the times of falling asleep and awakening, the number and duration of nocturnal disturbances of sleep and the number and duration of mid-day naps. A sample of 240 subjects (20 males and 20 females in each decade from the 20s to the 70s inclusive) was made consisting only of people who recorded for 50 or more days. These subjects were matched, as far as possible, in terms of neuroticism, temperament and intelligence.

It was found that although the average amount of sleep taken per day declined slightly from the 20s to the 50s, there was an increase in the 60s. This was partly due to an increase in the number of mid-day naps taken. The extraverts slept longer than the introverts. The incidence of nocturnal disturbances increased with advancing age, especially in females. These and other findings are discussed and it is suggested that in later years when social and occupational pressures are reduced, there is a tendency for a polycyclic sleep-wakefulness pattern to reappear.

INTRODUCTION

Attempts to measure the amount and quality of sleep a person takes have used five main methods; (a) continuous electroencephalographic recordings, (b) continuous or regular periodic observation by a trained person, (c) interviews, (d) questionnaires and (e) sleep charts. Although the first two methods can give virtually complete data they are time consuming and are more suitable for the intensive study of a few people. The third and fourth methods are less time consuming for the experimenter but yield subjective estimates of duration and mid-night disturbances etc., which are liable to error. The use of sleep charts (where the subject keeps his own record) has found some favour in the past decade since it proved useful in situations where subjects carried on with their daily activities (Ref. 13). Apart from giving detailed data about time of going to sleep, awakening, sleep disturbances and mid-day naps etc., the method gives the experimenter knowledge of the period of time over which the variables under consideration were measured, whereas most subjective methods leave this in doubt.

These methods have been used to measure both the duration and quality of sleep in both normals (Ref. 21) and abnormals (Refs. 5, 6, 16 and 23) and despite the difficulties inherent in measuring these aspects of behaviour, estimates have been reported and variations related to individual differences.

Best & Taylor (Ref. 2) stated that growing children need 10–12 hours sleep per 24 hours, while older people need rather less: 5–7 hours. These figures are rather broad and other investigators have been more specific. Andress, for example, showed that a group of 18–21 year old students took an average of 8·75 hours sleep (Ref. 1); other estimates differ widely.

Clemént & Bourlière (Ref. 4) interviewed 380 subjects (none of whom used sleeping pills) and were unable to find any great change in the amount of sleep taken over age (a mean of 7 hours 25 minutes was reported). Webb (Ref. 21), on the other hand, using a questionnaire found, surprisingly he thought, that the 50–89 year old group took slightly more sleep (7·39 hours) than the 30–49 year old group (7·23 hours). Laird's questionnaire survey of 509 men of distinction in American society also showed that subjects in the 80s took more sleep than those in younger age groups (Ref. 11). McGhie & Russell limited their attention to those people who claimed to sleep for 5 hours or less and found that the majority of these subjects were elderly (Ref. 17).

It might be thought that sex differences would exist in the total duration of sleep because of the continuing domestic duties of the female, throughout life, whereas the male would experience a sudden loss of activity on retirement, thus leaving him free to sleep if he so wished. Neither Webb (Ref. 21) nor McGhie & Russell (Ref. 17), however, found a sex difference at any age, while Clemént & Bourlière found that women slept only slightly longer (10 minutes) than men (Ref. 4).

The demands of a person's occupation do, it seems, affect the duration of their sleep. Using a sleep chart method with hospital staff, Masterton found differences between nursing and medical staff, the nurses sleeping longer hours and differences between physicians and surgeons in favour of the former (Refs. 14 and 15). The more senior also tended to sleep longer. All of these personnel and a group of schoolboys studied by similar means took more sleep during holidays possibly in an attempt to pay off an accumulated sleep debt. Despite these occupational differences, Clément & Bourlière (Ref. 4) found no relationship between intellectual level, as measured by the vocabulary score on the WAIS, and the duration of sleep. Vocabulary size, however, is not necessarily an index of occupational class. McGhie & Russell who used the Registrar General's classification found this more useful, for more subjects in Classes IV and V were reported to sleep for 5 hours or less than those in higher groups (Ref. 17).

There are some interesting incidental findings in this area. Lewis (Ref. 12) and Lewis & Masterton (Ref. 13) again using sleep charts, this time on scientists in polar areas, found that an average of 7·9 hours sleep was taken. This figure was remarkably constant over time despite periods of total darkness or daylight and despite the occasional fractioning of sleep into several shorter periods because of the demands of the job. Ross also working with scientists in Arctic conditions, found that slightly less sleep was taken in Oxford (7·6 hours), the 'home' of the expedition, than in Northeastern Norway (7·8 hours) where the scientists did their field work (Ref. 19). The effect of living at between 10,000 and 20,000ft in the Himalayas was much the same in that the expedition members took more sleep at altitude than when at home (Ref. 22).

An attempt to relate personality variables to duration of sleep was undertaken by Costello & Smith on patients who were observed discontinuously (Ref. 6). The extraverts slept considerably longer than the introverts both with (2·34 hours) and without medication (1·02 hours).

So far as the duration of sleep is concerned, then, it seems that despite different estimates of the mean figure, which may have arisen because of the differences in the data collecting methods used, there has been some success in associating individual differences with duration of sleep. A similar situation is apparent in the data which attempts to show how the quality of sleep depends upon age, sex and occupation, etc.

A frequently used indicator of the quality of sleep is how many times the person awakens having fallen asleep. Hobson & Pemberton in their extensive interviews of older people found that such disturbances were common in those aged 60 and over; 34·2 per cent of the males and 35·6 per cent of the females claimed to awaken several times per night (Ref. 9). The authors argued that even when allowances were made for those subjects who exhibited degenerative age changes there remained a substantial proportion of older people who suffered from severe sleep disturbances due to other causes. Webb noted that the frequency of admitted nocturnal disturbances rose with age: 16 per cent of the 9–29 year olds reported two or more disturbances per night, 39 per cent of the 30–49 year olds and 69 per cent of those aged 50 and over (Ref. 21). McGhie & Russell examined these complaints in more detail, taking only those persons who complained of mid-night disturbances occurring with 'great frequency' (Ref. 16). They found that women claimed the disturbances significantly more often than men and that while the incidence was unrelated to social class it increased rapidly with age.

It might be thought that subjects who suffered from poor quality sleep might be more prone to taking compensatory mid-day naps. Surprisingly little evidence is available on this, and comes from an incidental finding in the McGhie & Russell study which reported only 1·72 per cent of the subjects having admitted to taking mid-day sleep (Ref. 16).

It seems that the duration and quality of sleep varies widely between individuals when assessed by a variety of methods. The chief determinants of this variety, age, sex and occupation, are of obvious importance and it seems likely that temperament may have some influence. None of the studies examined possible interactions between variables, a situation which is hard to overcome without a large body of data on which the appropriate statistics may be performed. The present study was therefore undertaken in an attempt to examine three main variables, age, sex and temperament. The first two are known to be related to various dependent measures of sleep while there is suggestive evidence from Costello & Smith on the effect of temperament on duration of sleep (Ref. 6).

METHOD

625 members of the Medical Research Council Unit for Research on Occupational Aspects of Ageing panel of volunteers were sent sleep charts (Fig. 17). Printed instructions informed the subjects about the general nature of the study and gave information on how the charts were to be completed. A printed and partially completed specimen card was included. Because no reasonable check could be made on so many subjects the instructions asked for honesty and accuracy. It was emphasized that only the time actually spent asleep was to be recorded and not time spent awake in bed. Accuracy to the nearest half hour was demanded and if there was any difficulty in remembering times then the subjects

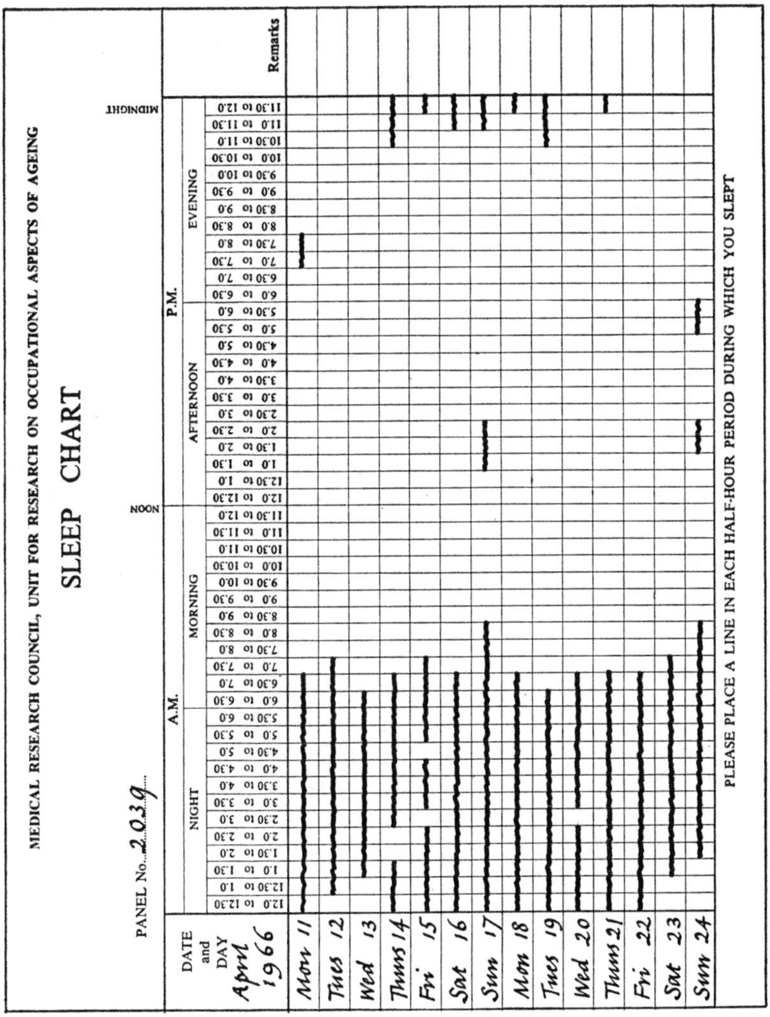

Figure 17.

were advised to leave the day in question blank. There was a remarks column into which details of medication and shift work or illness were to be placed. Each chart lasted for 14 days. Four successive charts were sent to each subject at two week intervals in an attempt to get a 56-day sample (Monday 11th April, 1966 to Sunday 6th June, 1966, inclusive) of data from each participant.

G

The design of the chart was based on similar ones used by the Medical Research Council's Human Physiology Section (Ref. 13) and consisted of a 10×8 in. yellow card on which the lines represented days. These were divided into two major areas, a.m. and p.m., subdivided into four six hour periods named 'morning', 'afternoon', 'evening' and 'night'. The final subdivision was into labelled half-hour periods. It was completed by having the subject draw a line through each half-hour period in which he subsequently judged himself to have been asleep for more than 15 minutes. Brief instructions were printed on the cover of the chart.

RESULTS

From each chart the following data were collected: (a) the mean duration of sleep per 24 hour period, (b) the mean time of falling asleep, (c) the mean awakening time, (d) the number of mid-night awakenings, (e) the mean duration of the mid-night awakenings, (f) the number of mid-day naps, (g) the mean duration of the mid-day naps.

271 men and 238 women (N = 509, 81·4 per cent) returned one or more of the charts sent to them. Not all subjects recorded their sleep habits for the same length of time (the mean number of days recorded was 51·8); however, from among those who recorded for 50 or more days (a mean of 55·7 days was found) a sample of 240 was made. This consisted of 20 males and 20 females in each decade from the 20s to the 70s inclusive. This was the maximum possible sample size because of a lack of subjects in the extreme age groups. So far as possible subjects were matched for temperament, by means of their scores on part 2 of the Heron Inventory, and for nonverbal intelligence. A description of the subjects is given in Table 1.

The data were classified by age (6 groups), sex (2 groups) and temperament (2 groups), these being achieved by ranking the subjects by their score on part 2 of the Heron Inventory (Ref. 8), within each age and sex group and dividing the population into 2 equal parts at the median score). The distributions of the data were plotted and analyses of variance performed on three variables (mean duration of sleep per 24 hour period, mean time of falling asleep and mean awakening time) which distributed relatively normally: the remaining variables were examined by a series of chi². The results of these are reported below and shown in Table 2.

TABLE 1

DESCRIPTION OF THE SUBJECTS USED IN THE STUDY (N = 240)

Age Group	Sex	N	Mean	SD	Heron Part 1 (Neuroticism)		Heron Part 2 (Sociability)		Raven's Matrices Score		Mill Hill Vocabulary Score	
					Mean	SD	Mean	SD	Mean	SD	Mean	SD
20–29	Male	20	25·45	2·37	8·05	4·21	6·65	2·54	52·90	5·62	31·30	9·46
	Female	20	23·95	2·98	9·40	3·15	5·20	2·57	52·20	3·92	31·70	4·59
30–39	Male	20	35·40	3·39	6·85	3·71	4·95	2·69	54·00	5·39	32·60	3·49
	Female	20	35·55	2·61	8·25	2·97	5·90	2·73	47·15	8·79	33·15	3·58
40–49	Male	20	44·50	3·20	7·65	4·27	5·70	2·76	48·95	5·92	35·15	5·60
	Female	20	45·00	3·45	7·60	3·62	6·25	2·40	47·70	4·88	35·70	4·34
50–59	Male	20	55·55	2·35	7·00	2·99	6·20	3·38	48·00	5·35	35·75	4·98
	Female	20	55·50	2·62	6·80	3·99	5·90	3·22	44·15	7·97	32·25	4·29
60–69	Male	20	64·55	3·21	5·75	3·07	5·65	2·52	44·65	7·96	37·45	4·28
	Female	20	64·70	2·97	6·90	3·51	5·95	3·24	37·80	9·09	32·90	5·34
70–79	Male	20	73·45	2·89	6·85	3·38	6·00	2·51	38·20	8·79	34·80	5·86
	Female	20	73·75	2·77	6·95	3·29	5·85	2·43	35·25	4·49	34·05	7·15
Totals/means		240	49·78	17·12	7·34	3·57	5·85	2·74	45·91	9·63	34·15	5·05

TABLE 2

MEANS AND STANDARD DEVIATIONS OF THE DEPENDENT VARIABLES (N = 240)

Age Group	Sex	Mean duration of Sleep/24 hr. (hrs.)		Mean time of falling asleep		Mean awakening time		No. of mid-night awakenings/8 weeks		Mean duration of mid-night awakenings		No. of mid-day naps/8 weeks		Mean duration of mid-day naps		N
		Mean	SD	Mean	SD	Mean	SD	Mean	SD	Mean	SD	Mean	SD	Mean	SD	
20–29	Male	7·65	1·60	12·20	1·94	7·93	1·33	2·70	4·41	0·68	1·03	0·45	0·68	0·38	1·76	20
	Female	7·72	1·59	12·25	1·48	8·05	1·47	4·95	6·22	0·66	1·60	2·15	6·17	0·44	1·95	20
30–39	Male	7·68	1·97	11·97	2·02	7·69	1·76	6·20	6·25	0·74	1·43	3·35	5·08	0·52	1·58	20
	Female	7·59	2·01	11·97	1·86	7·59	1·80	6·40	10·43	0·53	1·26	2·05	3·08	0·36	1·47	20
40–49	Male	7·38	1·80	12·07	1·63	7·38	1·88	5·80	6·75	0·60	1·26	6·10	8·88	0·59	2·16	20
	Female	7·61	1·92	12·10	1·39	7·64	1·76	3·55	4·06	0·58	1·16	4·45	5·70	0·45	1·68	20
50–59	Male	7·45	2·38	11·94	2·02	7·34	1·71	10·55	15·72	0·62	1·43	10·50	13·51	0·59	1·46	20
	Female	7·08	2·87	12·12	3·03	7·47	2·09	23·20	24·40	0·87	1·88	5·20	7·67	0·46	1·41	20
60–69	Male	7·81	2·98	11·66	2·44	7·46	2·31	10·90	21·78	0·49	1·58	12·40	12·64	0·72	2·66	20
	Female	7·93	3·76	11·60	2·78	7·62	2·84	16·35	18·25	0·74	1·40	12·45	13·82	0·63	1·55	20
70–79	Male	8·09	5·16	11·90	2·37	7·99	3·83	24·95	25·90	0·86	2·09	22·40	22·18	0·69	1·66	20
	Female	7·20	3·71	12·07	2·23	7·47	2·51	26·90	30·86	1·00	1·67	13·55	12·65	0·83	1·68	20
Totals/means		7·59	2·91	11·99	2·19	7·63	2·28	11·87	18·78	0·70	1·78	7·92	13·31	0·55	1·82	240

The Mean Duration of Sleep

The mean duration of sleep per 24 hour period was 7·59 hours. This varied, however, depending on age and temperament. There was a progressive decline in amount of sleep taken from the 20s to the 50s. In the 60s there was a sudden increase but a further decrease was evident in the 70s. From the analysis of variance, age was significant (F = 2·287, df = 5 and 216, p<0·05) as was temperament (F = 10·785, df = 1 and 216, p<0·001). The sex variable was not. On average the males took slightly more sleep (7·68 hours) than the females (7·52 hours), a difference of about 10 minutes. The introverted subjects in general took less sleep (7·38 hours) than the extraverted (7·78 hours) a difference of about 24 minutes, however there was an interaction of age and temperament (F = 3·437, df = 1 and 216, p<0·01) which is apparent in Fig. 18. This shows that the two temperament groups took approximately the same amount of sleep up until the 40s, but thereafter the extraverted tended to

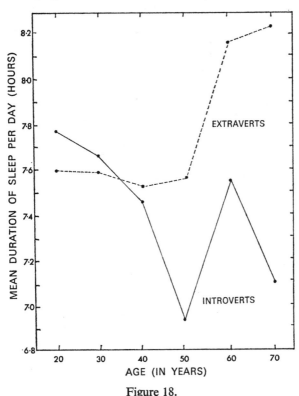

Figure 18.

sleep longer and, with some variation, the introverted rather less. A significant age by sex interaction (F = 2·586, df = 5 and 216, p<0·05) was apparently due to the erratic changes in the duration of sleep reported in the later decades by the females.

The Mean Time of Falling Asleep

The subjects were asked to record in which half-hour period they fell asleep rather than when they went to bed. The mean time of falling asleep for the entire population was 11·59 p.m. Older people tended to go to sleep rather earlier than the younger (F = 3·645, df = 5 and 216, p<0·01). Although the males tended to go to sleep earlier than the females and the extraverts earlier than the introverts these variables were not significant.

The Mean Awakening Time

The mean awakening time for the whole sample of 240 subjects was 7·63 a.m. Age was a significant variable (F = 3·885, 5 and 216, p<0·01) indicating that older people awoke earlier than younger. Within this

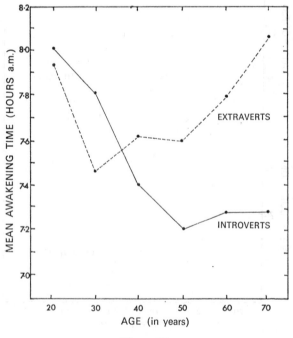

Figure 19.

general finding there were other influences at work. Even though sex was not a significant variable temperament was (F = 8·077, df = 1 and 216, p<0·01) and there was a significant age by temperament interaction (F = 3·709, df = 5 and 216, p<0·01) as Fig. 19 shows. The mean awakening time for the extraverted was 7·75 a.m. and for the introverted 7.50 a.m., a difference of 15 minutes. The trends are similar to those relating to the age by temperament interaction in the mean duration of sleep in that after the age of 40 the extraverts tended to awaken later and the introverts earlier.

The Frequency of Mid-Night Awakenings

There was rapid increase in the number of mid-night awakenings with age. In the 20s the reported frequency was about 1 per 2 weeks but by the 70s the figure was over 3 per week. Dividing the population at the median a chi² showed that a significantly large number of older people reported a high frequency of nocturnal disturbances (chi² = 16·178, p<0·001). Similar calculations showed that sex (chi² = 0·288) and temperament (chi² = 0·017) were not significant. There was a rapid increase in the number of disturbances the females reported from the 40s to the 50s. It seemed that in the menopausal years the female sleep pattern was severely disrupted and that the effects were not reversed in later years. Further chi² were calculated taking 10 disturbances as a cutoff point. From these it was clear that those subjects who suffered most from nocturnal disturbances were over 50 years of age (chi² = 28·174, p<0·001) and female (chi² = 18·870, p<0·001).

The Duration of the Mid-Night Awakenings

The mean duration of the mid-night awakenings was 0·70 hours (42 minutes). A series of chi² dividing the populations at the median scores showed that the durations remained constant with age (chi² = 1·667) and temperament (chi² = 0·068) whereas rather more females tended to be above the median duration (chi² = 3·267, p<0·10). The mean for the females was 0·73 hours and for the males, 0·64 hours. Taking a mean duration of 1·0 hour as a cutoff, rather than the median, the females again showed a significant tendency to report longer disturbances (chi² = 4·367, p<0·05).

The Frequency of Mid-Day Naps

The mean frequency with which mid-day naps were reported over the 8 week period of the study increased steadily with advancing age.

Significantly more old subjects (those aged 50 and over) reported taking more than the median number of naps (chi² = 21·293, p<0·001). No sex (chi² = 0·421) or temperament (chi² = 0·151) differences were apparent.

The mean number of mid-day naps reported by the sample was 7·92, or almost 1 per week. This figure, however, ranged from less than 1 per two weeks in the 20s to over 2 per week in the 70s. Some 62·9 per cent of the sample reported one or more mid-day nap during the eight weeks of the present study (62·5 per cent of the males and 60·8 per cent of the females). The effect of age is apparent and surprisingly regular in its increase from decade to decade, whereas one might have expected a sharp increase in the 60s, resulting from a lessening of activity on retirement.

The Duration of the Mid-Day Naps

The mean duration of mid-day naps was 0·55 hours (33 minutes). Significantly more older subjects reported naps longer than the median (chi²—12·235, p<0·001). There were no sex differences although there was a slightly significant temperament difference; the extraverts tending to take longer naps (0·59 hours) than the introverts (0·52 hours) (chi² = 2·836, p<0·10).

Mid-Day Naps as a Percentage of the Total Sleep

In view of the prevalence of mid-day naps, each subject's record was examined and the amount of sleep taken in naps expressed as a percentage of the total sleep taken. In the 20s, mid-day naps constituted a very small proportion of the total sleep taken (less than 1 per cent on average) but there was a steady rise in this figure with age (20s, 0·61 per cent; 30s, 1·05 per cent; 40s, 2·15 per cent; 50s, 2·45 per cent; 60s, 3·11 per cent and 70s, 5·44 per cent). The temperament differences are somewhat erratic with the extraverts tending to make more use of the device but the males make progressively more use of this device with age than the females. This analysis accounts, to some extent at least, for the rise in the total amount of sleep taken by older people in the 60s and 70s.

Additional Comments

Product moment correlations were calculated between the dependent and independent variables. These showed that neuroticism and verbal intelligence (Mill Hill Vocabulary score) were unrelated to any of the measures of sleep behaviour taken. Non-verbal intelligence was, apparently, related to the number of mid-night awakenings (r = −0·217, p$<$0·001) and mid-day naps (r $=$ $-$0·195, p$<$0·01). When partial correlations were computed, however, and age was held constant, these associations became insignificant.

The sample of 240 people was, in general, very healthy over the 8 weeks of the study. 36 (15 per cent) subjects mentioned medication on their charts. Of these subjects most (25) were women and 23 of these were aged 50 or over. Most of the medication was minor (aspirin) and for such complaints as headaches or influenza.

All shift workers were excluded from the sample and their results reported elsewhere (Ref. 20).

DISCUSSION

Apart from continuous EEG studies it is fair to say that all the other techniques mentioned rely on the subject's estimations of various times and durations. This poses the problem of how accurate is the subjective data in this study. There is virtually no evidence comparing subjective with objective measures of sleep, nor is there much evidence about the discrepancy between quantities estimated by any two subjective measures. Some indication of the importance of this comes from a comparison of the present study and that by McGhie & Russell (Ref. 17). These authors, using a questionnaire, reported that less than 2 per cent of their subjects admitted taking mid-day naps. The comparable figure from the present study, where subjects actually recorded their naps over 8 weeks, was 62·5 per cent for the males and 60·8 per cent for the females. Such a large difference may possibly be accounted for in terms of the phrasing in questionnaires which may imply that only habitual users of the device should reply in the affirmative.

The importance of comparing objective and subjective records in order that accurate data may be accumulated is obvious; yet there is no study doing this and until other methods (such as telemetered EEGs) become more readily available subjective methods will still find a place among the scientist's repertoire of techniques. Notwithstanding the shortcomings of the sleep chart method of studying sleep behaviour, the results of the present study may be discussed and compared with other findings.

With certain attitudes and exceptions the results of the present study confirm and extend other findings reviewed in the Introduction. It is clear, for example, that older people do, in fact, report taking more sleep than younger as Laird (Ref. 11) and Webb (Ref. 21) also found. Changes

G*

in the amount of sleep taken over the years are not, however, a simple function of age for there is an age by temperament interaction. The mean duration of sleep was around 7·5 hours, a figure which changed slightly with age and temperament and to a lesser extent with sex. The figure is within the ranges quoted by other authors (e.g., Ref. 10) and although it may reflect a seasonal influence, since the study was carried out in the late spring, is below the 8 hours common advice recommends. Over the population in general the duration of sleep distributed relatively normally around this mean, few achieving an average of over 10 hours or under 5. The data on the times of falling asleep and awakening are of some interest for age only affected the former whereas age, temperament and their interaction were significant determinants of the latter. This is consistent with the data on the duration of sleep and indicates that additional nocturnal sleep is achieved by awakening later rather than going to sleep earlier. The extraverts awoke later with increasing years and the introverts earlier. As reported by Costello & Smith there was no relationship between neuroticism and mean duration of sleep or any other dependent measure (Ref. 6). This finding does not, however, preclude the possibility that neurotics may complain of short or disturbed sleep more often than normals, even though their experience is the same as that of normal people.

By the usual criterion (the incidence of mid-night awakenings) the quality of sleep worsens with age as others have pointed out (Refs. 9, 16 & 21). The incidence of sleep disturbances is, however, a function of sex as well as age. Females reported awakening more often than males at almost all age groups and appeared to suffer most from this in the 50s where their sleep-wakefulness pattern became more irregular compared with previous decades. The females also reported an increased duration of these sleep disturbances with advancing age whereas the males estimated the durations as fairly constant in length.

These data may be an underestimate of the true picture, for subjects were asked to be accurate to the nearest half hour; thus disturbances of sleep lasting less than 15 minutes would not be reported.

It is feasible that a lack of nocturnal sleep may be compensated for, where it is practical, by mid-day naps for the incidence, duration and percentage of the population reporting mid-day naps increased with age. A further observation on the subject of mid-day naps is important, namely, that as age increased the contribution of these naps to the total amount of sleep taken assumed an increasing proportion, particularly in the males. If this is a compensatory device then more use is made of it by the older people on whom the demands of occupation and social pressures are less.

The impression left by these findings is that the sleep-waking cycle so laboriously acquired in the early years of life is progressively disrupted as life advances. Sleep is gradually reduced and fractioned into episodes up until the 50s or 60s when it increases slightly in duration, despite which the fractioning continues and an increasing proportion of sleep is taken during the daytime. Although most sleep is concentrated in the night hours, this is disturbed and taken in several episodes throughout the 24 hours of a day.

In trying to explain why the adult sleep-wakefulness pattern becomes more polycylic with age (Ref. 18) it is important to remember the factors which to some extent determine when a person may or may not sleep. It is likely that the sleep-wakefulness pattern learned during infancy is maintained in adult years largely because of social and occupational pressures. These encourage a person to sleep at night and not during the day, and require him, generally, to work during the daytime thus leaving the night hours free for sleeping. During pre-retirement years, however, sleep becomes disturbed, at first in the earlier years by the presence of small children, but increasingly by physical and psychosomatic illnesses which fraction nocturnal sleep into episodes. Occupational and social pressures leave little possibility for taking compensatory sleep, save the occasional mid-day nap, and hence there is a slight fall in the average amount of sleep taken from the 20s to the 50s.

Within this general description there is the important variation attributable to temperament: the extraverted tend to sleep longer and awaken later. These tendencies emerge only after the age of 40 and increase with age. Attempts have been made to explain such findings (Ref. 6) in theoretical terms (Ref. 7). Other explanations are permissible. The fact that younger extraverts and introverts behave similarly can be attributed to the effectiveness of social and occupational influences. After the age of 40 some occupational seniority is achieved and a more flexible personal routine may be established. It seems that the introverts did not take advantage of this for they continued to reduce their sleep and awaken earlier possibly because of their regard for punctuality and obligation: factors which could be achieved at the expense of less sleep. The extraverts, on the other hand, behaved quite differently, using the more permissive atmosphere as an opportunity to sleep more and get up later. This leads to the suspicion that the temperament differences are masked in the earlier adult years and emerge only when certain pressures are relaxed. Cooper & Payne have shown that extraverts go absent without leave more often than introverts and have worse time-keeping records than introverts (Ref. 3); findings which tend to support the present argument for temperament differences.

Retirement from full-time employment ostensibly permits a person to distribute his sleep as he wishes. This is more usual for males than females since the latter continue with their household duties although possibly at a more leisurely pace since they are no longer bound by their husband's working routine. This is reflected in the increase in the mean duration of sleep in the 60s. The story is not complete, however, for even though occupational pressures are relaxed others remain and increase. Illness which disturbs sleep, or any other activity, virtually compels sleep to be taken in episodes rather than in one continuous and uninterrupted stretch. Socially, it is still necessary to allocate the night hours for sleeping but an increasing percentage of sleep can be and is transferred to the daylight hours. Despite this increased flexibility, the duration of sleep fell again in the 70s, testifying perhaps to the severity of geriatric complaints.

The reversion to a more polycyclic sleep-wakefulness pattern in later adult life is not seen as a sudden occurrence emerging at retirement but as a gradual phenomenon developing over the years as various pressures permit or require. The problem of whether or not human beings prefer a polycyclic pattern cannot be answered from the present study.

REFERENCES

1. ANDRESS, J. M., An investigation of the sleep of normal school students. *J. educ. Psychol.*, **2**, 153–156, 1911.
2. BEST, C. H. & TAYLOR, N. B., *The Living Body* (4th edit.). London: Chapman & Hall, 1964.
3. COOPER, R. & PAYNE, R., Extraversion and some aspects of work behaviour. *Pers. Psychol.*, **20**, 45–57, 1967.
4. CLÉMENT, F. & BOURLIÈRE, F., Le sommeil chez l'adulte et les personnes âgées: facteure qui peuvent influer sur cet état. *Colloques Internationaux du C.E.R.S.*, **96**, 155–173.
5. COSTELLO, C. G. & SELBY, M. H., The relationships between sleep patterns and reactive and endogenous depressions. *Brit. J. Psychiat.*, **111**, 497–501, 1965.

6. —— & SMITH, C. M., The relationships between personality, sleep and the effects of sedatives. *Brit. J. Psychiat.*, **109**, 568–571, 1963.

7. EYSENCK, H. J., *Dynamics of Anxiety and Hysteria.* London: Routledge & Kegan Paul, 1957.

8. HERON, A., A two part personality inventory for use as a research criterion. *Brit. J. Psychol.*, **47**, 143–251, 1956.

9. HOBSON, W. & PEMBERTON, J., *The Health of the Elderly at Home.* London: Butterworth, 1955.

10. KLEITMAN, N., *Sleep and Wakefulness.* Chicago: Univ. Chicago Press, 1963.

11. LAIRD, D. A., A survey of the sleep habits of 509 men of distinction. *Amer. Med.*, **37**, 271–275, 1931.

12. LEWIS, H. E., Sleep patterns on polar expeditions. In *The Nature of Sleep* (eds. G. E. W. Wolstenholme & M. O. O'Connor). London: Churchill, 1961.

13. —— & MASTERTON, J. P., Sleep and wakefulness in the Arctic. *Lancet*, **1**, 1262–1266, 1957.

14. MASTERTON, J. P., Sleep of hospital medical staff. *Lancet*, **1**, 41–42, 1965.

15. ——, Patterns of sleep. In *The Physiology of Human Survival* (eds. O. G. Edholm & A. L. Bacharach). London: Academic Press, 1965.

16. McGHIE, A., The subjective assessment of sleep patterns in psychiatric illness. *Brit. J. med. Psychol.*, **39**, 221–230, 1966.

17. —— & RUSSELL, S. M., The subjective assessment of normal sleep patterns. *J. ment. Sci.*, **108**, 642–654, 1962.

18. MURRAY, E. J., *Sleep, Dreams, and Arousal.* New York: Appleton Century Crofts, 1965.

19. ROSS, H. E., Sleep and wakefulness in the Arctic under an irregular regime. *Biometeorology. Proc. 2nd International Bioclimatological Congress* (ed. S. W. Tromp). Oxford: Pergamon Press, 1962.

20. TUNE, G. S., A note on the sleep of shift workers. *Ergonomics*, **11**, 2, 183–184, 1968.

21. WEBB, W. B., Sleep characteristics of human subjects. *Bull. Brit. Psychol. Soc.*, **18**, 1–10, 1965.

22. WILLIAMS, E. S., Sleep and wakefulness at high altitudes. *Brit. med. J.*, **1**, 197–198, 1959.

23. WILLIS, J. H. P., Insomnia in psychiatric patients. *Guy's Hosp. Repts.*, **114**, 249–255, 1965.

Perceptual

Editor's Introduction

DIFFERENCES between extraverts and introverts are as well marked and numerous in the perceptual field as they were found to be in the sensory one—if indeed one can make a clear distinction between the two fields. There is no need to defend the differentiation here adopted; it is merely a matter of convenience, in which the simpler types of threshold and vigilance experiments are treated in one section, the more complex figural after-effects, constancy effects, perceptual fluctuations, masking effects and others in this section. Nothing more far-reaching is intended. However, with greater complexity comes greater difficulty in theoretical explanation and clear-cut deduction of experimental dependencies and it will be found that while on the whole results in this section are also favourable to some of the theoretical links suggested between personality and perception, unsolved problems still remain.

A particularly obscure result, for instance, is the dependence of kinaesthetic figural after-effects on the orientation of the wedge used to measure the effect; personality differences are in some way bound up with this (theoretically irrelevant) arrangement of the apparatus. As unpublished research in our own Department has verified Broadbent's finding, we must accept it, but the reasons for this curiosity are still obscure. A. Petrie, in her recent book (Ref. 2), has taken the general theory of personality correlates of figural after-effects a long way further; her work suggests that probably the whole theoretical basis of after-effects as satiation-produced (Köhler) is wrong and that some other theory is required. Perhaps many of these effects are nothing but negative time-errors; Claridge has shown, in a chapter contributed to the writer's *Experiments in Personality* (Ref. 1), that as expected extraverts show stronger negative time errors and this would explain many of the results observed by Petrie. However, at the moment all we can say is that the theoretical position is obscure.

Other complexities will be found in connection with such effects as the rotating spiral after-effect; here too both support and disproof of the theoretical prediction can be found, suggesting that there are still unrecognised factors in the situation which obscure the picture. Some of the other relationships posited and found appear more clear-cut—possibly because only a few investigators have worked with them, using only a few variations in the many parameters involved. Altogether

193

perceptual phenomena are among the most promising and interesting from the point of view of personality study; they are also among the most difficult, in view of the many complexities of decision-taking and other variables which almost invariably enter the situation and make it less obvious than it might be. No doubt the future will resolve many of our troubles in terms of better designs and more careful control of perceptual experiments.

H.J.E.

REFERENCES

1. CLARIDGE, G., The excitation–inhibition balance in neurotics, pp. 107–154. In *Experiments in Personality* (ed. H. J. Eysenck). London: Routledge & Kegan Paul, 1966.
2. PETRIE, A., *Individuality in Pain and Suffering*. Chicago: University of Chicago Press, 1968.

24

The Relation of Personality Trends to Degrees of Visual Constancy Correction for Size and Form

C. O. WEBER

First published in *Journal of Applied Psychology*, **23**, 703–708, 1939

THE inherent subjectivity of questionnaire tests of personality leads eventually to attempts to establish the existence of traits by means of objective laboratory methods. Without commenting on the validity of the results, we may illustrate the latter method by recalling a few familiar instances. Kretschmer's attempt to trace temperament to bodybuild (Ref. 6); the relationships established by J. W. Pinard (Ref. 7) and R. B. Cattell between character traits and laboratory tests of perseveration tendency (Ref. 1); Gatewood (Ref. 2), Hunt & Guilford's (Ref. 5) studies showing large day-to-day variations in mental output in schizoid personalities—all of these represent attempts to establish a psychology of traits on more secure foundations than are afforded by 'paper' tests, as we may call them.

In the class of such objective studies, there is one that has particularly attracted our attention. Robert H. Thouless, whose studies of the phenomena of visual constancy are suggestive, reports the following observation: during the course of an extended study of brightness, shape and size constancy, Thouless noted that extraverted or cycloid subjects tend to show larger amounts of visual constancy than do introverted or schizothymic subjects. That is, the schizothymic subject tends, as we would expect, to see external objects in terms of their stimulus character rather than in terms of their 'real' character. The paper in shadow, the distant object, the inclined circle impress him as having the stimulus properties of the moment. The introvert should find it quite natural to treat an external object as a sensation, as a phenomenon rather than as a real object. The object-directed extravert, on the other hand, because of an equally natural preference for practical articulations with external objects, will tend to see such objects in their real characters. In order to verify this casual observation, Thouless selected two groups of subjects of 14 members each, one group conforming as closely as possible to Kretschmer's description of the cyclothymic temperament, the other group to the schizoid temperament. The records of these subjects on the constancy tests show that the cyclothymic subjects show larger average indexes of constancy correction (or of 'phenomenal regression', as Thouless prefers to call it) for brightness, form and size (Ref. 8).

During the winter of 1937 we made an attempt to check the observation made by Thouless. 76 sophomores, all of them women, served as subjects. Each of them took Guilford & Guilford's new test, based on the new method of factor analysis and intended to measure three somewhat related attributes of personality: social introversion, emotionality and masculinity (Ref. 3). Since Guilford considers that masculinity as measured by this test is somewhat unsatisfactory as a definitive factor, we scored this test for social introversion and emotionality only. The author also made a personal attempt to rate the subjects on a seven-fold scale on Introversion-Extraversion, based on his personal acquaintance with them. Each subject also took the Allport A.S. Reaction Study.

The visual constancy tendencies of the subjects were determined by means of stereograms constructed by the author as a convenient and 'in-door' method of measuring degrees of size and form correction. The set of size constancy stereograms consists of 16 slides made up of paired photos of a round white disc photographed on an open lawn at four different distances (3, 6, 9, 12 metres), involving four degrees of disparition for each distance. The form constancy set consists of 15 similar slides made up of paired photographs of a table top tilted at five degrees of inclination from the vertical position (30, 40, 50, 60, 70 degrees) in the various slides. For each degree of inclination, again, there were slides representing three different degrees of disparition.

Each subject made but three observations for each slide, in each case gauging the size or form of the stereoscopic object and then selecting an equivalent object from charts of comparison areas (where size judgments were made) and from charts of comparison ellipses (where form judgments were required). For both the size and form series, control determinations were made by having the subjects gauge the sizes and forms of special slides made by cutting out the size discs and the table tops and mounting them on grey cardboards suitable for insertion in the stereoscope. Since the cues utilized in the constancy correction processes come from the field surrounding the object, the control slides seem suited for gauging the subject's natural tendencies to over- or under-estimate size and form when uninfluenced by the constancy tendencies. In this way it is possible to measure quantitatively the subject's tendency to make size and form corrections for the test objects in the photographed field, corrected by the measurements of mere tendencies to make errors of judgment of size and form as shown by the control slides.

Three observations on each slide may seem insufficient for measuring an individual's constancy tendencies. Actually, of course, since the sets of slides numbered 15 and 16, we have 45 and 48 observations from each subject. Moreover, repeated trials seem unnecessary because the deviations of an individual's judgments for a given slide are small. For instance, the correlation between the first and second choices of comparison areas for size slides, taking 200 judgments as material for the correlation, is $+0.954$ (± 0.005). For the form slides, first and second choices for identical slides show a correlation of $+0.984$ (± 0.001). Other correlations of this sort indicate that individual determinations vary very little during a given laboratory sitting. We are unable to state how constant such judgments are from day to day: Thouless reports that the day-to-day constancy of such judgments is high.

We used the critical ratio method as a means of determining the relations of visual constancy to personality traits. Since there were 76

TABLE 1

PERSONALITY TRAITS AND VISUAL CONSTANCY

Trait groups	N	Type C.C.	Av.C.C.	D.	D/S.E.d.	Prob-ability
1. Extravert-test	25	size	76.0			
Introvert-test	25	size	37.0	39.0	1.851	96.5
2. Extravert-rating	25	size	79.7			
Introvert-rating	25	size	29.0	50.7	2.136	98.4
3. Extravert-test	25	form	19.3			
Introvert-test	25	form	15.9	3.4	1.094	86.0
4. Extravert-test	25	size+form	46.6			
Introvert-test	25	size+form	27.4	19.0	1.713	96.0
5. Low emotionality	25	size	57.0			
High emotionality	25	size	52.2	4.8	0.276	61.0
6. Low emotionality	25	form	17.4			
High emotionality	25	form	16.6	0.8	0.244	59.0
7. Ascendancy	24	size	62.5			
Submission	24	size	59.3	3.2	0.141	55.0
8. Ascendancy	24	form	19.7			
Submission	24	form	17.5	2.2	0.586	72.0
9. Ascendancy	24	size+form	42.0			
Submission	24	size+form	38.3	3.7	1.532	93.0

subjects, we formed groups of the 25 most introvert and the 25 most extravert and then compared these opposed groups as regards visual constancy. The same procedure was followed in determining the differences in visual constancy in other personality trait groups. The results are given in Table 1.

The amount of average constancy correction for each group, whether for size, for form, or for both, is given under the caption 'C.C. Score' in the table. These values are percentages of the average excess of size (or of shape) of the experimental as compared with the control determinations. It will be seen that these corrections are large, especially for the size determinations. Thus, in the first line, the 25 most extraverted subjects tend to see the photographed discs as 76 per cent larger than the very same discs when cut out and mounted on the control slides.

GENERAL RESULTS

Introversion-extraversion appears to be the most definitely associated with visual constancy in this study. The last column to the right gives the probability that the differences found between groups are 'true differences' on the basis of 100. For size constancy, the ratios and probabilities are the best in the table and suggest that extraverts make reliably larger size corrections than do introverts. Judgments of form, however, give disappointing results. Perhaps to the introvert, traditionally supposed to be a good bookworm, the table-top is an especially 'real' object! In comparisons No. 4 and 9, size and form are averaged.

Guilford considers that subjects who earn high emotionality scores on his test are at once more emotional on the whole and exhibit a tendency to emotional dependency on others (Ref. 3). The differences between high and low emotionality groups are lowest of all. Psychologically, there is perhaps no reason for expecting that emotional traits should affect constancy corrections. Guilford's results as well as our own show that low emotionality correlates positively with extraversion, in our study to the extent of $+0.366$ (± 0.066). Hence, the slightly superior constancy correction of subjects with low emotionality is perhaps due to the positive association of low emotionality with extraversion. The differences between groups of ascendant and submissive subjects are of intermediate value. There is a tendency for ascendant subjects to show larger constancy corrections. Again, this may be due to the association of ascendancy with extraversion, which in the case of Guilford's test is $+0.697$ (± 0.039).

None of the critical ratios on our table indicates absolute reliability. However, in the case of introversion-extraversion, they are high enough to be significant. This study gives experimental support to the belief that the distinction between introversion and extraversion is somehow valid. It suggests also that introversion and extraversion are true personality traits in the sense that a true personality trait is not confined to one manifestation, but implies a stable organization of sub-traits. That extraverts should make larger constancy corrections is a natural inference from the prevalent conception of extraversion as a tendency to accept an object-directed attitude.

REFERENCES

1. CATTELL, R. B., On the measurement of perseveration. *Brit. J. educ. Psychol.*, **5,** 76–92, 1935.
2. GATEWOOD, L. C., An experimental study of dementia praecox. *Psychological Monographs*, **11,** whole No. 45, 1909.
3. GUILFORD, J. P. & GUILFORD, R. B., Personality factors S, E, and M, and their measurement, *J. Psychol.*, **2,** 109–127, 1936.
4. HUNT, J. McV., Psychological loss in paretics and schizophrenia. *Amer. J. Psychol.*, **47,** 458–463, 1935.
5. —— & GUILFORD, J. P., Fluctuation of an ambiguous figure in dementia praecox and in manic depressive patients. *J. abnorm. soc. Psychol.*, **27,** 443–452, 1933.
6. KRETSCHMER, E., *Physique and Character*. New York: Harcourt & Brace, 1926.
7. PINARD, J. W., Tests of perseveration: 1. Their relation to character. *Brit. J. Psychol.*, **23,** 5–19, 1932.
8. THOULESS, R. H., Individual differences in phenomenal regression. *Brit. J. Psychol.*, **22,** 216–241, 1931–32.

25

Personality and Perception:
The Constancy Effect and Introversion

J. AMOR ARDIS & ELIZABETH FRASER

First published in *British Journal of Psychology*, **48**, 48–54, 1957

AN investigation of the relationship between shape constancy and introversion-extraversion was carried out, using as subjects 24 first-year psychology students of Aberdeen University; 12 introverts and 12 extraverts, selected on the basis of the Minnesota TSE scale. Results showed (a) that introverts showed lower constancy effect than extraverts and (b) that there was a tendency for men to show greater constancy effect than women.

There was also some suggestion of the presence of a learning factor in the perceptual process which also distinguished introverts from extraverts. These results are discussed in the light of previous investigations. Hypotheses, which are shortly to be tested and which might account for the findings, are advanced.

INTRODUCTION

In the course of experiments with mescaline, it was noticed that the incidence and intensity of perceptual abnormalities varied with alterations in attention to the environment. On the one hand, so long as a practical, reality-orientated, extraverted attitude was maintained (often with difficulty), the environment would be made to appear approximately normal. On the other hand, when subjects lapsed into a dreamy preoccupied state, they experienced marked perceptual distortions. These included hallucinatory movement, tunnel vision, the appearance of networks superimposed on real objects and various other distortions which have been reported by many other workers with mescaline. The subject has recently been reviewed by Mayer-Gross (Ref. 8).

In our own experience, a regular feature of the distorted perceptions under mescaline was a reduction of the constancy effect—one important aspect of a more general disorganization of perception. For example, one subject, viewing a door somewhat obliquely, remarked that it seemed to be shaped like a wedge and that it required a definite effort to see it as he knew it to be, i.e., rectangular. This particular aspect of the disorganization, reduced constancy, or in Thouless's terminology reduced 'phenomenal regression to the real object' (Ref. 10), corresponded so closely to the presence of an introverted attitude that it was decided to investigate further the relationship, if any, existing between the constancy effect and the personality trait of introversion in normal individuals.

The role of personality factors in the perceptual process has received considerable attention in recent years. The work of Brunswik, Bruner & Postman, Frenkel-Brunswik, Klein & Schlesinger, and many others in this field, requires no exposition in this article. The area with which we are particularly concerned, the constancy phenomenon, has itself been the subject of a considerable literature. The factors affecting constancy (e.g., the number of cues present, the attitude of the observer, the role of learning and the developmental aspect of the phenomenon) have all been investigated and experiments on them have given rise to a number of controversial issues. The question of attitude, which is particularly relevant to our own research, has been studied by Klimpfinger (Ref. 6) and Holaday (Ref. 4) working under Brunswik. They demonstrated that the adoption of an analytical attitude on the part of the observer results in a marked reduction of both shape and size constancy.

Relatively few researches, however, have been carried out on the more specific question of how persons, who are known to differ on a given personality dimension, behave in a constancy experiment. Thouless did carry out one such investigation (Ref. 10). In the course of previous experiments, investigating individual differences in 'phenomenal regression', he had observed that 'those of introverted or schizothymic temperaments saw much more closely to the stimulus or perspective object[1] than did the extraverted or cyclothymic. It seemed even possible that this might be a measurable result of the greater interest in outside reality of the cyclothyme and in the subjective world of the schizothyme' (Ref. 10). An experiment in which 14 cyclothymes and 14 schizothymes (selected on the basis of Kretschmer's descriptions) were tested, gave results which, though they failed to reach significance, suggested nevertheless that schizothymes did experience phenomenal regression less markedly than cyclothymes.

In a later study, Weber, using stereoscopic material, confirmed that

---

[1] By this Thouless means the object as it appeared optically or in contradistinction to its true nature in objective reality.

extraverts showed greater size constancy than introverts, but reported non-significant results for shape constancy, although the tendency was in the expected direction (Ref. 11).

In our experiment we are concerned with shape constancy, and an attempt has been made to control experimentally, or partial out statistically, factors which are known, or thought, to influence the constancy effect. It was predicted that extraverts would show a more marked constancy effect in their perception than introverts.

CRITERIA OF INTROVERSION-EXTRAVERSION

For the purpose of this experiment, introverts are regarded as those individuals who have a low score and extraverts those with a high score on the Thinking dimension of the Minnesota TSE scale of introversion-extraversion devised and standardized by Evans & McConnell (Ref. 2). The authors constructed this scale to measure three types of introversion-extraversion, Thinking, Social and Emotional, which were isolated by Guilford in his factor analysis. This analysis yielded evidence that the available I-E tests were not measuring a single dimension of personality and Evans & McConnell devised three distinct sets of items in an effort to develop relatively independent tests dealing with thinking, social and emotional reactions. The result is a scale providing three measures of I-E, which have been shown by the authors to be almost uncorrelated. It was on the first of these, the Thinking I-E score, that our subjects were selected.

SUBJECTS

The subjects were drawn from the first-year class in psychology in Aberdeen University and their ages ranged from 17 to 24 years. Out of a group of 91 previously rated on the TSE Minnesota Scale, 24 students were selected: these comprised the 6 highest and 6 lowest scorers on the Thinking dimension among the men and the 6 highest and 6 lowest scorers among the women.

APPARATUS AND PROCEDURE

Three stimulus objects were employed; a disc 10 inches in diameter, a square of 10 inches diagonal and a rod 10 inches long and $\frac{1}{8}$ inch thick. All were of metal and painted white. They were supported by means of a clamp and stand and a rotating horizontal metal bar. They were presented to the subject either vertically—when the entire surface (or in the case of the rod the entire length) was visible—or horizontally, when only the edge of the circle or square (or the end of the rod) was visible, or in one of several intervening positions. The actual angle of inclination to the vertical was measured by a suitably attached protractor.

The subject was provided with a chin rest, adjusted to a comfortable height and the height of the first stimulus object, the metal disc, was adjusted to eye level so that, when it was in a horizontal position, it was seen by the subject as a straight line and, when vertical, as a complete circle. The subject was also provided with ten white cardboard ellipses, all with major axis 10 inches long and with minor axes ranging from 1 to 10 inches and numbered accordingly.

Instructions were standard for all subjects. It was pointed out that the circle, when tilted, would appear to the subject to be elliptical; he was to choose from the ten ellipses given to him, the one which looked nearest in shape to the tilted circle and call out its number. He was allowed to give intermediate values when the tilted circle seemed to him to fall between two of his ellipses. When inspecting the cardboard ellipses, he held these at right angles to his line of regard and at arm's length, the stimulus object being 7 feet away against a black background.

A similar procedure was followed with the square and the rod, the square being presented with its diagonals placed vertically and horizontally. In the case of the rod (which, in the horizontal position, was end on to the subject), he was provided with ten rods ranging from 1 to 10 inches in length from which he had to choose and for the square, a series of diamond-shaped pieces of cardboard, one diagonal always being 10 inch and the other 1 to 10 inches.

STATISTICAL TREATMENT OF RESULTS

The two estimates obtained for each presentation of each stimulus object were averaged for each subject and the final results, 7 readings for each of the 3 kinds of stimulus object for each of the 24 subjects (a total of 504 readings), were analysed. Analysis of variance was used, with four main variables: I-E, stimulus object, sex and angle. Results of this analysis are given in Table 1.

The main variable, I-E, gave highly significant results, with an F-ratio of 9·71 which with d.f. 1 and 420 gives $p < 0·001$. As predicted, introverts showed markedly less 'phenomenal regression' than extraverts and this was true for both sexes and for all three stimulus objects and at all

TABLE 1

Source	F-ratio	p
Introversion-Extraversion	9·71	0·001
Angle	198·70	0·001
Stimulus	<1	—
Sex	2·96	0·10
Sex × stimulus	1·99	—
I-E × stimulus	1·50	—

angles. The elicitation of this result, which was quite clear-cut, was the object of the experiment. Other findings will, however, be briefly mentioned.

Of the other three main variables, angles inevitably accounted for by far the largest proportion of total variance and gave a highly significant F-ratio. This was, of course, expected from the nature of the experimental procedure and is, from the point of view of this experiment, quite unimportant.

The different types of stimulus objects—disc, square and rod—had no noteworthy effect on the degree of phenomenal regression as the F-ratio for 'stimuli' was not significant.

There was a fairly strong tendency for women to exhibit less phenomenal regression (i.e., less perceptual constancy) than men. The F-ratio, however, just failed to reach the 0·05 level of significance.

Of the interactions, not one gave a significant F-ratio. There was a very slight suggestion of a differential reaction to the three stimulus-objects by (a) men as opposed to women and (b) introverts as opposed to extraverts. The probability of a chance result is too high, however ($p = $ about 0·20), for any importance to be attached to this result.

DISCUSSION

Introversion-Extraversion

The significant relationship, which we have found to exist in our subjects, between introversion as a personality trait and reduced constancy in perception of shape, is in general agreement with other workers (Refs. 4, 5, 6, 10 & 11). It is also, we feel, in accord with non-scientific everyday experience. It is somewhat surprising that Sheehan attached no great weight to the theory that personality might be one of the factors determining constancy (Ref. 9, p. 20, footnote).

One explanation of the non-significant results of both Thouless and Izzet may be that they were both ostensibly working with the schizo-thymic-cyclothymic dimension, subjects being selected on the basis of the authors' assessments. Thouless himself specifically equates schizo-thymia-cyclothymia with introversion-extraversion (Ref. 10), but we now have reason to doubt that, in their pure form, these dimensions are in any way related. Hence, it is not surprising that his results differ from ours, since he was not dealing with introversion-extraversion in as pure a form. Such correspondence as does exist between his results and ours may be attributed to the fact that, in his selection of schizothymes and cyclothymes, he was influenced by considerations of introversion and extraversion.

Weber's method bears superficial resemblances to ours, but his results are less highly significant. Three possible factors come to mind. First, the instructions given to our subjects were such as to motivate them to perceive phenomenologically rather than in terms of the real object. Though in our experiment extraverts and introverts were presumed to be equally motivated, the latter were probably less rigidly bound to customary perceptual patterns—to perception in terms of the real object. Sheehan has commented on the apparently greater flexibility in the perceptions of subjects showing low constancy (Ref. 9). Weber's subjects, on the other hand, were required to perceive in terms of a supposed real object. It appears to us that such a set is less likely to emphasize differences in personal perceptual patterns.

Secondly, Weber's subjects were American sophomores and, as a group, probably contained fewer really introverted individuals than did our group of Scottish students. Whereas the published norms show that 5 per cent of the American population have scores of less than 85, ten of our group (11 per cent) have scores below this level. On the other hand, at the extraverted end of the scale, no such difference was apparent. This implies that our group spread more widely over the scale; and selection of extremes may have resulted in a more marked contrast between our introverts and extraverts.

Thirdly, for our experiment, we selected as subjects 24 extremes out of a total of 91, while Weber chose 50 out of 75. It seems likely, therefore, that our introverts and extraverts were more distinct groups than Weber's and that this helps to account for the more significant results we obtained.

The Sex Difference
Our results which, though they fail to reach significance, suggest a

difference between the sexes, the women showing lower constancy than the men, do not agree with those of Thouless, who found a significant trend in the opposite direction. Methods of selection of subjects and the fact that, in his experiment, personality variables were not partialled out may account for the disagreement. Klimpfinger on the other hand, as we have mentioned, whose subjects ranged in age from 3-year-olds to adults, found that up to the age of 12, boys showed lower constancy and, thereafter, greater constancy, than girls (Ref. 7). There is no indication in her article of the significance or non-significance of these results and again personality variables were not controlled, but one might say that her results, in the relevant age-groups, agree with ours.

The Learning Factor in Perception

One interesting feature of our results, which just failed to be significant, was that the introverted group and particularly the male introverts, showed a progressive movement towards the low constancy end of the scale as the experiment proceeded, while the extraverts showed no tendency in any direction. Since the order of presentation of stimuli was not randomized (each subject was shown all positions of the disc, then the square and finally the rod), it is not possible at present to say whether this tendency is a function of the change of stimulus object or an indication of some learning process at work. An experiment, designed to answer this question, is in progress.

Theory

Before attempting to formulate any hypothesis to account for differences in constancy, it might be profitable to review briefly some of the main conditions and cases where low constancy is known to occur. These include (a) low illumination, (b) the use of a reduction screen, (c) monocular vision and (d) a relatively unstructured visual field, giving few cues. In addition, we have noted (e) that a phenomenologically directed attitude (as opposed to an object-directed one) results in reduced constancy and (f) that low constancy occurs in introverts. We have also found (g) that it is a frequent feature of mescaline intoxication.

We would suggest three possible types of reduced constancy: that due to sensory deprivation, that due to reduced attention to the environment and that due to a failure in the organizational process. The first calls for little comment; (a) to (d), mentioned above, are obvious examples.

A reduced attention to the environment appears the most plausible explanation of the reduced constancy we have been discussing in this paper. Though superficially similar to the 'sensory deprivation' type, because of the consequent reduction in amount of information being fed in, reduced constancy due to inattention may be more akin, from the point of view of neurological function, to the third type, presently to be mentioned. Experimental investigation of this second type of reduced constancy might well be carried out using 'latent learning' methods, or by 'attention-saturating' techniques, with particular emphasis on its relationship to speed of learning.

The third type of reduced constancy—organizational failure—is, we tentatively suggest, exemplified in mescaline intoxication. A hypothesis along these lines has already been presented elsewhere (Ref. 1). Therein, the concepts of Hebb (Ref. 3) were applied to certain phenomena of mescaline intoxication. The hypothesis may briefly be summarized thus:

The neuronal basis of perception is taken to be the activation of assemblies and phase-sequences of neurones. Activation, inhibition and modification of these complex spatio-temporal units are regarded as determined by (a) the nature of the stimulus and the resultant input to the central nervous system and (b) stored experience in a neuronal form. The latter might conveniently be labelled a 'reality-scheme', analogous to the 'body-scheme' postulated by neurologists and regarded as a vastly complex—and continually developing—type of phase sequence. The interaction between (a) and (b) might be expressed either as the shaping—by facilitation or inhibition—of the crude response to (a) by (b); or as the activation of fractions of (b) by (a). The distinction is verbal.

It is suggested that the interaction is disorganized by mescaline. One consequence of this may be the emergence of a more primitive, sensory-dominated, perception—one example of which is reduced constancy.

With other effects we are not at present concerned. But it may be suggested that mescaline disorganizes maximally those neuronal units which are the basis of complex, recently learned, responses. This subject may also be viewed from the standpoint of learning theory.

ACKNOWLEDGEMENTS

The authors of this article are members of a research group in Aberdeen investigating the Model Psychoses. They are indebted to Miss Sheila Fraser, M.A., Ed.B., who carried out the testing of subjects. She has presented a report of the experiments in a thesis, in part-fulfilment of the requirements of the Ed.B. degree. They would also like to thank Prof. Rex Knight for helpful comment and criticism.

REFERENCES

1. ARDIS, J. A. & DREWERY, J., Studies in the Model Psychoses. Communication to Scottish Branch of Royal Med. Psy. Ass, 1954.
2. EVANS, C. & MCCONNELL, T. R., A new measure of introversion-extraversion. *J. Psychol.*, **12**, 111–124, 1941.
3. HEBB, D. O., *The Organization of Behaviour*. New York: Wiley and Sons, 1949.
4. HOLADAY, B. E., Die Grössenkonstans der Sehdinge bei Variation der inneren und ausseren Wahrnehmungsbedingungen. *Arch. ges. Psychol.*, **88**, 418–486, 1933.
5. IZZET, T., Gewicht und Dichte als Gegenstande der Wahrnehmung. *Arch. ges. Psychol.*, **91**, 305–328, 1934.
6. KLIMPFINGER, S., Über den Einfluss von intentionaier Einstellung und Übung auf die Gestaltkonstans. *Arch. ges. Psychol.*, **88**, 551–598, 1933.
7. ——, Die Entwicklung der Gestaltkonstans vom Kind zum Erwachsenen. *Arch. ges. Psychol.*, **88**, 599–628, 1933.
8. MAYER-GROSS, W., Experimental psychosis and other mental abnormalities produced by drugs. *Brit. med. J.*, **2**, 317–321, 1951.
9. SHEEHAN, M. R., A study of individual consistency in phenomenal constancy. *Arch. Psychol.*, N.Y., **31**, no. 222, 1938.
10. THOULESS, R. H., Individual differences in phenomenal regression. *Brit. J. Psychol.*, **22**, 216–241, 1932.
11. WEBER, C. O., The relation of personality trends to degrees of visual constancy correction for size and form. *J. appl. Psychol.*, **23**, 703–708, 1939.

26

Cortical Inhibition, Figural Aftereffect
and Theory of Personality

H. J. EYSENCK[1]

First published in
Journal of Abnormal and Social Psychology, **51**, 94–106, 1955

THE formulation of a complete theory of personality must be based on the discovery of invariances of two rather different types. In the first place, what is required is *static* or *descriptive* invariance, i.e., the taxonomic, nosological, or dimensional analysis of personality. Work of this kind would result in a descriptive system of personality in terms of a limited number of abilities, traits and attitudes; in the exact sciences the most obvious analogue to this system would be the discovery of the Periodic Table of Elements. The statistical methods involved in studies of this kind would be those making use of analysis of interdependence (correlational analysis, component analysis, association and contingency analysis, factor analysis).

In the second place, what is required is *dynamic*, or *sequential* invariance, i.e., the analysis of lawful sequences of behaviour and the discovery of their causes. Work of this kind would result in a causal system of laws in terms of concepts such as conditioning, inhibition, oscillation, etc.; in the exact sciences the most obvious analogue to this would be the discovery of the laws of motion. The statistical methods involved in studies of this kind would be those making use of analysis of dependence (analysis of variance and covariance, regression analysis and confluence analysis).

As has been pointed out elsewhere (Ref. 5), a logical case can be made out for maintaining that the *static* type of analysis should precede the *dynamic*; before we can discover dynamic laws responsible for extra-

[1] The writer is indebted to the Bethlem Royal Hospital and the Maudsley Hospital Research Committee for a grant which made this study possible. Dr L. Minski, Superintendent of Belmont Hospital, and Dr M. Desai, Chief Psychologist, gave permission for patients to be tested and very kindly helped in the selection of patients, as did various psychiatrists at Belmont Hospital, to all of whom thanks are due. Numerous discussions with Mr M. B. Shapiro clarified many theoretical problems and the writer is indebted to Mr A. E. Maxwell for statistical help and advice.

H

209

version, say, or neuroticism, we must demonstrate that these concepts do in fact refer to measurable and operationally definable entities. Work summarized in *The Structure of Human Personality* has shown that many different investigators holding divergent points of view and making use of a great variety of test procedures can be found to agree with respect to their main conclusions in the taxonomic field. The following six points present a brief summary of the main areas of agreement:

1. Human conduct is not specific, but presents a certain amount of *generality*; in other words, conduct in one situation is predictable from conduct in other situations.

2. Different degrees of generality can be discerned, giving rise to different levels of personality organization of structure. It follows that our view of personality structure must be *hierarchical*.

3. Degrees of generality can be operationally defined in terms of correlations. The lowest level of generality is defined by test-retest correlations; the next level (trait level) by intercorrelations of tests purporting to be measures of the same trait, or the same primary ability; the highest level by correlations between different traits defining second-order concepts like g in the cognitive field and 'neuroticism' in the orectic field, or type concepts like extraversion-introversion.

4. Mental abnormality (mental deficiency, neurosis, psychosis) is not qualitatively different from normality, in the sense that a person with a broken arm, or a patient suffering from haemophilia, is different from someone not ill; different types of mental abnormality constitute the extreme ends of continuous variables which are probably orthogonal to each other.

5. It follows from the above that psychiatric diagnostic procedures are at fault in diagnosing categories, such as 'hysteria' or 'schizophrenia'; what is required is the determination of the main dimensions involved and a quantitative estimate of the patient's position on each of these dimensions (see example below).

6. The main dimensions involved in the analysis of personality for which sufficient experimental data are available to make possible a theoretical formulation are neuroticism and extraversion-introversion.

While the congruence of empirical findings in this field is welcome, it should not be allowed to disguise from us the fact that the task of personality theory cannot stop halfway. We would be well advised to regard traits, types, abilities, attitudes and 'factors' generally not as the end products of our investigation, but rather as the starting point for a more causal type of analysis. Thurstone has pointed out that a coefficient of correlation is a confession of ignorance (Ref. 44); it indicates the existence of a relation but leaves the causal problem quite indeterminate. Much the same is true of a statistical factor; based, as it is, on an analysis of a set of correlations, it still does not in itself reveal to us anything about the causal relations at work. In this paper, therefore, an attempt is made to go beyond the purely descriptive studies which have so far engaged the main attention of our laboratory and to attempt the construction of a causal hypothesis with respect to at least one of the main personality dimensions.

Extraversion and the Cortical Inhibition Hypothesis

A brief summary of an experimental investigation will indicate the type of fact calling for an explanation. Proceeding on the hypothesis that the test differences between hospitalized neurotics and nonhospitalized 'normals' (i.e., people without psychiatric involvement) would provide us with an outside criterion of 'neuroticism' and that test differences between hysterics (Jung's prototype group for the concept of 'extraversion') and dysthymics (patients suffering from anxiety, Jung's prototype group for the concept of 'introversion') would provide us with an outside criterion of 'extraversion-introversion', a battery of objective tests of persistence, suggestibility and other traits was administered to groups of hysterics, psychopaths, reactive depressives, obsessionals, anxiety states, mixed neurotics and normals (Ref. 13). Retaining the hysterics, anxiety states and normals as criterion groups, intercorrelations were calculated between tests for the subjects in the remaining groups, and a Lawley-type factor analysis was performed. Three clear-cut simple structure factors emerged, corresponding to intelligence, neuroticism and extraversion. Intelligence tests had high loadings on the intelligence factor; the tests differentiating between the normal and neurotic groups had high loadings on the neuroticism factor; the tests differentiating between the hysterics and anxiety states had high loadings on the extraversion-introversion factor.

Factor scores on the introversion-extraversion factor were then calculated for the persons in the various groups. Fig. 20 gives a diagrammatic indication of the results obtained. The line separating the neurotic groups from the normal subjects was drawn so as to put 10 per cent of the normal group on the neurotic side, this being the percentage found by R. Fraser to show debilitating neurotic tendencies in a normal working-class population (Ref. 8). It will be seen that psychopaths are slightly more extraverted than hysterics and that obsessionals and

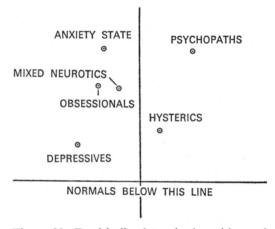

Figure 20. Empirically determined positions of group means for neurotic patients diagnosed as reactive depression, obsessional, anxiety state, mixed, hysteric, and psychopath, respectively.

depressives are about as introverted as anxiety states. Differences between extraverted groups and introverted groups are fully significant. Mixed neurotics are intermediate between the other groups; normals are very significantly lower on 'neuroticism' than any of the neurotic groups. These results allow us to use the hysteric-psychopath group on the one hand and the dysthymic group (anxiety state, reactive depression, obsessionals) on the other as criteria for any predictions made in terms of a theory of extraversion-introversion.

One further fact is relevant in connection with any hypothesis regarding extraversion-introversion. In a study of monozygotic and dyzygotic twins, McLeod has shown that a factor of extraversion-introversion (in addition to other factors) could be obtained from the intercorrelation of a large number of objective tests (Ref. 24); he also found that the intercorrelation of factor scores was very much higher for the monozygotic than for the dyzygotic twins. This indicates that extraversion is strongly based on an inherited disposition. If we are willing to use Holzinger's coefficient h^2 as a very rough index of the contribution of heredity to the variance of our extraversion measure in this sample, we would have to conclude that the contribution of heredity is very much stronger than that of environment.

This finding suggests that our search for a causal factor responsible for extraverted behaviour should be concentrated on properties of the central nervous system and more particularly the cortex, as it is unlikely that peripheral factors could be responsible for the far-reaching and complex differences observed between extraverts and introverts. Historically there have been several attempts in this direction; we need only mention the work of Gross on the primary and secondary function (Refs. 10 & 11) and that of Spearman on perseveration (Ref. 41). Experimental evidence is not lacking to show that these early attempts were quite unsuccessful; the recent work of Rim, for instance, has shown not only that there is no one general factor of perseveration but also that none of the 20 or so tests of perseveration used by him succeeded in differentiating at a reasonable level of significance between hysterics and dysthymics (Ref. 34).

More acceptable, perhaps, is a theory proposed by Pavlov, who considered the phenomena of hysteria to be closely linked with his concept of *inhibition*. Postulating excessive concentration of excitation in a weak nervous system, Pavlov argues that in the hysteric the process of negative induction should give rise to intense inhibition effects (Ref. 26). His theory is difficult to follow in detail and testable deductions cannot easily be made with any confidence. Further, Pavlov did not extend his tentative hypothesis to the typological field, nor did he himself carry out any experimental work on human beings to support or refute it. Nevertheless, the theory here presented is essentially a development and simplification of his. It bases itself on the concept of *reactive inhibition* developed by Hull (Ref. 17), rather than on that of *negative induction* developed by Pavlov (Ref. 27), because the evidence in favour of the former appears more conclusive than the evidence in favour of the latter and also because the former seems to lend itself more easily to the formulation of exact and testable predictions.

We may state this theory in three parts, dealing respectively with the general law, the postulation of individual differences and the typological postulate. The general law reads as follows:

A. *Whenever any stimulus-response connection is made in an organism (excitation), there also occurs simultaneously a reaction in the nervous structures mediating this connection which opposes its recurrence (inhibition).* This hypothesis is a more general formulation of Hull's first submolar principle; it states in effect, as he puts it, that

'all responses leave behind in the physical structures involved in the evocation, a state or substance which acts directly to inhibit the evocation of the activity in question. The hypothetical inhibitory condition or substance is observable only through its effect upon positive re-action potentials. This negative action is called *reaction inhibition*. An increment of reactive inhibition (ΔI_R) is assumed to be generated by every repetition of the response (R), whether reinforced or not and these increments are assumed to accumulate except as they spontaneously disintegrate with the passage of time.'

The second part of the hypothesis deals with the problem of individual differences adumbrated by Pavlov but almost completely neglected by Hull. A statement of this part of the hypothesis might be as follows:

B. *Human beings differ with respect to the speed with which reactive inhibition is produced, the strength of reactive inhibition and the speed with which reactive inhibition is dissipated. These differences themselves are properties of the physical structures involved in the evocation of responses.*

The third part of the hypothesis relates A and B to the results of taxonomic work summarized above and states:

C. *Individuals in whom reactive inhibition is generated quickly, in whom strong reactive inhibitions are generated and in whom reactive inhibition is dissipated slowly are thereby predisposed to develop extraverted patterns of behaviour and to develop hysterical disorders in cases of neurotic breakdown; conversely, individuals in whom reactive inhibition is generated slowly, in whom weak reactive inhibitions are generated and in whom reactive inhibition is dissipated quickly, are thereby predisposed to develop introverted patterns of behaviour and to develop dysthymic disorders in cases of neurotic breakdown.*

Comparatively little work has been done in this field since Pavlov's original fragmentary hypotheses were formulated. The experiments by Welsh & Kubis (Refs. 45 & 46) have lent some support to hypotheses of this type. In one experiment these investigators used PGR conditioning on 82 control subjects and 51 neurotic patients. They found, as could be predicted from the inhibition theory, that their patients, most of whom were of the dysthymic type, conditioned very much more quickly than did the controls (average number of repetitions required for the production of a conditioned response was $8 \cdot 6 \pm 3 \cdot 1$ in the patients and $23 \cdot 9 \pm 8 \cdot 2$ in the controls). Among the patients an attempt was made to rate the degree of anxiety from which they were suffering; it was found that the average number of repetitions required to produce a conditioned response in those with great and moderate anxiety was $7 \cdot 1$ and $8 \cdot 4$ respectively; in those with mild or no anxiety the number of repetitions required was $22 \cdot 2$ and $26 \cdot 3$. (Correlations between conditionability and age and intelligence were quite insignificant; test-retest reliability was 0·88 in the normal group.)

In another experiment 24 dysthymic patients were contrasted with 22 controls. Again the mean number of repetitions required was significantly different for the two groups, being $7·5\pm2·31$ for the dysthymic patients and $21·86\pm7·97$ for the controls. Some hysterics were also tested and were found difficult to condition.

The only investigation, however, to put the hypothesis to a proper test by including a matched group of hysterics as well as normal and dysthymic groups was carried out at the Maudsley Hospital by Franks (Ref. 7). Using the eyewink reflex to a puff of air as the response and a tone as the conditioned stimulus, he obtained unequivocal evidence that dysthymics condition more quickly than normals and normals more quickly than hysterics. (The normal group, being a random sample of the population, would include extraverts and introverts in roughly equal proportions and would therefore be ambivert on the average and consequently intermediate between the extravert-hysteric and the introvert-dysthymic groups.)

Among several other investigators who have succeeded in relating speed of conditioning to dysthymia, the work of Taylor (Ref. 42) and Taylor & Spence (Ref. 43) is of particular interest, as these investigators advance an explanation of the phenomenon which is somewhat different from our own.

Making use of Hull's formula $_sE_r = {_sH_r}\times D$, where $_sE_r$ represents excitatory potential, $_sH_r$ represents habit strength and D represents drive strength, they argue that anxiety is related to drive level and that consequently higher states of anxiety should lead to quicker conditioning ($_sE_r$) because of increases in drive strength (D). Their experiments do not provide crucial evidence with respect to the two theories involved as the same prediction would be made in terms of both hypotheses.[1] It

---

[1] Taylor and Spence (Ref. 43) use the Taylor Scale of Manifest Anxiety as a measure of anxiety in spite of the fact that little evidence is brought forward to support any assumption that it correlates with clinical estimates of anxiety. The work of Holtzman (Ref. 2), as well as that of Sampson & Bindra (Ref. 35), in which an attempt is made to link up scores on this scale and independent criteria, fails to support Taylor's hypothesis. Franks has shown that contrary to the Taylor and Spence hypothesis hysterics, whose scores on the Taylor scale are about as high as those of dysthymics, are more difficult to condition than members of a normal group, whose scores on the Taylor Scale are very much lower (Ref. 7). He also failed, as have other investigators (Refs. 2 & 14), to obtain a significant correlation between conditioning and score on the Taylor Scale. These findings throw considerable doubt on the Taylor-Spence hypothesis.

seemed necessary, therefore, to choose a prediction which would produce positive effects in terms of our hypothesis, but where no such prediction could reasonably be made in terms of the Taylor-Spence hypothesis. An attempt to formulate such a deduction will be made in the next section.

CORTICAL INHIBITION AND FIGURAL AFTEREFFECT

In searching for a phenomenon which would avoid the ambiguity of results encountered in the work of conditioning, it was found necessary to go back from Hull's development of learning theory to Pavlov's somewhat more fundamental position. Pavlov regarded the conditioned reflex as a tool for investigating the dynamics of cortical action rather than as a paradigm of learning. He considered that the laws discovered by him had perfectly general validity and were not restricted to the very special circumstances of the conditioning experiment; indeed, he suggested explicitly that perceptual and other phenomena could find an explanation in terms of inhibition, excitation, disinhibition, etc. It seems possible, therefore, that we may be successful in our search if we look for perceptual phenomena to which our general theory may be found applicable.

The phenomenon chosen for this purpose was the figural aftereffect discussed by Köhler & Wallach (Ref. 20), Gibson (Ref. 9), Luchins (Ref. 23) and others in a series of articles. Essentially, the effects observed showed beyond doubt that constant stimulation of parts of certain sensory surfaces, such as the retina, sets up states of inhibition in corresponding areas in the cortex which have measurable effects on the perception of stimuli later presented in the same region. If, for instance, a circle is fixated for a period of one or two minutes and is then withdrawn, other stimulus objects, such as a small square, appearing within that part of the retina and the cortex which had previously been surrounded by the circle, will appear smaller than a square of precisely the same size appearing elsewhere on the retina and the cortex.

Effects of this kind appear to be exactly in line with the statement quoted in explanation of Part A of our hypothesis to the effect that 'all responses leave behind in the physical structures involved in the evocation, a state or substance which acts directly to inhibit the evocation of the activity in question' (Ref. 17). It should be noted that in accepting the fact of the occurrence of figural aftereffects, we need not necessarily accept Köhler's theory regarding the origin of these aftereffects, just as in accepting the fact of Pavlovian inhibition we need not accept his theory of cortical inhibition. There is, indeed, a curious resemblance between the arch-atomist Pavlov, on the one hand and the arch-Gestaltist Köhler, on the other, in that both have proposed what are strictly physiological, molecular theories of brain action to account for their findings and that both theories are well outside orthodox neurology. Konorski has discussed the relationship between Pavlov's physiological and neurological theories and those of Sherrington and other orthodox workers in some detail and has attempted to account for Pavlov's experimental results in more acceptable terms (Ref. 21); Osgood and Heyer (Ref. 25) have attempted to do a similar service for Köhler's figural aftereffects.

While we need not deal in detail with Köhler's theories, we must note the terminology used by him, which is in part at least bound up with his theory. The reader will find a more extensive discussion in a recent paper by Luchins & Luchins (Ref. 23). Briefly, then, Köhler assumes that every visual figure is associated with currents in the visual sector of the nervous system, the currents being the results of a difference in density and brightness between figure and ground. (For ease of discussion we are presenting an example from the visual field, but the same arguments apply to all other sensory fields, and the experiment to be described shortly was, indeed, done in the kinaesthetic field rather than in the visual.) The visual sector is considered as a volume conductor and figure currents are assumed to polarize all surfaces through which they pass. This polarization and certain aftereffects in the affected cells are called *electrotonus* and it is known that this condition of electrotonus may proceed for some time after the polarizing current has ceased to flow. Köhler uses the term *satiation* to describe electrotonic effect of figure currents on the cortical sector; the term *figural aftereffects* is used to denote the alterations which test objects may show when their figure currents pass through a satiated region.

Satiation has as its main effect a localized inhibition in the sense that polarization of the affected cells increases their resistance to the passage of an electric current, thereby making the appearance of figure currents in that region more difficult, i.e., acting as an inhibiting agent. The main observable fact mediated in this way is the *displacement* of test objects from the affected region. This displacement is measurable, shows pronounced individual differences and may be used both as a measure and as an operational definition of cortical inhibition in the perceptual field.

The importance of these satiation phenomena in their own right will be obvious to anyone familiar with Köhler's highly original and brilliant

H*

work in this field. From the point of view of general psychology, they are of particular interest in that they form a bridge between two large fields of study which have hitherto remained either out of touch or else frankly antagonistic to each other. One of these is the field of conditioning and learning theory; the other is that of perception. In this work on figural aftereffects we find at long last a *rapprochement* between these large groups of workers and the sets of facts unearthed quite independently by them and it is encouraging to note that the general law of inhibition enunciated by Pavlov and more explicitly by Hull, appears to be formally identical with that advanced by Köhler in terms of perceptual satiation.[1] As long as we regard only the speculative brain theories of these writers, we will tend to miss the essential similarity of their formulations; once we concentrate on the molar rather than on the molecular parts of their theories the similarity will be striking.

The main aim of this section, however, is not to point to similarities between Pavlovian and Gestalt theories, but rather to link both of these with personality theory. From what has been said above it follows immediately that if our argument is sound and if the 'reactive inhibition' of Pavlov and Hull is indeed essentially identical with the factors involved in Köhler's 'satiation', then it would follow directly from Parts B and C of our theory that hysterics should show satiation effects more markedly than dysthymics. In fact, three quite specific predictions can be made. In the first place, satiation effects should appear *earlier* in the hysteric group; in the second place, they should appear more *strongly* in the hysteric group; and in the third place, they should disappear more *slowly* in the hysteric group. These are quite specific predictions which can be tested experimentally and it is only through such experimental verification that the theory can show its acceptability and usefulness. Our next section will, therefore, be concerned with certain empirical results obtained in comparing a group of hysterics and a group of dysthymics with respect to figural aftereffects.

AN EXPERIMENTAL TEST OF THE CORTICAL INHIBITION HYPOTHESIS: METHOD

Apparatus

The apparatus used in this experiment is an adaptation of that described by Köhler & Dinnerstein (Ref. 19); the exact form of apparatus

---

[1] Several workers in Great Britain have recently shown interest in attempts to bring together into one framework these two great fields (Refs. 1 & 3).

and procedure was taken from Klein & Krech (Ref. 18), who used it in their work on cortical conductivity in the brain-injured. As a full description and rationale are given by these authors, our own will be brief.

The apparatus consists of a comparison scale, a test object and a stimulus object. Movable riders are affixed to all three objects in such a way that the position of thumb and forefinger is fixed as the subject moves these two fingers up and down along the sides of the object. All objects are made of unpainted, smoothed hardwood. The apparatus is so arranged as to present the comparison scale to the left of the seated subject and either the test or stimulus object to his right.

Procedure

The subject (S) is blindfolded before he has an opportunity of viewing any part of the equipment. Having taken his seat in front of the apparatus, his task is explained in detail and a demonstration given. Then the experiment proper commences. Putting thumb and forefinger of his right hand into the rider on the test object and thumb and forefinger of his left hand into the rider on the comparison scale, S is required to adjust the position of the rider on the comparison scale until the distance between the fingers of his left hand feels equal to the distance between the fingers of his right hand. This is the point of subjective equality and all changes are measured from this point as the baseline. Four separate determinations are carried out and the results averaged, to make this baseline more reliable.

The next step in the experiment consists in providing S with varying periods of constant tactile stimulation. For this purpose he is instructed to put his fingers into the rider on the stimulus object, which is slightly broader than the test object ($2\frac{1}{2}$ in. as compared with $1\frac{1}{2}$ in.) and to rub the sides of the stimulus object at an even rate for periods of 30 sec, 60 sec and 120 sec, respectively. Four determinations of subjective equality are made after each period of rubbing, in order to obtain more reliable measures. In this way the effect of rubbing the stimulus object on the perception of the test object is ascertained. Finally, after 5 minutes rest and again after another 10 minutes rest, the subjective width of the test object is again ascertained in order to establish the perseverative effects of the stimulation periods. These two sets of judgments are again obtained four times each in order to increase reliability.

Scoring

The predicted aftereffect consequent upon the rubbing of a stimulus object *broader* than the test object is an apparent shrinking of the test object, which should manifest itself in terms of a decrement in the width on the comparison scale judged equal to the test object. For each subject this decrement is expressed in terms of his own original baseline, so that individual differences in perceived equality are taken into account in the score, which thus is essentially a percentage decrement score, i.e., an estimate of the shrinkage that has occurred as a percentage of the original width of the object as perceived by each subject.

The following scores will be reported in this paper: (1) average percentage decrement after 30 sec; (2) average percentage decrement after 60 sec; (3) average percentage decrement after 90 sec; (4) average percentage decrement after 120 sec; (5) sum of the above four scores; (6) maximum single percentage decrement obtained from any subject. In addition to these poststimulation aftereffects, the following recovery period scores were obtained: (a) average percentage decrement after a 5 minute rest; (b) average percentage decrement after (10 minutes+5 minutes =) 15 minutes rest; (c) sum of these two scores.

Subjects

The Ss used in this investigation were selected on the basis of two criteria. The first of these was that they should fall into the diagnostic groups of hysterics and dysthymics respectively. Diagnoses of conversion hysteria, hysteria and psychopathy were accepted as falling into the former group; diagnoses of anxiety state, reactive depression, obsessional and compulsive disorders were accepted as falling into the latter group.

In view of the known unreliability of psychiatric diagnosis, which has been demonstrated, for instance, in *The Scientific Study of Personality* (Ref. 4), it was considered advisable to have a second criterion which was independent of diagnosis. For this purpose a questionnaire was used which had been shown by Hildebrand to be a good measure of extraversion (Ref. 13). This questionnaire is Guilford's Rhathymia scale (Ref. 12) and the reader will find evidence regarding the adequacy of this scale as a measure of extraversion discussed elsewhere (Ref. 6). The procedure followed was that no one with a score below 31 was accepted as extraverted and no one with a score above 39 was accepted as introverted.[1] While it would have been desirable to have no overlap at all in

[1] Hysterics were found by Hildebrand to have an average score of 37 ± 12, dysthymics one of 28 ± 10 (Ref. 13). In our sample the means were 40 ± 12 and 25 ± 10 respectively.

the questionnaire scores of the two groups, it proved impossible to find a large enough group of subjects in the time available to reach this ideal. We can only suggest that the results found with the present groups would probably have been improved somewhat if a stricter criterion could have been employed.

TABLE 1

POSTSTIMULATION FIGURAL AFTEREFFECTS—DYSTHYMICS

Source	df	MS	F
Between times	3	116·0082	0·7752
Between people	13	2050·0241	13·7010
Residual	39	149·6416	
Total	55		

$r_{11} = 0.9270$

TABLE 2

RECOVERY PERIOD AFTEREFFECTS—DYSTHYMICS

Source	df	MS	F
Between times	1	1·9137	0·0541
Between people	13	642·1574	18·1429
Residual	13	35·3945	
Total	27		

$r_{11} = 0.9449$

There were fourteen subjects in each group, all of them males. The average ages of the two groups were 29·14 (hysterics) and 34·23 (dysthymics), an insignificant difference. Matrix IQ's were 100·86 and 104·92, Mill Hill Vocabulary IQ's 102·79 and 110·25; these differences also were insignificant.

Reliability of Scores

Granted that our methods of scoring, which we have taken over from Klein & Krech (Ref. 18), are the most obvious ones, we must first of all ask ourselves questions regarding their reliability and consistency. To our knowledge, there are no reports in the literature dealing with this question, which is of crucial importance whenever test results are to be used as psychometric scores. Consequently, two analyses of variance were carried out for each of the two groups with whom we are concerned, i.e., the hysterics and the dysthymics. The first analysis deals with the scores which we have called average poststimulation figural aftereffects; the second analysis deals with the scores from the two recovery periods. With the formula suggested by Hoyt (Ref. 16), reliabilities of 0·93 and 0·94 were found for the dysthymics; both of these were significant at the 0·001 level. For the hysterics the reliabilities are somewhat lower, being 0·78 and 0·86 respectively. Both of these however are significant at the 0·01 level. Full details are given in Tables 1, 2, 3 and 4.[1]

TABLE 3

POSTSTIMULATION FIGURAL AFTEREFFECT—HYSTERICS

Source	df	MS	F
Between times	3	38·5519	0·3895
Between people	13	443·9761	4·4860
Residual	39	98·9703	
Total	55		
$r_{11} = 0·7771$			

TABLE 4

RECOVERY PERIOD AFTEREFFECTS—HYSTERICS

Source	df	MS	F
Between times	1	53·8013	1·1749
Between people	13	319·8050	6·9837
Residual	13	45·7933	
Total	27		
$r_{11} = 0·8568$			

[1] This consistency in itself poses certain problems for the theoretical analysis of the figural aftereffect phenomenon. Some subjects consistently over-rate rather than under-rate the size of the test object after stimulation. This is very difficult to account for in terms of either the Gestalt or the statistical type of hypothesis. A survey of the literature on other types of inhibition phenomena (massed and spaced learning, reminiscence, etc.) indicates that while most people act in conformity with prediction, some consistently go counter to prediction, i.e., learn better with massed rather than with spaced practice, etc. Theorists usually deal with averages rather than with individual cases and traditionally disregard aberrations of this kind. It seems reasonable to ask that any adequate theory should be able to account for discordant cases as well as for the admittedly large number of concordant ones.

Having found dysthymics to be more consistent in their test performances than hysterics, we would expect to find the correlations among the six scores (four poststimulation scores and two recovery period scores) to be higher for the dysthymics than for the hysterics; this is indeed so. On comparison of the two sets of 15 correlations pair by pair, it was found that in 13 cases the dysthymic correlation was higher; in one case the two were equal; in one case the hysteric correlation was higher. Thus, our expectation is borne out that dysthymics would be more consistent than hysterics.

RESULTS

TABLE 5

	Poststimulation Figural Aftereffects						Recovery Period		
	30 sec	60 sec	90 sec	120 sec	ϵ	Max.	5 min	10 min	ϵ
	Hysterics								
Means	9·68	10·58	13·09	12·78	46·13	20·74	4·35	8·00	12·35
Variances	9·48	13·57	14·22	16·30	1775·90	97·58	14·65	12·94	645·70
	Dysthymics								
Means	1·70	6·21	2·98	7·96	18·85	15·32	0·89	0·36	1·52
Variances	12·97	21·95	32·83	27·77	8200·10	190·12	15·77	20·59	1284·31

We must next turn to the main differences between the groups. Means and variances for hysterics and dysthymics respectively are given in Table 5 for the four poststimulation aftereffects, the sum of the poststimulation aftereffects, the maximum poststimulation aftereffects, the five and ten minute recovery period aftereffects and the sum of the rest period aftereffects. Four poststimulation aftereffects and the two rest periods are plotted in Fig. 21. All the results will be seen to be in line with prediction. Figural aftereffects in the hysteric group appear more quickly, are more strongly marked and disappear more slowly than in the dysthymics.

The significance of the differences between the two groups was tested by means of Hotelling's T test (Ref. 15). This over-all test invalidated the null hypothesis at between the 0·01 and 0·05 levels of significance. Individual one-tail t tests applied to the 9 separate scores disclosed that only the 30 sec period gave results significant at below the 0·05 level of significance; the other scores were significant at approximately the 0·10 level only. It is suggested that in future work more attention be paid to short periods of stimulation (between 10 sec and 30 sec) as longer periods

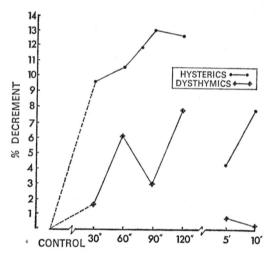

Figure 21. Amount of figural after-effect shown as percentage decrement after four different periods of stimulation and two different periods of rest.

of stimulation appear to increase variability without increasing differentiation. It might also prove useful to make use of more prolonged rest pauses; times of 15 minutes, 20 minutes and 30 minutes might give improved differentiation.

The calculation of differences between groups gives little idea of the strength of the relationship discovered. Accordingly product-moment correlations were calculated beween scores on the figural aftereffect test and the R scale. In addition to the 28 hysterics and dysthymics used for the group comparison, an additional seven neurotics were included in this calculation. These Ss had shown a discrepancy between diagnosis and score on the R scale and had therefore not been included in the group comparisons. Correlations for this group of altogether 35 neurotic subjects were as follows: 0·374 (30 sec); 0·252 (60 sec); 0·236 (90 sec);

0·218 (120 sec); 0·321 (5 minutes); 0·237 (10 minutes). It will be noted that with increasing periods of stimulation, correlations tend to fall off in a regular progression. As regards significance, the correlation for the 30 sec period almost reaches the 0·01 level; of the others only the correlation for the 5 minute rest period passes the 0·05 level of significance. The remaining correlations just fall short of the 0·05 level. Significance levels were of course calculated by using one-tailed tests, as follows from the logic of the experimental design.

It is interesting to note the fate of the seven individuals in whom diagnosis and R score disagreed. In each case where a patient was diagnosed hysteric but had an R score which put him on the introverted side, relatively small aftereffects were found. In each case where a patient was diagnosed dysthymic but had an R score which put him on the extraverted side, relatively large aftereffects were found. In other words, when diagnosis and questionnaire disagree, agreement of the experimental test is much closer with the questionnaire than with diagnosis. In view of the widespread habit of heaping contumely upon questionnaires, this fact may deserve stressing.

DISCUSSION

It will not require much discussion to establish the relevance of the results of our experiment to a theory of neurotic disorder. Psychoanalytic theories have usually played down differences between the various types of neurotic symptomatology as accidental, unimportant and variable; usually the implication has been that hysteria and the dysthymic disorders both lie close to each other along one single dimension of *regression* and that hysterical symptoms are in a sense merely a defence against the overt anxiety shown by the dysthymic. On the basis of this type of theory, no fundamental differences would be expected on psychophysiological measures of conditioning or of figural aftereffects. The fact that such differences are observed considerably weakens the Freudian theory and supports the dimensional theory outlined at the beginning of this paper. Another advantage of the dimensional theory appears to be that it can account for the similarities observed in the behaviour and the symptomatology of hysterics, brain-injured and leucotomized patients, a task not even attempted by psychoanalytic writers. A discussion of such an extension of our theory may be in order.

The experimental procedure adopted in Section 4 was taken over directly from Klein & Krech and a comparison of our results with theirs may be of some interest. They were concerned with differences between brain-injured patients and normals and found that figural aftereffect was much more strongly marked among the former than in the normal control group. The average size of the overall figural aftereffect was 12·08 per cent for the brain-injured and 6·25 per cent for the controls. The maximum degree of effect for the brain-injured averaged 19·50 per cent, for the controls, 13·00 per cent. Corresponding figures for hysterics and dysthymics are: 11·53 per cent and 4·71 per cent for average overall effect, 20·74 per cent and 15·32 per cent for maximum effect. There is thus a distinct similarity in the behaviour of the brain-injured in Klein & Krech's study and the hysterics in our own. The normal controls tested by Klein & Krech give results intermediate between our hysteric and dysthymic groups, though somewhat closer to the dysthymics.

These figures would seem to indicate similarities between hysteria and brain injury which are important from a theoretical point of view. In a series of studies (Refs. 28, 29, 30 & 31). Petrie has shown that one of the psychological aftereffects of leucotomy is an increase in extraversion, as measured by objective tests of personality similar to those used by Hildebrand in his factorial study (Ref. 13). The theory on which the prediction of a change toward extraversion after leucotomy was based was essentially one of increased cortical inhibition following brain injury.[1] Such an hypothesis is much too broad and general to account for all the known facts and will presumably require a good deal of detailed modification, particularly with respect to the differential activity of various parts of the brain and the effect of specific incisions and ablations. Thus, recent unpublished work by Petrie has shown that a change in the direction of increased extraversion is produced by all prefrontal operations involving the convexity (standard leucotomy, Rostral leucotomy and selective surgery of areas 9 and/or 10). On the other hand, cingulectomy and orbital undercutting, i.e., operations not involving the convexity, do not have aftereffects involving a shift toward extraversion on the tests used. If these results were to be confirmed, they would clearly indicate the need to make this general hypothesis much more specific.

Nevertheless, as a first approximation, this general hypothesis has

[1] Here again Pavlov's theory of negative induction has also been used to account for some of the observed effects (Refs. 36, 37, 38, 39 & 40); it is not clear to what extent negative induction and reactive inhibition can be identified with each other at the phenomenal level.

led to the prediction of the phenomena observed by Petrie (Ref. 28) and it does account similarly for the results of the Klein & Krech experiment. It would appear worthy of further investigation, particularly as it gives rise to very clear-cut predictions. Thus, we may predict that the formation of conditioned reflexes would be more difficult in the brain-injured than in the intact individual. Some evidence supporting this prediction has been published by Reese, Doss & Gantt (Ref. 33). After leucotomy, we would predict that inhibitory effects would be more strongly marked than before and we would also be able to make a number of predictions regarding the reactions of leucotomized patients on certain perceptual tests similar to those made in the concluding section of this paper with respect to hysterics.

Klein & Krech, in their paper, advance a somewhat different theory which, however, in most essentials appears to deviate but little from that used in our own work. They assume that

... 'transmission rate of excitation patterns varies from individual to individual, from time to time within the same individual and from area to area within a single cortical field at any time. With this assumption it is possible to appeal to *differential* cortical conductivity as a parameter which will help us understand inter- and intra-individual differences in cortical integration and therefore in behaviour' (Ref. 18, p. 118).

It may be worthwhile to indicate in just one sentence the essential difference between the conductivity hypothesis and the one advocated here. Klein & Krech postulate neural conductivity as a basic personality dimension, assuming that it may be high or low *prior to any stimulation.* We assume that individuals differ not with respect to conductivity, but with respect to the rate at which inhibition is aroused along cortical pathways by the passage of a neural impulse. The latter hypothesis seems to be more securely based on experimental findings, less subject to unprovable assumptions and more easily testable. It is for these reasons that it has been preferred in this paper. It should be added, however, that both the conductivity and the inhibition hypotheses give rise to similar predictions in the case of the degree of satiation to be expected in the brain-injured and hysterical patients and that the data reported here do not in any way disprove the conductivity hypothesis, any more than they prove the inhibition hypothesis.

It may be worthwhile, however, to indicate very briefly the type of prediction which our theory makes possible and to suggest lines along which it could be disproved.

1. If we accept Köhler's demonstration that the rate of disappearance with time of the Müller-Lyer and other illusions is a consequence of figural aftereffects, it can be predicted that the rate of disappearance of the illusion should be more rapid with hysterics than with dysthymics and in the brain-injured as compared with the normal.

2. If we accept Klein's interpretation of the phenomenon, it can be predicted that when the persistence of an afterimage is measured as a function of the duration of stimulus exposure, the duration of the after-image in hysterics should fall off significantly as compared with dysthymics. Klein has already shown that this is so when the brain-injured are compared with normal subjects (Ref. 18).

3. Phenomena of apparent motion may be reformulated in terms of the inhibition theory and it may be predicted that the optimal time interval for the perception of apparent movement would be decreased more in hysterics than in dysthymics after the introduction of some form of continuous stimulation in the path of the apparent movement. Shapiro has shown, in experiments using continuous stimulation in order to produce experimental inhibition effects in the occurrence of apparent movement, that under conditions of inhibition the time-interval threshold was 140 sigma, as compared with 250 sigma under noninhibition conditions (Ref. 40).

4. If a theory of satiation or inhibition be acceptable as accounting for reversal of perspective, then one would predict not only that the rate of reversal would increase in time as it is known to do but also that this increase in rate of reversal should be more marked among hysterics than among dysthymics. Our prediction here, as in the case of the experiment described in this paper, would relate more to a change of rate than to the initial rate of reversal, although the latter also should show differences in favour of the hysterics and the brain-injured.

5. Perceptual disinhibition phenomena of the type studied by Rawdon-Smith (Ref. 32) and others might be presumed also to show differences between hysterics and dysthymics. On the hypothesis that we are dealing with the inhibition of an inhibition in these cases, it might be predicted that disinhibition should be more pronounced among hysterics than among dysthymics.

6. Critical flicker fusion would be expected to be observed at different frequencies in hysterics and brain-injured, as compared with dysthymics and non-brain-injured. This follows directly from our interpretation of

the law of reactive inhibition. Some empirical data are available to support one of these predictions at least (Ref. 22).

7. Rotation phenomena, such as have been described by Shapiro (Ref. 40), have been explained by him in terms of inhibition (negative induction). If this hypothesis which has led to important discoveries in the field of brain injury, should prove acceptable, then we would expect a greater degree of rotation among hysterics than among dysthymics.

In making these predictions, we have purposely kept within the perceptual field, but it is clear that many other predictions could be made in the fields of learning, memory and motor behaviour. Phenomena of reminiscence, of massed and spaced learning, of vigilance, of blocking and many others have been interpreted in terms of inhibition. While it remains possible, of course, that in each separate case we must have recourse to a different type of inhibition, this does not seem a likely contingency and the hypothesis certainly appears worth testing that it is the same type of cortical inhibition which causes all these phenomena, as well as the perceptual ones discussed above. The obvious method of testing this hypothesis appears to be in terms of individual differences, i.e., in postulating that a person found to show a high degree of inhibition with respect to any one of these phenomena should also show a high degree of inhibition with respect to all the others. It is hoped to provide evidence with respect to this generalized inhibition hypothesis in the near future.

SUMMARY AND CONCLUSIONS

An attempt has been made in this paper to work out a dynamic theory to account for a number of experimental findings in the field of personality related to the concept of extraversion-introversion. Following Pavlov and Hull, a theory of cortical inhibition was developed to account for observed differences in behaviour and a deduction from this principle was made by extending it to the perceptual field. It was predicted that hysterics (as a prototype of the extraverted personality type) would be differentiated from dysthymics (as a prototype of the introverted personality type) in the *speed of arousal, strength and length of persistence* of figural aftereffects. A comparison of two groups of carefully selected subjects showed that (a) hysterics developed satiation and figural aftereffects more quickly than did dysthymics, (b) that hysterics developed stronger satiation and figural aftereffects than did dysthymics and (c) that hysterics developed more persistent satiation and figural aftereffects

230   *Bearings on Basic Psychological Processes*

than did dysthymics. The differences are statistically significant and are
in complete accord with prediction. In the discussion, certain parallels
were drawn between hysteria and brain injury in terms of the theory
outlined, with particular reference to the aftereffects of leucotomy.
Lastly, a number of predictions were made from the theory which should
permit of an experimental decision as to its validity.

REFERENCES

1. BERLYNE, D. E., Attention, perception and behaviour theory.
   Psychol. Rev., **58**, 137–146, 1951.
2. BITTERMAN, M. E. & HOLTZMAN, W. H., Conditioning and extinc
   tion of the galvanic skin response as a function of anxiety.
   J. abnorm. soc. Psychol., **47**, 615–623, 1952.
3. BROADBENT, D. E., Classical conditioning and human watch-keep
   ing. *Psychol. Rev.*, **60**, 331–339, 1953.
4. EYSENCK, H. J., *The Scientific Study of Personality*. London:
   Routledge & Kegan Paul, 1952.
5. ——, The logical basis of factor analysis. *Amer. Psychol.*, **8**, 105–
   114, 1953.
6. ——, *The Structure of Human Personality*. London: Methuen,
   1953.
7. FRANKS, C., An Experimental Study of Conditioning as Related to
   Mental Abnormality. Unpublished doctor's dissertation, Univer
   sity of London Library, 1954.
8. FRASER, R., *The Incidence of Neurosis among Factory Workers*.
   London: H.M.S.O., 1947.
9. GIBSON, J. J., Adaptation, after-effect and contrast in the perception
   of curved lines. *J. exp. Psychol.*, **16**, 1–51, 1933.
10. GROSS, O., *Die cerebrale Sekundärfunction*. Leipzig: Vogel, 1902.
11. ——, *Über psychopathologische Minderwertig-Keiten*. Leipzig:
    Vogel, 1909.
12. GUILFORD, J. P., *An Inventory of Factors STDCR*. Beverly Hills,
    California: Sheridan Supply Company, 1942.
13. HILDEBRAND, H. P., A Factorial Study of Introversion-Extraversion
    by Means of Objective Tests. Unpublished doctor's dissertation,
    University of London Library, 1953.
14. HILGARD, E. R., JONES, L. V. & KAPLAN, S. J., Conditioned dis

crimination as related to anxiety. *J. exp. Psychol.*, **42**, 94–99, 1951.

15. HOTELLING, H., The generalization of 'Student's' ratio. *Ann. math. Statist.*, **2**, 360–368, 1931.

16. HOYT, C., Test reliability obtained by analysis of variance. *Psychometrika*, **6**, 153–160, 1941.

17. HULL, C. L., *Principles of Behaviour*. New York: D. Appleton-Century, 1943.

18. KLEIN, G. S. & KRECH, D., Cortical conductivity in the brain-injured. *J. Pers.*, **21**, 118–148, 1952.

19. KÖHLER, W. & DINNERSTEIN, D., Figural aftereffects in kinesthesis. In: *Miscellanea Psychologica* (ed. Albert Michotte). Louvain: Institut Superieur de Philosophie, 1947.

20. —— & WALLACH, H., Figural after-effects: an investigation of visual processes. *Proc. Amer. phil. Soc.*, **88**, 269–357, 1944.

21. KONORSKI, J., *Conditioned Reflexes and Neuron Organization*. Cambridge: Cambridge University Press, 1948.

22. LANDIS, C., *An Annotated Bibliography of Flicker Fusion Phenomena*. Michigan: Michigan Armed Forces-National Research Council, 1953.

23. LUCHINS, A. S. & LUCHINS, E. H., The satiation theory of figural after-effects and Gestalt principles of perception. *J. Gen. Psychol.*, **49**, 3–29, 1953.

24. McLEOD, H., An Experimental Study of the Inheritance of Intro-version-Extraversion. Unpublished doctor's dissertation, University of London Library, 1954.

25. OSGOOD, C. E. & HEYER, A. W., A new interpretation of figural after-effects. *Psychol. Rev.*, **59**, 98–118, 1952.

26. PAVLOV, I. P., *Lectures on Conditioned Reflexes*. Vol. II. London: Lawrence & Wishart, 1941.

27. ——, *Conditioned Reflexes*. London: Oxford University Press, 1927.

28. PETRIE, A., *Personality and the Frontal Lobes*. London: Routledge & Kegan Paul, 1952.

29. —— & LE BEAU, J., A comparison of the personality changes after (1) prefrontal selective surgery for the relief of intractable pain and for the treatment of mental cases; (2) cingulectomy and topectomy. *J. ment. Sci.*, **99**, 53–61, 1935.

30. —— & ——, Études psychologiques des changements de la personalité produits par certaines opérations préfrontales sélèctives. *Rev. de Centre de Psychol. appl.*, **4**, No. 1, 1–16, 1953.

31. —— & ——, Psychological effects of selective frontal surgery including cingulectomy. *Proc. Vth Int. Congr. Neurol.*, Lisbon, **4**, 392–395, 1953.
32. RAWDON-SMITH, A. R. R., Experimental deafness. Further data upon the phenomenon of so-called auditory fatigue. *Brit. J. Psychol.*, **26**, 233–244, 1936.
33. REESE, W. G., DOSS, R. & GANTT, W. H., Autonomic responses in differential diagnoses of organic and psychogenic psychoses. *AMA Arch. Neurol. Psychiat.*, **70**, 778–793, 1953.
34. RIM, Y. S., Perseveration and Fluency as Measures of Extraversion-Introversion in Abnormal Subjects. Unpublished doctoral dissertation, University of London Library, 1953.
35. SAMPSON, H. & BINDRA, D., 'Manifest' anxiety, neurotic anxiety and the rate of conditioning. *J. abnorm. soc. Psychol.*, **49**, 256–259, 1954.
36. SHAPIRO, M. B., Experimental studies of a perceptual anomaly. *J. ment. Sci.*, **97**, 90–110, 1957.
37. ——, Experimental studies of a perceptual anomaly. II. Confirmatory and explanatory experiments. *J. ment. Sci.*, **98**, 605–617, 1951.
38. ——, Experimental studies of a perceptual anomaly. III. The testing of an explanatory theory. *J. ment. Sci.*, **99**, 393–410, 1953.
39. ——, An experimental investigation of the block design rotation effect. An analysis of psychological effect of brain damage. *Brit. J. med. Psychol.*, **27**, 84–88, 1954.
40. ——, A preliminary investigation of the effects of continuous stimulation on the perception of 'apparent motion'. *Brit. J. Gen. Psychol.*, **45**, 58–67, 1954.
41. SPEARMAN, C., *The Abilities of Man.* London: Macmillan, 1927.
42. TAYLOR, J. A., The relationship of anxiety to the conditioned eyelid response. *J. exp. Psychol.*, **41**, 81–92, 1951.
43. —— & SPENCE, K. W., The relationship of anxiety level to performance in serial learning. *J. exp. Psychol.*, **44**, 61–64, 1952.
44. THURSTONE, L. L., *Multiple Factor Analysis: a Development and Expansion of the Vectors of the Mind.* Chicago: University of Chicago Press, 1947.
45. WELCH, L. & KUBIS, J., The effect of anxiety on the conditioning rate and stability of the PGR. *J. Psychol.*, **23**, 83–91, 1947.
46. —— & ——, Conditioned PGR (psychogalvanic response) in states of pathological anxiety. *J. nerv. ment. Dis.*, **105**, 372–381, 1947.

27

Psychophysical Methods and Individual Differences in the Kinaesthetic Figural Aftereffect

D. E. BROADBENT

First published in *British Journal of Psychology*, **52**, 97–104, 1961

RECENTLY Eysenck found that hysterics displayed greater figural aftereffects than dysthymics do in a situation involving judgments of width of a wooden block by touch, before and after experience of a wider block. In the present research three groups of subjects were tested in a similar situation with some modifications. There was no correlation between extraversion and figural aftereffect. However, there was a correlation with one of the constant errors which might under some circumstances give rise to an apparent relation with figural aftereffect. Two other groups gave pseudo-figural aftereffects, although never exposed to a wider block. It was concluded that extraverts do not necessarily show larger figural aftereffects and that the exact method of determination of such effects is far more important than is generally assumed.

INTRODUCTION

A paper by Eysenck reported that hysteric neurotics showed larger kinaesthetic figural aftereffects than dysthymic neurotics did (Ref. 4). This is in accordance with the prediction from Eysenck's own theory that 'extraversion' (defined operationally as the group of qualities which amongst neurotics differentiate hysterics from dysthymics) is associated with a greater liability to reactive inhibition. There are, of course, several interpolated steps in the deduction, since it is not necessarily fair to identify figural aftereffects with reactive inhibition, despite certain similarities in the concepts. Moreover, one could equally well argue that a person with a greater liability to inhibition would show a rapid decay of perceptual (or neural) response as soon as the stimulus was removed and therefore a smaller figural aftereffect. Indeed Eysenck has himself used greater inhibition of a neural aftereffect as an explana-

233

tion of the effects of drugs on the 'Bidwell's ghost' phenomenon (Ref. 5, p. 241).

For these reasons any failure to confirm Eysenck's prediction would not have invalidated his general theory. But the connection between figural aftereffects and individual differences in other phenomena is of considerable interest. The following experiments were therefore intended to see how far the same findings would be obtained if the experimental conditions were slightly changed. As will be seen, it was found that the exact manner of presentation of the stimuli was crucial and one cannot therefore make the general statement that extraverts show larger figural aftereffects.

METHOD

The general procedure was the same as that used by Eysenck (Ref. 4) who very properly repeated the methods of Klein & Krech (Ref. 7) exactly; the earlier authors had shown a relation between aftereffects and brain injuries and it is therefore valuable that Eysenck's results were obtained by the same method. Broadly speaking, the technique is to sit the subject at a table, blindfolded and give him a standard block of wood to run along with his right hand. His left hand is placed on a wedge-shaped block and he moves that hand along the length of the block until he reaches the point on the wedge where its width feels identical to that of the standard block under the other hand. Four determinations of this point are made, thus giving an initial Point of Subjective Equality. The wedge is then removed and a block of different size presented to the right hand for a set period. After this the standard and the wedge are replaced and four more determinations made to find the new Point of Subjective Equality (P.S.E.). If the interpolated block was larger than the standard, the new P.S.E. is usually smaller than the initial value, showing the figural aftereffect. In Klein & Krech's method, fresh presentations (of different lengths of time) of the interpolated block are then made in order to study the aftereffect as a function of presentation time but this is a doubtful psychophysical procedure and was not adopted in the present case.

The main distinctive features of the present experiments were as follows: in the first three groups of subjects the wedge was presented with its narrow end alternately towards and away from the subject's body. In the procedure established by Klein & Krech the point of the wedge is always towards the body. Since the results of these groups showed a change in the bias towards the body between the first and second measurements of P.S.E., two more groups were tested with the point of the wedge always towards themselves but with no interpolated experience between the two measurements. These groups were intended to examine whether the results have anything at all to do with the interpolated experience, or whether they simply arise from the process of measurement itself.

The other respects in which the procedure was different from that of Eysenck are as follows:

1. The subjects were young men under 25 and formed a normal rather than neurotic population.

2. The length of the wedge was only 18 inches instead of 30 inches. It tapered from 4 inches to 1 inch, whereas that in the earlier experiments tapered from 4 inches to $\frac{1}{2}$ inch.

3. The questionnaire measure of extraversion applied was that of Heron (Ref. 6). This correlates highly with and is made up of similar questions to the Maudsley Inventory used by Eysenck.

4. The measure of size of figural aftereffect was not calculated as a proportion or percentage of the original size of P.S.E., but merely taken as the actual shift in inches of the P.S.E. along the wedge. This was because, as extraversion correlated slightly positively with initial P.S.E., the use of absolute scores gave the best possible chance of any correlation of extraversion and figural aftereffect. That is, a score was used which gave the benefit of any doubt to Eysenck's result.

5. The time of presentation of the interpolated block was only 20 sec whereas Eysenck's shortest time was 30 sec. This was in line with a suggestion made in the earlier paper that a shorter time was preferable.

In addition, each of the groups of subjects worked under its own individual conditions, as follows.

Orientation of Wedge

Groups 1, 2 and 3 (18, 16 and 17 subjects, respectively) made their judgments with the point of the wedge alternately towards and away from the body on successive determinations. Groups 1 and 2 made their first judgment with the point towards the body, the next with it away and so on. Group 3 made the first judgment with the point away from the body, the next with it towards and so on.

Groups 4 and 5 (22 and 38 subjects, respectively) had the point of the wedge always towards themselves, as in the procedure used by earlier workers.

Nature of Standard and Interpolated Blocks

Group 1 used a 3 inch wide block as its standard; all other groups used a 1½ inch block, which was the size used in the earlier papers. Group 1 had a 1 inch block as the interpolated one, whereas groups 2 and 3 used a 2½ inch interpolated block as earlier experiments did.

Groups 4 and 5 used no interpolated block whatever and merely rested for 20 sec between the two determinations of the P.S.E.

Pressure of Riders

The apparatus used by Klein & Krech and that of Eysenck, were fitted with 'riders', that is, with a kind of small carriage running along the top of each block. The fingers are inserted between guides and thus are held in a fixed relation to the longitudinal axis of the block. Furthermore, since the riders must start each run along the wedge from one end or the other, control is exercised over the end of the wedge from which the subject starts.

No riders were fitted to the present apparatus and all groups except 5 explored the blocks in a manner unprescribed by instructions. This meant that they usually started from the end of the wedge nearest themselves.

For group 5, riders were improvised by laying a ruler across wedge and standard block and requiring the subject to push it along with his fingers. It was started alternately from the near and the far ends of the wedge and no retracing was allowed, so that the subject made alternate ascending and descending judgments.

The various differences in procedure for each group are summarized in Table 1.

TABLE 1

THE CHARACTERISTICS OF PREVIOUS EXPERIMENTS AND OF
THE VARIOUS GROUPS IN THE PRESENT RESEARCH

	Orientation of wedge (point to or from the body)	Standard (judged) block (in.)	Interpolated block (in.)	Presence of rider
Klein & Krech, Eysenck	To throughout	1½	2½	Yes
Group 1	To, from, to, from	3	1	No
Group 2	To, from, to from	1½	2½	No
Group 3	From, to, from, to	1½	2½	No
Group 4	To throughout	1½	None	No
Group 5	To throughout	1½	None	Yes

RESULTS AND DISCUSSION

Groups 1, 2 and 3

These three groups, each of which received an interpolated block between the two groups of judgments, ought to have shown a correlation between extraversion and the size of shift in P.S.E. away from the interpolated block. That is, in group 1 extraversion should correlate with increase in P.S.E. and in groups 2 and 3 with decrease. The pooled τ correlation for all three groups (totalling 51 subjects) was however only 0·03, which is completely insignificant. It is important to note that the mean P.S.E. for groups 2 and 3 did nonetheless decrease, that is, the conditions were in fact such as to give a figural aftereffect (p<0·01 by sign test). In group 1 this was not so, probably because the difference in size of the standard and interpolated block was too great. But the low total correlation was not due to dilution by that group, which was in fact the group which gave the largest τ of the correct sign ($\tau = 0·15$). Groups 2 and 3 were less in accord with the inhibitory hypothesis, although they showed better figural aftereffect, τ being $-0·15$ and $0·08$ for the respective groups. (See Table 2 for a summary of all results obtained.)

This failure to reproduce Eysenck's results might of course be due to any or all of the differences in conditions already mentioned. It might also be due to an unfortunate sample of subjects, even though numerically it is larger than Eysenck's was; negative conclusions are hard to establish. There is, however, direct evidence that the discrepancy is due to the difference in orientation of the wedge. In the present experiment, as the initial and final P.S.E. are each the average of the two judgments with the point towards the body and two with it away, it is possible to detect any systematic bias of subjects. For instance, if the two 'point towards' judgments give larger values than the other two, the subject is biased in the direction away from his body. If we work out the size of this bias for each subject for his second set of judgments, we find that extraversion correlates with bias towards the body. τ (pooled for the three groups) $= 0·23$, p<0·05. For the first set of judgments this is not so: $\tau = 0·04$ which is quite insignificant. Thus it appears that in these results extraverts (a) do not show bigger figural aftereffects, (b) do not originally show more bias towards the body than intraverts do and (c) do show bias towards the body in the second series of judgments. Had the wedge-point been left pointing continuously towards the body, results (c) would have meant that extraverts would show a smaller P.S.E. in the second series. In the situation described by Eysenck (Ref. 4) this would

TABLE 2

SUMMARY OF RESULTS

	Variables correlated		τ	Effects over groups as a whole
Group I	Extraversion	Figural aftereffect	0·15	No figural aftereffect
II	Extraversion	Figural aftereffect	−0·15	Figural aftereffect
III	Extraversion	Figural aftereffect	0·08	Figural aftereffect†
Pooled I, II, III	Extraversion	Figural aftereffect	0·03	—
	Extraversion	Bias towards body, in first determination	0·04	—
	Extraversion	Bias in second determination	0·23*	—
IV	Extraversion	Pseudo-figural aftereffect	−0·06	Pseudo-figural aftereffect towards small end†
	Willingness to use extreme categories	Pseudo-figural aftereffect	−0·35*	—
V	Extraversion	Pseudo-figural aftereffect	−0·13	Pseudo-effect towards large end*

* p<0·05
† p<0·01

The significant in group IV is tested one-tailed; all other tests are two-tailed.

have indicated an apparently greater figural aftereffect for extraverts.

Group 4

The results of the first three groups did not appear very comprehensible. One possible explanation was that this type of situation is a persistence test, similar to that in which the subject holds out a leg parallel to the ground for as long as he is prepared to do so. Hysterics do worse on such tests than do dysthymics (Ref. 3) and it might be argued that the extraverted will therefore show a tendency to let their arms drop after a series of judgments, bringing their hands closer to their bodies. This explanation is not very plausible since leg persistence is also less in neurotics than in normals and the neuroticism scale of the Heron Inventory did not correlate with any of the effects here obtained. However, it was thought worthwhile to test some subjects without any interpolated experience at all and this was the purpose of group 4. This group showed a substantially lower P.S.E. on the second set of judgments than it did on the first. That is, a pseudo-figural aftereffect was obtained with no figure. (17 subjects reduced their P.S.E. and 4 increased it, so $p < 0.01$ by sign test.) This result confirms our suspicions of the method of leaving the wedge-point towards the body; but the pseudo-figural aftereffect does not correlate with extraversion ($\tau = 0.06$, which is insignificantly in the wrong direction). Thus the findings do not give any support to the theory that the extraverts become biased towards the body because of reluctance to hold their arms out straight.

At this point the chain of reasoning which led to the testing of group 5 should be explained. As has been said, all earlier groups tended to approach the wedge from the nearest end. In the case of group 4, this meant the smaller end. Now the subjects never saw the wedge before they began feeling it and therefore began the experiment with no idea of the range of values that were in fact available for them to choose. Initially, therefore, they would produce a P.S.E. unmodified by the effects of this range. In repeated trials, however, they would become familiar with the part of the wedge lying between the P.S.E. and the point; and this would be for them the range of possible judgments which they could make. Now there is a well-known central tendency in judgment situations (e.g. Ref. 8, p. 56) which makes subjects give judgments unduly biased towards the middle of the range they have available. If this tendency were operative, the original P.S.E. would shift towards the centre of the range with which the subject was familiar, that is, in group 4, towards the small end. This would produce our pseudo aftereffect.

To give some support to this interpretation, results were examined from a weight-lifting experiment which happened to have involved 17 of the subjects in group 4. Ten weights were judged using an arbitrary scale from 1 to 5; some people were more ready to use the categories 1 and 5 than others were. A score of 'willingness to use extremes' was obtained for each subject by counting the number of times that categories 1 and 5 were used. This quantity is correlated with the size of the pseudo-figural aftereffect, $\tau = 0.35$, which is comfortably significant at the 0.05 level by a one-tail test and almost so by a two-tail test (critical ratio = 1.91). So we have some tentative grounds for believing that the subjects who show the pseudo-figural aftereffect most strongly are those who most object to using extreme categories of judgment.

Group 5

If the suggestion just made is correct, then a group of subjects whose experience of the wedge was deliberately broadened, to include the entire array of possible widths available for judgment, would not show the pseudo-figural aftereffect of group 4. On the contrary, any of them who avoided extremes of judgment would in this situation tend to make judgments biased towards the centre of the wedge rather than towards one end of it (because the P.S.E. is on the small side of the centre of the wedge). Thus the trend of judgments should be away from the body rather than towards it, giving a pseudo-figural aftereffect in the opposite direction to that found in group 4. This finding was indeed obtained: group 5 were made to explore the wedge from both ends so that they became familiar with all its length. Their second set of judgments gave a P.S.E. which was larger than their initial one: 26 showed the effect and 11 the opposite, so $p < 0.05$. Thus they showed a pseudo-figural aftereffect in the opposite direction to that of group 4. Once again there was no significant correlation between extraversion and the size of this pseudo-effect: $= -0.13$ for which $p < 0.05$. Nevertheless, the results of this group support the view that the tendency to avoid extreme judgments causes a trend in the P.S.E. which will appear even in the absence of any distorting experience.

CONCLUSIONS

Individual Differences

So far as individual differences are concerned, these experiments are unfortunately purely destructive. They cast doubt upon the correlation between extraversion and figural aftereffect and suggest rather that extraverts develop a peculiar form of bias during the course of the psychophysical procedure used by Klein & Krech and therefore by Eysenck. But they afford no clue to the mechanism of this bias. If we adopt Eysenck's approach for a moment, we might perhaps argue that the establishment of a stable and accurate subjective scale of judgment requires that the person concerned should not suffer from too rapid an inhibition of the internal responses resulting from the earlier stimulation in the sequence. People who did inhibit such responses and thus forgot the available range of judgments might show relatively more bias in later measurements than less forgetful people do. Such a view might reconcile the reactive inhibition theory with the present results, but it would do so in a rather different way from the original theory. There would no longer be any connection postulated between reactive inhibition and figural aftereffect; merely between the former concept and particular psychophysical procedures.

Another, not necessarily incompatible, point of view would be to take up some form of the theory put forward by Broadbent according to which intraversion is characterized by the use of information from a long sample of past events (Ref. 1, p. 167). On this view the intraverts, when making their second set of judgments after experiencing the inter-polated block, would still make use of the past information concerning the range of possible judgments available. But the extraverts would, at the same stage in the experiment, be influenced purely by the present situation and so would be biased by the central tendency effect towards the end of the wedge which they met first in making their judgment. A difficulty for this point of view is that tests of long- and short-sampling still do not appear to correlate with questionnaire measures of extra-version: this rather ominous point has been made previously (Ref. 1, p. 147) and further unpublished investigations made since that time have failed to show any correlation. It would therefore be unwise to press any explanation in terms of long- and short-sampling too far.

Furthermore, both the above theories suffer from the weakness that groups 4 and 5 showed no correlation between extraversion and 'pseudo-figural aftereffect'. Yet if the individual differences appearing in the other groups were due purely to reactive inhibition of previous judgments, or to short-sampling, there ought to be similar correlations even when no interpolated experience is given. A possible escape from this criticism is that the interpolated experience causes forgetting of events occurring before it, that is, forgetting of the first series of judgments. But this is an *ad hoc* assumption and not predicted from either theory.

Even though these results do not support any general characterization of extraverts as 'short-sampling' or 'inhibited', it may still be a positive contribution to suggest that aspects of personality may reveal themselves in certain methods of making psychophysical measurements no matter what the quantity measured. We have seen some evidence that an individual with a strong tendency to avoid extreme categories of judgment may show a characteristic trend in the mean of his judgments throughout a series of measurements: the same might conceivably be true if we were studying differential thresholds in hearing, or the ability to make time estimations, provided that the psychophysical procedures were the same. Such a possibility would provide an underlying link between the oddly disparate characteristics sometimes reported as distinguishing particular kinds of personality.

Figural Aftereffects in General

It is difficult to resist the feeling that the normal precautions of psychophysics have not been sufficiently applied in experiments on the kinaesthetic figural aftereffect. Some papers do not state whether subjects explored the wedge at will or whether they were started systematically from either end. Yet the present results show that these two procedures will increase or decrease the aftereffect, the direction of the error depending on the position of the P.S.E. on the wedge. It is quite rare to find researches in which a control group is tested without an interpolated experience, but this is clearly an essential precaution. Two investigations should be noted in which the precaution was taken: those of Wertheimer & Leventhal (Ref. 9) and of Charles & Duncan (Ref. 2). In the first of these it was found that the initial P.S.E. was lower than the P.S.E. in later determinations, even although there was a very long interval, between the presentation of the block whose aftereffect was being measured and the taking of the later measurements. Thus if the aftereffect is ascribed to neural satiation, the latter process must to some extent be supposed permanent. But a similar effect appeared on a smaller scale even in a group who received no interpolated experience and who therefore were showing a 'pseudo-effect' like those found in groups 4 and 5 of the present experiment. Wertheimer & Leventhal explain this pseudo-effect by ascribing it to a genuine effect appearing on the wrong hand: since the hand sliding along the wedge experiences mostly parts larger than the P.S.E. and so the part of the wedge which is originally at the P.S.E. begins to feel too small. The new P.S.E. is therefore larger. It will be noted that this explanation is consistent with the finding in the present experiment that people who experience only the small end of the wedge show their pseudo-effect in the opposite direction. But if this explanation is adopted we must suppose that the genuine figural after-effect is indeed to some extent permanent: and the present writer thinks it more reasonable to regard this permanent effect as the building up of a scale of judgment, the temporary effect being of a quite different nature. Various experimental tests of this point suggest themselves: for example, the two effects should be in opposite directions if the interpolated block was of a size between the P.S.E. and the middle of the wedge.

The experiment of Charles & Duncan had as its primary purpose the evaluation of figural aftereffect as a function of the difference in size between original and interpolated blocks. The control group with no interpolated block showed no pseudo-effect. This is not surprising from our present point of view, since it appears that the authors took a set of four measurements of P.S.E. as practice before any of the experimental determinations were made, and required the subjects to approach P.S.E. alternately from either end of the wedge. The pseudo-effect should therefore have been complete by the time the experiment proper began. Furthermore, subjects were instructed to use a method of overshooting P.S.E. and returning to it, which might possibly minimize such effects. It would perhaps be desirable for future workers on this aftereffect to consult the methods employed by Charles & Duncan.

REFERENCES

1. BROADBENT, D. E., *Perception and Communication*. Oxford: Pergamon Press, 1958.
2. CHARLES, J. P. & DUNCAN, C. P., The distance gradient in kinesthetic figural aftereffect. *J. exp. Psychol.*, **57**, 164–170, 1959.
3. EYSENCK, H. J., *Dimensions of Personality*. London: Routledge & Kegan Paul, 1947.
4. ——, Cortical inhibition, figural aftereffect and theory of personality. *J. abnorm. soc. Psychol.*, **51**, 94–106, 1955.
5. ——, *The Dynamics of Anxiety and Hysteria*. London: Routledge & Kegan Paul, 1957.
6. HERON, A., A two-part personality inventory for use as a research criterion. *Brit. J. Psychol.*, **47**, 243–251, 1956.
7. KLEIN, G. S. & KRECH, D., Cortical conductivity in the brain-injured. *J. Pers.*, **21**, 118–148, 1952.

8. OSGOOD, C. E., *Method and Theory in Experimental Psychology.* New York: Oxford University Press, 1953.

9. WERTHEIMER, M. & LEVENTHAL, C. M., 'Permanent' satiation phenomena with kinesthetic figural aftereffects. *J. exp. Psychol.,* **55,** 255–257, 1958.

28

Introversion-Extraversion and Figural Aftereffect[1]

C. R. PARAMESH

First published in *Indian Journal of Psychology*, **38**, 93–97, 1963

INTRODUCTION

In recent years, a number of experimental studies have been reported on the relationship between the personality dimension of introversion-extraversion and figural aftereffects for vision. While the findings o Eysenck (Ref. 2) and Holland (Ref. 5) demonstrate the existence of a positive relation between degree of introversion and persistence of aftereffects, Rechtschaffen (Ref. 7) and Norcross *et al*. (Ref. 6) report studies which do not support the hypothesis that the amount of aftereffect is related to introversion-extraversion. Eysenck's hypothesis that introverts show a greater persistence of aftereffects than extraverts follows from a postulate involving these personality factors.

According to Eysenck, 'Individuals in whom reactive inhibition is generated quickly, in whom strong reactive inhibitions are generated and in whom reactive inhibition is dissipated slowly, are thereby predisposed to develop extraverted patterns of behaviour and to develop hysterical disorders in cases of neurotic break-down: conversely, individuals in whom reactive inhibition is generated slowly, in whom weak reactive inhibitions are generated and in whom reactive inhibition is dissipated quickly, are thereby predisposed to develop introverted patterns of behaviour and to develop dysthymic disorders in cases of neurotic break-down' (Ref. 1).

The purpose of the present study was to explore the relationship between introversion-extraversion and figural aftereffects for vision, using the Spiral After-Effects Test (SAT).

METHOD

The Archimedes Spiral test used in the present investigation was similar

[1] Based on a thesis approved by the University of Madras for the degree of Master of Letters (M. Litt). The research work was done under the supervision of Major S. Parthasarathy, Professor of Psychology, S. V. University, Tirupathi.

to the one illustrated by Eysenck (Ref. 2) except for minor changes. It consisted of a 4-throw spiral of 180° and it was 8 inches in diameter. It was mounted on a spindle, driven by a fractional H.P. electric motor. The speed of rotation of the disc could be varied by a rheostat adjustment. The provision of a reversal switch allowed the rotation of the disc to be stopped abruptly. It also enabled the spiral to be rotated in both clock-wise and counter clock-wise directions. The motor, with all its accessories, except the spiral disc and the switch to operate, was enclosed in a compact mazonite box. The spiral was kept outside the box thus enabling the subject to concentrate his attention on the disc.

The experiment was conducted in a dark room. The subjects were tested individually. The spiral was illuminated by a 60w bulb. It was rotated at 100 rpm. The subject, seated 3ft from the spiral, was instructed to concentrate on the central point on the spiral while it was being rotated and to report immediately when the apparent movements ceased after the rotation was stopped. Each subject was given two trials of one minute each rotating the disc in clock-wise and counter clock-wise directions. A rest pause of one minute was given between one trial and another. The mean duration of aftereffects for the two trials was obtained for each individual. Preceding the test proper, each subject was given a practice trial of a short duration to ascertain that he understood the nature of the aftereffects.

SUBJECTS

The sample for this study consisted of college male students. A questionnaire consisting of 60 items was used for measuring extraversion-introversion. This questionnaire was validated against teachers' ratings on a five-point scale and was tested for its reliability by the split-half method. It was administered to 325 male students belonging to two colleges in the city of Madras. All the subjects fell in the age range 16–20 years. From this group of 325 subjects, two extreme groups, extraverts and introverts, representing 25 per cent of the total population were selected. Those who obtained E scores of 44 and above comprised the extravert group and those who obtained E scores of 28 and below on the questionnaire comprised the introvert group.

Although this criterion yielded 44 extraverts and 47 introverts, in the final stage only 25 subjects representing each group were given the Spiral aftereffects test.

RESULTS

The main results obtained in the present experiment are given in Table 1 below.

TABLE 1

MEAN DURATION OF SPIRAL AFTEREFFECTS

	Extravert	Introvert
N	25	25
Mean	12·82 sec	18·74 sec
SD	4·9 sec	8·94 sec

To determine the effect of direction of rotation of the spiral on the length of aftereffects, analysis of variance was applied and the results are given in Tables 2 and 3 for the extravert and introvert groups, respectively.

TABLE 2

ANALYSIS OF VARIANCE OF SPIRAL AFTEREFFECTS OF THE EXTRAVERT GROUP

Source	Sum of squares	df	Mean square variance	F
Between classes	353·78	1	353·78	11·5
Within classes	1483·60	48	30·98	(p<0·01)
Total	1837·38	49		

TABLE 3

ANALYSIS OF VARIANCE OF SPIRAL AFTEREFFECTS OF THE INTROVERT GROUP

Source	Sum of squares	df	Mean square variance	F
Between classes	165·62	1	165·62	1·89 (not significant)
Within classes	4245·80	48	88·44	
Total	4411·42	49		

DISCUSSION

A number of theories have been offered to explain the phenomenon of 'figural aftereffects'. The term 'aftereffects' is used for the Köhler-type satiation effects, which Eysenck equates with inhibition. The term is also used for quite a different phenomenon, namely 'after-images' such as the spiral aftereffects. Of the various hypotheses that have been postulated, the present study has attempted only to verify Eysenck's hypothesis, namely that the amount of aftereffect is related to introversion-extraversion. Eysenck has explained this phenomenon in terms of the postulate of individual differences and the typological postulate. He identifies figural aftereffects with reactive inhibition. According to him, human beings differ in the rate at which reactive inhibition is generated and dissipated and the strength of the inhibition produced. These differences predispose individuals to develop introverted and extraverted patterns of behaviour. Similarly individuals also differ with respect to the speed and strength of excitation produced. Since in the case of the extravert personality, weak excitatory potentials are generated slowly and strong inhibitory potentials are generated quickly, they should have shorter duration of aftereffects than introverts. The findings of the present study confirm this.

The raw data for the mean duration of aftereffects for the extraverted individuals and introverted individuals obtained in the present study showed wide individual differences within each group. The scores ranged from 2·0 to 23·5 and from 10·0 to 58·0 seconds for the extravert and introvert groups, respectively. The mean scores were 12·82 and 18·74 for the extravert and introvert groups, respectively. This mean difference was found to be significant at the 0·01 level of probability. Hence the alternative hypothesis that introverts are given to longer persistence of aftereffects than extraverts can be accepted. The findings of this study therefore confirm the earlier results of Eysenck.

In addition to the main findings, some comment would appear to be of interest on the results regarding the direction of rotation of the spiral. It has been reported by Holland (Ref. 3) that illumination visual angle and speed of rotation (50 to 150 rpm) contribute little to the total effect. According to Holland length of stimulation is the only major factor influencing the duration of aftereffect (Ref. 4). But, the results of the present study (Tables 2 and 3) regarding the direction of rotation of the spiral indicated that the length of aftereffect is greater in the case of clock-wise rotation than in the case of counter clock-wise rotation. This difference between directions of rotation was found to be significant at 0·01 level for the extravert group, while the introvert group also showed the same tendency as the extravert group but was not significant at any acceptable level of confidence. Hence the direction of rotation of the spiral as a factor in determining the response to the spiral test could be investigated further.

REFERENCES

1. EYSENCK, H. J., Cortical inhibition, figural aftereffect and theory of personality. *J. abnorm. soc. Psychol.*, **51,** 94–106, 1955.
2. ——, *Dynamics of Anxiety and Hysteria.* London: Routledge & Kegan Paul, 1957.
3. HOLLAND, H. C., The Archimedes Spiral. *Nature,* **179,** 432–433, 1957.
4. ——, Some determinants of seen aftermovement in the Archimedes Spiral. *Acta. Psychol.*, **14,** 215–222, 1958.
5. ——, Measures of perceptual functions. In *Experiments in Personality,* Vol. II (ed. Eysenck, H. J.). London: Routledge & Kegan Paul, 1960.
6. NORCROSS, K. J., LIPMAN, R. S. & SPITZ, H. H., The relationship of extraversion-introversion to visual and kinesthetic aftereffects. *J. abnorm. soc. Psychol.*, **63,** 210–211, 1961.
7. RECHTSCHAFFEN, A., Neural satiation, reactive inhibition and introversion-extraversion. *J. abnorm. soc. Psychol.*, **57,** 283–291, 1958.

29

Extraversion and Duration of the Archimedes Spiral Aftereffect[1]

JOHN B. KNOWLES[2] & LEONARD KRASNER[3]

First published in *Perceptual and Motor Skills*, **20,** 997–1000, 1965

Two studies are reported testing the relationship between reported duration of the Archimedes Spiral Aftereffect (SAE) and the interaction between the personality variables of neuroticism and extraversion as measured by Eysenck's MPI. In both studies SAE was related to an interaction between neuroticism and extraversion, but in opposite directions in each. Because of the different attitudes towards Ss' task in the two studies, it was concluded that the personality variables interacted with each other and with a third variable, that of 'task-motivation'.

INTRODUCTION

Repeated attempts to test Eysenck's prediction that the duration of the Archimedes Spiral Aftereffect (SAE) is inversely related to extraversion (Ref. 1) have met with varying success. The inconsistencies between various studies are not surprising since the data to be presented here suggest that the SAE report is a complex phenomenon dependent upon an interaction between extraversion, the additional personality variable of neuroticism and at least one other factor, which we have tentatively identified as 'task-motivation'.

STUDY 1

Method

Our first set of data was obtained from a sample of 80 female volunteer Ss (M_{age} = 31·59, SD = 4·88) who were paid $2.00 each for their

[1] This study was supported by Research Grant M–6191 from the National Institute of Mental Health, USPHS, through Stanford University.

[2] The study was completed while the first author was on leave of absence from the Medical Research Council Clinical Psychiatry Research Unit, Graylingwell Hospital, Chichester, Sussex, England.

[3] USPHS Visiting Scholar, Educational Testing Service, Princeton, N.J., 1964–65.

participation in a study (Ref. 7) during which they were given, among other tests, the short form of the Maudsley Personality Inventory (Ref. 2) and the Archimedes spiral.

The spiral, reproduced from Robbins *et al.* (Ref. 8), was rotated in a clockwise direction at approximately 100 rpm for 30 sec under the prevailing conditions of illumination. Following a demonstration of the effect, S, seated 8ft from the spiral, was instructed to concentrate on the centre of the spiral, to report the direction of apparent movement during rotation (expansion) and to say 'now' when the aftereffect (contraction) appeared to stop. This procedure was followed for two sets of four trials separated by approximately 15 minutes, the intertrial interval being 10 sec within each block of trials.

Measures of neuroticism (N) and extraversion (E) were obtained from the 12 items of the shortened form of the MPI. Scores were obtained following Eysenck's procedure by crediting a score of $+1$ for a response in the keyed direction and a score of -1 for the converse response (Ref. 2).

Results

Preliminary inspection of the data suggested an interaction between SAE, neuroticism and extraversion and thus we examined the mean SAE averaged over the 8 trials in 4 groups of Ss: 'Stable Introverts' (SI), 'Neurotic Introverts' (NI), 'Stable Extraverts' (SE) and 'Neurotic Extraverts' (NE). The criteria for 'extraversion' and 'neuroticism' were a positive total score on the E and N scales of the MPI, respectively. Three Ss for whom either personality or SAE records were incomplete were omitted prior to analysis, as were 14 Ss with zero N scores; these latter Ss were omitted to produce more extreme 'neurotic' and 'stable'

TABLE 1

MEAN DURATION OF SPIRAL AFTEREFFECT (SEC) IN PERSONALITY
GROUPS DEFINED BY SHORT FORM OF MPI (FEMALE Ss, N = 63)

	'Stable': Negative N Scores	'Neurotic': Positive N Scores	t	p
Introvert: Zero and Negative E score	10·38 (n = 14)	16·28 (n = 13)	3·20	<0·01
Extravert: Positive E score	12·25 (n = 16)	12·31 (n = 20)		
t	1·07	2·33 (p<0·05)		

groups. Of the remaining 63 Ss, 14 were in the SI group, 13 in the NI group, 20 in the NE group and 16 in the SE group.

Analysis of the SAE data by an analysis of variance appropriate to the unequal cell frequencies showed a significant interaction between the stability-neuroticism and introversion-extraversion factors ($F = 5.72$, $p<0.025$, df = 1/59).

Table 1 shows that the nature of the interaction was such that introversion-extraversion was a significant factor determining SAE only in the case of 'neurotic' Ss ($t = 2.32$, $p<0.05$).

STUDY 2

Method

Data generously made available to us by Dr H. Holland enabled us to undertake a similar analysis in a second series of Ss. These were 75 male industrial apprentices, between the ages of 16 and 19, tested during their normal working hours as part of a wider study of personality and perceptual functions (Ref. 6). As part of this study, they were required to concentrate on an illuminated spiral rotated at 100 rpm for 15, 30, 50, 80 and 100 sec. For our purpose, we selected the measures of SAE taken following 30 sec of stimulation as being closest to our conditions of administration.

These Ss had been given the full version of the MPI (Ref. 2) and thus, as before, we were able to define four personality groups; the criteria were, for neuroticism, a score in excess of 20 (approximately the mean of the scale) and, for extraversion, a score in excess of 33.

RESULTS

TABLE 2

Mean Duration of Spiral Aftereffect (Sec) in Personality Groups Defined by Standard Form of MPI (Male Apprentices, $N = 75$)

	'Stable': N Score, 0–20	'Neurotic': N Score, 21–48	t	p
Introvert (10–32)	20.30 (n = 20)	17.82 (n = 22)	1.46	
Extravert (33–48)	15.06 (n = 18)	19.67 (n = 15)	2.39	<0.05
t	2.93 (p<0.01)	1.00		

An analysis of variance, similar to that previously used, indicated once again a highly significant interaction between the two personality variables (F $= 7.59$, p<0.01, df $= 1/71$). However, on this occasion, a significant difference in favour of the introverts occurred only in the 'stable' groups; in contrast to our own study, the *neurotic* introverts tended to report shorter SAE than did the neurotic extraverts.[1]

DISCUSSION

Our first finding was that in both samples the duration of the SAE was dependent upon an interaction between neuroticism and extraversion. However, in addition, we found that the directions of the interaction were strikingly different in the two samples. We must conclude, therefore, that the duration of the SAE is determined by a complex interaction between these two personality factors and at least one other unidentified variable.

Although either sex or age characteristics may be the variable in question, we are more inclined to identify the variable as being S's attitude toward the task, or 'task-motivation'. By design, and for reasons which do not concern us here, the importance of the study and E's prestige were both emphasized in our own study (i.e., Study 1) whereas, in contrast, the apprentice group was tested under conditions which Eysenck & Willett conceive of as being of 'low drive' (Ref. 4). These experimental manipulations could have contributed to differences in 'task-motivation'. This variable is of potential significance since the duration of the SAE *reported by S* is largely dependent upon compliance with E's instructions to fixate the spiral and upon S's manner of judgment concerning the rather ambiguous end-point of the aftereffect.

A somewhat similar observation is reported by Eysenck & Warwick, who found that the correlation between extraversion and Critical Flicker Frequency threshold (CFF) was positive (r $= 0.32$) in their high-drive group (applicant apprentices) but negative (r $= 0.12$) in their low-drive group (apprentices accepted for training) (Ref. 3). Their suggestion that 'the fickle nature of the relationship observed in the past between personality and CFF may be due in part to a neglect of the drive aspect' (Ref. 3, p. 160) appears equally applicable to the investigation of SAE phenomena. It is, as they write, 'tempting to argue that we are here

[1] From the data presented, it is apparent that there was a substantial difference in the overall mean SAE between the two samples, which we attribute to some presumably stable difference in testing procedures. In any event, since we are concerned with the interactions *within* each sample, such overall differences, although of interest, are not immediately relevant.

dealing with an interplay between personality and drive along the lines of the Yerkes-Dodson Law' but we would also agree that 'the data are too slight to bear any such interpretations, except in terms of a speculative aside' (Ref. 3, p. 160). Finally, additional confirmatory evidence as to the relationship between motivation and report of length of spiral aftereffect has been reported by Eysenck, Willett & Slater (Ref. 5).

REFERENCES

1. EYSENCK, H. J., *The Dynamics of Anxiety and Hysteria*. London: Routledge & Kegan Paul, 1957.
2. ——, A short questionnaire for the measurement of two dimensions of personality. *J. appl. Psychol.*, **42**, 14–17, 1958.
3. —— & WARWICK, K. M., Situationally determined drive and the concept of 'arousal'. In *Experiments in Motivation* (ed. H. J. Eysenck). Oxford: Pergamon, 1964.
4. —— & WILLETT, R. A., Introduction. In *Experiments in Motivation* (ed. H. J. Eysenck). Oxford: Pergamon, 1964.
5. ——, —— & SLATER, P., Drive, direction of rotation and massing of practice as determinants of the duration of the aftereffects from the rotating spiral. *Amer. J. Psychol.*, **75**, 127–133, 1962.
6. HOLLAND, H., Measures of perceptual functions. In *Experiments in Personality* (ed. H. J. Eysenck). London: Routledge & Kegan Paul, 1960.
7. KRASNER, L., KNOWLES, J. B. & ULLMANN, L. P., The effect of verbal conditioning of attitudes on subsequent motor performance. *J. pers. soc. Psychol.*, **1**, No. 5, 1965.
8. ROBBINS, E. S., WEINSTEIN, S., BERG, S., RIFKIN, A., WECHSLER, D. & OXLEY, B., The effect of electroconvulsive treatment upon the perception of the spiral aftereffect: a presumed measure of cerebral dysfunction. *J. nerv. ment. Dis.*, **128**, 239–242, 1959.

30

Activation, Control, and the Spiral Aftermovement[1]

PAUL LEVY & PETER J. LANG[2]

First published in
Journal of Personality and Social Psychology, **3,** 105–112, 1966

SIXTY college students were selected on the basis of anxiety and impulsivity questionnaires. They were then tested for duration of the spiral aftermovement and resting cardiac rate. Longer aftermovements were found for high-anxious Ss than for low-anxious Ss; impulsive students showed shorter aftermovements than nonimpulsives. Aftermovement duration was significantly related to an interaction between heart rate and heart-rate variability. It was concluded that individual differences in the aftermovement are explained in part by different levels of activation and control, as these constructs are assessed through personality questionnaires and by cardiovascular activity.

INTRODUCTION

Individual differences in the duration of the spiral aftermovement have been observed by many investigators and both personality constructs and hypothesized physiological states have served in theoretical explanations. Eysenck, Holland & Trouton observed a decrease in aftermovement following the administration of sodium amytal (Ref. 8). Costello found that meprobamate, another central nervous system depressant, yielded a similar effect (Ref. 5). Eysenck attributed these results and the reduced aftermovement sometimes observed in brain-damaged subjects to a hypothetical 'cortical inhibition' (Ref. 6). Furthermore, this inhibitory state was held to be high in subjects diagnosed hysteric or psychopathic and in subjects with high scores on the Maudsley Extraversion scale. Claridge reported data consistent with

[1] These data were collected by the first author in preparing a master's thesis at the University of Pittsburgh, 1964. The research was directed by the second author, and supported by Grant M–3880, from the National Institute of Mental Health, United States Public Health Service.
[2] Now at the University of Wisconsin.

the last hypothesis (Ref. 4). However, Holland & Eysenck observed no relationship between the aftermovement and extraversion in a study of industrial apprentices (Ref. 12). Furthermore, Mayer & Coons have presented findings which question the hypothesis of short aftermovement in brain-damaged subjects (Ref. 17). They found no aftermovement differences between functional and organic patients when the instructions were reassuring.

Claridge failed to find that hysterics report significantly shorter aftermovement than normals (Ref. 4). However, dysthymics and schizophrenics did have longer than normal aftermovements. Anxiety characterizes the former diagnosis and Lang & Buss present strong evidence that schizophrenics are chronically hyperaroused (Ref. 15). These results, considered together with the studies of depressant drugs, suggest an alternative hypothesis: long spiral aftermovements are related to high levels of arousal or activation. Eysenck & Holland reported negatively on this proposition in a study of drive and the Archimedes spiral (Ref. 7). However, their experimental manipulation had questionable validity: low-drive subjects were simply applicants being evaluated for the same job.

The relationship between the aftermovement and activation deserves further exploration. The Taylor Manifest Anxiety (MA) scale (Ref. 22) is a useful questionnaire measure of the latter construct. While it is by no means factorially pure, there is evidence that this scale correlates both with physiological indices of arousal (Ref. 2) and the clinical analogue of arousal, anxiety (Refs. 3 & 20).

Pavlovian cortical inhibition seems to have little value as an explanation of aftermovement findings. However, length of aftermovement may well be related to behavioural inhibition or impulsivity. Although the subject is instructed to report on the presence or absence of a subjective phenomenon, it is the latency of the verbal report that is actually measured. The subject's basic capacity to delay responding could contribute importantly to this measure. Eysenck & Eysenck report that their extraversion scale includes subfactors of sociability and impulsivity (Ref. 9), but the latter trait has not been separately assessed in previous studies of the aftermovement.

Despite the organismic tack taken by interpreters of the aftermovement phenomenon, little effort has been made directly to measure relevant somatic activity. However, activation has frequently been identified with high activity levels in the autonomic nervous system (Refs. 10 & 16). If long aftermovement is related to a high level of arousal, a positive correlation with heart rate would be anticipated. Furthermore, Lacey & Lacey suggest that variability in autonomically mediated responses is characteristic of impulsive individuals (Ref. 14). They suggest that feedback via blood pressure sensitive receptors in the carotid artery causes momentary changes in cortical activity and associated motor behaviour. These authors speculate that perceptual-motor processes may be greatly influenced by this phenomenon and that these effects are most readily seen in subjects with highly variable cardiac rate. In support of this position, they have demonstrated a negative relationship between the ability to inhibit erroneous responses in a reaction-time situation and cardiac rate lability (Refs. 13 & 14).

Cardiac rate variability and average cardiac rate are relatively un-correlated (Ref. 14). In this they parallel the questionnaire-derived traits of impulsivity and anxiety (Ref. 1). These pairs of dimensions may be brought together under the broader constructs of activation and control. The former refers in a general way to the amplitude or intensity of behaviour; the latter describes the efficiency with which behaviour is focused or directed. It is suggested that these two factors are important contributors to individual differences in the duration of the spiral after-movement.

The Problem

1. The proposed experiment was designed to evaluate the relationship of the aftermovement phenomenon to the concepts of activation and control. Both psychophysiological and questionnaire measures of these constructs were employed in the experiment. Initially, the subjects were divided into four questionnaire subgroups according to their anxiety and impulsivity scale scores. Subgroup aftermovement durations were then compared. Next, the subjects were reassigned to different subgroups, according to their average heart rate and heart-rate variability measures. Again the subgroup aftermovement durations were analysed. It was held that individual differences in aftermovement duration are attributable to both the questionnaire and psychophysiological indices of the activation and control constructs. Relationships between the questionnaire and physiological measures were also investigated.

2. Spigel studied the effects on the aftermovement of an interval of darkness immediately following the rotation of the spiral and preceding the presentation of the stationary image (Ref. 21). He found that the aftermovement became shorter with longer intervals. He also showed that when a nonhomogeneous perceptual field was presented during the

interpolated period (rather than darkness) the mean aftermovement was further reduced. In the present experiment both the nondelayed aftermovement and darkness interval aftermovement were evaluated. It was suggested that afferent feedback from the cardiovascular system may have affects similar to external stimulation. Thus, constant high or low heart rate might not greatly effect the length of the aftermovement. However, high cardiovascular variability during the darkness interval would act in the same way as a variable external field and induce a shorter aftermovement. Paralleling this hypothesis, impulsive subjects (who are held to have high resting cardiac variability) would be expected to show greater aftermovement reduction associated with the darkness interval than nonimpulsives.

METHOD

Subjects

Personality Measures: 60 male undergraduates, chosen over a period of three semesters from the introductory psychology course at the University of Pittsburgh, participated in this experiment. They were selected on the basis of scores obtained on the Taylor MA scale (Ref. 22) and a 24-item impulsivity scale developed by Wilkinson (Ref. 23). The latter scale defines impulsivity as the inability to tolerate delay. The following are sample items: 'I find my snap judgments tend to be good ones'; 'I am rather cautious in my reactions to unexpected situations'; 'I tend to respond quickly to most situations'. The Wilkinson scale has a high degree of internal consistency—the biserial correlations range from 0·45 to 0·75 with a median coefficient of 0·57. Furthermore, little relationship exists between the Wilkinson and Taylor scales. A nonsignificant correlation of 0·14 was obtained from a random selection of introductory psychology students ($N = 60$), not employed in this experiment.

Subjects who had received scores falling within the extreme quadrants of both scales were assigned to four experimental groups (subgroup $n = 15$): high anxious–high impulsive, high anxious–low impulsive, low anxious–high impulsive, low anxious–low impulsive. Table 1 gives the ranges and mean scores of the four subgroups on the anxiety and impulsivity scales. An analysis of variance did not reveal significant differences between highs or between lows in different subgroups.

Cardiac Activity Scores: Subjects were assigned to new groups on the basis of their average heart rate and heart-rate variability. Average rate

TABLE 1

ANXIETY AND IMPULSIVITY MEAN SCORES AND RANGES
FOR THE PERSONALITY INVENTORY SUBGROUPS

	Group			
	1	2	3	4
Anxiety				
M	24·53	23·80	8·60	8·40
Range	22–28	21–28	4–11	3–11
Impulsivity				
M	18·27	6·07	17·53	5·20
Range	16–21	1–8	16–22	2–8

was determined in the following manner: each subject's cardiac activity was recorded for 15 minutes and a count was made of the total number of beats occurring during this period. From this data, each subject's mean number of beats per minute was determined. The measure of heart variability employed was similar to that employed by Lacey.[1] For the last 5 minutes of the 15–minute rest interval, peak to trough heart rate differences were taken from the cardiotachometer record and a frequency distribution of these differences charted for each subject. The median of the distribution was the subject's variability score.

Mean heart rate and median heart variability scores for all subjects were cast into two separate distributions. Subjects were then assigned to one of four groups, depending on whether they fell above or below the median on each of the two distributions. Table 2 indicates the range, mean heart rate and heart-rate variability of the four cardiac subgroups. As before, analysis of variance revealed no significant differences between either highs or lows in different groups.

Apparatus

Heart rate was recorded by a Fels cardiotachometer with write-out on a Grass polygraph. The standard EKG lead II was employed, with electrode placements on the right wrist and left calf. Raw EKG, muscle potentials from the right forearm, GSR (Fels dermohmmeter) and respiration data were also written out on the Grass instrument.

---

[1] John I. Lacey described a similar method based on a 15-minute sample in a personal communication, 1964. However, analysis of 8 records randomly selected from the 60 subjects used here indicated that the 5-minute distributions were essentially the same as those obtained for the entire 15-minute rest interval.

TABLE 2

HEART RATE AND VARIABILITY MEAN SCORES AND RANGES FOR THE
CARDIAC SUBGROUPS

	Group A (n = 16) Below median HR-below median HV	Group B (n = 14) Below median HR-above median HV	Group C (n = 14) Above median HR-below median HV	Group D (n = 16) Above median HR-below median HV
Rate				
M	61·8	64·4	77·4	76·7
Range	54·4–66·8	55·0–69·0	69·8–91·0	69·0–90·6
Variability				
M	4·83	8·83	5·54	9·64
Range	3·0–7·2	7·4–12·0	4·0–7·3	7·5–17·0

The stimulus employed in obtaining the aftermovement was a small circular disc 6 inches in diameter with a radial, spiral pattern printed on it. From a darkened room, the subject observed a 14-inch, reverse projected image of the disc. In an adjacent apparatus cubicle, a Hurst 12 rpm synchronous motor with instantaneous stop rotated the pattern at a constant speed. The cubicle also contained the polygraph, a timing circuit with several switches which control the polygraph marking pen, the projector, rotation of the disc and a Standard Electric timer. A subject switch was wired to the marking pen and also stopped the timer.

Procedure

The experiment consisted of three parts: (a) Five 30-second presentations of the rotating spiral. At the end of each presentation the projector was turned off for 0·10 second. When the image was reprojected, it was physically stationary. Coincident with the reillumination of the disc, the timer was activated and the polygraph paper marked. When the subject no longer saw the aftermovement he pressed a button under his right hand, again marking the polygraph paper and also terminating the timer. For all of these presentations the mean lengths of the aftermovements (in 1/100s of a second) were calculated. (b) There was a 15-minute rest interval, during which time somatic activity was continuously recorded. (c) Five more trials were presented and the mean length of aftermovement was calculated. During these latter trials, rather than a momentary hiatus, a 30-second darkness interval was interpolated between presentations of the rotating and stationary spiral.

TABLE 3

MEAN INITIAL AND FINAL TRIAL AFTERMOVEMENT DURATIONS FOR
EACH OF THE PERSONALITY INVENTORY SUBGROUPS

| | Initial | | Final | |
	Low anxious	High anxious	Low anxious	High anxious
Low impulsivity	18·90	27·40	18·15	24·50
High impulsivity	11·06	15·67	8·37	13·46

The procedure was the same for all subjects regardless of experimental group. The subject was seated in a comfortable lounge chair and the electrodes and respiration bellows were secured. The lights in the experimental room were turned off and the rotating spiral was projected onto the screen approximately 4ft directly in front of the subject. Following a brief explanation, the subject was instructed to fixate on the centre of the disc and administered one practice trial. The subject was then told:

In a few moments, the procedure will be repeated. You are to do exactly as you did before. Remember, press the button when you can no longer perceive any movement. It is very important that you do not move your eyes but continue to concentrate on the centre metallic part of the disc. Except for the necessary movement of your right hand, you are to remain as motionless as possible so that an accurate biological record may be obtained. Everyone sees the movement for different lengths—try to do your best.

After the five experimental trials, the screen was closed. The room remained dark. The subject was told to relax and for the next 15 minutes somatic activity was continuously recorded. At the end of the 15 minute period, the screen was opened and the subject was told that the disc would again be presented, but between rotating and stationary images the projector light would be off for a longer duration than before. Five experimental trials were then presented. The intertrial interval was again 2 minutes. Somatic activity was recorded continuously during the interpolated 30–second intervals of darkness.

RESULTS

Personality Inventory Subgroups
1. Table 3 gives the mean aftermovement durations for each of the

personality inventory subgroups. The patterns of means are similar in the initial and final trials. Although the initial durations seem to be larger than those of their corresponding final trials, a t test detected no significant difference.

The effects of impulsivity and anxiety on perceived length of after-movements were tested by an analysis of variance (2×2 factorial design). A summary of the results for the initial and final trial test periods is presented in Table 4. The differences in mean aftermovement duration were significant at the 0·01 level for the impulsivity variable in both the initial and final trials. Those subjects who, as a group, had low impulsivity scores perceived aftermovement for a longer period of time than the high impulsives.

The differences in mean aftermovement duration were significant at the 0·05 level for the anxiety variable in the initial trial period. A similar trend (though not significant) was obtained for the final aftermovement trials. In neither analysis was a significant interaction obtained.

TABLE 4

ANALYSIS OF VARIANCE OF MEAN INITIAL AND FINAL AFTERMOVEMENT
FOR THE FOUR PERSONALITY INVENTORY SUBGROUPS

Source	SS	df	MS	F
Initial				
Anxiety (A)	643·94	1	643·94	4·90*
Impulsivity (B)	1437·46	1	1437·46	10·93†
A × B	56·41	1	56·41	0·43
Within error	7361·64	56	131·50	
Final				
A	490·50	1	490·50	3·00
B	1625·00	1	1625·00	9·949†
A × B	5·92	1	5·92	0·36
Within error	9146·69	56	163·33	

* $p < 0.05$
† $p < 0.01$

2. F tests of the mean absolute change and percentage change (Ref. 21) from initial to final trials, yielded no significant differences among the four personality scale subgroups. However, Spigel's data suggest that there is no substantial decay of the aftermovement unless the inter-polated darkness interval is at least two times the subject's mean aftermovement. Since the interpolated darkness interval was held con-

stant at 30 sec, it is possible that only subjects having initial mean after-movements of 15 sec or less would show substantial decay. They alone experienced a darkness interval long enough to cause a significant shortening of the aftermovement. Hence it was reasoned that if postulated differences between low and high impulsives' percentage scores were to appear in the data, the differences would be most likely to occur for these particular subjects. In point of fact, the overall, average percentage of change for the above 15-sec group was somewhat smaller (0·01) than for the 15-sec or less group (0·08, N = 31). Furthermore, the mean percentage reduction for the high impulsives of the 15-sec or less group was 0·21 and the mean percentage reduction for the low impulsives was −0·27 (initial score and absolute change yielded an r of 0·66). A test of this difference in percentage of reduction resulted in a t of 2·05, p < 0·03 (high- and low-anxious subjects were about equally represented in these two impulsivity subgroups).

TABLE 5

MEAN INITIAL AND FINAL AFTERMOVEMENT DURATIONS FOR THE FOUR
CARDIAC SUBGROUPS

Group	Heart rate		Aftermovement	
	Variability	Average	Initial	Final
B	High	Low	11·9	9·9
D	High	High	23·3	20·3
A	Low	Low	19·8	17·4
C	Low	High	17·2	16·1

Note: Subjects were assigned to groups on the basis of the cardiac rate and variability measures as obtained during the 15–minute rest interval.

3. The analysis of variance (2 × 2 factorial design) of differences in the mean heart rate of the four questionnaire subgroups (as recorded both during the last 5 minutes of the rest interval and the average of the 30-sec interpolated darkness intervals) did not yield significant differences either for the impulsivity or anxiety scales. No interaction effect was obtained. Similar analyses of differences in the mean heart variability scores of the four subgroups did not yield significant main effects or interactions.

Cardiac Rate Subgroups
1. The four subgroups were classified on the basis of the 15-minute

rest interval, rate and variability measures. Table 5 shows their initial and final mean movements. An analysis of variance (2×2 factorial design, method of unweighted means) of differences in the mean length of the initial aftermovement, yielded an interaction effect between heart rate and heart variability that was significant at the 0·05 level. Table 6 presents a summary of this analysis. Although no difference in mean length of initial aftermovement was found between high and low heart-rate groups with low variability, a t test revealed that the difference in lengths of mean aftermovement for the two high variability groups apparent in Table 5 was significant at the 0·005 level (t = 2·86). A similar analysis of the final aftermovement data did not prove significant.

TABLE 6

ANALYSIS OF VARIANCE OF MEAN INITIAL AFTERMOVEMENTS FOR THE FOUR CARDIAC SUBGROUPS

Source	Uncorrected SS	df	Corrected SS	MS	F
Heart rate (A)	19·339	1	288·63	288·63	1·91
Heart variability (B)	0·807	1	12·04	12·04	
A×B	49·808	1	743·38	743·38	4·92*
Within error		56	8461·51	151·10	

*$p < 0.05$

TABLE 7

MEAN IMPULSIVITY AND ANXIETY TEST SCORES FOR THE FOUR CARDIAC SUBGROUPS

Group	Variability	Heart rate Average	Impulsivity	Anxiety
B	High	Low	14·29	16·14
D	High	High	9·38	18·00
A	Low	Low	11·38	14·31
C	Low	High	12·43	16·93

Furthermore, regrouping the subjects on the basis of average cardiac rate and variability for the 30-sec darkness intervals, yielded no significant results.[1] F tests of the differences in mean percentage change

[1] Rate and variability were calculated for the five 30–sec darkness intervals, during the final aftermovement trials. Based on these scores, subjects were reassigned to cardiac subgroups in the same manner as in the main heart-rate analysis.

among the four cardiac subgroups, defined both by the last 5 minutes of rest or the 30-sec interpolated darkness intervals were not significant.

2. Table 7 gives the mean anxiety and impulsivity test scores for each of the four cardiac subgroups.

The analysis of variance (2×2 factorial design, method of unweighted means) of differences in anxiety scores for the four subgroups did not yield any significant differences. However, in a similar F test of differences in impulsivity scores for the four subgroups, the probability of the obtained interaction (between cardiac rate and cardiac variability) was less than $0 \cdot 08$ (F = $3 \cdot 23$). No difference in impulsivity was found between high and low heart-rate groups with low variability. However a t test revealed that the difference between high and low heart-rate groups with high variability apparent in Table 7, was significant at the $0 \cdot 01$ level (t = $2 \cdot 47$).

DISCUSSION

These results indicate that high-impulsive subjects as a group report shorter aftermovements than do low impulsives. It was further found that high-anxious subjects report longer aftermovements than low-anxious subjects. Finally, these variables appear to assert effects additive to each other, since the longest average aftermovement was seen in the high anxious–low impulsive subgroups and the shortest aftermovements were obtained in the low anxious–high impulsive subgroup.

As measured here, impulsivity appeared to be the more influential variable. Low impulsives showed significantly shorter aftermovements than high impulsives on *both* initial and final trials. Furthermore, among impulsive subjects with short initial aftermovements, high impulsives showed a significantly greater percentage of reduction in aftermovement than low impulsives on the darkness interval trials. Aftermovement differences between the anxiety groups achieved a less stringent confidence level ($p < 0 \cdot 05$) on initial trials and they were not significant on the second group of trials. Furthermore, no relationship was found between the Taylor scale and cardiac rate.

The relationship between heart rate and the aftermovement is complex. Neither average rate nor variability may be considered separately and furthermore, differences in the average rate of low-variable subjects were unrelated to the aftermovement. However, within high-variability subjects, rate did parallel aftermovement duration in the manner suggested by the activation hypothesis, that is, subjects with a rapid pulse reported significantly longer aftermovement. The variability-impulsivity relationship also proved to be more complex than was anticipated. Again no differences were found within low-variable subjects. However, slow-pulse individuals tended to have high scores on the Wilkinson impulsivity scale; variable, rapid-pulsed subjects generally achieved lower scores.

The heart-rate interaction described above was unanticipated and will be explored further. It is important to point out that it was not one-sided: the low-variable subgroup means fell between those achieved by the high-variable groups (see Table 5). Rate interacted with high variability to produce aftermovement lengths at the extremes. A similar result was obtained for the Wilkinson scale. It will be interesting to discover if these effects can be obtained with other tasks.

Whereas the impulsivity scale directly predicted both the initial and final afterimages, the cardiac rate interaction only related to the initial afterimage. The physiological relationships are thus both more complex and less strong than those defined by at least one of the personality questionnaires. Furthermore, when the other organismic events recorded during this experiment were added to the cardiac measures, no improvement in aftermovement prediction was obtained.[1] In part this result may be attributed to an experimental design in which extremes were selected by questionnaire, while no special care was taken to assure disparity along physiological dimensions. A replication should either employ a large group of randomly selected subjects, or base subject participation on cardiac activity.

It is important to consider possible differences between *reported* and *perceived* aftermovement. It is not clear from these data whether impulsive subjects saw shorter aftermovements, or simply could not delay the button press, despite a continuing aftermovement. No subject reported this phenomenon and in a sense the question is not meaningful, that is, a subjective state cannot be measured independent of behaviour. However, one may ask if there were inconsistencies in the different response systems involved. As one check on this hypothesis, electrical potentials were recorded from the muscle group involved in the button

---

[1] A multiple correlation analysis of the relationship between initial aftermovement and six physiological variables (heart rate, heart-rate variability, respiration rate, average conductance, number of GSRs, and bursts of muscle activity) was performed on the IBM 7090 computer at the University of Pittsburgh Data Processing Center. None of the obtained correlations approached an acceptable confidence level. Furthermore, the afterimage was evaluated for GSR level and variability groups in an analysis of variance similar to that reported here for the cardiac subgroups. No significant main effects or interactions were obtained.

press. It was suggested that if high impulsives were pressing before the aftermovement stopped, they would also show a greater number of partial, anticipatory presses than low impulsives. No significant difference between these groups was observed, either in the number of EMG bursts or tension level during the prepress period.

The general hypothesis that activation and control constructs are related to individual differences in the aftermovement received considerable support. Subjects who may be described as chronically anxious, or who characteristically find it difficult to delay responses, reported aftermovement durations consistent with these characteristics. Furthermore, at least one autonomic response system bore a relationship to both the aftermovement and to the questionnaire estimate of behaviour control. Future work should be focused on the direct manipulation of these variables. At the somatic level, subjects could be trained to alter heart rate prior to aftermovement judgments. The technology is available: operant control of heart-rate acceleration (Ref. 19) and heart-rate variability (Ref. 11) have both been demonstrated.

Cognitive factors and set also deserve more consideration. Mayer & Coons have shown that not only the length, but also the presence or absence of the aftermovement phenomenon may be manipulated by instructions and that these effects interact with pathology (Ref. 17). In the present experiment the instructions suggested that all would see an aftermovement and no valence was assigned to duration. A different preparatory set would undoubtedly alter results.

The interaction between cognitive factors and physiological state is also of considerable importance. While Eysenck and his associates obtained reduced aftermovement following the administration of sodium amytal, longer aftermovements were not associated with the stimulant d-amphetamine (Ref. 7). Schachter & Singer suggest that emotional states involve both a physiological state of arousal and an appropriate cognition (Ref. 18). It would be useful to study the effects of amphetamine on the aftermovement when subjects are uninformed about the drug's effects and anxious cognitions are encouraged, as opposed to a condition in which the drug action is explained. The separate effects of anxiety and physiological arousal could thus be assessed. In summary, the present results suggest provocative new directions for the study of the relationship between perceptual, somatic and verbal responses.

REFERENCES

1. BARRATT, E. S., ANS Activity Related to Intra-Individual Variability. Final report to the National Institute of Mental Health, United States Public Health Service, Project M-4534, 1961.

2. BARRATT, E. S., An intraindividual study of some ANS correlates. *Amer. Psychologist*, **17,** 361, 1962.

3. BUSS, A. H., WIENER, M., DURKEE, ANN & BAER, M., The measurement of anxiety in clinical situations. *J. consult. Psychol.*, **19,** 125–129, 1955.

4. CLARIDGE, G., The excitation-inhibition balance in neurotics. In *Experiments in Personality* (ed. H. J. Eysenck). Vol. 2. *Psychodynamics and Psychodiagnostics.* London: Routledge & Kegan Paul, 1960.

5. COSTELLO, C. G., The effects of meprobamate on perception: 3. The spiral aftereffect. *J. ment. Sci.*, **106,** 331–336, 1960.

6. EYSENCK, H. J., *The Dynamics of Anxiety and Hysteria.* London: Routledge & Kegan Paul, 1957.

7. —— & HOLLAND, H., Length of spiral aftereffects as a function of drive. *Percept. mot. Skills*, **11,** 129–130, 1960.

8. ——, —— & TROUTON, D. S., Drugs and personality: 3. The effects of stimulating and depressant drugs on visual aftereffects. *J. ment. Sci.*, **103,** 650–655, 1957.

9. EYSENCK, S. B. G. & EYSENCK, H. J., On the dual nature of extraversion. *Brit. J. soc. clin. Psychol.*, **2,** 46–55, 1963.

10. FREEMAN, G. L., *The Energetics of Human Behaviour.* Ithaca: Cornell University Press, 1948.

11. HNATIOW, M. & LANG, P. J., Learned stabilization of cardiac rate. *Psychophysiology*, **1,** 330–336, 1961.

12. HOLLAND, H. & EYSENCK, H. J., Spiral aftereffect as a function of length of stimulation. *Percept. mot. Skills*, **11,** 228, 1960.

13. LACEY, J., Psychophysiological approaches to evaluation of psychotherapeutic process and outcome. In *Research in Psychotherapy* (ed. E. A. Rubenstein & M. B. Parloff). Washington, D.C.: National Publishing Company, 1959.

14. —— & LACEY, BEATRICE, The relationship of resting autonomic activity to motor impulsivity. In *The Brain and Human Behaviour* (ed. H. Solomon, S. Cobb & W. Penfield). Baltimore: Williams & Wilkins, 1958.

15. LANG, P. J. & BUSS, A. H., Psychological deficit in schizophrenia: 2. Interference and activation. *J. abnorm. Psychol.*, **70,** 77–106, 1965.
16. MALMO, R. B., Measurement of drive: An unsolved problem in psychology. In *Nebraska Symposium on Motivation: 1958* (ed. M. R. Jones). Lincoln: University of Nebraska Press, 1958.
17. MAYER, E. & COONS, W. H., Motivation and the spiral aftereffect with schizophrenic and brain-damaged patients. *Can. J. Psychol.*, **14,** 269–273, 1960.
18. SCHACHTER, S. & SINGER, J. E., Cognitive, social and physiological determinants of emotional state. *Psychol. Rev.*, **69,** 379–399, 1962.
19. SHEARN, D. W., Operant conditioning of heart rate. *Science*, **137,** 530–531, 1962.
20. SIEGMAN, A. W., Cognitive, affective and psychopathological correlates of the Taylor manifest anxiety scale. *J. consult. Psychol.*, **20,** 137–141, 1956.
21. SPIGEL, I., The Effects of Differential Post-Exposure Stimulation on the Decay of the Aftereffect of Visually Perceived Movement. Unpublished doctoral dissertation, Temple University Library, 1961.
22. TAYLOR, JANET A., A personality scale of manifest anxiety. *J. abnorm. soc. Psychol.*, **48,** 285–290, 1953.
23. WILKINSON, H. J. F., Impulsivity-Deliberativeness and Time Estimation. Unpublished doctoral dissertation, University of Pittsburgh Library, 1962.

Extraversion and Rate of Fluctuation of the Necker Cube

CYRIL M. FRANKS & L. E. H. LINDAHL[1]

First published in *Perceptual and Motor Skills*, **16**, 131–137, 1963

INTRODUCTION

JUNG attempted to define two types, the introvert and the extravert (Ref. 17). But his conceptualization of these terms was unclear and his prototypes dependent almost entirely upon colourful descriptions for their identification. For example, he identified introverts with William James' tender-minded thinkers and with Ostwald's 'classics' and extraverts with James' tough-minded thinkers and with Ostwald's 'romantics'. Although Jung seemed to regard introversion and extraversion as personality traits rooted in the very structure of personality, his notions in this respect are confusing and unsatisfactory. His apparently fixed belief that the conscious and unconscious parts of the personality are *always* opposite with respect to their introversive and extraversive qualities makes it difficult to postulate any causal physical basis within the nervous system.

McDougall considerably simplified Jung's experimentally unworkable framework by postulating a single personality dimension of introversion-extraversion along which all individuals can be ranged in a line or scale according to the degree with which this normally distributed component of their personality is present in their constitutional make-up, most people occupying the middle ranges (Ref. 19). Citing much inferential but little experimental evidence, he attempted to explain this distribution by the influence of a chemical factor generated within the body and exerting a specific influence upon the nervous system in proportion both to the quality and quantity that is produced and liberated into the blood stream. According to McDougall, phylogenetic and ontogenetic development alike bring with them both increasing dominance and inhibition by the cortex of the lower brain-levels and also increasing behavioural introversion. It is suggested that introversion is a fundamental property of the nervous system and that increasing introversion

[1] Now at the University of London Institute of Psychiatry, Maudsley Hospital.

parallels the growing dominance of the lower brain-levels by the cortex. This trend is supposed to be counteracted by some natural biochemical compensating factor termed by McDougall 'substance X'. This mysterious 'substance X' is supposed to prevent, or diminish, the inhibitory influence of the cortex upon these more primitive lower-level functions of the nervous system. It is supposed to achieve this by increasing the resistance of the synapses to the passage or discharge of nervous current, and it is the extravert who is supposed to be constitutionally provided with a large amount of this substance. In developing this argument in defence of extreme extraversion as a consequence of excessive 'substance X' and extreme introversion as a consequence of a defect in, or lack of, this substance McDougall overlooked the perhaps equally plausible and at least equally logical possibility that introversion itself might be the product of some biochemical causative agent. Nevertheless, it is possible from McDougall's theory to generate testable predictions concerning possible relationships between behavioural extraversion and performance on certain psychophysiological tests presumed to be fairly directly mediated via central processes. One such prediction made by McDougall is that the increased synaptic resistance brought about by 'substance X' would result in a decrease in the rate of fluctuation of perspective of certain two-dimensional ambiguous figures. Therefore, the more slowly such a figure fluctuates, the more extraverted the individual is; the more rapidly it fluctuates the more introverted he is.

Eysenck has made predictions which are diametrically opposed to those of McDougall; extraverts should show both a faster rate of fluctuation and also a faster rate of change of fluctuation with time than introverts (Ref. 7). Eysenck based this prediction upon two contingencies, that reversible perspective alternation is essentially central in origin and determined in part by the process of neural satiation (a concept regarded by Eysenck as similar to that of reactive inhibition) and that extraverts show quicker and stronger satiation effects than do introverts. Although apparent interocular transfer has been shown to be inadequate evidence that certain visual phenomena are central in origin (Ref. 6), there is acceptable evidence that the process underlying alternation in perspective of simple two-dimensional figures is of a central rather than a peripheral nature (Ref. 2). Köhler & Wallach were probably the first to include fluctuation in reversible perspective as part of the general range of satiation phenomena (Ref. 18) and recent investigators have tended to agree (e.g. Refs. 4, 9 & 16) although the issue is far from resolved (see Refs. 3, 15 & 21). Eysenck himself, it should be noted, still remains unconvinced that this explanation is, in fact, the correct one (Ref. 10).

The second contingency, that extraverts manifest quicker and stronger satiation effects than do introverts has been demonstrated by Eysenck on more than one occasion. This finding, predicted by Eysenck in terms of his theory, is itself dependent upon the questionable assumption that neural satiation and reactive inhibition are identical or similar phenomena (see Ref. 8). The more any one perspective abates, the greater the opportunity, and hence likelihood, for the alternative perspective to emerge. The increased rate of change of fluctuation with time is supposed to be due to the accumulating effects of incompletely dissipated satiation.

Numerous investigators have tested McDougall's predictions using various devices for estimating extraversion; very few have as yet explicitly examined those of Eysenck. Such available evidence as there is remains largely inconclusive either on methodological grounds, such as inadequate testing procedures or lack of controls, or because of inappropriate measures of extraversion. Therefore, it is hardly surprising that no relationship between introversion-extraversion and rate of fluctuation has been reported (e.g., Ref. 14), introverts have been shown to report fluctuations more frequently than extraverts (e.g., Ref. 22) and introverts have been shown to fluctuate less often than extraverts (e.g., Ref. 5).

METHOD

To set up a crucial experiment the Necker Cube was selected as the ambiguous figure and the Maudsley Personality Inventory (MPI) as the measure of introversion-extraversion. The Necker Cube offers two advantages: first, it has been shown to be superior to a wide variety of other such figures with respect to reliability of fluctuation rate, range of scores, variability of pattern and ease of testing (Ref. 22); second, both Eysenck and McDougall have made their predictions with respect to the Necker Cube.[1] The MPI has been the subject of criticism but there is

[1] It should be noted that although, for a variety of reasons, McDougall explicitly preferred and made frequent use of the windmill illusion, he made special mention of the fact that 'observations were made also upon the alternation of phases of the ambiguous cube figure (drawn on the flat) under the various conditions described below. The rate of alternations of this figure ran closely parallel to those of the windmill under all conditions'.

good reason to believe that it is an effective self-rating measure of extraversion (E) if used with normal Ss (Ref. 11). Because it is reasonable to believe that blinking or its avoidance, either spontaneous or deliberate and either with or without Ss awareness, is likely to modify the rate of fluctuation (e.g., Refs. 1 & 23), it was decided to record and measure the rate of simple blinking of all Ss during a period as near to the actual time of the experiment as possible.

Ss were 92 normal adult male psychologically naïve volunteers. So far as interview and medical examination could ascertain no S had ever received any form of CNS impairment, no S had been recently receiving any drugs likely to produce even temporary CNS changes and none had taken any stimulant or depressant beverages for at least 3 hours prior to the experiment, or any form of alcohol in the preceding 12 hours.

Continuous and discontinuous extraneous stimuli in any modality are likely to modify the central processes under examination in ways which may be neither predictable nor even measurable. To reduce such eventualities to a minimum the experiment was carried out in a sound-proof room and the cube itself enclosed in a specially constructed restrictive viewing box. A two-dimensional cube was slit out of a sheet of black art paper cemented to the polished face of a frosted glass plate. The viewing box in which this cube was enclosed was adjustable in height, lightproof and painted flat black inside and outside. The cube was illuminated by a $7\frac{1}{2}$w frosted bulb placed behind a frosted glass plate and viewed through a pair of close-fitting rubber goggles attached to one end of the apparatus. Fluctuations in perspective could be recorded by a light touch on a silent telegraph key attached to a Gorrell & Gorrell operations recorder housed in a sound-proof container. To synchronize events and thus facilitate scoring, power was delivered to the chart drive motor through the cube illumination switch. Eyeblinks were recorded by means of a pair of photoelectrically equipped spectacles (Ref. 12).

Having completed the MPI each S was brought into the sound-proof room, seated comfortably and asked to gaze at a picture on the wall for about 5 minutes while wearing the spectacles. S was unaware that his rate of blinking was being continuously recorded.

After removing the spectacles S was given some minimal standardized instruction and training in the nature of the Necker Cube phenomenon and the use of the recording key. He was told to depress the key whenever the lower square of the cube appeared to be nearer him and to permit the key to raise when it appeared farther away. Two viewing conditions

K

were utilized, a passive *natural* condition in which S was instructed to relax and let any changes occur naturally and an active *hold* condition in which S was instructed to try to hold any one percept as long as possible, resisting all attempts to change. The scored part of the experiment consisted of six 1-minute viewing periods separated by 30 sec rest periods. Three periods were under *natural* conditions, followed by three under *hold* conditions (in a subsidiary experiment, in which half the Ss received *hold* trials first while half received *natural* trials first, the order of presentation of the two sets of trials was found to produce no pertinent differences in rates of fluctuation).

RESULTS AND DISCUSSION

To construct six-point curves for each of the *natural* and *hold* viewing periods, the data were scored in terms of the number of fluctuations per successive 10-sec period. Blink rate was related neither to extraversion nor to rate of fluctuation. To estimate reliabilities within any one viewing condition first and third minute fluctuation rates were correlated. These Pearson product-moment correlations are 0·48 and 0·82 for the *natural* and *hold* conditions, respectively. The correlation

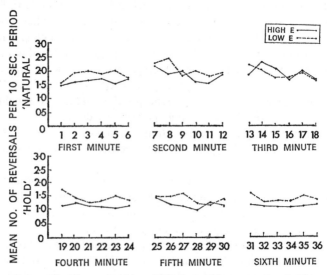

Figure 22. Mean number of Necker Cube reversals of 46 introverts and 46 extraverts per 10-sec period under *natural* and *hold* conditions.

between total numbers of fluctuations under these two conditions is 0·62.

The 92 Ss were then divided into two groups consisting of the 46 most and the 46 least extraverted Ss, respectively, according to their scores on the MPI and the 10-sec course of fluctuation plotted for each group for each of the six 1-minute viewing sessions (Fig. 23). Table 1 compares the over-all reversal rates of these Ss during each minute. Introverts reversed at a more rapid rate in five out of the six sessions, these differences being statistically significant (two-tailed t tests) for all three *hold* sessions, but for only one of the *natural* sessions. It appears, therefore, that the *hold* measure is more reliable and that it differentiates more effectively between introverts and extraverts. Introverts and extraverts are equally effective in deliberately reducing the rate of fluctuation when so requested ($p < 0.01$). They do not appear to differ with respect to rate of *change* of fluctuation with time, as predicted by Eysenck.

TABLE 1

MEAN NUMBER OF REVERSALS PER MINUTE-SESSION FOR 46 INTROVERTS
AND 46 EXTRAVERTS UNDER NATURAL AND HOLD CONDITIONS

Min	Natural				Min	Hold			
	High E	Low E	t	p		High E	Low E	t	p
1	9·78	11·28	2·95	<0·02	4	6·84	8·52	4·18	<0·01
2	11·04	12·12	1·30	ns	5	6·96	8·10	2·35	<0·05
3	11·46	11·28	0·24	ns	6	6·60	7·98	3·61	<0·01

According to Eysenck & Slater the concept of reminiscence is applicable in perceptual tasks involving fluctuation (Ref. 11). To provide estimates of reminiscence within each viewing condition the mean fluctuation rate for all Ss for the last 10-sec period in any minute session was compared with the corresponding rate for these Ss in the first 10-sec period in the following session. The only significant reminiscence effect was between the first and second minutes under *natural* conditions ($p < 0.01$). Eysenck's theory predicts that extraverts should have a higher reminiscence score than introverts (Ref. 7). The present data, which yield no apparent relationship between extraversion and reminiscence, fail to substantiate this prediction in the present perceptual situation. One possible explanation is that the Necker Cube phenomenon cannot satisfactorily be accounted for in terms of an inhibition-satiation type process.

So far as the *hold* condition is concerned, these data appear to confirm

McDougall's general prediction and seemingly fail to support that of Eysenck. However, in evaluating these results in terms of the validity of Eysenck's general theory, certain limitations must be observed. Eysenck's prediction is contingent upon the tenability of the hypothesis that fluctuation in visual perspective can be totally or at least partially accounted for in terms of Köhler-type satiation. The tenability of this hypothesis is at best questionable. Furthermore, as in other tasks requiring perceptual concentration, the increasing tendency of the extravert not to concentrate as time proceeds may complicate the generation of testable predictions over and above the expected differential rates of change in fluctuation. This effect may be present in addition to individual differences in rates of oscillation which are probably dependent not upon cortical inhibition *per se* but upon certain neural speed variables. Therefore the present data, although certainly inconsistent with Eysenck's original, conditional and unmodified prediction, are in no way crucial to Eysenck's theory. Indeed, if Ammons' concept of a learning theory of depth perception (Ref. 1) is applicable, then, in terms of Eysenck's theory, it would be the *introverts* who would learn to fluctuate more rapidly. Although the present data yield no indication of such a learning effect, it could be that differential learning had taken place very rapidly in the brief training period. The fact that, apart from the first minute, the *natural* condition produced insignificant differences seemingly weakens the evidence in favour of McDougall's prediction. Again, it is possible that, perhaps for some of the reasons suggested and depending upon the conditions, it is the early test period which is sometimes the more crucial. Further investigation of these possibilities is required.

SUMMARY

Based on the notion of a synaptic-resistance increasing substance abundantly present in extraverts, McDougall characterized introverts as possessing a more rapid rate of reversal than extraverts when presented with ambiguous perceptual figures. Eysenck, provisionally accepting the questionable assumption that this rate of reversal is indeed due to a Köhler-type of satiation, deduced an exactly opposing outcome. Although an experiment using 92 normal Ss, the Necker Cube and the Maudsley Personality Inventory, apparently supports McDougall's position, the data need not be inconsistent with Eysenck's theory if certain limitations and suggested modifications are taken into consideration.

REFERENCES

1. AMMONS, R. B., ULRICH, P. & AMMONS, C. H., Voluntary control of perception of depth in a two-dimensional drawing. *Proc. Mont. Acad. Sci.*, **19**, 160–168, 1959.
2. BROWN, K. J., Studies of apparent change as a function of observation time, using a new type of dynamic ambiguous figure. *WADC Tech. Rep.*, 54–139, 1954.
3. CARLSON, V. R., Satiation in a reversible perspective figure. *J. exp. Psychol.*, **45**, 442–448, 1953.
4. COHEN, L., Rate of apparent change of a Necker Cube as a function of prior stimulation. *Amer. J. Psychol.*, **72**, 327–344, 1959.
5. COSTELLO, C. G., The control of visual imagery in mental disorder. *J. ment. Sci.*, **103**, 840–849, 1957.
6. DAY, R. H., On interocular transfer and the central origin of visual aftereffect. *Amer. J. Psychol.*, **71**, 784–789, 1958.
7. EYSENCK, H. J., *The Dynamics of Anxiety and Hysteria.* London: Routledge & Kegan Paul, 1957.
8. ——, A factor analysis of selected tests. In *Experiments in Personality* (ed. H. J. Eysenck). Vol. 2. London: Routledge & Kegan Paul, 1960.
9. —— & EYSENCK, S. B. G., Reminiscence on the spiral aftereffect as a function of length of rest and number of pre-test trials. *Percept. mot. Skills*, **10**, 93–94, 1960.
10. ——, HOLLAND, H. & TROUTON, D. S., Drugs and personality. 4. The effects of stimulant and depressant drugs on the rate of fluctuation of a reversible perspective figure. *J. ment. Sci.*, **103**, 656–660, 1957.
11. —— & SLATER, P., Effects of practice and rest on fluctuations in the Mueller-Lyer illusion. *Brit. J. Psychol.*, **49**, 246–256, 1958.
12. —— & WITHERS, W. C. R., Photo-electric recording of eyelid movements. *Amer. J. Psychol.*, **68**, 467–471, 1955.
13. FRANKS, C. M., HOLDEN, E. A. & PHILLIPS, M., Eysenck's 'stratification' theory and the questionnaire method of measuring personality. *J. clin. Psychol.*, **17**, 248–253, 1961.
14. FREDERIKSEN, N. O. & GUILFORD, J. P., Personality traits and fluctuation of the outline cube. *Amer. J. Psychol.*, **46**, 470–474, 1934.
15. HOCHBERG, J. E., Figure-ground reversal as a function of visual satiation. *J. exp. Psychol.*, **40**, 682–686, 1950.

16. HOWARD, I. P., An investigation of a satiation process in the reversible perspective of revolving skeletal shapes. *Quart. J. exp. Psychol.*, **13**, 19–33, 1961.

17. JUNG, C. G., *Psychological types*. London: Kegan Paul, 1924.

18. KÖHLER, W. & WALLACH, H., Figural aftereffects: investigation of visual processes. *Proc. Amer. phil. Soc.*, **88**, 269–357, 1944.

19. MCDOUGALL, W., The chemical theory of temperament applied to introversion and extraversion. *J. abnorm. soc. Psychol.*, **24**, 293–309, 1929.

20. —— & SMITH, M., *The Effects of Alcohol and some other Drugs during Normal and Fatigued Conditions*. Med. Res. Council, Spec. Rep. No. 56. London: HMSO, 1920.

21. MCEWEN, P., Figural aftereffects. *Brit. J. Psychol. Monogr. Suppl.*, No. 31, 1958.

22. PORTER, E. L. H., Factors in the fluctuation of fifteen ambiguous figures. *Psychol. Rec.*, **2**, 231–253, 1938.

23. WASHBURN, M. F. & GILLETTE, A., Studies from the Psychological Laboratory of Vassar College: 62. Motor factors in voluntary control of cube perspective fluctuations and retinal rivalry fluctuations. *Amer. J. Psychol.*, **45**, 315–319, 1933.

32

Visual Masking as a Function of Personality

R. J. MCLAUGHLIN[1] & H. J. EYSENCK

First published in *British Journal of Psychology*, **57**, 393–396, 1966

VISUAL masking was related to the personality dimensions of intro-version-extraversion and neuroticism. It was predicted and found that extraverts have a higher masking threshold than introverts. The function of reticulo-cortical arousal and inhibition mechanisms is discussed in relation to extraversion-introversion as a possible source for an explanation of this phenomenon.

INTRODUCTION

Visual masking, meta-contrast, or the suppression of the primary visual stimulus, are terms which have been applied to a phenomenon in which one visual stimulus (S_1) is applied for a brief period (10–30 m/sec) and followed by another brief visual stimulus (S_2) after a variable inter-stimulus interval (ISI). With ISI of 40 m/sec or less only S_2 is seen and S_1 is suppressed or 'masked'; with ISI of 100 m/sec or more, both stimuli are seen. For most subjects there is an intermediate value of the ISI (masking threshold) at which S_1 ceases to be suppressed and is seen. This threshold can be established with considerable accuracy (Refs. 11 & 13) and forced-choice methods do not seem to have any advantage over conventional procedures (Ref. 10). Other phenomena of a similar kind, such as the Bidwell effect (Refs. 1 & 7) appear to obey similar laws and visually evoked potentials have been shown to correlate with the psychological events of visual masking (Ref. 2).

Since S_2 appears to *inhibit* the perception of S_1, it has been argued that personality differences in inhibitory potential should be relevant to this phenomenon, as should CNS stimulant and depressant drugs (Ref. 3). In terms of physiological arousal theory, introverts are postulated to be in a state of higher cortical arousal than extraverts (Refs. 4 & 5) and

---

[1] Now at Saint Louis University, Saint Louis, Missouri.

should thus be able to maintain the discrimination between S_1 and S_2 more efficiently than extraverts. Similarly, stimulant drugs, by increasing cortical arousal, should increase discrimination, while depressant drugs, by decreasing arousal, should have the opposite effect. It was predicted therefore that introverts (and persons given stimulant drugs) would have lower masking thresholds than extraverts (and persons given depressant drugs). The drug prediction has been verified several times (Refs. 1, 3 & 11) and the purpose of the present investigation was to test the personality prediction.

METHOD

Subjects

64 paid volunteers were tested on the Eysenck Personality Inventory (EPI) and put into 4 groups: neurotic extraverts (NE), stable extraverts (SE), neurotic introverts (NI) and stable introverts. 8 subjects were eliminated from further testing because they obtained scores from 11 to 13 on the E–I scale (mean = 12·0) and were thus not easily classifiable as either introverted or extraverted. One other subject was eliminated at this point because his 'lie scale' score was too high (L = 6) for his personality score to be accepted as valid.

7 subjects were eliminated during the experiment, 5 for having an error rate above 10 per cent, indicating that they were reporting the test stimulus when it was not being presented and a further 2 subjects for not reporting the presence of the test stimulus below an ISI of 130 m/sec, which might be an indication that the subject did not have normal visual acuity.

The remaining 48 subjects, 11 females and 37 males, were equally divided, 12 in each of the 4 personality groups. The mean age of subjects was 25·71 years (S.D. = 8·29) and all reported that they had normal or corrected-to-normal visual acuity.

Apparatus

The instrument, previously described by Holland (Ref. 11, pp. 72–75), was an electronic Dodge-type tachistoscope with variable exposure and interval between exposures. The exposed fields were illuminated at 0·155 log. L by four 9-inch 6w fluorescent tubes arranged around a rectangle and shaded to illuminate a 7-inch square. The stimuli presented were a 20mm black disc (visual angle 0·46°) and a black annulus with inner and outer diameters of 20mm and 58mm (visual angle 1·26°) both presented on a white ground. The disc was viewed binocularly through, and the annulus reflected from, a half-silvered mirror placed at 45° to the line of regard. The sequence of stimulus presentations was: (1) test figure 15 m/sec; (2) ISI, variable; (3) masking figure 15 m/sec. The darkened fields between the trials contained a pin-point source of red light superimposed on the centre where the disc and annulus appeared. This point served as a focusing stimulus when the subject was told that the lights were to be flashed.

The tachistoscope was modified to carry two display wheels which could easily be rotated into position and held by a spring-loaded ball-bearing and dimple giving very accurate positioning. Hence it was easy to select between a present or absent masking stimulus within a matter of 2 or 3 sec.

Procedure

Each subject was tested individually. The procedure followed that reported by Holland (Ref. 11) with sometimes two exceptions. First, a measurement of the subject's responses was made on trials in which the annulus was shown but the disc was not (to establish error rate). Secondly, subjects were required to rate on a three-point scale (1 = 'positive'; 2 = 'fairly certain'; 3 = 'not sure') their confidence in having seen the disc on those trials in which they reported its appearance. An ascending method of limits was used proceeding from an ISI of 40 m/sec and increasing in steps of 5 m/sec until the subject responded correctly on two consecutive trials that he was positive (saying '1') that he had seen the test stimulus. It was necessary to limit the range of ISI tested and only to test in a series of ascending limits to maximize the reliability of the measure, because of the limited availability of subjects and the problems of fatigue that would be expected if the session exceeded 45 minutes. After five consecutive threshold measurements the subject was given a rest period of approximately 5 minutes before a final series of five further threshold measurements was made.

RESULTS

The masking threshold was computed for each subject by averaging the ISI of the first response, for each of the ten trials, for which the subject correctly reported that he was positive the disc appeared. Table 1 summarizes the masking thresholds for the four personality groups. A 2×2 analysis of variance was applied to the thresholds, comparing extraversion-introversion with high and low levels of neuroticism. The

K*

comparison of introversion with extraversion yielded the only significant effect ($F = 4\cdot21$; D.F. 1, 44; $p < 0\cdot05$) with extraverts having a higher threshold than introverts. Bartlett's test showed no significant heterogeneity of variance.

TABLE 1

MEAN MASKING THRESHOLDS (AND S.D.) FOR EACH OF THE FOUR PERSONALITY GROUPS (N = 12); FOR ALL FOUR GROUPS COMBINED, MEAN THRESHOLD = 71·11 (S.D. = 12·26, N = 48)

	Stable		Neurotic	
	Mean	S.D.	Mean	S.D.
Extraverts	74·33	12·73	75·04	13·19
Introverts	68·83	10·68	66·25	11·50

The correlation between the threshold for the first five trials and the second five was 0·96 for all subjects, showing high intra-subject reliability of the masking threshold measurements.

DISCUSSION

A possible explanation of masking phenomena may be found in Granit's concept (Ref. 9) of pre-excitatory inhibition (Ref. 3); it seems likely that higher centres play an important part in this activity (Ref. 1). Donchin & Lindsley, who have studied averaged evoked cortical potentials to pairs of flash stimuli and who found that physiological masking occurred with short ISI, have raised the question of the localization of the stage in the visual system at which the neural effect produced by S_2 interferes with the effect elicited by S_1; they consider four possibilities: (1) retina (receptor cell layer to ganglion cell layer), (2) lateral geniculate body (relay and other functions), (3) cortical structures (primary and secondary) and (4) non-specific sensory system (reticular and thalamic) (Ref. 2). Eysenck has argued for the relevance of the reticular system in connection with personality differences along the extraversion-introversion axis and data from experiments with drugs are in good agreement with this hypothesis (Ref. 12).

The work of Shagass & Schwartz (Refs. 14 & 15) appears to be relevant. They administered pairs of stimuli and recorded the evoked potentials, thus making it possible to plot the cycle of recovery of responsiveness. They found that the early portion of the recovery cycle for the primary somatosensory response tended to be biphasic in form. The first phase of recovery occurs very early, the amplitude of the second response equalling that of the first, or exceeding it before 20 m/sec. There is then a phase of diminished responsiveness, followed by a longer phase of full recovery, usually reaching a peak at about 100–130 m/sec. Dysthymics (introverted neurotics) were found to have higher recovery ratios than psychopaths (personality disorders—neurotic extraverts), i.e. they recovered more quickly. These data are in good agreement with those reported here and suggest that the processes involved are essentially similar.

Another phenomenon which appears closely relevant is critical flicker fusion (Ref. 3). There is evidence that introverts have higher C.F.F. thresholds (i.e. discriminate better between flashes at high frequencies) than extraverts and that stimulant drugs improve discrimination, while depressant drugs have an opposite effect (Ref. 6). Aiba has compared C.F.F. with masking and has drawn attention to some of the similarities and to the possibilities of accounting for both along similar theoretical lines (Ref. 1). It cannot be said that any particular theory in this field is at present clearly indicated as more correct than any of the others; indeed, it seems likely that these phenomena represent the confluence of neural impulses originating from several different points. Nevertheless, there is increasing evidence (a) that reticulo-cortico arousal and inhibition mechanisms play a part in the causation of the phenomena themselves and (b) that personality differences along the extraversion-introversion axis are meaningfully related to masking and to C.F.F. effects through the mediation of the reticular system.

We are indebted to the Maudsley and Bethlem Royal Research Fund for financial assistance.

REFERENCES

1. AIBA, S., The suppression of the primary visual stimulus. In *Experiments with Drugs* (ed. H. J. Eysenck). Oxford: Pergamon Press, 1963.
2. DONCHIN, E. & LINDSLEY, D. B., Visually evoked response correlates of perceptual masking and enhancement. *Electroenceph. clin. Neurophysiol.*, **19**, 325, 1965.
3. EYSENCK, H. J., *Dynamics of Anxiety and Hysteria.* London: Routledge & Kegan Paul, 1957.

4. ——, The biological basis of personality. *Nature*, **199**, 1031–1034, 1963.
5. ——, Biological factors in neurosis and crime. *Scientia*, **58**, 1–11 1964.
6. ——, *The Biological Basis of Personality*. Springfield: C. C. Thomas, 1967.
7. —— & AIBA, S., Drugs and personality. 5. The effects of stimulant and depressant drugs on the suppression of the primary visual stimulus. *J. ment. Sci.*, **103**, 661–665, 1957.
8. —— & EYSENCK, S. B. G., *Manual of the Eysenck Personality Inventory*. London: University of London Press, 1964.
9. GRANIT, R., *Receptors and Sensory Perception*. New Haven: Yale University Press, 1955.
10. HECKENMUELLER, E. G. & DEMBER, W. N., A forced-choice indicator for use with Werner's ring pattern in studies of backward masking. *Psychonom. Sci.*, **3**, 167–168, 1965.
11. HOLLAND, H. C., 'Visual masking' and the effect of stimulant and depressant drugs. In *Experiments with Drugs* (ed. H. J. Eysenck). Oxford: Pergamon Press, 1963.
12. KILLAM, E. K., Drug action on the brain stem reticular formation. *Pharmacol. Rev.*, **14**, 175–224, 1962.
13. POLLACK, R. H., Backward figural masking as a function of chronological age and intelligence. *Psychonom. Sci.*, **3**, 65–66, 1965.
14. SHAGASS, C. & SCHWARTZ, M., Cerebral responsiveness in psychiatric patients. *A.M.A. Arch. Gen. Psychiat.*, **8**, 177–189, 1963.
15. SHAGASS, C. & SCHWARTZ, M., Neurophysiological dysfunctions associated with psychiatric disorders. *Psychiat. Res. Rep.*, **17**, 130–152, 1963.

33

Internalization Ratio, Accuracy, and Variability of Judgments of the Vertical

BERNARD J. FINE & ALEXANDER COHEN

First published in *Perceptual and Motor Skills*, **16,** 138, 1963

IN an unpublished study (which yielded equivocal results) investigating the relationship between auditory stimulation and perception of the vertical, a subsidiary hypothesis was made pertinent to the relationship between Welsh's MMPI-derived Internalization Ratio (IR) (Ref. 4) and the accuracy and variability of judgments of the vertical.

Following Fine's usage of the IR (Refs. 2 & 3), Ss scoring 0·88 or below on the IR (extraverts) were expected to be less accurate and more variable in their judgments of true vertical than Ss scoring above 0·88 (intermediates and introverts). The hypothesis was derived from the work of Eysenck and others (summarized in Ref. 1) which indicates that extraverts are more dependent than introverts upon external cues when making judgments, are more variable in their responses than introverts and prefer speed to accuracy when performing specific tasks. Since external cues were minimal in the present study, it was felt that differences in accuracy and variability of judgments between introverts and extraverts would be maximized.

The data[1] presented here represent only the control trials (those with no auditory stimulation) of the experiment proper. A total of 32 judgments of the vertical (16 with the rod starting from 85° to the left of true vertical and 16 starting from 85° to the right) were obtained for each of the 32 Ss. Two measures were calculated for each S: the mean deviation from true vertical (regardless of the direction of the deviation) over 32 trials and the standard deviation of the mean. Medians for each of the two distributions of scores thus obtained were determined and median tests calculated.

[1] A transcript of raw scores (Document No. 7386) may be ordered from the American Documentation Institute, Auxiliary Publications Project, Photoduplication Service, Library of Congress, Washington 25, D.C. Remit $1.25 for photocopies or 35mm. microfilm.

Of the 18 extraverts, 12 were above the median in their deviations from true vertical, whereas only 4 of the 14 introverts and intermediates had deviations above the median. The median test yielded a chi² of 3·17 (df = 1) which is statistically significant (p<0·05, 1-tail). With regard to variability, 13 of the 18 extraverts had standard deviations above the median, whereas only 3 of the 14 intermediates and introverts were above the median. The median test yielded chi² of 6·22 (df = 1) which is significant (p<0·01, 1-tail). The data support the hypothesis that there is a relationship between the IR and the accuracy and variability of judgments of the vertical.

REFERENCES

1. EYSENCK, H. J., *Handbook of Abnormal Psychology*. New York: Basic Books, 1961.
2. FINE, B. J., Welsh's Internalization Ratio as a behavioural index. *J. appl. Psychol.*, **45**, 117–119, 1961.
3. ——, Introversion-extraversion and motor vehicle driver behaviour. *Percept. mot. Skills*, **16**, 95–100, 1963.
4. WELSH, G. S., An anxiety index and internalization ratio for the MMPI. In *Basic Readings on the MMPI in Psychology and Medicine* (ed. G. S. Welsh & W. G. Dahlstrom). Minneapolis: University of Minnesota Press, 1956.

34

Some Factors Affecting the Hearing of Words Presented Dichotically [1]

P. C. DODWELL

First published in *Canadian Journal of Psychology*, **18**, 72–91, 1964

INTRODUCTION

LISTENING to two things at once has been investigated under a variety of different conditions. Broadbent's findings and those of Cherry are by now too well known to require yet another exposition (Refs. 2 & 6). Broadbent's explanation of sequential reproduction has been questioned (Ref. 19) and this has led to intermodality studies (Ref. 3). Dichotic listening has been studied in elderly psychiatric patients with memory disorder (Ref. 12) and in patients with temporal-lobe damage (Ref. 15). Most of this work has been done using groups of digits as stimuli, or with continuous prose passages (e.g., Refs. 18 & 28). In the one case we have very 'neutral' stimuli, in the other very 'meaningful' ones. There is an extensive continuum of verbal materials between these two extremes and it would be of interest to know, whatever the filter and storage system for hearing may be, to what extent such characteristics as frequency and meaningfulness of words are factors in their perceivability under dichotic stimulation.

It has been shown, under dichotomous binocular presentation, that suppression of one of a pair of words can occur as a function of emotional significance, that is, perceptual defence can be demonstrated under dichotomous visual stimulation (Refs. 7 & 30). It seems quite possible that a similar effect can be demonstrated in dichotomous listening. If it can be, then any postulated filter must be thought of as something rather more elaborate than a simple block to prevent informational overloading of the perceptual system.

The experiments reported below attempt to clarify some of the variables which affect the perception of words under dichotic stimulation.

[1] This research was supported by a grant from the Arts Research Committee of Queen's University, whose support is gratefully acknowledged. Thanks are also due to Miss Dawn Campbell, M.A., for her assistance in the project.

METHOD

The procedure was nearly identical for Experiments 1 to 4. Tapes were prepared in such a way that pairs of words occurred simultaneously on two channels, at the rate of one pair every four seconds (a pilot experiment showed that this allowed sufficient time between pairs for S to respond to both words fairly comfortably. A Heathkit model TR-IAQ tape recorder was used. With this machine it is possible to record on one track, then play back on that track whilst recording on the other. The recorder timed herself by watching the rotating spot on a decade counter (Hunter Klockounter) and speaking at every fourth rotation. As the second channel was being taped she both watched the rotating spot on the decade tube and also listened to the first channel. Some care was taken to make the presentations simultaneous and the loudness, emphasis and speed of enunciation the same for each pair of words (every pair of words contained equal numbers of syllables): tapes were accepted for use in the experiments only when the matching appeared to be good. Of course one cannot control all these factors rigidly with spoken words but it is felt that they probably had little effect on the experimental results.

Every experimental list was preceded by a practice list, which served to accustom Ss to the experimental situation and, during the recording session, presented an opportunity for the recorder to synchronize words as well as possible prior to the recording of the Experimental lists.

A set of instructions was read out to each S before an experimental session:

> 'This is an experiment in hearing. When the experiment starts, you will hear words spoken into these headphones. First of all you will hear the words 'now listen now' spoken into both ears. Then there will be a series of words, spoken in pairs, one word to the right ear, and a *different* word to the left at the same instant.
>
> 'The first thing I want you to do is to make the words in the two ears sound equally distinct, as far as you can, by turning the volume knobs whenever necessary. The upper knob controls the volume in your right ear and the lower knob controls the left ear.
>
> 'There will be 10 pairs of words to start with, as a practice list, during which you can make adjustments, but I should also like you to report as many of these words as you can recognise.
>
> 'Then, after a pause, you will again hear "now listen now", followed

by pairs of different words to the left and right ears. Listen carefully to these words and report as many of them as you can. If at any time the words in one ear appear to be clearer or louder than the words in the other, you should make an adjustment of the knob, so they become equally distinct.

'Altogether there are ( ) lists of words. Only the first one is preceded by a short practice list.[1] There will be a pause between lists and I shall tell you when the next list is about to begin'.

S was then seated in a small, sound-deadened cubicle with the experimenter (a personable young woman), listened to the lists of words through headphones in the usual way, reported as many words as possible and the experimenter noted down all omissions or misperceptions. Each S listened to several lists (four, five, or six depending on the experiment) and in between lists rested for about one minute.

Ss for the experiment were young adults, both men and women, mainly graduate students in psychology in Experiments 1 and 2, and summer school students who knew nothing about experiments in dichotic stimulation in the remaining experiments.

EXPERIMENT 1

This experiment aimed at establishing the effect of frequency of words in written English, as assessed in the Thorndike-Lorge word count, on their perceivability. Six lists were prepared and the frequencies of the words in the lists are shown in Table 1. Each list contained 30 pairs of words. The words of different frequencies were assigned randomly to the two channels, but with the restriction that there was an equal number of more and less frequent words in each list on each channel and each pair consisted of one more and one less frequent word. Six subjects took part in the experiment, each one assigned to the row of a Latin square. The columns of the square correspond to order of presentation, the letters to lists, so that each list occurred once for each subject and once in each position. The numbers of correct and incorrect responses for each list were recorded and the score for each list was the number of more frequent words correctly perceived minus the number of less frequent words correctly perceived. No account was taken of differences in sensitivity

[1] Although a practice list was recorded before each experimental list, only one practice list was played to a subject, the practice list preceding the particular list which they heard first. Order of presentation of lists was varied between subjects (see below).

TABLE 1

WORD LIST FOR EXPERIMENT

List	More frequent	Less frequent
A	1000 most frequent	1 in 4×10^6
B	1000 most frequent	1 in 10^6
C	1000 most frequent	10 in 10^6
D	50 in 10^6	1 in 4×10^6
E	50 in 10^6	1 in 10^6
F	50 in 10^6	10 in 10^6

Frequencies of words in the lists used in Experiment 1. The words of each pair had equal numbers of syllables, and all words were of one, two or three syllables.

for the two ears (except that each subject set a volume control so that the words in the two ears appeared to be 'equally distinct', and could reset this control at any time, which in fact happened quite infrequently) but this should not affect the scores, since the more frequent words occurred equally often for both ears. Analysis of variance of the results showed that 'treatments', that is, lists, was the only significant source of variation ($F = 2 \cdot 79$, $p < 0 \cdot 05$ for 5 and 20 df). The experiment was replicated with six different subjects, but using the same Latin square, in order to test for a possible effect of the six different orders of presen-

TABLE 2

ANALYSIS OF RESULTS FOR EXPERIMENT 1, BOTH RUNS

Source	df	MS	VR
Orders	5	$25 \cdot 2$	$1 \cdot 07$
Residual (a)	6	$23 \cdot 67$	
Total between rows (individuals)	11		
Treatments (lists)	5	$115 \cdot 6$	7*
Trials	5	$22 \cdot 6$	$1 \cdot 36$
Residual (b)	50	$16 \cdot 6$	
Total	71		

* $p < 0 \cdot 01$

The analysis shows that the only significant source of variance is between lists, that is between words of different frequencies (see Table 3a).

tation. The result was essentially the same as in the first run, except that the treatment effect was significant at the 1 per cent level (F = 4·25). The analysis of the combined sets of data is shown in Table 2: 'treatments' is still the only significant factor.

TABLE 3A

AVERAGE SCORES ON EACH LIST OF WORDS, BOTH RUNS COMBINED

List A	7·3	List D	8·8
List B	5·0	List E	3·9
List C	2·8	List F	0·5

TABLE 3B

PERCENTAGE OF WORDS CORRECTLY PERCEIVED,
AS A FUNCTION OF FREQUENCY, BOTH RUNS COMBINED

Frequency	Percentage
1000 most frequent	69·8
50 in 10^6	70·2
10 in 10^6	67·7
1 in 10^6	58·6
1 in 4×10^6	48·4

TABLE 3C

PERCENTAGE OF WORDS CORRECTLY PERCEIVED
AS A FUNCTION OF NUMBER OF SYLLABLES AND FREQUENCY

	1000 m.f.	$50/10^6$	$10/10^6$	$1/10^6$	$1/4 \times 10^6$
1 syllable	59·4	48·6	40·5	30·5	37·4
2 syllables	71·6	73·6	69·9	55·2	50·9
3 syllables	69·2	71·9	74·0	65·1	50·3

Table 3a shows that the greater the difference in frequency between words on the lists, the more likely it is that the frequent words will be perceived correctly more often. Table 3b shows that, overall, frequent words are perceived correctly more often than infrequent words. Table 3c shows that words of one syllable tend to be harder to perceive than words of two or three syllables.

Table 3a shows the mean scores obtained for the different lists. Recalling that two different frequencies of 'frequent' words were used (Table 1) it can be seen that as the frequencies of the pairs of words within a list become more similar, so does the preponderance of correct perception of the more frequent words become less. Table 3b shows the extent to which, over-all, frequent words are perceived more often than infrequent ones. It appears that the number of syllables in a word affects its detectability. Table 3c shows that words of one syllable tend to be harder to perceive than words of two or three syllables. This should not, of course, constitute an important source of variability in the analysis of Table 2, since 'number of syllables per word' was matched for pairs of words within a list. It could be argued that the effects shown in Experiment 1 are simply well-known monaural effects (cf., for example, Ref. 27) measured in an unusual situation. To find out more precisely what is happening in this situation, the perception of more frequent words was analysed separately from the perception of less frequent. The analyses were performed on the two runs combined. Fig. 23 shows the percentages of more and less frequently heard words over both runs: it is clear that the effect described above is entirely due to performance on the 'less frequent' ear. Analysing the same data in two different ways may raise some doubts in the purist's mind, but here the procedure seems reasonable since a different question is being asked in the two analyses. Analysis of both the more frequent and the less frequent words was done as a 2×3 factorial, with two levels of the more frequent word (lists A, B, C *versus* D, E, F) and three levels of the competing less frequent word (A, D *versus* B, E *versus* C, F). The response on the more frequent word was statistically flat, no matter what the frequency of the competing word

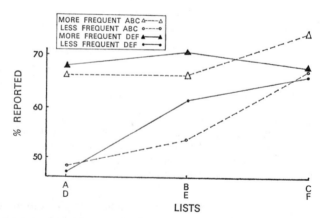

Figure 23. Percentages of words heard correctly in Experiment 1, more and less frequent words shown separately for the two groups of three lists given in Table 1.

and there was no difference between performance on the two levels of the more frequent word. In fact all the F ratios were less than one. However, the frequency effect on the less frequent ear was reliable ($p < 0.01$) and, as Fig. 23 shows, performance improves as the frequency becomes larger. The other effects were not significant.

The frequency effect may obviously be due in part, at least, to response bias. The point of the experiment (as a preliminary to Experiments 4 and 5) is simply to show that there is a strong frequency effect on correct report.

EXPERIMENT 2

Since a number of studies have shown that meaningfulness of words is a factor in speed of learning (e.g., Ref. 21) and perceptual redintegration (Ref. 22) it would seem desirable to know whether meaningfulness is an important factor in perception under the conditions of dichotic stimulation. 'Meaningfulness' is here used in Noble's operationally defined sense of the mean number of associations evoked from subjects by the word in a set time interval. Meaningfulness and frequency are of course closely related (Ref. 29) but a recent study by Johnson, Frincke & Martin has shown that, using words matched in frequency but varying in meaningfulness (m), an effect of meaningfulness on visual duration thresholds (VDTs) can be demonstrated, although the effect is small (Ref. 14). They also found that frequency was essentially unrelated to VDTs when meaningfulness was controlled. It has also been found that goodness-badness of words, as rated on the semantic differential (Ref. 24), affects perceptual redintegration (Ref. 22) and VDTs (Ref. 14).

The aim of the present experiment is to assess the effects of frequency, meaningfulness and goodness-badness on the perceivability of words presented dichotically. Three lists of words were used, being the lists presented by Johnson, *et al.* (Ref. 14). List 1 contained sixteen pairs of words, matched in frequency but varying in m (Ref. 14, Table II, first list). List 2 contained seven pairs of two-syllable words, matched in frequency and m, one of each pair being a 'good' word, the other 'bad' (Ref. 14, Table II, second list). List 3 also contained sixteen pairs of two-syllable words matched in m and varying in frequency (Ref. 14, Table II, third list).

The same 12 subjects took part in this experiment (it having been established in Experiment 1 that serial effects were negligible). All subjects heard all three lists, the order of presentation of lists being randomized. The scores in this experiment were simply the numbers of words in the two different categories of the non-matched variable correctly perceived (for example, the high m and low m categories for List 1). By t-tests for correlated means, between the numbers of words in the two categories correctly perceived, it was established that there were significant differences for each list: more meaningful words are perceived more readily than less meaningful ones (List 1), 'good' words are perceived more readily than 'bad' ones (List 2) and more frequent words are better perceived than infrequent ones (List 3). The significance levels for these differences were 2, 5 and 2 per cent respectively.

Johnson, Frincke & Martin point out that their list of words matched in m and varying in frequency (List 3 in this study) is not entirely adequate, since goodness is not well controlled in it. Also, the list of words matched in both frequency and m, varying in 'goodness', is small.

EXPERIMENT 3

To assess further the role of 'goodness' as a factor in perceivability a new list of words was prepared. Originally the intention was to take 30 pairs of words, one 'good' and one 'bad', from the atlas of semantic profiles (Ref. 13), which could be matched on the Thorndike-Lorge word count. Unfortunately an insufficient number of the 360 words in the atlas could be found at the extremes of 'goodness' and 'badness' which could also be matched for frequency, so eventually a list of 30 pairs was made up, with 15 'good' and 15 'bad' words, each matched for frequency with a 'neutral' word (also from the atlas). These words and their ratings and frequencies, are shown in Table 4a. It should be noted that they have not been equated for meaningfulness.

Two classes of summer school students in psychology at Queen's University, who had completed the Maudsley Personality Inventory, served as volunteer subjects in this experiment. Inglis has suggested that there may be characteristic differences in the sorts of response given by introverts and extraverts to 'threatening' or 'taboo' words and he has used this hypothesis to attempt to explain some of the rather confusing results of experiments on perceptual defence (Ref. 11). Although the 'bad' words in the present list can only be considered mildly 'threatening' in character, it would nevertheless seem possible that differences in response patterns might appear as a function of introversion-extraversion. In the present instance subjects were classified in a sixfold manner, as shown in Tables 5a and 5b which also gives Maudsley Personality Inventory norms for a young adult Canadian population. The criterion used for classification was that a 'neurotic' was a person whose N score was at least 1 s.d. above the mean N score and that similarly an 'introvert' or 'extravert' was a person whose score was at least 1 s.d. below, or above, the E score mean.

TABLE 4A

LISTS OF GOOD AND BAD WORDS MATCHED WITH NEUTRAL
WORDS OF THE SAME FREQUENCY

	Frequency	Rating		Frequency	Rating
Good			*Neutral*		
Butter	100	197	Sudden	100	383
Truth	100	143	Small	100	350
Peace	100	130	Square	100	350
Eat	100	190	Run	100	387
Study	100	180	Army	100	367
Light	100	183	Short	100	330
Sweet	100	193	Dream	100	337
Happy	100	153	Easy	100	340
Car	100	197	Far	100	340
Flower	100	187	City	100	353
Church	100	180	Box	100	363
Justice	50	167	Wagon	50	330
Sunday	50	193	Negro	47	363
Bible	25	187	Lemon	27	307
Patriot	17	190	Elegant	13	300
Bad					
Hate	50	653	Block	50	367
Steal	50	667	Jump	50	337
Grief	45	560	Pig	44	310
Criminal	31	643	Lingering	26	397
Inferior	19	580	Obvious	23	353
Crooked	18	593	Lofty	19	350
Indifferent	15	580	Millionaire	14	300
Dreary	14	563	Shady	12	367
Fraud	10	637	Snail	8	347
Scorching	9	620	Spanking	9	367
Nasty	7	600	Frosty	8	373
Scalding	6	567	Dusky	8	340
Stagnant	4	627	Pigment	4	303
Heartless	3	637	Mallet	3	380
Putrid	1	637	Fervid	1	367

Frequencies are measured per million words. Goodness-badness ratings are those obtained by Jenkins, Russell & Suci (Ref. 13).

TABLE 4B

TABOO WORDS AND MATCHED NEUTRAL WORDS

	Lists				
Taboo	1	2	3	4	5
Vagina	Chicago	Forgotten	Partition	Mimosa	Subpoena
Intercourse	Company	Reproduce	Tearfully	Pirouette	Character
Orgasm	Pitiful	Shareholder	Rosewater	Government	Indicate
Whore	Rife	Fugue	Fool	Hung	Kite
Masturbate	Fraternize	Gentleman	Hospital	Emphasis	Insecure

The same five frequency classes as are shown in Table 1 are represented once each in each row of neutral words in this table.

TABLE 5A

CHARACTERISTICS OF MAUDSLEY PERSONALITY INVENTORY SCORES

	Neuroticism (N)	Extraversion (E)
Mean	24·99	26·80
S.D.	9·56	9·22

Number in sample = 107
Mean age = 30·7, range = 19–51
Correlation of N and E scores: −0·084

TABLE 5B

MEAN SCORES FOR DIFFERENT GROUPS IN EXPERIMENT 3

	Low E	Normal E	High E
High N	1 (N = 4)	5 (N = 5)	—
Normal N	1 (N = 7)	−0·5 (N = 31)	−3·7 (N = 14)

Table 5a shows Maudsley Personality Inventory score characteristics for a young adult Canadian population. Table 5b shows the mean scores obtained in an experiment on perceivability of words with different degrees of emotional tone (see text).

Since both 'good' and 'bad' words appear in the list, each matched against a 'neutral' word, the scoring procedure adopted was to count the number of times a 'good' word was heard but not its 'bad' counterpart. Similarly the number of times the opposite effect occurred (the 'better' of the two was not heard but the 'worse' was) was counted. The final score for a subject was the first of these numbers minus the second, so a positive score indicates that a person tends to hear the 'better' of a pair, a negative score indicates the opposite. Table 5b shows the mean scores for the different groups of subjects; unfortunately there were no high-E, high-N scorers in the sample. A simple analysis of variance indicated that the variance of group means was not significant at the 5 per cent level, but was not far from being so (m = 2·1, 4 and 56 df). The result is suggestive, since the result is in the direction predicted by Inglis, namely that introverts should tend to 'defend', or not hear 'bad' words, more often than extraverts. The effects of emotional tone were quite small, as the means in Table 5b demonstrate. In the previous experiment it was shown that goodness-badness was a relevant factor, but in that case the good words were matched against bad ones. When good or bad words are matched against neutral words, it is perhaps not surprising that the effects are less clear. Unfortunately no Maudsley Personality Inventory scores were available for subjects in the previous experiment, so that differences in these scores as a function of E and N scores could not be examined.

EXPERIMENT 4

To examine more adequately the phenomenon of perceptual defence in dichotic listening, the same group of subjects as was used in the previous experiment listened to a further set of lists in which there occurred some 'taboo' words. Very few such words occur in the Thorndike-Lorge count and, bearing in mind some evidence given in *The Trial of Lady Chatterley* (Ref. 26), one imagines that if they did, their frequency in written English might not reflect too reliably their frequency in the spoken language, a point also made by Postman, *et al.* (Ref. 25). At all events, it was not possible to match a group of taboo words against others of equal frequency, so the following procedure was adopted: each taboo word was paired in turn with a word from one of five frequency classes and placed in one of five lists of 20 pairs of words. Thus, each taboo word appeared once in each list, paired with a word of a particular frequency. The five taboo words in any one list were paired with five words, one from each of the different frequency classes, and different matching words were used for each list (see Table 4b). The pairings were chosen using a Latin square, in which rows represent taboo words, columns order of occurrence and letters frequencies. The remaining 15 pairs of words in each list were also chosen from the same five frequency classes but different frequencies were represented in each word-pair. To assess whether the taboo words were perceived less often than others, the frequency of hearing taboo words in a list was counted for each subject as well as the frequency of hearing neutral words. The ratio of taboo to neutral words was multiplied by seven (since there are seven times as many neutral as taboo words) and this number was the subject's 'defence' score. If the number is less than one, it means that he tends to defend, or not hear the taboo words; if it is greater than one, it means the opposite. A value of one, of course, means that taboo words are heard just as frequently as others. For List 1, the mean score for 61 subjects was 0·88, and on a t-test this differs significantly from a value of 1 ($t = 2·2$, $p < 0·025$ on a one-tailed test). The mean score for introverts in this sample was not significantly different from the mean score for extraverts and since the difference was in the opposite direction to that predicted by Inglis (the introverts tending to defend slightly less than the extraverts) this experiment lends no support to his hypothesis. This statement must be qualified, however (see Experiment 5 below).

The results for the remaining four lists are essentially similar to those for List 1, the taboo words still being 'defended' against, even though they had been heard several times. In some cases there was clear misapprehension of the taboo word over several lists, such as hearing 'Regina' for 'vagina' (a hardly surprising mistake for Canadians) and 'poor' for 'whore'. This last was the least often perceived of the taboo words, no doubt because it is a word of only one syllable. It could be argued that the taboo words were not heard simply because they are less frequent than the neutral ones. No direct refutation of this suggestion is at present possible, since the frequency of the taboo words is not known. However, separate analyses of the frequency of perceiving taboo words and of perceiving the non-taboo words paired with them, indicated that the taboo words behave rather as if they were all in the same (low) frequency class.

A rather crude analysis of variance of the total number of times each taboo word was heard against other words, one from each of the five frequency classes, yields a 5×5 design, with one reading per cell. Differences in perceivability between taboo words were highly significant ($p < 0·01$) but effects of the competing word were not. That is to say, the response on the taboo word was essentially the same, no matter what the frequency of the competing word.

On the other hand, analysis of the non-taboo words in the five frequency classes by the same method indicated that there were no significant differences between competing (taboo) words in their effects on the non-taboo words and the effect of the frequency of the non-taboo words on their own perceivability was in the same direction as was found in Experiment 1, although here the effect was not reliable (F = 2·2, 4 and 16 df).

If the 'defence' effect demonstrated in Experiment 4 is purely a frequency effect, it indicates that the frequency of taboo words is low and that it is somewhere between 1 in 10^6 and 1 in $2·5 \times 10^7$, since the proportion of taboo words heard falls between the proportions for these two frequency classes. This point is not too well established, however, (a) because one does not know whether there is some residual 'defence' effect as well as a frequency effect and (b) because Experiment 1 only demonstrated an even response for the *more frequent* class, against competing words of a lower frequency.

Since word frequency, response bias and similar factors have been invoked to explain away perceptual defence (and indeed the result of Experiment 4 looks as if it may well be due to frequency alone) it is desirable to try to measure *changes* in 'defence' behaviour within individuals, a procedure which at least rules out some of the alternative explanations, should an effect be produced.

EXPERIMENT 5

It was stated above that no support for Inglis' hypothesis was obtained in Experiment 5, whereas, in fact, Inglis predicted that introverts would defend more than extraverts under low stress but the reverse would be true under high stress (Ref. 11). It could be argued that the experimental arrangements represented a situation of high stress for the subjects, so that the hypothesis may still hold good. To test this possibility, an attempt was made to manipulate the level of stress, to see what effect it might have on responses of introverts and extraverts respectively. Since the defence effect has been shown to be quite small (Experiment 4), a design was used in which changes in defence under different stress conditions were examined within individuals. Clearly if one attempts to increase stress for a subject in the experimental situation it is unlikely that, for the same subject, the stress level can subsequently be reduced in that situation. Hence, a design in which the only order of treatments is from low stress to high stress is required. An appropriate design has been devised by Cox and is described by Maxwell (Ref. 16); this involves four subjects per experimental group. The design is shown in Tables 6a and 6b, together with six experimental groups chosen from the summer school students who had answered the Maudsley Personality Inventory. The reason for picking these six groups (none of these subjects had taken part in Experiment 4) will become clear from inspection of Fig. 24, which shows Inglis' hypothesized relation between introversion-

TABLE 6A

COX'S DESIGN FOR EXPERIMENT 5

	First condition	Second condition
S_1	Not anxious	Not anxious
S_2	Not anxious	Anxious
S_3	Not anxious	Anxious
S_4	Anxious	Anxious

Each subject is tested under the two conditions shown. A special form of analysis of covariance allows one to estimate the 'treatment' (change from Not anxious to Anxious) effect independently of an overall change in scores between first and second testings.

TABLE 6B

GROUPS OF SUBJECTS FOR EXPERIMENT 5

	Description	
Group	N score	E score
NE	High	High
SE	Normal	High
S	Normal	Normal
NS	High	Normal
SI	Normal	Low
NI	High	Low

Each group consists of four persons.

extraversion and neuroticism, level of stress and degree of perceptual defence. The prediction can be made that there will be a change to less defence amongst introverts subjected to high stress, but a change to more defence amongst extraverts, the changes being most extreme for those who also have high N scores. Four of the five lists containing taboo words were used with each experimental group and since the four lists for any experimental group were presented in an order determined by arranging the lists in a 4×4 Latin square (with rows representing subjects, columns order of testing), no differences in defence scores can be atttributed to differences between lists. Also, the argument about possible effects of word frequency becomes irrelevant, since the only measure of interest is the *change* in degree of perceptual defence with changing stress.

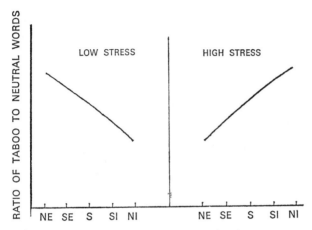

Figure 24. The relation between perceivability of taboo words, introversion-extraversion, and level of stress, according to the theory of Inglis. (N=neurotic, S=stable, E=extravert, I=introvert).

Unfortunately not all of the volunteers for this experiment turned up, so that only five of the projected seven groups of four (six shown in Table 6b and one replication of group S) could be completed, since most possible replacements had already been used in Experiment 4.

With volunteer subjects of the type available, it is not possible to induce high stress in too unpleasant a fashion, so the procedure adopted was as follows: under the low-stress condition the following instruction, in addition to the general instructions mentioned earlier, was read out:

'This experiment is simply to test how well these words can be heard. Don't worry if you miss some words, or if you think you may not have recognized them correctly'.

For the high-stress condition the instruction was:

'Now for these lists I would like to compare your performance with what we know about what other people hear. I will let you know when you are wrong by flashing this red light. I want you to try as hard as you can to report everything you hear correctly.'

In fact the red light was flashed at predetermined points in the different lists; none was an occasion when a taboo word had been presented.

Each subject within a group was assigned at random to one of the four orders of treatment shown in Table 6a (two lists being heard by each subject under each condition). At the end of the experimental session each subject was asked not to talk to anyone about the experiment.

TABLE 7

ANALYSIS OF PERCEPTUAL DEFENCE SCORES, EXPERIMENT 5

Group	Predicted change	Obtained change (t, estimating effect of increasing stress)	Significance level
NE	Negative	−4·56	$p<0.05$*
S	None	4·21	N.S.
S	None	1·24	N.S.
NS	None	3·47	N.S.
NI	Positive	9·31	$p<0.02$

* Each t has 2 df.

The 'treatment' effect is estimated independently of any overall change from first to second condition. Thus, although the NE group's 'defence' scores increased considerably from the first condition to the second, the two subjects' scores for whom the first and second conditions are identical (NA–NA, and A–A) increased significantly more than the scores of the two subjects for whom there was a change in condition (NA–A).

The results of this experiment are shown in Table 7 and Fig. 24. The analysis of the Cox design estimates the treatment effect (low-stress to high stress) independently of treatment order over the four subjects in each group. Originally, simply the numbers of taboo words heard under each condition (two lists per condition) were analysed and no significant changes demonstrated. However, it was also noticed that the total number of words perceived tended to fluctuate with the changing stress level (Fig. 25), so the results were reanalysed, using the proportion of taboo to neutral words as before (Experiment 4). It is these results that are shown in Table 7 and they confirm the hypothesis Inglis quite clearly, although the actual changes in proportions were small. It is unfortunate that the high E and high I groups with normal N scores were

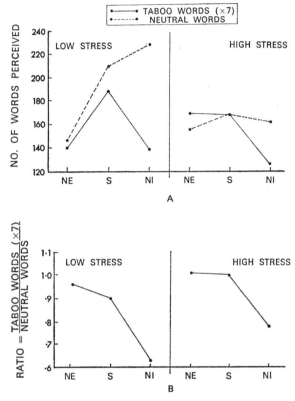

Figure 25. A: Numbers of taboo and neutral words perceived under different levels of stress. B: the same data expressed as ratios.

incomplete and hence no analysis for these groups is possible, but it seems reasonable to suppose that the changes in perceptual defence demonstrated are associated with E scores rather than with N scores, since the effects are opposite to one another for scores at the two ends of the E-score continuum. This interpretation is also supported by the finding that the high N, normal E scores did not show a significant change in defence with changed level of stress.

DISCUSSION

The findings here reported demonstrate unequivocally the importance of frequency, meaningfulness and emotional tone as factors in the perceivability of pairs of words presented dichotically. They throw no particular light on what the sensory storage and/or filtering system may be that mediates hearing under the given conditions, except to suggest (a) that it is a system sensitive to more variables than mere 'information content' as this is defined technically and (b) that, if the system is one of limited capacity, there is surprisingly little interaction between the two ears, in the sense that detection on the 'more frequent' ear in Experiment 1 seemed to be unaffected by the detectability of words on the 'less frequent' ear.

The results of Experiments 1–4 are not really surprising in view of earlier work on the importance of word frequency, meaningfulness and emotional tone in perception and verbal learning. Indeed, it could be argued that the effects shown are not different from already known monaural effects. The confirmation of an hypothesized difference in perceptual defence for introverts and extraverts under different levels of stress is perhaps more striking, especially as a number of attempts to correlate behavioural factors with E scores on the Maudsley Personality Inventory have been unsuccessful, or have not demonstrated the relations postulated by Eysenck (Refs. 4, 9, 17 & 31). It may be noted that the result was obtained in this instance with what can probably be regarded as quite a small change in level of stress and with subjects who were not extreme types in the sense of displaying clinical symptoms, for example, of hysteria or dysthymia. (At least such symptoms were not detected at the time of testing.) It would seem worthwhile to extend the same investigations to some clinically defined groups, as well as to extreme scorers on the Maudsley Personality Inventory E scale who have normal N scores. If Inglis' theory about perceptual defence was found to be generally confirmed in such studies, this would add to our understanding of these personality dimensions, as well as to our understanding of the process of perceptual defence itself.

Since the experiments here reported were performed, an extensive review of work on perceptual defence has been published (Ref. 5). Brown attempts to reconcile various apparently contradictory findings on the basis of a curvilinear relation between degree of perceptual defence (more precisely, thresholds for emotionally toned words) and degree of emotionality of the words, namely that the threshold rises for increasing emotionality up to a certain point, but then descends until 'perceptual vigilance' occurs. He hypothesizes that the point of 'maximum defence' will be at a higher level of emotionality for extraverts than for introverts.

The suggested relations (for which some empirical evidence has been obtained by Brown) are shown in Fig. 26. At first sight, these relations seem to be different from those suggested by Inglis. However, if we make the assumption that changing the level of stress has approximately the same effect as increasing the level of emotionality of words (and in terms of 'arousal' (Ref. 10) this seems a reasonable assumption to make) we see that Inglis' hypothetical relations would coincide with the central part of Brown's curves, where the two cross. This is demonstrated in Fig. 27, where Inglis' relation is presented in the same form as Brown's. Further confirmation for this idea comes from Experiment 3, where it was found (although the finding was not quite statistically reliable) that extraverts tended to hear more 'bad' words than did introverts, whereas in other cases (e.g., Ref. 8) the reverse has been found. These findings are consonant with the probability that the words used in Experiment 3 fall at the low end of the emotionality continuum (Fig. 26).

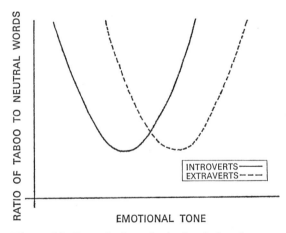

Figure 26. Brown's hypothesized relation between perceivability of words of different degrees of emotionality and personality characteristics.

In conclusion, it may be noted that the design used in Experiment 5 allows one to draw conclusions about changes in perceptual defence which are not open to many of the objections concerning such things as response hierarchies, word frequencies, response sets and the like, which have been raised against many of the conclusions drawn from other experiments on perceptual defence, since the changes are demon-

L

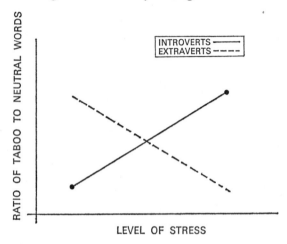

Figure 27. Inglis' relation expressed in the same form
as Brown's relation in Figure 26.

strated within individuals. To the writer it seems that this type of
design, and related ones, are likely to command increasing attention as a
useful means of unravelling the problems, both theoretical and practical,
in the understanding of perceptual defence.

REFERENCES

1. BROADBENT, D. E., Successive responses to simultaneous stimuli.
   Quart. J. exp. Psychol., **8,** 145–152, 1956.
2. ——, *Perception and Communication.* Oxford: Pergamon Press,
   1958.
3. —— & GREGORY, MARGARET, On the recall of stimuli presented
   alternately to two sense-organs. *Quart. J. exp. Psychol.*, **13,**
   103–109, 1961.
4. BRONZAFT, A., HAYES, R., WELCH, L. & KOLTUV, M., Relationship
   between PGR and measures of extraversion, ascendance and
   neuroticism. *J. Psychol.*, **50,** 193–195, 1960.
5. BROWN, W. P., Conceptions of perceptual defence. *Brit. J. Psychol.,
   Monogr. Supplement*, No. 35, 1961.
6. CHERRY, E. C., Experiments on the recognition of speech with one
   or two ears. *J. Acoust. Soc. Amer.*, **25,** 975–979, 1953.

7. DAVIS, J. M., Personality, perceptual defence and stereoscopic perception. *J. abnorm. soc. Psychol.*, **58**, 398–402, 1959.
8. ERIKSEN, C. W., Psychological defences and 'ego strength' in the recall of completed and incompleted tasks. *J. abnorm. soc. Psychol.*, **49**, 45–50, 1954.
9. HAMILTON, V., Theories of anxiety and hysteria—a rejoinder to Hans Eysenck. *Brit. J. Psychol.*, **50**, 276–280, 1959.
10. HEBB, D. O., Drives and the C.N.S. (conceptual nervous system). *Psychol. Rev.*, **62**, 259–274, 1955.
11. INGLIS, J., Abnormalities of motivation and 'ego functions'. In *Handbook of Abnormal Psychology* (ed. H. J. Eysenck). London: Pitman, 1960.
12. —— & SANDERSON, R. E., Successive responses to simultaneous stimulation in elderly patients with memory disorder. *J. abnorm. soc. Psychol.*, **62**, 709–712, 1961.
13. JENKINS, J. J., RUSSELL, W. A. & SUCI, G. J., An atlas of semantic profiles of 360 words. *Amer. J. Psychol.*, **71**, 688–699, 1958.
14. JOHNSON, R. C., FRINCKE, G. & MARTIN, L., Meaningfulness, frequency and affective character of words as related to visual duration threshold. *Can. J. Psychol.*, 199–204, 1961.
15. KIMURA, DOREEN, Some effects of temporal-lobe damage on auditory perception. *Can. J. Psychol.*, **15**, 156–165, 1961.
16. MAXWELL, A. E., *Experimental Design in Psychology and the Medical Sciences*. London: Methuen, 1958.
17. MCDONELL, C. & INGLIS, J., Verbal conditioning and personality. *Psychol. Rep.*, **10**, 374, 1962.
18. MILLER, G. A., The magical number seven, plus or minus two: some limits on our capacity for processing information. *Psychol. Rev.*, **63**, 81–97, 1956.
19. MORAY, N., Attention in dichotic listening: affective cues and the influence of instructions. *Quart. J. exp. Psychol.*, **4**, 56–60, 1959.
20. ——, Broadbent's filter theory: postulate H and the problem of switching time. *Quart. J. exp. Psychol.*, **12**, 214–220, 1960.
21. NOBLE, C. E., The role of stimulus meaning (m) in serial verbal learning. *J. exp. Psychol.*, **43**, 437–446, 1952.
22. NEWBIGGING, P. L., The perceptual redintegration of frequent and infrequent words. *Can. J. Psychol.*, **15**, 123–132, 1961.
23. ——, The perceptual redintegration of words which differ in connotative meaning. *Can. J. Psychol.*, **15**, 133–142, 1961.

308   *Bearings on Basic Psychological Processes*

24. Osgood, C. E., Suci, G. J. & Tannenbaum, P. H., *The Measurement of Meaning*. Urbana, Ill.: University of Illinois Press, 1957.
25. Postman, L. J., Bronson, Wander C. & Gropper, G. L., Is there a mechanism of perceptual defence? *J. abnorm. soc. Psychol.*, **48**, 215–224, 1953.
26. Rolph, C. H., *The Trial of Lady Chatterley*. London: Penguin Books, 1961.
27. Savin, H. B., Word-frequency effect and errors in the perception of speech. *J. Accoust. Soc. Amer.*, **35**, 200–206, 1963.
28. Treisman, A. M., Contextual cues in selective listening. *Quart. J. Exper. Psychol.*, **12**, 242–248, 1960.
29. Underwood, B. J., Verbal learning and the educative process. *Harvard educ. Rev.*, **29**, 107–117, 1959.
30. Van de Castle, R. L., Perceptual defense in a binocular rivalry situation. *J. Pers.*, **28**, 448–462, 1960.
31. Willett, R., Measures of learning and conditioning. In *Experiments in Personality* (ed. H. J. Eysenck). London: Routledge & Kegan Paul, 1960.

35

Field Dependence and the Maudsley Personality Inventory[1]

FREDERICK J. EVANS

First published in *Perceptual and Motor Skills*, **24**, 526, 1967

THIS report describes the relation of the cognitive style of field dependence (FD)—field independence (psychological differentiation) to the Maudsley Personality Inventory (MPI) dimensions of neuroticism (N) and extraversion (E). There have been few attempts to relate this cognitive dimension (Ref. 5) to the standard paper-and-pencil psychological inventories. Bound found no relationship between objective test measures of N and the embedded figures test (EFT) (Ref. 2). Franks found no relationship between FD (rod-and-frame test) and either N or E (Ref. 3). From a consideration of the face validity of the MPI scales and from the concept of global versus analytical modes of behaviour underlying FD, a positive correlation was predicted between FD and E but no significant relationship between FD and N.

The MPI (Ref. 4), an 8-item form of the EFT (Ref. 1) and the draw-a-person (DAP) test were administered to 59 college undergraduates (40 males).[2] Standardized scores for DAP (scored according to instructions found in Witkin, *et al.* (Ref. 5)) and EFT were summed to produce an index of FD.[3]

Pearson correlations between MPI:E and the three measures of FD were: EFT = 0·39 (p<0·005); DAP = 0·21 (p<0·05); EFT+DAP = 0·39 (p<0·005). Correlations between MPI:N and measures of FD were insignificant: EFT = −0·12; DAP = 0·08; EFT+DAP = 0·11.[4] As predicted, there is some relation between field dependence and extraversion.

---

[1] This research was supported in part by Contract No. Nonr–4731 (00) from the Office of Naval Research.

[2] Sex differences were not found for the MPI and FD variables.

[3] A high score on the measures of FD indicates field dependence. Significance levels reported are one-tailed.

[4] The correlations between the MPI Lie Scale and FD were insignificant (EFT = 0·06; DAP = −0·02; EFT+DPA = 0·03).

REFERENCES

1. BIERI, J. & MESSERLEY, S., Differences in perceptual and cognitive behaviour as a function of experience type. *J. consult. Psychol.*, **21,** 217–221, 1957.
2. BOUND, M. M., A Study of the Relationship Between Witkin's Indices of Field Dependency and Eysenck's Indices of Neuroticism. Unpublished doctoral dissertation, Purdue University Library, 1957.
3. FRANKS, C. M., Differences determinées par la personnalité dans la perception visuelle de la verticalité. *Rev. Psychol. appl.*, **6,** 235–246, 1956.
4. EYSENCK, H. J., *Manual of the Maudsley Personality Inventory.* London: University of London Press, 1959.
5. WITKIN, H. A., DYK, R. B., FATHERSON, H. F., GOODENOUGH, D. R. & KARP, S. A., *Psychological Differentiation.* New York: Wiley & Sons, 1962.

36

Relationship between Sharpening and Extraversion

D. W. FORREST

First published in *Psychological Reports*, **13**, 564, 1963

DURING the course of a recent investigation (Ref. 2) Ss were asked to remember a series of 10 drawings depicting 'stick men' engaged in various activities representative of certain of the needs in Murray's system. It was noticed, *en passant*, that the ways in which Ss described these drawings in their efforts at recall seemed to be related to a personality characteristic which might be termed 'social extraversion'. Those Ss who were lively and sociable in the testing situation appeared to exaggerate their descriptions of the activities portrayed in the drawings, e.g., in recalling a drawing designed to represent n Aggression, which was usually described as 'Two men fighting a duel', such Ss might say, 'One man running his sword through and killing his opponent'. This type of exaggeration in which the activity is expressed in a stronger or more violent form than usual resembles the 'sharpening' found by Allport & Postman (Ref. 1) in their study of rumour and we followed their usage in terming such descriptions 'sharpened'.

The object of the present experiment was to put this incidental observation to a more exact test by noting the number of sharpened descriptions given to the recalled pictures by a group of 40 Ss drawn from the same population of British undergraduate women and by subsequently obtaining their extraversion (E) scores from the Maudsley Personality Inventory (MPI).

Ss were classified as 'extreme sharpeners' if they gave four or more sharpened responses out of the 10 possible, while those who gave none were termed 'levellers'. This procedure led to 12 Ss falling in each of these categories, the remaining 16 Ss with 1, 2 or 3 sharpened responses being termed 'average sharpeners'.

The extreme sharpeners had a mean E score of 33·1; the average sharpeners, 31·3; and the levellers, 18·9. An analysis of variance gives an F of 20 (p < 0·05) and t tests run between the three pairs of means reveal that the levellers differ significantly from both groups of sharpeners at

$p < 0.001$, there being no significant difference between the extreme and average sharpeners.

Thus the original observation seems to have been supported: those who gave sharpened descriptions of these pictures in a recall situation were more extraverted than those who were unable or unwilling to provide such redundancy. Such a finding needs to be further generalized before any definite rationale can be offered. It is tentatively suggested that the extraverts' tendency to sharpen is an aspect of their greater verbal fluency in a test situation (cf. Ref. 3).

REFERENCES

1. ALLPORT, G. W. & POSTMAN, L., *The Psychology of Rumour*. New York: Holt, 1947.
2. FORREST, D. W. & LEE, S. G., Sensitization and defense in perception and recall. *Psychol. Monogr.*, **76,** No. 4 (Whole No. 523), 1962.
3. FOULDS, G. A., A method of scoring the TAT applied to psycho-neurotics. *J. ment. Sci.*, **99,** 235–246, 1953.

37

Introversion-Extraversion Differences in
Judgments of Time

R. LYNN

First published in
Journal of Abnormal and Social Psychology, **63,** 457–458, 1961

INTRODUCTION

AN attempt has been made by Claridge to apply Eysenck's theory of introversion-extraversion (Ref. 1) to the problem of time errors (Ref. 2). The time error is a constant error that occurs in psychophysical judgments and consists of systematic overestimation (negative time errors) or underestimation (positive time errors) of the second of two identical stimuli. The hypothesis advanced by Claridge is as follows: the first stimulus produces both excitatory and inhibitory effects, the inhibitory effects reducing its perceived intensity or duration. This hypothesis accounts for the preponderance of negative time errors that most investigators have reported. When this hypothesis is taken in conjunction with Eysenck's postulate that extraverts generate reactive inhibition more quickly and dissipate it more slowly than introverts, it also follows that extraverts should show larger negative time errors than introverts. Claridge verified this hypothesis using judgments of intensity of sound and duration of time. A tendency for hysterics (extraverted neurotics) to show greater negative time errors than dysthymics (introverted neurotics) in judgments of time intervals has also been reported by Eysenck (Ref. 4).

Llewellyn-Thomas has published a new procedure for obtaining time judgments designed to maximize individual differences (Ref. 5). This procedure involves the use of a positive feed-back technique in which the subject is required to make a judgment of a standard and is then presented with his judgment as his new standard and so on over a number of trials. Any tendency to error becomes cumulative with this method. The present paper reports the results of an investigation designed to examine introversion-extraversion differences in estimations of time using the Llewellyn-Thomas technique.

METHOD

The subjects were two groups of 20 introverted and 20 extraverted male university students. Introversion-extraversion was assessed by the Maudsley Personality Inventory (Ref. 3). The introverts scored between 6–18 on this scale and the extraverts between 29–44.

The procedure follows that of Llewellyn-Thomas. The apparatus consisted of a light that could be switched on with two keys, one of which was held by the experimenter and the other by the subject. The experimenter told the subject that he would switch on the light for a brief interval and following this the subject should switch on the light and attempt to keep it on for the same interval of time. The subject was told that there would be a number of trials which might differ in length and he was asked not to count or use any other aids to time estimation. The first standard was 15 seconds and there were nine further trials in which the subject was successively given his last judgment as his new standard. The interval between trials was approximately 5 seconds.

TABLE 1

MEAN TIME ESTIMATIONS OF INTROVERT AND EXTRAVERT GROUPS USING THE LLEWELLYN-THOMAS POSITIVE FEEDBACK TECHNIQUE

	Trials									
	1	2	3	4	5	6	7	8	9	10
Introverts										
M	15·2	14·5	14·2	12·7	12·3	13·9	15·5	17·7	17·5	18·4
SD	4·2	2·6	6·3	4·1	6·5	6·3	7·6	7·0	9·4	11·4
Extraverts										
M	15·4	15·0	13·5	13·0	12·5	11·8	11·6	11·3	10·4	10·2
SD	5·3	4·5	5·1	7·3	7·3	8·7	8·7	8·9	8·7	9·6
Value of t	*ns*	*ns*	*ns*	*ns*	*ns*	*ns*	*ns*	2·46*	2·21*	2·40*

* Significant at the 0·05 level.

RESULTS

The results are given in Table 1. It will be noted that there are no differences between introverts and extraverts on the first five trials, but that differences in the direction predicted by Eysenck's theory emerge from Trial 6 and become statistically significant at the 0·05 level on the last three trials. The results do not replicate the findings of Claridge and

Eysenck exactly, since they found significant introversion-extraversion differences on a single trial. It is not easy to account for this discrepancy, since the procedures used appear to have been the same. Nevertheless, the hypothesis that introversion-extraversion differences in time judgments do exist receives some support from the present experiment. Further, Eysenck's theory that these introversion-extraversion differences reflect differences in the generation of reactive inhibition entails the prediction that the differences would become greater as the trials proceed, since reactive inhibition would not dissipate fully in the intertrial interval; and it is evident from inspection of the table that this also occurred.

REFERENCES

1. CLARIDGE, G. S., The excitation-inhibition balance in neurotics. In *Experiments in Personality* (ed. H. J. Eysenck). London: Routledge & Kegan Paul, 1960.
2. EYSENCK, H. J., *The Dynamics of Anxiety and Hysteria*. London: Routledge & Kegan Paul, 1957.
3. ——, *The Maudsley Personality Inventory*. London: University of London Press, 1959.
4. ——, Personality and the estimation of time. *Percept. mot. Skills*, **9**, 405–406, 1959.
5. LLEWELLYN-THOMAS, E., Successive time estimation during automatic positive feedback. *Percept. mot. Skills*, **9**, 219–224, 1959.

38

Personality Factors and Preference Judgements

H. J. EYSENCK

First published in *Nature*, **148**, 346, 1941

INTRODUCTION

IN a previous paper, certain correlations were reported between the temperamental characteristics of a number of observers and their scores on a test of aesthetic appreciation, the K test (Ref. 2). As these correlations were based on a comparatively small number of cases and as the temperament test used was not quite in line with recent developments, the experiment was repeated with certain modifications.

METHOD

The form of the K test used consisted of 15 pairs of pictures (12 pairs of landscapes and 3 pairs of portraits) chosen in such a way that the two pictures forming each pair dealt with much the same subject but in two different ways. One treated the subject in the modern, colourful way associated with Cezanne, van Gogh and Modigliani, the other in the more academic manner of Hobbema, Constable and Wilson. The test is scored in terms of preference for the modern school.

The Nebraska Personality Inventory was used in this investigation. This test was constructed by Guilford on the basis of his work on personality factors S, E and M (Ref. 3). For reasons which will become apparent later, it was decided not to use Guilford's scoring key, but rather to derive a scoring key from a reanalysis of the original correlations on which Guilford's personality factors are based. (I am very much indebted to Prof. Guilford for his kindness in sending me his original data and other material, without which such an analysis would not have been possible).

The observers taking part were university students, W.E.A. students and 'middle-class' people unconnected with academic life. Their ages ranged from seventeen to around fifty; sexes were distributed roughly equally. (I want to record my gratitude to Dr P. E. Vernon, who very kindly gave the tests to a number of Scottish students.)

RESULTS

Most modern workers seem to regard some such general dichotomy as introversion-extraversion as definitely established in the temperamental field. Guilford's analyses, which revealed no trace of such a general factor, were therefore received with some surprise. It would appear that the explanation of the absence of a general factor of this kind lies in the method of analysis he adopted; by using Thurstone's principle of rotation even a very strong general factor is invariably obliterated. In fact, the situation seems to be exactly parallel to that which prevails in the analysis of cognitive tests, where also the existence of a general factor is disputed by the adherents of Prof. Thurstone.

In the field of cognition it has been shown that the use of Prof. Burt's group-factor method makes it possible to arrive at a compromise between the claims of the 'general factorists' and the 'group factorists' (Ref. 1); this method enables us to assess quantitatively the relative importance of these various factors. It appeared reasonable to expect that an application of this method to the data collected by Guilford would lead to a similar compromise between those who claimed to have proved the existence of a general factor of introversion-extraversion and those who favoured analysis into group-factors only. When an analysis by means of Burt's formula was carried out, a comparatively strong general factor appeared which accounted for 9·5 per cent of the variance and could easily be identified with introversion-extraversion; in addition, three group factors were extracted which accounted for 3·9, 6·4 and 3·5 per cent of the variance respectively. These group factors resembled closely Guilford's personality factors S, E and M.

(A similar result appeared when another research of Guilford's was reanalysed (Ref. 4). Here, because of a great deal of overlap, Burt's group-factor method did not seem applicable and his general-factor method was used. A general introversion-extraversion factor was found to account for 14·8 per cent of the variance, while two other factors accounted for 8·7 per cent and 5·5 per cent respectively. The first of these factors opposed traits characteristic of *depression* and of what Guilford calls *rhathymia*; the second factor opposed traits concerned with *thinking* and traits concerned with *feeling*.)

The correlation between the *K* test and extraversion, as tested by those items in the Nebraska Inventory for which scores could be derived from our analysis, was highly significant, being more than five times its probable error. For fifty observers it was 0·43±0·08. This confirms the results reported earlier.

Only one of the correlations between the K test and the three group factors S, E and M even approaches significance (according to Fisher's test of significance for small samples, a correlation of 0·27 would be significant). These correlations are: K and S = −0·26, K and E = −0·05, and K and M = 0·08.

The observers were asked whether they were conservative or radical politically; it was found that radicalism correlated with the K test to the extent of 0·34±0·08, which is definitely significant and also supports a previous finding (Ref. 2).

One further point may be worth noting. Dr P. E. Vernon, who had quite independently found evidence for a factor of the kind described earlier (Ref. 2), found that those observers who had 'good taste' in painting tended to prefer the modern works, while the others tended to prefer the older artists. The observers in this experiment were asked if they were very much interested in art, or not at all interested in art. The average scores of these three groups in the K test were respectively 8·8, 5·9 and 4·0, thus indicating that those who were very much interested in art tended to prefer modern art and that lesser degrees of interest in art were accompanied by less liking for modern art. It cannot be maintained, of course, that those who say that they are very much interested in art are *eo ipso* those who have good taste, but so far as we can deduce anything at all from these results, they would seem to bear out Dr Vernon's observation.

CONCLUSIONS

It has been confirmed that the K test correlates positively with extraversion and with radicalism. No significant correlations were found with personality factors S, E or M, although a negative correlation with S approached significance. Preference for modern art tended to be associated with general interest in art.

REFERENCES

1. EYSENCK, H. J., *Brit. J. educ. Psychol.*, **9,** 270, 1939.
2. ——, *Brit. J. Psychol.*, **31,** 262, 1941.
3. GUILFORD, J. P. & GUILFORD, R. B., *J. Psychol.*, **2,** 109, 1936.
4. —— & ——, *J. abnorm. soc. Psychol.*, **34,** 21–36, 1939.

39

Introversion and the Arousal Jag

R. LYNN & J. BUTLER

First published by
British Journal of Social and Clinical Psychology, **1,** 150–151, 1962

THE present note reports two tests of Berlyne's theory of the 'arousal jag' (Ref. 1), taken in conjunction with Eysenck's theory of individual differences. Berlyne's theory postulates that small increases in arousal—'arousal jags'—are pleasurable, but large increases unpleasant and hence avoided. Among the wide range of phenomena to which he applies this theory are gambling and looking at paintings, the explanation of these activities being that they provide arousal jags. Berlyne has himself made explicit the implications of his theory for individual differences in the size of arousal jags different individuals will seek. His theory assumes that different determinants of arousal summate, so that individuals who are characterized by chronic high levels of arousal, or in whom arousal is quickly mobilized, will be inclined to seek less violent arousal jags than those in whom arousal is low or mobilized slowly. The reason for this is that individuals with high levels of arousal are nearer to the critical point at which arousal becomes unpleasantly high and hence will be comparatively less able to tolerate increases in arousal. If we follow Claridge and assume that introverts have higher levels of arousal than extraverts (Ref. 2), it becomes possible to make a number of predictions.

Our first test of this theory was concerned with individual differences in gambling. Berlyne's theory of gambling is as follows. Gambling causes anxiety and a rise in arousal—'an arousal jag'—and hence is pleasurable as long as the anxiety is not too great. It is reasonable to assume that the size of arousal jag provided by gambling is related to the size of the sum of money involved, large sums of money causing more anxiety and larger arousal jags. Our prediction is therefore that individuals who score high on introversion are less able to tolerate large arousal jags and hence will be less inclined to gamble large sums of money.

This prediction was tested in the following way. One hundred and eighteen students were used as subjects for the experiment. Neuroticism and introversion-extraversion were measured with the Maudsley Personality Inventory. Inclinations for gambling were assessed by giving subjects the following instructions:

> 'Imagine that you have £100 and that the necessities of life are cared for by a weekly income. Someone now makes you an offer to gamble with your £100. The terms are that whatever sum you put forward will be covered by an equal amount, a coin will then be spun and either you lose your money, or you double it. You have only one chance. Now please write down on a piece of paper how much you would gamble in response to this offer.'

Those subjects who refused to gamble were then asked to state whether this was because they disliked risk taking or because they had moral objections to gambling. Six subjects stated that they had moral objections to gambling and these were eliminated in the calculation of the results. (These subjects scored somewhat higher than average on neuroticism and introversion and if they had been included the correlations would have been higher.) There was a positive and statistically significant product moment correlation between the sum gambled and extraversion ($r = +0.27$, $p = <0.05$) (however, it might possibly be argued that this result would be predicted on the basis of introversion-extraversion differences in socialization). There was also a negative and statistically significant correlation between neuroticism and the amount gambled ($r = -0.19$, $p<0.5$). This result suggests that individuals who score high on neuroticism may be high on arousal, a hypothesis which is in line with the greater sympathetic reactivity of neurotics.

The second experiment concerned individual differences in aesthetic preferences. Berlyne's theory of aesthetic preferences makes use of a simplicity-complexity dimension in preferences for visual forms which various investigators have identified (e.g., Ref. 3). Since there is evidence that complex figures induce more arousal than simpler ones, Berlyne argues that individuals who like large arousal jags will tend to prefer the more complex pictures. If our initial hypothesis is correct, it follows that individuals who score highly on introversion should prefer simple pictures to complex ones.

There is already some evidence available on this point. Eysenck (Ref. 3) reported a correlation between a preference for simple paintings in bright colours and extraversion and again a preference for simple bright paintings by neurotic extraverts (Ref. 4). It should be noted that these findings are in the opposite direction from those demanded by our extension of Berlyne's theory. In view of these puzzling findings we decided to repeat Eysenck's investigation using a more recent and reliable measure of introversion-extraversion (Eysenck's measure of extraversion was an early questionnaire devised by Heidbreder.) Accordingly, Eysenck's K test and the MPI were given to 40 female students. The product moment correlation between introversion and score on the K test was <0.46 ($p < 0.05$), i.e., subjects scoring introverted tended to prefer the less bright and more complex paintings; the correlation between neuroticism and the K test was $+0.12$, which is not statistically significant. These results therefore replicate and support Eysenck's earlier work and confirm that the relationship is an embarrassment to Berlyne's theory as it is formulated at present.

In considering ways of salvaging the theory, it should be observed that Eysenck himself regarded his K test as a measure of colour preferences (Refs. 3 and 4) and not, as Berlyne interprets it, a measure of preferences for simplicity or complexity. If we accept Eysenck's interpretation of his test, then it would be expected that extraverts would prefer the bright paintings and introverts the subdued ones since bright colours give greater arousal jags. This is in fact the direction in which the correlation lies, so that the theory can be salvaged by accepting Eysenck's interpretation of the K test as a measure of preferences for colour brightness. It is hoped that the findings will appear sufficiently promising to stimulate further interest in the possibility of an integration of the concepts of arousal and personality theory.

REFERENCES

1. BERLYNE, D. E., *Conflict, Arousal and Curiosity*. New York: McGraw-Hill, 1960.
2. CLARIDGE, G. S., Arousal and inhibition as determinants of the performance of neurotics. *Brit. J. Psychol.*, **52,** 53–63, 1961.
3. EYSENCK, H. J., Type-factors in aesthetic appreciation. *Brit. J. Psychol.*, **31,** 262–270, 1941.
4. ——, *Dimensions of Personality*. London: Routledge & Kegan Paul, 1947.

40

Personality and Extra-Sensory Perception[1]

H. J. EYSENCK

First published in
Journal of the Society for Psychical Research, **44**, 55–71, 1967

AMONG the phenomena characteristic of ESP is considerable individual variability; some well-known individuals have possessed remarkable ability in this respect, at least for certain periods of time, while others have none, or may tend to give significantly negative results, i.e., deviate from chance in a negative direction. Individual differences form the subject matter of personality study and a number of attempts have been made to correlate extra-sensory ability with various personality traits. Rao has summarized these studies by saying that they

'provide little convincing rationale for a basis of understanding the nature of psi in its relation to human personality . . . there is no intrinsic reason why personality differences should help or hinder psi if it is like other abilities such as perception or memory' (Ref. 33).

It is the purpose of this article to advocate a rather more optimistic view and to argue that our knowledge of personality and of psi permits us to put forward certain hypotheses which can be subjected to experimental test and which in fact have already found some tentative support in past research.

Consider first of all certain points about psi which are widely accepted, even though definitive support has not yet been forthcoming. In the first place, it is often argued that psi is a very ancient and primitive form of perception, possibly antedating cortical developments in the course of evolution. This would lead one to the deduction that cortical arousal might be an actual disadvantage in relation to psi, which might be more easily discovered in a state of relaxation or cortical inhibition. Sinclair (Ref. 38), Thouless (Ref. 43), Gerber & Schmeidler (Ref. 14) and Rao (Ref. 31) have provided some evidence in this connection and electro-

[1] This paper is based on a lecture given to the Society for Psychical Research on 29th November, 1966.

physical studies such as those of Otani (Refs. 28 & 29) on GSR and Stanford (Ref. 40) on EEG alpha activity have furnished further support for such a thesis. The evidence is not by any means unanimous, as Rao has pointed out in his summary (Ref. 33), but on the whole tends to favour the hypothesis. If we can lend credence to this conclusion, we would have here an important clue to the nature of psi, because ordinary sensory thresholds are *raised* in relaxation and *lowered* in conditions of cortical arousal; psi behaves in an opposite direction, thus emphasizing its *extra*-sensory nature.

In the second place, psi appears to be characterized by a decline of performance over time. This decline may occur within a run, or within a specific unit of experimentation, larger than a run, or it may be chronological, i.e., extending over long periods (Ref. 33). In the third

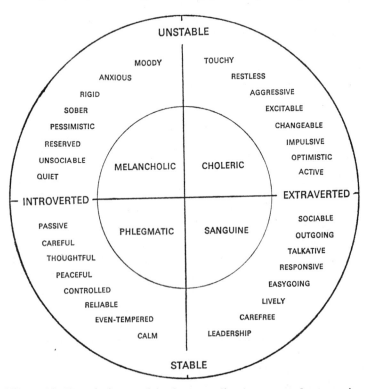

Figure 28. Descriptive model of personality in terms of two major factors: Extraversion-Introversion (N), and emotionality, instability or neuroticism (E).

place, performance may be improved by the factor of novelty; as Pratt & Woodruff have shown, when subjects shifted from working with large symbols to small ones or vice versa, there was a substantial rise in their scoring level (Ref. 30). And last, conditions of spontaneity seem to favour high scoring in ESP work as compared with less spontaneous, more rigid conditions (Ref. 34).

Keeping in mind these considerations, let us now turn to personality theory. There is considerable agreement that a large portion of those individual differences in behaviour which we subsume under the heading of 'personality' can be related to two main dimensions of personality which may be called extraversion-introversion the one and emotionality, instability or neuroticism the other (Ref. 9). Fig. 28 shows in diagrammatic form the relation between these two dimensions, as well as the traits which characterize individuals respectively high or low on either of these dimensions. Inside the circle are given the names of the 'four temperaments' which traditionally have been used to describe the four 'types' which are created by combining high extraversion and high emotionality (choleric), high introversion and high emotionality (melancholic), low extraversion and low emotionality (phlegmatic) and high extraversion and low emotionality (sanguine). Descriptively these dimensions of personality are derived from the observed intercorrelations between certain traits; Fig. 29 shows how extraversion is derived from the empirical correlations between sociability, impulsiveness, activity, liveliness and excitability.

Both extraversion and emotionality are normally distributed in the population and both are firmly based on constitutional factors. Eysenck has surveyed the evidence in considerable detail (Ref. 11) and no attempt

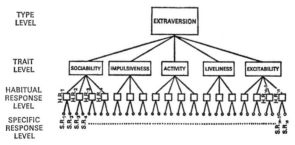

Figure 29. Diagrammatic representation of the extravert type, which has been deduced from the observed correlations between traits like sociability, impulsiveness, activity, liveliness, and excitability.

will be made here to discuss this point in any detail. It is important, however, to note that what is inherited must be structure, not function, so that we are faced with the problem of linking extraverted, or emotional, behaviour with some neurological, physiological or anatomical structure. We shall here be concerned in particular with the factor of extraversion and in this connection Eysenck has suggested the *reticular formation* (ascending reticular activity system) as the most likely source of individual differences between introverts and extraverts (Ref. 11) (Fig. 30). This structure receives collaterals from the long ascending sensory pathways which lead to cortical projection areas; its function is to produce cortical arousal through neurons relaying to the particular projection areas in question, as well as to other parts of the cortex. The link with introversion is furnished by the hypothesis that introverts

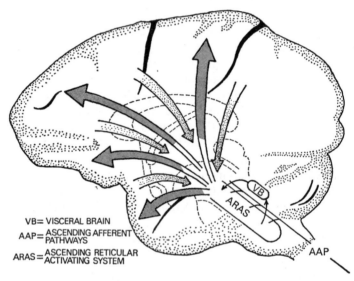

VB = VISCERAL BRAIN
AAP = ASCENDING AFFERENT PATHWAYS
ARAS = ASCENDING RETICULAR ACTIVATING SYSTEM
AAP

Figure 30. Location and function of the ascending reticular activating system. Arrows going to the different parts of the cortex symbolize cortical arousal produced by the reticular formation; arrows going from the cortex towards the reticular formation indicate reciprocal cortical influence on the ARAS.

have lower reticular formation thresholds, so that they are characterized by a higher degree of arousal. Physiological studies using the EEG have indeed shown higher degrees of arousal in introverts under resting ('idling') conditions; thus extraverts show greater alpha amplitude and lower alpha frequency, both of which are signs of low arousal, while introverts show low alpha amplitude and high alpha frequency. Much other work is reviewed in *The Biological Basis of Personality* (Ref. 11), to which the reader must be referred for further detail. Among the psychological findings which are relevant to our hypothesis are the following: (1) introverts have lower sensory thresholds; (2) extraverts are more susceptible to monotony (decline in performance); (3) extraverts respond more favourably to novel stimuli; (4) extraverts perform better under group than under individual conditions.

If we may regard it as permissible to assume (a) that conditions of high cortical arousal are unfavourable to ESP and (b) that introverts are habitually in a state of greater arousal than ambiverts and ambiverts than extraverts, then we may make the deduction that, other things being equal, extraverts should do better on psi tests than introverts. With this hypothesis in mind, we may now search the literature in order to find support or disproof.

Rao has summarized early impressions:

'Several of these outstanding subjects seem to be sociable or extraverted. Rhine's subjects were sociable. The Jones boys, according to Soal, were also extraverts; and Bo was a hyperactive extravert.'

Rao also noted that

'the artistic characteristic seems to be another fairly common feature. Rhine noted this characteristic among all his major subjects. Shackleton was an artist by profession. After leaving her academic environment, Miss S. "occupied herself with music, giving lessons and attending concerts". Miss J.K. was much interested in music and was an accomplished pianist' (Ref. 33).

This stress on the 'artistic temperament' is interesting, because in our work (unpublished) we have found that students registered in fine arts courses tend to have very high extraversion scores (as well as high N scores).[1]

Along more rigorous lines of research, Humphrey used the Bernreuter

---

[1] A similar impression of extraverted, choleric personality is given in a similar survey of Continental paragnosts published by Tenhaeff (Ref. 42); he has also given personality tests to such persons which reinforce this impression of somewhat unstable extraversion. However, the tests used in his research are entirely of a very subjective, interpretive character, and it would not be wise to accept their evidence without many qualifications.

Personality Inventory and found that extraverts scored above chance expectation, while introverts obtained below chance scores (Ref. 21). Two separate series of experiments were carried out and in both groups statistically significant results were obtained. Casper repeated Humphrey's experiment and obtained suggestive results in the same direction (Ref. 7). Black obtained a negative correlation between social introversion, as measured by the MMPI and the ESP scores of his subjects. None of these investigators used properly constructed and validated scales for the measurement of extraversion-introversion, but the measures employed would undoubtedly correlate reasonably well with such more modern devices as the MPI or the EPI (Ref. 12).

Aström used the MPI on 19 university students and 29 nursing students, each of whom was given five runs through the ESP pack of cards under group testing conditions, where each card was given a 5 second exposure to the agent. The total number of runs (240) gave 1317 hits, which is significant at beyond the $0 \cdot 001$ level of probability. There was no correlation with N, but introverts (defined as being more than 1 SD below average on the E scale) scored an average of $24 \cdot 00$ hits, while extraverts (defined as being more than 1 SD above average on the E scale) scored an average of $33 \cdot 27$ hits; the difference is statistically significant (Refs. 1 & 2). Fig. 31 shows his results in detail.

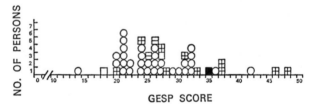

Figure 31. GESP scores of 48 subjects. Very extravert subjects are indicated by black squares, extravert subjects by squares with a cross inside. Very introverted subjects are shown by white squares, introverted subjects by a square with a horizontal line. Subjects within $\pm$ 1 SD are shown as circles. Quoted with permission from Åström (Ref. 1).

Green failed on two occasions to find any correlation between psi and extraversion or neuroticism (Refs. 16 & 17). On both occasions she used binary random series of Zener cards (star or cross), employing 108 Ss in the first study and 40 undergraduates in the second. A possible explanation of this failure may lie in the fact that overall scores on psi did not reach an extra-chance level and it seems reasonable to assume that when there is no evidence of psi in the totality of runs, then no significant correlations will be found between sub-sets of runs and an external like E or N.

Green was more successful in a later experiment (Ref. 18), using 100 cards which were either red or black. 184 students were group-tested, conditions being arranged in such a way that they were separated by a corridor from experimenter and agent, who in turn sat in separate rooms. Sets of 10 guesses were run in sequence in such a way that during alternate sets Ss could or could not see E on television closed circuit; they could never see the agent. Overall results were significant only for

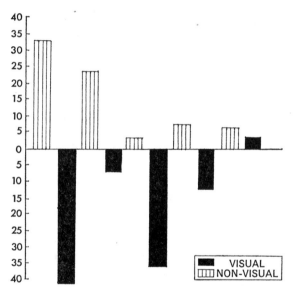

Figure 32. Deviation from chance scores of subjects in pre-cognition tests under visual and non-visual conditions. Quoted with permission from Green (Ref. 18).

1+ target scores, i.e. when the first guess was matched with the second target, etc. Under these conditions the non-visual runs gave above-chance scores, the visual runs below-chance scores (Fig. 32). In the non-visual condition, the mean E score of those (N = 21) who made 28 or more correct guesses was 28·19, while the mean E scores of those (N = 14) who made 17 or fewer correct guesses was 19·86. The extraverts are superior at a level of significance which approaches a p-value of 0·01. Under visual conditions, this tendency was reversed; high scorers had an E score of 22·67, low scorers one of 28·39. This difference in favour of the introverts was significant at the 0·04 level. The reversal was significant at beyond the 0·01 level. N failed to show significant results throughout. (These p values are uncorrected for the fact that the 1+ runs only were analysed, not the O or the 1− runs, which showed no overall deviation from chance. However, overall deviation does not of course imply significant correlations with external criteria, such as Personality Inventories.)

In addition to these studies which used measures of E directly, there are a few which are relevant because of their use of indirect evidence. Schmeidler divided her Ss in two groups on the basis of their work habits and found that 'ego-involved' Ss scored below chance expectation, while 'task-oriented' Ss gave positive scores, a difference which proved significant (Ref. 35). This is relevant because introverts tend to be more easily 'ego-involved' in their work than extraverts. Nicol & Humphrey found that Ss who rated themselves as self-confident on the Guilford-Martin Inventory tended to score positively, while those obtaining low ratings tended to obtain fewer successes (Ref. 27). Extraverts, on the whole, tend to have higher scores on self-confidence than do introverts. Van de Castle found a suggestive correlation between PK ability and spontaneity (Ref. 44); again extraverts tend to be more spontaneous than introverts. (This study, it should be noted, used the Rorschach test, which is of doubtful reliability and validity, so that the results reported should not be taken too seriously.) Shields, working with children, found significant differences in psi ability between withdrawn and sociable children, with the latter but not the former scoring significantly on an ESP test (Ref. 37). (Sociability is of course one of the most prominent traits characterizing the extravert.) Carpenter found that low perceptual defensiveness correlated with high ESP (Ref. 5), the correlation amounting to 0·79! Perceptual defence has been shown to be correlated with introversion, although the task used by Carpenter is different from those used in relation to personality study (Ref. 11). Last, Rao found a significantly negative correlation between Taylor's MAS and ESP (Ref. 32); this is relevant because it is well known that the MAS is not only a measure of neuroticism, but also has a component of introversion. (Freeman & Nielsen failed to discover a correlation between the MAS and psi, but they were working with precognition (Ref. 13)).

Work on positive and negative attitude to ESP and the scores produced by 'sheep' and 'goats', may also be relevant because introverts tend to be characterized by scientific, cautious and doubting tendencies which would seem to predispose them to become 'goats', while extraverts are more characterized by artistic tendencies and to be less resistant to such group pressures as often exist (or may be imagined to exist) in ESP experimental circles. Schmeidler (Ref. 35), Bevan (Ref. 3), Schmeidler & McConnell (Ref. 36), Muso (Ref. 24). Bhadra & Parthasarathy (Ref. 4) and others have found that indeed goats score poorly, sheep well, when compared with each other. It would seem desirable, however, before adducing this evidence in favour of our hypothesis to correlate attitudes with extraversion-introversion directly; only if a positive relation could be established between extraversion and favourable attitudes towards ESP could we regard these studies as relevant.

Expansiveness and compressiveness of drawings has also been used as a personality measure to differentiate good and poor scorers in ESP experiments, following Humphrey's early work (Refs. 19 & 20). McMahan (Ref. 23), Smith & Humphrey (Ref. 39), Stuart (Ref. 41), West (Ref. 45), Casper (Ref. 6), Kahn (Ref. 22), Nash (Ref. 25) and others have brought forward contradictory evidence, some finding positive correlations between high scoring and expansiveness, others finding negative correlations, others yet finding none at all. This is not surprising; Eysenck has summarized the literature to show that there is an *interaction* effect between extraversion and neuroticism in determining expansiveness of drawings; no predictions or conclusions are possible when N scores are not available (Ref. 11). This area of research might with advantage be opened up again in connection with E or N scores used in combination.

On the whole, there is thus remarkable unanimity among research workers who have addressed themselves to this problem; in no case where there is evidence of psi in the total record has there been found a tendency for introverts to score better than extraverts and in practically every case examined has there been a significant or near-significant tendency for extraverts to do better than introverts. The correlations are not usually very high, but of course the obtained figures should be corrected for attenuation in the criterion, i.e., for the presumably rather low reliability of the ESP scores used. Surprisingly no study has been found which even attempted to calculate these reliabilities, or correct for them. This should always be done, as without such information the closeness of the association cannot be ascertained.

It is interesting to note that the factors enumerated as characterizing psi performance, such as decline in performance, improvement through novelty and the positive influence of spontaneity, have particular relevance to extravert performance. It is extraverts who are particularly susceptible to monotony, show loss of vigilance and respond favourably to changes in conditions. Here again, therefore, we appear to have a connecting link between ESP and personality.

A number of points arise from this discussion, relating either to the interpretation of data or to the design and analysis of future research. The first point, already alluded to above, relates to the analysis of ESP data. The almost universal practice in the studies summarized has been to treat performance on the ESP test as evidence of some sort of psi ability which gives rise to a score, usually simply made up by summing or averaging the total number of hits for each person. From the psychometric point of view this is a very elementary method which leaves much to be desired. In the construction of any personality or ability test, the psychologist puts great emphasis on the *reliability* of his instrument, i.e., he investigates the extent to which his subjects produce respectable scores. Only if reliabilities are reasonably high is it worth his while to continue investigating the validity of his instrument, i.e., to discover whether it measures what it is supposed to measure, or to use it in studies of a correlational kind. Clearly, if a test does not correlate with itself, i.e., does not give reproducible results, it would be absurd to expect it to correlate with any other measure whatever and its failure to do so could not be interpreted as indicating the absence of a true relation between the ability which the test attempts (but apparently does not succeed) to measure and the other measure. Conversely, of course, if a test does consistently correlate with some outside measure, such as a test of extraversion, then the test must clearly possess some minimum degree of reliability.

It should clearly have been one of the first tasks of workers in the ESP field to establish the reliability of their scores, rather than to use these scores in various ways which *assume* the existence of reliability. It is sometimes argued that the demonstration of extra-chance results proves the reliability of the test, but this is not so. Consider Table 1a and Table 1b. The former shows the (imaginary) scores of 12 people on two GESP runs through a Zener pack; it will be seen that they score well above chance expectation, but they completely fail to show any evidence of reliability: a person scoring high on Run 1 does not necessarily score high on run 2, and a person scoring low on run 1 does not necessarily score low on run 2. In Table 1a, therefore, there is evidence for ESP, but none for reliability of individual differences and it would be idle to imagine that one could usefully correlate a person's score with some outside criterion. If run 1 doesn't correlate with run 2, why should either be expected to correlate with any other type of test, such as a personality test?

TABLE 1

A

	A	B	C	D	E	F	G	H	I	J	K	L
Run 1	5	4	6	9	8	5	7	9	15	11	14	10
Run 2	14	11	15	7	9	8	5	6	9	4	5	14

B

	A	B	C	D	E	F	G	H	I	J	K	L
Run 1	0	7	6	4	5	5	4	6	7	3	10	3
Run 2	1	7	5	3	6	5	4	7	8	3	9	2

In Table 1b there is no evidence of ESP in the means of the 12 subjects, which add up to 5 on either run. There is, however, considerable evidence of reliability; those who score above chance on one run score above chance on the other and vice versa. This reliability in scoring would furnish us with evidence of the existence of ESP equally as strong as and possibly more impressive than, that furnished by differences in means. Given that the experiment was properly controlled, the reliability of the performance of the subjects can only be ascribed to the action of ESP; the failure of the mean scores to exceed the chance level would be ascribed to the fact that while some people (sheep?) consistently scored above chance, others (goats?) consistently scored below chance. The study of reliability thus furnishes us with a second, independent means of searching for evidence of the existence of psi and it seems possible that many unsuccessful studies, discarded because of a failure to show above-chance mean scores, might contain convincing evidence of ESP had only the reliabilities been studied by means of one of the many available statistical techniques.

If consistency of scoring thus gives evidence of ESP, so does consistency of correlation of scores with an outside criterion and the fact that so many different studies, using different measures of extraversion, different measures of psi, carried out in different countries and by different investigators, all converge on agreement with the hypothesis stated at the beginning of this paper furnishes strong evidence for the existence of psi, evidence all the stronger because (1) it could not have been faked, as the investigators did not know of the hypothesis in question, or of the theoretical relevance of their particular study and (2) it shows regularity of functioning of psi ability over and above simple mean differences. (In addition, (3), the hypothesis brings ESP results in line with knowledge obtained and theories elaborated in the general field of psychology.) We would conclude, therefore, that in future work in ESP, reliabilities of the scores used should always be computed as a matter of routine and published in addition to means and averages and that correlations with other types of data, such as personality inventories or intelligence tests, should be corrected for attenuation due to unreliability of the ESP score.

The second point relates to the design of ESP experiments. In fact, there are several related points.

(a) The evidence suggests that extraverts score above chance, while introverts score at or below the chance level, in GESP experiments. If this be so, then it seems clear that personality inventories such as the M.P.I. or the E.P.I. should always be included in ESP experiments. The negative contribution of introverts to the total score can obscure or may completely cancel out the positive contribution of extraverts; it seems possible to suggest that many negative outcomes of experimental studies might have been avoided if positive and negative scorers could have been identified through the use of a personality inventory. Where the phenomenon under observation is clearly capricious to an unprecedented extent, we cannot afford to neglect any means of bringing order into this chaos and to sort out potential 'good' subjects from potential 'poor' subjects. (The same argument holds of course in relation to the 'sheep vs. goats' distinction; questions to ascertain subjects' attitudes towards ESP in general and the experiment in which they serve in particular should form part of the routine in every experimental enquiry of this nature.) Present practice resembles too closely for comfort the old navy doctrine of 'some like two lumps of sugar, others like none, so give everybody one lump in their tea!'. It is meaningless to average scores across groups which are non-homogeneous with respect to some variable which is correlated with the experimental measure employed and the evidence suggests strongly that extraversion-introversion is such a variable. Such averaging throws out much valuable evidence which we can ill afford to lose.

(b) The fact that in nearly all the studies noted the differences observed favoured the extraverts should not be taken to mean that here we have the much sought-after 'reproducible ESP experiment'. It seems likely that the repeatability of the findings is related to the similarity of conditions under which the studies quoted were carried out; it will be remembered that when Green changed her conditions from non-visual to visual, the correlation with personality was reversed. The whole situation is complicated by the existence and possible relevance of the so-called Yerkes-Dodson Law to research in this area. This well-documented law states two things. In the first place, it states that the relation between performance and arousal or drive is curvilinear; with very low arousal performance is poor, but it improves as arousal increases until an optimal level is reached beyond which performance declines again. In the second place, the law states that this optimum level of arousal is high for simple tasks and low for complex tasks. It seems likely that for ESP too there is an optimal level of arousal and that the actual conditions of the experiment interact with the arousal level of the individuals taking part. Thus it may be that (in Green's experiment) under non-visual conditions the relatively low arousal of the extraverts was near the optimum, while the rather higher arousal level of the introverts was above the optimum. Change to visual conditions might have lowered the general arousal level, bringing the extraverts below optimum and the introverts to optimum. (It is unlikely that this simple hypothesis would in fact account for all the facts of the case; it is put forward simply to illustrate the kind of complex situation which might easily arise.) In order to test hypotheses of this kind it would of course be necessary to monitor the arousal level of each subject, a task which in principle is not beyond our technical ability, but which is in practice rather difficult to carry out, particularly when dealing with groups of subjects all at the same time.

(c) Even apart from the question of correlations with personality, it seems likely that our argument that a well-controlled study of the conditions under which experiments are carried out, together with properly planned changes in the various parameters involved, would throw much light on various areas hitherto curiously neglected. ESP tests are carried out in groups or on individuals, but little attempt has been made to investigate changes in performance due to this factor. Changes in motivation due to instructions, to offers of reward, or to other manipulations of the environment are likely to change the arousal pattern of subjects in ways which are likely to affect performance. Even time of day has been shown to affect arousal. Most of these factors have been allowed to obscure the measurement of ESP, rather than being used for the purpose of clarifying the nature of ESP and facilitating its measurement; it is suggested that more energy could with advantage be devoted to their experimental study.

In making this suggestion, however, one proviso is necessary. Conditions inevitably interact with personality, so that a simple study of the influence of conditions, uncontrolled for extraversion-introversion, would not be very informative. As an example consider some of the work on the effects of time of day on performance (Ref. 8). Introverts performed better in the morning than extraverts but extraverts performed better in the afternoon. A study of performance pure and simple would have found no difference between morning and afternoon; it required the interaction analysis of personality to bring out the very marked differences. Similarly in relation to performance alone or in groups; there is no overall effect but introverts do better in the former condition and extraverts in the latter (Ref. 8). It seems likely that the indefinite and conflicting results reported in the literature when experimental conditions have been studied with reference to their effect on psi have been due to the neglect of personality as a modifier variable. The suggestion again must therefore be that investigation of parameter changes should be accompanied by the application of personality inventories for the measurement of E and N.

SUMMARY

(1) The hypothesis has been deduced from facts and theories in general psychology, personality theory and the body of knowledge comprising ESP research, that introverts would make relatively poor psi subjects, while extraverts would make relatively good psi subjects. (2) A survey of the literature showed surprising agreement on the better performance of extraverted subjects as compared with introverted subjects on GESP tests. (3) It was argued that for a proper understanding of the relation between psi performance and personality it would be necessary to apply standard psychometric methods to psi scores; in particular the absence of any knowledge regarding the reliability of these scores was deplored. (4) It was argued that experimental studies varying the arousal level of subjects would give additional information of great interest to the general hypothesis advanced and it was suggested that such studies would require the inclusion of personality inventories, as personality traits such as extraversion and emotionality would act as modifier variables. (5) It was suggested that the search for evidence in favour of the existence of ESP had concentrated too much on differences from chance of mean or

average scores and that alternative statistical methods were available which might in fact show significance even where traditional methods had failed to find any significance.

REFERENCES

1. Aström, J., GESP i belysring ar Eysenck's personlighetsteori. *Varld och vetande*, **9**, 281–286, 1964.
2. ——, GESP and the MPI measures. Paper read at 8th Ann. Conv. in Parapsychol., New York, 1965. Abstract published in *J. Parapsychol.*, **29**, 292–293, 1965.
3. Bevan, J. M., The relation of attitude to success in ESP scoring. *J. Parapsychol.*, **11**, 296–309, 1947.
4. Bhadra, B. R. & Parthasarathy, S., ESP and attitudes. Quoted by Rao, K. R. (Ref. 33).
5. Carpenter, J. C., An exploratory test of ESP in relation to anxiety proneness. In *Parapsychology from Duke to FRNM* (ed. J. B. Rhine *et al.*). Durham, North Carolina: Parapsychology Press, 1965.
6. Casper, G. W., A further study of the relation of attitude to success in ESP scoring. *J. Parapsychol.*, **15**, 139–145, 1951.
7. ——, Affect of receiver's attitude towards sender in ESP tests. *J. Parapsychol.*, **16**, 212–218, 1952.
8. Colquhoun, W. P. & Corcoran, D. V. J., The effects of time of day and social isolation on the relationship between temperament and performance. *Brit. J. soc. clin. Psychol.*, **3**, 226–231, 1964.
9. Eysenck, H. J., *The Structure of Human Personality*. London: Methuen, 1960.
10. ——, *The Maudsley Personality Inventory*. London: University of London Press, 1965.
11. ——, *The Biological Basis of Personality*. Springfield, Ill.: C. C. Thomas, 1967.
12. —— & Eysenck, S. B. G., *The Eysenck Personality Inventory*. London: University of London Press, 1965.
13. Freeman, J. A. & Nielsen, Winnifred, Precognition score deviations as related to anxiety levels. *J. Parapsychol.*, **28**, 239–249, 1964.
14. Gerber, Rebecca & Schmeidler, Gertrude R., An investigation of relaxation and of acceptance of the experimental situations as

M

related to ESP scores in maternity patients. *J. Parapsychol.*, **21**, 47–57, 1957.

15. GILBERT, L. & SCHMEIDLER, G. R., A study of certain psychological factors in relation to ESP performance. *J. Parapsychol.*, **14**, 53–74, 1950.

16. GREEN, C. E., Extra-sensory perception and the extraversion scale of the Maudsley Personality Inventory. *J. Soc. Psychical Res.*, **43**, 728, 1966.

17. ——, Extra-sensory perception and the Maudsley Personality Inventory. *J. Soc. Psychical Res.*, **43**, 727, 1966.

18. ——, The Maudsley Personality Inventory and Differential Scoring in a Card-Guessing Situation. Unpublished papers from Psychophys. Res. Unit, Oxford, 1967.

19. HUMPHREY, B. M., Success in ESP as related to form of response drawings. I. Clairvoyance experiments. *J. Parapsychol.*, **10**, 78–106, 1946.

20. ——, Success in ESP as related to forms of response drawings. II. GESP experiments. *J. Parapsychol.*, **10**, 181–196, 1946.

21. ——, Introversion-extraversion ratings in relation to scores in ESP tests. *J. Parapsychol.*, **18**, 252–262, 1957.

22. KAHN, S. D., Studies in extra-sensory perception: experiments utilizing an electronic scoring device. *Proc. Amer. Soc. Psychical Res.*, **25**, 1–48, 1952.

23. MCMAHAN, E. A., An experiment in pure telepathy. *J. Parapsychol.*, **10**, 224–242, 1946.

24. MUSO, J. R., ESP experiments with primary school children. *J. Parapsychol.*, **29**, 115–121, 1965.

25. NASH, C. B., Negative correlation between the scores of subjects in two contemporaneous ESP experiments. *J. Amer. Soc. Psychical Res.*, **56**, 80–83, 1962.

26. ——, Relations between ESP scoring level and the Minnesota Multiphasic Personality Inventory. Paper read at the Sixth Ann. Conv. of the Parapsychol. Ass., New York, 1963. Abstract in *J. Parapsychol.*, **27**, 274, 1963.

27. NICOL, J. F. & HUMPHREY, BETTY M., The exploration of ESP and human personality. *J. Amer. Soc. Psychical Res.*, **47**, 133–178, 1953.

28. OTANI, S., Relations of mental set and change of skin resistance to ESP. *J. Parapsychol.*, **19**, 164–170, 1955.

29. ——, Some relations of ESP scores to change in skin resistance.

In *Parapsychology from Duke to FRNM* (ed. J. B. Rhine *et al.*). Durham, North Carolina: Parapsychology Press, 1965.
30. PRATT, J. G. & WOODRUFF, J. L., Size of stimulus symbols in extra-sensory perception. *J. Parapsychol.*, **3**, 121–158, 1939.
31. RAO, K. R., The differential response in three new situations. *J. Parapsychol.*, **28**, 81–92, 1964.
32. ——, ESP and the manifest anxiety scale. *J. Parapsychol.*, **29**, 12–18, 1965.
33. ——, *Experimental Parapsychology*. Springfield: C. C. Thomas, 1966.
34. SCHERER, W. B., Spontaneity as a factor in ESP. *J. Parapsychol.*, **12**, 126–147, 1948.
35. SCHMEIDLER, G. R., Separating the sheep from the goats. *J. Amer. Soc. Psychical Res.*, **39**, 47–49, 1945.
36. —— & MCCONNELL, R. A. *ESP and Personality Patterns*. New Haven: Yale University Press, 1958.
37. SHIELDS, ELOISE, Comparison of children's guessing ability (ESP) with personality characteristics. *J. Parapsychol.*, **26**, 200–210, 1962.
38. SINCLAIR, U., *Mental radio*. Springfield: C. C. Thomas, 1962.
39. SMITH, B. M. & HUMPHREY, B. M., Some personality characteristics related to ESP performance. *J. Parapsychol.*, **10**, 169–189, 1946.
40. STANFORD, R. G., A study of the relationships between ESP scoring and brainwaves. In *Parapsychology from Duke to FRNM* (ed. J. B. Rhine *et al.*). Durham, North Carolina: Parapsychology Press, 1965.
41. STUART, C. E., HUMPHREY, B. M., SMITH, B. M. & MCMAHAN, E., Personality measurements and ESP tests with cards and drawings. *J. Parapsychol.*, **11**, 118–146, 1947.
42. TENHAEFF, W. H. C., On the personality structure of paragnosts. *Proc. Parapsychol. Inst., State Univ., Utrecht*, **2**, 1–79, 1962.
43. THOULESS, R. H., A report on an experiment in psychokinesis with dice and a discussion on psychological factors favouring success. *J. Parapsychol.*, **15**, 89–102, 1951.
44. VAN DE CASTLE, R. L., An exploratory study of some personality correlates associated with PK performance. *J. Amer. Soc. Psychical Res.*, **52**, 139–150, 1958.
45. WEST, D. J., ESP performance and the expansion-compression rating. *J. Soc. Psychical Res.*, **35**, 295–308, 1949–50.

Motor Movements

Editor's Introduction

THERE are direct connections between the reticular formation (R.F.) and motor neurons such that excitatory and inhibitory impulses can be passed directly to the motor units in questions and consequently one would expect that motor activity would show clearly the effects of differential R.F. thresholds. In most experiments, of course, cortical loops are involved, complicating the relationships involved, but nonetheless making possible certain types of prediction. A varied list of articles is given here, representing the main lines of work which have been done in the past. Many interesting differences between extraverts and introverts have in fact been found, ranging from size of doodles to differential behaviour in hypnosis.

Of particular interest in this set of studies is the emergence of the importance of moderator variables, as they are styled in the American work, or of zone analysis, as this is referred to by British workers. In either case, what has been shown is that simple comparisons between extraverts and introverts may be misleading; neuroticism as a personality variable, or stressful experimental conditions, may interact with E–I in such a way that differences are obscured unless these disturbing factors are taken into account. This interaction effect, which had first been shown by Venables in a paper here reprinted, is apparently much more widespread than had been realised and in future work it seems almost mandatory that some form of zone analysis must be employed. The nature of the moderator variables in question must of course depend on the theoretical assumptions made and the particular questions asked; neuroticism and intelligence are the most obvious ones, but other variables may in due course have to be considered.

The allocation to this section of some of the papers reprinted may seem almost haphazard; why for instance should a paper on speech patterns (emphasizing the length and distribution of silences!) be included here? The answer of course is (a) that allocation of papers to one of several very broad categories must inevitably be somewhat subjective and even haphazard and (b) that speaking is a motor task and that attention may with advantage be paid, not only to what is being said, but also to the timing and other non-cognitive aspects of the simple muscular act of speaking—or not speaking! Behaviouristically-oriented psychologists should not require apologies for concentration on objectively measurable aspects of activities usually regarded more from a subjective point of view.   H.J.E.

343

41

Changes in Motor Response with Increase and Decrease in Task Difficulty in Normal Industrial and Psychiatric Patient Subjects[1]

PETER H. VENABLES

First published in *British Journal of Psychology*, **46,** 101–110, 1955

INTRODUCTION

CLINICAL observation led Bleuler to describe two classes of people (Ref. 2). In one, where 'sanguine' temperament is displayed, there is a quick and intensive reaction to emotional impression, in the other the affect is suppressed, leading to displacements and conversions. Nunberg produced experimental evidence for these two types in work on motor movement in response to word association (Ref. 12). The first type made excessive and the second decreased motor movement under affect. Berrien found evidence of two extreme types of reaction to emotion-provoking stimuli in rhythmical finger movement of psychotic patients (Ref. 1). He described these as excitatory and inhibitory in nature.

In work on the performance of pilots in a simulated aircraft cockpit, Davis observed two sorts of errors, those of overaction and those of inertia (Ref. 4). Subjects displaying overactivity reaction made larger control movements and excessive reaction to instrument deviation; the extent and gradient of movement was greatly increased and over-correcting frequent. Subjects showing inertia reaction made errors which were large and of long duration; control movements were relatively small and were less disturbed by restless movement than those in the performance of subjects showing overactivity reaction. As a further test of this finding of an 'overactivity-inertia' continuum, Davis devised a less complicated task involving pointer alignment. Similar reactions were observed on this task. The relationship of these reactions to personality type was found to confirm previous work. Anxious subjects were found to show overactive and hysterics inert reactions.

[1] Based on part of a thesis approved for the degree of Ph.D. in the University of London.

The present experiment was designed to provide further data bearing on the hypothesis that (a) behaviour on a task may vary on a continuum ranging from overactive to inert and (b) that this behaviour is related to personality factors in such a way that when the task is made more difficult dysthymics tend to show modification of performance in the overactive direction, while hysterics change to a more inert form of behaviour. In addition, further evidence was sought on the direction of change of behaviour when task difficulty is decreased.

METHOD

The experiment was conducted as part of a larger investigation into the effects of psychological handicap. It occupied approximately 8 minutes during a session lasting 1½ hours during which the subject completed a battery of intelligence and personality tests. The short duration of the experiment was not deemed to be a disadvantage in that it offered a possibility to test previous workers' findings under conditions not previously employed and provided a test of the possibility of generalization.

The type of experiment employed was dictated by the practical aim of simulating the stimulus conditions met with by a bus conductor in the course of his job. It provided a means of measuring the subject's reaction to an increase or decrease in the rate of presentation, or in complexity of stimuli. This was an attempt to parallel change in 'load' conditions imposed by an increase or decrease in the number of passengers boarding the bus.

Subjects
Sample 1 consisted of 210 male trainees for the job of bus conductor. Their age range was 18–46 years, mean $28 \cdot 1 \pm 7 \cdot 5$. Data were available for each subject to enable factor scores of Intelligence, Neuroticism and Introversion-Extraversion to be allocated to him. These scores were derived from the analysis of results on 15 psychometric tests.

Sample 2 had the purpose of providing validation groups to substantiate findings obtained on sample 1. The subjects in sample 2 consisted of 11 showing anxiety states (age range 21–48 years, mean $30 \cdot 7 \pm 7 \cdot 3$) and 11 hysterics (age range 21–46 years, mean $32 \cdot 8 \pm 8 \cdot 5$) selected from a population of 52 male psychoneurotic patients interviewed at a psychiatric hospital. The selection was made by taking those subjects where clear psychiatric diagnoses showing absence of features

M*

other than anxiety or hysteria were confirmed by scores obtained on a questionnaire which had been found previously (Ref. 8) to differentiate anxiety states from hysterics. The two groups are known as Anxious (A) and Hysterics (H) for purposes of reference in the text. To enable results from samples 1 and 2 to be compared, two groups of 11 subjects each from sample 1 were selected on the basis of high scores on the neuroticism factor and extreme scores on the introversion-extraversion factor; these groups, chosen to have characteristics which tended to approach those of the anxious and hysteric hospital patient groups, may be called quasi-anxious (QA) and quasi-hysteric (QH). The terms quasi-hysteric and quasi-anxious have been adopted in view of the possibly misleading connotation of other labels which might have been used, e.g., industrial hysteric. The groups should be considered to be operationally defined, although it is hoped that they have some resemblance to those from sample 2.

Apparatus

From the subjects' viewpoint the apparatus consisted of a milk-white screen $8\frac{3}{4} \times 5\frac{1}{2}$ inches, set in a brass frame, at an angle of 45° from the base. On either side of the centre line of the frame and at $2\frac{3}{8}$ inches from it were two marks over which the stimulus lights appeared. In the horizontal shelf in front of the display screen was a slot $8\frac{1}{2}$ inches long through which a knob protruded. A pointer attached to the knob indicated its position against the marks on the display panel. Five stimulus lights were set vertically behind the display panel above each lateral mark. Their position was not visible until alight. Reading from the bottom the stimuli were (1) white, (2) green, (3) red, (4) showing the word 'yes', (5) showing the word 'no'.

The subject was given the following instructions:

' "When your hear this click" (a signal indicating that a new stimulus was being presented), "move the pointer from the mark in the centre to the mark under the white light, if it is on its own, or has green, or 'yes' over it. However, if it has red or 'no' over it move it to the mark on the opposite side. After this, move the pointer as quickly as possible to the centre mark.' "

The pointer was attached to a lever controlling a pen which recorded the subject's movement on a moving paper. The stimuli were automatically presented in predetermined sequence via the contacts of three uniselectors. The presentation of stimuli was divided into three consecutive periods of 50 displays each. In the first easy period A, white lights only were used at a 2-sec periodicity; this was followed by a difficult period B, using all the lights as 1·5 sec per display and a final easy period C, identical with A. The whole task thus took 275 sec to complete. The order of presentation of lights was such that each direction of movement to each type of display was balanced. Every fifth response in the difficult period B was to a simple white light stimulus. This scheme was adopted as it was required to measure characteristics of response which were not themselves reactions to difficult stimuli, but were set in an environment of difficult stimuli. By this means it was hoped to measure not the immediate effect of distraction, but the effect on response to a standard stimulus of the emotional condition produced by having to respond to more complex stimuli.

Procedure

The subject was seated in front of the apparatus which was placed on a low table, so that this forearm was parallel to the ground; he was asked to use his preferred hand. The task was explained to the subject, who was allowed to practise at his own speed whilst 50 displays were presented. It was then explained that his responses would be recorded and that he should expect a period of white lights only at a slow speed, a period using all the lights at a slightly faster speed, and finally white lights only again at a slow speed, there being no break between the periods.

The Scoring of the Records

Thirty of the 150 responses recorded for each subject were used for measurement. These were every fifth response and were to simple white light stimuli throughout. The method of marking is shown in Fig. 33. The following measures were used and are designated by symbols used throughout the remainder of the paper:

R   Maximum extent of response.
W   Width of response measured at a fixed distance (10 arbitrary units) from the centre line.
M   The deviation from the centre line of the point of return after each response.

Ten responses were measured in each period A, B and C and means and standard deviations were calculated for each variable. The means were designated $\bar{R}$, $\bar{W}$ and $\bar{M}$, and the standard deviations, giving

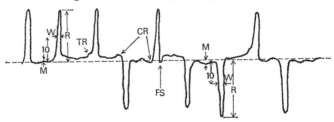

Figure 33. Artificial example showing method of scoring psychomotor task records.

measures of variability within each period, were denoted by S_R, S_W
and S_M.

In addition to this, measurement of selected responses secondary
features of all the responses in each period were counted. These were:

FS False starts, where the subject started initially in wrong direction.
TR Trailing returns, where the subject did not make a simple direct
    return movement to the centre line after a response.
CR Corrected returns, where the return movement overshot the
    centre mark and had to be corrected.

RESULTS

Establishment of a Method of Measuring the Overactive-Inert Continuum

Prior to the commencement of any measurement, examination of
records of the subjects in sample 1 showed that they ranged from those
showing extensive responses of short duration with considerable overshooting and subsequent correction, to those showing short responses
lasting some length of time. These were thought to represent opposite
poles of the overactive-inert continuum. A period of 25 typical responses
(numbers 10–34) in period A was rated for this feature on a five-point
scale by the writer and an assistant. The correlation between the ratings
was 0·807. There was thus a feature of the records which could be determined with reasonable reliability. The problem was to decide how this
feature might best be measured so that changes between the different
periods of the task could be followed. The possible measures of activity
could be derived from those measures already outlined; these were:

(1) The amount of response per unit time, measured by $\overline{R}/\overline{W}$.
(2) The magnitude of the response, measured by $\overline{R} \times \overline{W}$.

The term magnitude of response is somewhat ambiguous and needs further explanation. Measured by $\bar{R} \times \bar{W}$, it is proportional to the area of the response. Thus a response of small magnitude is one of small extent, or one which is completed quickly, or both. The other measure $\bar{R}/,\bar{W}$ where the extent of response is divided by the time taken for it, gives a measure which is of course related to 'magnitude' but is not identical. A response showing 'large response per unit time' is one where a response of large extent is completed quickly. We should expect a positive correlation between small magnitude of response and large response per unit time, although in so far as there is a difficulty of choice between the two measures this correlation should depart from unity. The problem of deciding which of these measures was more suitable was tackled in the following way.

It was thought that use could be made of the secondary features of responses along with the rating determined above to provide evidence on which a decision might be made. It was hypothesized that an 'active' subject might show a greater number of false starts (FS) and corrected returns (CR) and a smaller number of trailing returns (TR) than an inert subject. With this in mind $\bar{R}/\bar{W}$, $\bar{R} \times \bar{W}$, FS, TR, CR and the rating of overactivity-inertia (Rat. 0–1), scores for period A were intercorrelated. The table of intercorrelations (Table 1) shows that R/W with FS, TR and CR follows more closely that of the rating with these variables than does that of $R \times W$. These factors determined the choice of R/W as a suitable measure of 'activity'. To add further confirmation a Lawley maximum likelihood type factor analysis (Ref. 10) was carried out on the intercorrelation between R/W_A, FS_A, TR_A, CR_A and the rating. The result is shown in Table 2.

The first unrotated factor accounts for 41·18 per cent of the variance and is most highly loaded on R/W and the rating. It was not possible to identify the second factor nor was it thought worthwhile to extract further factors which were shown to be present in the residual matrix by Lawley's test of significance.

The variable R/W_A resulted from measures taken on responses 1, 6, 11, 16, etc. A measure of reliability can be calculated by comparing this score with a similar one taken from responses 3, 8, 13, . . ., etc. When this was done a reliability coefficient of 0·970 was obtained. It is clear from this work that a factor of overactivity-inertia was present in the records and that it could be reliably measured.

It was hoped that a measure of 'disorganization of behaviour' independent of the 'activity' factor described above might be developed. The hypothesis could be advanced that a record showing organization was

TABLE 1

INTERCORRELATION OF HYPOTHESIZED MEASURES OF
OVERACTIVITY-INERTIA, SAMPLE 1, N = 210

		R/W$_A$	R×W$_A$	FS$_A$	RT$_A$	CR$_A$	Rat. 0–1
Large response per unit time	R/W$_A$	—	—	—	—	—	—
Small magnitude of response	R×W$_A$	0·694	—	—	—	—	—
Many false starts	FS$_A$	0·081	0·500	—	—	—	—
Few trailing returns	TR$_A$	0·221	−0·078	0·337	—	—	—
Many corrected returns	CR$_A$	0·491	0·237	0·040	0·129	—	—
Overactivity	Rat. 0–1	0·858	0·618	0·001	0·379	0·437	—

Note: A correlation of 0·136 is significant at the 0·05 level.

TABLE 2

UNROTATED FACTOR LOADINGS OF HYPOTHESIZED
MEASURES OF OVERACTIVITY-INERTIA

		I°	II°
Large response per unit time	R/W$_A$	0·924	0·269
Many false starts	FS$_A$	0·089	−0·226
Few trailing returns	TR$_A$	0·342	−0·231
Many corrected returns	CR$_A$	0·511	0·023
Overactivity	Rat. 0–1	0·905	0·184
	Per cent variance accounted for	41·18	4·4

one where the responses, however large or small, were of even length and
width and showing accuracy of alignment to the centre line. Disorganization would then be characterized by high M, S$_R$, S$_W$ and S$_M$ scores.
Following the previous procedure the records were rated on a 5-point
scale for 'disorganization of response'. The reliability of the rating was
0·667. Measures S$_R$, S$_W$, S$_M$, M and the rating were intercorrelated,
with R/W as a marker for the activity factor. The factor analysis of the
matrix yielded a first factor accounting for 23·5 per cent of the variance.
This having its highest loading on R/W was again clearly an activity
factor, the second factor could not be interpreted in an orthogonal
position and when an oblique solution through the cluster S$_R$, S$_M$ and
the rating was adopted, the correlation between the factors was approxi-

mately 0·87. It was therefore apparent that no measure of disorganization could be developed independently of the 'Activity' factor.

*Determination of the Relation of the Overactive-Inertia Continuum of
Motor Behaviour to Personality Classification*
Five types of measures were calculated for each subject for each of the
nine variables outlined earlier and for the index R/W. These were:

(1) Performance in period A, e.g. R/W_A.
(2) Performance in period B, e.g. R/W_B.
(3) Performance in period C, e.g. R/W_C.
(4) Change in performance between periods A and B, e.g., R/W_{A-B}.
(5) Change in performance between periods B and C, e.g., R/W_{B-C}.

These measures were correlated with factor scores measuring Intelligence, Neuroticism and Introversion-Extraversion for the group of 210
normal subjects, sample 1.
It was found that increase in Inertia from period A to period B
measured by R/W_{A-B} was positively correlated with the factor of
Extraversion at a significant level ($r = +0·141$, $p<0·05$) and that
increase in inertia between period B and period C (R/W_{B-C}) was negatively correlated with Extraversion ($r = 0·147$, $p<0·05$). No significant
correlations with the other two personality factors were obtained.
In the case of the neurotic group, sample 2, rank correlations between
the same variables and the anxious-hysteric dichotomy were calculated.
It was found that inertia in period A (R/W_A) was significantly correlated
with hysteria ($r = +0·36$, $p<0·05$) and that increase in inertia from
period B to C was negatively correlated with hysteria ($r = -0·41$,
$p<0·05$).
The results from 22 subjects from sample 1 selected to be comparable
with the anxious and hysteric groups showed that, as in the parent
population, increase in inertia from periods A to B, was correlated with
hysteria (neurotic-extraversion) ($r = +0·57$, $p<0·05$) and increase in
inertia from periods B to C was negatively correlated with hysteria
($r = -0·63$, $p<0·05$).
The rank correlation method used is that developed by Whitfield
(Ref. 16) from Kendall's work (Ref. 9), for use where one variable is
ranked and the other dichotomous. It should be interpreted in this case
in the same manner as a biserial coefficient. The use of this method was
dictated by the non-normal distribution resulting from the examination
of extreme cases.

Mean scores for R/W, R and W for periods A, B and C and for change in performance between periods A and B and B and C are given in Table 3. These are shown for the total normal sample for groups QA and QH derived from it and for groups A and H from the psychiatric patient sample, sample 2. Mean scores which are significantly different in groups QA and QH and groups A and H in italics. The significance of the difference between scores on these sub-groups was tested by the median method (Ref. 11); in view of the non-normal distribution of measures. Fig. 34 shows in graphic form the relationships outlined above and shown in the upper part of Table 3.

If we examine the results from either the whole of sample 1 or the subgroups drawn from it, it is seen that extravert and quasi-hysteric subjects show a significant tendency to change their performance in the inert direction under increased difficulty. The reverse tendency is shown in introvert, quasi-anxious and anxious subjects. The hospitalized, hysteric patient presents an initially inert type of response. Commencing performance on this level he does not change his performance which is substantially similar to his starting performance.

TABLE 3

MEAN PERFORMANCE SCORES OF SUBJECTS FROM SAMPLES 1 AND 2 ON
VARIABLES R/W, R AND W, FOR PERIODS A, B AND C

	Sample 1			Sample 2	
Variable	Total	QA	QH	A	H
R/W_A	5·93	5·32	6·05	*6·09*	*4·33*
R/W_B	5·38	5·71	5·59	7·03	4·39
R/W_C	5·58	4·82	6·00	6·08	4·72
R/W_{A-B}	+0·55	−0·39	*+0·46*	−0·94	−0·06
R/W_{B-C}	−0·20	+0·89	*−0·41*	*+0·95*	−0·33
R_A	21·37	20·97	21·68	*20·66*	*19·35*
R_B	20·62	20·50	20·73	19·84	19·10
R_C	21·40	21·38	21·78	20·55	19·76
R_{A-B}	+0·75	+0·47	+0·95	+0·82	+0·25
R_{B-C}	−0·78	−0·88	−1·05	−0·71	−0·66
W_A	3·93	4·33	3·76	4·30	4·95
W_B	4·18	3·83	3·92	*3·76*	*4·83*
W_C	4·17	4·66	3·82	4·56	4·57
W_{A-B}	−0·25	+0·50	*−0·16*	+0·54	+0·12
W_{B-C}	+0·01	−0·83	*−0·10*	−0·80	*+0·26*
N	210	11	11	11	11

Differences significant at less than the 0·05 level of confidence are in italic.

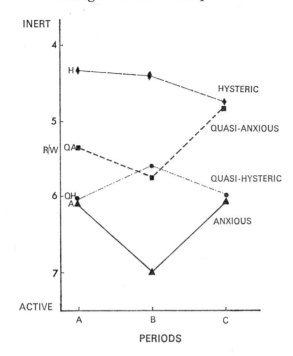

Figure 34. Changes in activity of response (r/w)
between periods a, b, and c in groups A, H, QA
and QH.

With decrease in task difficulty there is in all cases a significant
tendency for the extravert or hysteric subject to perform more actively
whilst the introverted or anxious patient subject shows a decrease in
activity.

On examination of the measures which make up the index R/W it is
seen that response length tends to shorten in the difficult period and
lengthen subsequently, although to different extents, in different groups of
subjects. On decrease of difficulty there is a general lengthening of response in all groups. It is the measure W, the time for which the response
lasts, that seems to be responsible to a greater extent for differential behaviour between the groups. In both dysthymic groups there is a speed up
of response under difficulty followed by a slowing down with decrease in
difficulty. In the hysteric patient group performance is slow initially
whilst in the extraverted group drawn from sample 1 there is a slowing

down on increase of difficulty. In both of these groups there is a speed up on decrease of difficulty.

While W, measuring speed of response, appears to parallel many of the findings of R/W in dysthymic-hysteric group differentiation it is felt that the latter measure does operate sufficiently differently to justify the reasons for its original inclusion. Evidence is given when motor task variables are related to G.S.R. measures. The work of White (Ref. 15), Freeman & Simpson (Ref. 6) and Staudt & Kubis (Ref. 13) shows that increase in G.S.R. conductance accompanies increase in muscular tension. Other work reported elsewhere (Ref. 14), indicates that increase in 'activity' measured by R/W_{A-B} is significantly correlated ($p = 0.045$ and 0.03) with increase in conductance, in both normal and neurotic groups. Increase in speed measured by W_{A-B} does not show significant correlations with increase in conductance. The work of Freeman & Pathman (Ref. 5) and Champion (Ref. 3) would lead us to expect that an increase in motor movement would result in a dissipation of autonomic disturbance. In the case of G.S.R. response after the difficult period, it is the measure W_{B-C} and not R/W_{B-C} which shows a significant correlation with decrease in conductance supporting Freeman & Pathman's and Champion's work. It would thus seem that there is a useful differentiation between the measures R/W and W and that the former may measure behaviourally something akin to muscular tension, whilst the latter measures speed of response.

Correlations of task variables with Intelligence and Neuroticism show that they are in general independent of these factors. If a group of subjects from sample 1 having ambivert and low neuroticism factor scores are compared with the two patient groups the finding of independence of the overactivity-inert continuum from neuroticism is supported by insignificant rank correlations of $+0.05$, $+0.18$ and 0.00 with R/W_A, R/W_{A-B}, and R/W_{B-C} respectively. Independence from age is shown by correlations of $+0.09$, $+0.01$ and $+0.01$ with the same variables.

DISCUSSION

In the work described an attempt has been made to provide further data bearing on the relation between motor performance and personality. The work of previous writers has been largely confirmed and additional findings showing evidence of regulatory behaviour after task difficulty has ceased have been given. It is of some interest that in many ways it is the change in performance when the stimulus situation changes from difficult to easy, which seems to be the most valuable indicator of different functions in different types of personality. Whilst in the hysteric group there was little change when the task difficulty increased, it was the marked change in the direction of overactivity on decrease of difficulty which differentiated this group from the anxious patients.

An external source of evidence on this point is given when the performance scores of 18 subjects in sample 1 who were discharged (largely for dishonesty) are examined. The scores for these subjects are compared with those resigning or remaining in employment in the same period of six months. It was found that the measure R/W_{B-C} differentiated the discharged from the rest at a significant level ($p < 0.01$). This was not, however, the case with R/W_{A-B} where a quite insignificant F-ratio was obtained. The discharges show behaviour which was in many ways similar to that of extraverted subjects.

The results of this work have some similarities to those of Foulds (Ref. 7) although he used a very different type of experiment. Foulds found that distraction produced a speed up of performance of dysthymics on the Porteus Maze, whilst speed up, although shown in non-dysthymics, was not significant. Examination of Table 3 shows a very similar state of affairs in the performance of our anxious and hysteric groups on periods A and B.

Also shown in the data presented is some indication of the difference between the performance of hospitalized and non-hospitalized groups of tentatively similar personality type. This is particularly striking in the case of the hysterics and quasi-hysterics, where the initial performance of the hysteric in hospital is so inert that no change in the inert direction seems possible. On the other hand, the quasi-hysteric in industry presents an initially quite active performance. These differences should not be pursued too far in view of the present unsatisfactoriness of tests with which it is hoped to measure in a normal population the counterpart of anxiety-hysteria in a hospital population.

The findings quoted indicate that performance is by no means a static phenomenon and that perhaps greater attention should be given in industrial situations to the maintenance of an even level of difficulty of work, in order to avoid alteration of performance due to interaction effects with features of the operatives' 'personality' in its narrowest sense.

Any attempt to present a theoretical basis for these findings is at the moment considered premature; further experimentation to test various hypotheses is proceeding.

SUMMARY

A motor task, involving the movement of a pointer in relation to stimulus lights under easy, difficult and subsequently easy conditions was performed by 210 male subjects consisting of a random selection of trainee bus conductors, age range 18–46 and by 22 male patients, age range 21–48, in a psychiatric hospital, selected from a group of 52 patients as having clear-cut psychiatric and questionnaire diagnosis.

Performance on the motor task could be described as falling on a continuum of overactivity-inertia. In general, under conditions of increased task difficulty, extraverted subjects showed a tendency to increased inertia of performance and introverted subjects to increased activity. When the task became easier the reverse relationship was found to hold true.

ACKNOWLEDGEMENTS

The author wishes to acknowledge the valuable assistance from Dr H. J. Eysenck and Mr M. B. Shapiro and his colleagues Drs Eisler, Heron, Markowe, O'Connor and Tizard. The psychiatric patient subjects were made available through the co-operation of Dr M. Desai.

REFERENCES

1. BERRIEN, F. K., Finger oscillations as indices of emotion. 1. Preliminary validation. *J. exp. Psychol.*, **24**, 485–498, 1939.
2. BLEULER, E., *Affektivitat, Suggestibilitat, Paranoia.* Halle: Verlag Carl Marhold, 1906.
3. CHAMPION, R. A., Studies of experimentally induced disturbance. *Austral. J. Psychol.*, **2**, 90–99, 1950.
4. DAVIS, D. R., *Pilot Error—Some Laboratory Experiments.* London: HMSO, 1948.
5. FREEMAN, G. L. & PATHMAN, J. H., The relation of overt muscular discharge to physiological recovery from experimentally induced displacement. *J. exp. Psychol.*, **30**, 161–174, 1942.
6. —— & SIMPSON, R. M., The effects of experimentally induced muscular tension upon palmar skin resistance. *J. Gen. Psychol.*, **18**, 319–326, 1938.
7. FOULDS, G. A., Temperamental differences in maze performance.

Part II. The effect of distraction and of electro-convulsive therapy on psychomotor retardation. *Brit. J. Psychol.*, **43**, 33–41, 1952.

8. HILDEBRAND, H. P., A Factorial Study of Introversion-Extraversion by Means of Objective Tests. Unpublished Ph.D. thesis, University of London Library, 1953.

9. KENDALL, M. G., A new measure of rank correlation. *Biometrika*, **30**, 81–93, 1938.

10. LAWLEY, D. N., The application of the Maximum Likelihood Method of Factor Analysis. *Brit. J. Psychol.*, **33**, 172–175, 1943.

11. MOSES, L. E., Non-parametric statistics for psychological research. *Psychol. Bull.*, **49**, 122–143, 1952.

12. NUNBERG, H., On the physical accompaniments of association processes. In Jung, C. G., *Studies in Word Association*. London: Heinemann, 1918.

13. STAUDT, V. & KUBIS, J. F., The psychogalvanic response and its relation to changes in tension and relaxation. *J. Psychol.*, **25**, 443–453, 1948.

14. VENABLES, P. H., Some findings on the relationship between G.S.R. and motor task variables. *J. Gen. Psychol.*, **55**, 199–202, 1956.

15. WHITE, M. M., Relation of bodily tension to electrical resistance. *J. exp. Psychol.*, **13**, 267–277, 1930.

16. WHITFIELD, J. W., Rank correlation between two variables one of which is ranked, the other dichotomous. *Biometrika*, **34**, 292–296, 1947.

42

Personality Functions of Graphic Constriction and Expansiveness[1]

MICHAEL A. WALLACH & RUTHELLEN C. GAHM

First published in *Journal of Personality*, **28**, 73–88, 1960

INTRODUCTION

IT is widely assumed that the constriction or expansiveness of a person's graphic expression is in some sense indicative of his personality. Consider, for example, the modern artists Jackson Pollock (Ref. 13) and Paul Klee (Ref. 16). Although, to be sure, there are numerous dimensions along which their works differ, one striking difference is in the size of their paintings. Pollock's canvases are immense—one even being approximately 9 by 18 feet. He spread the canvas out on his studio floor and walked over and around it as he worked, dropping the paint in great splashes with wide, sweeping movements. Even then the limitation of a single painting's possible size was too restricting. He could satisfy his desire for graphic expansion only by unrolling huge areas of canvas and painting one giant picture after another serially as if they were one work, with but narrow separations between them. And his personality? According to such biographers as Hunter and Willing, Pollock was taciturn and ascetic, but outwardly anguished—his behaviour reflecting anxiety (Refs. 13 and 22).

Different from Pollock, both in his art and in his nature, was Klee. His pictures were tiny—four by six inches was not an atypical size—and they were worked on painstakingly and slowly. Klee often would observe a painting of his for hours while silently smoking his pipe, then walk to it and add a line or dot of colour and resume his observation. Klee too was an introvert, but with a higher wall between himself and the world.

[1] This study is part of a research project supported by a grant (M–269) to the senior author from the National Institute of Mental Health, United States Public Health Service, conducted under the auspices of the Age Center of New England, Inc. Grateful thanks are due Donald S. Dunbar of Simmons College for making classes available. Nathan Kogan and Lise Wallach made invaluable critical comments on the manuscript.

His appearance was one of self-containment, his behaviour not reflecting the disturbance that, from the accounts of Miller (Ref. 16), Baynes (Ref. 5) and other biographers, we judge to have been present.

Perhaps the most extensive clinical attempt to assess the relationship between painting and personality has been the study of children by Alschuler & Hattwick (Ref. 3). Their work led them to decide that graphic expression of spatial expansiveness tends to reflect not the child's isolated emotional state, but rather how the child relates to his social environment. Children who were very restrictive spatially in their paintings often seemed more socially withdrawn. This same general finding of a relationship between social introversion and the use of less space in children's paintings was reported by Elkisch (Ref. 9). Precker (Ref. 17) has reviewed much of this literature.

While a similar interpretation of graphic constriction and expansiveness also is offered in much of the work on handwriting interpretation (e.g. Ref. 24) and on the consistency shown among various kinds of expressive behaviour in the same individual (e.g. Refs. 1 & 2), it is often argued that just the reverse can occur. Alschuler & Hattwick, for example, report that

'. . . some children conceal their true feelings in their overt behaviour but express them in their easel painting. In such cases, paintings and overt behaviour are likely to reflect contrasting, rather than similar, drives' (Ref. 3, Vol. 1, pp. 4–5).

Such contrast, indeed, is a decisive reason for using projective techniques: they are expected to reveal tendencies that are not permitted overt expression (Ref. 7). Graphic constriction or expansiveness may indicate just the opposite of what the individual allows himself at an overt level, his fear of direct expression permitting him only this indirect compensation or displacement. This would certainly seem to be the case, for instance, with Pollock in contrast to Klee. While Klee *reflects* his introversion by painting in a very constricted space, Pollock *compensates* for his introversion by painting over a huge area.

Graphic constriction or expansiveness, then, may serve either as a reflection of social introversion-extraversion tendencies, or, alternatively, as a safe level on which to displace behaviour tendencies undergoing overt inhibition. We may label these 'reflections' and 'displacement' functions respectively—emphasis on the first being more congenial to the general idea that personality expresses itself in a consistent manner at all levels; emphasis on the second, to the idea that personality may express covertly or implicitly tendencies that are contrary to overt conduct.

To leave the matter at this, however, hardly would be satisfying. We would find ourselves able to 'explain' any overt adaptation as symptomatic either of a parallel or a contradictory covert need. That is, we could invoke the 'reaction formation clause' whenever it suited our fancy. The present research hence aimed at resolving these interpretations by proposing that each of the two suggested functions becomes the crucial one under different conditions. Our objective was to test hypotheses concerning the particular conditions under which reflection and displacement functions would be served. The hypotheses arise from an approach and findings discussed elsewhere (Refs. 20 and 21) and hinge on the following proposals.

A person's claiming to want isolation from others (social introversion) may be viewed as one adaptation to the presence of others in his surroundings. As Wallach & Greenberg have suggested, a general indication of the extent to which this sort of adaptation functions successfully for the individual is whether he shows a low or high level of anxiety. If a person's overt attitude of moving away from people is accompanied by strong anxiety, the preference that he claims for social isolation has failed to defend him against anxiety and we may assume that he still possesses a strong need for others. If, on the other hand, a minimum of anxiety is found for an individual professing social introversion, then his mode of adaptation seems to be working. There is no reason in this latter case to expect strong, unconscious needs running counter to the social introversion that he claims to find congenial. Rather, we would expect consistency between the person's overt expression and implicit needs.

These views suggest the conditions that should promote functions of reflection vs. displacement in the personality's expressive behaviour. If the individual's adaptation of social introversion is successful, as indicated by an absence of anxiety, then such introversion should be reflected in his covert behaviour too, since no strong contrary need is being inhibited from the sphere of overt conduct. Consistency between explicit and implicit expressive behaviour is predicted. If, on the other hand, the person's social-isolation adaptation is accompanied by a high level of anxiety, this implies the continued existence of an inhibited need pressing for overt expression. We hence expect it to be displaced to the level of covert behaviour, making for an inconsistency between the directions of conscious and covert conduct.

The relations between social extraversion and anxiety, on the other hand, do not seem amenable to a parallel interpretation. Wallach & Greenberg's findings suggested that extraversion is a more 'normal' adaptation than introversion, so that the meaning of anxiety for social extraverts seemed difficult to fathom (Ref. 21). All one could predict from the research just cited was that covert expression of extraversion might well be expected to accompany its overt expression. This covert extraversion should be less intense than the covert extraversion shown by anxious social introverts, however, since such implicit expression of extraversion is the only channel open for persons of the latter sort, while social extraverts also permit themselves an overt display of social involvement.

Where does graphic constriction and expansiveness enter this picture? It enters as one mode of covert expressive behaviour related to social introversion-extraversion tendencies. Moving toward other people may be covertly expressed by an expansiveness in the area covered by one's graphic movements, while moving away from others and back to the self may be covertly expressed by a constriction in this area (as suggested, for example, by Alschuler & Hattwick (Ref. 3) and by Wolff & Precker (Ref. 23)). Since degree of graphic constriction thus would be a covert rather than direct indication of social tendencies, it could function either to express attitudes also shared at the conscious level, or as a channel for the displacement of attitudes denied conscious admission.

Our earlier discussion suggests that the first of these possibilities should occur when a consciously held attitude of introversion is a successful mode of social adaptation, thus leading to graphic constriction (as, for example, in the non-anxious social introversion of Klee). The second possibility, on the other hand, should occur when the introversion attitude fails as a means of adaptation, thus resulting in a push toward graphic expansiveness (as, for instance, in the anxious social introversion of Pollock). Success or failure of an introversion adaptation (as defined in terms of anxiety level) thus would constitute the conditions under which graphic constriction-expansiveness would serve reflection or displacement functions for the personality. Extraversion attitudes, on the other hand, should lead to a middling degree of graphic expansiveness, since the graphic medium reflects an extraversion part of which also is manifested overtly. In this latter case, covert means—for example, graphic expansiveness—are not the only channel available for extraversion's expression, as in the situation for anxious social introverts.

In short, the following particular hypotheses were derived for evaluation in the present experiment:

(1) When an overt adaptation of social introversion is accompanied by high anxiety, S's graphic expression will be *more* expansive than that of social extraverts and nonanxious social introverts.

(2) When an overt adaptation of social introversion is not accompanied by high anxiety, S's graphic expression will be *less* expansive than that of social extraverts and anxious social introverts.

METHOD

Subjects

Women students in introductory psychology classes at Simmons College participated in two group administration sessions separated by a two months' interval. The first was devoted to a doodling procedure; the second, to the taking of a personality inventory. The total number of Ss present during both sessions was 76 and they identified themselves by name in the case of each procedure.

Doodling Procedures

Measuring the area of paper covered by a person's free doodling seemed to constitute a straightforward way of assessing tendencies toward constriction or expansiveness in graphic style. But if one tries to induce students in a classroom to doodle simply by asking them, one usually meets with a high proportion of refusals. On the other hand, it is just as inappropriate for our purposes to force 'doodling' by asking S to transcribe designs revealed to view under minimal perceptual conditions. This latter method was used by Aronson, who tachistoscopically exposed a slide showing various 'basic' doodle patterns and requested S to draw what he saw (Ref. 4)—a procedure which really is closer to selective copying than to doodling.

The approach adopted in the present experiment lay mid-way between these two extremes. Its aim was to provide a setting which easily would induce everyone to doodle, but would introduce as little visual stimulus constraint as possible. In addition, it was recognized that doodling requested in a classroom situation is a novel task likely to reflect random variability from short-run practice effects as well as the influence of personality. It therefore was necessary to construct a situation which would let S gain familiarity with what was required of her and to measure doodling after familiarity with the task had been achieved—i.e., after random effects from settling down into the task had washed out.

Toward these ends, the following procedure was designed. Doodling was elicited under the guise of a test of creative imagination in which S was to doodle in the manner she thought would best express music that she heard. The S first would listen to a musical selection without doodling and then doodle while hearing it a second time. Between these two hearings of a single piece, the creative imagination aspect of the procedure was reinforced by asking S to write a story suggested to her by the music. Three such pairs of musical selections were presented in succession. They were all jazz recordings, 185, 147 and 146 seconds in length respectively and were heard in the same order by everyone.

Presenting the doodling task as a test of one's imaginativeness in responding to music made it difficult for anyone to refuse on the ground of being without an idea. On the other hand, maximum freedom in doodling was provided since no visual stimulus constraint was present at all. Finally, random variability was minimized by repeating the doodling task three times and taking as one's measure only the final (i.e., third) set of doodles—the one that should be as free as possible from random variability due to settling down into the task.

The following instructions were read to S after she had heard the first piece once without doodling (and without knowing yet that she would be asked to doodle):

'Now we will replay the musical selection. Once more, let the mood really come over you. But this time, I'd like you to draw doodles on this page *while* you listen to the music. Doodle in whatever way you think best expresses the music to which you are listening. Just draw whatever doodles you want, in whatever way you want; but all your doodling should be directly inspired by the mood of the music to which you are listening.

'One important thing: your doodles should not show any recognizable animals, people or things in them. Don't draw people, animals, houses, or anything like that. Just draw designs—whatever kind of designs the music inspires you to draw. Your doodling should be inspired by the music and should be designs rather than anything specific. You have already heard this selection. When I play it again, start doodling in whatever way the music makes you feel.'

After hearing the second piece once and again after hearing the third piece once, a slightly abridged form of the above was read again.

Doodling was permitted only during the second hearing of a piece and the doodling to each selection was done on a separate blank sheet of $8\frac{1}{2}$ by 11 inch white paper. The S's doodling pad was turned to a blank sheet of this paper during the first hearing of a piece. The instructions specifically asked S to draw designs rather than representations of animate or inanimate objects, because it was felt that the particular representational content chosen could itself act as one influence on the area of the drawing made—an influence not relevant to the present study. All the Ss complied with this request.

Scoring of the Doodles

The final set of doodles produced by each S was scored for graphic constriction vs. expansiveness in the following way. An 8 by 10 inch cross-grid consisting of 20 squares, each two inches on a side, was laid out on a sheet of tracing paper, there being four squares across and five down the sheet. The grid was placed over a page of doodles. Keeping the grid's edges parallel to the edges of the page of doodles at all times and keeping the long dimension of the grid parallel to the long dimension of the page of doodles, the grid was adjusted until the number of squares into which doodling fell was minimized. This minimum number of squares covering the doodling was then counted, a person's possible graphic constriction-expansiveness score hence ranging from 1 to 20.

This measure of graphic expansiveness was obtained by each of two independent scorers, neither of whom knew the personality scores of the Ss when assessing graphic expansiveness. Interscorer reliability for the final doodle set was calculated by summing the number of agreements on squares and dividing by this sum plus the sum of the number of disagreements on squares. In more detail, the number of agreements on squares for a page of doodles was the smaller number of squares scored by one of the two judges. When the two judges agreed on the number of squares, then all the squares represented 'agreements'. The number of disagreements on squares for a page of doodles was the difference between the smaller and the larger number of squares which the respective judges scored, when the two judges differed. These agreement and disagreement figures each were summed across Ss, the final reliability quotient being sum agreements over sum agreements plus sum disagreements, expressed as a decimal. This reliability was 0·96.[1] One of the

[1] The reliability quotient was based on the 98 Ss who attended the doodling session a larger N than the 76 who attended both doodling and personality test sessions.

scorers resolved those cases in which disagreements of scoring had occurred.

Personality Assessment Procedure

The untitled paper-and-pencil questionnaire administered during the second class session consisted of the Neuroticism and Extraversion scales from Eysenck's Maudsley Personality Inventory (Refs. 11 & 14) and the Emotional Extraversion scale from the Minnesota T–S–E Inventory (Ref. 10). The items from these three scales were randomly interspersed and the scales were scored in the ways described by their authors.

The rationale for using this questionnaire is as follows. The propositions and hypotheses presented earlier led us to be concerned with two personality variables: a person's level of manifest anxiety and her overt attitude of social introversion or extraversion (social isolation vs. expressed desire for the company of others). These are the two personality dimensions that emerge in a majority of factor analyses of paper-and-pencil personality tests. Eysenck's Neuroticism scale provides an index of Ss' admitted anxiety, correlating highly with the Taylor Manifest Anxiety Scale (Ref. 19). His Extraversion scale, on the other hand, correlates strongly with the Social Extraversion scale of the Minnesota T-S-E and only to a small extent with the latter's Emotional Extraversion scale. The Eysenck scales were preferred because of the thorough investigation that has been made of their relations with other instruments.

The Emotional Extraversion scale from the Minnesota T-S-E was added because, although our theory and hypotheses specifically concerned social introversion-extraversion and manifest anxiety, Allport & Vernon's work on expressive consistency (Ref. 2) suggested that one might expect a relation between avowed openness of emotional expression and expansiveness of graphic expression.

RESULTS AND DISCUSSION

Analysis Techniques

The two-way analyses of variance reported below each involved some two of the three personality dimensions as treatment variables whose effects on graphic expansiveness were to be examined. In each analysis four groups were constructed, representing the high–high, high–low, low–high and low–low combinations of any two of these personality variables. Each variable therefore was dichotomized by a split of the sample into high and low scorers. For none of the three variables could the split be exactly at the median, because a number of Ss were tied for a score overlapping the median in the case of each variable. In each of the three cases, most Ss tied for that score were on one side of the median and only a few on the other.

Since it was inadvisable to reduce the sample size by dropping the whole group of Ss whose score value fell at the median of the distribution, the split on each variable was made in such a manner as to yield upper and lower halves that were as close as possible to equality. In fact, the extent of the cutting point's variation from half-and-half never exceeded a 46–54 per cent split and was closer than that to half-and-half in two of the three splits.[1]

In order to equalize the cell sizes in any two-by-two analysis, the cell size for an analysis was taken as the smallest number of Ss in any cell and Ss beyond that number were removed from the other three cells by random elimination. Bartlett's test for homogeneity (Ref. 18, pp. 249–250) was made for the variances in each analysis and the variances were homogeneous. Since none of the bases of classification involved random sampling, the fixed constants model (Ref. 15, pp. 304–306) was used for choosing the error term in calculating F ratios.

Anxiety Level, Social Introversion-Extraversion and Graphic Expansiveness

Before turning to the test of our hypotheses on the interaction between anxiety level and social introversion-extraversion, let us consider the anxiety and social introversion-extraversion variables separately. While the correlation between level of manifest anxiety and degree of graphic expansiveness is -0.03 (insignificant for our sample of 76), that between social introversion-extraversion and graphic expansiveness is 0.36 (significant beyond the 0.01 level for an N of 76)—the individual who is more extraverted socially also being more expansive in her graphic productions. These trends are reflected in the row and column effects for the joint analysis of these variables presented in Tables 1 and 2. While the F for anxiety level is not at all significant, that for social introversion-extraversion exceeds the 0.08 level.[2] The correlation between

[1] The most deviant break, that of 46–54 per cent, occurred in the case of the emotional extraversion variable.

[2] The social introversion-extraversion effect reaches a lower level of significance in this analysis of variance than in the Pearson correlation statistic, because some Ss were lost in the analysis of variance due to their random elimination from oversized cells. Thus, while the total N in the correlation computation was 76, that for the analysis of variance was 60.

the manifest anxiety and social introversion-extraversion scales, by the way, is a nonsignificant −0·15 (for an N of 88 including the above 76).

TABLE 1

MEAN DEGREES OF GRAPHIC EXPANSIVENESS FOR
SOCIAL EXTRAVERSION AND ANXIETY GROUPS
(N = 15 per Cell)

	High social extraversion	High social introversion
High anxiety	8·67	11·33
Low anxiety	14·20	6·73

TABLE 2

ANALYSIS OF VARIANCE, GRAPHIC EXPANSIVENESS FOR
SOCIAL EXTRAVERSION AND ANXIETY GROUPS
(N = 60)

	df	Mean square	F	$p<$
Social extraversion	1	86·40	3·36	<0·08
Anxiety	1	3·26	0·13	n.s.
Interaction	1	385·07	14·99	<0·001
Within cells	56	25·68		

But our hypotheses concerned not the direct but the interactive effects of these personality variables on graphic constriction-expansiveness. This interaction, as shown in Tables 1 and 2, is significant beyond the 0·001 level. The lack of correlation between anxiety level alone and graphic expansiveness, then, comes about because presence or absence of anxiety has a different kind of effect on graphic expression depending on whether the individual in question is a social introvert or extravert. To explore this finding further, separate t tests were calculated for high- vs. low-anxiety extraverts and for high- vs. low-anxiety introverts. For the extraverts, where the mean for high anxiety Ss is 8·67 and that for low-anxiety Ss is 14·20, t is 2·94 (p<0·01 for Ns of 15 each). For the introverts, where the mean for high-anxiety Ss is 11·33 and that for low-anxiety Ss is 6·73, t is 2·53 (p<0·02 for Ns of 15 each).

While the general directions of the present interaction parallel those found in the Wallach & Greenberg study on symbolic sexual arousal

(Ref. 21), there are certain differences between the two sets of results. In the present study it was predicted that non-anxious introverts would show the greatest graphic constriction and inspection of Table 1 indicates this to be the case. It was also predicted that anxious introverts would show the greatest graphic expansiveness and the results show that they indeed are high in expansiveness. However, they are exceeded by one other group: non-anxious extraverts. In short, the theory's predictions were verified concerning the personality functions of graphic expansiveness for anxious vs. non-anxious social introverts. Its prediction, however, that both extravert groups would fall in the middle of the constriction-expansiveness continuum was not borne out, for while the anxious social extravert group is indeed in the middle, as expected, the non-anxious social extravert group falls at the high expansiveness extreme.

The latter result may be understood, however, if we simply extend our proposals concerning anxiety level and social introversion and apply them also to anxiety level and social extraversion. Our initial view about extraversion assumed it to be a more 'normal' adaptation than introversion and hence one to which our reasoning concerning anxiety as indicative of a defence's failure vs. success was inapplicable. The compulsive sociability frequently found in our culture makes it reasonable, however, to propose that an overt attitude of social extraversion may function in just as defensive a manner as one of social introversion. Just as we postulated that an anxious social introvert would really like to move toward others, so also we might expect that an anxious social extravert—a compulsive social mixer—would really be happier if he could avoid others. Since such a need to move away from others is denied overt expression, it should appear covertly in the form of greater graphic constriction than is found for non-anxious social extraverts. This in fact is the case.

In sum, the findings suggest an extension to extraversion of our views concerning introversion. Success or failure of a mode of overt social adaptation may be judged from the attendant anxiety level in the case not only of introversion but also extraversion, high anxiety indicating a failure of the adaptation. If overt introversion *or* extraversion is unaccompanied by anxiety, then its covert expression should be consistent in direction—the non-anxious introvert being more constricted graphically and the non-anxious extravert more expansive. Graphic constriction-expansiveness serves a reflection function. On the other hand, if overt introversion *or* extraversion is accompanied by a high anxiety level, thus indicating its failure as a mode of adaptation, then we expect there to be a strong implicit need running in a contrary direction—the anxious introvert covertly seeking to move toward others and hence being more expansive graphically, the anxious extravert covertly seeking to move away from others and hence being more constricted graphically. Graphic constriction-expansiveness serves a displacement function of permitting the expression of needs inhibited from explicit recognition.

A further point requires discussion in comparing the present results with those of the Wallach & Greenberg experiment. In the present study, the highest degree of graphic expansiveness is found in the case of non-anxious social extraverts (the mean score being 14·20), anxious social introverts being next in order (11·33). On the other hand, in the research by Wallach & Greenberg concerning symbolic sexual arousal and using the same Ss, these two groups are reversed: the highest degree of such arousal is found for anxious social introverts (a mean score of 6·13), with the non-anxious social extraverts being next (3·93). The orderings of the remaining two groups are the same in both studies—anxious social extraverts being next-to-lowest and non-anxious social introverts being lowest on both arousal and graphic indices. Since symbolic arousal and graphic expansiveness perform a reflection function for the non-anxious social extraverts and a displacement function for the anxious social introverts, these findings indicate that the function of displacement is stronger than that of reflection in the case of symbolic sexual arousal, but the function of reflection is stronger than that of displacement in the case of graphic expansiveness.

Freud proposes that use of a covert form of expression for the displacement of needs denied overt expression becomes more possible as that covert channel lies at a greater distance, in some sense, from the relevant overt form (Refs. 6 and 12). The findings of our two studies hence lead to the suggestion that the index of graphic constriction-expansiveness in the present experiment is psychologically closer to professed attitudes of introversion-extraversion than the index of symbolic sexual arousal in the Wallach & Greenberg research. The graphic constriction-expansiveness variable would seem closer to the individual's surface and hence more reflective of the individual's general expressive style. It is more suitable for the reflection of attitudes permitted overt outlet. The symbolic sexual arousal index, on the other hand, would seem further from the surface and hence more suitable for the displacement of attitudes denied overt outlet. This reasoning suggests why reflection for non-anxious extraverts is stronger than displacement for anxious

N

introverts is stronger than reflection for non-anxious extraverts in the symbolic sexual arousal study. Such an interpretation would render understandable both the similarities and the differences between the two studies' findings.

Further Findings

Several questions remain concerning the possible range of psychological meaning that may be given to the graphic constriction-expansiveness variable. Our results led to the suggestion, for example, that the graphic variable, as a covert form of avowed social introversion-extraversion lies closer to the latter than does the index of symbolic sexual arousal used in the Wallach & Greenberg experiment. Two further possible relations of graphic expansiveness were explored in the present study: ones concerning emotional expansiveness and the tendency to agree.

Emotional Expansiveness

There is evidence of a moderate relationship between openness of emotional expression as measured by the emotional introversion-extraversion scale administered to our Ss and graphic expansiveness; the correlation between these two variables being 0.24 (significant beyond the 0.05 level with an N of 76). That this relationship is not strong, however, is indicated from further two-way analyses of variance. In one, examining emotional introversion-extraversion and social introversion-extraversion in relation to the graphic measure, the only significant or near-significant effect was caused by social introversion-extraversion. Social introverts again were more constricted ($F = 4.45$; $df = 1, 64$; $p < 0.05$). In another, examining emotional introversion-extraversion and high vs. low manifest anxiety, none of the effects on the graphic index approached significance. As regards the suggestion drawn from Allport & Vernon's research, then, our results indicate that there indeed is some—but not a high degree—of expressive consistency between a person's graphic constriction-expansiveness and her degree of emotional openness.

While the emotional and social introversion-extraversion scales of our personality inventory are not significantly related ($r = 0.16$, which is not significant for the sample of 88 who took the questionnaire), there is a moderate relationship between this inventory's emotional introversion-extraversion and manifest anxiety scales ($r = 0.23$, $p < 0.05$ with an N of 88). If anything, emotional introversion-extraversion—the tendency to express all kinds of emotional states, including negative ones—thus has something in common not with social intraversion-extraversion but with manifest anxiety—the tendency to express negative emotional states in particular. The degree of commonality is not sufficient, however, to cause an interaction effect between social and emotional introversion-extraversion for the graphic variable. It is of interest that this same interaction approaches significance for these Ss ($p < 0.07$) when symbolic sexual arousal is the dependent variable and that this effect results solely from a heightened mean for the cell of Ss who are emotional extraverts and social introverts. These are the people for whom heightened arousal or graphic expansiveness would constitute a displacement of social tendencies which are denied at the overt level. Once again, then, we see that symbolic sexual arousal is more suitable for this function of displacement than is graphic expansion.

Tendency to Agree

Since all the manifest anxiety scale items are keyed so that 'yes' responses yield a high anxiety score and two-thirds of the social extraversion scale items are keyed so that 'yes' responses result in a high social extraversion score, it is necessary to consider whether the simple tendency to agree with test items (Ref. 8) exerts an effect on graphic constriction-expansiveness. That it does not is evident from a consideration of the yes-no preferences being shown by our four groups of anxious or non-anxious social introverts and extraverts. Both the anxious social extraverts and non-anxious social introverts are graphically constricted: yet the former group is answering most items 'yes', while the latter group answers most items 'no'. If anything, this would lead one to think that Ss who consistently agreed or disagreed in their questionnaire responses were more constricted graphically than those who sometimes agreed and sometimes did not.

But on the hypothesis of a response-set bias, most people should exhibit such agreement or disagreement consistency. The existence of anxious social introvert and non-anxious extravert groups—each of whom must be marking 'yes' about half the time and 'no' the other half—shows that at least half the Ss are inconsistent. Further, a general predominance of inconsistency is indicated by the following. If a general agreement consistency effect were operating to a significant degree, then there should be a significant positive correlation between the two scales, since an agreement-biased person would score high in manifest anxiety and in the middle on social extraversion. A correlation of

−0·15 was found (N = 88), which is nonsignificant and even negative in direction.

SUMMARY AND CONCLUSIONS

An experiment was devised to explore the personality functions of graphic constriction and expansiveness. We began with a proposal concerning the conditions under which graphic constriction-expansiveness should be reflective of overt social introversion or extraversion tendencies respectively, in contrast to the conditions under which this graphic variable should serve as a displacement for the expression of social tendencies denied overt outlet. With female undergraduates as Ss, graphic constriction-expansiveness was measured in terms of the amount of area filled with doodling in a procedure designed to elicit expressive graphic designs and aspects of personality relevant to our hypotheses were assessed with a paper-and-pencil inventory.

The main results were as follows: Social introverts high in anxiety level were more expansive graphically than non-anxious social introverts, while social extraverts high in anxiety were more constricted graphically than non-anxious social extraverts. Non-anxious extraverts were also more expansive graphically than non-anxious introverts, while anxious extraverts were more constricted graphically than anxious introverts.

These findings led to the following conclusions: graphic constriction or expansiveness may serve as a covert expression of tendencies to move away from (social introversion) or toward others (social extraversion) respectively. Success or failure of each of these modes of overt social adaptation may be judged from the attendant anxiety level of the individual, high anxiety indicating a failure of the adaptation. If overt introversion or extraversion is unaccompanied by anxiety, then its covert expression will be consistent in direction—the non-anxious introvert being more constricted graphically, the non-anxious extravert more expansive. Under these conditions, graphic constriction-expansiveness serves a reflection function. But if overt introversion or extraversion is accompanied by a high level of anxiety, thus indicating its failure as a mode of adaptation, then there is a strong covert need running in an opposite direction—the anxious introvert covertly seeking to move toward others and therefore being more expansive graphically, the anxious extravert covertly seeking to move away from others and therefore being more constricted graphically. Under these conditions, the person's overt and implicit levels of expression are inconsistent in direction and graphic constriction-expansiveness serves a displacement function of permitting the expression of needs denied explicit recognition.

Further discussion compared the present findings with a study by Wallach & Greenberg on symbolic sexual arousal to music (Ref. 21) and considered additional results on emotional expansiveness and the tendency to agree.

REFERENCES

1. ALLPORT, G. W., *Personality*. New York: Holt, 1937.
2. —— & VERNON, P. E. *Studies in Expressive Movement*. New York: Macmillan, 1933.
3. ALSCHULER, ROSE H. & HATTWICK, LA BERTA W., *Painting and Personality*. Chicago: University of Chicago Press, 1947.
4. ARONSON, E., The need for achievement as measured by graphic expression. In *Motives in Fantasy, Action and Society* (ed. J. W. Atkinson). New York: Van Nostrand, 1958.
5. BAYNES, H. G., *Mythology of the Soul*. Baltimore: Williams & Wilkins, 1940.
6. BREUER, J. & FREUD, S., *Studies in Hysteria*. New York: Nervous and Mental Disease Publishing Co., 1936.
7. CATTELL, R. B., Principles of design in 'projective' or misperceptive tests of personality. In *An Introduction to Projective Techniques* (ed. H. H. Anderson & Gladys L. Anderson). New York: Prentice-Hall, 1951.
8. COUCH, A. & KENISTON, K., Yeasayers and Naysayers: Agreeing Response Set as a Personality Variable. *J. abnorm. soc. Psychol.*, **60,** 151–174, 1960.
9. ELKISCH, PAULA, Children's drawings in a projective technique. *Psychological Monographs*, **58,** No. 1 (Whole No. 266), 1945.
10. EVANS, CATHERINE & MCCONNELL, T. R., *Minnesota T-S-E Inventory*. (Rev. ed.) Princeton: Educational Testing Service, 1957.
11. EYSENCK, H. J., The questionnaire measurement of neuroticism and extraversion. *Rev. Psicol.*, **54,** 113–140, 1956.
12. FREUD, S., Repression. In *Collected papers*. Vol. 4. London: Hogarth Press, 1925.

13. HUNTER, S., *Jackson Pollock*. New York: Museum of Modern Art, 1956.
14. JENSEN, A. R., The Maudsley personality inventory. *Acta Psychol.*, **14**, 314–325, 1958.
15. McNEMAR, Q., *Psychological Statistics*. (Rev. ed.) New York: Wiley & Sons, 1955.
16. MILLER, MARGARET (ed.), *Paul Klee*. New York: Museum of Modern Art, 1946.
17. PRECKER, J. A., Painting and drawing in personality assessment. *J. proj. Tech.*, **14**, 262–286, 1950.
18. SNEDECOR, G. W., *Statistical Methods*. Ames, Iowa: Iowa State Coll. Press, 1946.
19. TAYLOR, JANET A., A personality scale of manifest anxiety. *J. abnorm. soc. Psychol.*, **48**, 285–290, 1953.
20. WALLACH, M. A., Art, science and representation: toward an experimental psychology of aesthetics. *J. Aesthet. & Art Crit.*, **18**, 159–173, 1959.
21. —— & GREENBERG, CAROL, Personality functions of symbolic sexual arousal to music. *Psychol. Monogr.*, **74**, Whole No. 494, 1960.
22. WILLING, V., Thoughts after a car crash. *Encounter*, **7**, 66–68, 1956.
23. WOLFF, W. & PRECKER, J. A., Expressive movement and the methods of experimental depth psychology. In *An Introduction to Projective Techniques* (ed. H. H. Anderson & Gladys L. Anderson). New York: Prentice-Hall, 1951.
24. WOLFSON, ROSE, Graphology. In *An Introduction to Projective Techniques* (ed. H. H. Anderson & Gladys L. Anderson). New York: Prentice-Hall, 1951.

43

Extraversion, Neuroticism, and Expressive Behaviour: an Application of Wallach's Moderator Effect to Handwriting Analysis

RONALD TAFT[1]

First published in *Journal of Personality*, **35**, 570–584, 1967

PERSONALITY traits are dimensions that represent the characteristic behavioural unities of an individual. The behaviour concerned is mainly instrumental, that is, directed toward the achievement of goals and the traits are, to a large extent, an inference from the type of goals sought. Thus, many trait descriptions can be translated into goal descriptions; for example, the trait of gregariousness could otherwise be described as a desire for affiliation with people. Personality is to some extent, then, reflected in the individual's choice of goals. But it also is reflected in the characteristic way in which he pursues the goals, i.e., his 'expressive style'. A similar distinction has been made by Guilford between 'hormetic' and 'temperament' traits (Ref. 12). For example, a person who typically acts out his impulses may express his need for affiliation by showing initiative in actively seeking social interactions. Or, a person who has a nervous, moody temperament may manifest considerable fluctuations in his pursuit of affiliative relationships. Such differences in style represent personality traits and provide a source from which these traits can be inferred.

Because of the unity of personality functioning it has been assumed that some expressive traits and even certain goal-directed ones, such as the need for affiliation, can be inferred from expressive movements. The most widely used source of this type used for personality assessment is handwriting because of several practical advantages. It provides a permanent record which can be obtained from the subject without his knowing the use to which it will be put and its form is sufficiently standardized to permit a comparison between the performance of different individuals. In addition, handwriting, in contrast with most other

[1] The author thanks Valerie Yule for her assistance in the collection and analysis of the data.

expressive movements, represents a communication and it therefore also permits the interpretation of variations in the movements in relation to the content.

The traditional methods used for interpreting personality from handwriting have been complex signs, unanalysed intuitions and inferences by analogy. Graphologists have objected to attempts to relate simple objective signs in the handwriting to single personality traits on the grounds that such attempts violate the complexities of the relationship. (See, for instance, the criticism by Meloun (Ref. 17), of such a study by Harvey (Ref. 13). Atomistic studies, however, are necessary if we are to advance our understanding of *how* personality characteristics are reflected in handwriting, rather than the more general question of *whether* they are.

The present study investigates the relationship between the expression of tempo and expansiveness in handwriting and two temperamental traits—extraversion and neuroticism—that have been claimed by Eysenck to be basic dimensions in personality (Ref. 8). These traits have been operationally defined for this study as the scores on the E and N scales of Eysenck's MPI (Ref. 7). The Extraversion items refer to such topics as liveliness ('Would you rate yourself as a lively individual?'), social initiative, gregariousness and a preference for action over thought. In other words, persons who score high on the E scale could be expected to invest more energy into external activities than those who score low.[1]

Among the characteristics which graphologists traditionally look for in handwriting are signs of the degree to which the writer constricts or releases the investment of energy in his activities. For example, Jacoby claims that writers with wide movements are 'genuinely forgetful of themselves, feel drawn to the wide world', while writers with narrow movements 'seek to keep to themselves, to preserve themselves and not to lose themselves to the world' (Ref. 14, p. 42). Some slight empirical support is provided for such interpretations by Meredith's finding that Cattell's UI 21 factor ('exuberance vs. restraint') has loadings on measures of speed and expansiveness of expressive movements (Ref. 18). Cattell for a positive loading of expansiveness on this factor (Ref. 2, p. 247) cites evidence. Wallach & Gahm also found a positive correlation between extraversion and a measure of the expansiveness of 'doodles' drawn to accompany various pieces of music (Ref. 23).

---

[1] This inference is based on the manifest content of the inventory items, and it is not necessarily contradictory to Eysenck's argument that extraverts generate central inhibition at a faster rate than introverts (Ref. 6).

On the basis of such findings and the prima facie analysis of extraversion, a positive relationship between extraversion and size and speed of handwriting is hypothesized.

The Neuroticism items on the MPI relate to topics such as moodiness, depression, guilt, worry, tension, restlessness and lack of concentration. The N scale has been demonstrated to distinguish neurotic patients from normals (Ref. 7) and has a correlation of 0·77 with the Taylor MAS.[1] According to the Spence-Taylor hypothesis that manifest anxiety is an indicator of generalized drive (Ref. 22), it might be expected that persons high on anxiety (or neuroticism) would be more energetic than the low anxious. On the other hand, anxiety could be associated with defensiveness and inhibition so that the higher energy level would not be manifest in expressive behaviour. Energy output is not necessarily expressed in external modes; as Freud has stated for the case of libido, energy can be used in repression and other defensive processes and would therefore not be manifested through direct expression (Ref. 11). The amount of energy invested in actual motor behaviour is thus a function both of the typical energy level of the individual and of the amount that is available after the operation of defensive diversions.

Cattell & Scheier found no relationship between 'Anxiety' (UI 24) or 'Neural Reserves' (UI 23) and indicators of generalized drive (Ref. 3). If anything UI 24 is associated with less energetic expressive behaviour (low writing pressure and slow tempo in various performances) and UI 23, while unrelated to those measures, is associated with constricted expressive movements. Eysenck also found that various measures of tempo, including speed of writing numbers, loaded negatively on the neuroticism factor (Ref. 4).

In the light of both the theory and the above evidence, no hypothesis is proposed concerning the relationship between N and size and speed of handwriting. The scale is included in the study both for an additional investigation of the matter and in order to study its interactive effects when taken together with extraversion.

Several studies have been made of the relationship between questionnaire measures, peer ratings of personality traits and various handwriting characteristics (e.g. Refs. 1, 13, 16 & 20). These studies have failed to find any consistent association between measures of size of handwriting and indicators of extraversion or neuroticism. None of the studies,

---

[1] The N scale of the MPI has been used as the measure of anxiety rather than the MAS in order to make the present study parallel with that of Wallach & Gahm (Ref. 23).

N*

however, used any direct measures of speed.[1] They also reported most of their results in the form of generalizations about factor clusterings or ratio indices which do not provide sufficient information on the individual correlations for a check to be made on the findings for individual variables.

After summarizing the literature on experimental graphological research, Fluckiger, Tripp & Weinberg concluded that some traits, such as anxiety and feelings of dominance and impulsiveness, can be successfully predicted from handwriting (Ref. 10) but the case for direct relationships with actual handwriting signs is not a strong one.

METHOD

Subjects

The subjects were 86 senior psychology students, 32 males and 54 females, who were tested in three groups as part of their regular laboratory sessions.

Procedure

Observation Test: Without preliminary explanation, the subjects were given blank sheets of unruled foolscap paper and the following instructions:

'The first test is an observation test. When you are asked to start, on the first sheet of paper list as many objects as you can that you noticed between the hours of eight and nine this morning. Write across the paper and raise your hand when you have finished.'

After one minute the subjects were told to mark the point that they had reached; they were then instructed to continue until they had finished.

Printing: The instructions were:

'The next test, on the next sheet of paper, is a speed test of printing. When you are asked to begin, print as fast as you can the words FASTER AND FASTER AND FASTER until you are told to stop, just keeping on going across the page.'

After one minute the subjects were told to mark the point reached and then to continue. One more minute was allowed.

[1] Eysenck measured speed of writing but his study was aimed at discrimination between schizophrenics, depressives and normals, and did not use any direct measures of personality traits (Ref. 5).

Diagram Copying:

'On the next sheet of paper, copy the diagram on the board freehand. Draw it freehand, don't rub out or take another sheet of paper. This is not a speed test, you will not be timed.'

Friends:

'Now take the next sheet of paper and print across the page the initials of all the people you would count as your friends. Put your pencils down when you finish' (two minutes were allowed).

Dot Joining: The subjects were given two minutes to join dots as slowly as they could while still keeping the pencil moving.

Maudsley Personality Inventory: This test was presented with a minimum of introduction. Subjects were asked to answer it honestly 'for the sake of the experiment'. There was no mention of speed but at the end of one minute the subjects were instructed to mark the item reached and then to continue.

Introspective Report: Subjects were asked to write a report on their reactions to the previous tests. There was no hint of speed in the instructions but the subjects were stopped after three minutes.

Scores

The following scores were derived from the tests (the figures in parentheses represent the mean and standard deviation for each score).

1. MPI E scale: (28·1, 8·9).
2. MPI N scale: (23·7, 10·0).
3. Observation speed: number of words written in first minute (25·1, 13·8).
4. Printing speed first minute: number of letters printed in first minute (27·7, 3·9).
5. Printing speed second minute: (26·4, 3·4).
6. Introspective report speed: number of words in three minutes (76·0, 21·9).
7. Observation width: number of letters per line of writing, i.e., narrowness of letters (40·3, 13·3).

8. Printing width: number of letters printed per line in the full test (38·1, 10·1).
9. Friends width: number of letters per line (20·0, 5·6).
10. Introspective report width: number of letters per line (35·6, 12·3).
11. Lecture notes width: subjects provided a page of their lecture notes for this measure; score was the number of letters per line (39·1, 13·2).[1]
12. Observation density: number of letters in densest square inch (24·3, 8·6).
13. Printing density: number of letters in densest square inch (21·0, 7·2).
14. Good friends density: number of letters in densest square inch (9·9, 3·9).
15. Introspective report density: number of letters in densest square inch (22·2, 7·7).

In all computations concerning expansiveness variables (scores 7–15), signs were reversed so that a high score referred to large writing.

Five additional scores were obtained from the tests but were not relevant to the present variables. Fluency scores were derived from the number of responses given to the Observations and Friends tests and these correlated positively and significantly with extraversion. Speed of responding to the MPI, speed on the Dot Joining test and the size of the Diagram Copying were all unrelated to any of the other measures and were not used further.

RESULTS

Speed

The intercorrelation matrix of the four remaining measures of speed of writing (Table 1) indicates a clustering of three of them: the two measures of printing speed (variables 5 and 6) and the speed of writing the observations (variable 4). Speed in the introspective report may have been affected as much by thinking time as by speed of writing and there was also no speed pressure of any sort. The correlation of 0·82 between the two printing speed measures is a good indication of the reliability of this measure.

E was uncorrelated with the measures of writing speed, but N correlated significantly with speed of observations. The correlations between

---

[1] Measures 11–15 were available for only 59 cases.

N and the two measures of printing speed were also positive, but not significant.

TABLE 1

INTERCORRELATIONS OF EXTRAVERSION, NEUROTICISM AND SPEED (N = 86)

Measures	1	2	3	4	5
MPI					
1. Extraversion	—				
2. Neuroticism	−0·04	—			
Speed					
3. Observation	0·17	0·40*	—		
4. Printing (first minute)	0·03	0·12	0·27*	—	
5. Printing (second minute)	0·00	0·11	0·23*	0·82*	—
6. Introspective report	0·00	0·02	−0·02	−0·09	−0·07

* p<0·01

Expansiveness

The 9 measures of expansiveness of handwriting clustered together irrespective of whether they referred to printing or handwriting, width of letters or density of writing. The correlations ranged from 0·20 (variables 13, 14 and 15) to 0·78 (variables 12 and 14) with a median of 0·57. Thus, expansiveness was a comparatively consistent characteristic.

E failed to correlate significantly with any of the measures of expansiveness. N also was uncorrelated with the width of writing, but it was correlated negatively with all of the measures of density of writing: i.e., the higher the neuroticism the more letters per square inch. The correlations were significant (p<0·05) for density of observations (variable 11) and density of lecture notes (variable 15). Since these correlations with N did not occur for length of writing, the effect must have been due to narrow spacing of the lines. This could be the result of writing quickly and thus smaller, or of the bunching up of the writing due to constriction which in turn might account for the speed.

Disregarding probable interactive effects between expansiveness and speed, let us consider now whether there is any consistent relationship between the personality traits and indices of energy output. To compute this each subject was scored on every relevant measure according to whether they scored above or below the median. Those who scored above the median on at least two of the three measures of speed (omitting Introspection report) were classified as 'fast', and the others as 'slow'. Those who scored above the median on the majority of the expansiveness variables were classified as 'large' writers and the others as 'small'. (Note that the signs of the measures were reversed so that more dense writing was described as small.)

The subjects were also divided into those who were high and those who were low on E and N, respectively. There were no differences for any of these groups between the number of subjects who wrote slow and small and those who wrote fast and large. Thus, there seemed to be no relationship between the traits and energy output as expressed in a combination of expansiveness and speed.

Our conclusions for this initial part of the analysis are that extraversion is not related to either expansiveness or speed of writing but that neuroticism is slightly related to speed and also to density of writing although not to width. On the whole, these results seem to confirm previous findings that graphological signs do not relate directly to personality traits, with some possible minor exceptions.

APPLICATION OF WALLACH'S MODERATOR HYPOTHESIS

A new approach to the study of expressive behaviour by Wallach & Gahm employs anxiety as a moderator variable (Ref. 23). These investigators found that for subjects (female psychology students) who were low on anxiety (Neuroticism), extraverts tended to be expansive in graphic expression, while introverts were constrictive. For highly anxious subjects the relationships were reversed. The rank order of the four groups on expansiveness (from most to least) was: E low N; I high N; E high N; I low N. The measure of expansiveness was derived from the size of physiognomic representations ('doodling') to music. Wallach & Gahm state, 'Graphic constriction or expansiveness may indicate just the opposite of what the individual allows himself at an overt level, his fear of direct expression permitting him only this direct compensation or displacement' (Ref. 23, p. 74). They explain the constriction in the graphic expression of highly anxious extraverts and the expansiveness of the highly anxious introverts as attempts to defend themselves against anxiety.

On the basis of Wallach & Gahm's findings we propose the following hypotheses: (a) Low neurotic extraverts (ELN) will write larger than high neurotic extraverts (EHN), (b) high neurotic introverts (IHN) will write larger than low neurotic introverts (ILN) and (c) low neurotic extraverts (ELN) will write larger than low neurotic introverts (ILN).

Wallach & Gahm did not employ tempo as a variable and it is difficult to predict whether neuroticism would act as a defensive variable in this respect in view of the complication that anxiety may reflect generalized drive as well as defensiveness. The only prediction that we can make is that: (d) low neurotic extraverts (ELN) will write faster than low neurotic introverts (ILN).

RESULTS

To test these hypotheses, the subjects were divided into extreme scorers on each of the four interactions (ELN, EHN, ILN, IHN). The 15 most extreme cases were selected for each group. There were 5 males and 10 females in each, excepting for IHN in which it was possible to find only two males. The mean scores on the two personality scales for the four groups are listed in Table 2. Comparing these scores with those published in the MPI manual, the IHNs were similar to hospitalized dysthymics, only less highly neurotic and the EHNs were like hospitalized psychopaths or psychosomatic cases, only more highly extraverted. In short, they truly represented extreme groups. For this reason we shall present results also for the middle 26 subjects who do not fall into any of the extremes. This is a prudent control to apply when using extreme groups in order to check on the interpretation of trends (Ref. 9).

The modal method of probing the scores already described in the first part of this report was applied in order to dichotomize the subjects on the expansiveness and speed of their writing. The analysis is presented in Table 3.

On size of writing, the ELNs wrote larger than the EHNs. (Hypothesis a confirmed; chi^2 is significant at 0·01 level.)

The IHNs wrote larger than the ILNs, but this was not significant. (Hypothesis b not confirmed, but the trend is in the predicted direction.)

TABLE 2

MEAN SCORES OF INTERACTION GROUPS ON MPI

	Low Neurotic		High Neurotic		Middle group	U.S. student norms[1]
	Extravert	Introvert	Extravert	Introvert		
E	36·5	18·6	35·5	17·5	30·2	28·5
N	12·5	14·0	33·6	34·6	23·9	20·9

[1] From MPI manual

TABLE 3

DISTRIBUTION OF THE INTERACTIVE PERSONALITY GROUPS ON THE HANDWRITING VARIABLES

	Low Neurotic		High Neurotic		Middle group	Total
	Extravert	Introvert	Extravert	Introvert		
Size (variables 7 to 15)						
Large	12	5	4	7	14	42
Small	3	10	11	8	12	44
Percentage large	80	33	27	47	54	49
Speed (variables 3, 4, 5)						
Fast	6	8	11	8	10	45
Slow	9	7	4	7	16	41
Percentage fast	40	53	73	53	38	52

TABLE 4

INTERACTION GROUPS AND EXPENDITURE OF ENERGY

	Low Neurotic		High Neurotic		Middle group	Total
	Extravert	Introvert	Extravert	Introvert		
Slow and small	3	4	3	5	6	21
Slow and large	6	3	1	3	8	21
Fast and small	0	6	8	2	8	24
Fast and large	6	2	3	5	4	20
Total	15	15	15	15	26	86

The ELNs wrote larger than ILNs. (Hypothesis c confirmed; chi^2 of 4·7 is significant at 0·05 level.)

On the speed dimension, there was no difference for the low neurotics between the E and I subjects. (Hypothesis d not confirmed.) There was also no difference between the IHNs and ILNs. The only clear trend in the speed tests was the faster writing of the EHNs. This group was faster than any other group (including the middle group) on each one of the three tests of speed.

Before discussing the findings we shall also complete the picture by presenting the scores on the interaction groups for the various combinations of size and speed (Table 4). The low neurotic and high neurotic extraverts differed significantly (chi² 21·6, p<0·01, df = 6): the EHNs tended to write fast and small, while the ELNs tended to write either slow and large or fast and large.

DISCUSSION

The results of the interaction analyses appear to confirm the value of considering the effect of extraversion on handwriting in conjunction with neuroticism rather than on its own. Considering size also, we have confirmed Wallach & Gahm's findings that those most expansive in graphic expression are the low anxiety extraverts who are more expansive than high anxiety introverts. The low anxiety extraverts were also more expansive in their handwriting than the low anxiety introverts, thus confirming the general expectation for extraverts where this orientation is uncomplicated by defensive processes. Wallach & Gahm also found that low anxiety introverts wrote less expansively than high anxiety introverts and our own results support this finding, although the differences were not statistically significant.

Although Wallach & Gahm did not study tempo as another dimension of expressive behaviour, we found for this a similar moderator effect with extraversion: the highly anxious extraverts wrote much faster than the low anxious extraverts. Degree of anxiety, however, played no role in the handwriting speed of the introverts whose speed was in between the two extraverted groups. Unlike the results on expansiveness, the middle group on extraversion and neuroticism were not in the middle on speed of writing. This variable therefore is not linear and it appears that a certain degree of extraversion and neuroticism has to be reached before the combined effect on speed starts to operate.

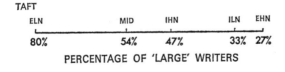

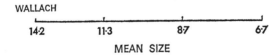

Figure 35. A proportional rank ordering of the results on expansiveness.

Thus, in our study, the two major effects of anxiety were on extraversion rather than introversion. In formulating their study, Wallach & Gahm had expected the major effect to occur with introversion, on the grounds that extraversion is a more socially normal form of behaviour than introversion and therefore evokes less need in anxious persons to defend themselves by disguising its outward manifestation. Wallach & Gahm were surprised at their finding that this defensive process also applied to anxious extraverts and they had to postulate that 'an anxious social introvert . . . would really be happier if he could avoid others' (Ref. 23, p. 82). As shown in Fig. 35, the differences between the high and low extraverts on expansiveness were even greater in our study than in that of Wallach & Gahm. The differences could possibly be due to a lesser valuation in Australia of extraverted traits than in the United States. This possibility, however, is not substantiated by empirical evidence comparing the two cultures (e.g. Ref. 21 and Gruen[1]). A more likely explanation is that, while anxiety-prompted defensiveness could be expected to operate in both extraverts and introverts, it would be more strongly induced in those whose behaviour brings them more into contact with people, i.e., the extraverts. The stronger effect of anxiety on extraverts in our study compared with that of Wallach & Gahm could have been due to the type of activity involved in the experiment. The difference could also be due to the different tasks involved. Handwriting is probably a much more practiced and automatic activity than doodling which was consciously directed to the expression of moods. The handwriting was therefore more likely to reflect the unconscious attitudes of the subject than were the directed doodles.

Defensiveness was more likely to be shown by the subjects in their responses to the MPI and in the social behaviour on which those responses were based than in their handwriting.[2] In the highly anxious subjects, the extraversion or introversion revealed in their handwriting expression is assumed to be closer to their unconscious, basic attitudes than are responses to the inventory which could even be consciously

---

[1] Personal communication from Dr W. Gruen, Veterans Administration Hospital, Canandaigna, N.Y., based on his American Core Culture Inventory.

[2] Jung has pointed out that neurosis can be the result of social pressures on a person that make him behave overtly in a manner that 'violates his individual disposition'. 'As a rule, whenever such falsification of type takes place as a result of internal influence, the individual becomes neurotic later, and a cure can successfully be sought only in development of that attitude which corresponds with the individual's natural way' (Ref. 15, pp. 415–16).

falsified as well as unconsciously distorted. It seems especially likely that the handwriting (or the doodling) was not defensively distorted since the experimental situations to which the various form of handwriting were collected kept any possible stress to a minimum. Further research could investigate defensiveness more directly by using some independent measure of defensiveness. As shown by Ruebush, such a test, while it may be correlated with anxiety, makes an independent contribution to the understanding of behaviour (Ref. 19). Further experiments on expressive productions, including handwriting, are also required in order to test the effect of various types of manipulated stress.

In conclusion, some comments should be made on the implications of this study for graphology. First, our findings support the contention of graphologists that a single-sign, single-trait approach is limited. Not only is it necessary in interpretation to consider a combination of signs in the handwriting but it is also clear that it is necessary to consider patterns of traits as well. Presumably a graphologist is able to use a combination of various signs of extraversion and anxiety in addition to the ones tested in this study, but these must still be regarded as unvalidated. Some hints arising from this study are that large writing, the least efficient but the most effective way of communicating, is likely to be produced by a low anxious extravert and unlikely to be produced by a high anxious extravert. Fast and small writing, the most efficient but least effective way of communicating, is unlikely to be produced by a low anxious extravert or by a high anxious introvert. Nevertheless, individual predictions on this basis are risky. But this minute graphological payoff is only a by-product of this study and it does little to assist in the conversion of graphology from an 'intuitive' art to a set of articulated and validated scientific inferences.

SUMMARY

Self-report measures of extraversion and neuroticism were correlated with speed and expansiveness in writing and printing on various writing tasks. Extraversion was uncorrelated with any of the measures of speed and expansiveness but neuroticism showed a small positive relationship to speed. Following a lead from Wallach & Gahm, neuroticism was used as a moderator in the relationship between extraversion and the handwriting variables, with fruitful results. The largest writers and the ones who wrote the least in any given space were the low neurotic extraverts, while the smallest writers were the high neurotic extraverts.

In the low neurotic group of subjects the extraverts wrote larger than the introverts. The fastest writers were the high neurotic extraverts, who exceeded the three other interaction groups.

It was thus confirmed that interactions between self-reported extraversion and neuroticism are related to handwriting characteristics. Wallach & Gahm's study had indicated that the interaction was related to the expansiveness of 'doodles'. The present study confirms this finding for handwriting and extends it to tempo as well as size of expressive movements. The possibility is suggested for further study that handwriting reflects the basic temperamental qualities of the person, but that in highly defensive persons (neurotic) their overt behaviour tends to reflect the type of temperament that is opposite to their basic type.

REFERENCES

1. BIRGE, W. R., An experimental inquiry into the measurable handwriting correlates of five personality traits. *J. Pers.*, **23**, 215–223, 1954.
2. CATTELL, R. B., *Personality and Motivation Structure and Measurement*. New York: World, 1957.
3. —— & SCHEIER, I. H., *The Meaning and Measurement of Neuroticism and Anxiety*. New York: Ronald, 1961.
4. EYSENCK, H. J., Criterion analysis—an application of the hypothetico-deductive method to factor analysis. *Psychol. Rev.*, **57**, 38–53, 1950.
5. ——, Schizothymia-cyclothymia as a dimension of personality. *J. Pers.*, **20**, 345–384, 1952.
6. ——, *The Dynamics of Anxiety and Hysteria*. London: Routledge & Kegan Paul, 1957.
7. ——, *Manual of the Maudsley Personality Inventory*. Univ. of London Press, 1959.
8. ——, *The Structure of Human Personality*. (2nd ed.) London: Methuen, 1960.
9. ——, Personality and experimental psychology. *Bull. Brit. Psychol. Soc.*, **19**, 1–28, 1966.
10. FLUCKIGER, F. A., TRIPP, C. A. & WEINBERG, G. H., A review of experimental research in graphology: 1933–60. *Percept. mot. Skills*, **12**, 67–90, 1961.

11. FREUD, S., Formulations regarding the two principles in mental functioning in *Collected Papers*, Vol. 4. London: Hogarth Press, 1924.
12. GUILFORD, J. P., *Personality*. New York: McGraw-Hill, 1959.
13. HARVEY, O. L., The measurement of handwriting considered as a form of expressive movement. *Charac. Pers.*, **2**, 310–321, 1934.
14. JACOBY, H. J., *Self-knowledge Through Handwriting*. London: Dent, 1941.
15. JUNG, C. G., *Psychological Types*. New York: Harcourt, 1923.
16. LORR, M., LEPINE, L. T. & GOLDEN, J. V., A factor analysis of some handwriting characteristics. *J. Pers.*, **22**, 348–353, 1954.
17. MELOUN, J., Handwriting measurement and personality tests. *Charac. Pers.*, **2**, 322–330, 1934.
18. MEREDITH, G. M., Contending hypotheses of ontogenesis for the exuberance-restraint personality factor UI 21. *J. genet. Psychol.*, **108**, 89–104, 1966.
19. RUEBUSH, B. K., Anxiety. In *Child Psychology* (ed. H. W. Stevenson). Chicago: University of Chicago Press, 1963.
20. SECORD, P. F., Studies of the relationship of handwriting to personality. *J. Pers.*, **17**, 430–448, 1949.
21. TAFT, R., Opinion convergence in the assimilation of immigrants. *Austral. J. Psychol.*, **14**, 41–54, 1962.
22. TAYLOR, JANET A., A personality scale of manifest anxiety. *J. abnorm. soc. Psychol.*, **48**, 285–290, 1953.
23. WALLACH, M. A. & GAHM, RUTHELLEN, C., Personality functions of graphic constriction and expansiveness. *J. Pers.*, **28**, 73–88, 1960.

44

Personality Trait Deduced from Behaviour Theory (1): Mirror Drawing Measures on the Vertivity Dimension

EIICHI OKAMOTO

First published in
Japanese Journal of Psychological Research, **6**, 99–107, 1964

VARIOUS aspects of mirror-drawing were analysed in relation to the vertivity scale (extraversion-introversion). A new measuring method was tried to turn out more information on the locus of mirror-drawing than the conventional method. The subjects were divided into three groups according to their response to a questionnaire. Being viewed in terms of a model of automatic control theory, the result has shown that vertivity had a close relationship to the feedback mechanism. In addition, some reference has been made to Eysenck's typological postulate.

INTRODUCTION

The present study is an attempt to fill the gap between behaviour theory and personality theory. In the theory of behaviour or learning there has been a trend to look after an equation of the organism in general and wilfully to neglect the difference between individuals; usually the data of many subjects are pooled together and then one has to fit the data to a certain behavioural equation. The theory of personality, on the other hand, is concerned with the details of traits or types and rarely applies the principles of behaviour to the individual person; a single person or animal can be analysed in many ways from each personality dimension and therefore we cannot expect exactly the same pattern of behaviour between individuals. It is necessary that efforts be made to inter-relate these two theories in order to develop a more integrated theory.

A few authors have made such efforts (Refs. 3, 7 & 14). Their studies have contributed a great deal but still more systematic elaborations are needed. This is the reason why a new approach was tried from a different angle in this experiment. An instrumental concept to intervene between personality trait and behaviour equation is the 'feedback' mechanism in an automatic control system which has been playing a prominent role in cybernetics. An organism can be considered as such a system with many kinds of feedback-loop.

It is needless to say that 'learning' is a process of negative feedback. In the sequence of learning, the process of feedback toward a given goal repeatedly operates from output to input. From the viewpoint of learning theory, the component of feedback circuit is proposed to be equal to each individual. In fact, it nevertheless differs from person to person. This difference comprises one of personality traits.

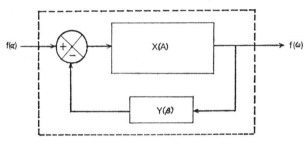

Figure 36. Feedback diagram in an automatic control system.

Along with this line we can imagine a typical block diagram like Fig. 36. It is a basic process of an automatic control system. The inside of the broken line indicates a complicated personality structure—the so-called 'black box'. The traits of personality depend upon the differences of circuit elements in two block components $X(A)$ and $Y(\beta)$. $X(A)$ is the main component and $Y(\beta)$ is the feedback component. Significant stimuli come into the box through the perceptual process (input), are transformed there quasi-linearly and discharge themselves through the effector (output). The behaviour of the organism should be recognized as such a quasi-linear system in which the feedback processes operate in a way that the higher fidelity of response is attained (Ref. 13, p. 109).

A number of personality traits have been enumerated in various theories of personality. From them we take up the trait of 'vertivity', a dimension of introversion-extraversion. There are reasons for assuming that this dimension is related to the feedback element—$Y(\beta)$ component. Also Eysenck hypothesized that learning speed is correlated with vertivity; the introverts are conditioned more effectively than the extraverts (Ref. 3, p. 114). He verified this relationship experimentally although the present writer reserves a certain objection against his hypothesis.

The characteristics of the feedback-vertivity relation also appear in the principal items of the vertivity questionnaire. For instance, the following questions especially suggest that they contain feedback properties:

'Are you a careful individual?'
'Are you inclined to be slow and deliberate in movement?'
'Would you rate yourself an impulsive person?'

Being judged from these items, the extraverts on the one hand tend to react strongly to the signals which are coming in (impulses) and often overshoot the target carelessly. On the other hand it is clear that the introverts respond carefully and integrate the signals coming from outside. This difference in their behaviour patterns is chiefly due to the difference of the feedback mechanism by which the individual's speed of learning is affected, whether accelerated or not, as Eysenck assumed. Using these terms, we define the dimension of vertivity as the time-lag of feedback which characterizes the introvert and the time-lead of feedback which characterizes the extravert. In a more abstract sense, we may use a mathematical analogy and say that the extraverts have 'differential' properties and the introverts 'integral' properties. These properties will be discussed later in more detail.

There are two important points to be considered. One is that the items of the vertivity questionnaire are not perfectly homogeneous. They are also loaded on factors other than vertivity. This fact is, so to speak, the existence of the noise in the input which causes 'equivocation'. Redundancy of these items is related to 'equivocation' in information theory.

Another is the 'ambiguity' of response which is to be conceived as the noise in the output (Ref. 1). In Garner 'equivocation' is called the stimulus-equivocation and 'ambiguity' is called the response-equivocation (Ref. 6). 'Equivocation' causes some awkwardness in interpretation of questionnaire items. The subjects are therefore apt to misunderstand the meanings of items. The first point, 'equivocation', thus affects the level of stimulus validity. On the contrary the second point, 'ambiguity', depends upon circumstantial factors leading to biased answers. For example, suppose there is a person who is objectively located at about the middle of the vertivity scale and yet in his living environment belongs to a subgroup of markedly introvert people. His behaviour will exhibit more extraversive characteristics as compared to his behaviour in normal subgroup (Fig. 37).

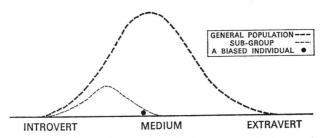

Figure 37. Biased distribution of sub-group against general population.

Thus an innate introvert may acquire an extraversive response habit through conditioning processes in the course of his personal history (vice versa with an innate extravert). The second point therefore affects the level of response reliability.

We have to correct these two misleading points. In addition, personality measurement is usually based on verbal tests. It is desirable to add some manual tests of personality as in the case of intelligence scales. The discrepancies between verbal questionnaire and manual performance may be worth scrutinizing.

For this reason, we need to find a suitable manual test which corresponds to a verbal one. In the present study we define 'vertivity' in accordance with the feedback component. We believe that mirror-drawing is the most suitable test for this purpose. In mirror drawing, the past experiences of the subjects hardly help and various kinds of responses appear in the acquisition process (transitory period). It is the main problem of this experiment to see how responses are related to vertivity.

METHOD

We employed a modification of the traditional mirror-drawing experiment. All the preceding mirror-drawing experiments had their subjects trace on a track (between two lines) and recorded only two measures; errors and time. However, they neglected additional useful information (Refs. 10, 11 and 17). In the present study the subjects were required to trace on a line. As we shall describe later, this technique provided richer information as to the characteristics of the S's response.

Mirror-drawing is a typical activity of feedback mechanism. One cannot respond without feedback. A preceding response becomes a stimulus to the next response; if he overshoots the line he has at once to correct his own response. This sequence continues incessantly. The fluctuation of drawing activities makes wavelike displacements against the base-line. This must be a 'simular' process to oscillation in physics, i.e., a kind of composed harmonic movement; to be plotted against the ordinates is the distance from base-line (amplitude) and the abscissa represents the time.

We can apply this wave-like displacement not only to such a physical 'simulation' but also to the principles of behaviour (Ref. 9). The amplitude (the ordinate value) of the locus would correspond to Hullian inhibitory potential. The greater amplitude of the locus indicates the stronger potential of the subject. At the limit point, the locus shows feedback and converts toward the base-line.

The base-line is the homeostatic level (zero potential). It means that the attainment of the base-line from divergence serves as reinforcement to the subject and the reactive inhibitory potential is discharged at that time and point. This corresponds to a 'compensatory task' in automatic control theory.

Like the Skinner-box, mirror drawing is a typical situation of free responding where CR itself is the significant independent variable and the subject can operantly regulate CR for him. This self-producing response becomes the CS for the next response. In contrast to this, the pursuit-rotor experiment resembles a situation of restricted responding

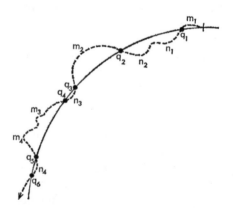

Figure 38. New measures of the mirror-
drawing on a base-line.

like Pavlovian conditioning, where CS is important as an independent variable and the subject is restricted by CS. This of course corresponds to a 'pursuit task' in automatic control theory.

The subjects were 60 female college students. They had two trials of mirror-drawing. A questionnaire of vertivity (Tanaka Kosei Kensa) was administered between the two trials and for which the subjects were divided in 3 groups—the introvert, the medium and the extravert—each containing 20 Ss each. In mirror drawing the subjects are asked to trace a circle of 10 cm diameter.

Five measures (P, Q, R, S and T) were taken as criteria for comparing between groups. At least three of them have never been used before.

P: Frequencies of fluctuation M and N were at first counted as shown in Fig 38 on the outside and the inside. The P-values are calculated by the following formulas.

when $M > N$, $p = 1 - \dfrac{N}{M}$,

and $M < N$, $-p = 1 - \dfrac{M}{N}$,

where $M = m_1 + m_2 + \ldots + m_l$
$N = n_1 + n_2 + \ldots + n_l$

The equation of the p-value has a double meaning: the redundancy of information theory *and* also the relative discriminative threshold. The range of p-value is $-1 < p < +1$. The p-value is continuous from its positive side to its negative side.[1]

Q: The frequency of attaining the base-line (zero potential) and the effect of spontaneous reinforcement. Each one is indicated by $q_1, q_2 \ldots q_k$.

R: Distance from the base-line, classified into six categories; -3, -2, -1, $+1$, $+2$, $+3$. The unit of category is 3 mm.

S: The frequency of distracted or entangled responses during a trial. This measure almost corresponds to the number of errors in the usual measure on a track.

---

[1] It is possible that the ratio of M to N is represented in another way; e.g. $\hat{P} = (M-N)/(M+N)$. But we can easily transform P into $\hat{P}$ by the following equation; $\hat{P} = P/(2 \pm p)$, where negative in M N, and positive in M N. We preferred P to $\hat{P}$, because P can detect rather fine changes of fluctuation than $\hat{P}$, and also covers the meanings of redundancy of information and Weber's fraction.

T: The time required for tracing the circle. This is not a new measure but in the present study it means the sum of differentiated time (τ_1, τ_2, . . .). The $_k$ is the time required for tracing from q_{k-1} to q_k. Other things being equal, the greater T indicates the lower potential.

The schematic models of mirror-drawing are shown in Fig. 39. All of them are the same in p-value but are different in Q- and R-values.

The average values in each group are shown in the following table. For example, P_1 means the value on the 1st trial, P_2 on the 2nd, $_1P_2$ the average of the 1st and 2nd, dP the difference between P_1 and P_2 in the absolute value ($|P_1|-|P_2|$). Notations for the other measures accord this.

TABLE 1

THE COMPARISON OF THE MIRROR-DRAWING MEASURES AMONG THREE LEVELS OF VERTIVITY SCALE

Groups Mean	Introvert (81)	Medium (108)	Extravert (138)	Average (109)
P_1	0·126	0·124	0·222	0·158
P_2	0·167	0·111	0·294	0·191
$_1P_2$	0·147	0·118	0·258	0·174
$SD(_1P_2)$	0·31	0·32	0·39	0·33
dP	0·048	0·018	−0·035	0·010
Q_1	15·85	15·35	14·75	15·32
Q_2	13·10	14·45	13·70	13·75
$_1Q_2$	14·48	14·90	14·23	14·54
dQ	2·75	0·90	1·05	1·57
R_1	3·60	3·70	3·05	3·45
	(1·85: 1·75)	(2·00: 1·70)	(1·80: 1·25)	(1·88: 1·67)
R_2	3·00	3·05	2·90	2·84
	(1·45: 1·55)	(1·60: 1·45)	(1·60: 1·30)	(1·55: 1·29)
$_1R_2$	3·30	3·33	2·98	3·20
dR	0·60	0·65	0·15	0·45
S_1	2·10	1·35	2·20	1·88
S_2	0·90	1·45	0·90	1·08
$_1S_2$	1·50	1·40	1·55	1·48
dS	1·20	−0·10	1·30	0·80
T_1	51·75	49·25	54·25	51·75
T_2	43·75	38·00	46·50	42·75
$_1T_2$	47·75	43·63	50·38	47·25
dT	8·00	10·75	8·75	9·00

The values in the first row show the mean of vertivity scores, and the ratios below R-values show outward versus inward amplitude.

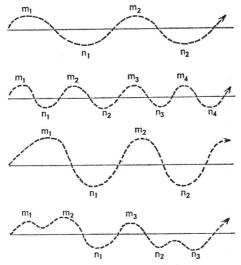

Figure 39. Various phases of the same p-value different in Q- and R-values.

The P-value forms a binomial-like distribution (Fig. 40). The Q-, R- and T-values form the normal distribution (Fig. 41).The distribution of the S-value fits an exponential one (Fig. 42). The data plotted between two broken lines means negative stable feedback (Ref. 12). These fittings were based on the average of two trials.

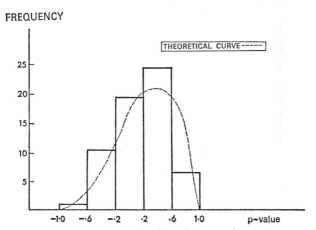

Figure 40. Distribution of the p-value.

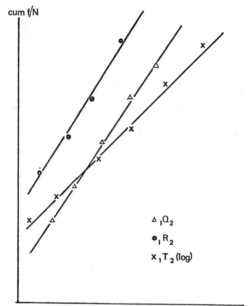

Figure 41. Linearities of Q-, R-, and T-value on the normal provability paper.

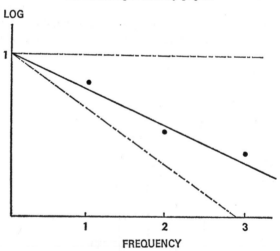

Figure 42. Linearity of the s-value on the half log. paper.

$$S(x) = A\lambda e^{-\lambda x}$$

where

$$A = 1, \lambda = 0\cdot674$$

RESULTS

When analysing a mirror drawing of a circle, it is possible, if necessary, for us to make use of a rectangular vector diagram like Fig. 43. There are two directions of force; one component is a tangential vector and another is a centripetal vector. If the locus is situated at point A (vector OA), another vector OB is required in order to attain a fitted vector OC (when the distance is small, a chord OC is almost equal to an arc OC).

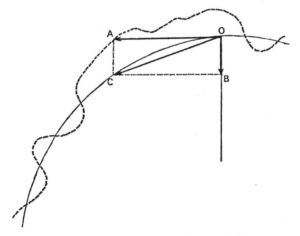

Figure 43. Vector diagram on a point A of divergence.

Usually, a subject at first has a tendency to overshoot outwardly due to the curvature of the circle. This outward response functions as a stimulus (input). It has to be fed back negatively to the opposite direction in the inverse phase. This process occurs in and out of the base-line. In the last stage of habit formation (stationary state) the P-value becomes zero (i.e. $N/M = 1$). This means that there is only random fluctuation in and out of the base-line. In the initial stage (transitory state) all the groups will show positive P-values as was the case in this experiment.

The Introvert Group: The results for this group tend to show a smaller p-value than those of the extraverts, but not so much as that of the mediums. This difference influences the ratio of the R-value (in and outward amplitude). They showed the reversal ratio in R (1·45: 1·55); the inward amplitude is larger than the outward one. These facts mean that the centripetal vector is more dominant in the extraverts than in the

introverts. We can observe that their dP-value is distinctly larger than
the other ones and this positive value is due to the calculation of the
absolute values in P_1 and P_2. This may verify Eysenck's typological
postulate. The largest value of dQ in this group may reflect Eysenck's
postulate that the introverts are more conditionable than the extraverts.

The Extravert Group: The results for this group show significant
differences in P- and P-values from those of the introvert group. Particularly, the value of dp shows negative acceleration. It can be expected
from Eysenck's postulate that strong reactive inhibitions (I_r) are quickly
generated and slowly dissipated in the extraverts. In other words it
corresponds to reminiscence but a better interpretation is that stimulus
aggregates overcharged above the limit of one's channel capacity have
some time-lag in terms of the feedback mechanism.

The Medium Group (*Control*): It has the least values of P, S and T.
This means that the mediums demonstrated the most adaptive activity
in mirror-drawing. The largest dT, the largest difference between T_1 and
T_2, also shows their highly adaptable aspect. At any rate it can be said
that this group shows the most efficient process of learning. The only
exception is that dS takes on negative values in this group. This may
have something to do with the neurotic dimension, though we have of
course not dealt with this in the present experiment.

General Points of View: It can be observed that the P-value indicates a
u-shaped distribution though the introverts show lower value than the
extraverts. The introverts and the extraverts both have higher values
than the mediums. This result can be interpreted as an excess of feedback, whether of time-lag or time-lead. In order to detect more meaningful information we took up the difference between P_1 and P_2 in absolute
value: $dP = |P_1| - |P_2|$. For instance, when in a subject P_1 is (-0.23)
and P_2 is (0.09), dP is (0.140). We can see an almost linear relationship
in dP from the introverts through the mediums to the extraverts—
positive to negative.

In the Q-values, we cannot observe any systematic difference among
the three groups though dQ shows a high value in the introverts as we
observed before. In the R-values, there is no difference between the
introverts and the mediums but the extraverts show somewhat lower
values than the other two groups. In the S- and T-values, we can easily
see that the mediums show differences from the other groups.

DISCUSSION

In the limit of learning, habit strength ($_sH_r$) reaches the maximum and only the muscles necessary to trace the figure are activated. In an early period of learning, on the other hand, inhibitory potential ($_sI_r$) is at the maximum and the unnecessary muscles are activated and hence the trace is apt to deviate from the base-line. The present author takes a slightly different position from the Hullian system. As trials are repeated, the response is modified to inhibit the movement of unnecessary muscles and facilitate that of necessary muscles. Doubtlessly this modification depends upon the reorganization of the dynamic structure in the sensory motor system toward the fidelity of the response.

In these sequences of transitory state, the individual difference in response, if there are any, would indicate the differences within the dynamic system in the brain. Such dynamic change is similar to the functioning of the so-called automatic control system in electronics. This relation is not only recognizable in an analogical process but also in a mathematical equation which is expressed as a certain exponential function. Here we want to discuss two important problems. The first one is an analogical inference between psychology and electronics. The exponential function in Hull means that a rectangular wave input as the stimulus (step function—this means that a certain constant stimulus constellation is given during the experiment) is transformed into Laplace image function (Fig. 44).

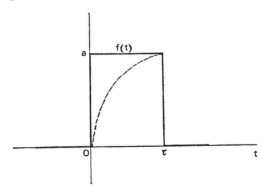

Figure 44. Laplace Transform of rectangular impulse.

$$f(t) = aE(t) - aE(t - \tau)$$
$$f(t) \supset \frac{a}{s}(1 - e^{-s\tau})$$

o

Further, from this 'simulation' it can be assumed that the introverts have a greater time-lag element (integral component) and the extraverts have a greater time-lead element (differential component), whereas the normals are balanced. It can be a definition of vertivity in behaviour theory.

The combination of the time-lag and the time-lead elements in feedback $Y(\beta)$ has a compensating balance and maintains high fidelity of the transfer function. Thus various divergences in a given response will be 'automatically' eliminated in the course of repetitive trials. We will discuss these theoretical issues at a future time.

The second problem is a sophisticated syllogism of Eysenck (Ref. 3). He assumes that in introverts the conditioned response is easily obtained while in extraverts it is not. This assumption depends upon the following syllogism: (1) Strong excitatory potential and weak inhibitory potential occur in introverts, (2) this combination makes the subjects easily conditionable and (3) introverts are, thus, easily conditioned. Certainly he verified this assumption in several experiments but Eysenck's typological postulate also reveals the opposite picture!

The crucial experiments, cited by Eysenck as positive evidence, deal with negative learning in eye blink and accompanying GSR (Refs. 4 & 5). In positive learning some other aspects may appear. Our hypothesis is that just the converse is the case in positive learning; the extraverts are easily conditioned and the introverts are not. The present study does not test this assumption, however, because the focus of the present experiment is on the momentary differences in the initial phase of learning and mirror drawing is considered a negative learning.

If our hypothesis is true, it is possible to interpret more comprehensively various behaviours which are related to the vertivity dimension. Then it will also become necessary to explore the other dimensions of personality in the light of dynamic analysis of behaviour.

SUMMARY

There are two purposes in the present study. The first one is an attempt to bridge the gap between personality trait theory and behaviour theory by means of the concepts of the automatic control system. The main concept used here is the mechanism of feedback (negative in this case). This feedback property relates to the vertivity dimension (introversion-extraversion).

The second purpose is to measure personality traits not only by verbal

Personality Trait Deduced from Behaviour Theory 403

questionnaire but also in terms of manual performance. Mirror-drawing performance was taken as a suitable measure which is related to vertivity because of its excellent reference to feedback mechanism. Conversely, this means that the dimension of vertivity can be defined in terms of feedback properties in personality. Thus we can eliminate both 'equivoca-tion' and 'ambiguity', two factors which cause misleading answers to questionnaire. They correspond to validity of stimulus and reliability of response. A new method of recording was attempted using mirror-drawing data, which made dynamic analysis of drawing locus possible. Out of five measures taken, three of them were new. Especially, the p-value has an important significance representing 'redundancy' and the relative discriminative threshold.

The results show that the introvert group tends to be conditioned more effectively than the extraverts, but it is noteworthy that the medium group is the most efficient in P- and T-values.

Electro-dynamic and mathematical interpretations were applied to these results. The introverts exhibit the dominance of 'integral' properties and the extraverts exhibit the dominance of 'differential' properties when simulated in terms of the feedback component of automatic control system. Eysenck's typological postulate can be accepted as valid provided that learning is of a negative kind. In this way the present study serves to unify behaviour and personality theories by using concepts of electro-dynamic simulation.

REFERENCES

1. ATTNEAVE, F., *Applications of Information Theory to Psychology.* New York: Holt, Rinehart & Winston, 1959.
2. COOK, T. W., Mirror position and negative transfer. *J. exp. Psychol.*, **29**, 155–160, 1941.
3. EYSENCK, H. J., *The Dynamics of Anxiety and Hysteria.* London: Routledge & Kegan Paul, 1957.
4. FRANKS, C. M., An Experimental Study of Conditioning as Related to Mental Abnormality. Unpublished Ph.D. thesis, University of London Library, 1954.
5. ——, Conditioning and personality; a study of normal and neurotic subjects. *J. abnorm. soc. Psychol.*, **52**, 143–150, 1956.
6. GARNER, W. R., *Uncertainty and Structure as Psychological Concepts.* New York: Wiley & Sons, 1962.

7. GUILFORD, J. P., *Personality*. New York: McGraw-Hill, 1959.

8. —— & MARTIN, H. G., Age and sex differences in some introvertive and emotional traits. *J. Gen. Psychol.*, **31,** 219–229, 1944.

9. HULL, C. L., *Principles of Behaviour*. New York: Appleton-Century, 1943.

10. KINCAID, M., A study of individual differences in learning. *Psychol. Rev.*, **32,** 34–53, 1925.

11. KINGSLEY, H. L., *The Nature and Conditions of Learning*. New York: Prentice Hall, 1946.

12. KUO, B., *Automatic Control Systems*. New York: Prentice Hall, 1962.

13. LUCE, R. D., *Developments in Mathematical Psychology*. Glencoe, Ill.: Free Press, 1960.

14. LUNDIN, L. W., *Personality: An Experimental Approach*. New York: Macmillan, 1961.

15. McGEOCH, J. A., *Psychology of Human Learning*. New York: Longmans, 1942.

16. QUASTLER, H., *Information Theory in Psychology*. Glencoe, Ill.: Free Press, 1955.

17. STARCH, D., A demonstration of the trial and error method of learning. *Psychol. Bull.*, **7,** 20–23, 1910.

45

Individual Differences in Free Response-Speed

FRANK H. FARLEY

First published in *Perceptual and Motor Skills*, **22**, 557–558, 1966

THE response-speed (covertly timed) of 30 Ss on a simple printing task under unstressful conditions was correlated with their Maudsley Personality Inventory extraversion scores, Manifest Anxiety Scale scores and need-achievement scores from the Edwards Personality Preference Schedule. Extraversion correlated $-0·42$ ($p<0·02$) with log speed, the MAS correlated $0·11$ and need-achievement $-0·20$ (both non-significant).

INTRODUCTION

Contemporary personality research concerned with the response characteristics of Ss along an extraversion-introversion dimension (Refs. 2 & 3) has suggested that extraverts may be characterized by a greater response-speed than introverts. The evidence has been of two types. Where speed and accuracy were involved, extraverts tended to sacrifice accuracy for greater speed, i.e., they demonstrated a higher speed/accuracy ratio than introverts (Refs. 3 & 6). Where speed only was primarily involved, extraverts appeared to perform more quickly than introverts (Ref. 2). Evidence for the latter differentiation is not as extensive as that involving the speed/accuracy ratio.

The present study has attempted to extend the information on simple speed by specifically examining the relationship between free untimed (not-overtly-timed) responding on a simple task and the extraversion-introversion dimension. The suggested greater response-speed of extraverts over introverts is considered to be a general attitude or enduring behavioural characteristic which is largely independent of particular task characteristics or instructions. Generally, the response-speed of introverts would be expected to be impaired in relation to that of extraverts except under conditions of massed and extended practice, where reactive inhibition could develop (Ref. 2). Under experimental conditions in which free, self-paced responding on a short, simple task was required, it was expected therefore that extraverted Ss would take less time to emit a given number of responses than would introverted Ss.

In order to extend the investigation of individual differences in such free response-speed to personality characteristics other than extraversion, the personality variables of anxiety and need-achievement were considered. Anxiety as operationally defined by the Manifest Anxiety Scale (MAS) (Ref. 10) is a personality variable that has received wide-spread attention in relation to learning and performance (Ref. 9). The same may be said of need-achievement (Ref. 7), which has in common with manifest anxiety hypothetical 'energizing' properties. The writer knows of no research that has related the MAS or need-achievement to free response-speed, as such, on a simple task, though Reynolds, Blau & Hurlbut, using a simple addition task administered under timed conditions and instructions that S perform as rapidly as possible during 1-minute trials, found a non-significant superiority of high MAS Ss over low MAS Ss (Ref. 8). These authors also employed another simple task involving drawing a line above Xs and below Os, in which Ss were given 2 minutes to complete as many responses as possible. On this task, the high MAS group was significantly superior to the low MAS scores and performance on a digit symbol task.

METHOD

Ss in the present study were 30 nurses, orderlies, domestic hospital staff and university undergraduates. 16 were male and 14 female, with a mean age of 29·37 years, SD = 11·14.

They were administered the Maudsley Personality Inventory (Ref. 4) to obtain an extraversion measure (MPI–E), the Taylor MAS and the need-achievement scale of the Edwards Personality Preference Schedule (Ref. 1) and were tested on the experimental task without E's knowledge of their personality scores. The task employed required the free copying of 4 simple two-line figures or symbols on a prepared sheet ruled in rows of $\frac{1}{2}$ inch squares.[1] The 4 example symbols were drawn on an index card mounted on a stand in front in front of S. The task was administered under neutral (non-anxiety-evoking) instructions. Ss were requested simply to print the 4 symbols repeatedly, one symbol per square, until they had completed three rows. It was possible to record covertly the

---

[1] This task was based on one designed by Dr W. J. Craig, University Hospital, Saskatoon, Canada, as part of a larger project. The author expresses his appreciation to Dr Craig for allowing him to employ this task in his own research.

total time taken by each S to complete the necessary number of responses.

RESULTS

A log transformation was performed on the time scores and product-moment correlations were computed between each S's log time and his MPI–E, MAS and need-achievement scores. The Pearson correlation of log time with MPI–E was -0.042 ($p < 0.02$), a non-significant 0.11 with MAS and -0.20 with need-achievement. Scatter plots for each correlation revealed no curvilinearity.

CONCLUSIONS

Given the limitations on generality imposed by the present sample size, the results suggest that the personality dimension of extraversion influences free response-speed in simple task performance and that anxiety and achievement motivation, as measured, bear no relationship to such speed under the present (non-anxiety-evoking) conditions.

REFERENCES

1. EDWARDS, A. L., *Personal Preference Schedule, Test Manual.* (Rev. ed.) New York: Psychological Corp., 1959.
2. EYSENCK, H. J., *The Dynamics of Anxiety and Hysteria* London: Routledge & Kegan Paul, 1957.
3. ——, *The Structure of Human Personality.* New York: Macmillan, 1960.
4. ——, *Maudsley Personality Inventory.* San Diego, Calif.: Educational & Industrial Testing Service, 1962.
5. GOODSTEIN, L. D. & FABER, I. E., On the relation between Taylor scale scores and digit symbol performance. *J. consult. Psychol.,* **21,** 152–154, 1957.
6. HIMMELWEIT, H. T., Speed and accuracy of work as related to temperament. *Brit. J. Psychol.,* **36,** 132–144, 1946.
7. MCCLELLAND, D. C., ATKINSON, J. W., CLARK, R. A. & LOWELL, E. L. *The Achievement Motive.* New York: Appleton-Century, 1953.

8. REYNOLDS, W. F., BLAU, B. I. & HURLBUT, B., Speed in simple tasks as a function of MAS score. *Psychol. Rep.*, **8,** 341–344, 1961.

9. SPENCE, J. T., Learning theory and personality. In *Concepts of Personality* (eds. J. M. Wepman & R. W. Heine), Chicago: Aldine, 1963.

10. TAYLOR, J. A., A personality scale of manifest anxiety. *J. abnorm. soc. Psychol.*, **48,** 285–290, 1953.

46

The Speed and Accuracy Characteristics of Neurotics

HARRY BRIERLEY

First published in *British Journal of Psychology*, **52,** 273–280, 1961

THIS experiment tests the psychiatric observation that the different groups of neurotics can be distinguished by their speed and accuracy. It is shown that introverted neurotics are characterized by low speed and extraverted neurotics by low accuracy. If regarded as measuring an aspect of personality, speed-accuracy patterns may be specially valuable because of their sensitivity to variations in time.

INTRODUCTION

Factorial investigations over the last 25 years have recognized individual differences in speed. Thurstone found three speed factors, involving fitting words into categories, arithmetical computation and perceptual tasks (Ref. 32). The Spearman-Holzinger Unitary Traits Study found a general speed factor over and above 'g' (Ref. 19). Woodrow (Ref. 35), Davidson & Carroll (Ref. 8) and Tate (Ref. 31) have also demonstrated an ability or preference for speed, using a variety of different methods of investigation. The problem now becomes one of deciding whether or not these speed differences have any importance. That is to say, it is necessary to find out whether measures of speed have any special value in predicting any aspect of human behaviour distinct from the arbitrarily mixed speed and accuracy scores of common intelligence tests and the like.

Baxter defined 'speed', operationally, as the time taken by a subject to finish the Otis Intelligence Test and 'level' as the number of items correct in unlimited time, these being crude estimates of speed and accuracy (Ref. 2). He found that the multiple correlation of academic rating with these scores was higher than the correlation with the normal Otis time-limit score. Myers also showed that there seemed to be an optimum value for the speeding of tests when they were used to predict naval academy results (Ref. 22). In this limited field, therefore, there seems evidence of the utility of distinct speed and accuracy measurements.

Some investigations have found that the speed of mental functioning differs according to group and individual testing conditions (Refs. 5 & 20). This may well be a result of the imposition of group speed standards by such slight cues as the sound of scratching pencils or of pages being turned. In some investigations the group speed standards would be clearly observable, as in the well known Ruch & Koerth experiment when subjects were allowed to leave once they had finished the tests (Ref. 26). It also appears that the transient factors, such as change of tester and the rewards offered for success (Refs. 6 & 29) or the minor cultural differences which might arise between one school and another (Ref. 5) might influence the balance of speed and accuracy of mental performance. It seems, therefore, that research into mental speed and accuracy requires specially carefully controlled conditions of testing which have not often obtained in past researches.

Three relevant variables—difficulty, accuracy and persistence—have also been ignored at various times. There is little purpose in deriving a speed score without specifying the difficulty of the tasks involved. On the whole harder tasks take longer; but the relationship is not a perfect one as Cane & Horn showed (Ref. 4). It may be that the relationship between speed and difficulty is not the same for all individuals and this could be one of the reasons why speed differences have always been more easily observed when the tasks are limited to those of low difficulty (see, for example, Ref. 30).

There is some evidence that speed and accuracy are interchangeable (Refs. 29 & 34, p. 32), but again accuracy has often been left un-controlled in studies of speed. Peak & Boring (Ref. 25), McFarland (Ref. 21) and others have controlled accuracy to some extent by rejecting all incorrect responses and rejecting items which have been answered with less than a standard level of success by the group as a whole. This sort of method probably provides as near a measure of control as is practicable at the moment; but it should be noted that a correct response might follow inaccurate, but aborted, attempts at solution.

Many researches on mental speed have employed tests such as dotting and letter cancellation. There is a strong suggestion in the work of Studman (Ref. 28) that such tests are better regarded as measuring 'perseverance-industry-tenacity' or Webb's 'w' factor (Ref. 33) than speed. Studman found that hysterics scored lower on these tests than did patients with anxiety states, whilst Himmelweit found that hysterics showed lower persistence than dysthymics (Ref. 18). This is in contrast with the fact that in such researches as have been carried out into the speed characteristics of neurotics, hysterics seem to be the faster. Thus, if left uncontrolled, persistence differences can counteract speed differences.

Psychiatric literature abounds in references to speed of thinking in mental illness. For example, Curran & Partridge (Ref. 7) describe the slowness of thinking in depression (p. 53), the quick thinking of manic patients (p. 54) and the thoughts 'rushing' through the mind of the schizophrenic. The obsessional personality is usually described as slow and ponderous in his attempts to maintain high accuracy, whilst the hysteric is impulsive and erratic. Few of these clinical observations have been accurately examined by experiment, although Ogilvie (Ref. 24), Eysenck (Ref. 9) and Broadhurst (Ref. 3) report loss of intellectual speed in schizophrenia. Hetherington's work on the effects of E.C.T. leads him to suggest that depression is associated more with motor retardation than with psychic retardation (Ref. 16).

Slater compared the test responses of different neurotic groups and concluded that, given time, the obsessional would score more highly than the hysteric on common intelligence tests (Ref. 27). Himmelweit investigated the speed differences between hysterics and dysthymics as diagnosed by psychiatrists (Ref. 18). Subjects were instructed to work as quickly and accurately as possible on tests of hidden words, cancellation, adding 7s, measurement and the track tracer. The dysthymics were slower and more accurate than the hysterics; but the only speed difference for the groups to prove statistically significant was that derived from the track tracer. Nevertheless, Himmelweit concluded 'it has been possible to show that hysterics belong to the speed preference and dysthymics to the accuracy preference type'. Nelson applied the Nufferno Speed Test to groups of mentally ill patients including one group of 20 neurotics (Ref. 23). Speed as measured by this test did not differentiate either between the abnormal groups themselves or between the abnormal and control groups. This seems rather contrary to general expectation as well as to the findings of such workers as Studman, Ogilvie and others mentioned above. Nelson's groups were, however, selected to include only those patients who were fully co-operative and, in the writer's experience, only a fraction of psychotic patients, and not all neurotics, are able to respond adequately to this test. Whatever standards of full co-operation were accepted, it is quite possible that this selection vitiated the results of the experiment.

A series of studies by Foulds (Ref. 11) and Foulds & Caine (Refs. 12 and 13) have considered the speed of response of neurotic patients on the Porteus Maze Test in particular. In the earliest of these Foulds showed that the speed of starting and tracing the mazes decreased in the order: psychopaths, hysterics, anxiety states, obsessionals and reactive depressions. In the later studies, Foulds & Caine found that timed test responses were more closely related to personality type than to diagnostic category. They showed that obsessive personalities take longer on the Mazes and Matrices than hysteroids. This finding is somewhat complicated by the fact that they employed a Hysteroid-Obsessive Rating Scale of their own design, based on psychiatric texts. (In this experiment psychiatrists' ratings on this scale correlated 0·40 with neuroticism but only 0·21 with introversion-extraversion, both as measured by the Heron Questionnaire (Ref. 15).) These findings led them to the prediction that obsessives would show lower speed and higher accuracy than hysteroids in performance on the Nufferno Tests.

Intellectual speed or speed of thinking are used in this paper to refer to observable problem-solving behaviour. It may well be that this does not reliably indicate the actual mental processes taking place. For example, Hetherington found that electro-convulsive therapy reduced the output of depressives on tests of adding and letter substitution (Ref. 16). He concluded from this that loss of thinking speed was a therapeutic effect of E.C.T. in depression and that this was consistent with the hypothesis that depressive psychic retardation was not a simple slowing of thoughts, but was due to the interference of a 'constant surge' of painful thoughts. The loss of output was not statistically significant on either test used, however, in contrast with the significant increases of speed in the later stages of treatment and the period following. Further, if output on tests of this type did measure an aspect of thinking speed, it was only a very limited one.

The evidence of speed differences between hysterics and dysthymics, presented above, is fairly strong when tasks which demand largely motor responses are concerned, i.e., the track tracer and maze tracing. There is no strong evidence that speed of thinking or problem solving, as distinct from motor performance, differentiates the groups. Moreover, persistence, accuracy and difficulty of task are not controlled variables in any of the investigations which have studied the time of response to tests of the intelligence test type. There are features of the Nufferno Speed Tests which make them specially suitable for an investigation of the intellectual speed of neurotics, whilst controlling these three variables.

METHOD

The Nufferno Speed Tests consist of eighteen scored items, all of similar difficulty level and all of the Thurstone letter-series type. The speed score is derived from the mean of the log times for each item correctly solved. The reason for this scoring is discussed by Furneaux (Ref. 14). The subject is timed by a concealed stop watch and performs the test under the instruction to work at his own rate with 'no need at all to hurry'. All incorrectly solved or abandoned items are rejected for the speed scoring but the number correct is taken as an accuracy score. Thus accuracy is controlled in the manner used by previous workers. The tests are available at two levels of difficulty; test B 1 consists of items which are harder than those in test A 2, but as all the items in a test are of similar difficulty, difficulty is a controlled variable when comparing the groups on that test. Furneaux considers the problem of persistence and concludes that it is possible to measure speed at the level of difficulty involved in these tests, as distinct from the effects of persistence limits (Ref. 14). Therefore, the three important variables appear to be satisfactorily controlled when speed is measured by this method.

The testing was carried out individually by the same examiner for all subjects. The testing situation was maintained as uniform as possible and all the subjects were instructed that the tests were purely for research purposes and would not help them in any way. In view of a work decrement effect reported by Eysenck on a similar test (Ref. 10), rest pauses of one minute were introduced before each speed test. The subjects were instructed to sit quietly with their eyes closed and to try not to think about the testing.

Forty neurotic subjects of average or above-average intelligence were referred by the consultants of the hospital for the purposes of the research. Patients undergoing treatment with E.C.T. were avoided and those being treated with appreciable doses of drugs such as 'Largactil' which might have a serious effect on mental functioning were not considered. The neurotic group was divided equally into introvert and extravert personality types according to their scores on the Heron Sociability Test (Ref. 15), the median score being 6·5. This division significantly differentiated the anxiety and obsessive-compulsive diagnostic groups from the remaining neuroses (Table 1). On this evidence the two groups will be described as Dysthymics and Hysterics in accordance with Eysenck (e.g. Ref. 10, p. 26).

The age range for the neurotic subjects was 16–53 years with a mean age of 32 years.

A control group of 20 normal subjects was drawn from hospital medical, clerical and artisan staff, and each was matched for age with

TABLE 1

ASSOCIATION BETWEEN PSYCHIATRIC DIAGNOSIS
AND QUESTIONNAIRE CLASSIFICATION

	Questionnaire classification	
	Extravert	Introvert
Hysteria	6	3
Hypochondriasis	4	1
Phobic states	2	1
Psychopathic personality	3	2
Total	15	7
Anxiety states	4	9
Obsessive compulsive	1	4
Total	5	13

chi² for 2×2 table is 4·5. $0.05 > p > 0.02$.

one hysteric and one dysthymic subject. The maximum age range in each trio was 4 years. To effect this matching it was necessary to select patients, according to age only, to fill the last five places. The groups did not differ significantly in their scores on the Mill Hill Vocabulary Scale. This was accepted as indicating that they were of similar premorbid intelligence. The control group and the hysteric group included 11 males and 9 females, the dysthymic group 9 males and 11 females. Himmelweit suggested that females are quicker than males, therefore the bias in these groups would be contrary to the experimental hypothesis (Ref. 18). Actually there were differences in intelligence between Himmelweit's male and female groups and it is not clear whether she had taken this into consideration in arriving at her conclusion.

RESULTS

The distribution of scores in this investigation sometimes becomes seriously non-normal and for this reason, especially, non-parametric statistics have been applied.

Table 2 summarizes the results and shows that the speed and accuracy differences are entirely as expected. At both levels of difficulty the dysthymic group is significantly slower than the control group in solving problems. The hysteric group also appears somewhat slower although not to a statistically significant degree, but is also apparently faster than

TABLE 2

SPEED AND ACCURACY SCORES

Group	Mean speed score*	Wilcoxon T Dysthymics	Wilcoxon T Hysterics	Mean accuracy score	Wilcoxon T Dysthymics	Wilcoxon T Hysterics
		Test A2 (low difficulty)				
Controls	193·2	42 N = 19 0·025 > p > 0·01 (one-tailed test)	97·5 (not sig.)	16·3	33 N = 17 0·025 > p > 0·01 (one-tailed test)	31 N = 19 p = 0·005 (one-tailed test)
Dysthymics	181·3	—	64·0 (not sig.)	13·8	—	93 (not sig.)
Hysterics	189·7	—	—	13·3	—	—
		Test B1 (higher difficulty)				
Controls	197·3	39 N = 20 0·01 > p > 0·005 (one-tailed test)	83·5 (not sig.)	15·1	44·5 N = 17 p = 0·072 (not sig.)	13·5 N = 18 p = 0·005 (one-tailed test)
Dysthymics	181·1	—	66·0 (not sig.)	13·3	—	55·5 N = 20 p = 0·032 (one-tailed test)
Hysterics	190·8	—	—	11·3	—	—

* The speed scores are stated as Nufferno Corrected Speed Scores

dysthymics. In accuracy the result is that the hysteric group shows the lowest score at both levels of difficulty and is significantly lower than the controls. Dysthymics also appear to be rather less accurate than controls, in fact significantly so at the lower level of difficulty. Moreover, it is only at the higher level of difficulty that the hysteric-dysthymic accuracy difference becomes statistically significant.

The pattern of speed and accuracy in problem solving is thus shown to be that hysterics are characterized by low accuracy and dysthymics by low speed. Each of the groups tends to be both slower and less accurate than the control group however.

DISCUSSION

The primary aim of this investigation was that of testing out a hypothesis derived from clinical observation. It is one of the important functions of clinical psychologists to attempt to find objective validity for such observations. In this case the psychiatric observations and the psychological experiment are in agreement. The outcome of this can be greater subjective confidence in psychiatric recommendations, as for example where the solution of employment problems in rehabilitation is based on clinical diagnosis. This sort of consideration is probably less important than the broader implications. The researches into skilled performance, e.g., those of Welford (Ref. 34), have emphasized the fundamental importance of speed. It is curious, therefore, that untimed, leisurely tests often seem intuitively preferred to time-limited tests. It may be that the attempt to remove time limits in psychological tests is to turn a blind eye to a crucial factor. In this investigation neurotic subjects were shown to be effectively inferior to normal persons either in speed or accuracy. The immediate question which arises is what the nature of this inferiority is. It may be that this is a real limitation in ability, or alternatively it could be more akin to a preference for a different pace of work or accuracy of response. The solution might be found in attempts to pace performance so as to find out if neurotics are capable of adopting the normal pattern of performance and of becoming as quick and accurate as normals when the conditions demand it.

If these deficiencies are true limitations of ability, then either they may be of the nature of an impairment resulting from neurotic illness, or factors in the patient's personality which predispose him to neurosis. In the former case speed and accuracy may be associated with progress of treatment rather as Hetherington inferred (Ref. 16) but in the latter case the predisposing factors may remain unrelated to the course of treatment. Framed in other terms, one is led to ask how far these speed and accuracy defects are the cause of neurotic breakdown and how far the result of it. If they are the result, do they form part of a neurotic defence against more radical breakdown?

In this investigation, as in some of those referred to earlier, there is a clear relationship between patterns of speed and accuracy and questionnaire measures of introversion—extraversion for neurotic patients. As they are consistent in many different types of material, they are likely to have some degree of stability in time. That is, a person showing high accuracy and low speed at one period will tend to show the same pattern at a later period when re-tested. There is, however, an important difference between these speed and accuracy testing methods and questionnaire methods. Investigations such as that of Bartholomew & Marley emphasize the temporal stability of questionnaire introversion-extraversion scores and that 'treatment in hospital has little effect on questionnaire response' (Ref. 1). Demonstrations of this kind of reliability also indicate insensitivity to variations which might occur and this is what one would expect from the content of many questionnaires. One of the major difficulties patients raise in completing questionnaires of this type is that they seem to be able to answer in different ways according to whether they take them as referring to one period or another. In few, if any, questionnaires can the responses be made applicable to the here and now situation, although it is true that they will to some extent reflect present perception of a state of affairs which existed in the past. This sort of insensitivity is not a defect of the speed and accuracy test which can be used to assess the state of the patient at a well-defined and short period in time. Moreover, it seems that speed and accuracy testing is likely to be repeatable without serious re-test effects. There are many fields of research in which such methods of personality measurement may be useful to describe a situation existing at a particular instant in time and where methods with high temporal stability would be unsuitable.

ACKNOWLEDGEMENTS

This paper is an extract from an M.A. thesis presented by the author to Liverpool University. The help of the staff of the Department of Psychology is very gratefully acknowledged, as is the assistance of the hospital staff and patients.

REFERENCES

1. BARTHOLOMEW, A. A. & MARLEY, E., The temporal reliability of the Maudsley Personality Inventory. *J. ment. Sci.*, **105,** 238–240, 1959.
2. BAXTER, B., An experimental analysis of the contributions of speed and level in an intelligence test. *J. educ. Psychol.*, **32,** 285–296, 1941.
3. BROADHURST, A., Experimental studies of the mental speed of schizophrenics. II. *J. ment. Sci.*, **104,** 1130–1136, 1958.
4. CANE, V. R. & HORN, V., The timing of responses to spatial perception questions. *Quart. J. exp. Psychol.*, **3,** 133–145, 1951.
5. CHAPMAN, J. C., Persistence, success and speed in a mental test. *Ped. Sem.*, **31,** 276–284, 1924.
6. COURTIS, S. A., The relation between speed and quality in educational measurement. *J. educ. Res.*, **10,** 110–131, 1927.
7. CURRAN, D. & PARTRIDGE, M., *Psychological Medicine* (4th ed.). London: Livingstone, 1957.
8. DAVIDSON, W. M. & CARROLL, J. B., Speed and level in time-limit scores—a factor analysis. *Educ. Psychol. Measmt.*, **5,** 411–427, 1945.
9. EYSENCK, H. J., Differential Cognitive Tests. Office of Naval Research Report, Contract no. N 625585, Bur. Med. Surg., U.S. Navy, London Branch, 1953.
10. ——, *The Dynamics of Anxiety and Hysteria.* London: Routledge & Kegan Paul, 1957.
11. FOULDS, G. A., Temperamental differences in maze performance. II. *Brit. J. Psychol.*, **43,** 33–42, 1952.
12. —— & CAINE, T. M., Personality factors and performance on timed tests of ability. *Occup. Psychol.*, **32,** 102–105, 1958.
13. —— & ——, Psychoneurotic symptom clusters, trait clusters and psychological tests. *J. ment. Sci.*, **104,** 722–732, 1958.
14. FURNEAUX, W. D., The Determinants of Success in Intelligence Tests. Paper read at the Bristol meeting. British Association for the Advancement of Science, 1955.
15. HERON, A., A two-part personality measure for use as a research criterion. *Brit. J. Psychol.*, **47,** 243–251, 1956.
16. HETHERINGTON, R., Efficiency and retentivity of depressed patients. *Brit. J. med. Psychol.*, **29,** 258–269, 1956.
17. HIMMELWEIT, H. T., Speed and accuracy of work as related to temperament. *Brit. J. Psychol.*, **36,** 132–144, 1946.

18. ——, The level of aspiration of normal and neurotic persons. *Brit. J. Psychol.*, **37**, 41–59, 1947.

19. HOLZINGER, K. J., *Preliminary Report on the Spearman-Holzinger Unitary Traits Study*. Chicago: Statist. Lab., Dept. Educ., Univ. Chicago, 1934.

20. HUNSICKER, L. M., *A Study of the Relationship Between Rate and Ability*. New York: Teachers' College, Columbia University, 1925.

21. MCFARLAND, R. A., An experimental study of the relationship between speed and mental ability. *J. Gen. Psychol.*, **3**, 67–97, 1930.

22. MYERS, C. T., The factorial composition and validity of differentially speeded tests. *Psychometrika*, **17**, 347–352, 1952.

23. NELSON, E. H., An Experimental Investigation of Intellectual Speed and Power in Mental Disorders. Unpublished Ph.D. thesis, University of London Library, 1953.

24. OGILVIE, B. C., A Study of Intellectual Slowness in Schizophrenia. Unpublished Ph.D. thesis, University of London Library, 1954.

25. PEAK, H. & BORING, E. G., The factor of speed in intelligence. *J. exp. Psychol.*, **9**, 71–94, 1926.

26. RUCH, C. M. & KOERTH, W., 'Power' vs. 'Speed' in Army Alpha. *J. educ. Psychol.*, **14**, 193–208, 1923.

27. SLATER, P., Scores of different types of neurotics on tests of intelligence. *Brit. J. Psychol.*, **35**, 40–42, 1944.

28. STUDMAN, G., The measurement of speed and flow of mental activity. *J. ment. Sci.*, **81**, 107–137, 1935.

29. STURT, M., A comparison of speed with accuracy in the learning process. *Brit. J. Psychol.*, **12**, 289–309, 1921.

30. SUTHERLAND, J. D., The speed factor in intelligent reactions. *Brit. J. Psychol.*, **24**, 276–294, 1934.

31. TATE, M. W., Individual differences in speed of response in mental test materials of varying degrees of difficulty. *Educ. Psychol. Measmt.*, **8**, 353–374, 1948.

32. THURSTONE, L. L., *Primary Mental Abilities*. Chicago: University Press, 1938.

33. WEBB, E., Character and intelligence. *Brit. J. Psychol. Monogr. Suppl.*, no. **3**, 1918.

34. WELFORD, A. T., *Ageing and Human Skill*. Oxford: Oxford University Press, 1958.

35. WOODROW, H., The relation between abilities and improvement with practice. *J. educ. Psychol.*, **29**, 215–230, 1938.

47

Involuntary Rest Pauses in Tapping as a Function
of Drive and Personality

H. J. EYSENCK[1]

First published in *Perceptual and Motor Skills*, **18**, 173–174, 1964

THE hypothesis was tested that involuntary rest pauses occurring during massed practice on a tapping task would be more numerous for extraverted Ss; significant correlations in the predicted direction were obtained. It was also predicted that involuntary rests would be less numerous under conditions of high drive than under conditions of low drive; support for this hypothesis was suggested by the results of an analysis of covariance, but not at a statistically significant level. As anticipated, high-drive Ss produced a greater number of taps than did low-drive Ss.

INTRODUCTION

Recent personality theory links the growth of reactive inhibition with extraverted personality patterns (Ref. 1). According to Hull (Ref. 5) and Kimble (Ref. 6), I_R produces blocks or involuntary rest pauses during massed practice and it would follow therefore that such involuntary rests should be more frequent for extraverts than for introverts, as well as appearing earlier in their practice. Direct measurement of such rests is difficult on the pursuit rotor and other hypothetical consequences of the build-up of inhibition have been used, such as reminiscence (Ref. 3). Recently, efforts have been made to design tasks which would permit direct measurement of involuntary rests and Spielman has shown on a tapping task that extraverted Ss produced almost 20 times as many such rests as did introverted Ss and also produced them earlier (Ref. 7). (Personality was measured on the M.P.I.; Ss were working-class people taken at random from a factory job. The 9 most introverted and the 9 most extraverted Ss of a total group of 90 were administered the tapping test.) The present paper reports an attempt to check this finding.

[1] The writer is indebted to the Research Fund of the Maudsley and Bethlem Royal Hospital for support.

Kimble has also predicted that reminiscence scores would increase with increases in drive, high drive preventing the occurrence of many involuntary rests and Eysenck has shown that reminiscence is indeed a function of drive (Ref. 4). The present experiment uses high-drive and low-drive groups to test directly the assumption that high-drive Ss would have fewer involuntary rests. The method used for manipulating drive has been explained in detail elsewhere (Ref. 4). Ss were 78 industrial apprentices, half tested under conditions where they thought that their scores would be taken into consideration in determining their admission to a training course important for their future advance (high drive), half tested after admission (low drive). All Ss were male, ages varying between 16 and 18.

METHOD

Ss were instructed to tap as fast as possible for 1 minute on a metal board with a metal stylus. Through a transistor switch and oscillator, the exact duration of each tap, i.e., the length of time the stylus was in touch with the plate, was transferred to a magnetic tape running through a tape recorder. Gap duration, i.e., the length of time the stylus was *not* in touch with the plate, was similarly recorded. The tape was then fed into a sequential event timer and recorded, which causes events to be recorded to operate one or more of its eight high speed input relays, subsequent registration and transfer being effected by cold cathode trigger tubes. Clock pulses are also counted on three counter tubes, which can be reset to zero electronically when an event is recorded. Settings are read out via the store unit into the output unit, which operates a punch. Tape from the output unit can then be fed directly into electronic computers for detailed analysis.

RESULTS

(1) High-drive boys have shorter mean gap time (t = 3·78), but only insignificantly shorter mean tap time (t = 1·39) than low-drive boys. High drive thus produces a greater number of taps during practice.

(2) Extraversion, measured on the M.P.I. (Ref. 2), correlates positively with the number of involuntary rests, when these are defined as gaps more than 3 SDs longer than the mean for any particular S. The product-moment correlations were 0·24 and 0·23 for the high-drive and the low-drive groups, respectively. Separately these correlations fall

422 Bearings on Basic Psychological Processes

short of statistical significance but jointly they are significant ($p < 0.05$).

(3) Involuntary rests are insignificantly more numerous in the high-drive groups ($t = 1.20$); but this cannot be taken as counter to prediction as the number of taps too is significantly higher in this group. An analysis of covariance shows that for equal number of taps the high-drive group has fewer involuntary rests, although the F of 3·64 falls just short of significance ($F = 3.98$ at $p < 0.05$).

DISCUSSION

We have concentrated more on gaps than on taps, following Spielman (Ref. 7), because gaps appear to give more relevant information. This may be due to the fact that the inevitable rebound of the metal stylus from the metal plate makes it inherently unlikely that involuntary rests could be taken during the tap; they are much more likely to be taken during the gap. It would require a voluntary act by S to force the stylus during a tap to remain in contact with the board, rather than to rebound. The data for taps show tendencies similar to those for gaps, but results are not significant.

REFERENCES

1. EYSENCK, H. J., *Dynamics of Anxiety and Hysteria*. London: Routledge & Kegan Paul, 1957.
2. ——, *Maudsley Personality Inventory*. San Diego: Educ. Indust. Testing Service, 1962.
3. ——, Reminiscence, drive and personality—revision and extension of a theory. *Brit. J. soc. clin. Psychol.*, **1**, 127–140, 1962.
4. ——, *Experiments in Motivation*. New York: Macmillan, 1964.
5. HULL, C. L., *Principles of Behaviour*. New York: Appleton-Century, 1943.
6. KIMBLE, G. A., An experimental test of a two-factor theory of inhibition. *J. exp. Psychol.*, **39**, 15–23, 1949.
7. SPIELMAN, I., The Relation Between Personality and the Frequency and Duration of Involuntary Rest Pauses During Massed Practice. Unpublished Ph.D. thesis, University of London Library, 1963.

48

Ocular Movements and Spontaneous Blink Rate as Functions of Personality

CYRIL M. FRANKS

First published in *Perceptual Motor Skills*, **16,** 178, 1963

INTRODUCTION

ALTHOUGH the importance of both deliberate and spontaneous blinking and eye movements in the study of certain perceptual phenomena has been stressed repeatedly, the circumstances surrounding the relative contributions for these two variables remain open to question. Meredith & Meredith have suggested that differential eye movements and blink rates may be associated with different types of viewing instructions (Ref. 3). This could partially account for recently reported differences among Necker cube fluctuation data obtained under different viewing instructions (Ref. 1). In this study, in which eye movements *per se* were not investigated, blinking was unrelated either to extraversion or to fluctuation.

METHOD

In a subsequent investigation eye movements and blink rates were related to the extraversion scores of 39 normal adult males. Spontaneous blinking was recorded photoelectrically while Ss sat in a soundproof room gazing at a 600 rpm rotating spiral for two 1-minute viewing periods, separated by a 3-minute interval. Extraversion scores were then obtained by having Ss complete the E scale of the Maudsley Personality Inventory (MPI). Spontaneous eye movements were investigated by a technique which required Ss to keep their heads still and report any fleeting 'flashes' obtruding upon the otherwise uniform grey appearance at the same high speed (Ref. 2). This effect, which also occurs when certain blinks occur, is supposed to be stable and reliable. After a brief explanation and practice period Ss were given two trials of 1 minute separated by a 3 minute interval, all flashes being recorded by a light

423

touch on a silent telegraph key attached to a counter. For 20 Ss the blink test followed the questionnaire.

RESULTS AND DISCUSSION

The order of presentation was found to produce no pertinent differences in either rate of blinking or report of flashes. Pearson product-moment test-retest correlations were 0·72 and 0·84 for the blinks and flashes, respectively. Correlations among mean blink rate, mean flash rate and E were as follows: blink-E, $r = 0·10$; blink-flash, $r = 0·22$; E-flash, $r = 0·42$. If flash rate does indeed measure certain eye movements, then these data suggest that eye movements may be of greater pertinence than eye blinks in studies involving visual fixation and extraversion. These data also provide some support for Eysenck's contention that extraverts are poorer at visual fixation than are introverts (see Ref. 2).

REFERENCES

1. FRANKS, C. M. & LINDAHL, L. E. H., Extraversion and rate of fluctuation of the Necker cube. *Percept. mot. Skills*, **16,** 131–137, 1963.
2. HOLLAND, H. C., Measures of perceptual function. In *Experiments in Personality* (ed. H. J. Eysenck), 193–233. London: Routledge & Kegan Paul, 1960.
3. MEREDITH, G. M. & MEREDITH, C. G. W., Effect of instructional conditions on rate of binocular rivalry. *Percept. mot. Skills*, **15,** 655–664, 1962.

49

Alternation in Choice Behaviour and Extraversion

H. J. EYSENCK & A. LEVEY[1]

First published in *Life Sciences*, **4,** 115–119, 1965

INTRODUCTION AND METHOD

IT may be deduced from Eysenck's general theory relating extraversion to exaggerated inhibitory effects that alternation would occur with greater frequency in extraverted Ss as compared with introverted Ss; the assumption is of course made in this context that alternation behaviour is due to central inhibition or satiation (Ref. 1). Some animal experiments, using Eysenck's drug postulate, have given support to this general view (Ref. 3) but no direct experimental evidence seems to be available regarding human Ss. In the present experiment, 48 army volunteers of between 20 and 30 years of age were tested, their personality assessments being obtained with the newly developed Eysenck Personality Inventory (Ref. 2), which gives scores for Extraversion (E), Neuroticism (N) and a Lie scale (L). The distribution of these scores was not dissimilar to that found with the standardization group.

The alternation test itself consisted of two parts. In the first of these Ss sorted 100 picture postcards into five piles according to their individual preferences; the pictures were all by recognized painters and ranged from classical through impressionistic to ultra modern. Each person then chose the two best-liked pictures (first pair) and also the two next-best liked (second pair). He was then seated in front of a specially constructed tachistoscope which allowed him to view one or the other picture in a given pair; and was told that he could alter the picture seen by pushing a button. His score was (a) the number of alternations made and (b) the average time in seconds each picture was looked at before changing; as the latter score is more informative, it has been used in this report. Two 5-minute tests were performed on each person, the second pair of

[1] We are indebted to a grant from the M.R.C. for the support of this investigation. We are grateful to Dr S. B. G. Eysenck for preliminary experimentation with this test, which led to improvements in design.

425

pictures following the first after an average of 5 minutes. The test-retest correlation (product-moment) for mean time was 0·81, which is significant at $p < 0.01$.

RESULTS

Inspection of the results suggested that times for viewing increase from first to second test and that this increase might be different at different points of the practice curve. In order to assess this observation statistically performance scores were Vincentized in a rough and ready fashion by averaging scores over the first observation period (A), the midmost (B) and the last (C); this obviates the difficulty created by the fact that different observers have different numbers of observation periods (Fig. 45). Analysis of variance was done separately for the A, B and C scores, both for tests (first against second) and for personality (E, Intermediate and I). No significant interactions were observed; person-

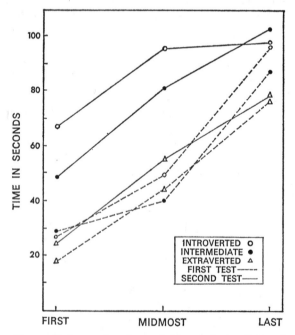

Figure 45. Inspection times of pictures during first and second test, and at first, midmost and last exposure, given separately for introverts, extraverts and intermediate subjects.

ality differences were significant (p <0·05) for A, but not for B or C and period differences were significant (p <0·01) for A and B, but not for C. We may conclude that extraverts alternate more (have shorter inspection periods) at the beginning of the test, but that this superiority wears off; and that alternation periods are longer during the second test as compared with the first, except toward the end of the test.

Correlations (product-moment) were run between test scores and personality scales; neither N nor L gave significant results. E correlated −0·20 with total length of inspection times, summed for tests 1 and 2; this is significant (p <0·05) for a one-tailed test. The correlation for test 1 alone is equally significant, while that for test 2 just fails to be significant. When A, B and C scores were correlated with E, correlations at the p <0·01 level (one-tail) are observed for A_2 and B_2; all the other correlations are negative as predicted but fall short of significance. (r_E; $_{A_2}$ = −0·31; r_E; $_{B_2}$ = −0·29).

DISCUSSION

The results on the whole bear out the hypothesis that inspection periods will be shorter for extraverted than for introverted Ss. Whether this finding can be interpreted in terms of inhibition/satiation producing alternation must of course remain doubtful; it is to be noted that contrary to expectation alternation periods lengthened during the course of the test, a finding observed both from test 1 to test 2, and also from period A through B to C. Inhibition/satiation might have been expected to have shown cumulative results, with a shortening rather than a lengthening of alternation periods. Observation of the conduct of Ss, discussion with some and reports of introspections suggest that the experimental conditions permit of other ways of dissipating inhibition besides alternation behaviour. Thus S might 'go outside the situation' by looking away altogether from the picture in the tachistoscope; he might try to engage E in a discussion; or he might play some form of game with the cards, such as counting items in the pictures, or weaving stories around them. Two Ss (both extraverts) found the task so 'boring' that they gave up without completing it; they are of course not included in this account. It seems reasonable to speculate that alternative ways of dissipating inhibition were increasingly and differentially resorted to as the experiment progressed, thus increasing alternation times and decreasing the amount of correlation with E. Future experiments might with advantage attempt to control or at least measure inhibition-produced behaviour of this kind, in order to test the truth of these hypotheses.

SUMMARY

A reliable choice alternation test was given to 48 Ss in which S could alternate looking at one or other of two picture postcards (paintings) chosen by him from 100 cards. He was scored for average time spent on each presentation, both on the original test and on a repetition, using two other pictures chosen in a similar manner. Extraverted Ss were expected and found to have shorter alternation periods, particularly at the beginning of each test; alternation periods lengthened during each test, from test 1 to test 2 and correlations between E and alternation period decreased as the test went on. An hypothesis is presented to account for these additional facts.

REFERENCES

1. EYSENCK, H. J., *The Dynamics of Anxiety and Hysteria*. New York: Praeger, 1957.
2. —— & EYSENCK, S. B. G., *Manual of the Eysenck Personality Inventory*. San Diego: Educ. Indust. Test. Serv., 1963.
3. SINHA, S. N., FRANKS, C. M. & BROADHURST, P. L., The effect of a stimulant and a depressant drug on a measure of reactive inhibition. *J. exp. Psychol.*, **56**, 349–354, 1958.

50

Speech Patterns and Personality[1]

R. W. RAMSAY

First published in *Language and Speech*, **11**, 54–63, 1968

THIS study reviews briefly the literature on the relation between non-content aspects of speech and personality variables. Data on lengths of sound, silence, units and sound/silence ratio are then presented showing that in general speech patterns of Dutch Ss are similar to English-speaking Ss. There is also confirmation of some differences in speech patterns between extraverts and introverts and some differences were found due to sex and intelligence.

This study sets out to review briefly the literature on some non-content aspects of speech which have been related to personality variables and then to give the results of some experiments in this area.

INTRODUCTION

There are some early studies relating vocal behaviour to personality, but little has been done in recent years. Pear (Ref. 18) and Herzog (Ref. 14) found that listeners were able to judge correctly the sex of a speaker and were moderately good at estimating the speaker's occupation, his height, weight and appearance. Other studies also had moderate success in making statements about a speaker's appearance (Refs. 1, 24 & 27). Cantril & Allport reported on a series of 14 experiments which involved 24 speakers and 600 judges. Judges were asked to match voices with 12 features of personality: age, height, complexion, photographic appearance, appearance in person, handwriting, vocation, political preference, extraversion-introversion, ascendence-submission, dominant values and a summary sketch of personality. Some success was obtained but no characteristic was always revealed correctly and in general judges agreed with each other in excess of their accuracy (Ref. 2). A series of studies by Fay & Middleton investigated judgments of a number of personality characteristics from voices transmitted over a public address

[1] This is part of a study presented as a doctoral dissertation at the University of London and was supported by a scholarship from the Canada Council.

system. Among those characteristics judged with success were Spranger's personality types (Ref. 7), but they had little success with such attributes as sociability (Ref. 8) and extraversion-introversion (Ref. 9). Sanford (Ref. 21) and Licklider & Miller (Ref. 15) in reviewing these studies point out the operation of stereotypes in judgments, a condition which produces agreement among judges more often than agreement with external criteria.

Most of the studies attempting to relate vocal behaviour with personality have made use of the judgment of human listeners. The listener must make a decision about what he hears and very often he must be specially trained to describe a certain aspect in a limited situation. After a review of this literature on judging personality from speech, Starkweather states that he is pessimistic about the general utility of listening to a voice in order to assess directly the personality of the speaker (Ref. 26).

Chapple investigated one aspect of vocal behaviour, the duration of utterances, and introduced a more objective method of measuring individual differences by means of the Interaction Chronograph (Refs. 3 & 4). He claimed that stable differences exist between Ss in the characteristics of the distribution of the durations of speech units, but his method still relied to some extent on judgments and decisions made by the operator of the Interaction Chronograph. Saslow *et al.* define a number of variables that can be obtained from the Interaction Chronograph (Ref. 22) and Matarazzo & Saslow by means of factor analysis identify two strong and three weak factors in vocal behaviour (Ref. 16). The strong factors were (a) how long an individual waits or remains silent before communicating and (b) the number and average duration of each communicative interaction.

Matarazzo *et al.* in a study attempting to relate a number of variables to vocal patterns obtained from the Interaction Chronograph, found positive correlations between lengths of action (time spent in actual speech) and silence with intelligence (Ref. 17). These correlations did not reach significance but nevertheless indicate that intelligence as a personality factor may be of importance. Goldman-Eisler has related speech duration and information about the speaker. She divided short silences and short actions from long silences and long actions, with a dividing line of 20 seconds. She found that of the 4 measures obtained, the frequency of long silences seemed most consistent and indicative of an individual's style of talking (Ref. 10). In another study, using psychiatric interviews as data, the division into long and short actions and silences was 5 seconds (Ref. 11). A ratio of short to long silences was here a consistent description of vocal activity for both physicians and patients. In most of her studies Goldman-Eisler has concentrated on measurement of the silence periods rather than on the action periods, the former being in her opinion of more psychological importance. Ref. 12 is a good review of the relevant findings from her studies over the last few years.

Starkweather studied the duration of vocal speech patterns in role-playing situations where different Ss played a pre-arranged part opposite a standard role-player who was the same person for each S (Ref. 25). Two situations were studied in which it was possible to obtain utterance duration measures for the standard role-player speaking to many different Ss in the same situations and also for different Ss speaking to the same standard role-player. Overall curves of the distribution of durations did not reveal much, but the distributions were then divided into four parts to discover which portions might vary with the three dimensions of situation, speaker and listener. Very short utterances of less than one second were interpreted as providing feedback and reinforcement from the listener to the speaker. The production of long utterances, greater than 20 seconds, was a relatively stable characteristic of the speaker and not easily influenced by the activity of the listener.

Most of the studies using the Interaction Chronograph have been devoted to finding which measures given by the chronograph are stable and could possibly reveal personality characteristics of the speaker. Few studies have set out to relate the measures to specific personality traits. One such study is that done by Matarazzo *et al.* (Ref. 17) mentioned above; another is a recent investigation by Siegman & Pope in which they found a significant negative correlation between extraversion and duration of silence in an interview situation (Ref. 23). More recently, Ramsay found significant differences between extraverts and introverts in the lengths of sound and silence over a number of verbal tasks (Ref. 19).

Studies using the Interaction Chronograph have taken measures during interviews between two or more people, for the obvious reason that speech is a social phenomenon usually occurring between two or more persons. But in attempting to assess personality aspects of a speaker, this approach can be criticized on two counts. First, the reliability of the measures could be improved. Secondly, the effect on personality assessment of two or more different persons interacting is unknown. Starkweather's role-playing experiments have attempted to minimize this effect by having a standard role-player, but most studies have not controlled this interaction variable.

The purpose of the present study was to refine the techniques of measurement of speech patterns, and to relate these speech patterns to some variables within Eysenck's framework of personality (Ref. 5).

METHOD

The complete operation for continuous speech measurement (given in detail in Ref. 20) consists of recording a S's verbalizations by means of a throat microphone onto magnetic tape at a constant volume. The taped verbalizations are then passed at a constant volume through a relay. A recording device then registers the time during which the relay is closed (speech) and open (silence) correct to 0·01 second and punches this information on 5-hole tape. The tape is then processed by a computer.

The Ss in this study consisted of three groups: 29 female first-year university students, 28 female students of low intelligence from a technical school and 28 male first-year university students. The average age for each group was 19·0, 16·25 and 20·5 respectively. All Ss were living in Amsterdam and all testing was conducted in Dutch. All Ss completed a questionnaire (Ref. 28) from which extraversion and neuroticism scores could be obtained.

The verbal tasks were:

(a) an initial unrecorded reading task to get the Ss used to the microphone and to allow the Ss to habituate to some extent to the testing situation. This also gave the E a chance to get a general level of voice loudness for recording.

(b) reading a short passage of prose (average time taken approximately one minute).

(c) reading a longer passage of more difficult prose (average time taken approximately three minutes).

(d) a conversation with the E lasting at least three minutes.

(e) a description of the pictures on three T.A.T. cards, with no time limit.

(f) stories made up about three different T.A.T. cards, with no time limit.

The data obtained consisted of four measures:

(a) the mean of the lengths of utterances.

(b) the mean of the lengths of silences.

(c) the mean of the lengths of units (sound plus subsequent silence).

(d) a sound/silence ratio (the ratio of the total period of sound over the total period of silence in a task).

Each measure was taken separately for each verbal task, so for each S there were four scores for each of the five verbal tasks, a total of 20 scores per S. The type of analysis used was a split plot design with repeated measurements. Factor A corresponded to groups or samples, with three levels; Factor B with two levels corresponded to extraversion-introversion; Factor C with two levels corresponded to high and low neuroticism; Ss were nested within factors A, B and C; and factor D corresponded to tasks, with five levels. All probability values in the results were evaluated in terms of the conservative test suggested by Greenhouse & Geisser (Ref. 13).

RESULTS

The results of the analyses of variance for the three samples are summarized in Table 1.

Sound

Taking sound first, there is a highly significant difference between tasks and the linear trend[1] is negative and highly significant (Fig. 46).

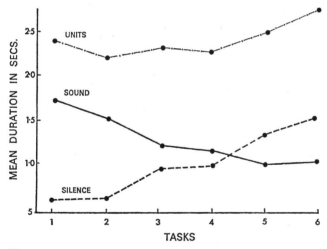

Figure 46. Distribution of sound, silence and units over tasks
in the three samples combined.

[1] A significant linear trend denotes a systematic linear relationship between the dependent and independent variables. A significant difference between linear components of the trend denotes a significant difference between the slopes of the trends.

P

TABLE 1

SUMMARY OF THE ANALYSES OF VARIANCE OF THE THREE SAMPLES COMBINED

Source	df	Sound M.S.	Sound F	Silence M.S.	Silence F	Units M.S.	Units F	Sound/Silence Ratio M.S.	Sound/Silence Ratio F
Groups	2	685,531	50·18‡	20,822		147,319	13·82‡	11,093	14·30‡
Extraversion	1	162		241,391	5·36*	70,031	6·58*	717	
Neuroticism	1	10,514		80		13,259		1,002	
G×E	2	3,508		3,797		2,644		318	
G×N	2	5,067		7,124		3,364		457	
E×N	1	972		1,406		1,155		78	
G×E×N	2	10,392		10,893		5,019		322	
Between Ss	72	13,674		45,019		10,699		776	
Tasks	5	620,906	135·21‡	2,055,702	185·25‡	96,453	24·33‡	59,137	277·13‡
G×T	10	19,944	4·16*	64,317	5·80*	34,472	8·52†	1,266	5·93*
E×T	5	6,716		25,165		4,589		334	
N×T	5	2,462		8,094		2,295		135	
G×E×T	10	4,794		5,354		2,727		276	
G×N×T	10	2,103		12,054		3,654		125	
E×N×T	5	10,475		10,428		6,686		472	
G×E×N×T	10	3,279		7,584		2,884		61	
Ss within groups	360	4,584		11,097		4,048		213	
Linear Trends									
Tasks	1	2,831,857	617·77‡	9,847,578	887·41‡	247,664	61·18‡	273,929	1,283·72‡
E×T	1	16,540		66,364	5·98*	4,501		834	
N×T	1	6,677		850		152		318	
E×N×T	1	23,314	5·09*	207		8,548		872	4·08*
G×E×T	1	22,496		1,152		11,089		993	4·65*

* p<0.05   † p<0.01   ‡ p<0.005

There is a highly significant difference between groups, the female high-intelligence group having the highest mean score ($\overline{X} = 1\cdot49$ seconds), the female low-intelligence group being next ($\overline{X} = 1\cdot25$ seconds) and the male high-intelligence group having the lowest mean length of sound ($\overline{X} = 1\cdot11$ seconds). Thus there are differences between the groups due to intelligence and due to sex. There is a significant difference in the linear trend for the extraversion-introversion by neuroticism interaction over tasks and a significant groups by extraversion-introversion by task linear interaction, but these do not appear to be meaningful.

Silence

The overall analysis of silence shows highly significant differences and a positive linear trend over tasks (Fig. 46). Unlike sound, there are no significant differences between groups, except over tasks and this interaction is small. There are significant differences between extraverts and introverts and the linear trend of extraversion-introversion by tasks is significant. The mean length of silence for introverts is $1\cdot03$ seconds, compared with $0\cdot93$ seconds for extraverts. This difference is negligible for reading tasks, but increases with increasing complexity of task, as shown in Fig. 47.

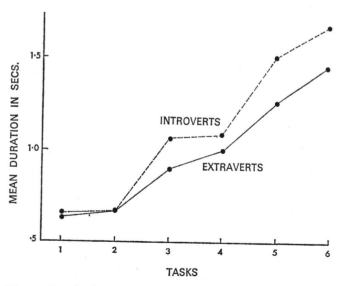

Figure 47. Distribution of extravert-intravert differences over tasks in duration of silence in the three samples combined.

Units

The analysis of units shows a highly significant difference between tasks, overall and in linear trend, but in comparison with the differences between tasks in sound and silence, the units difference is small (Fig. 46). Thus, where the mean length of sound decreases with task complexity and the mean length of silence increases with task complexity, the mean length of units tends to remain almost the same over tasks. There is a highly significant difference between groups, which is probably due to the differences found between groups in the length of sound.

Sound/Silence Ratio

The analysis of sound/silence ratio shows a highly significant difference between tasks: as the complexity of the task increases, the ratio drops from an average of 2·85 to 0·79. There is also a highly significant difference between groups, the female high intelligence group having a mean ratio of 1·88, the female low intelligence group a mean of 1·60 and the male high intelligence group a mean of 1·37. Thus the males spend less proportion of time in speaking and more time in silence. The extraversion by neuroticism by tasks linear trend is significant and the groups by extraversion by tasks linear trend is significant, but these are not discussed.

DISCUSSION

General Aspects of Speech Patterns

In all the results reported, including a previous study (Ref. 19), the lengths of sound and silence differ over tasks: as the complexity of the verbal task increases, the length of time spent in speech decreases and the length of time spent in silence increases. This is not a new finding. Goldman-Eisler has reported this in a number of publications and she concludes that silence is used for higher cognitive activity. This study supports this conclusion and also shows that this finding holds up cross-culturally.

The length of units (speech plus subsequent silence) does not seem to change much over tasks (Fig. 46) and the mean square for Ss within groups is lower than that of either sound or silence. Where the F ratios for the linear trend of sound and silence are 617·77 and 887·41 respectively, the linear trend for units is only 61·18. Thus it is reasonable to state that there is little difference between the length of units over tasks, compared with differences in sound and silence. This finding has not been evident from other studies and would indicate that there is a stable pattern or rhythm in speech, regardless of the complexity of the task. As the task becomes more complex, the speech becomes more internalized, external speech decreases and internal thought processes increase. Goldman-Eisler and co-workers have recently come up with similar findings and their work will be investigating this rhythm in more detail.[1]

Extraversion-Introversion Differences in Speech Patterns

Turning now to the personality factors, it is clear that extraverts and introverts differ in non-content aspects of speech. In a previous study the extraverts produced longer bursts of sound but in these and other unpublished data there were small differences between extraverts and introverts in sound (Ref. 19). Thus it seems that there are no real differences in length of utterances correlated with the personality factor of extraversion-introversion. This would tend to confirm Goldman-Eisler's findings that the action part of speech is not as important for psychological study as the pauses within speech.

There are significant differences between extraverts and introverts in the length of silence between utterances. In general, introverts use longer silences between utterances. If silence is used for higher cognitive activity then the results support the idea that the introvert is the thoughtful type: he thinks before acting and weighs his words more than the extravert. Eysenck & Eysenck describe the extravert as 'sociable, likes parties, has many friends, needs to have people to talk to and does not like reading or studying by himself'. The introvert is described as 'a quiet retiring sort of person, introspective, fond of books rather than people; he is reserved and distant except to intimate friends. He tends to plan ahead, "looks before he leaps" and distrusts the impulse of the moment' (Ref. 6). The results of this study show that this description is valid for speech patterns, as other studies have shown it to be valid in other aspects of behaviour.

Further support for the introvert being the thoughtful type can be found in Fig. 47. In reading, which is a well-practiced habit requiring little higher cognitive activity, the pauses are short and extraverts and introverts are much alike. But as the verbal tasks become more difficult the pauses increase in length and the introvert's pauses increase even more than the extravert's: a significant linear trend of interaction.

---

[1] From a personal communication.

Neuroticism Differences in Speech Patterns

The effect of neuroticism on speech patterns seems to be small and inconsistent. There were some significant interactions, but the results do not show any consistent pattern and therefore no interpretation can be made concerning the neuroticism effect.

Male-Female Differences in Speech Pattern

The data comparing the male and female Dutch groups bring out clearly and at an acceptable level of significance sex differences that were suggested by some unpublished data. There is no significant difference between the male and female groups in length of silence, but there are highly significant differences in lengths of sound, units and in sound/silence ratio. Although the actual difference in average length of sound between males and females is small (0·26 seconds), when it is considered that this is 28 per cent of the average length over all three samples, this is a not inconsiderable difference. It cannot be determined from the data whether females talk *more* than males—the verbal tasks were not in the nature of normal free-flowing communication—but females spend a higher proportion of speech time in sound compared with males.

Intelligence Differences in Speech Patterns

In the Matarazzo *et al.* study a correlation between speech patterns and intelligence was suggested (Ref. 17). In the data presented in this study there are significant differences between the high and low intelligence groups in sound but not in silence, the high intelligence female group speaking in longer bursts of sound than the low intelligence group. But there is also an interaction with the male-female differences between groups in length of sound: the male high intelligence group has the shortest length of sound of all three groups. This intelligence difference is therefore difficult to interpret.

REFERENCES

1. BONAVENTURA, M., Ausdruck der personlichkeit in der sprechs-timme und im photogramm. *Arch. ges. Psychol.*, **94**, 501–570, 1935.
2. CANTRIL, H. & ALLPORT, G. W., *The Psychology of Radio*. New York: Appleton Century, 1935.

3. CHAPPLE, E. D., Quantitative analysis of the interaction of individuals. *Proc. Nat. Acad. Sci.*, **25**, 58, 1939.

4. ——, Personality differences as described by invariant properties of individuals in interaction. *Proc. Nat. Acad. Sci.*, **26**, 10–16, 1940.

5. EYSENCK, H. J., *The Structure of Human Personality*. London: Methuen, 1960.

6. EYSENCK, S. B. G. & EYSENCK, H. J., The validity of the questionnaire and rating assessment of extraversion and neuroticism and their factorial stability. *Brit. J. Psychol.*, **54**, 51–62, 1963.

7. FAY, P. J. & MIDDLETON, W. C., Judgement of Spranger personality types from the voice as transmitted over a public address system. *Charac. Pers.*, **8**, 144–155, 1939.

8. —— & ——, The ability to judge sociability from the voice as transmitted over a public address system. *J. soc. Psychol.*, **13**, 303–309, 1941.

9. —— & ——, Judgment of introversion from the transcribed voice. *Quart. J. Speech*, **28**, 226–228, 1942.

10. GOLDMAN-EISLER, F., The measurement of time sequences in conversational behaviour. *Brit. J. Psychol.*, **42**, 355–362, 1951.

11. ——, Individual differences between interviewers and their effects on interviewees' conversational behaviour. *J. ment. Sci.*, **98**, 660–670, 1952.

12. ——, Hesitation, information and levels of speech production. In *Disorders of Language* (ed. A. V. S. de Reuch and M. O'Connor). London: Churchill, 1964.

13. GREENHOUSE, S. W. & GEISSER, S., On methods in the analysis of profile data. *Psychometrika*, **24**, 95–112, 1956.

14. HERZOG, H., Stimme und personlichkeit. *Z. Psychol.*, **130**, 300–379, 1933.

15. LICKLIDER, J. C. R. & MILLER, G. A., The perception of speech. In *Handbook of Experimental Psychology*. (ed. S. S. Stevens). New York: Wiley & Sons, 1951.

16. MATARAZZO, J. D. & SASLOW, G., Factor analysis of interview interaction behaviour. *J. consult. Psychol.*, **22**, 419–429, 1958.

17. MATARAZZO, R. G., MATARAZZO, J. D., SASLOW, G. & PHILLIPS, J. S., Psychological test and organismic correlates of interview interaction patterns. *J. abnorm. soc. Psychol.*, **56**, 329–338, 1958.

18. PEAR, T. H., *Voice and Personality*. New York: Wiley & Sons, 1931.

19. RAMSAY, R. W., Personality and speech. *J. Pers. soc. Psychol.*, **4**, 116–118, 1966.

20. —— & LAW, L. N., The measurement of duration of speech. *Language and Speech*, **9,** 96–102, 1966.
21. SANFORD, F. H., Speech and personality. *Psychol. Bull.*, **39,** 811–845, 1942.
22. SASLOW, G., MATARAZZO, J. D. & GUZE, S. B., The stability of Interaction Chronograph patterns in psychiatric interviews. *J. consult. Psychol.*, **19,** 417–430, 1955.
23. SIEGMAN, A. W. & POPE, B., Personality variables associated with productivity and verbal fluency in the initial interview. *Proc. Ann. Con. Amer. Psychol. Assoc.*, **73,** 273–274, 1965.
24. STAGNER, R., Judgements of voice and personality. *J. educ. Psychol.*, **27,** 272–277, 1936.
25. STARKWEATHER, J. A., Vocal behaviour: the duration of speech units. *Language and Speech*, **2,** 146–153, 1959.
26. ——, *Proceedings of the Association for Research in Nervous and Mental Disease*. Baltimore: Williams & Wilkins, 1964.
27. TAYLOR, H. C., Social agreement on personality traits as judged from speech. *J. soc. Psychol.*, **5,** 244–248, 1933.
28. WILDE, G. J. S., *Neurotische Labiliteit gemeten volgens de Vrangenlijstmethode*. Amsterdam: van Rossen, 1962.

51

Persistence, Personality and Motivation

C. G. COSTELLO & H. J. EYSENCK[1]

First published in *Perceptual and Motor Skills*, **12,** 169–170, 1961

INTRODUCTION

A REVIEW of the literature on persistence discloses confusion in relating objective measures of this trait to personality (Ref. 3). Theoretically, we may subdivide persistence tests according to the negative drive which opposes continuation, i.e., 'pain' in the case of physical tests (Refs. 7, 8 and 9), 'boredom' in the case of ideational tests and according to the positive drive which motivates continuation, i.e., 'group prestige' or 'self-motivation' (Refs. 5 & 7). It may be predicted from the general theory of Eysenck (Refs. 1 & 2) that these positive sources of motivation will apply more strongly to extraverts and introverts, respectively; it may similarly be predicted that *pain* will be a stronger negative drive for introverts, who would be expected to be less persistent on physical tasks, while boredom will be a stronger negative drive in extraverts, who would be expected to be less persistent on mental tasks. The argument in favour of this prediction has been presented elsewhere (Ref. 6) and the greater pain tolerance of extraverts has been demonstrated.

METHOD

In the present study 8 groups of 9 children between 14 and 17 years were selected on the basis of the Junior M.P.I. (Ref. 4) such that extreme high and low scorers on neuroticism and extraversion were selected, giving four combinations. Sex was an additional variable. Each S was given 3 trials of strength on a dynamometer with 20 sec intervals between trials, in the order R, L, R; 13 minutes later 3 more trials were given in the order L, R, L. Two-thirds of the mean strength of each hand was calculated and S given 2 trials of persistence at this setting, S being instructed to keep the pointer as long as possible at this setting for his

[1] We are indebted to the Society for Research in Human Ecology for a grant which made this study possible.

P*   441

right hand with his right hand and at this setting for his left hand with his left hand. The two trials correlated 0·80 and their mean was S's persistence score.

RESULTS

The mean persistence scores for extraverts and introverts were 39·30 and 30·06, respectively; those for males and females were 34·97 and 34·40, respectively; and those for low and high N scores were 35·93 and 33·44, respectively. Analysis of variance disclosed significance at the 0·02 level for extraversion-introversion; none of the other main effects, and none of the interactions, approached significance. It may be noted that extraverts and introverts did not differ in their prepersistence strength records or in their age. The results support the original hypothesis, extraverts being roughly 30 per cent more persistent than introverts.

SUMMARY

In a study of persistence on the dynamometer of 72 children, the more extraverted were found to be significantly more persistent. No differences were found with respect to neuroticism or sex.

REFERENCES

1. EYSENCK, H. J., *Dynamics of Anxiety and Hysteria.* New York: Praeger, 1957.
2. ——, (ed.) *Experiments in Personality* (2 vols.). London: Routledge & Kegan Paul, 1960.
3. ——, *The Structure of Human Personality.* New York: Wiley & Sons, 1960.
4. FURNEAUX, W. D. & GIBSON, H. B., A children's personality inventory designed to measure neuroticism and extraversion. *Brit. J. educ. Psychol.,* **31,** 204–207, 1961.
5. KREMER, A. H., The nature of persistence. *Stud. Psychol. & Psychiat.,* **5,** 1–40, 1942.
6. LYNN, R. & EYSENCK, H. J., Tolerance for pain, extraversion and neuroticism. *Percept. mot. Skills,* **12,** 161–162, 1961.
7. MACARTHUR, R. S., An experimental investigation of persistence in secondary schoolboys. *Can. J. Psychol.,* **9,** 47–54, 1955.

8. RETHLINGSHAFER, D., The relationship of tests of persistence to other measures of continuance of activities. *J. abnorm. soc. Psychol.*, **37**, 71–82, 1942.

9. THORNTON, G. R., A factor analysis of tests designed to measure persistence. *Psychological Monographs*, **51**, 1–42, 1939.

52

Neuroticism, Extraversion, Drive, and Suggestibility

W. D. FURNEAUX

First published in
International Journal of Clinical and Experimental Hypnosis, **9**,
195–214, 1961

INTRODUCTION

IN a recent communication the relationships between some personality characteristics and response to tests of suggestibility have been considered and some of the relevant evidence reviewed (Ref. 4). In the view of the present writer, the kind of conflict of evidence which was revealed by this review frequently arises as the result of attempts to analyse data in terms of assumptions which are not, in fact, justified. The assumptions of linearity and additivity, which are often made quite unwittingly when the multiple-correlation technique is employed, for example, are particularly suspect. If they had been imposed in the study mentioned above (Ref. 4) no useful result at all would have emerged. As it was, however, it proved to be possible to adduce evidence for the view that susceptibility to hypnosis correlates negatively with MPI neuroticism in the more extraverted section of the population and negatively with extraversion in the more neurotic section. In the present paper an attempt is made to determine the personality correlates of postural-sway and chevreul-pendulum responses, using techniques of analysis which involve as few *a priori* assumptions as possible. The results have proved to be of such a nature as to suggest a particular drive-model, which can usefully be applied to the analysis of test responses in situations of an inter-personal kind.

DETAILS OF EXPERIMENT AND SUBJECTS

Some of the subjects for investigation were university students, others were adult readers of a radical journal, more than half of whom scored above the 95th percentile on Raven's Progressive-Matrices test. Each S completed a version of the Maudsley Personality Inventory (MPI)

444

Neuroticism, Extraversion, Drive and Suggestibility 445

which included a lie scale and from which scores for neuroticism, extraversion and 'lying', were obtained. All those obtaining lie scores (L) of ten or more were designated as 'liars'. There is evidence that the MPI neuroticism scores of liars are highly suspect, but that their E scores may be reasonably valid.

Each S was exposed to recorded postural sway suggestion (falling forward) for a period of two and a half minutes, during which time a continuous record of sway was obtained. Immediately preceding the period of suggestion a record was obtained of the amount of sway occurring while the subject was encouraged to relax and to stand in a comfortable although upright posture, for 30 seconds. Scores for sway under suggestion were obtained by noting the largest forward or backward departure from the base line obtained during the last 5 seconds of this pre-suggestion recording. If both backward and forward movements occurred, sway was scored in the direction of the largest movement. Some individuals thus obtained negative (i.e. backward) sway scores, either because the magnitude of their backward oscillations exceeded that of the forward ones, or because they displayed *only* backward movement.

All the students fell into the age range of 18–25 years, while for the radicals the mean age was nearly 34 with a standard deviation of 10·7 and a range from 21–75. Some information as to the numbers of subjects falling into various categories is set out in Table 1.

TABLE 1

NUMBERS OF SUBJECTS AND THEIR TEST RESPONSES

	Students		Radicals		Total	
	M	F	M	F	M	F
Total Liars	10	4	7	1	17	5
Total negative sway	4	1	3	1	7	2
Negative sway, not liars	1	0	0	1	1	1
Liars and negative sway	3	1	3	0	6	1
Liars not negative sway	7	3	4	1	11	4
Total liars and/or negative sway	11	4	7	2	18	6
Neither negative sway nor liars	26	14	29	6	55	20
Total experimental group	37	18	36	8	73	26
Liars falling completely	3	2	0	0	3	2
Non-liars falling completely	14	5	12	1	26	6
Total falls	17	7	12	1	29	8

The Correlation of Sway with Extraversion and Neuroticism

Since the questionnaire responses of the liars must be suspect it seems reasonable to exclude them at first from analyses which are concerned with measurements of N or E. Subjects who obtained negative sway scores also comprise an ambiguous group. It hardly seems justifiable to treat them as if they were less suggestible than those not swaying at all. On the other hand, there is no evidence that they should be scored as if they had swayed forwards. This group, therefore, will also be excluded from the initial analysis. Negative-sway and lying are so highly correlated that of the 7 males showing the former characteristic, 6 would have been excluded if lying was the only ground for elimination.

Within the remaining group of 55 males the product-moment correlation between SW and E is -0.02 and for SW and N it is -0.29, i.e., there is a slight tendency for the more stable subjects to sway the most ($p = 0.05$). For the women the correlation between SW and E is $+0.05$ and for SW and N it is almost exactly zero.

The distributions of E scores for the positive-sway and negative-sway males are set out in Table 2. The number of negative swayers is of course too small for it to be justifiable to draw any confident conclusions, but there is clearly no large difference between the two groups and it is worth noting that significance at the 0.05 level would only be achieved if the observed differences in the proportions falling into each range of E scores had occurred with a negative sway group numbering rather more than 50.

Since 6 of the 7 backward swaying males were also liars, then because the N scores of liars are suspect, little purpose would be served by comparing the N distributions of forward and backward swayers. No conclusions are possible as to the N and E characteristics of backward swaying females since only two such responses were observed.

In summary, therefore, the use of conventional forms of analysis seems to lead to the conclusions that, for males:

(a) Extraversion is not a determinant of body-sway response, either within the forward or backward swaying groups.

(b) There is a slight association ($r = 0.29$) between low N and high SW.

For females:

(c) Neither N, nor E, is related to SW.

TABLE 2

EXTRAVERSION DISTRIBUTION OF POSITIVE AND NEGATIVE SWAY GROUPS
(MALES)

Sway groups	E score category										
	0–4	5–9	10–14	15–19	20–24	25–29	30–34	35–39	40–45	>45	Total
Positive swayers	0	3	4	11	9	21	12	3	3	0	66
Negative swayers	0	0	0	21	1	1	2	1	0	0	26

ZONE ANALYSIS

Within a total test-space, defined for example by orthogonal axes of
N and E, any circumscribed area may be specified as a 'zone'. Every
member of an experimental sample will have a position within the test-
space which is determined by the N and E scores he obtains. All individuals who fall within some defined zone may be said to *inhabit* that
zone. If the zone covers only a small fraction of the total test-space, it of
course follows that all Ss who inhabit it must have combinations of N
and E scores which are rather similar. The object of *zone-analysis*, the
technique which is now to be described, is to determine whether there is
any evidence that membership of circumscribed zones within a total
test-space is associated with the possession of unusual characteristics of
some kind.

The analysis should clearly treat males and females as separate subgroups. If this is not done, then if there are sex-differences associated
with the characteristics being studied and if the distribution of males
within the test-space differs from that of females, then apparent between-
zone differences in the characteristics will be generated as artefacts.

In the present case the test-space is that enclosed by orthogonal axes
of N and E and the characteristic to be considered is that of postural-
sway (SW). The most obvious way of defining the zones which are to be
studied, within the total NE space, is to take the four quadrants which
arise when the subjects are divided thus:

(i) Group *ni*, i.e. those with high scores for N but low scores for E
(neurotic introverts).

(ii) Group *ne*, i.e. those with high scores on both N and E (neurotic
extraverts).

(iii and iv) Groups *si* and *se*, defined in an analogous fashion (i.e., stable introverts and stable extraverts).

This method of sub-division has previously been shown to lead to fruitful results in other investigations (Ref. 3).

The number of women available for study was 21. This is a large enough number to generate artefacts, based on sex-differences, if the female group is combined with the male group for purposes of analysis. It is too small a number, however, to sub-divide further, in terms of quadrant membership, if statistically significant results are to be hoped for. When the present analysis was designed, therefore, it was decided to use the females, at first, purely as an inspection group, by studying which it was hoped that specific hypotheses might be developed which could then be tested in terms of the data from the males. Since one-tailed tests could thus be used, the male data would be utilized very efficiently. If these hypotheses proved to be supported at an acceptable level of significance, when thus tested within the male group, there would be at least a strong presumption that they were equally valid for the females, rather than the result of sampling artefacts. If they should not survive such testing, however, it would still be possible to evolve fresh hypotheses with the data from the male group (which is much larger).

If the female group is sub-divided into quadrants by cutting the N and E scales as near as possible to the mean scores which were observed within the English MPI Standardization Sample (i.e. at N = 20 and E = 25), the numbers of subjects exhibiting low, medium and high sway within each quadrant are as set out in Table 3. The cutting points for defining the sway categories were chosen so as to divide the females into three sub-groups as nearly equal in number as possible (see Table 4). It is clear from Table 3 that this female sample is more neurotic and more extraverted than the MPI Standardization Sample. The figures also show that the inhabitants of quadrants *si* and *ne* swayed less than did those of *se* and *ni*, but the difference is not statistically significant. The last column of Table 3 sets out the number of males who inhabit each of the quadrants which have been defined for the females and it will be noted that the male sample is much more neurotic than was the MPI Standardization group and very slightly more extraverted. Comparing the males and females of this experiment, the largest difference is in the proportions inhabiting quadrant *ni*, i.e., 38 per cent of the men but only 14 per cent of the women. There is also a marked surplus of women in *se*, i.e., 24 per cent as compared with 9 per cent of the men.

A disproportionately large number of males thus fall into a quadrant associated with high sway for the women and a disproportionately small number into one associated with low sway. If men and women with the same quadrant membership were to demonstrate equal degrees of sway, then these differences in the NE distribution-characteristics of the male and female sub-groups would generate a difference in their overall SW distributions also, the men appearing to be the more suggestible. Such a difference does in fact differentiate the men from the women in the present experiment, as has already been remarked (Table 1). If it is assumed that the proportion of women who fell during the sway test, in each quadrant, gives a valid estimate of the proportion of men in the same quadrant who will fall, then from Table 3 can be computed the proportion of the total male group (liars and negative sway excluded) who would be expected to fall. The relevant figure comes out to be 40 per cent, which agrees quite well with that of 47 per cent actually observed (Table 4). Without considering at all the actual sway distributions characterizing the males inhabiting the various quadrants, we are thus led to consider the following hypotheses:

(H_1) Within any quadrant the distribution of SW for males is indistinguishable from that for females.

(H_2) When the distribution of SW scores for males in *se* is compared with that for males in either *ne* or *si* the former group will prove to be the more suggestible.

(H_3) When the distribution of SW scores for males in *ni* is compared with that for males in either *ne* or *si*, the former group will prove to be the more suggestible.

It is clear from Table 4 that the SW distribution for the males is J-shaped, as a result of the large number of cases in the 'fall' category, which cannot further be subdivided. This circumstance greatly complicates the use of any of the parametric tests which might otherwise have been used for purposes of analysis. A powerful non-parametric procedure for testing distribution differences is available in the Kolmogorov-Smirnov test (Ref. 5). The cumulative frequency distributions which are needed in order to apply this test to the hypotheses H_1 to H_3 are set out in Table 4, rows 1 to 4.

If, in Table 4, the cumulative distributions for *se* and *si* are compared it will be observed that whereas 60 per cent of the men in *si* swayed 2 inches or less, none of those in *se* had so low a score. The largest difference between the two cumulative distributions occurs at 4 inches of

TABLE 3

NUMBER OF FEMALES WITH VARIOUS DEGREES OF SWAY, BY NE QUADRANT
AND NUMBER OF MALES IN EACH QUADRANT

Quadrant	Amount of sway in inches			Total females	No. of males in quadrant
	0–4·0	4·1–9·0	Fall		
se	2	0	2	4	7
ne	6	1	2	9	22
si	0	4	0	4	5
ni	1	0	2	3	21
Total	9	5	6	20	55

Note: The one female who swayed backwards is not included.

TABLE 4

CUMULATIVE PERCENTILE FREQUENCY DISTRIBUTIONS OF SWAY, BY QUADRANT,
FOR MALES AND FEMALES SEPARATELY, EXCLUDING LIARS AND BACKWARDS SWAY

Row No.	Sex	Quadrant	SW Score											N
			0	1	2	3	4	5	6	7	8	9	Fall	
1	Male	se	00	00	00	14	14	14	14	14	14	14	100	7
2		si	60	60	60	60	80	80	80	80	80	80	100	5
3		ne	5	9	23	23	36	45	55	59	59	64	100	22
4		ni	5	5	5	5	14	19	19	33	38	48	100	21
5		si+ne	15	19	30	30	44	52	59	63	63	67	100	27
6		se+ni	4	4	4	7	14	18	18	29	32	39	100	28
7		Total	9	11	16	18	29	34	38	45	47	53	100	55
8	Female	se	25	25	25	50	50	50	50	50	50	50	100	4
9		si	0	0	0	0	0	25	75	100	100	100	100	4
10		ne	0	22	22	67	67	67	67	78	78	78	100	9
11		ni	33	33	33	33	33	33	33	33	33	33	100	3
12		si+ne	0	13	13	46	46	54	69	85	85	85	100	13
13		se+ni	29	29	29	43	43	43	43	43	43	43	100	7
14		Total	10	20	20	45	45	50	60	70	70	70	100	20
15	Male &	se	9	9	9	27	27	27	27	27	27	27	100	11
16	Female	si	33	33	33	33	44	56	78	89	89	89	100	9
17		ne	3	13	23	35	42	52	58	65	65	68	100	31
18		ni	8	8	8	8	17	21	21	33	38	46	100	24
19		si+ne	10	17	25	35	42	52	62	70	70	72	100	40
20		se+ni	9	9	9	14	20	23	23	31	34	40	100	35
21		Total	9	13	17	25	32	39	44	52	53	57	100	75

sway and is maintained right up to 9 inches. 80 per cent of the men in *si* sway 9 inches or less, but only 14 per cent of those in *se* fail to achieve a higher score, a difference of 66 per cent. It is this difference which has been entered as a decimal in the column headed D_{max} in Table 5, in the row which has been allocated to the comparison now being made (row 1). The nature of the difference between the two cumulative distributions is clearly of such a kind as to support the hypothesis H_2, i.e., that males in *se* will prove to be more suggestible than those in *si*. The direction of this observed difference is summarized in the column headed 'Direction' in Table 5 and in the column following this is recorded the fact that the observed difference was in the direction predicted. Since a prediction as to the direction of difference was made before examining the data, a one-tailed test of significance is appropriate as is indicated in the column headed 'Test'. The relevant application of the KS test to the observed value of D_{max} gives rise to a value of p of 0·075.

The results of making the other, similar, comparisons which are called for by hypotheses H_2 and H_3 are set out in rows 2, 3 and 4 of Table 5. All four comparisons give differences which are in the predicted direction and the chance probability of such an occurrence is only about 0·06. It is clear that the null hypothesis can be rejected decisively on the results of the comparison between *ni* and *si* and that it is hardly tenable in the case of the other three comparisons.

Neither of the hypotheses H_2 and H_3 implies any prediction as to the relative suggestibility of males in *si* as compared with *ne*, or in *se* as compared with *ni*. These comparisons can easily be made (Table 4) and rows 5 and 6 of Table 5 summarize the relevant results. It is clear that there is no justification at all for making any distinction between *se* and *ni* and the null hypothesis is clearly tenable at a lower level of confidence in respect of the comparison between *si* and *ne* also. These results suggest that quadrants *se* and *ni* can legitimately be combined, so that comparisons may be made in terms of groups involving larger numbers than are available when each quadrant is considered separately. If this is done then H_2 and H_3 require modification, i.e.:

(H_4) When the distribution of SW scores for males in *si* is compared with that for males in (*se+ni*), the latter group will prove to be the more suggestible.

(H_5) When the distribution of SW scores for males in *ne* is compared with that for males in (*se+ni*), the latter group will prove to be the more suggestible.

The comparisons relevant to H_4 and H_5 can be made from Table 4 and the results obtained are summarized in rows 7 and 8 of Table 5, from which it will be observed that both predictions are borne out at a high level of confidence.

Rows 9 to 12 in Table 5 set out the results of comparisons relevant to H_1 and it will be observed that the data provide no significant evidence against the hypothesis. It would be unwise to accept it too uncritically at this stage, however, in view of the small number of women available within the various subgroups. If quadrants *se* and *ni* are combined, as seems to be justifiable from the evidence considered above, it will be observed that the hypothesis of equal suggestibility as between men and women continues to be tenable within the larger sample thus afforded (row 13, Table 5). There is perhaps a little less justification for combining *ne* and *si*, but the results of comparing males and females within such a combined group are set out in row 14 of Table 5. Once again it is clear that the null hypothesis continues to be tenable within the larger group.

In summary, therefore, the comparisons set out in Table 5 seem to establish fairly conclusively that, liars and negative sway being excluded, the males in quadrants *si* and *ne* tend to exhibit lower SW scores than do those in $(se+ni)$. There is no reason to believe that there are any differences in the SW distributions characterizing males in *se* as compared with *ni*, nor that there are any differences in suggestibility when males and females having the same quadrant membership are compared. The apparently greater suggestibility of the males, considered as a single group, when they are compared with all the females together, can be accounted for in terms of the different NE distributions characterizing the two sexes. It is possible, however, that these latter conclusions, concerning male/female comparisons, may need to be modified when greater numbers of women have been tested.

The results summarized above are based on a group of subjects from which liars and individuals exhibiting negative sway have been excluded. It is clear from Table 1 that the distribution of SW scores within the group omitted from the analysis differs in the direction of low suggestibility from that found for those included. Whereas nearly 50 per cent of the included subjects fell outright, only about 25 per cent of those omitted from the analysis reacted so strongly. Now suppose, as an example, that the depleted individuals were predominantly members of one quadrant, say *ni*. Under these circumstances the deletion of liars and negative-sway reactors would itself necessarily generate the relative

TABLE 5

BETWEEN-ZONE COMPARISONS OF SW DISTRIBUTIONS

Row No.	Comparison	D_{max}	Direction	Predicted Direction	Test	p	Hypothesis
	Males						
1	*se* v. *si*	0·66	*se* > *si*	As found	One-tailed	0·075	H_2
2	*se* v. *ne*	0·50	*se* > *ne*	As found	One-tailed	0·075	H_2
3	*ni* v. *si*	0·66	*ni* > *si*	As found	One-tailed	0·035	H_3
4	*ni* v. *ne*	0·36	*ni* > *ne*	As found	One-tailed	0·072	H_3
5	*si* v. *ne*	0·55	*ne* > *si*	No prediction	Two-tailed	0·168	—
6	*se* v. *ni*	0·34	*se* > *ni*	No prediction	Two-tailed	0·600	—
7	(*se*+*ni*) v. *si*	0·66	(*se*+*ni*) > *si*	As found	One-tailed	0·028	H_4
8	(*se*+*ni*) v. *ne*	0·37	(*se*+*ni*) > *ne*	As found	One-tailed	0·034	H_5
	Males v. Females						
9	*se* quadrant	0·36	Male > Female	No prediction	Two-tailed	0·97	H_1
10	*si* quadrant	0·80	Female > Male	No prediction	Two-tailed	0·10	H_1
11	*ne* quadrant	0·44	Male > Female	No prediction	Two-tailed	0·18	H_1
12	*ni* quadrant	0·28	Male > Female	No prediction	Two-tailed	0·98	H_1
13	(*se*+*ni*)	0·36	Male > Female	No prediction	Two-tailed	0·46	H_1
14	(*si*+*ne*)	0·22	Male > Female	No prediction	Two-tailed	0·83	H_1

scarcity of low SW responses which was found to characterize members of the quadrant concerned (Table 4). It is thus, in theory, possible that at least some of the differences of SW distribution which appear to have been demonstrated might be artefacts, arising from the fact that a subgroup of individuals having particular NE membership and also unusual sway characteristics has been deleted from the sample examined. The need to take account of this complication will be considered further on a subsequent page.

If the demonstrated differences in SW distributions are accepted at their face value, it is necessary to try to explain them and the hypothesis which will now be described has been designed to that end.

SUGGESTIBILITY AS A FUNCTION OF DRIVE

There is by now much evidence that the behaviour of an organism in any situation is determined in part by its drive-state at the time (e.g., Ref. 6). As drive increases, both the strength and the quality of performance in what may be called the 'relevant task' increase. This simple relationship, however, is complicated by the existence of the Yerkes-Dodson law, which states that for the performance of a task of any given complexity there is an optimum drive-level (Ref. 7). When this optimal level is exceeded, although the total energy output from the organism may continue to rise, it becomes maladaptive. Pre-potent response tendencies of a competitive or irrelevant nature are activated and performance in the 'relevant task' declines progressively with further drive increments.

There seems to be no reason why the phenomenon of suggestibility should not be examined in terms of this kind of formulation. In these terms one would expect that an individual generating a high level of drive in a suggestibility-test situation, other things being equal, would react more strongly to the suggestions than another person generating less drive. It would also be expected that there might be some subjects who generate supra-optimal drive in some suggestibility-test situations and whose response is therefore small and accompanied perhaps by reactions of an irrelevant or bizarre kind. In order to test such a hypothesis it is necessary to have some measure of drive strength. This can probably be made available by using GSR recordings, but these were not employed during the course of the experiments with which this paper is concerned. An alternative approach is however possible.

It will be useful at this stage to introduce the concept of *habitual drive level* (D$_h$). This is concerned with the notion that, although in a particular individual different situations will tend to evoke differing degrees of drive, yet over a sufficiently wide and representative range of situations the within-person variance of drive-level will be less than that between persons. In so far as this is true, the concept that a person tends to be characterized by a certain drive-level clearly has a meaning and it is this which is implied by the symbol D$_h$. The concept of *chronic drive state*, as used by Spence, is concerned with precisely the same idea, but it is now very closely associated with the idea that the drive concerned is some form of tendency to become anxious, of the kind which it is claimed can be measured by the Taylor Anxiety Scale. For reasons that will become apparent, any sort of identification of anxiety and drive must specifically be excluded in the present context and for this reason it seems justifiable to coin a new term and a new symbol. Hull's use of the idea of *generalized drive*, or a non-specific drive-factor, also relates to the same type of concept.

HABITUAL DRIVE LEVEL AND NEUROTICISM

It is now possible to take a further step in the development of the argument and to postulate that individuals in whom high drive is frequently and easily generated, i.e., those with high D$_h$, are more likely to develop neurotic symptoms than are those in whom it is low. This view seems to be justifiable on several grounds. Some neurotic symptoms, for example, can themselves be regarded as manifestations of maladaptive responses produced during states of high drive. Again, the frequent occurrence of conditions of high drive will presumably increase the probability of mal-adaptive, one-trial learning. The notion is presented here simply as one which seems to have a certain plausibility, and no attempt will be made to justify it in detail. In so far as it is well founded, however, it clearly suggests that the dimension of Neuroticism in classificatory systems such as that developed by Eysenck might with advantage be replaced by a dimension of Drive, but that measures of N may provide a convenient, if approximate, score for D$_h$. The assertion that neuroticism acts *as* a drive is of course familiar within the context of Hullian learning theory, but it will be appreciated that this formulation differs in important ways from that which is now being proposed.

If an indirect score for D$_h$ can be obtained by measuring N, then there should be a relationship between N and suggestibility of the same kind as the one which might be expected to relate drive and suggestibility, i.e., other things being equal, response to tests of suggestibility should be greatest in subjects having high N scores, save that, because of the effect of the Yerkes-Dodson law, a decrement might be observed for values of N increasing beyond the value associated with optimal D_h for the particular test being investigated. It is clear, however, that the data on body-sway which are set out in Table 4 cannot be accounted for in terms of such a simple hypothesis.

EXTRAVERSION, D_h AND EFFECTIVE DRIVE

In order to account for the experimental data it is in fact necessary to introduce a further postulate, i.e., that the actual drive generated by a person in any situation is a function not only of D_h but also of the strength of his predisposition to attend to the stimuli characterizing that situation. This predisposition will in part depend on the subject's previous experiences in similar situations, but also, one would expect, on the more or less consistent response tendencies which are associated with intro-version-extraversion. It is entirely consistent with the known character-istics of the extravert to assert that he has a strong and continuing set to attend to stimuli associated with the activities of other people and that the situations which lead him to enter states of high-drive are predom-inantly interpersonal in character. Since suggestibility tests, and also hypnotic induction procedures, provide the very epitome of an inter-personal situation, one would thus predict that as between two indi-viduals of equal D_h, both in the same suggestibility-test situation, the one who is the more extraverted will produce the greatest amount of drive. It is probably permissible, here, to use Hull's term *effective drive* (D) to denote the drive strength actually produced by the interaction of D_h and extraversion (E).

In summary therefore, the assertion now is that

$$D = f(D_h, E, K, P)$$

where K includes all determinants of drive which are specific to the particular test situation concerned and P all those which are specific to the momentary state of the subject. If neuroticism is now used to esti-mate D_h, then the actual response of a subject can be expressed

$$R = f(N, E, K, P, {}_sH_R)$$

In the present context habit strength (${}_sH_R$) can probably be equated with the subject's ideo-motor tendency (Ref. 1) and if this is denoted by H_m then the final form for the functional relationship becomes

$$R = f(N, E, K, P, H_m).$$

In terms of this model and on the assumption that D is either an additive or a multiplicative function of N and E, a number of easily tested predictions can be made. In a reasonably well standardized test situation it can be assumed that K is substantially constant. A group of subjects selected for both low N and low E, but heterogeneous in other respects, will probably contain individuals characterized by a wide range of values of H_m, but since for all of them the value of effective drive will be low, then none will exhibit a great response to suggestion. In a similarly introverted group for whom N is high, however, the effective drive will be much stronger and although zero values of H_m will still be associated with zero response, both the mean and the variance of response scores for the group as a whole will be substantially higher than that observed in the more stable group. Within a sufficiently introverted group it seems unlikely that even the highest values of N will be associated with supra-optimal values of effective drive and it seems plausible to assume that both the mean and the variance of test scores (R) should increase progressively within sub-groups selected for progressively increasing values of N.

Within a sample selected for high E, however, the relationship between N and R must be quite different. At very low values of N the effective drive will be close to zero, so that response will be minimal even in subjects with high H_m. Because of the high values of E, however, the value of D associated with quite moderate values of N will be substantial, so that both the mean and the variance of R scores must increase very rapidly within sub-groups selected to display progressively increasing values of N. As a result it seems likely that D might attain a Yerkes-Dodson optimum at quite a moderate value of N and that in sub-groups selected to display even higher values of this parameter both the mean and variance of R should progressively decline. The net outcome of these interactions will be that stable introverts and neurotic extraverts should both display poor reactions to suggestibility tests, whereas neurotic introverts and stable extraverts should both show a strong response. This of course is precisely the picture presented by the data set out in Table 4.

CHEVREUL-PENDULUM

All subjects who took the postural-sway test, as described in the opening pages of this paper, were also tested with the chevreul-pendu-lum, using the same method as has been described elsewhere (Ref. 2). Relationships involving pendulum scores are easier to handle than those for postural-sway, since there is no negative response category. The problem of the MPI 'liars' still remains, however. Fortunately, it does seem to be possible to apply to the N score actually obtained by an MPI liar a correction of a reasonably plausible kind, in terms of which his true N score may be estimated, while the evidence suggests that the E scores obtained by liars can fairly safely be used without correction. The evidence for these assertions will be presented elsewhere.

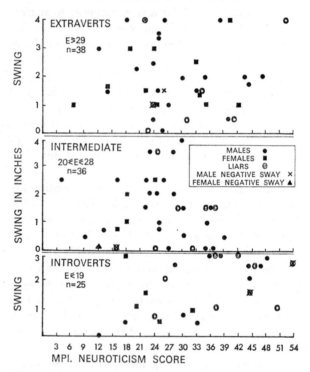

Figure 48. Neuroticisms, Extraversion, and Chevreul-Swing.

In Fig. 48 is set out a set of three graphs. One of these is concerned only with those individuals who obtained E scores of 19 or less and displays chevreul-pendulum swing (PS) as a function of N. It is obvious that in this sub-group PS increases with N up to values of at least 42;

beyond which point there may be some slight decline. If the apparent slight fall of PS at very high values of N is assumed to result only from sampling errors, then the relationship between the two variables in this introverted group can be expressed as a linear regression, the relevant correlation coefficient being about 0·70 (p<0·001). The trend of the data is, however, in every way consistent with the existence of a Yerkes-Dodson optimum at, or near to, the top of the N scale. It should be noted that a distinctive symbol has been used to indicate MPI liars, all of whom have been allocated N scores corrected in terms of the relevant lie-score. Different symbols have also been used for males and females. In so far as can be judged on the basis of the rather small number of individuals falling into each category the nature of the general relationship between N and PS is of much the same kind for male liars and non-liars and also for females. Additional symbols have also been used to denote those individuals who gave negative responses in the postural-sway test and these individuals will be discussed at a later stage.

In the same Figure a separate graph is devoted to an 'intermediate' group, made up of individuals having E scores between 20 and 28 inclusive. Here, the relationship between N and PS is obviously curvilinear, the magnitude of response reaching a maximum for N scores in the region of about 23 to 25. For subjects with N scores of 24 or less the correlation between N and PS is plus 0·55, whereas for those with N values above this cutting point it is minus 0·50. For both the positive and negative correlation the relevant null hypothesis could have been rejected at about the 0·02 level of confidence but for the fact that the cutting point for defining the dichotomy was not determined in advance of the inspection of the data. Within this intermediate group also it will be noted that the trend of the data would not greatly be affected by removing either the females or the male liars. This trend is entirely in accord with what would be expected in terms of the drive-model which is under consideration. As N increases, so does PS, until a Yerkes-Dodson optimum is reached at an N value of about 25, after which there is a decline. This optimum occurs at a lower value of N than was observed in the case of the more introverted group previously discussed, as is required by hypothesis.

Finally, the same relationship is displayed for those individuals having E scores of 29 or more. This curve shows a clear decrement of response from N values in the region of 18 up to the maximum of the N scale. There are only four points below N = 15 and their position is consistent with the hypothesis that in this region the relationship between

N and PS is expressed by a positive correlation. This apparent effect may, however, represent only the effect of sampling errors and if it is assumed that all the data for the extraverts should be summarized in terms of a single linear regression, then the relevant correlation co-efficient has the value of minus 0·48 (p <0·01). However, in terms of the drive-model under discussion, one would expect a Yerkes-Dodson optimum at a low value of N and the evidence can certainly be con-strued as implying that one exists at about N = 18, i.e., at a lower value than that found for either the intermediate or the introverted sub-groups. Once again, there seems to be no reason to believe that the removal of either the liars or the females would in any way alter the nature of the apparent relationships.

Fig. 48 thus reveals precisely those forms of interaction between N, E and PS, which would be expected in terms of the theoretical analysis set out in the preceding section of this paper. It is a matter of very consider-able interest that the only two subjects who displayed large negative responses in the postural-sway test were individuals whose drive in the chevreul situation was clearly supra-optimal as judged from Fig. 48. This suggests that negative reactions in the body-sway situation may be explained as pre-potent opposing response tendencies which can be activated by a drive level which is too high. Of the seven individuals (including one woman) who displayed small values of negative sway, two appear to have been working under very low drive in the chevreul situation, four at above optimal values and one just about at the optimum. Because all assessments of response are subject to error of measurement, it is clear that some subjects whose true sway-score should be zero, either because of low-drive, or low sH_R, will in fact be allo-cated a slight negative score and the two low-drive negative body-sway reactors (both of whom are members of the intermediate group in Fig. 48) can be explained in these terms. The drive level which is associated with a Yerkes-Dodson optimum will of course vary from one test situation to another and the greater the task-complexity, the lower will it be. It seems highly probably that the postural-sway test involves a higher level of task-complexity than does the chevreul and if this is true one would expect that values of N which are associated with optimum drive in the case of the latter situation may well be supra-optimal in the former. The single negative-reactor in the body-sway situation whose drive under chevreul conditions seems to have been close to the optimum, may well therefore have been functioning under supra-optimal drive in the body-sway situation. In summary therefore; of the nine subjects who exhibited negative sway, seven were probably working under conditions of supra-optimal drive, while the other two can be explained as being low-drive subjects who should really have been classified as zero swayers. All the nine subjects exhibiting negative sway are distinguished by special symbols in Fig. 48.

Some Further Considerations

The model which has now been described, and to some degree justified, generates a number of further predictions and suggestions.

In suggestibility-test situations it appears that stable introverts are functioning under conditions of sub-optimal drive and it should be possible to increase their response to tests of this kind by techniques which raise the situation-drive-level, K. It should also be possible to achieve the same result by increasing P, the drive-component which reflects a specific personal reaction to the test-situation. The use of drugs immediately suggests itself in this connection.

On the other hand, since neurotic extraverts appear to be functioning at drive-levels which are supra-optimal, their suggestibility-test responses can be increased by reducing the effective drive. This need to differentiate between personality-types when attempting to produce a particular end result may help to account for the ambiguous and contradictory findings which have so frequently been reported in connection with attempts to manipulate suggestibility and in particular with those involving the use of drugs.

Since $_sH_R$ plays a part in determining test response, then it should be possible to manipulate test scores by using various forms of practice and pre-test training. Here again, however, paradoxical effects might be expected, for the training concerned might itself alter the value of K associated with the test situation and this might serve to produce a differential reaction as between stable introverts and neurotic extraverts.

The effect of supra-optimal drive on test response will presumably vary as between tests, as will also the drive level which represents the Yerkes-Dodson optimum. One would therefore predict that the inter-correlations among suggestibility-test responses might be greater in samples from which subjects liable to experience supra-optimal effective drive levels have been deleted, than for the population at large. Differences of sampling in terms of NE distributions may therefore help to account for the apparent differences in the 'structure' of suggestibility which have been reported by various investigators.

Perhaps the most intriguing, although also the most speculative suggestion which can be made on the basis of this drive-model, is one concerned with the astonishing divergence of opinion which is found among workers in this field as to the suggestibility of hysterics. If one accepts the characterization of the hysteric as a neurotic extravert, then there is clearly a sense in which his response-tendencies in suggestibility type situations are stronger than those of individuals of any other personality type. If the total situation is of such kind as to involve a high level of K, however, then the hysteric will be functioning under a very high effective drive. Such 'relevant' responses as he does make within the situation will therefore tend to be small and there will in addition appear a whole range of irrelevant and possibly bizarre forms of behaviour. If, however, the situation can be manipulated so that it involves a low K, then under these circumstances the response of the hysteric should be greater than that of any other individual. On the whole, the divergence of opinion as to the suggestibility of hysterics involves a conflict between therapists on the one hand and experimentalists on the other. It seems very probable that the value of K associated with therapeutic situations, in which the subject has formed a relationship with an operator to whom he has become habituated, is much lower than that which arises when a person is suddenly precipitated into an experimental situation of a novel kind. A whole range of experiments on the suggestibility of hysterics, involving, for example, habituation to the test situation, seems to be called for by considerations of this kind.

The evidence presented in this paper suggests that in situations of an inter-personal kind a higher drive is generated by extraverts than by introverts. The balance of evidence from other studies suggests that precisely the opposite is true in circumstances where the interpersonal element is lacking, such as in the majority of the conditioning and learning situations which are used by learning theorists. It seems likely that neurotic introverts will tend to generate quite a high level of effective drive in virtually any kind of test-situation, whether it involves interpersonal components or not and that this high drive-level will in some way be associated with manifest anxiety. The neurotic-extravert, on the other hand, will experience similarly high levels of effective drive only under circumstances such that the interpersonal element is decisively important. The difference between the two groups would lead one to expect that extraversion might be associated with successful learning and task performance in situations which involve a definite pupil/teacher relationship of a continuous kind. The introvert, on the other hand, will be at an advantage when there is hardly any pupil/teacher interaction at all. In examination situations it might be expected that the introvert will always generate the greater degree of drive and this might sometimes be associated with a high level of performance, but also with poor results if supra-optimal levels should be produced. These speculations are hardly relevant to the field of suggestibility, but they do serve to illustrate that attempts to apply any drive-model to a wide range of differing situations may frequently involve the need to take account of the effects of rather complicated interactions.

SUMMARY

An examination of the body-sway responses of an adult sample suggests that men who are characterized by any particular combination of N and E scores exhibit test responses which are approximately equal to those given by women having the same score combinations. The apparently greater suggestibility of the males, within the group studied, can be explained in terms of male/female differences in NE distributions. It seems likely that most attempts to compare the suggestibility of men and women are meaningless and that the results obtained reflect only differences of NE distributions arising during sampling.

In the group studied, the body-sway scores of stable extraverts and neurotic introverts tended to be large, whereas they were smaller for stable introverts and neurotic extraverts. This result can be explained in terms of a theoretical model in which the effective drive produced in a subject by a test-situation is a multiplicative or additive function of both his neuroticism and his extraversion. It is suggested that in tests of a predominantly inter-personal type the extravert's predisposition to attend to stimuli associated with the activities of other people leads him to generate a higher level of drive than that which is produced in introverts characterized by the same degree of neuroticism. In terms of such a model it would be predicted that stable introverts will show little response to suggestibility tests because they generate little drive, whereas neurotic extraverts will react poorly because their level is so high as to exceed the Yerkes-Dodson optimum for tasks of the relevant kinds. The appearance of contra-suggestibility in the body-sway situation can be explained as one of the effects of the activation of pre-potent opposing reaction tendencies which is known to occur under conditions of supra-optimal drive.

The theoretical model concerned provides a satisfactory explanation of the chevreul-pendulum responses which were observed in the same group of subjects. In addition it generates a number of predictions and suggestions which can serve to guide future experimental work in this field.

REFERENCES

1. EYSENCK, H. J., *Dimensions of Personality*. London: Routledge & Kegan Paul, 1947.
2. —— & FURNEAUX, W. D., Primary and secondary suggestibility: an experimental and statistical study. *J. exp. Psychol.*, **35**, 485–503, 1945.
3. FURNEAUX, W. D., Psychological Tests for the Selection of University Students. Report to the Imperial College of Science and Technology, University of London, 1957.
4. —— & GIBSON, H. B., The Maudsley Personality Inventory as a predictor of susceptibility to hypnosis. *Int. J. clin. exp. Hypnosis*, **9**, 3, 1961.
5. SEIGEL, S., *Nonparametric Statistics for the Behavioural Sciences*. New York: McGraw-Hill, 1956.
6. SPENCE, K. W., *Behaviour Theory and Conditioning*. Newhaven: Yale University Press, 1956.
7. YERKES, R. M. & DODSON, J. D., The relation of strength of stimulus to rapidity of habit-formation. *J. comp. Neurol. Psychol.*, **18**, 459–482, 1908.

Conditioning and Learning

Editor's Introduction

THE studies in this section deal with activities of even greater complexity than those discussed in the sections on perception and motor movement and it is small wonder that many difficulties still remain unresolved. However, it seems that recent theories have improved upon the rather elementary notions which gave rise to earlier papers and it remains to be seen whether this degree of cautious optimism is supported by the bulk of ongoing work.

There are three main groups of studies in this section. The first consists of experiments involving the formation of conditioned responses, particularly the eyeblink reflex. The outcome of the great volume of work that has been done in response to the early studies of Franks appears to be that relations between personality and conditioning depend entirely on the choice of parameters—type of reinforcement, length of CS-UCS interval, strength of UCS and so forth. Fortunately it seems possible to specify the appropriate choice of parameter by reference to the general theory of extraversion-introversion, so that we can with some confidence predict the type and size of correlation to be expected from a given combination of parameters.

The second group of studies consists of experiments involving learning rather than conditioning. These studies are rather heterogeneous and it seems difficult to give any meaningful short summary, other than to say that they clearly implicate extraversion-introversion as an important factor in predicting size and direction of results. One study at least also shows again the importance of zone analysis, i.e., the interaction effects of extraversion and neuroticism.

The third group of studies relates to reminiscence and in some ways these studies are of particular interest because they show the interaction between theory and experiment exceptionally clearly. The writer originally suggested that if, as Hull (Ref. 3) & Kimble (Ref. 4) had argued, reminiscence was due to dissipation of reactive inhibition, then extraverts should show greater reminiscence; this was found to be in fact so in some two dozen studies. However, as one of the papers reprinted here makes clear, the Hull-Kimble theory is almost certainly erroneous, at least in part, and reactive inhibition cannot be the active agent in mediating the personality correlations found. The writer suggested as a possible alternative conditioned inhibition, but this suggestion is perhaps intrinsically not a very happy one. Quite recently a third hypothesis was

467

advanced (Ref. 1) which suggests that reminiscence is due to consolidation of the memory trace; that this consolidation is a direct function of cortical arousal; and that hence introverts would show better memory, and greater reminiscence, *in the long run*. The italicised words are important because the theory also specifies that while consolidation is going on it interferes with performance, which accordingly suffers; hence *in the short run* extraverts will show better memory and greater reminiscence. It appears that the length of the rest pause interpolated between performances is of crucial importance—extraverts should show greater reminiscence with short rest pauses, introverts with longer ones. An unpublished experiment by A. M. Clark has shown the expected crossover for high- vs. low-arousal subjects when 10 minutes and 24 hour rest periods were used. In another recent experiment, E. Howarth and the writer (Ref. 2) had different groups of introverted and extraverted sub-

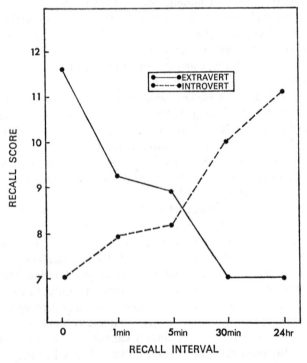

Figure 49. Recall scores of different groups of introverted and extraverted subjects after different recall intervals.

jects learn paired CVC nonsense syllables to a criterion and then retested them after different rest periods; the Fig. 49 shows clearly the expected cross-over. It may be that at long last we are approaching a better understanding of the dynamics of learning and conditioning as related to personality.

H.J.E.

REFERENCES

1. EYSENCK, H. J., A three-factor theory of reminiscence. *Brit. J. Psychol.*, **56,** 163–181, 1965.
2. HOWARTH, E. & EYSENK, H. J., Extraversion, arousal, and paired-associates recall. *J. exp. Res. in Personal.*, **3,** 114–116, 1968.
3. HULL, C. L., *Principles of Behaviour*. New York: Appleton-Century-Crofts, 1943.
4. KIMBLE, G. A., An experimental test of a two-factor theory of inhibition. *J. exp. Psychol.*, **39,** 163–189, 1949.

53

Conditioning and Personality: A Study of Normal and Neurotic Subjects[1]

CYRIL M. FRANKS

First published in
Journal of Abnormal and Social Psychology, **52**, 143–150, 1956

PAVLOV'S theory of cortical functioning (Refs. 24, 25 & 26) emphasizes two basic cortical processes, *excitation* and *inhibition*. The term *inhibition* is unfortunately used in at least three different senses. There is the general psychiatric usage of the word, as applied to the introverted, withdrawn personality; there is the neurophysiological use of the word; there is the Pavlovian usage. It must be stressed that cortical inhibition in the Pavlovian sense (which is how it is used in the present paper) should be associated with the *absence* of behavioural inhibition in the psychiatric sense. Pavlov has produced ample evidence to suggest that both *excitation* and *inhibition* are positive and molar cortical processes (Refs. 24, 25 and 26). However, any further assumptions about the physiological nature of these two processes would be largely speculative; it must be sufficient for the present to regard them both as hypothetical constructs and not merely as intervening variables (Ref. 23).

During his experiments, Pavlov observed large individual differences in the behaviour of his dogs. Certain dogs (which he called the excitatory kind) developed stable positive conditioned responses with ease and retained these responses for a long time during extinction. Other dogs (which he called the inhibitory kind) developed positive conditioned responses very poorly, which, once formed, were easily disrupted and soon extinguished. After a discussion of experimentally produced 'neuroses' in animals and in man, Pavlov wrote as follows:

'It has been seen that the above-mentioned method may lead to different forms of disturbance, depending on the type of nervous system of the animal. In dogs with the more resistant nervous system

[1] This research was aided by a grant from the Central Research Fund of the University of London.

it leads to a predominance of excitation; in dogs with the less resistant nervous system, to a predominance of inhibition. So far as can be judged on the basis of casual observation I believe that these two variations in the pathological disturbance of the cortical activity in animals are comparable to the two forms of neurosis in man—in the pre-Freudian terminology *neurasthenia* and *hysteria*—the first with exaggeration of the excitatory and weakness of the inhibitory process, the second with a predominance of the inhibitory and weakness of the excitatory process' (Ref. 24, p. 397f.).

Pavlov never followed up this observation and it has been neglected ever since. From this observation, however, it is possible to predict that neurotics of the neurasthenic type should form conditioned reflexes rapidly and that these reflexes should be slow to extinguish, whereas neurotics of the hysteric type should form conditioned reflexes slowly and that these reflexes should extinguish readily. Since the term *neurasthenic* is ill-defined and rarely used in contemporary psychology, it would seem better to examine both *neurasthenia* and *hysteria* more carefully in an attempt to discover how they differ rather than to test the above prediction immediately. Both neurasthenia and hysteria are generally regarded as forms of neuroses, so it is along a dimension other than neuroticism that differences must be sought. Pavlov himself has implicitly suggested the dimension of excitation—inhibition, the neurasthenic being at the excitation end of the continuum and the hysteric at the inhibition end.

In seeking another dimension, Eysenck pointed out (Ref. 1, p. 52f.) that Jung (Ref. 21, p. 421) suggested that the characteristic neurosis of the extravert is hysteria, whereas that of the introvert is psychasthenia. Jung also emphasized the independence of introversion and neuroticism and this independence has been experimentally confirmed by Eysenck and his co-workers (Refs. 1, 2 & 3). They have demonstrated the existence of two orthogonal factors, introversion-extraversion and neuroticism and have shown that anxiety neurotics, obsessive-compulsives and depressives typically have high scores on tests of neuroticism *and* high scores on tests of introversion (with correspondingly low scores on tests of extraversion). To these introverted neurotics Eysenck has given the name of dysthymics. He has also shown that hysterics and psychopaths have high scores on tests of neuroticism and high scores on tests of extraversion (with correspondingly low scores on tests of introversion).

The neurasthenic type of neurotic would seem to be subsumed under the heading of *dysthymia* and the hysteric under the heading of *hysteria* (used here in Eysenck's sense to include both hysteria and psychopathy). Furthermore, an examination of patients usually included in these categories suggests that dysthymia is related to Pavlov's concept of excitation and hysteria to inhibition. Thus, the dysthymic usually presents overt physical and mental characteristics of anxiety, obsessions, compulsions, or ruminations. He may be irritable, introspective, ill at ease with people, very much aware of himself and of others. He is often overconscientious and highly sensitive to his environment. He may be agitated, hyperactive and tense, or he may be reflective in his thought, overcautious and hesitant. All these characteristics are consistent with a presumed state of cortical excitation.

The hysteric group presents very different characteristics. They may develop 'escape mechanisms' such as fugues, amnesia, or gross conversion symptoms. They tend to be insensitive, irresponsible, unreliable and little concerned about other people. Most of these characteristics seem to involve some form of dissociation and may hence be reasonably conceived as associated with a state of cortical inhibition.

Pavlov's original observation may, therefore, be slightly revised in the form of the following hypothesis:

> 'Neurotics of the dysthymic type form conditioned reflexes rapidly and these reflexes are difficult to extinguish; neurotics of the hysteric type form conditioned reflexes slowly and these reflexes are easy to extinguish.'

PREVIOUS STUDIES

There have been many experimental studies on the conditionability of neurotics (e.g., Refs. 5 and 31). Most workers have found that 'neurotics' as a group condition better than normals. They have usually made no attempt, however, to classify the neurotics into dysthymics and hysterics. Since more patients are of the dysthymic variety than the hysteric, these findings are probably more accurately interpreted as indicating that dysthymic neurotics condition better than normals. More recently, Taylor & Spence compared the conditionability of anxious neurotics with 'other neurotics' and failed to find any statistically significant differences (Ref. 35). It is significant, however, that the diagnoses represented in the general category of 'other neurotics' included reactive depression, alcoholism, psychopathy, character disorders, obsessive compulsions, compulsions, etc. In other words, this classification of 'other neurotics' included large numbers of both the dysthymic and hysteric types of neurotics. Thus, the relative conditionability of dysthymic as compared with hysteric neurotics remains an open question.

Many studies, however, have been made of the conditionability of *one kind* of dysthymia, the anxiety states. Using the PGR, for example, it has been shown that anxious subjects condition better than normals (Refs. 28, 36 & 37) and similar results have been obtained with the eyeblink reflex (Refs. 18, 29, 30 & 32).

Thus, since dysthymics and hysterics appear to differ along the dimension of introversion-extraversion and since it seems reasonable to associate dysthymia with excitation and hysteria with inhibition, it is probable that excitation is associated with introversion and inhibition with extraversion. If this argument is sound, then conditionability is more a function of introversion-extraversion than of neuroticism. None of the studies cited bears on this hypothesis since they were concerned with the conditionability of only one group, the anxiety states. Such Ss would form conditioned responses more readily than non-anxious Ss either because they were more neurotic or because they were more introverted. A crucial experiment would have to examine the conditionability of both dysthymics and hysterics and also of normals. If the ease of conditionability of the dysthymics is related to their neuroticism, then hysterics and dysthymics should condition equally well and the normals should condition less well than either neurotic group. If, however, the ease of conditionability of the dysthymics is related to their degree of introversion (i.e., to their degree of excitation), then it follows that the hysteric group would condition the least, the dysthymic group the most and the normals in between. Furthermore, if conditionability is related to introversion-extraversion, then within the normal group there should be no correlation between conditionability and a test of neuroticism, but a significant negative correlation between conditionability and a test of extraversion.

THE PRESENT EXPERIMENT

20 dysthymic patients, 20 hysteric patients and 20 normals were tested in a specially constructed soundproof conditioning laboratory (Ref. 7). The unconditioned stimulus (US) was a puff of air, the conditioned stimulus (CS) a tone administered through a pair of headphones and the unconditioned (UR) and conditioned (CR) responses were both eye-

Q*

blinks and PGR changes. Partial conditioning was used, each S being given 30 reinforcements, interspersed with 18 test trials and 10 extinction trials. All conditioning was carried out in one session, taking approximately half an hour per S. The 20 normal Ss were retested after an interval of 14–21 days. All Ss were given personality questionnaires defining neuroticism and introversion-extraversion, together with Taylor's Manifest Anxiety Scale (Ref. 33) and the Maudsley Medical Questionnaire (MMQ).

Subjects

All Ss were aged between 17 and 47 years. Although the normal group was significantly younger than the two neurotic groups, the neurotic groups did not differ significantly in age. The groups were not matched for sex since there is some evidence to suggest that there is no relationship between sex and eyeblink conditionability and there are no reasons for suspecting that sex differences exist with respect to PGR conditioning (Ref. 22). According to Hilgard & Marquis (Ref. 19, p. 303), there is little correlation between intelligence and conditionability; consequently, no attempt was made to match the 3 groups on this variable other than to exclude any Ss of low intelligence, the criterion being a raw score of less than 29[1] on the Raven Matrices non-verbal test of intelligence (Ref. 27). All 3 groups happen to be significantly different from each other in intelligence. The data relating to age, sex, intelligence and extraversion are presented in Table 1.

TABLE 1

DATA ON AGE, SEX, INTELLIGENCE, AND EXTRAVERSION SCORES
(N=20 in each group)

Group	Age in years		Sex (No. of Subjects)		Matrices Raw Score		R Score	
	Mean	SD	M	F	Mean	SD	Mean	SD
Hysterics	28·8	7·1	7	13	44·6	9·0	49·6	11·2
Normals	24·3	4·9	6	14	57·0	3·0	40·5	11·6
Dysthymics	31·3	8·2	15	5	50·2	6·7	20·6	6·3

[1] In terms of the Wechsler-Bellevue scale, this would mean very approximately that Ss with an IQ below 90 would be excluded. However, concern here was not with an S's IQ but with his absolute amount of intelligence, his raw score on the test concerned irrespective of age, sex, etc.

The 20 Normal Subjects

The normal Ss consisted of Occupational Therapy students, student male nurses and Occupation Centre student teachers. All were naive with respect to psychology and all were volunteers. They were requested to avoid discussing the experiment with friends. 23 Ss were originally tested, of whom one was rejected because she blinked excessively; one was rejected because he did not know sufficient English to answer the personality questionnaires and one was rejected because he had recently been discharged from a mental hospital.

The 40 Neurotic Subjects (20 Dysthymics, 20 Hysterics)

All the neurotic Ss were residential or outpatients at the Maudsley Hospital. No patient was used who had any evidence or history of psychotic features, brain injury, or epilepsy, or who had received any form of psychosurgery. No S was used who had any physical treatment such as ECT or insulin during the previous eight weeks or who had been recently receiving such medication as sodium amytal. (All Ss were denied any drugs for the preceding 24 hours.)

The Ss were included in the hysteric group if the psychiatrist concerned could diagnose them as having one or more of the following character-istics: hysterical personality, conversion symptoms, hysteria, psycho-pathic personality, psychopathic features. Furthermore, the psychiatrist was requested to select those Ss with a minimum of obsessive-com-pulsive features, manifest anxiety or depression.

The Ss were included in the dysthymic group if they could be diagnosed as having one or more of the following characteristics: manifest anxiety, reactive depression, obsessive-compulsive features. They also had to show a minimum of hysteric and psychopathic characteristics.

One final criterion was used in selecting the two neurotic groups. All hysteric patients with a score of less than 33 on Guilford's R Scale (Ref. 13) were rejected and all dysthymic patients having an R score of above 32 were also rejected. This criterion was included since it has been shown that Guilford's R Scale is one of the best available measures of extraversion (Refs. 3 and 17). Thus, the two neurotic groups were deliberately chosen to minimize overlap along the dimension of intro-version-extraversion. By this means, any differences in conditionability between introverted and extraverted neurotics should become more readily apparent with a relatively small number of cases. The means and SDs for the three neurotic and normal groups are presented in Table 1. Although all 3 groups are significantly different from each other with respect to their R scores, the normal group tends to resemble the hysterics more than they do the dysthymics in this respect.

28 hysteric patients were originally tested, of whom 8 had to be rejected because seven had R scores below 33 and because of a major error by the experimenter during conditioning with one. The final group of 20 hysterics were diagnostically constituted as follows: 8, hysteria; 2, hysterical features in an immature personality; 2, conversion hysteria; 1, anorexia nervosa hysteria; 1, hysteria plus mixed neurotic reactions; 1, hysterical palsy; 3, sexual psychopathy; 1, chronic alcoholism in a psychopathic personality; 1, delinquency in a psychopathic personality.

27 dysthymic patients were originally tested of whom seven had to be rejected for the following reasons: 4 had R scores above 32; 2 had changed diagnoses; 1 was initially sensitive to the sound, giving both a blink and a PGR to a sound stimulus. The final group of 20 dysthymics were diagnostically constituted as follows: 11, mainly obsessional and compulsive features; 5, mainly anxiety features; 4, mainly depressive features. In most cases the diagnoses were mixed, including more than one of these features.

The Personality Questionnaires

Guilford's scales STDCR (Ref. 13) and the Guilford-Martin scales G and A (Ref. 16) were typed on cards, one item to each card, and the S required to 'mail' each card into one of three slotted boxes labelled YES, NO and ?. The 237 cards were presented to the Ss in random order. The seven traits are described in the test manuals as follows:

S   social introversion: shyness, seclusiveness, etc.
T   thinking introversion: an inclination toward meditative or reflective thinking, self analysis, etc.
D   depression: habitually gloomy, pessimistic with guilt feelings, etc.
C   cycloid disposition: strong emotional fluctuations, emotional instability, etc.
R   rhathymia: happy-go-lucky, carefree, lively, impulsive, etc.
G   general activity: a general pressure to engage in overt activity, etc.
A   ascendancy: leadership qualities; social ascendancy, etc.

The Guilfords identified these traits by factor analysis studies (Ref. 14 & 15). There is, however, some evidence to suggest that C and D are largely measures of the factor of neuroticism and that R is a good measure of the introversion-extraversion dimension, a high R score characterizing the extravert end of the dimension (Ref. 3, p. 106ff.; Ref. 17).

Taylor's Manifest Anxiety Scale and the MMQ were also typed on cards and the S requested to 'mail' each card into one of two boxes labelled TRUE and FALSE. Taylor's scale normally consists of 50 anxiety items and 175 buffer items but here the original 175 buffer items were omitted and in their place was substituted the 48 items of the MMQ. These 98 items were administered in random order.

Taylor's anxiety scale has been used extensively in conditioning studies (e.g., Refs. 29, 30 & 32) and is supposed to discriminate the anxious from the nonanxious Ss. The MMQ consists of a 40-item neuroticism scale together with 18 'Lie' items. It is discussed in detail by Eysenck (Ref. 2, p. 94ff.) and there is little doubt that, given good subject motivation, it discriminates well between neurotics and normals.

Conditioning Sequence, Apparatus and Method of Recording

Before the conditioning session was begun, each S was given 3 tone stimuli, followed by 3 air puff stimuli (*not* paired with the CS) and then 3 more tone stimuli. Only Ss who did not give PGR or eyeblink responses to the last three tone stimuli were included in the conditioning study. The purposes of these trials were to eliminate those Ss who showed any evidence of pseudo-conditioning (Refs. 11 & 12) or original sensitivity to the tone.

The conditioning session consisted of 30 reinforced trials, randomly interspersed with 18 test trials (called acquisition trials). The US consisted of an air puff, lasting 500 msec, delivered at a pressure of 65 mm. of mercury from a 2·5 mm. internal diameter polythene tube at approximately 2 cm. from the right eye. The CS was a pure tone, delivered to both ears through a pair of padded high quality earphones at a frequency of 1100 cycles per sec for a duration of 800 msec after the tone was presented. The time intervals were accurately controlled by means of an electronic timer. Finally, each S was given ten consecutive test trials (called extinction trials).

The air was supplied from a compressed air cylinder and puffed into the eye by means of an electronically operated gas valve. The polythene tube ran from the gas valve to a pair of plain glass spectacles worn by the S. The right spectacle lens had a small aperture into which the plastic tube was attached. The eyelid movements were recorded by means of a photoelectric cell attached to the same lens as the polythene tube. This photoelectric method of recording the eyelid movements has been described in detail elsewhere (Ref. 10). It is particularly suitable for working with patients since it does not require any electrodes or artificial eyelashes to be attached directly to S and S does not have to keep his head rigidly still. Briefly, it consists of a small photoelectric cell and a linear amplifier, the amplifier EMF being used to drive the pen of a recording milliameter. The milliameter was equipped with several channels so that eyelid movements, PGR trace and the occurrence of the CS and the US all appeared on the same record.

Procedure

The Ss were told that they were to be tested in a quiet room where measures could be made of how well they were able to relax under various conditions. As detailed elsewhere (Ref. 6), the conditioning laboratory can be partitioned into two by means of a sliding curtain. The S was seated comfortably in an armchair in one half of the laboratory, facing a small table so arranged that his field of vision was largely confined to the plain walls of a booth constructed around this table. His head rested against an adjustable padded headrest and his feet were supported by a footstool. The E and the apparatus occupied the other half of the room. Once the test was ready to begin, the curtains could be drawn together, leaving a small gap just sufficient for E to see S (but S was unable to see E).

The spectacles, headphones and PGR electrodes were fitted on S; and after a suitable interval, S's hearing threshold was measured for the frequency of 1100 cycles per second (both ears simultaneously). Any S whose hearing threshold was below -20 db was excluded from the study. In the middle of the booth was a small red light (6·3v., 0·5 amp.) which S was instructed to look at whenever it was on. The red light was switched on 5 to 10 seconds before any stimulus was delivered and switched off a few seconds afterward. It was found that this procedure reduced strain in S and ensured that his eyes were open during the critical period just before any stimulus was delivered without having to tell him to keep his eyes open. It also reduced eye movements and spontaneous blinking during this critical period. The nine sensitization and pseudo-conditioning stimuli were then given, followed by the conditioning and extinction session.

The S was then asked such questions as, 'Did you find the air puff bearable or unpleasant?' and 'Did you feel sleepy?' Finally, he was requested to sort the personality items. The intelligence test had been given to most Ss upon an earlier occasion. For the 20 normal Ss, the whole procedure, except the intelligence testing, was repeated after an interval of 14–21 days.

A CR was recorded whenever the record showed a deflection of 1·27 mm. (0·05 inch) or more during a latency of between 156 and 625msec after the onset of the CS for the eyeblink and a latency of between 0·5 and 8·0 seconds after the onset of the CS for the PGR.

RESULTS

Table 2 gives the mean number of conditioned responses during the 18 acquisition test trials and the 10 extinction test trials for both PGR and eyeblink reflexes in all three groups.

From the data presented in Table 2 it may be concluded for both eyeblink and PGR reflexes that:

1. Dysthymics give significantly more CRs than hysterics both for the acquisition trials and for the extinction trials (one-tailed t test: $p < 0.0005$ for the eyeblink acquisition and extinction trials; $p < 0.005$ for the PGR acquisition trials and $p < 0.025$ for the PGR extinction trials).

2. The normals give significantly less CR than the dysthymics for both acquisition and extinction trials (one-tailed t test: $p < 0.0025$ for the eyeblink acquisition trials; $p < 0.01$ for the eyeblink extinction trials; $p < 0.025$ for the PGR extinction trials).

3. When the normals are compared with the neurotics as a combined group, there are no significant differences in the number of CRs produced.

The differences are not so marked for the PGR as for the eyeblink reflex, probably because of the low intensity of the US. It was noticed that an air puff at a pressure of only 65 mm. of mercury was in several cases insufficient to produce even an unconditioned PGR after the first few trials.

Fig. 50 shows the histograms for the acquisition of CRs for the eyeblink reflex. If eight CRs are chosen as the cutoff score, then the classification error is 20 per cent for the hysteric group and 10 per cent for the dysthymic group, giving a total misclassification of only 15 per cent.[1] In Fig. 51, the total number of eyeblink CRs given by each of these

---

[1] When similar histograms are plotted for the PGR data using a cutoff of 3 CRs, the total misclassification is 30 per cent. When a double criterion is used, however, in which to be classified as hysteric the patient must have 8 or less eyeblink CRs *and* also 3 or less PGR CR's, then the two groups may be separated with no misclassification whatsoever.

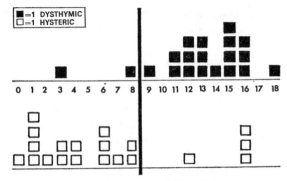

NO. OF ACQUISITION CRs

Figure 50. Number of hysterics and dysthymics mis-classified using the frequency of eyeblink conditioned reflexes as a measure.

groups is plotted for each of the 18 acquisition test trials and the ten extinction test trials.

TABLE 2

MEAN NUMBER OF CR's GIVEN BY EACH GROUP

(N = 20 per group; maximum acquisition score = 18; maximum extinction score = 19)

Group	Eyeblink				PGR			
	Acquisition		Extinction		Acquisition		Extinction	
	Mean	SD	Mean	SD	Mean	SD	Mean	SD
Hysterics	6·7	5·9	2·7	2·7	2·3	2·7	0·8	1·7
Normals	7·9	5·4	3·7	2·7	2·4	3·3	0·6	1·7
Dysthymics	12·4	4·1	6·3	3·2	5·4	4·0	2·1	2·3

As indicated in Table 2 and Fig. 51, there are no statistically significant differences in conditionability between normals and hysterics. In accordance with the theory presented in this paper, it is to be expected that normals would differ with respect to conditionability from both hysterics and dysthymics to approximately the same extent that they differed from these two neurotic groups in extraversion. In the present study the extraversion scores of the normal group (see Table 1) are more like those of the hysteric group than of the dysthymics. This state of affairs probably occurred because, although the normal group was chosen at random, it was, naturally enough, the extraverted rather than the introverted subjects who volunteered for the experiment. This situation

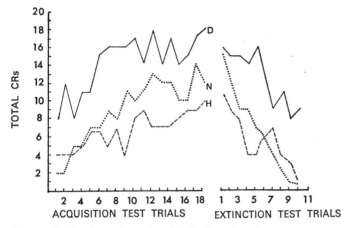

Figure 51. Total number of eyeblink CRs given by each group at each test trial (N = 20 in each group).

possibly accounts for the findings that the conditioned response behaviour of the normals is somewhat similar to that of the hysterics although the differences in conditionability between these two groups are not statistically significant.

Similar results were obtained for PGR conditioning; here also the dysthymics conditioned much more strongly than the hysterics and than the normals and the hysterics and the normals behaved very much the same. Both the hysterics and the normals seemed to adapt to the PGR fairly rapidly and the normals tended to resemble the hysterics more than the dysthymics with respect to their extraversion scores.

Another measure of conditionability was the number of reinforcements necessary to achieve a criterion of three successive CRs. This index gave a correlation with the acquisition score of 0·80 for the eyeblink reflex and 0·78 for the PGR reflex, which is in agreement with the finding of Humphreys, who concluded that to report a criterion score and an acquisition score is superfluous since the correlation between these two scores is as high as the reliability of the conditioning measures will allow (Ref. 20).

For the normal group, the test-retest reliability over the period of 14–21 days was 0·52 for the eyeblink acquisition score, 0·37 for the eyeblink extinction score and 0·40 for the PGR acquisition score. The PGR Pearson product-moment coefficient for the extinction data could not meaningfully be calculated because there were too many zero values

on retest. The PGR correlation is low when compared with that of
Welch & Kubis, who obtained a test-retest reliability of 0·88 (Refs. 36
& 37), but they used electric shock as the US.

When corrected for attenuation (a procedure carried out only where
reliability data existed, i.e., for the normal group), the correlation
between the PGR and eyeblink acquisition scores was 0·53. For none
of the groups were there any significant correlations between any measure
of conditioning and age, sex, or intelligence.

TABLE 3

CORRELATIONS AMONG CONDITIONING AND GUILFORD'S R SCALE,
TAYLOR'S ANXIETY SCALE AND THE MMQ FOR ALL Ss
(N = 60)

Scale	Eyeblink Conditioning		PGR Conditioning
	Acquisition	Extinction	Acquisition
R	−0·48	−0·37	−0·25
Anxiety	+0·15	+0·16	+0·17
MMQ	+0·08	+0·04	+0·20

Table 3 presents the Pearson product-moment correlations between
conditioning and Guilford's R Scale, Taylor's Manifest Anxiety Scale
and the MMQ for the number of eyeblink CRs during acquisition and
extinction. For the PGR only the acquisition CRs were considered,
since adaptation proceeded too rapidly during extinction. The correlations between R and the conditioning measures are, of course, negative
because rhathymia is a measure of extraversion. Using a one-tailed test
of significance, all three correlations between R and the conditioning
measures are highly significant, whereas the correlations between
conditioning and the MMQ are insignificant in all cases. Similar results
were considered separately. Furthermore, for each of the three conditioning measures in Table 3, the correlation between conditioning and R is
significantly greater (p < 0·02) than the correlation between conditioning
and the Taylor score and the correlation between conditioning and the
MMQ.

That the D and C scales are also measures of neuroticism is suggested
by the high correlation (0·88) between D+C combined and the MMQ.
Taylor's Anxiety Scale correlated 0·86 with D+C combined and 0·92
with the MMQ (for all 60 Ss). As elaborated elsewhere (Ref. 8), these
intercorrelations strongly suggest that these three scales all essentially

are measures of neuroticism; hence, the insignificant correlations of both the anxiety and the MMQ scales with conditioning.

There were several other relevant findings. The hysterics tended to give fewer unconditioned PGR responses to the air puffs than the dysthymics. When the replies to the postconditioning questions were analysed, it was found that the dysthymics reported the air puffs as being disturbing significantly more often than did the hysterics. Although not significant, the hysterics appeared to report that they felt sleepy during the session more often than did the dysthymics.

DISCUSSION

These results would indicate very strongly so far as the eyeblink reflex is concerned, and very possibly for the PGR reflex, that conditionability is related to introversion-extraversion and not to neuroticism, the extraverted subjects tending to condition much less well than the introverted ones. The results also suggest that manifest anxiety is related to strong conditionability only to the extent that anxious people are introverted. Taylor's Anxiety Scale differentiates those subjects who condition well from those who condition poorly only to the extent that it fails to measure neuroticism. Since this scale has a very large projection on the neuroticism dimension and only a small projection on the introversion dimension, it is probably an extremely poor diagnostic measure of conditionability. This explains the very low correlation between this scale and conditionability obtained in the present study and also the only slight successes obtained by Spence and his colleagues and by Hilgard, Jones & Kaplan in their attempts to obtain positive correlations between the Taylor scale and conditionability (Ref. 18).

The poor conditionability of the hysterics, their more rapid PGR adaptation to the air puffs, their subjective reports that the air puffs were not very disturbing and perhaps their reports of feeling sleepy all support the hypothesis that hysterics are in a state of cortical inhibition in which dissociation phenomena predominate; in a similar manner, the results obtained for the dysthymic group support the hypothesis that dysthymics are in a state of cortical excitation. Since conditionability in both neurotics and in normals is apparently related to introversion-extraversion and not to neuroticism, it would seem very probable that excitation-inhibition is closely related to introversion-extraversion.[1] This conclusion,

---

[1] This is in agreement with the finding that sodium amytal, an inhibitory drug, decreases conditionability and increases extraversion (Ref. 9).

if correct, is of considerable theoretical and practical interest and together with other experimental findings, should help to generate a dynamic and physiologically based theory of personality structure (Ref. 4) in which the behaviour of both the dysthymic and the introverted individual is described in terms of over-conditioning and cortical excitation and the behaviour of both the hysteric and the extraverted individual is described in terms of underconditioning and cortical inhibition.

SUMMARY

Pavlov's concepts of excitation and inhibition were related to the dimension of introversion-extraversion in normal and neurotic subjects. Normal and neurotic subjects were conditioned, using the eyeblink and PGR reflexes. It was found that (a) anxiety states conditioned much better than hysterics and (b) conditionability is related to introversion-extraversion and not to neuroticism.

REFERENCES

1. EYSENCK, H. J., *Dimensions of Personality*. London: Routledge & Kegan Paul, 1947.
2. ——, *The Scientific Study of Personality*. London: Routledge & Kegan Paul, 1952.
3. ——, *The Structure of Human Personality*. London: Methuen, 1953.
4. ——, A dynamic theory of anxiety and hysteria. *J. ment. Sci.*, **101**, 28–51, 1955.
5. FINESINGER, J. E., SUTHERLAND, G. F. & McGUIRE, FRANCES F., The positive conditioned salivary reflex in psychoneurotic patients. *Amer. J. Psychiat.*, **99**, 61–74, 1942.
6. FRANKS, C. M., An Experimental Study of Conditioning as Related to Mental Abnormality. Unpublished doctor's dissertation, University of London Library, 1954.
7. ——, The establishment of a conditioning laboratory for the investigation of personality and cortical functioning. *Nature*, **175**, 984–985, 1955.
8. ——, The Taylor scale and the dimensional analysis of anxiety. *Rev. Psychol. appl.*, **6**, 35–44, 1956.
9. —— & LAVERTY, S. G., Sodium amytal and eyelid conditioning. *J. ment. Sci.*, **101**, 654–663, 1955.

10. —— & WITHERS, W. C. R., Photoelectric recording of eyelid movements. *Amer. J. Psychol.*, **68,** 467–471, 1955.
11. GRANT, D. A., The pseudo-conditional eyelid response. *J. exp. Psychol.*, **32,** 139–149, 1943.
12. GRETHER, W. F., Pseudo-conditioning without paired stimulation encountered in attempted backward conditioning. *J. comp. Psychol.*, **25,** 91–96, 1938.
13. GUILFORD, J. P., *Inventory of Factors STDCR.* Beverly Hills, Calif.; Sheridan Supply Co., 1940.
14. —— & GUILFORD, RUTH B., Personality factors S, E and M and their measurement. *J. Psychol.*, **2,** 109–127, 1936.
15. —— & ——, Personality factors D, R, T and A. *J. abnorm. soc. Psychol.*, **34,** 21–36, 1939.
16. —— & MARTIN, H. G., *The Guilford-Martin Inventory of Factors GAMIN, Manual of Directions and Norms.* Beverly Hills, Calif.; Sheridan Supply Co., 1945.
17. HILDEBRAND, H. P., A Factorial Study of Introversion-Extraversion by Means of Objective Tests. Unpublished doctor's dissertation, University of London Library, 1953.
18. HILGARD, E. R., JONES, L. V. & KAPLAN, S. J., Conditioned discrimination as related to anxiety. *J. exp. Psychol.*, **42,** 94–99, 1951.
19. —— & MARQUIS, D. G., *Conditioning and Learning.* New York: Appleton-Century, 1940.
20. HUMPHREYS, L. G., Measures of strength of conditioned eyelid responses. *J. Gen. Psychol.*, **29,** 101–111, 1943.
21. JUNG, C. G., *Psychological Types.* London: Routledge & Kegan Paul, 1924.
22. McALLISTER, W. R., Eyelid conditioning as a function of the CS-US interval. *J. exp. Psychol.*, **45,** 417–422, 1953.
23. MacCORQUODALE, K. & MEEHL, P. E., On a distinction between hypothetical constructs and intervening variables. *Psychol. Rev.*, **55,** 95–107, 1948.
24. PAVLOV, I. P., *Conditioned Reflexes.* (Trans. G. V. Anrep). Oxford: Oxford University Press, 1927.
25. ——, *Lectures on Conditioned Reflexes. Vol. 1. The Higher Nervous Activity (Behaviour) of Animals.* (Trans. W. H. Gantt). London: Lawrence & Wishart, 1928.
26. ——, *Lectures on Conditioned Reflexes. Conditioned Reflexes and Psychiatry.* (Trans. W. H. Gantt). New York: International Publishers, 1941.

27. RAVEN, J. C. R., *Progressive Matrices*. London: H. K. Lewis, 1948.

28. SCHIFF, ETHEL, DOUGAN, CATHERINE & WELCH, L., The conditioned PGR and the EEG as indicators of anxiety. *J. abnorm. soc. Psychol.*, **44**, 549–552, 1949.

29. SPENCE, K. W. & FABER, I. E., Conditioning and extinction as a function of anxiety. *J. exp. Psychol.*, **45**, 116–119, 1953.

30. —— & TAYLOR, JANET A., Anxiety and strength of the UCS as determiners of the amount of eyelid conditioning. *J. exp. Psychol.*, **42**, 183–188, 1951.

31. —— & ——, The relation of conditioned response strength to anxiety in normal, neurotic and psychotic subjects. *J. exp. Psychol.*, **45**, 265–272, 1952.

32. TAYLOR, JANET A., The relationship of anxiety to the conditioned eyelid response. *J. exp. Psychol.*, **41**, 81–92, 1951.

33. ——, A personality scale of manifest anxiety. *J. abnorm. soc. Psychol.*, **48**, 285–290, 1953.

34. —— & SPENCE, K. W., The relationship of anxiety level to performance in serial learning. *J. exp. Psychol.*, **44**, 61–64, 1952.

35. —— & ——, Conditioning level in the behaviour disorders. *J. abnorm. soc. Psychol.*, **49**, 497–503, 1954.

36. WELCH, L. & KUBIS, J., The effect of anxiety on the conditioning rate and stability of the PGR. *J. Psychol.*, **23**, 83–91, 1947.

37. —— & ——, Conditioned PGR (psychogalvanic response) in states of pathological anxiety. *J. nerv. ment. Dis.*, **105**, 372–381, 1947.

Personality Factors and the Rate of Conditioning

CYRIL M. FRANKS

First published in *British Journal of Psychology*, **48,** 119–126, 1957

60 NORMAL male students were conditioned, using the eyeblink reflex. It was found (1) that those students who were introverted conditioned considerably better than those who were extraverted and (2) that there was no correlation between conditioning and neuroticism. This experiment was designed primarily to provide support for an introversion-extraversion theory of conditioning as opposed to Spence's drive theory. The implications of the experiment are discussed and related to other experiments designed to show that Hull's Seventh Postulate, as used by Spence, leads to erroneous deductions. It would seem that conditioning is independent of drive level where the drive is a secondary factor in the conditioning situation.

INTRODUCTION

Hull offers evidence to suggest that behaviour is a function of two principal classes of variable—learning and motivation (Ref. 21, p. 240f.). These two variables are supported to combine multiplicatively according to the formula, response $= f(sE_R) = f(D \times sH_R)$, where sE_R, D and sH_R represent three theoretical constructs, namely, reaction potential, drive strength and habit strength (Postulate no. 7). According to Hull sH_R is a dependent hypothetical learning variable and its value can be calculated (Ref. 21, p. 178f.); in practice this would seem to be impossible since it is neither clear what his four critical constructs (k, j, u and i) are, nor how they should be determined. In addition, Hull states that there are some other independent variables which may affect the value of sH_R and which cannot at present be defined. D is also a hypothetical construct and is supposed to represent the total drive strength operating in the organism at a given moment, thus in any specific situation the value of D is assumed to be determined by both relevant needs and the total aggregate strength of existing irrelevant needs.

Spence and his colleagues (e.g., Refs. 26, 27 & 28) have adapted

Hull's model, in particular the above equation, to make predictions about eyelid conditioning. They argue that the total effective drive strength (D) is in part a function of the level of internal anxiety or emotionality of the subject; consequently subjects with a greater degree of anxiety would possess more drive and therefore form conditioned responses better than subjects with a lesser degree of anxiety. They have used Taylor's Manifest Anxiety Scale (Ref. 29) as their measure of anxiety and claim that, in general, this prediction has been confirmed. (This scale and its relationship to conditioning is discussed elsewhere in this paper.)

An entirely different theory (Refs. 4 & 5) has been developed by Eysenck on the basis of certain Pavlovian concepts and hypotheses. (Pavlov's original observation (Ref. 24, p. 397f.) was to the effect that neurasthenics possessed an exaggeration of the excitatory process and hysterics an exaggeration of the inhibitory process.) Retaining the notion of excitation and inhibition potentials as determining $_sE_R$, Eysenck has postulated individual differences in the development of these two potentials and linked these differences with personality development according to the following postulate:

'Individuals in whom reactive inhibition is generated quickly, in whom strong reactive inhibitions are generated and in whom reactive inhibition is dissipated slowly are thereby predisposed to develop extraverted patterns of behaviour and to develop hysterico-psychopathic disorders in cases of neurotic breakdown; conversely, individuals in whom reactive inhibition has developed slowly, in whom weak reactive inhibitions are generated and in whom reactive inhibition is dissipated quickly, are thereby predisposed to develop introverted patterns of behaviour and to develop dysthymic disorders in cases of neurotic breakdown' (Ref. 4, p. 35).

The well-established finding (e.g., Spence and his colleagues; Welch and his colleagues, Refs. 30 & 31) that anxious subjects condition better than non-anxious may be explained either in terms of Spence's theory of superior drive level or in terms of Eysenck's theory of inhibition-excitation and extraversion-introversion. (Eysenck has established that anxious subjects are more introverted and more neurotic than normal subjects (Refs. 2 & 3).) A crucial experiment would be one for which each theory would predict different results. One such experiment is that in which drive is manipulated, while introversion-extraversion remains unaltered; Spence's theory would predict a change in conditionability, Eysenck's theory would predict no change. To increase drive a group of normal male subjects were deprived of food, drink and tobacco for 24 hours, while another similar group were allowed to eat, drink and smoke in their usual manner. It was found that both groups conditioned equally well (Ref. 12).

Another crucial experiment would be one which examined the conditionability of three groups, namely, normals, introverted neurotics (anxiety states) and extraverted neurotics (hysterics and psychopaths). Spence's theory would presumably predict that both groups of neurotics would condition better than the normal group (the assumption being that high neuroticism, or high emotionality, may be associated with high drive). Eysenck's theory would predict that the introverted neurotics would condition best, the extraverted neurotic worst and that the normals—being as a group neither introverted nor extraverted—would be intermediate in their ease and strength of conditioning. Such an experiment was carried out by the present writer (Ref. 10). It was found, using both the eyeblink reflex and the PGR, that patients diagnosed as anxiety states conditioned readily and that patients diagnosed as hysterics or psychopaths conditioned poorly, the normals being in between. Several other findings are of relevance, in particular, that both neurotic groups had high scores on Taylor's anxiety scale, whereas the normal group had a low score on this scale. Furthermore, like other workers (Refs. 1 and 20), the writer found no significant correlation between conditioning and Taylor's scale. It was also found that conditionability was unrelated to neuroticism as measured by the Maudsley Medical Questionnaire or by Guilford's D and C Scales (Ref. 15) but was closely related to introversion-extraversion, as measured by Guilford's rhathymia scale, R (Ref. 15). (The evidence for the Maudsley Medical Questionnaire and Guilford's D and C scales being measures of general neuroticism and Guilford's rhathymia scale being a measure of extraversion is presented by Eysenck together with a general discussion of these scales (Refs. 2 & 3). Guilford's scales are also discussed elsewhere in the present article.) Spence's hypothesis, therefore, appears to gain no support from the experimental findings detailed above; and it seems reasonable to conclude that when Hull's equation, *as used by Spence*, is applied to conditioning situations where the drive is irrelevant, then conditioning is dependent not upon the drive component but only upon the excitation component, i.e., upon $_sH_R$.

Two objections to these findings may be raised. First, whereas Spence and his colleagues worked mainly with normal student volunteers, the writer used mainly hospitalized neurotic patients. Secondly, since it was impossible to avoid knowing or guessing into which of the two categories each patient fell it could be possible that attitudinal factors were systematically influencing the results. Therefore it would seem desirable to carry out a similar study on a group of normal student volunteers about whom nothing relevant was known and, as a further precaution, have a different experimenter administer the questionnaires.

PLAN OF PRESENT EXPERIMENT

Subjects

60 paid undergraduate male volunteers were used ranging in age from 18 to 26 years. All subjects were given a meal allowance and travelling expenses. None of them was studying psychology as a main subject and all of them were naive with respect to experimental methods in psychology.

Conditioning apparatus

The conditioning apparatus and laboratory has been described in detail elsewhere (Ref. 10). Briefly, the unconditioned stimulus was an air puff of 500msec duration and pressure 65 mm. of mercury, delivered from a 2·5 mm., internal diameter polythene tube situated approximately 2 cm. from the right eye. The conditioned stimulus was a pure tone, delivered to both ears through a pair of high-quality padded earphones; its frequency was 1100 cycles per sec and its duration 800 msec, at an intensity of 65 db above the frequency threshold and so arranged that the air-puff began 350 msec after the start of the tone. All time intervals were accurately controlled by means of a small photoelectric cell (Ref. 14) mounted upon the same lens as supported the air-puff delivery tube. The air was supplied from an electronically operated gas cylinder and the recording milliammeter was so arranged that eyelid movements and the occurrences of the various stimuli all appeared on the same record. The experiment took place in a soundproof laboratory (Ref. 9) so arranged that the apparatus and experimenter were in one half of the room and the subjects being conditioned in the other half, the two parts of the room being separated by a sliding curtain.

Personality Questionnaire

All subjects were given a new questionnaire, the Maudsley Personality Inventory (Ref. 6), recently developed by Eysenck from the questionnaires of Guilford & Guilford (Refs. 16, 17, 18 & 19) and from the Maudsley Medical Questionnaire. The need for a new questionnaire arose because the Guilford scales, although they can be used to measure the two orthogonal dimensions of introversion-extraversion and neuroticism, have been observed to possess certain limitations. First, it would seem that in the derivation of these scales little attention has been paid to sex differences; working with these scales suggests that some items in each scale are more predictive of a high score on that scale in the case of men than for women and vice versa. Secondly, the claim by the Guilfords that each of the scales measures a unitary factor is dubious; it would seem that certain scales are far from unitary and can be resolved into two unrelated components. There is good evidence (Ref. 3) to indicate that when a factor analysis of the intercorrelations between the Guilford scales is carried out two clear-cut orthogonal factors emerge, these two factors being identifiable as neuroticism and introversion-extraversion respectively, scales C (cycloid disposition) and D (depression) most characterizing neuroticism and scales R (rhathymia) and—to a lesser extent—G (general activity) and A (ascendancy) characterizing introversion-extraversion. Other studies strongly support these conclusions (Refs. 4 & 5). Thirdly, although the R scale has a low correlation with both the C and the D scales, an item analysis showed that certain individual items in the R scale correlated more highly with the total score on the C scale or the D scale than with the total score on the R scale. A similar deficiency was found in some of the D and C items.

The new scale was constructed in such a way that these limitations were largely obviated. The neuroticism scale (N) and the introversion-extraversion scale (E) each contains 24 items, so that the test is considerably easier to give and to score than the earlier questionnaires. All items in the N scale have significant relations with Guilford's C and D scales, for both men and women and insignificant relations with Guilford's R scale. All items in the E scale have significant relations with Guilford's R scale, for both men and women and insignificant relations with Guilford's D and C scales (Ref. 6). Sex differences are small for both E and N scales and the intercorrelation between the two scales is -0.048 for a sample of 200 men and 200 women. The split half reliabilities of both scales are high.

METHOD

The subject was first given the Maudsley Personality Inventory by an independent experimenter. He was then told that records would be made of how well he 'relaxed under various conditions when in a quiet room' and brought to the conditioning laboratory, where he was seated in an armchair, complete with padded head and foot rest. This chair was arranged so that his field of vision was almost completely confined to a small booth immediately in front of him. After the subject was made comfortable, the apparatus was fitted, his hearing threshold taken and the intensity of the tone stimulus adjusted accordingly. Before commencing the conditioning session proper, brief tests were carried out for initial eyeblink sensitivity to sound and for pseudo-conditioning. A technique of partial reinforcement was used, consisting of 30 reinforced trials, interspersed with 18 test trials (called acquisition trials) consisting of only the conditioned stimulus. After the sequence of 30 reinforcement trials and 18 acquisition test trials had been given, the subject received a further series of 10 successive test trials (called extinction trials). The intertrial interval varied from 20 to 30 sec and the complete session lasted approximately half an hour.

RESULTS AND DISCUSSION

Of the 60 subjects 5 had to be rejected for the following reasons: 2 because of excessive blinking, rendering the records unscorable; 1 because only irregular unconditioned responses were obtained; 1 because of an experimental error during testing; and 1 because the questionnaire was incomplete. For the remaining 55 subjects the correlations between conditioning and introversion-extraversion (E) were -0.46 for the number of acquisition conditioned responses and -0.34 for the number of extinction conditioned responses. These correlations are negative because E is a measure of extraversion and the theory requires the prediction that introverts would condition well and extraverts relatively poorly. The correlations are very similar to those reported between eyeblink conditioning and Guilford's R scale of extraversion for a group of 60 subjects consisting mainly of hospitalized neurotics, namely, -0.48 for the acquisition scores and -0.37 for the extinction scores (Ref. 10). The correlations between conditioning and neuroticism, as measured by the N scale of the Maudsley Personality Inventory, were 0.04 for the acquisition measure and 0.15 for the extinction measure. Using a one-tailed test of significance, the two correlations between conditioning and extraversion are highly significant ($p < 0.01$), whereas the two correlations between conditioning and neuroticism are insignificant. These results strongly suggest that in normal subjects also conditionability is related to introversion-extraversion and not to neuroticism.

TABLE 1

CONDITIONING AND PERSONALITY SCORES

| | | Conditioning | | Extraversion (E) | Neuroticism (N) |
		Acquisition	Extinction		
All 55 subjects:	Mean	7·18	2·57	13·09	8·90
	S.D.	5·12	2·65	4·49	5·65
High extraversion					
(15 most extraverted):	Mean	3·73	0·60	18·40*	8·27
	S.D.	3·64	1·14		5·57
Low extraversion					
(15 least extraverted):	Mean	9·87	3·53	7·53†	9·13
	S.D.	4·87	2·75		4·06
High neuroticism					
(15 most neurotic):	Mean	5·73	2·27	14·47	16·27‡
	S.D.	5·15	2·85	3·86	
Low neuroticism					
(15 least neurotic):	Mean	6·00	2·20	13·60	2·60§
	S.D.	4·02	2·16	3·89	

* This is the mean extraversion score of the top 15 subjects on the extraversion scale, the range of their scores being from 17 to 22.

† This is the mean extraversion score of the bottom 15 subjects on the extraversion scale, the range of their scores being from 10 to 3.

‡ This is the mean neuroticism scale of the top 15 subjects on the neuroticism scale, the range of their scores being from 12 to 22.

§ This is the mean neuroticism score of the bottom 15 subjects on the neuroticism scale, the range of their scores being from 5 to 0.

Table 1 presents the mean number of acquisition conditioned responses given by the 55 subjects, together with the mean number of extinction conditioned responses. The mean extraversion score (E) and the mean neuroticism score (N) are also given. Similar data are provided for the 15 subjects scoring highest on the extraversion scale and the 15 subjects scoring lowest on this scale and for the 15 subjects scoring highest on the neuroticism scale and the 15 subjects scoring lowest on this scale. Applying t-tests to these data produces the following results:

High Versus Low Extraversion

The high extraversion group give significantly fewer acquisition conditioned responses than the low extraversion group (t = 3·79; p< 0·0005). Similar results were obtained for the extinction conditioning scores (t = 3·71, p<0·0005). The high and low extraversion groups are very similar in their neuroticism scores and certainly are not significantly different in this respect (t = 0·47).

High Versus Low Neuroticism

The high and low neuroticism groups are very similar in their ease of conditioning and certainly are not significantly different (acquisition, t = 0·155; extinction, t = 0·073). These two groups are also very similar in their extraversion scores (t = 0·59).

Figs. 52 and 53 present the data of Table 1 in a different manner. In Fig. 52, the total number of conditioned eyeblink responses given by the most extraverted 15 subjects and by the least extraverted 15 subjects is plotted for each of the 18 acquisition test trials and each of the 10 extinction test trials. It is clear from this figure that the 15 subjects with the lowest extraversion scores condition much better than the 15 subjects with the highest extraversion scores. (It might be argued, from Fig. 52, that the more introverted group condition better because they start off better. However, by test trial no. 7 both groups condition equally readily; from then onwards the more introverted group condition far better and furthermore are not completely extinguished after ten successive extinction trials, as are the more extraverted group.) In Fig. 53, the high and low neuroticism groups are compared with respect to their condition-ability. It is clear that the 15 most neurotic subjects closely resemble the 15 least neurotic subjects in their conditioned response behaviour.

From these results it would seem reasonable to conclude that conditionability is closely related to introversion-extraversion and not at all related to neuroticism, as these two personality dimensions are measured here. Two conclusions would seem to follow from the experiments discussed so far. First, that drive does not affect conditioning in situations where the drive is an irrelevant one. Secondly, that conditioning is unrelated to neuroticism, but closely related to the personality dimension of introversion-extraversion.

The first conclusion requires some elaboration. It is, for example, clear that drives may increase the learning of instrumental responses (e.g., see Ref. 23, p. 305f.), but it would seem difficult to conceive of eyelid conditioning in the present series of experiments as primarily and consistently instrumental. It is also clear that under certain circumstances, drives increase conditioning when the drives are directly relevant

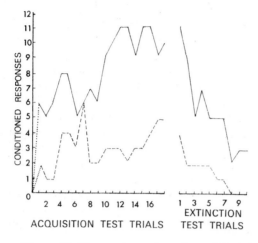

Figure 52. The total number of conditioned eyeblink responses given by the fifteen most extraverted subjects (broken line) and by the fifteen least extraverted subjects (solid line).

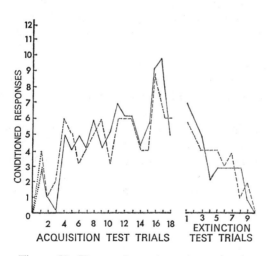

Figure 53. The total number of conditioned responses given by the fifteen most neurotic subjects (broken line) and by the fifteen least neurotic subjects (solid line).

to the conditioning stimuli, thus Zener & McCurdy (Ref. 33) found that hungry dogs yield a greater conditioned salivary response than non-hungry dogs and Lashley and Winsor obtained similar results with humans (Refs. 22 and 32).

The second conclusion is, in part, related to the first, since neuroticism is often regarded as a state of heightened emotionality and it is not unreasonable to regard emotionality as a form of drive. The second conclusion is of interest also because many workers—quite independent of any drive theory—have expected neurotics to condition better than normals (e.g., Refs. 7, 8 & 25). Further evidence supporting the relationship between conditioning and introversion-extraversion is the finding that sodium amytal, a cortical depressant, reduces conditionability and at the same time increases the degree of extraversion (Ref. 13). This finding is in accord with the general formulation that Pavlov's cortical processes of excitation and inhibition underlie the personality dimension of introversion-extraversion.

If conditioning is closely related to introversion, then it would be expected that a clear positive relationship between conditionability and anxiety would emerge, since anxious subjects have been shown to be introverted. However, Spence and his colleagues obtained only poor relationships between anxiety and eyelid conditioning—their correlations, although positive, were sometimes insignificant and always slight. The explanation would seem to be (Ref. 11) that their measure of anxiety, the Taylor Anxiety Scale, has an extremely high correlation with the Maudsley Medical Questionnaire, which has been found (Ref. 3) to be an adequate measure of general neuroticism. At the same time, Taylor's scale has a considerably smaller correlation with introversion, this correlation being sufficient to account for the positive but poor results obtained by Spence and his associates. It would seem, then, from the above conclusions and the evidence presented, that Spence's use of Hull's Seventh Postulate leads to erroneous deductions and is, in fact, incorrect in situations where the drive concerned is a secondary factor in the condition situation; what appear to be the determining factors are individual differences in the cortical processes of excitation and inhibition.

REFERENCES

1. BITTERMAN, M. E. & HOLTZMAN, W. H., Conditioning and extinction of the galvanic skin response as a function of anxiety. *J. abnorm. soc. Psychol.*, **47**, 615–623, 1952.
2. EYSENCK, H. J., *The Scientific Study of Personality*. London: Routledge & Kegan Paul, 1952.
3. ——, *The Structure of Human Personality*. London: Methuen, 1953.
4. ——, A dynamic theory of anxiety and hysteria. *J. ment. Sci.*, **101**, 28–51, 1955.
5. ——, Cortical inhibition, figural aftereffect and the theory of personality. *J. abnorm. soc. Psychol.*, **51**, 94–106, 1955.
6. ——, The questionnaire measurement of neuroticism and extraversion. *Riv. Psichol.*, **54**, 113–140, 1956.
7. FINESINGER, J. E., SUTHERLAND, G. F. & McGUIRE, F. F., The positive conditioned salivary reflex in psychoneurotic patients. *Amer. J. Psychiat.*, **99**, 61–74, 1942.
8. FINK, D. H., *Release from Nervous Tension*. New York: Simon & Shuster, 1943.
9. FRANKS, C. M., The establishment of a conditioning laboratory for the investigation of personality and cortical functioning. *Nature*, **175**, 984–985, 1955.
10. ——, Conditioning and personality. *J. abnorm. soc. Psychol.*, **52**, 143–150, 1956.
11. ——, The Taylor scale and the dimensional analysis of anxiety. *Rev. Psychol. appl.*, **6**, 35–44, 1956.
12. ——, The effect of food, drink and tobacco deprivation upon the conditioned eyeblink response in normal subjects. *J. exp. Psychol.*, **53**, 117–120, 1957.
13. —— & LAVERTY, S. G., Sodium amytal and eyelid conditioning. *J. ment. Sci.*, **101**, 654–663, 1955.
14. —— & WITHERS, W. C. R., Photoelectric recording of eyelid movements. *Amer. J. Psychol.*, **68**, 467–471, 1955.
15. GUILFORD, J. P., *An Inventory of Factors STDCR*. Stanford, California: Sheridan Supply Co., 1940.
16. —— & GUILFORD, R. B., An analysis of the factors in a typical test of introversion-extraversion. *J. abnorm. soc. Psychol.*, **28**, 377–399, 1934.
17. —— & ——, Personality factors S, E and M and their measurement. *J. Psychol.*, **2**, 109–127, 1936.

R

18. —— & ——, Personality factors D, R, T and A. *J. abnorm. soc. Psychol.*, **34**, 21–36, 1939.
19. —— & ——, Personality factors N and GD. *J. abnorm. soc. Psychol.*, **34,** 239–248, 1939.
20. HILGARD, E. R., JONES, L. V. & KAPLAN, S. J., Conditioned discrimination as related to anxiety. *J. exp. Psychol.*, **42,** 94–100, 1951.
21. HULL, C. L., *Principles of Behaviour.* New York: D. Appleton-Century, 1943.
22. LASHLEY, K., Reflex secretion of the human parotid gland. *J. exp. Psychol.*, **1,** 461–493, 1916.
23. MUNN, L. M., *Handbook of Psychological Research on the Rat.* Cambridge, Mass.: Houghton-Mifflin, 1950.
24. PAVLOV, I. P., *Conditioned Reflexes* (trans. G. V. Anrep). Oxford: Oxford University Press, 1927.
25. SCHILDER, P., The somatic basis of the neurosis. *J. nerv. ment. Dis.*, **70,** 502–519, 1929.
26. SPENCE, K. W. & FABER, I. E., Conditioning and extinction as a function of anxiety. *J. exp. Psychol.*, **45,** 116–119, 1953.
27. —— & TAYLOR, J. A., Anxiety and strength of the UCS as determiners of the amount of eyelid conditioning. *J. exp. Psychol.*, **42,** 183–188, 1951.
28. TAYLOR, J. A., The relationship of anxiety to the conditioned eyelid response. *J. exp. Psychol.*, **41,** 81–92, 1951.
29. ——, A personality scale of manifest anxiety. *J. abnorm. soc. Psychol.*, **48,** 285–290, 1953.
30. WELCH, L. & KUBIS, J., The effect of anxiety on the conditioning rate and stability of the P.G.R. *J. Psychol.*, **23,** 83–91, 1947.
31. —— & ——, Conditioned PGR (Psychogalvanic response) in states of pathological anxiety. *J. nerv. ment. Dis.*, **105,** 372–381, 1947.
32. WINSOR, A. L., Conditions affecting human parotid secretion. *J. exp. Psychol.*, **11,** 355–363, 1928.
33. ZENER, K. & McCURDY, H. G., Analysis of motivational factors in conditioned behaviour. 1. The differential effect of changes in hunger upon conditioned, unconditioned and spontaneous salivary secretions. *J. Psychol.*, **8,** 321–350, 1939.

55

Conditioning, Introversion-Extraversion and the Strength of the Nervous System

H. J. EYSENCK[1]

First published in
Proceedings of the 18th International Congress of Psychology,
9th Symposium, 1966

TEPLOV'S main contribution to psychology consisted of the systematic working out of the relations obtaining between personality on the one hand and the concepts of excitation and inhibition on the other (Ref. 10). The work carried out in our laboratories, too, has concerned itself very much with these relations (Ref. 1) and in spite of obvious differences in approach there have also been certain interesting similarities. In particular, it would seem that the Pavlovian notion of 'strong' and 'weak' nervous systems, which has formed the basis for most of Teplov's experimental work, bears a striking similarity to the notions of extraverted and introverted personality types, as they emerge from our own. The 'weak' personality type appears to resemble the introvert, the 'strong' personality type the extravert. Even if it is admitted that similarity does not imply identity, it is certainly striking that two quite independent approaches should issue in such closely related concepts (Ref. 6).

This similarity becomes even more apparent when we consider these personality types in terms of physiological and neurological concepts. Gray has translated the concepts used by Pavlov and Teplov into the language of modern neurophysiology and has shown that different degrees of arousal of the reticular formation can mediate all or most of the experimentally ascertained differences between 'weak' and 'strong' nervous systems (Ref. 10). In a similar manner, Eysenck has suggested a close relationship between reticular formation arousal thresholds and introversion-extraversion (Ref. 7). According to these theories, low thresholds of the ascending reticular activating system would be

[1] Thanks are due to the M.R.C. for the support of this investigation.

499

characteristic of the 'weak' nervous system and the introvert, high thresholds of the 'strong' nervous system and the extravert. Again, the synchronizing part of the reticular formation exerts an inhibitory influence on cortical activity and it may be supposed that low thresholds of this system characterize the extravert and the 'strong' nervous system. Little direct evidence is unfortunately available relating to these theories, but work on the E.E.G. (Ref. 6), on critical flicker fusion (Ref. 12) and in particular on drugs known to affect the reticular formation (Ref. 12) has on the whole borne out the general theory in a rather striking manner (Ref. 4).

Among the similarities resulting from experimental work perhaps the most impressive is that relating to sensory thresholds. The lower thresholds found in persons possessing a 'weak' nervous system constitute one of the most important proofs of the Teplov school for the correctness of their theories. As a direct consequence of their work and the hypothesis relating introversion to a 'weak' nervous system, several studies have recently been carried out in England to study sensory thresholds in introverts and extraverts. Using the Maudsley Personality Inventory (Ref. 2) as the measure of personality, Haslam has several times found a significantly lower pain threshold in introverts as compared with extraverts and Smith has similarly discovered lower auditory thresholds in introverts using the usual psychophysical methods as well as a forced-choice technique. These and other experiments, too numerous to mention, make it likely that the conceptions of our two schools are in fact closely related and that empirical work directly devoted to a verification of this hypothesis would be of considerable value.

One interesting contrast between the Russian and the English work has been the comparative neglect of direct measures of conditioning by Teplov, as compared with the large body of work reported on this topic by the Maudsley group (Ref. 6). We have used in the main the eyeblink conditioning experiment, in which a puff of air to the eye is the unconditioned stimulus (UCS) and a tone delivered over ear-phones the conditioned stimulus (CS). A summary of the work on this test and on GSR conditioning, carried out by us and also by various other experimenters, has shown that different investigators have reported very divergent results, some producing the predicted positive correlation between introversion and conditionability, others failing to find such a correlation. The failure of so many experiments to duplicate the results of our early studies, which gave very positive results, would appear to be due to their failure to duplicate the exact conditions of the tests carried out; as will be shown below, the general theory linking intro-version with greater cortical arousal ('excitation') predicts in some detail the exact choice of parameters which alone would be expected to generate positive correlations between introversion and conditioning. In particular, it is proposed that the following three parameters are crucial and must be carefully selected and controlled in order to obtain positive results.

(1) Partial reinforcement favours introverts; 100 per cent reinforce-ment does not.

(2) Weak unconditioned stimuli favour introverts; strong UCS do not.

(3) Small CS–UCS intervals favour introverts; large US–UCS intervals do not.

Partial Reinforcement

Pavlov already pointed out that unreinforced trials produced inhibi-tion and if we link the growth of inhibition with extraversion in particu-lar, then clearly partial reinforcement will impede conditioning more in extraverts than in introverts (Ref. 1). Furthermore, there is direct evi-dence to link partial reinforcement with cortical inhibition along neurophysiological lines; as Magoun has pointed out:

'In each of the several categories of conditioned reflex performance in which Pavlov found internal inhibition to occur . . . recent electro-physiological studies have revealed features of hypersynchronisation and/or spindle bursting in the E.E.G.' (Ref. 14).

UCS Strength

It is well known that conditioning is in part a function of the strength of the UCS (and possibly of the CS also—Ref. 13). Given that introverts have lower sensory thresholds (and probably smaller difference thresh-olds as well) than extraverts, then objectively identical UCS would be subjectively stronger for them and should therefore produce stronger conditioned responses. UCS of too great strength, on the other hand, should produce 'protective inhibition' much earlier in introverts than in extraverts. It may further be surmised that UCS of low strength adapt quickly and thus produce inhibition; this growth of inhibition again should be stronger in extraverts than in introverts. There is direct experimental backing for the inhibitory action of weak UCS and of partial reinforcement in the work of Ross & Spence who conclude:

'Inhibition of performance is more readily accomplished under conditions of low puff strengths . . . The differences between the 100 per cent and 50 per cent reinforcement groups at high levels of puff strength require that considerable "inhibition" still be present with such puffs' (Ref. 15).

CS–UCS Interval

It is well known that optimal CS–UCS intervals in eye-blink conditioning centre around 500 msec, but no work appears to have been done on individual differences in this respect. The concept of reaction time is clearly relevant here; Gray has summarized the work of the Teplov school by saying that 'at stimulus intensities below that at which asymptotic reaction time is reached, the weaker the nervous system, the faster the reaction time'. By going below the 500 msec mark, we can insure that we go below the asymptotic value for conditioning, and under those conditions, particularly when allied with weak UCS, we would expect introverts to react better to short CS–UCS intervals than extraverts. Gray has reviewed the whole literature on these relations quite exhaustively (Ref. 10), including the work of Fuster (Ref. 9) and of Issac (Ref. 11) on the association with the reticular formation and there seems little doubt that the experimental findings mediate a relationship such as that proposed.

It follows from what has been said that the very divergent findings with respect to the proposed relationship between introversion and eyeblink conditioning which form such a prominent feature of the literature, including the Russian, are only to be expected, considering that many different variations of type of reinforcement, CS–UCS interval and strength of UCS and CS have been employed. The experiment to be reported here, which was carried out by A. Levey in the Maudsley Laboratory, was specially designed to throw light on the hypotheses outlined above, relating to the change in the relation between conditioning and introversion with change in the conditions of the experiment. Subjects were tested under all possible combinations of two conditions of reinforcement, two CS–UCS intervals and two UCS strengths; for each pair of conditions a prediction was made (which has already been outlined) as to which condition would favour the introverts as compared with the extraverts. The detailed conditions of testing were as follows: *Reinforcement schedule*—100 per cent reinforcement against 67 per cent reinforcement. *CS–UCS interval:* 500 msec vs. 400 msec. *UCS strength:* 6 pounds per square inch vs. 3 pounds per square inch.

Subjects were selected on the basis of the Maudsley Personality

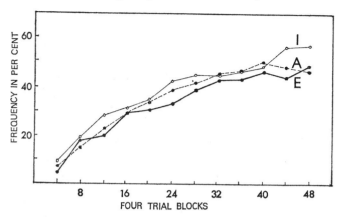

Figure 54. Rate of eyelid conditioning in extraverts, introverts and ambiverts under combination of all parameters.

Inventory and categorized as extraverted, introverted or intermediate (ambivert); they were also categorized as high, low or average on neuroticism. Equal numbers were then chosen from each of these categories, until 18 subjects had been included in each of the 8 experimental groups (combinations of reinforcement schedule, CS–UCS interval and UCS strength), making a total of 144 subjects in all; all of these were male. Fig. 54 shows the growth, over 48 acquisition trials, of conditioned habit strength for the extraverted, introverted and ambivert groups; there is a slight superiority of the introvert group over the extravert group in this overall comparison, amounting to some 20 per cent on the last few trials; the ambivert group is situated in between the other two groups most of the time, although it overlaps with both other groups on occasion. The differences are not significant on an analysis of variance, largely because of the tremendous size of the variances; this of course is not unexpected because of the variations in testing conditions imposed by our general scheme. Figs. 55 and 56 show the results for weak and strong UCS respectively; as expected the weak UCS shows introverts much more conditionable, while the strong UCS shows extraverts more conditionable. Ambiverts are intermediate between the two extreme groups. This reversal is quite dramatic and supports the prediction.

The results for the 400 and 800 msec CS–UCS interval show, as expected, that the short interval favours the introverts; for the long interval there is very little difference between the groups (Figs. 57 and 58). The

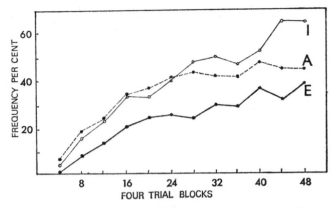

Figure 55. Rate of eyelid conditioning for introverts, ambiverts and extraverts under weak UCS conditions.

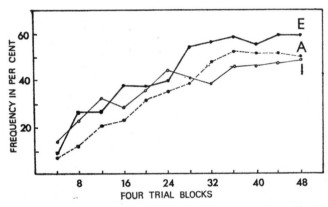

Figure 56. Rate of eyelid conditioning for extraverts, ambiverts and introverts under strong UCS conditions.

results for partial and continuous reinforcement show that there is a slight tendency for partial reinforcement to favour the introverts, but this tendency is not strong enough to give much support to our hypothesis (Figs. 59 and 60). If the results of this experiment can be taken as representative, we might conclude that strength of UCS was the most important parameter, followed by CS–UCS interval, with reinforcement schedule last. However, any such generalization would of course be restricted to the values of UCS strength, interval duration and reinforcement schedule adopted in this experiment; there is no reason to suppose that these are in any sense optimal. It seems very likely that much greater differences between introverts and extraverts could be demonstrated with better choice of parameter values. In particular, pressures of less than 3 pounds per square inch as UCS strength and intervals even shorter than 400 msec, present good prospects of improving discrimination.

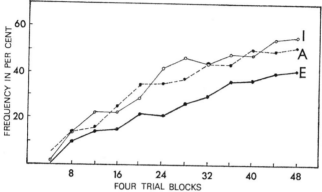

Figure 57. Rate of eyelid conditioning for introverts, ambiverts and extraverts under short CS-UCS interval conditions.

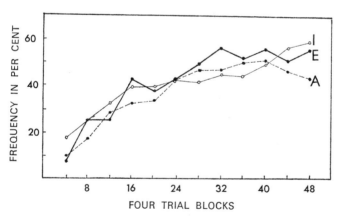

Figure 58. Rate of eyelid conditioning for extraverts, ambiverts and introverts under long CS-UCS interval conditions.

Figs. 61 and 62 present results for optimal and worst combinations of conditions respectively, i.e., weak UCS, short CS–UCS interval and partial reinforcement (Fig. 61) as against strong UCS, long CS–UCS

R*

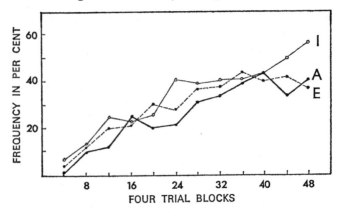

Figure 59. Rate of eyelid conditioning for introverts, ambiverts and extraverts under partial reinforcement conditions.

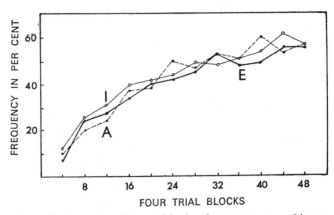

Figure 60. Rate of eyelid conditioning for extraverts, ambiverts and introverts under 100 per cent reinforcement conditions.

interval and continuous reinforcement (Fig. 62). The difference is obvious and may be summed up in the intra-group correlations. For the optimal conditions, the correlation between introversion and conditioning is $+0.40$, while for the worst conditions it is -0.31; this difference is significant at the 1 per cent level on a one-tail test. In the combination of conditions favourable, according to theory, to the introverts, we find that after 30 trials the extraverts show no evidence of any conditioning at all, while the introverts have reached a level of conditioning at which 46 per cent of responses are in fact conditioned. Conversely, under conditions favouring the extraverts, these produce after 30 trials almost twice as many conditioned responses as do the introverts.

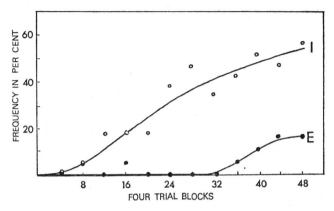

Figure 61. Rate of eyelid conditioning for introverts and extraverts under conditions of partial reinforcement, weak UCS, and short CS-UCS interval.

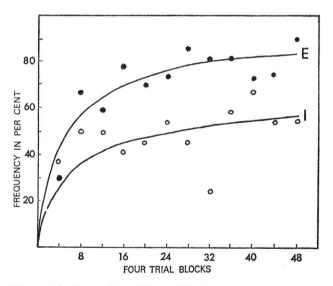

Figure 62. Rate of eyelid conditioning for extraverts and introverts under conditions of 100 per cent reinforcement, strong UCS, and long CS-UCS interval.

When we say that conditions are favourable to the introverted or the extraverted group, we are of course speaking in terms of comparison of the one group with the other. In fact there are many interesting comparisons to be made taking into account absolute levels of conditioning. Thus introverts achieve identical levels of conditioning at the end of the experiment (54 per cent), but they reach this end along quite different paths. (Fig. 63).

The introverts working under unfavourable conditions (as compared with extraverts) achieve a high level of conditioning very early (after 4 trials only) and do not change much after that; under favourable conditions (as compared to extraverts) they show a regular increase which gradually brings them up to the same level. Extraverts under favourable and unfavourable conditions behave quite differently (Fig. 64), as shown by the fact that the terminal values reached by them after 48 trials differ sharply; under unfavourable conditions, only 12 per cent condition, under favourable conditions, 92 per cent! If these data can be assumed to be generally valid, then it would seem that extraverts are much more at the mercy of conditions, while introverts ultimately reach reasonable levels of conditioning regardless of conditions. Replication of these results would seem to be desirable before too much effort is spent on explanations along theoretical lines. (It is interesting to note that the ambivert group shows very similar growth patterns under both conditions, namely the usual gradual increment in number of conditioned responses (Fig. 65). As might have been expected, the strong

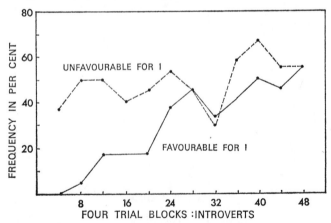

Figure 63. Rate of eyelid conditioning for introverts under conditions favourable and unfavourable for introverts.

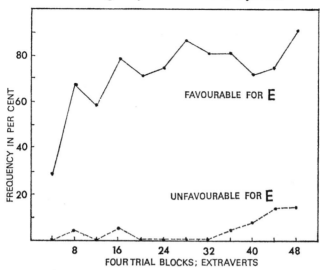

Figure 64. Rate of eyelid conditioning for extraverts under conditions favourable and unfavourable for extraverts.

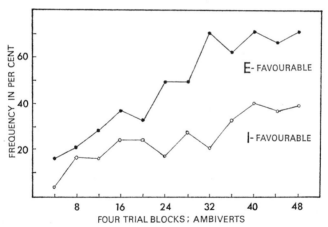

Figure 65. Rate of eyelid conditioning for ambiverts under conditions favourable for introverts and extraverts, respectively.

UCS-continuous reinforcement conditions result in better conditioning, but there is no dramatic difference in the shape of the curves; all that is apparent is a lower starting point and a less marked slope for the weak UCS-partial reinforcement conditions.)

In this case conditions may be said to be *overall* favourable or un-favourable according to the total amount of conditioning that takes place under these conditions for the total population tested. Thus strong UCS intensity produces quicker conditioning than does weak UCS intensity; 800 msec CS–UCS intervals are somewhat better than 400 msec intervals; continuous reinforcement is better than partial reinforcement. The results clearly show that the conditions which are favourable for the formation of conditioned responses *on the whole*, are, in this experiment at least, also those which are favourable to extraverts and unfavourable to introverts, respectively. One might be tempted to argue from these facts towards some general law of the kind: introverts form conditioned responses even under objectively unfavourable conditions; extraverts only form conditioned responses when conditions are optimal. Such a statement is in line with our results, but much more work along these lines will be required before we can regard it as well supported; clearly the particular selection of conditions of this one experiment and the inevitably small number of subjects tested, restrict the generality of our findings. Nevertheless, it may be useful to restate our major finding in this form, if only to suggest a possible link with clinical, penological and other applied fields (Refs. 1 & 5).

SUMMARY

It is now time to summarize the results obtained. As has been stressed before (Ref. 3), it is meaningless to compare groups of persons on a test of conditioning unless parameters are precisely specified and if individual differences are the subject matter of the experiment, then such para-meters must be chosen in accordance with a specific theory. The fact that the literature is full of contradictory results, achieved with appar-ently random selection of parameters, reinforces this point. Our data show that it is possible to choose conditions which give results favouring introverted subjects or extraverted subjects; what is interesting and important is that these conditions could be formulated and stated on theoretical grounds, so that the experimental results serve to support and verify the theory. The overall failure of the experiment to show differences between introverts and extraverts at a reasonable level of significance is also in line with the hypothesis; when conditions are evenly balanced between favouring one group or the other, then averag-ing results over all conditions should not give results strikingly favouring one side. It should be noted that the conditions chosen were by no means extreme; it will be interesting to continue experimentation with more extreme conditions and thus render the differentiation of introverts and extraverts even more clear-cut and obvious than has been possible in the present experiment. It should also be interesting to continue work on eyeblink conditioning by linking it up with experimental measures of the Pavlov-Teplov dimension of weak-strong nervous system; predictions here are in general very similar to those made in connection with introversion-extraversion. Altogether it is believed that Pavlov was right in pointing out the fact that individual differences in conditioning are extremely prominent in work in this field and that these differences hold much promise in mediating predictions and explanations of human conduct, neurosis and crime. Efforts to do so (Refs. 1, 6 & 8) can only benefit from more intensive study of the relation between personality and different parameters of eyeblink conditioning.

REFERENCES

1. EYSENCK, H. J., *The Dynamics of Anxiety and Hysteria*. London: Routledge & Kegan Paul, 1957.
2. ——, Conditioning and personality, *Brit. J. Psychol.*, **53**, 299–305, 1962.
3. ——, *The Maudsley Personality Inventory*. San Diego: Educ. Indust. Testing Service, 1959.
4. ——, The biological basis of personality. *Nature*, **199**, 1031–1034, 1963.
5. ——, *Crime and Personality*. Boston: Houghton-Mifflin, 1964.
6. ——, Extraversion and the acquisition of eyeblink and GSR conditioned responses. *Psychol. Bull.*, **63**, 258–270, 1965.
7. ——, *The Biological Basis of Personality*. Springfield: C. C. Thomas, 1967.
8. —— & RACHMAN, S., *Causes and Cures of Neurosis*. San Diego: R. R. Knapp, 1965.
9. FUSTER, J. M., Effects of stimulation of brain stem on tachistoscopic perception. *Science*, **127**, 150, 1958.
10. GRAY, J., *Pavlov's Typology*. Oxford: Pergamon Press, 1965.
11. ISAAC, W., Arousal and reaction times in cats. *J. comp. physiol. Psychol.*, **53**, 234–236, 1960.

12. KILLAM, E. K., Drug actions on the brain stem reticular formation. *Pharmacol. Per.*, **14**, 175–224, 1962.
13. KIMBLE, G. A., *Hilgard and Marquis' Conditioning and Learning.* New York: Appleton-Century, 1961.
14. MAGOUN, H., *The Waking Brain.* Springfield: C. C. Thomas, 1963.
15. ROSS, L. E. & SPENCE, K. W., Eyelid conditioning performance under partial reinforcement as a function of UCS intensity. *J. exp. Psychol.*, **59**, 379–382, 1960.
16. SAVAGE, R. D., Electro-cerebral activity, extraversion and neuroticism. *Brit. J. Psychiat.*, **110**, 98–100, 1964.

56

Pupillary Response, Conditioning and Personality

DAVID S. HOLMES[1]

First published in
Journal of Personality and Social Psychology, **5**, 98–103, 1967

THIS research tested the relationship of levels of acetylcholine and norepinephrine (as inferred from speed of pupillary constriction and dilation) to awareness of an environmental contingency, performance on a verbal conditioning task and personality. High levels of acetylcholine, inferred from rapid constriction, were found to be significantly related to greater awareness of an environmental contingency, superior performance in verbal conditioning and to introverted personality traits as measured by self-report and peer ratings. Relationships between levels of norepinephrine, inferred from speed of dilation, awareness, conditioning and personality were for the most part inconsistent and non-significant. The conclusion was that speed or efficiency of neural transmission at cholinergic synapses, where acetylcholine is the transmitter substance, was related to conditioning and personality. The lack of significant findings regarding norepinephrine was attributed to the probable limitation of this mediator to synapses of the autonomic system.

INTRODUCTION

In the past few years a number of important findings have been reported relating brain chemistry to learning. Rosenzweig, Krech & Bennett have shown that rats which performed better in three different types of situations had greater amounts of cholinesterase (ChE) in the cerebral cortex (Refs. 14 & 15). It has been known for some time that acetylcholine (ACh) is important in facilitating neural transmission at the synapses (Ref. 2) and since ChE breaks up or hydrolyzes ACh after the transmission of the impulse, ChE was used as an indicator of the amount of ACh available; that is, better learning was accompanied by higher

---

[1] The author wishes to express his appreciation to Lee Sechrest for his assistance in the design of the research and to E. Femme for her assistance throughout the project.

levels of ChE and, inferentially, higher levels of ACh. In another approach to the study of neural transmission and learning, Russell, Watson & Frankenhaeuser have shown that animals fed a ChE inhibitor, Systox, which consequently reduced the hydrolysis of ACh, showed slower extinction than normal animals (Ref. 18). All of these data suggest that there is an important relationship between speed or efficiency of neural transmission and learning.

The application of this work to humans was retarded by the lack of appropriate techniques for measuring ACh or ChE levels. Recently, however, Rubin proposed that speed of pupillary constriction may be taken as an indicator of the amount of the cholinergic mediator (ACh) present (Ref. 16). It should be recalled that synapses employing ACh as a transmitter are called cholinergic, while those employing norepinephrine are called adrenergic (Ref. 4). The pupillary response provided a good measure of cholinergic mediator, because, as Rubin pointed out, 'the magnitude of constriction is an increasing monotonic function of the amount of the cholinergic mediator liberated' (Ref. 17, p. 567); that is, faster constriction is indicative of greater amounts of ACh at cholinergic synapses. In like manner, Rubin suggested that speed of pupillary dilation be used as a measure of the amount of the adrenergic mediator (norepinephrine) present at the synapses, for again it seemed justified to assume a monotonic relationship (Ref. 17). The introduction of these measures has thus provided what seems to be simple and reliable measures of the transmitter substances and, consequently, predictors of learning.

If pupillary response is a predictor of learning in the human, then the application of this predictor might be carried one step further, into the area of personality. It has been theorized that an individual who learns or conditions rapidly tends to be highly sensitive to his environment, anxious, inhibited, compulsive, introspective and often ill at ease. Conversely, the individual who conditions slowly would tend to be impulsive, irresponsible, unreliable and insensitive to the environment and to the feelings of others. A considerable amount of research has been accumulated which supports the relationship between this dimension of personality and speed of conditioning (Refs. 7, 9, 11 & 13). Eysenck has referred to easily conditioned individuals as introverts and to less easily conditioned individuals as extraverts; he has subsequently developed a scale to measure these characteristics (Ref. 6).

The present study was an attempt to test the relationships between speed of neural transmission, conditionability and personality. On the basis of earlier work with animals and the theoretical extrapolation to personality, it was predicted that subjects with inferred higher levels of the transmitter substances, as measured by the pupillary responses, would (a) be more aware of an environmental contingency, (b) evidence superior performance in verbal conditioning and (c) rate themselves and be rated by peers as generally more introverted in personality.

METHOD

The subjects were 49 women in an introductory psychology class at Northwestern University. The first part of the experiment consisted of a verbal conditioning procedure similar to the one reported by Taffel (Ref. 20). Each subject was given 80 3×5 inch cards. On each card was typed a different past-tense verb. Below the verb were the pronouns I, we, you, he, she and they. The pronouns appeared in a different order on each card. The subject's task was to make up a sentence using the verb and the pronoun of her choice. The experimenter sat behind a screen which separated him from the subject and recorded the pronouns used. The experimenter did not reinforce any of the subject's responses on trials 1 through 20. For trials 21 through 80, the experimenter responded with the word 'good' in a flat, unemotional tone at the end of any sentence starting with the pronouns I or we. After completing the conditioning procedure, each subject was questioned concerning her awareness of the reinforcement contingency, according to a modified form of the inquiry schedule developed by DeNike & Spielberger (Ref. 1). In addition to assessing awareness, two items of the inquiry were used to determine the subject's behavioural intentions; that is, if the subject was aware of the reinforcement contingency, did the knowledge have a conscious effect on her behaviour?

Following the verbal conditioning procedure, photographic measurements were taken of pupillary dilation and constriction. During the photographic procedure, the subject sat in a chair with her head held firmly in a Bausch and Lomb chin rest and forehead brace. The photographs of the eyes were taken with an Asahi Pentax single-lens reflex camera which was fitted with an extension bellows and an f4·5, 105 mm lens. The lens was 16 inches from the subject's eyes. The adapting light used to constrict the pupils was placed 9 inches from the subject's eyes, at a point 5 inches below the plane between the subject's eyes and the camera lens. This light source consisted of a 3·5-inch square of white frosted glass which was illuminated from behind by a 100w white bulb.

The lens of this light source was tilted so that the light was aimed directly at the subject's eyes. 8½ inches to either side of the camera lens and 14 inches from the subject's eyes were the infrared light sources, which were 2·75-inch squares. The illumination for these lights was provided by 200w bulbs which were housed in 10-inch photoflood reflectors. The light exposed to the subject was filtered through a Kodak Wratten filter No. 87. Consequently, the only light visible to the subject during the photographing of the dilating pupils was a dull red glow on either side of her field of vision. The intensity of the visible light was less than 0·5 footcandle.

All subjects were given the following explanation of the apparatus and procedure:

'This apparatus will be used for taking photographic measurements of your eye. During the time the photographs are being taken, I will want you to keep your chin firmly in the chin rest and your forehead against the metal brace. While in this position, look straight forward at the lens of the camera. If you cannot see the lens because it is too dark, look straight forward at the point at which you think the lens should be. A series of photographs will be taken with this white light on and a series of photographs will be taken with this light off. When the light is off, you may notice a very dim red glow on each side of the side panels. Ignore these and continue to look straight ahead.'

After the subject had her head positioned in the head rest, the room light was extinguished. Ten seconds later the adapting light and the infrared lights were turned on for 15 seconds to maximally constrict the pupil. At the end of this interval, the adapting light was turned off. Photographs of the dilating pupils were taken after intervals of 5, 10, 15, 30, 45 and 60 seconds. Prior to photographing the constricting pupils, the pupils were dark adapted for 1 minute. After 1 minute of complete darkness the adapting light and the infrared lights were turned on. The constricting pupils were photographed after intervals of 1, 2, 3, 4 and 5 seconds with a different trial being used for each measurement. The time intervals were controlled by a Hunter interval timer. Pupillary size after the various intervals of time was determined by projecting the developed negatives on a screen and measuring the diameter of the pupil with a millimeter ruler. The negatives were projected from a distance of 17 feet with a 5-inch lens. Since the photographs of the pupil carried only an identification number and the measurements were recorded on numbered data sheets, the experimenter did not know the identity of the subject who was being measured.

After completion of the photographic procedures, the subjects filled out a questionnaire which contained the Extraversion (E) and Neuroticism (N) scales from the Maudsley Personality Inventory and the A, R and MA scales from the MMPI.

Before leaving the laboratory, each subject was given three peer-rating forms and three envelopes. She was instructed to give one form and envelope to each of the three girls whom she felt knew her best and ask them to rate her on the various items. The form consisted of 16 descriptive statements about personality characteristics. All of the items were worded in the positive direction. 8 items described introverted characteristics and 8, extraverted characteristics. Within each set of 8 items, half were socially desirable and half less desirable, though none were completely undesirable. Rating of a subject on this form was done by placing an X on a 9-inch graphic scale beneath each item. The scale had end points labelled 'Very Descriptive' and 'Not Descriptive'. All rating forms were returned to the experimenter in sealed, self-addressed envelopes. The scoring key was constructed so that extraverted descriptions received higher scores. The final score on the peer-rating form was the sum of the ratings given by all three judges.

RESULTS

Speed of Pupillary Constriction

The mean and SD of the proportion of constriction after each interval are presented in Table 1. It should be pointed out that 100 per cent constriction was not reported in this table because of what might be called a 'bounce effect'; that is, some subjects reached maximal constriction in 3 or 4 seconds and then dilated slightly, which caused a drop in the constriction curve for these subjects and lowered the overall mean proportion of constriction after 4 and 5 seconds. Because of this bounce, the measurement after 4 and 5 seconds for some subjects was not an accurate measure of the speed of constriction and therefore the measures taken after 1, 2 and 3 seconds were judged to be most accurate for comparing rates of constriction.

Extreme subjects (fast and slow) were identified as those whose proportion of constriction after at least two of the three intervals was plus or minus one SD from the mean of the distribution for each respective interval. Intermediate subjects were identified as those whose propor-

TABLE 1

PROPORTION OF CONSTRICTION AFTER INTERVALS OF TIME

Sec	M	SD
1·0	63·69	10·15
2·0	82·73	8·07
3·0	92·76	5·35
4·0	98·10	2·57
5·0	98·10	4·78

Note: N = 49

tion of constriction was within plus or minus one SD of the mean of each respective distribution. 8 subjects were identified as fast constrictors, 17 as intermediate speed constrictors and 8 as slow constrictors.

Speed of Pupillary Constriction and Awareness: On the basis of their responses to the awareness inquiry, the subjects were classified as either aware or not aware of the reinforcement contingency. (It should be noted that there was 98 per cent agreement between two independent judges with regard to classifying the subjects on awareness or behavioural intentions.) To test the hypotheses relating increased awareness and high ACh levels, the proportions of aware and not aware subjects within the fast and slow constricting groups were compared. A Fisher test of exact probability indicated that there was a significant (0·05) relationship between fast constriction and awareness. Of the fast constrictors, 62·5 per cent were aware, while 12·5 per cent of the slow constrictors were aware.

Speed of Pupillary Constriction and Verbal Conditioning: Before discussing the relationship between speed of constriction and performance curves in verbal conditioning, some comment should be made concerning the subjects' conscious attitude toward performance on this task. When the postconditioning inquiries were scored for behavioural intentions, it was found that some of the aware subjects had consciously fought against giving conditioned responses. This tendency on the part of some subjects and the effect it had on the data has been noted and reported earlier (Refs. 8 & 10). Since the use of subjects who reported consciously resisting the giving of conditioned responses would distort any relationship between performance and speed of constriction, in Fig. 66 where performance curves for fast, intermediate and slow

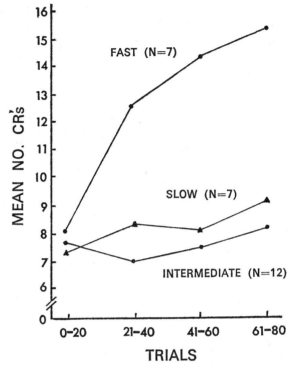

Figure 66. Verbal conditioning performance curves
for subjects with fast, intermediate, and slow pupillary
constriction.

constrictors are plotted, only those subjects who did not resist conditioning were used.

Analysis of variance for repeated measures (Ref. 3) indicated that
there were significant differences between the groups ($F = 53·54$,
$df = 2·23$, $p < 0·01$) across blocks of trials ($F = 5·11$, $df = 3·69$,
$p < 0·01$) and the Groups × Trials interaction was significant ($F = 3·57$,
$df = 6·69$, $p < 0·01$). The correlations between the total number of
conditioned responses given on trials 21–80 and the proportion of
constriction after intervals of 1, 2 and 3 seconds were 0·33 ($p < 0·05$),
0·44 ($p = < 0·005$) and 0·52 ($p < 0·005$), respectively. All of these
results clearly indicated that there was a significant relationship between
fast pupillary constriction, which was indicative of an inferred high
ACh level and performance on a verbal conditioning task. (It should be

noted that since awareness is related to verbal conditioning performance—Refs. 8, 10 & 19—the findings relating the pupillary response to awareness and to verbal conditioning performance are not completely independent. They were presented separately in this paper because, while related, they represented different types of functioning and behaviour which have been of interest to psychologists.)

Speed of Pupillary Constriction and Personality Measures: When the fast and slow constrictors were compared over the personality measures, the slow constrictors were found to be more extraverted than fast constrictors, as measured both by the E scale (t = 3·09, df = 14, p<0·01) and by the peer-rating form (t = 1·78, df = 14, p<0·10). Fast and slow constrictors did not differ significantly on the measures of general maladjustment, that is, the A, MA and N scales (t = 0·41, 0·83, 0·43, respectively; df = 14).

In summary, fast pupillary constriction which is indicative of high levels of ACh was significantly related (a) to the development of awareness of a reinforcement contingency, (b) to superior performance on a verbal conditioning task and (c) to the personality characteristics of introversion.

Speed of Pupillary Dilation

The mean and SD of the proportion of dilation after each of 6 intervals are presented in Table 2. Because there was only limited variability in the subjects' responses after the intervals of 30, 45 and 60 seconds, extreme subjects were selected on the basis of their dilation after 5, 10 and 15 seconds. Fast (N = 8), intermediate (N = 19) and slow (N = 6) dilators were then selected in the same way as extreme constrictors.

TABLE 2

PROPORTION OF DILATION AFTER SIX INTERVALS OF TIME

Sec	M	SD
5	77·55	8·74
10	87·86	6·99
15	92·45	5·85
30	95·94	4·43
45	97·59	3·97
60	98·86	1·81

Note: N = 49

Speed of Pupillary Dilation and Awareness: A Fisher test of exact probabilities comparing the frequencies of aware and not aware subjects within the fast and slow dilating groups indicated that the distribution was well within the limits of chance occurrence.

Speed of Pupillary Dilation and Verbal Conditioning: When comparing the performance curves of the fast, intermediate and slow dilators, the data from aware subjects who consciously resisted conditioning were not used. Analysis of variance indicated that there was a significant increase in conditioned responses over trials (F = 5·56, df = 3·63, p<0·01), but that there were no significant differences between the groups (F = 0·06, df = 2·21).

Speed of Pupillary Dilation and Personality Measures: When the fast and slow dilators were compared over the personality measures, the fast dilators evidenced significantly higher E-scale scores (t = 2·70, df = 12, p<0·05), but the groups did not differ on the peer-rating form measure of extraversion (t = 0·51, df = 12). As was the case with subjects differing in speed of constriction, the fast and slow dilators did not differ on the A, N or MA scales (t = 1·4, 1·62, 1·54, respectively; df = 14).

DISCUSSION

The results of the present study clearly related the speed of pupillary constriction to awareness of an environmental contingency, susceptibility to verbal conditioning and to personality in terms of the introversion-extraversion dimension. Since more rapid constriction is supposedly indicative of greater amounts of ACh at the cholinergic synapses, the results of this study were in agreement with earlier findings on animals where subjects with an inferred higher level of ACh evidenced better performance. The results of the present study, however, extended the findings to the area of personality and offered support for the hypothesis relating high levels of ACh to environmental awareness, rapid conditioning and consequently to introverted personality characteristics. That is, subjects with inferred high ACh levels who are more aware and more easily conditioned by environmental contingencies would be more likely to learn, or introject, the rules, restraints and anxieties of the environment than would their low ACh counterparts. The differences in neural conductivity and the concomitant differences in reactions and conditioning, would therefore play a major role in their personality characteristics with regard to the dimension of introversion and extraversion.

Some comments might be made in regard to the personality differences which the present author found to be associated with fast and slow constriction. Rubin recently reported differences in constriction between normals and neurotics (Ref. 17). The points on his Fig. 2 (p. 564) indicated that after each interval the neurotics had evidenced *more* constriction than had the normals; that is, the neurotics were faster constrictors. Though consistent, the differences were not significant. When the diagnoses of the neurotic subjects were checked (p. 563), it was found that all of these subjects could be classified as suffering from *introverted* disorders. In the present study fast constrictors were significantly more introverted. The independent-dependent variables have been reversed in the two studies but when Rubin's neurotics are seen as introverted, the results of the two studies are consistent. The fact that Rubin's findings were not significant could be attributed to the fact that his introverted neurotics were compared to an unselected sample of normals, a sample which, it is fairly certain, would have included introverted normals who would thus have decreased the differences between the groups.

The results using speed of dilation, the measure of the adrenergic mediator, were for the most part inconsistent and nonsignificant. This probably stemmed from the fact that 'only the cholinergic transmitters have been proved to be transmitters within the brain', while the adrenergic transmitters may be limited to the autonomic system (Ref. 12, p. 554); that is, adrenergic synapses may not have played a role in the responses measured in this study.

The consistency of the findings within this study, as well as the agreement between the results of this project and earlier research on animals, was very encouraging. It seems clear that if the pupillary response is in fact a function of ACh, the level of this transmitter substance is an important determinant of psychological functioning.

REFERENCES

1. DeNike, L. & Spielberger, C., Induced mediating states in verbal conditioning. *Journal of Verbal Learning & Verbal Behaviour*, **1,** 339–345, 1963.

2. ECCLES, J., *The Physiology of Nerve Cells*. Baltimore: Johns Hopkins Press, 1957.

3. EDWARDS, A., *Experimental Design in Psychological Research*. New York: Holt, Rinehart & Winston, 1960.

4. EULER, U. VON, Autonomic neuroeffector transmission. In *Handbook of Physiology* (ed. J. Field, H. Magoun & V. Hall). Vol. 1. Washington, D.C.: American Physiological Society, 1959.

5. EYSENCK, H. J., *Dimensions of Personality*. London: Routledge & Kegan Paul, 1947.

6. ——, The questionnaire measurement of neuroticism and extraversion. *Riv. Psicol.*, **50**, 113–140, 1956.

7. ——, *Experiments in Personality*. London: Routledge & Kegan Paul, 1960.

8. FARBER, I., The things people say to themselves. *Amer. Psychol.*, **18**, 185–197, 1963.

9. FRANKS, C., Conditioning and personality: a study of normal and neurotic subjects. *J. abnorm. soc. Psychol.*, **52**, 143–150, 1956.

10. HOLMES, D., Awareness, Intentions and Verbal Conditioning Performance. Paper read at Midwestern Psychological Association, Chicago, May 1966.

11. JOHNS, J. & QUAY, H., The effect of social reward on verbal conditioning in psychopathic neurotic military offenders. *J. consult. Psychol.*, **26**, 217–220, 1962.

12. MORGAN, C., *Physiological Psychology*. New York: McGraw-Hill, 1965.

13. QUAY, H. C. & HUNT, W. A., Psychopathy, neuroticism and verbal conditioning: a replication and extension. *J. consult. Psychol.*, **29**, 283, 1965.

14. ROSENZWEIG, M., KRECH, D. & BENNETT, E., Brain chemistry and adaptive behaviour. In *Biological and Biochemical Bases of Behaviour* (ed. H. Harlow and C. Woolsey). Madison: University of Wisconsin Press, 1958.

15. ——, —— & ——, Heredity, environment, brain chemistry and learning. In *Current Trends in Psychological Theory: A Bicentennial Programme* (ed. R. Patton). Pittsburgh: University of Pittsburgh Press, 1961.

16. RUBIN, L., Pupillary reactivity as a measure of adrenergic-cholinergic mechanisms in the study of psychotic behaviour. *J. nerv. ment. Dis.*, **130**, 386–400, 1960.

17. RUBIN, L., Autonomic dysfunction as a concomitant of neurotic behaviour. *J. nerv. ment. Dis.*, **138**, 558–574, 1964.
18. RUSSELL, R., WATSON, R. & FRANKENHAEUSER, M., Effects of chronic reductions in brain cholinesterase activity on acquisition and extinction of a conditioned avoidance response. *Scand. J. Psychol.*, **2**, 21–29, 1961.
19. SPIELBERGER, C., Theoretical and epistemological issues in verbal conditioning. In *Directions in Psycholinguistics* (ed. S. Rosenberg). New York: Macmillan, 1965.
20. TAFFEL, C., Anxiety and the conditioning of verbal behaviour. *J. abnorm. soc. Psychol.*, **51**, 496–501, 1955.

57

GSR Conditioning and Personality Factors in Alcoholics and Normals[1]

MURIEL D. VOGEL[2]

First published in
Journal of Abnormal and Social Psychology, **6**, 417–421, 1961

INTRODUCTION

EYSENCK has suggested that the ease with which CRs are acquired and retained is dependent upon the personality factor of introversion-extraversion (Ref. 2). Franks has examined this hypothesis by comparing eyeblink conditioning of clinically diagnosed hysterics with that of 'dysthymics' (i.e., patients suffering from anxiety, reactive depressions and obsessions or compulsions) (Ref. 3). These two groups are identified as 'neurotic extraverts' and 'neurotic introverts', respectively, in Eysenck's personality schema. The hysterics were found to acquire the conditioned eyeblink more slowly than the dysthymics, who conditioned quickly. No difference in conditioning was found between a normal group and a neurotic group containing hysterics and dysthymics. Similar results also were obtained in another study which examined the conditioned eyeblink of paid normal subjects in relation to personality tests of extraversion and neuroticism (Ref. 4). More extraversive subjects, defined in terms of higher test scores on the Maudsley Personality Inventory (MPI), acquired the CR more slowly and extinguished this response more quickly than did less extraversive (i.e., more introversive) subjects, but no relation between conditioning and neuroticism test scores was observed.

The conditioned galvanic skin reflex (GSR) was recorded simultaneously with conditioned eyeblink in Franks' study (Ref. 3). GSR

[1] This paper is adapted from a dissertation submitted in partial fulfilment of the requirements for the PhD degree at the University of Toronto.

[2] The author wishes to express her appreciation to A. H. Shephard for his advice in connection with this study and to R. H. Walters for assistance in the preparation of the paper.

conditioning was developed more slowly in hysterics than in dysthymics, but the differences between the two groups were slight and extinction could not be examined because GSR adaptation occurred too rapidly under Franks' testing procedures. He suggested that the difference between the groups in GSR conditioning might be reduced because of the low intensity airpuff which was employed as the UCS. He noted that this weak UCS sometimes failed to elicit the unconditioned GSR after the first few trials. Vogel, using a bell as the UCS, examined GSR conditioning of alcoholics in relation to the personality variables of extraversion and neuroticism (Ref. 8). Although acquisition and extinction of the conditioned GSR was found to relate as predicted to extraversion scores on the MPI, the rate of CR acquisition was observed also to correlate with neuroticism scores. Vogel's observations (Ref. 8) appear to contradict Eysenck's theory, which holds extraversion and neuroticism to be independent with extraversion as the variable relevant to conditioning behaviour.

Since there has been no research specifically designed to compare alcoholics and non-alcoholics in GSR conditioning, the correlations reported by Vogel between conditioning and personality may apply only to alcoholics (Ref. 8). This possibility was investigated in the present study. GSR conditioning was conducted with alcoholics and with non-alcoholic 'normals' (i.e., subjects not hospitalized for alcoholism or other psychiatric disorder). Because these two groups could be expected to differ in neuroticism and because the author's previous study found alcoholics' neuroticism scores correlated with speed of acquisition, covariance analyses were employed to permit an examination of GSR conditioning in relation to extraversion, statistically free from possible influence by differing neuroticism scores. The experimental hypothesis, in accord with Eysenck's theory, was formulated as follows:

1. When differences in neuroticism are controlled in alcoholic and non-alcoholic groups, the conditioned GSR is elicited in fewer trials and is more resistant to extinction in introversive than in extraversive subjects.

In addition to the finding that, among alcoholics, extraversion was associated with slower acquisition of the conditioned GSR, Vogel also noted that some alcoholics failed to display the conditioned response within the maximum number of trials permitted in her procedure (Ref. 8). On the assumption that slower conditioning is related solely to the extraversion variable, the following hypothesis was set forth:

2. Alcoholic and nonalcoholic individuals with extraversive test scores more frequently fail to display a conditioned GSR than those with introversive scores.

METHOD

Subjects

The sample of alcoholics consisted of 48 males, all of whom were admitted to the Alcoholism Research Foundation Clinic during the time the study was being conducted. All male patients in the clinic were tested, provided they could read English sufficiently to complete a questionnaire. Conditioning data could not be obtained for 8 subjects who failed to condition within the maximum number of trials permitted in the conditioning procedure. These subjects were considered separately for investigation of the second experimental hypothesis.

The control group contained 41 adult male volunteers who were not hospitalized for alcoholism. The majority of these subjects were first and second year University of Toronto summer school students. Volunteers were obtained also from the Ontario College of Education summer school course and from professional and technical personnel who visited the building where the experiment was being conducted. One subject in this group failed to display conditioning in the maximum number of acquisition trials allowed and was used only in the testing of the second hypothesis.

Procedure

All subjects completed the MPI (Ref. 1) and the alcoholics also reported on certain drinking behaviour. The latter data were obtained for another study reported elsewhere (Ref. 9).

The short term of hospitalization and the small patient population of the clinic made selection of only extremely high and low extraversion (E) score subjects highly impractical. For this reason, all available subjects were employed in this study. E scores on the MPI from both university students and alcoholic patients of the Alcoholism Research Foundation Clinic had been found previously (Ref. 7) not to differ significantly from the mean score of 24·6 reported by Eysenck for normal males (Ref. 1). The score of 24·6 was selected, therefore, as a measure of central tendency in E scores appropriate to samples of both alcoholics and non-alcoholics. Subjects were dichotomized into two categories— those below and those above 24·6. For convenience, these two categories are identified, respectively, as 'introversive' and 'extraversive'.

In the alcoholic sample of 40 cases, the mean E score was 20·98 (SD = 9·42) and the mean neuroticism (N) score was 35·85 (SD = 11·19). 20 subjects had E scores less than 24·6 and the remaining alcoholics had E scores greater than 24·6. The non-alcoholic group was also composed of 20 subjects in each of these two categories. The mean E score for the 40 non-alcoholics was 23·77 (SD = 9·42); the mean N score was 20·98 (SD = 11·59).

The GSR conditioning procedure and measures have been fully described elsewhere (Ref. 7) and may be summarized briefly. Subjects were tested individually for conditioning in a semi-soundproof room. The subject was told that the test was one of relaxation or repose and that his task was to spell the syllables which were presented to him by a memory drum.

The CS was a nonsense syllable, LAJ, which appeared 16 times, randomly placed among 35 other low association value syllables (Ref. 5). The memory drum presented a different syllable every 6 seconds. The UCS was an unpleasantly loud doorbell buzzer which reliably elicited the UCR of abrupt change in skin conductance. The first presentation of the CS was followed in 0·5 second by the UCS. A 50 per cent reinforcement schedule was employed so that alternate presentations of the CS were reinforced. Skin resistance was measured by a Lafayette 601-A GSR amplifier, using finger clamp electrodes and an Esterline-Angus pen recorder which traced the GSR continuously. Every 6 seconds, immediately before presentation of a new syllable by the memory drum, the GSR amplifier was balanced to the subject's skin resistance at that moment. This procedure automatically centred the Esterline-Angus pen at 0 on the record chart and permitted an easy comparison of GSR responses to each syllable during the conditioning procedure. Accurate identification of response to the CS and UCS was permitted by a side pen which automatically marked the chart when these stimuli were presented.

The criterion of conditioning was similar to that employed by Welch & Kubis (Refs. 11 & 12), which required three consecutive GSR reactions to the CS (LAJ) when unaccompanied by the UCS (bell). A GSR reaction was defined as a change in skin resistance to the CS which was larger than the subject's largest GSR occurring to the intervening buffer syllables. The number of reinforcements (i.e., the number of times the bell was presented) prior to achievement of this criterion constituted the count of trials to acquire the CR. A larger score thus indicated slower conditioning.

Vogel noted that this conditioning procedure could not satisfactorily be continued much longer than 20 minutes because of increasing boredom or restlessness on the part of the subject (Ref. 8). Slight shifts in posture, sighs, or comments aside to the experimenter all altered skin conductance somewhat and under such conditions a record of conditioning could not reliably be obtained. For this reason, a limit of 15 minutes was placed on acquisition trials. This duration permitted 24 presentations of the CS accompanied by UCS and 24 unreinforced presentations. The maximum possible score for a subject was thus 24 and if conditioning had not then been achieved, the subject was grouped with the others who 'failed to condition'.

Extinction trials commenced immediately after the subject displayed the CR. The UCS was no longer presented and the subject continued to spell syllables as they were presented by the memory drum. His GSR responses were recorded and the number of CRs to the first 10 unreinforced presentations of the CS were counted. A CR was defined as a GSR to the CS which was larger than the subject's largest GSR to the intervening neutral syllables. This score indicated the number of CRs during 10 extinction trials. The subject thereafter continued spelling syllables until 'extinction' occurred. 'Extinction' in this case was defined as 3 consecutive presentations of the unreinforced CS, all of which failed to elicit a CR. In many cases, this had occurred by the time the 10 standard extinction trials were completed. Two scores on extinction were thus obtained for each subject: the number of CRs displayed in 10 unreinforced trials and the number of CRs prior to extinction. In both cases, a larger score was considered to indicate greater CR resistance to extinction.

RESULTS

To examine GSR conditioning of alcoholic and non-alcoholic subjects in relation to extraversion, 2×2 covariance analyses were performed.[1] This technique was employed to adjust the conditioning scores for any influence attributed to neuroticism (N) score differences in these two groups.

[1] A detailed covariance analysis table for each conditioning measure has been deposited with the American Documentation Institute. Order Document No. 6868 from ADI Auxiliary Publications Project, Photoduplication Service, Library of Congress; Washington 25, D.C., remitting in advance $1.25 for microfilm or $1.25 for photocopies. Make checks payable to: Chief, Photoduplication Service, Library of Congress.

The covariance analysis of acquisition scores from alcoholic and non-alcoholic subjects is summarized in Table 1. After adjusting scores for the effect attributable to neuroticism, interaction effects were non-significant. Alcoholic and non-alcoholic groups do not appear to differ in the number of acquisition trials, but a significant effect for personality is obtained (F = 78·58, df = 1/75, p<0·01). Introversive subjects in alcoholic and non-alcoholic groups displayed the conditioned response in an average of 6·12 trials, whereas extraversive subjects averaged 13·05 trials before the CR was displayed.

Table 2 summarizes the covariance analysis of CRs displayed in 10 extinction trials. No significant interaction effect was obtained and no significant difference was observed between alcoholic and non-alcoholic subjects. The significant effect for personality (F = 43·56, df = 1/75, p<0·01) indicates that introversive alcoholics and non-alcoholics displayed more conditioned responses (mean score of 5·82) during 10 extinction trials than did extraversive subjects in these two groups (mean score of 3·20).

The covariance analysis of number of conditioned GSRs observed prior to extinction is summarized in Table 3. The only significant effect

TABLE 1

COVARIANCE ANALYSIS OF NUMBER OF TRIALS TO ACQUIRE A
CONDITIONED GSR WITH N SCORES OF THE MPI AS COVARIANT

Source	df	Adjusted MS	F	p
Group	1	7·9	0·65	>0·10
Personality	1	950·8	78·58	<0·01
Group × Personality interaction	1	20·7	1·71	>0·10
Within cells	75	12·1		

TABLE 2

COVARIANCE ANALYSIS OF NUMBER OF CONDITIONED GSRs OBSERVED DURING TEN
EXTINCTION TRIALS WITH N SCALE SCORES OF THE MPI AS COVARIANT

Source	df	Adjusted MS	F	p
Group	1	0·7	0·21	>0·10
Personality	1	148·1	43·56	<0·01
Group × Personality interaction	1	6·2	1·80	>0·10
Within cells	75	3·4		

TABLE 3

COVARIANCE ANALYSIS OF NUMBER OF CONDITIONED GSRs OBSERVED PRIOR TO
EXTINCTION WITH N SCALE SCORES OF THE MPI AS COVARIANT

Source	df	Adjusted MS	F	p
Group	1	8·15	0·55	>0·10
Personality	1	572·33	38·33	<0·01
Group × Personality interaction	1	6·61	0·44	>0·10
Within cells	75	14·93		

observed is that attributable to personality ($F = 38·22$, df $= 1/75$, $p < 0·01$). Introversive subjects displayed an average of 8·67 CRs prior to extinction, but extraversive subjects averaged only 3·47. The evidence from the analyses presented in Tables 2 and 3 both indicate that the conditioned GSR was more resistant to extinction in alcoholic and non-alcoholic subjects having introversive test scores than in those having extraversive scores.

An examination of personality test scores obtained in the group of 9 subjects who did not display conditioning in the maximum number of acquisition trials allowed revealed a striking agreement with the experimental hypothesis. All subjects who 'failed to condition' had E scores greater than 24·6 and thus would be categorized 'extraversive' in this study.

DISCUSSION

Introversive alcoholics and non-alcoholics displayed a conditioned GSR which was more quickly elicited and more resistant to extinction than that displayed by extraversive subjects. Since covariance analyses were performed in this study, the differences in GSR conditioning observed between introversive and extraversive subjects are statistically independent of differing neuroticism scores. This finding is in accord with Franks' studies of conditioned eyeblink (Refs. 3 & 4) and may be interpreted to support Eysenck's theory which asserts that condition-ability is dependent upon extraversion and is unrelated to neuroticism. An explanation for the seemingly contradictory observation of an association between neuroticism and GSR conditioning in alcoholics (Ref. 8) is suggested in Eysenck's recently revised MPI manual. He reports that while extraversion and neuroticism scales are almost entirely independent, a slight negative correlation is obtained, particularly if the sample contains only subjects with high neuroticism scores. Since alcoholics are found to have high neuroticism scores, such a correlation could be expected in Vogel's sample (Ref. 8) and may explain her observed correlation between neuroticism and GSR conditionability.

The prediction that alcoholic and non-alcoholic subjects failing to display a conditioned GSR tend to have personality test scores classified as extraversive rather than introversive was supported by the observation that all 9 non-conditioned subjects had extraversive scores. Since 8 of these were alcoholics, this finding could suggest that difficulty in GSR conditioning under the procedures of this study is more typical of alcoholics than of individuals not hospitalized for alcoholism. In contrast to a mean extraversion score of 29·05 obtained by the 20 extraversive alcoholics who displayed GSR conditioning, the alcoholics who did not condition had a mean score of 32·38. This might also suggest that failure to display GSR conditioning is associated with an extreme degree of extraversion, indicated by unusually high scores on the MPI.

Some of the subjects who displayed the conditioning pattern verbalized no awareness of the systematic presentation of the bell with the CS, in many instances identifying the bell as a ringing telephone. Although it is almost certain that the academic backgrounds of some of the non-alcoholics would make them sophisticated in terms of conditioning techniques, these subjects were not observed to condition in consistently fewer trials than those who were completely naive to this procedure. Speed of acquisition and extinction of the CR appeared to be unrelated to the subject's prior knowledge of conditioning principles or to his failure to associate the occurrence of the bell with the CS. This observation is in accord with results from other studies of GSR conditioning (Ref. 10) and of conditioning the autonomic finger twitch response (Ref. 6), indicating that verbal instructions or prior knowledge of the required response did not influence the speed with which the CR was established or extinguished.

SUMMARY

Measures of GSR conditioning were obtained from 40 in-patients of an alcoholism clinic and from 40 non-alcoholic males. These subjects also completed the Maudsley Personality Inventory (MPI) which contains an introversion-extraversion scale. In accord with the experimental hypothesis, the CR was found to be more quickly acquired and more resistant to extinction in introversive than in extraversive subjects. Alcoholics and non-alcoholics did not differ either in mean extraversion scores or in mean rate of establishing and extinguishing the CR. In accord with the hypothesis that more extraversion is associated with poorer condition-ability, subjects who failed to display conditioning within the maximum number of training trials allowed were found to have extraversive test scores. It was noted that these results are consistent with some other eyeblink conditioning studies and might be interpreted as lending support to Eysenck's personality theory.

REFERENCES

1. EYSENCK, H. J., The questionnaire measurement of neuroticism and extraversion. *Riv. Psicol.*, **50**, 113–140, 1956.
2. ——, *Dynamics of Anxiety and Hysteria.* London: Routledge & Kegan Paul, 1957.
3. FRANKS, C. M., Conditioning and personality: a study of normal and neurotic subjects. *J. abnorm. soc. Psychol.*, **52**, 143–150, 1956.
4. ——, Personality factors and the rate of conditioning. *Brit. J. Psychol.*, **48**, 119–126, 1957.
5. GLAZE, J. A., The association value of nonsense syllables. *J. genet. Psychol.*, **35**, 255, 1928.
6. HEFFERLINE, R., KEENAN, B. & HARFORD, R., Escape and avoidance conditioning in human subjects without their observation of the response. *Science*, **130**, 1338–1339, 1959.
7. VOGEL, MURIEL D., Alcohol Drinking Behaviour Related to GSR Conditioning and Personality Factors in Alcoholics. Unpublished doctoral dissertation, University of Toronto Library, 1960.
8. ——, The relation of personality factors to GSR conditioning of alcoholics: an exploratory study. *Can. J. Psychol.*, **14**, 275–280, 1960.
9. ——, The relationship of personality factors to drinking patterns of alcoholics. *Quart. J. Stud. Alcohol.*, **22**, 394–400, 1961.
10. WALL, H. W. & GUTHRIE, G. M., Extinction of responses to sub-ceived stimuli. *J. genet. Psychol.*, **60**, 203–210, 1959.
11. WELCH, L. & KUBIS, J., Conditioned PGR in states of pathological anxiety. *J. nerv. ment. Dis.*, **105**, 372–381, 1947.
12. —— & ——, Effect of anxiety on conditioning rate and stability of PGR. *J. Psychol.*, **23**, 83–91, 1947.

58

Effects of Anxiety Level and Extraversion-Introversion on Probability Learning[1]

MICHAEL A. WALLACH & RUTHELLEN C. GAHM

First published in *Psychological Reports*, **7**, 387–398, 1960

INTRODUCTION

SUPPOSE an individual has to predict which of two events will occur on each of a series of tries and one of these events is more likely than the other although both in fact occur in a random sequence. How often will the rare event be predicted? Two factors might conceivably make for a high rate of predicting the rare event. It is the purpose of this study to separate them and examine their possible relationships to aspects of personality in an older sample.

A high rate of predicting the rare event will result if the person assumes there is some pattern to the rare event's occurrence and tries to solve the problem of accurately predicting when the rare event will occur (the 'problem' approach). For such a person, trying to 'catch' the rare event's occurrence is a challenge which he accepts: being correct in predicting the rare event is more important to him than being correct in predicting the frequent event. On the other hand, a high rate of predicting the rare event also will result if the person simply isn't sensitive to the infrequency of the rare event and hence treats it as if it occurs more often than it does (the '50:50' approach).

Although both 'problem' and '50:50' approaches lead to more frequent prediction of the rare alternative, the former is a much more 'thoughtful' approach to the task than the latter. Can we distinguish the two in terms of some additional response measure? Latency of predicting the rare alternative seems to provide a method. If high frequency of choosing the rare alternative is due to the 'problem' approach, then

[1] This investigation was supported by a research grant (M–2269) from the National Institute of Mental Health, Public Health Service, conducted under the auspices of The Age Center of New England, Inc. Grateful thanks are due Marguerite Braun, Leonard R. Green and Lynne Hamilton, for aid in data analysis.

choice of the rare alternative should be preceded by a longer latency than choice of the frequent alternative: S should be especially thoughtful before predicting the rare event since its accurate prediction is the challenge for him; it is the rare event with which his hypotheses specifically are concerned. Predicting the frequent event, on the other hand, is more likely to be correct and hence poses less of a problem. If, on the other hand, high choice frequency for the rare event is due to the '50:50' approach, then S should be about as fast in predicting the rare alternative as he is in predicting the frequent one since he is insensitive to the difference between them. Although a frequency measure alone, then, is not sufficient to distinguish the 'problem' and '50:50' approaches, measuring latencies as well as frequencies seem to provide a way of making this discrimination. We hence may operationally define the 'problem' approach in terms of high choice frequency for the rare event and also a longer latency of choice for the rare event than for the frequent one. The '50:50' approach, on the other hand, may be defined in terms of high choice frequency for the rare event and also as short a latency of choice for the rare event as for the frequent one.

While clear relationships have been found between probability learning performance and stimulus condition independent variables (such as the degree of deviation from 50:50 in the relative frequencies of the two events),[1] little understanding has been obtained of how probability learning performance may vary with personality when stimulus conditions are held constant. Fillenbaum, for instance, using young adult males, found no correlations beyond what might be expected by chance between scores on MMPI scales and individual differences in choice frequency for a rare alternative occurring in a random sequence with 67:33 as the actual relative frequencies (Ref. 7). However, variability for young adults in cognitive performances of the kind just cited typically is not large. It may be especially difficult to obtain relationships between personality and probability learning among younger Ss, therefore, because of an insufficient range of individual differences in the probability learning measures.

The impetus to the present research was the view that work with an older male sample well might cast light on these apparently elusive relationships between personality and probability learning. The greater variability in cognitive performances found, on the average, among older as compared with younger Ss, might reveal relationships between probability

---

[1] See Feather for a review of such stimulus condition variables (Ref. 6), and see Bruner, Goodnow & Austin for some relevant experiments (Ref. 1).

learning and personality that remain concealed in younger individuals.

In particular, it was desired to investigate two aspects of personality which might be expected to influence the use of the more deliberative 'problem' approach to probability learning versus the more thoughtless '50:50' approach. These aspects are manifest anxiety level and extra-version-introversion. A high level of anxiety has been found to disrupt attempts at rational, deliberative solving of complex problems (see, e.g., Ref. 4). So also we well might expect extraverts to be more impulsive and less contemplative than introverts. In sum, the presence for older Ss both of high anxiety and of extraversion might be expected to favour the occurrence of the thoughtless '50:50' approach. On the other hand, the presence for older Ss both of low anxiety and of introversion might be expected to favour the occurrence of the thoughtful, deliberative 'problem' approach.

The hypotheses under examination in the present research, then, are that (a) high anxiety extraverts in an older male sample will be most likely to show a '50:50' approach to probability learning, while (b) low anxiety introverts in an older male sample will be most likely to show a 'problem' approach.[1]

METHOD

The Experimental Situation

A simple binary choice situation was arranged, analogous to ones used with young adult males by Goodnow (Ref. 9) and others. On each of 100 trials, S had to predict which of two lights would appear. He made his prediction by pressing the button under the light on which he was betting. After each prediction, the left- or right-hand light immediately went one for on second, thus informing S which side was correct on that trial.

In actuality the left-hand light was correct on 70 trials and the right-hand light on 30, with this 70:30 probability being present and order randomized within each block of 10 trials. Which button S pushed on a trial and which light was illuminated on that trial from the automatic programme sequence, were recorded by pen marks on the channels of an Esterline-Angus moving tape. Later reading of the tape permitted us to count the number of times the right-hand button was pushed within a series of trials and to measure, in terms of length of tape, the latency

[1] Examples of analysing the personality variables of manifest anxiety and extra-version-introversion in combination may be seen in research by Wallach & Gahm (Ref. 25) and Wallach & Greenberg (Ref. 26).

between a light's going off and S's next push of the left- or right-hand button. Because an initial period of familiarization with the pay-off schedule was necessary before scores would become meaningful, it was decided beforehand to consider frequency and latency measures for the last 20 trials: that is, Trials 81–100.

The latency score used was a ratio consisting of the mean of S's latencies for right-hand choices, divided by the mean of that S's latencies for left-hand choices. Mean latency for right-hand choices indicated S's reaction speed when predicting the rare alternative, while mean latency for left-hand choices indicated the same S's reaction speed when predicting the frequent alternative. Dividing the former mean by the latter mean hence provided an index of S's latency in predicting the rare alternative compared to his latency in predicting the frequent one.

Instructions to S directed him to predict which of the two lights would go on for each trial. S knew that the machine was programmed, so he couldn't alter or control the lights in any way. His only job was to predict, by pushing the appropriate button, which light would come on next. The main object of the test, S was told, was to predict correctly as often as possible.

Personality Variables of Manifest Anxiety and Extraversion-Introversion

The group form of the MMPI (Ref. 12) was individually administered to each S some time before he went through the probability-learning task. Scale scores then were obtained for each of the MMPI scales listed by Kassebaum, Couch & Slater (Ref. 14, p. 228), plus certain others which are of too specialized interest to report here but are described by Slater in 1958 (Ref. 20).[1] Scores for these MMPI scales were intercorrelated for a sample of 129 older males, including Ss in the present study plus additional Ss from the same population. The correlation matrix was factor analysed by Thurstone's complete centroid method (Ref. 23) and orthogonal rotations carried out with the aim of maximizing the similarity of the two largest factors to the comparable two largest factors in the parallel MMPI study by Kassebaum, Couch & Slater using male college students (Ref. 14).

The two factors, each accounting for more of the total variance than any other factor, had to do with manifest anxiety and extraversion-

[1] All statistical treatment of these MMPI data, the factor analysis, and computation of factor scores, were carried out by Philip E. Slater, to whom we are greatly indebted for aid in facilitating the present research. These data were processed at the MIT Computation Center.

S*

introversion. It is of interest that the two largest factors emerging in the present older sample closely matched the two largest factors that emerged from the study of college students just cited. This finding provides evidence that these aspects of personality structure do not change with increasing age.

On the first factor, which accounted for about 32 per cent of the total variance, those scales that were highest loading (0·74 or better) were 'admission of weaknesses' (Ref. 20), 'anxiety' (Ref. 28, pp. 264–281), 'caudality' (Ref. 29), 'dependency' (Ref. 16), 'hypertension correction scale' (Ref. 20), 'neuroticism' (Ref. 30), 'parietal' scale (Ref. 8), 'psychasthenia' and 'schizophrenia' (Ref. 13), with negative loadings for 'ego functioning' (Ref. 13) and 'leadership' (Ref. 17). The 'admission of weaknesses' scale, developed by Slater, contains those items from the MMPI for which a 'yes' response means that S admits there is something psychologically or physically wrong with him. The presence of this scale, the Welsh 'anxiety' scale and Winne's 'neuroticism' scale, plus the fact that most of the other scales noted above also are indicative of manifest feelings of 'disturbance', seemed to make 'manifest anxiety' the most appropriate label for this first factor.[1]

On the second factor, which accounted for about 10 per cent of the total variance, those scales that were highest loading (0·60 or better) were 'agreement with general assertions' (Ref. 20), an 'extraversion index' consisting of hypomania score minus depression score (Ref. 20), 'hypomania' (Ref. 13) and 'sociability' (Ref. 11), with negative loadings for 'repression, denial' (Ref. 28, pp. 264–281) and 'social introversion' (Ref. 13). Slater's 1958 scale for 'agreement with general assertions' contains those items from the MMPI for which agreement means adherence to generally held preferences, interests and beliefs about people and things. The nature of the various scales loading highly on this second factor seemed to make 'extraversion-introversion' the most appropriate label for it.

Ss' anxiety and extraversion-introversion scores were based on these respective factors rather than on single scales, in order to enhance the reliability of the measures employed. Individual factor scores were obtained by a method described in detail by Kassebaum, Couch & Slater (Ref. 14). In brief, the variables included for computation of factor scores on each of the two factors were so selected as to satisfy the following double criterion: (a) maximizing the communality of the factor measure in question and (b) minimizing the saturation on the remaining

[1] It might also be called 'neuroticism' (see Ref. 5) or 'ego weakness' (see Ref. 14).

factors by equalizing the positive and negative loadings of these variables on each of the remaining factors. When the set of variables was found which satisfied this double criterion for a factor measure, the individual scores for each variable (i.e., scale) in the set were converted into standard scores so that score distributions on the variables in question could be treated as equivalent. An individual's factor score for anxiety or extraversion then consisted of the algebraic sum of his standard scores for the variables included in the factor measure in question. The correlation between anxiety factor scores and extraversion factor scores was −0·09 for the 52 older males in the present study, thus indicating the orthogonality of these two score dimensions.

Ss were separated into extraverts and introverts by dichotomizing the distribution of extraversion factor scores as close to the median as possible. Similarly, Ss were separated into high and low anxiety groups by dichotomizing the distribution of anxiety factor scores as close to the median as possible.[1] Four groups of Ss resulted from these dichotomizations: high anxiety extraverts, high anxiety introverts, low anxiety extraverts and low anxiety introverts. As expected from the orthogonality of these two factors, a similar, although not identical, number of Ss fell into each of these four groups. These groups contained not the extremes of the anxiety and extraversion-introversion factor score distribution, but rather all of the cases.

These two dichotomized personality dimensions constituted our treatment variables. Their effects on the dependent variables of frequency and latency of choice were investigated by 2-by-2 analyses of variance. Because of some inequalities in the cell sizes for each analysis, Snedecor's Method of Unweighted Means (Ref. 21, pp. 385–388; Ref. 10) was used in the computation. Since none of the bases of classification involved random sampling, the fixed constants model (Ref. 15, pp. 304–306) provided the suitable method for selecting the error term in computation of F ratios.

Control Variables

It was desirable to insure that any frequency and latency differences among the personality groups were not artifacts of intelligence, education, or age differences among these same groups. The intelligence

---

[1] Splits could not occur exactly at the median because, for each of the two distributions of factor scores, a score for which several Ss were tied overlapped the median, with a majority of the tied Ss falling on one side of it. Each split was made by assigning all tied Ss to this majority side.

measure used was the vocabulary subtest from the Wechsler intelligence test for adults (Ref. 27). A vocabulary index was chosen to assess intelligence for two reasons. First of all, the vocabulary subtest of the Wechsler groups has a very high correlation with the score based on the complete Wechsler battery of 11 subtests. Secondly, vocabulary scores have been reported to show the least decrement with age of any intelligence test measure (see, for instance, Refs. 3 and 22). Since our Ss were of an older age group and we wished to determine their intellectual comparability to young adults, vocabulary score seemed to be the most appropriate way of doing so.

The vocabulary test was administered individually after S went through the probability-learning task. Vocabulary scoring was done according to Wechsler's manual of instructions by each of two independent judges. The score used was the sum numerical value of S's vocabulary credits. Reliability of the two judges' sum scores, as determined by an intraclass correlation coefficient (Refs. 18 & 19) was 0·95 for a larger sample of older males and females including the 52 older males of the present study. Disagreements were resolved by taking the average of the two discrepant sum scores in question.

Highest attained level of education and date of birth also were known for all Ss. Education level was measured in terms of years of schooling. Age was determined to the nearest year by taking an arbitrary current date (the same date for all Ss) and subtracting from it each S's date of birth.

Subjects

The participants in the present study were 52 older males.[1] Their high intellectual and educational status made them comparable in these respects to male college students. Mean age was 70·6 (SD = 7·0). With regard to Wechsler vocabulary test score, the mean was 34·8 (SD = 5·0).[2] Finally, mean level of education was 13·6 years of schooling (SD = 3·0), or an average of 1·6 years of college.

---

[1] While the work cited by Fillenbaum, Goodnow, and other researchers on probability learning has focused on young adult males, the present research thus utilizes a sample of older males. That research on probability learning has focused on males probably reflects the difficulty of inducing females to understand the nature of the probability learning task. Indeed, attempts by the present investigators to use older females proved infeasible for just this reason: interviews indicated that older females were unable to understand the nature of the experimental task.

[2] Data on college students reported by Dana (Ref. 2) and others indicate that our older Ss' scores tend, if anything, to exceed those of young adult college students.

RESULTS AND DISCUSSION

TABLE 1

MEAN FREQUENCIES OF CHOICE OF RARE ALTERNATIVE DURING
THE LAST 20 TRIALS FOR PERSONALITY GROUPS (N = 52)[1]

Groups	Extraversion	Introversion
High anxiety	8·07	4·67
Low anxiety	6·33	8·14

[1] Group sizes in this and all following tables are 12, 14, 14 and 12, for high anxiety introverts, high anxiety extraverts, low anxiety introverts and low anxiety extraverts, respectively.

Table 1 presents the means and Table 2 the analysis of variance for frequency of choice of the rare alternative during the last 20 trials, i.e., Trials 81–100, for the four personality groups. Scores are approximately normally distributed and variances are homogeneous by Bartlett's test (Ref. 24, pp. 193–194). The only significant F value is for the interaction of anxiety and extraversion. Frequency of choice of the rare alternative is higher for anxious extraverts and non-anxious introverts than the frequency of the rare alternative's actual occurrence. For the remaining two personality groups, however, frequency of choice of the rare alternative matches or is lower than the frequency of its actual occurrence. With 1 and 48 degrees of freedom, the F for this interaction is 5·92 ($p < 0.03$).

TABLE 2

ANALYSIS OF VARIANCE, FREQUENCIES OF CHOICE OF RARE ALTERNATIVE DURING
THE LAST 20 TRIALS FOR PERSONALITY GROUPS (N = 52)

Source	df	Mean square	F	p
Extraversion	1	8·02	0·54	n.s.
Anxiety	1	9·83	0·66	n.s.
Interaction	1	87·79	5·92	<0.03
Within cells	48	14·83		

The latency ratio score means and analysis of variance are presented in Tables 3 and 4, respectively, for the four personality groups during the last 20 trials. S's latency ratio score is the mean latency of his right-hand responses during those 20 trials divided by the mean latency of his

TABLE 3

MEAN LATENCY RATIO SCORES FOR SPEED OF CHOICE OF THE ALTERNATIVES
DURING THE LAST 20 TRIALS FOR PERSONALITY GROUPS (N = 52)[1]

Groups	Extraversion	Introversion
High anxiety	1·01	1·27
Low anxiety	1·08	1·53

[1] Each S's ratio score consists of the mean latency of his right-hand responses divided by the mean latency of his left-hand responses during these 20 trials.

TABLE 4

ANALYSIS OF VARIANCE, LATENCY RATIO SCORES FOR SPEED OF CHOICE OF THE
ALTERNATIVES DURING THE LAST 20 TRIALS FOR PERSONALITY GROUPS (N = 52)[1]

Source	df	Mean square	F	p
Extraversion	1	2·70	6·21	<0.03
Anxiety	1	0·69	1·58	n.s.
Interaction	1	0·24	0·54	n.s.
Within cells	48	0·43		

[1] While the means in Table 3 are raw scores, a square root transformation was applied for the analysis of variance in order to avoid heterogeneity of variances. Before the transformation, decimal points were moved one digit to the right and scores carried out to two figures beyond the new decimal point.

left-hand responses during the same series of 20 trials.[1] The more a latency ratio score exceeds one, the greater is S's latency in predicting the rare in contrast to the frequent alternative. We find a significant effect for the extraversion-introversion dimension, introverts being slower in predictions of the rare in contrast to the frequent alternative than extraverts. As variances proved heterogeneous by Bartlett's test, a square root transformation was applied and led to homogeneous variances by that test. The analysis of variance on transformed scores, which were approximately normally distributed, yielded an F of 6·21 (1 and 48 df, $p<0.03$) for extraversion-introversion, with no other effect signifi-

[1] In the case of two Ss (one in each of two groups), no right-hand responses were given during Trials 81 to 100. The mean right-hand latency term for their latency ratio score was estimated as the grand mean of the mean right-hand latency scores for all Ss during Trials 81 to 100. Such a procedure provides the most conservative estimate one could make.

cant. The finding of larger latency ratio scores for introverts is heavily contributed to by the low-anxiety introverts, who show the largest latency ratios of all four groups. High-anxiety extraverts, on the other hand, show the smallest latency ratios of all the groups.

These frequency and latency results constitute our main findings. What light do they shed on our initial questions of separating 'problem' and '50:50' approaches to the probability-learning task and finding hypothesized personality correlates of each? From the means of Table 1, we note that high anxiety extraverts and low anxiety introverts both predict the rare alternative more frequently than it occurs and more often than the other groups. Turning now to the means of Table 3, we find that a sizeable difference in latency ratio scores discriminates high-anxiety extraverts from low-anxiety introverts, even though both predict the rare event very often. High-anxiety extraverts have the smallest latency ratio scores of all four groups; indeed, they predict the rare alternative just about as quickly as they predict the frequent alternative. Low-anxiety introverts, on the other hand, have the largest latency ratio scores of all four groups, taking about 50 per cent longer in predicting the rare alternative than they do in predicting the frequent one.

The probability-learning behaviours of high-anxiety extraverts and low-anxiety introverts thus meet our operational definitions for the '50:50' and 'problem' approaches, respectively. While high anxiety extraverts predict the rare event with high frequency, their latency in predicting it is short—no longer than when they predict the frequent event. This is the behaviour in terms of which we defined the '50:50' approach. According to this approach, S simply isn't sensitive to the infrequency of the rare event and treats it as if it occurs more often than it does because, in effect, he doesn't really know any better. On the other hand, while low-anxiety introverts also predict the rare event with just as high a frequency, their latency in predicting it is long—half again longer than when they predict the frequent event. This is the behaviour in terms of which we defined the 'problem' approach, according to which S assumes the rare event occurs in some pattern and tries to solve the problem of accurately predicting when the rare event will occur.

Our expectations were confirmed, furthermore, with regard to which personality group would exhibit each approach. High anxiety should disrupt attempts at problem-solving and extraversion should represent a relatively impulsive, non-contemplative attitude also inimical to problem-solving. Ss for whom both high anxiety and extraversion are present hence should be most likely to exhibit the impulsive, thoughtless behaviour of the '50:50' approach and this was the case. On the other hand, low anxiety should provide a supportive context for attempts at problem-solving and introversion should represent an attitude of deliberation and contemplation also favourable to problem-solving. Ss who are low in anxiety and introverted hence should be most likely to show the deliberative, thoughtful behaviour of the 'problem' approach and this too was the case.

In order to determine whether the relationships we have reported were influenced by intelligence, education or age differences, analyses of variance were performed using the same four personality groups. The dependent variables tested were vocabulary score, education and age, respectively, in three separate two-way analyses of variance. In none of the analyses did the F for interaction, rows or columns even approach significance. We therefore may conclude that no vocabulary score, education, or age differences are influencing the relationships obtained.

SUMMARY AND CONCLUSIONS

The purpose of the present research was to use older males as Ss in an attempt to determine relationships between personality and approaches to a probability-learning situation. While attempts to obtain such relationships with young adult males have met with little success, it was felt that the wider range of individual differences in cognitive performances typically found in older as compared with younger Ss might reveal relationships between personality and probability learning that remain concealed in younger adults.

The probability-learning situation required S to predict which of two alternatives would occur on each of many tries, one of these alternatives occurring less frequently than the other but in a random sequence. Two approaches which involved a high rate of predicting the rare event were isolated as dependent variables whose relations with personality were to be assessed. In one approach, S supposes that there is some pattern to the rare alternative's occurrence and tries to solve the problem of accurately predicting when the rare event will occur (the 'problem' approach); while in the other, S simply fails to discriminate just how infrequently the rare event occurs (the '50:50' approach). Although both approaches should lead to high frequency of predicting the rare event, we reasoned that the 'problem' approach should result in longer latencies for predicting the rare event than for predicting the frequent event (since accurate prediction of the rare event is perceived as the main challenge), while the '50:50' approach should result in about the same latencies for predicting the rare as for predicting the frequent event (since S is insensitive to the difference between them).

High manifest anxiety was expected to disrupt and low manifest anxiety to facilitate, attempts at deliberative problem-solving. So also extraverts were expected to be more impulsive and thoughtless, introverts more contemplative and thoughtful. Presence both of high anxiety and extraversion hence was expected to favour the occurrence of the thoughtless '50:50' approach to the probability learning task, while presence both of low anxiety and introversion was expected to favour the occurrence of the more thoughtful 'problem' approach. These expectations were confirmed in an experiment with 52 older males.

Our main conclusions are as follows:

(a) Light can be shed on relationships between personality and probability learning by using an age sample whose probability-learning performances provide a wider range of individual differences than typically is the case with young adults.

(b) It is of importance to use combined rather than single procedures for the assessment of probability learning and of personality.

In the present study, frequency and latency of choice were jointly used as probability learning indices; and manifest anxiety and extraversion-introversion were jointly used as personality indices.

REFERENCES

1. BRUNER, J. S., GOODNOW, J. J. & AUSTIN, G. A., *A Study of Thinking*. New York: Wiley & Sons, 1956.
2. DANA, R. H., A comparison of four verbal subtests on the Wechsler-Bellevue, Form 1 and the WAIS. *J. clin. Psychol.*, **13**, 70–71, 1957.
3. DOPPELT, J. E. & WALLACH, W. L., Standardization of the Wechsler Adult Intelligence Scale for older persons. *J. abnorm. soc. Psychol.*, **51**, 312–330, 1955.
4. EASTERBROOK, J. A., The effect of emotion on cue utilization and the organization of behaviour. *Psychol. Rev.*, **66**, 183–201, 1959.
5. EYSENCK, H. J., The questionnaire measurement of neuroticism and extraversion. *Riv. Psicol.*, **54**, 113–140, 1956.
6. FEATHER, N. T., Subjective probability and decision under uncertainty. *Psychol. Rev.*, **66**, 150–164, 1959.

7. FILLENBAUM, S., Some stylistic aspects of categorizing behaviour. *J. Pers.*, **27**, 187–195, 1959.

8. FRIEDMAN, S. H., Psychometric Effects of Frontal and Parietal Lobe Brain Damage. Unpublished doctoral dissertation, University of Minnesota Library, 1950.

9. GOODNOW, J. J., Determinants of choice-distribution in two choice situations. *Amer. J. Psychol.*, **58**, 106–117, 1955.

10. GOSSLEE, D. G., Level of Significance and Power of the Unweighted Means Test. Paper read at Amer. Statist. Assn., Chicago, 1959.

11. GOUGH, H. G., *Manual for the California Psychological Inventory*. Palo Alto, Calif.: Consulting Psychologists Press, 1957.

12. HATHAWAY, S. R. & McKINLEY, J. C., A multiphasic personality schedule (Minnesota): I. Construction of the schedule. *J. Psychol.*, **10**, 249–254, 1940.

13. —— & ——, *Manual for the Minnesota Multiphasic Personality Inventory*. (Rev. ed.). New York: Psychological Corp., 1943.

14. KASSEBAUM, G. G., COUCH, A. S. & SLATER, P. E., The factorial dimensions of the MMPI. *J. consult. Psychol.*, **23**, 226–236, 1959.

15. McNEMAR, Q., *Psychological Statistics*. (Rev. ed.). New York: Wiley & Sons, 1955.

16. NAVRAN, L., A rationally derived MMPI scale to measure dependence. *J. consult. Psychol.*, **18**, 192, 1954.

17. OETTEL, A., Leadership: a Psychological Analysis. Unpublished doctoral dissertation, University of California Library, 1952.

18. ROBINSON, W. S., The statistical measurement of agreement. *Amer. sociol. Rev.*, **22**, 17–25, 1957.

19. ——, The geometric interpretation of agreement. *Amer. sociol. Rev.*, **24**, 338–345, 1959.

20. SLATER, P. E., Preliminary Report of Progress on "Correlates of Anxiety". Unpublished manuscript, 1958.

21. SNEDECOR, G. W., *Statistical Methods*. (5th ed.). Ames, Iowa: Iowa State Coll. Press, 1956.

22. STROTHER, C. R., SCHAIE, K. W. & HORST, P., The relationship between advanced age and mental abilities. *J. abnorm. soc. Psychol.*, **55**, 166–170, 1957.

23. THURSTONE, L. L., *Multiple Factor Analysis*. Chicago: University of Chicago Press, 1947.

24. WALKER, H. M. & LEV, J., *Statistical Inference*. New York: Holt, 1953.

25. WALLACH, M. A. & GAHM, R. C., Personality functions of graphic constriction and expansiveness. *J. Pers.*, **28,** 73–88, 1960.

26. —— & GREENBERG, C., Personality functions of symbolic sexual arousal to music. *Psychological Monographs*, **74,** No. 7 (Whole No. 494), 1960.

27. WECHSLER, D., *The Measurement of Adult Intelligence.* Baltimore: Williams & Wilkins, 1944.

28. WELSH, G. S. & DAHLSTROM, W. G., *Basic Readings on the MMPI in Psychology and Medicine.* Minneapolis: University of Minnesota Press, 1956.

29. WILLIAMS, H. L., The development of a caudality scale for the MMPI. *J. clin. Psychol.*, **8,** 293–297, 1952.

30. WINNE, J. F., A scale of neuroticism: an adaptation of the MMPI. *J. clin. Psychol.*, **7,** 117–122, 1951.

59

Introversion, Neuroticism, Rigidity and Dogmatism[1]

DAVID WATSON

First published in *Journal of Consulting Psychology*, **31,** 105, 1967

IN a 2×2 design—high or low neuroticism and introvert or extravert—four groups of subjects were given a problem-solving task which makes it possible to differentiate a subject's ability to produce novel responses from his ability to utilize such responses. No differences were found between groups in their ability to produce novel responses, but there was a significant interaction of neuroticism and introversion-extraversion in the subject's ability to utilize novel responses. The results are discussed in terms of the relative inflexibility of the organized response sequences of certain subjects.

INTRODUCTION

A great many people talk about the relation between neuroticism and rigidity but few have done a great deal about it. Pervin pointed out that, prior to his study, there were apparently only three experimental investigations of the relationship (Ref. 7). In a review article, Wilson indicated that a number of studies of experimentally induced 'neurosis' in infra-human animals have led to the observation of stereotyped, repetitive or rigid behaviour in the 'neurotic' animals (Ref. 12) and a number of clinical observations on human neurotics have pointed to the same kind of behaviour. At one time or another most of the major theorists seem to have had something to say about the rigidity manifested by neurotics (cf., Refs. 1, 7 & 12).

Pervin found that, on several different kinds of tasks, hospitalized neurotics were more rigid than hospitalized normals. Rigidity was defined as the perseveration of some behaviour no longer appropriate to a changed task. As Chown has pointed out, there is no clear definition

[1] This research was supported by a grant from the President's Committee on Research in the Humanities and Social Sciences of the University of Toronto. Gerald B. Glass ran the subjects and aided in the analyses. His help is gratefully acknowledged.

of rigidity (Ref. 1). Theorists have spoken of such things as an 'inability to change one's set when the objective conditions demand it' (Ref. 8) or a 'lack of variability of response' (Ref. 11). In other words, rigidity can be defined as an inability to employ novel or changed responses when such would be adaptive to a situation. This seems to be what personality theorists have meant when they spoke of the neurotic as rigid.

These considerations point up two problems concerning the relationship between neuroticism and rigidity. First, are there personality dimensions other than neuroticism which affect the relationship? Pervin suggested, for example, that different types of neurotics differed in rigidity on various kinds of tasks. Eysenck hypothesized that introverted neurotics were rigid but that extraverted neurotics were not (Ref. 2). One purpose of this study was to test Eysenck's hypothesis.

The second problem concerns a behavioural definition of rigidity. In any situation which demands novel or changed responses, the rigid person fails. But he may fail for one or the other of two reasons: (a) he may not be able to produce the necessary novel response or (b) he may be able to produce the novel response but not be able to utilize it in an adaptive manner. In other words, people can appear to be rigid—in terms of their performance on some task—either because they cannot generate novel responses or because they cannot utilize effectively whatever novel responses they do generate.

Rokeach has offered a distinction, supported by experimental data, between rigidity and dogmatism (Ref. 9). Rigidity he defined as 'the resistance to change of *single* beliefs' while dogmatism is the 'resistance to change of *systems* of beliefs' (italics in original). While these definitions may be appropriate to Rokeach's theory, it seems more appropriate for the purposes of this study to use a similar, but somewhat changed, distinction. This study used the same task employed by Rokeach (Refs. 9 and 10). A behavioural description of the kind of behaviour Rokeach observed on his experimental task, the Doodlebug problem, is this: in attempting to solve the problem, some subjects seemed never to overcome a wrong set, while others did overcome the set but still did not utilize the newly acquired set to solve the problem. Using this description, we can define rigidity as the inability to produce novel or changed responses, while dogmatism is the inability to utilize novel responses which have been produced.

This descriptive distinction has apparently not been made in discussions of the relationship between neuroticism and rigidity. Thus, if neurotics are 'rigid', we don't know whether this apparent inflexibility is due to their inability to produce or generate novel responses, or to their inability to utilize novel responses which they may be able to produce. A second purpose of this study, therefore, was to investigate the inflexibility of neurotics' problem-solving behaviour to determine which, or both, of the two kinds of inflexibility they exhibited.

The third purpose of the study was to test an inference from Rokeach that people who are dogmatic on the task—as defined by their performance—would be more likely to reject, or be hostile toward, the task than would people who are not dogmatic (Ref. 9).

The 2×2 design of the study included two degrees of neuroticism, high and low, and two groups selected for their introversion scores. The dependent variables were two performance indices, one measuring rigidity and one, dogmatism, and a set of questions designed to measure hostility or rejection.

METHOD

Subjects

The Maudsley Personality Inventory (Ref. 3) was administered to 194 male and female students in an introductory psychology course. The scale gives two scores, one for neuroticism and one for introversion-extraversion. The correlation between the two sets of scores was almost zero ($r = 0.01$, $N = 194$), which supports Eysenck's contention that they are uncorrelated. Four extreme groups were isolated: High Neuroticism-Introvert (HN-I), High Neuroticism-Extravert (HN-E), Low Neuroticism-Introvert (LN-I) and Low Neuroticism-Extravert (LN-E). The LN Ss all had scores below the 18th percentile of the neuroticism dimension; the HN Ss' scores were above the 73rd percentile. The I Ss' scores were below the 22nd percentile on the introversion-extraversion dimension and the E Ss' scores were above the 65th percentile. From each of the four groups, 10 Ss were randomly selected.

Procedure

Subjects participated in the experiment singly, with only the experimenter (E) in a room with them. The same E was used for all Ss. The E did not know in what group any of the Ss belonged. The Ss were given the instructions to the Doodlebug problem and worked at it for 30 minutes, or until they had correctly solved it. The problem has been described in detail by Rokeach (Ref. 9). Briefly, it presents S with a hypothetical situation in which Joe Doodlebug finds himself. Food has been placed east of Joe, but he cannot jump directly to it. He has to jump exactly four times to reach it. The S's task is to figure out why it is that Joe must jump four times to reach the food. Certain rules must be observed. In order to solve the problem, S must realize three things: (a) the bug does not have to face the food in order to eat it, (b) he can jump sideways, (c) he was already involved in a series of jumps when the food was placed beside him and must complete that series before changing direction to jump to the food. These three statements constitute the solution to three wrong sets which the S is likely to adopt. The problem for S is that, as the situation is described to him, the bug is facing in the wrong direction, cannot possibly manoeuvre to face the food in four jumps. Only if S can overcome the three erroneous assumptions which he is likely to make and then integrate his novel ideas, can he solve the problem.[1]

The Ss first read the instructions and then began working. They were asked to think out loud while working at the problem; during the experimental period they were frequently reminded to do this. The Ss' verbalizations, which were recorded and timed by E, indicated whether they had or had not overcome each of the three assumptions which it is necessary to overcome if the problem is to be solved. After beginning the task, S was allowed ten minutes to work at the problem. If he had not solved it in 10 minutes, he was given a hint. There were three hints, corresponding to the three statements listed above and arranged hierarchically, as they are above. After 10 minutes, S was given the first hint—that the bug could jump sideways—or a second if he had already verbalized the first, or a third if he had verbalized the first two. Thus all Ss were given some hint after 10 minutes, depending upon which hints they had spontaneously verbalized previously. If necessary, Ss were given a second hint after 15 minutes and a third after 20 minutes. At the third hint, E also read over the problem with S. If S had not solved the problem after thirty minutes he was stopped and the solution explained to him. At the end of the period S answered a six-item questionnaire while E was out of the room.

During the experimental period, E answered any direct questions which S put to him. If S asked, for example, 'Can he jump sideways?', E answered yes. E recorded and timed any remarks S made which indicated that S had spontaneously overcome any one of the beliefs. Thus E

---

[1] The solution to the problem is that Joe was moving west but facing north when the food was placed down. He must jump three more times to the west, however, as one rule requires him always to jump four times in any direction before changing directions, and then once sideways to the east to reach the food.

knew which and how many of the beliefs were spontaneously overcome by S.[1] Rokeach operationally defined rigidity as the number of beliefs spontaneously overcome and dogmatism as the time to solution after the beliefs were overcome (Ref. 9). Overcoming the beliefs, Rokeach feels, is an act of analysis, while solving the problem once the beliefs are overcome is an act of synthesis. In this study, overcoming the beliefs was defined as producing novel responses, while solving the problem was defined as utilizing novel responses which had been produced.

The Doodlebug problem, then, generates two separate scores: one for producing novel responses—the number of beliefs spontaneously overcome—and one for utilizing them—time to solution after they are overcome. A third measure is total time to solution, a measure of general inflexibility.

RESULTS

The first data to be analysed were those for general inflexibility, total time to solution. If any group was generally more inflexible than other groups, the relevant analysis should be significant. These data were extremely skewed, a Pearson type-III distribution: 15 of the 40 Ss did not solve the problem in the allotted time period. Because of the extreme skew, analysis of variance was inappropriate. To analyse the data, the grand median for scores over all four conditions was obtained and a $2 \times 2 \times 2$ table was constructed. Two dimensions of the table were the N and I-E dimensions; the third was the number of scores falling above or below the grand median for each of the other two dimensions. Analysis was performed by partition of chi² (Ref. 13). The overall analysis was significant (chi² (1df) = 7·2, p<0·01), but none of the chi² values for the constituent parts of the analysis was significant. In other words, neither the N nor the I-E dimensions, nor their interaction, had significant effects. From this analysis, one would have to conclude that there were no specifiable differences between groups in general inflexibility.

It was pointed out earlier that the groups might not differ in overall inflexibility, but could differ either in their ability to produce new responses—what Rokeach called rigidity—or in their ability to utilize

---

[1] By means of a one-way mirror and intercom arrangement, the reliability of E's judgements concerning when beliefs had been overcome was checked by a second E. After 10 pre-experimental, practice Ss, the mean difference between the two Es was four seconds, which was sufficiently accurate, since the time measures were taken in minutes.

novel responses which might have been generated—Rokeach's dogmatism. Rigidity was analysed as it has been by Rokeach (Ref. 9): a chi^2 test was applied to the number of beliefs spontaneously overcome by each group in the first ten and in the first 15 minutes of the task. There were no differences in the number of beliefs overcome in ten minutes (chi^2 (1df) = 0·01), nor in the number overcome within 15 minutes (chi^2 (1df) = 0·64). Thus the groups did not differ in their ability to generate novel responses.

To analyse the subjects' ability to utilize novel responses which they might have produced, Rokeach used the time to solution after the first, second and third beliefs had been overcome, either spontaneously by the subject or following a hint. The reasoning is that if Ss differ in the time required to solve the problem after they have overcome a belief, then some are not utilizing the new responses available to them. Similar analyses were used in this study. Since the groups in this study did not differ in the number of beliefs spontaneously overcome, any differences in time to solution after overcoming beliefs would indicate differences in the utilization of new responses.

The data were, again, extremely skewed and partition of chi^2 of the N by I-E by median split design was the method of analysis employed, i.e., the analyses were identical to that of the total time to solution. The time to solution after the first belief did not indicate any significant differences between groups, although the chi^2 value for the interaction of N and I-E almost reached an acceptable level, chi^2 (1df) = 3·60, p<0·10. Tables 1 and 2 present the number of scores falling above or below the median for time to solution after the second and third beliefs, two $2 \times 2 \times 2$ tables. The overall chi^2 was significant only for time to solution after the second belief, but there was a significant interaction of N and I-E after the second and third beliefs. There were no significant main effects. Since the overall chi^2 is significant only for time to solution after the second belief, the interaction which was partitioned there should be given more weight. Table 2 can be seen as offering tentative confirmation for the significant effect in Table 1.

Inspection of Table 1 will indicate that most of the interaction effect is due to the large difference between the two HN groups. The HN-I group was unable to utilize novel responses, while the HN-E group was as proficient—perhaps even more so—as the two LN groups. From these and the above analyses, we may conclude that the groups were not different in their ability to produce novel responses, but that the HN-I group was relatively inferior in its ability to utilize such responses.

TABLE 1

NUMBER OF SCORES ABOVE AND BELOW THE GRAND MEDIAN FOR
TIME TO SOLUTION AFTER THE SECOND BELIEF

	Above Median		Below Median	
	Introvert	Extravert	Introvert	Extravert
High Neuroticism	9	1	1	9
Low Neuroticism	4	6	6	4
	df	chi²	p	
Overall	4	13·60	<0·10	
Neuroticism (N) × Introversion				
Extraversion (I–E)[1]	1	0		
N × Median Split (MS)	1	0		
I–E × MS	1	3·60	<0·10	
N × I–E × MS	1	10·00	<0·01	

[1] $N \times I–E$ is necessarily zero, as each cell entry summed over MS is $n = 10$, i.e., all scores are either above or below the median.

TABLE 2

NUMBER OF SCORES ABOVE AND BELOW THE GRAND MEDIAN
FOR TIME TO SOLUTION AFTER THE THIRD BELIEF

	Above Median		Below Median	
	Introvert	Extravert	Introvert	Extravert
High Neuroticism	8	3	2	7
Low Neuroticism	3	7	7	3
	df	chi²	p	
Overall	4	8·40	<0·10	
N × I–E[1]	1	0		
N × MS	1	0·20		
I–E × MS	1	0·20		
N × I–E × MS	1	8·00	<0·01	

[1] See note to Table 1

Following the task, the Ss were given a six-item questionnaire designed to measure Ss' rejection of, or hostility toward, the task. The questions were: (a) How much did you enjoy working on the Doodlebug problem? (b) How much would you enjoy working on similar problems? (c) How much do you like Joe Doodlebug? (d) How *sensible* do you think the problem is? (e) How *reasonable* is it to ask subjects to work on such a problem? (f) How relevant were the experimenter's answers to your spoken thoughts and questions? These questions were all taken from the phrases used by Rokeach to describe the reaction of dogmatic Ss to the problem (Ref. 9). Since there were significant differences between groups on Rokeach's measure of dogmatism, one could expect similar differences in response to the present questionnaire. Using analysis of variance, there were, however, no significant differences on any of the six questions. It cannot be concluded then, that—to use Rokeach's terms—those Ss who are more dogmatic are more likely to be hostile or rejecting toward the task.

DISCUSSION

Two conclusions follow from this study. The first is that it is inappropriate to speak loosely of the 'rigidity' or 'inflexibility' of neurotic behaviour, as it was shown that neurotics are not different from non-neurotics in their ability to produce novel responses, but rather in their ability to utilize such responses. The second conclusion is that not all neurotics manifest this inability to utilize novel responses: it is shown by introverted neurotics only.

Pervin found general differences in inflexibility between hospitalized neurotics and others (Ref. 7). There are at least two possible reasons why his results and those of this study are only partially in agreement. First, Pervin's Ss were hospitalized, while those in this study were defined as neurotic on the basis of their responses to the MPI. The differences in results could be due to possible variations in the severity of the disorder, or to the differential methods of diagnosis employed. Second, Pervin did not distinguish introverted and extraverted neurotics. Perhaps only introverted neurotics are hospitalized, or perhaps, when hospitalized, only people in that category are categorized as neurotic.

Eysenck had predicted differences between HN-I and HN-E Ss on general inflexibility and the present results tend to confirm and extend his hypothesis. The difference between the two groups is in their ability to utilize novel responses. The fact that there was only a significant interaction of N and I-E and no main effects rules out the possibility of explaining these results on the assumption that the I-E dimension is merely another measure of dogmatism, or that the E Ss tried harder in the social situation of the experiment. Clearly, studies using other measures of the I-E dimension should be tried. It is possible that the HN-I Ss may have been more anxious or distressed than the HN-E Ss. The possibility was mentioned above that Pervin's Ss were more severely disordered than most of the Ss in this study and it may be that the I-E dimension reflects differences in anxiety or severity of disorder. Clearly, future studies of the relationship of neuroticism and problem-solving inflexibility should consider the I-E dimension as well as some measure of neuroticism.

Previous studies have shown neurotics to be inflexible in their problem-solving. In this study it was shown that such overall inflexibility is not due to the neurotics' inability to produce novel responses, but in their inability to utilize such responses once produced. In other words, the inflexible Ss were not able to integrate the novel responses they produced into organized response sequences to solve the problem. It has been suggested that, with practice, responses become organized in sequences which have a unitary nature (Ref. 4) and it seems likely that in this study the Ss' approaches to problem-solving were well-organized response sequences. If one conceives of the Ss' approach to the problem as being the execution of certain organized sequences, then it is possible to discuss the relative flexibility of such sequences (Refs. 5 & 6). Seen from this point of view, the inflexibility of the HN-I Ss is conceived of as an inability to modify organized response sequences. They are able to produce the units required for a new, more effective, sequence, but are unable to interrupt their previously organized sequences; hence their overall performance remains inflexible. The reasons why the modification of organized sequences should be more difficult for some Ss than others is not clearly understood. Mandler and Mandler & Watson have shown, however, that the interruption of organized response sequences can be anxiety-producing (Refs. 5 & 6) and it may be that the HN-I Ss were either experiencing greater distress or have less tolerance for it; or both. Alternatively, they may have highly overlearned sequences which they execute whenever faced with any type of problem. Clearly the variables which produce the inflexibility of the organized sequences of the HN-I Ss are not elucidated in this study. The point here has been to show that the difference between groups is due to an inability to fit novel responses into old sequences, rather than an inability to produce the new responses.

REFERENCES

1. CHOWN, SHEILA, Rigidity—a flexible concept. *Psychol. Bull.*, **56**, 195–223, 1959.

2. EYSENCK, H. J., *Dimensions of Personality*. London: Routledge & Kegan Paul, 1947.

3. ——, *Manual of the Maudsley Personality Inventory*. London: University of London Press, 1959.

4. MANDLER, G., From association to structure. *Psychol. Rev.*, **69**, 415–427, 1962.

5. ——, The interruption of behaviour. *The Nebraska Symposium on Motivation*, **12**, 163–219, 1964.

6. —— & WATSON, D., Anxiety and the interruption of behaviour. In *Anxiety and Behaviour* (ed. C. Spielberger). Lincoln, Nebraska: Nebraska University Press.

7. PERVIN, L. A., Rigidity in neurosis and general personality functioning. *J. abnorm. soc. Psychol.*, **61**, 389–395, 1960.

8. ROKEACH, M., Generalized rigidity as a factor of ethnocentricism. *J. abnorm. soc. Psychol.*, **43**, 259–277, 1948.

9. ——, *The Open and Closed Mind*. New York: Basic Books, 1960.

10. ——, MCGOVNEY, W. & DENNY, M., A distinction between dogmatic and rigid thinking. *J. abnorm. soc. Psychol.*, **51**, 87–93, 1955.

11. WERNER, H., The concept of rigidity—a critical evaluation. *Psychol. Rev.*, **53**, 43–52, 1946.

12. WILSON, R., On behaviour pathology. *Psychol. Bull.*, **60**, 130–146, 1963.

13. WINER, B., *Statistical Principles in Experimental Design*. New York: McGraw-Hill, 1962.

60

Conscious and Preconscious Influences on Recall:
a Reassessment and Extension[1]

STEVEN H. STEIN & ROBERT H. HARRISON
First published in *Psychological Reports*, **20,** 963–974, 1967

IN an attempt to replicate the Spence finding that primary recall hinders the recall of primary associates (Ref. 15), an experiment controlling for serial position and associative clustering effects was performed. Results were obtained which indicate facilitation rather than restriction of associate recall after primary recall. Spence-type results were obtained, however, with Ss whose scores were above the sample mean on the Extraversion scale of the Maudsley Personality Inventory. In addition, hypotheses based on Eysenck's theories concerning introversion-extraversion and anxiety were tested as to their efficacy in predicting the amount and pattern of primary associate (associates to the primary of a word list) and control word associate (associates related to a primary which does not appear in the word list) recall. As predicted, extraversion correlated with the degree to which S alternated between primary associates and control associates during recall. Anxiety was not related to any of the experimental measures.

INTRODUCTION

The purpose of the present study was to investigate some of the stimulus determinants and personality dimensions underlying the response organization of words in a particular kind of free recall task. In this type of task the effect of presenting a key stimulus word (primary) on recall of other related stimulus words (associates) can be assessed.

---

[1] This study is based upon a Master's thesis submitted by the senior author to the University of Massachusetts. The study was carried out under the supervision of the junior author. Acknowledgement is extended to Dr William E. Broen for his advice and discerning criticism. This research was conducted while the senior author was a National Institute of Mental Health Predoctoral Fellow at the University of Massachusetts.

Spence presented Ss with a list consisting of one primary word, 10 associates to the primary and 10 control words (matched to associates in terms of Thorndike-Lorge frequency of occurrence in the English language) and asked them to recall as many words as possible (Ref. 15). The primary, *cheese*, was placed at the centre of the list. His data demonstrated that: (1) there were significantly more associates than control words recalled *before* the primary was recalled; (2) *after* primary recall there were no significant differences in number of associates and number of control words recalled; and (3) combined analysis of the difference scores also showed that there were more associates recalled than control words before rather than after the primary was recalled. Spence reasoned that before *cheese* was recalled, it was held in a pre-conscious state in which it could activate a wider range of associates than in a conscious (having-been-recalled) state. This preconscious state was hypothesized to be similar to that induced by the subliminal perception of *cheese* in an earlier study by Spence & Holland using the same recall list (Ref. 16). Subliminal (but not supraliminal) perception of cheese also produced activation of cheese associates. In addition, Spence found that 'early recallers' of cheese tended to have lower associate-minus-control-word differential recall indices than 'late recallers' of cheese (Ref. 15). Hence, the supraliminal and subliminal groups in the Spence & Holland study had associate recall indices similar to those of early and late recallers of the Spence study (Ref. 15).

Spence claims these studies demonstrate that semi-awareness of the primary activates recall of its associates better than full awareness. Thus, they serve to reinforce several Freudian notions concerning preconscious thought. Freud considered thoughts which are beyond an individual's awareness but available for immediate recall to be 'preconscious'. He characterized pre-conscious thinking as fanning out over a wide range of associative connections as opposed to conscious thought which is more direct and restricted. Spence used the Freudian preconscious model to account for the 'silent' influence the primary has over a wide network of associations, facilitating associate recall prior to recall of the primary itself.

Objections to the 1964 Spence study have been manifold. Worell & Worell modified the Spence paradigm by using a different word list in which the imbedded primary word was either related or unrelated to the associate words (Ref. 18). With this design the Spence results of superior associate word recall prior to primary recall were replicated. However, they obtained the Spence results even when the primary was *not* related to the associates as well as when it was, indicating that the primary had very little to do with increased associate recall in either study. They accounted for their results by invoking a general associative cluster hypothesis (Refs. 2 & 5).[1] Worell & Worell argue that the experimental words are inter-related whereas the control words are not. Clusters of experimental (inter-related) words tend to be recalled before non-associated control words. Thus, more primary associates than control words will be recalled early. Other things being equal, the primary itself will be recalled in the middle of the list (having been presented in the middle) and the Spence results (more associates than controls before primary recall) will then follow. To meet this objection in a new experiment, control words should be as interrelated as the primary's associates.

In another critical study, Jung points out that 6 of the 10 outermost items (excluding buffers) in the Spence experimental word list were associates (Ref. 13). Since Deese & Kaufman found highest recall for items at the beginning and end of the list as opposed to those in the middle (Ref. 6), the Spence results could have also been due to associate words having occupied favoured positions. Jung found no difference between associate and control word recall prior to recall of the primary using a list in which the control words occupied the most favourable recall positions. A second necessary control, then, is for serial position effects.

While the above two studies suggest explanations which *might* account for the Spence results, neither study answers the quantitative question: are Spence's results *completely* accounted for by clustering and serial order effects? Is there some residue of support for Spence's hypothesis? A close replication of Spence's experiment seems called for, controlling for serial position and clustering effects. In the present experiment, word lists were presented which contained a primary, associates to this primary (primary associates, PA) and control word associates (CA). Both sets of associates were matched in terms of associative connection to their respective primaries (the primary to the primary associates was presented in the word lists whereas the primary to the control word associates was omitted from the word lists) to eliminate associative cluster effects. Many recall lists were used and serial-position-bias effects among lists were controlled by interchanging primaries. For one group, two matched sets of associates were presented with the primary for only

---

[1] The Bousfield hypothesis is based on item clustering within a superordinate category rather than 'free association' clustering.

one of the sets. An equivalent group was presented with the same sets of associates but with the other primary.

The first purpose of the experiment, then, was to replicate Spence's study with proper controls. Hypothesis 1 stated that, in accord with Spence's findings, more primary associates than control words would be remembered before primary recall, but not after primary recall.

The other purpose of this study was to evaluate the ability of Eysenck's use of Hullian reactive inhibition to predict certain characteristics of the recall data. Eysenck considers generation of inhibition in relationship to excitation to be the major variable differentiating 'extraverts' from 'introverts', 'Individuals in whom reactive inhibition is generated quickly, in whom strong reactive inhibitions are generated and in whom reactive inhibition is dissipated slowly are thereby predisposed to develop extraverted patterns of behaviour and to develop hysterical disorders in cases of neurotic breakdown; conversely, individuals in whom reactive inhibition is generated slowly, in whom weak reactive inhibitions are generated and in whom reactive inhibition is dissipated quickly, are thereby predisposed to develop introverted patterns of behaviour and to develop dysthymic (obsessive-compulsive) disorders in cases of neurotic breakdown' (Ref. 8).

We assume that in the present experimental paradigm all word cues presented to S induce both inhibition and excitation which respectively limit and facilitate his recall of them. Three hypotheses emerge from Eysenck's theory:

(2a) Since introverts generate reactive inhibition slowly and dissipate it rapidly, they should show greater recall of both primary and control word associates than extraverts.

(2b) Assuming that both excitation and inhibition generalize from associates to primary and also from primary to associates, introverts' recall of primary associates should be greater than their recall of control word associates. They should be able to take advantage of the generalized excitatory increments provided by the primary to its associates, while dissipating the primary's inhibitory effects. Extraverts, on the other hand, should have greater difficulty in recalling primary associates than control word associates since they should build up greater amounts of reactive inhibition to the primary and its associates than will the introverts.

(2c) Extraverts should show greater alternation of recall between the primary associates and the control word associates; this shifting should be due to the rapid development of mediated reactive inhibition

T

to both the presented primary and the missing primary, resulting in a change from one set of associates to the other.[1]

Although Eysenck considers the generation and dissipation of reactive inhibition to be a function of the introversion-extraversion dimension, he also notes that tolerance of this inhibition increases as a function of drive level (Ref. 7). It should be mentioned that Eysenck regards neuroticism as a drive and thus establishes a given S's drive level in terms of Maudsley Personality Inventory (MPI) neuroticism score. He also uses the terms 'anxiety' and 'neuroticism' interchangeably; Franks in fact has found a correlation of 0·92 between neuroticism as measured by the Maudsley Medical Questionnaire and the Taylor Anxiety Scale which has been used as an operational definition of anxiety (Ref. 12). Thus Hypothesis 3 predicts that correlations between anxiety and the recall measures should parallel those found for introversion.

METHOD

Subjects

Subject sample included 26 male and 34 female students, with a mean age of 19·3 years, who were enrolled in sections of the introductory psychology courses at the University of Massachusetts. They participated in order to fulfil part of their course assignments. Three Ss completed the recall task but not the personality questionnaires.

Test Materials

All Ss filled out a questionnaire containing the Maudsley Personality Inventory (MPI) extraversion (E) and neuroticism (N) scales, the Bendig short form to the Manifest Anxiety Scale (MAS) (Ref. 1) and the MMPI Lie (L) Scale.

Experimental Stimuli

Six word lists each containing a primary, 10 primary associates (PA), 10 control word associates (CA) and three buffer words at the top and bottom of the list were used in the free-recall task. All six lists were administered to each S. Table 1 presents these lists. The reader should note that *two* primaries and associates to those primaries are presented

[1] An additional independent measure of the tendency to alternate can be derived by asking Ss to generate a random series of heads and tails based on 100 tosses of an imaginary coin. Thus, alternation behaviour is also reflected by the number of alternations between heads and tails in the particular head-tail sequence used by S.

TABLE 1

EXPERIMENTAL WORD LISTS SHOWING SERIAL POSITION IN LISTS AND
ASSOCIATIVE STRENGTH

	Position	R–Jf[1]		Position	R–Jf[1]
	Word List 1			Word List 2	
DEEP*			EAGLE*		
shallow	4	318	bird	1	550
sea	20	76	scout	16	34
hole	8	24	bald	12	16
pit	16	11	high	3	10
purple	14	9	emblem	2	8
far	3	7	claw	14	6
voice	18	4	air	19	4
steep	5	3	lion	7	3
snow	15	2	liberty	18	2
valley	6	1	cliff	5	1
SHORT†			DREAM†		
tall	9	397	sleep	15	453
fat	12	76	wish	9	35
small	1	21	boat	8	17
hair	11	11	vision	17	10
stout	2	9	sweet	4	8
pants	19	6	Freud	13	6
stubby	7	4	world	11	4
stop	13	3	time	6	3
time	10	2	delight	20	2
beer	17	1	lazy	10	1
	Word List 3			Word List 4	
COLD*			BUTTERFLY*		
hot	9	348	moth	4	144
winter	11	66	fly	16	78
ice	4	29	yellow	8	62
wet	19	13	net	11	42
dark	2	10	flower	19	33
hard	1	6	cocoon	6	23
sneeze	13	5	summer	13	22
coat	15	3	worm	2	9
sweat	10	2	madam	7	4
slaw	17	1	flutter	17	3

* A primary
† B primary
[1] R–Jf = Russell-Jenkins normative frequencies

TABLE 1—CONTINUED

EXPERIMENTAL WORD LISTS SHOWING SERIAL POSITION IN LISTS AND
ASSOCIATIVE STRENGTH

	Position	R–Jf[1]		Position	R–Jf[1]
	Word List 3			Word List 4	
FRUIT†			WHISTLE†		
apple	5	378	stop	9	131
fly	18	63	train	10	89
cake	12	23	noise	15	73
tree	3	13	tune	12	49
salad	6	11	song	20	33
candy	14	6	man	5	24
bowl	16	5	lips	1	21
queer	7	3	horn	18	8
jello	8	2	talk	3	4
cocktail	20	1	tweet	14	3
	Word List 5			Word List 6	
SWEET*			DOCTOR*		
sour	9	434	nurse	3	238
candy	12	162	sick	14	146
music	13	33	hospital	12	24
good	15	15	patient	1	11
tooth	8	13	stethoscope	10	7
low	2	8	cure	7	6
honey	11	7	pill	13	4
chocolate	17	5	bill	19	3
smile	6	2	pain	15	2
potato	10	1	fee	9	1
CHAIR†			THIEF†		
table	16	493	steal	6	286
sit	19	205	robber	4	138
seat	14	38	money	11	37
arm	4	15	gun	18	12
sofa	20	12	river	5	7
cushion	7	8	jewels	2	6
stool	3	7	sneak	16	4
back	1	3	stop	8	3
study	18	2	sly	20	2
magazine	5	1	flee	17	1

* A primary
† B primary
[1] R–Jf = Russell-Jenkins normative frequencies

in Table 1 for each of the six word lists. Only one of the two primaries in a list was presented to a given S. The associates of the omitted primary are control associates for that S. Half of the Ss were presented the A* primaries, the other half received the B† primaries. Thus, control word associates (CA) for half of the Ss were primary associates (PA) for the other half and vice versa. Serial position and associative strengths (to the primary) for both sets of associates are also listed in Table 1. Positions of the PAs and CAs in the list were randomly determined. The primary was always placed in the middle of the list. Since the primary and control associates were interchanged, serial position bias was controlled in the experiment.[1]

Procedure

The free-recall task was administered to all Ss before they received the personality questionnaire. E gave the following instructions adapted from Spence & Holland (Ref. 16) prior to presentation of the first list:

'You are going to hear a list of 27 words. Later on I will ask you to reproduce them from memory. This is not a test, for it is quite impossible to remember all the words. Just relax and listen closely. The word lists will be played through once.'

In order to control E bias, the word lists were tape recorded by a college freshman who had no knowledge of the experiment's purpose. They were spoken at a rate of one per second. A Revere T1500 model tape recorder was used for recording and administering the experimental task.

After the recall task, Ss were asked to generate a random series of heads and tails with these instructions (adapted from Ref. 4):

'I want you to make believe that an imaginary coin is being tossed 100 consecutive times. The likelihood of a head on any one toss is the same as the likelihood of a tail. Also, the outcome of any one toss has no relationship to the outcome of the following or preceding tosses. With these factors in mind, I want you to generate a random series of heads and tails such as you might expect to occur with the 100 tosses. By random, I mean 50 per cent heads and 50 per cent tails. Indicate a

---

[1] The associative values were obtained from the Russell-Jenkins normative sample (Ref. 14). Thus, the term Russell-Jenkins frequency (see Table 1) refers to the number of Ss in the associative norm sample (N = 1,008) giving the associate as a first response to the primary. Inspection of Table 1 shows that both sets of associates are closely matched in terms of Russell-Jenkins associative frequency. We assume this matching controls for associative clustering.

head by H and a tail by T. Work as quickly as you can and continue to work until all 100 blanks are filled'.

Following the head-tail alternation task, Ss were asked to fill out the personality questionnaires.

Experimental Design

The six experimental word lists were presented (to six different groups) in six different orders controlling for ordinal position effects and for sequence (each list followed every other list once) effects. The groups were further subdivided into those who received only 'A' primaries and those who received only 'B' primaries. Primaries were arbitrarily assigned to 'A' and 'B' categories. Five Ss were randomly assigned to each of the 12 subgroups.

RESULTS

Comparability of Different Subgroups

An analysis of variance was performed in order to establish the comparability of the 12 subgroups with respect to the following measures:

1. PA minus CA difference score *before* primary recall.
2. PA minus CA difference score *after* primary recall.
3. Combined difference score *before* (PA−CA) *minus* after (PA−CA).
4. Number of PA recalled.
5. Number of CA recalled.
6. Rank of primary position in recall (when it was recalled).
7. Primary associate recall per cent (PA/(PA+CA)).
8. PA−CA run per cent. A run was defined as a sequence of PAs in which CAs did not appear or vice versa. Buffer words and intrusions were not considered to have interrupted a run. The PA−CA run per cent is computed as the number of PA−CA runs divided by the number of PAs and CAs recalled plus one. Given a random series this index has an expected value of 0·5 regardless of number of relevant words (PA+CA) recalled.

Since subjects' scores on these variables were pooled over word lists, only the between-subject variance components are central to the results of the current study. With only the exceptions listed below, the total score on each measure for each S across word lists was tabulated and these scores were used in generating an inter-correlation matrix relating all personality and experimental measures.

The between-subjects analysis of all the experimental measures yielded only 2 F ratios out of 24 significant at the 0·05 level. These ratios referred to the difference between primary type A versus primary type B for: (1) the number of CA recalled (F = 5·70, df = 1/48, p<0·05) and (2) the combined difference scores (F = 4·41, df = 1/48, p<0·05). To correct for these effects, mean CA scores for each of the 12 subgroups were calculated. Then deviation scores based on the difference between S's raw score and his subgroup mean were determined. These deviation scores were used in place of the raw scores (number of CA recalled) in the inter-correlation matrix. The combined difference scores were not similarly corrected. However, for testing of the Spence hypothesis, two analyses were performed, one for all groups receiving A primaries and one for all groups receiving B primaries.

Replication of Spence

The present findings concerning the pattern of PA and CA recall before and after primary recall are in opposition to those of Spence relating to associates and control words. Hypothesis 1 was not supported by the data.

1. There were significantly more PAs recalled than CAs *after* primary recall (two-tailed Wilcoxon test; T = 410·5, N = 60, p<0·005). Spence failed to find any difference.

2. The difference between PA and CA recall was insignificant prior to primary recall (two-tailed Wilcoxon test; T = 865·5, n.s.). Spence's data shows this to be highly significant in favour of PA.

3. Analysis of the difference between number of PA and number of CA recalled before and after recall (combined difference score) showed that there were greater 'after' (PA—CA) scores than before (PA—CA) scores (two-tailed Wilcoxon test; T = 366·3, N = 60, p<0·002). Spence's data were significant in the opposite direction. Results based on separate analysis of each primary group were similar to the above findings (two-tailed Wilcoxon tests; 'A' primary: T = 114·5, N = 30, p<0·02 and 'B' primary: T = 92, N = 30, p.<0·001).

Personality Factors in Recall

Hypothesis 2a was rejected since PA, CA and total number of words recalled were not significantly related to the MPI-E scale (r = 0·087, n.s.; r = 0·020, n.s.; and r = 0·022, n.s., respectively).

Hypothesis 2b was partially confirmed. The correlation between the

TABLE 2

INTER-CORRELATION MATRIX RELATING PERSONALITY AND EXPERIMENTAL MEASURES

	1	2	3	4	5	6	7	8	9	10	11	12	13	14	15	16	M	SD
1. MPI—N																	25·90	9·77
2. MPI—E	-17																26·44	8·64
3. MAS	-76	-22															16·23	7·75
4. MMPI—L	-30	-10	-16														6·83	4·02
5. PA recalled	-10	-09	-15	05													25·84	6·73
6. CA recalled (Deviation Scores)	-09	02	-13	12	60												20·74	7·27
7. Buffers recalled	-32	-09	16	28	44	44											19·61	4·47
8. Intrusions	-19	-01	15	-00	-19	12	-31										14·16	6·55
9. Total words recalled	-10	-02	-10	15	82	69	58	16									84·16	16·42
10. PA% [PA/(PA+CA)]	-21	-22	-10	-02	-07	-35	-33	20	-31								0·52	0·26
11. Rank of recalled primary	-08	-13	-21	-22	41	32	56	-18	49	-30							7·84	2·37
12. Number of primaries recalled	-09	-01	14	-08	50	54	21	-01	49	-20	25						3·81	1·29
13. PA—CA run %	06	-24	-06	19	-36	-22	-29	-10	-43	19	-19	-27					0·46	0·22
14. Number of head-tail runs	-08	-09	01	-17	17	22	11	02	26	-32	11	35	-31				57·61	9·21
15. Before minus after (PA—CA) difference score	07	32	-07	-30	-07	-11	-20	07	-10	-04	-20	-15	07	05			-2·30	0·32
16. After (PA—CA) difference score	-03	-27	01	26	34	07	27	-09	22	15	30	09	-17	-05	-64		1·80	0·37
17. Before (PA—CA) difference score		20	-17	-24	11	-14	-15	09	-04	26	10	-03	64	-23	72	-11	0·49	0·35

E-I scale and the proportion of primary associates recalled to total associates recalled (PA/PA+CA) is -0.168 (p<0.11, one-tailed). If one considers the data only *after* primary recall, when reactive inhibition to the primary is expected to be high, the correlation between the E-1 scale and PA—CA is significant (r = -0.265, p<0.025, one-tailed); in addition, the correlation between these two measures before primary recall when reactive inhibition to the primary is low is again in the predicted direction although not significant (r = 0.20, p<0.08, one-tailed).

Hypothesis 2c was confirmed. The predicted positive correlation between PA—CA run per cent and extraversion score (r = 0.242, p<0.05, one-tailed) was obtained. Extraversion did not, however, correlate positively with HT runs as we had anticipated (r = 0.087, n.s.).

All portions of Hypothesis 3 were rejected. (a) The correlations between total number of words recalled and anxiety scores were in the opposite direction to that predicted (MAS, r = -0.104, n.s.; MPI-N, r = -0.097, n.s.). (b) The correlations between PA/(PA+CA) score and the two anxiety scales were in the opposite direction to that predicted (MAS, r = -0.21, n.s.; MPI-N, r = 0.096, n.s.). The correlation of PA—CA after primary recall with the anxiety scales is in the direction predicted but not significant (MAS, r = $+0.005$, n.s.; MPI-N, r = $+0.067$, n.s.). (c) The correlations between PA—CA run per cent and anxiety were also in the predicted direction but not significant (MAS, r = -0.06, n.s.; MPI-N, r = -0.09, n.s.).

DISCUSSION

The results clearly demonstrate that there is an increment in primary association recall *after* the primary is recalled. Such results are contradictory to: (1) the Spence results of greater associate-minus-control-word difference scores (measure of relative primary associate activation) before primary recall rather than after primary recall; (2) Deese's findings that free recall is solely based on inter-item associative clustering and independent of primary induced activation; and (3) the Worell & Worell's demonstration (Studies 2, 3, 4) that their Spence-type results were independent of primary word relatedness to the associates (Ref. 18). Thus the present investigators, using control word associates in place of unrelated control words, found that there is a primary associate activation effect after primary recall in contradistinction to the Spence results.

T*

Spence's findings may, however, apply to a select population. Out of 57 Ss, 18 showed relatively higher PA—CA scores prior to primary recall and thus paralleled the Spence data. 14 of these 18 Ss had extraversion scale scores which were above the sample mean (26·4); the remaining 4 Ss had MPI-E scores within one standard deviation below the mean. In addition, the positive correlation between the combined difference (before (PA—CA) minus after (PA—CA)) with the MPI-E scale ($r = 0.324$, $p < 0.025$) also indicates that *extraverts* have the tendency to exhibit the Spence recall pattern whereas *introverts* display the reverse pattern. It should be noted that Spence's hypotheses about the preconscious were derived from Freud's earlier theoretical writings. Freud's unconscious, pre-conscious and conscious model was being formulated during the writing of *Studies on Hysteria* and a great deal of his early theorizing is based on hysterics. Eysenck's evidence on the close relationship between extraversion and hysteria suggests that this model of the mind may be meaningful for the type of patients Freud was dealing with.

The Eysenck introversion-extraversion model was partially successful in predicting the experimental results. It operated most successfully in differentiating those who conformed to the Spence results from those who did not and predicted alternation between CA and PA fairly well. It was poor in predicting alternation in the imaginary coin tossing task. This may be explained by the fact that S was instructed to devise a random sequence rather than instructed to do a task (e.g., recalling words) in which alternation could occur spontaneously. The Eysenck model is also partially successful in predicting the degree to which primary associates (as opposed to control associates) can be recalled. It is particularly successful in predicting this after the primary has been recalled and has theoretically created a fair amount of reactive inhibition. The model failed to predict overall ability to recall words. Curiously, the amount of alternation in the imaginary coin tossing task predicted total recall better than any other nonrecall variable.

In general, then, the present study, using proper controls, suggests that the primary is more effective after it has been recalled rather than before, as implied in Spence's work. The association between extraversion-introversion and influence of the primary before rather than after its recall suggests that there is a sub-population for whom the Spence hypothesis applies.

REFERENCES

1. BENDIG, A. W., The development of a short-form of the MAS. *J. consult. Psychol.*, **20**, 384–386, 1956.
2. BOUSFIELD, W. A., The occurrence of clustering in the recall of randomly arranged associates. *J. Gen. Psychol.*, **49**, 229–240, 1953.
3. BRUEL, I., GINSBERG, S., LUCKOMNIK, M. & SCHMEIDLER, G., An unsuccessful attempt to replicate Spence's experiment on the restricting effects of awareness. *J. Pers. soc. Psychol.*, **3**, 128–130, 1966.
4. CLAPP, R., The Effect of Stress and Subject Anxiety on the Ability to Produce Random Series. Unpublished master's thesis, University of Massachusetts Library, 1966.
5. DEESE, J., Influence of inter-item associative strength upon immediate free recall. *Psychol. Rep.*, **5**, 305–312, 1959.
6. —— & KAUFMAN, R. A., Serial effects in recall of unorganized and sequentially organized verbal material. *J. exp. Psychol.*, **54**, 180–187, 1957.
7. EYSENCK, H. J., Cortical inhibition, figural aftereffect and theory of personality. *J. abnorm. soc. Psychol.*, **51**, 94–106, 1955.
8. ——, A dynamic theory of anxiety and hysteria. *J. ment. Sci.*, **101**, 28–51, 1955.
9. ——, The questionnaire measurement of neuroticism and extraversion. *Riv. Psicol.*, **54**, 113–140, 1956.
10. ——, Comments on a test of the personality-satiation-inhibition theory. *Psychol. Rep.*, **5**, 395–396, 1959.
11. ——, *Manual of the Maudsley Personality Inventory*. London: University of London Press, 1959.
12. FRANKS, C. M., The Taylor Scale and the dimensional analysis of anxiety. *Rev. Psychol. appl.*, **6**, 35–44, 1956.
13. JUNG, J., Restricting effects of awareness?: Serial position bias in Spence's study. *J. Pers. soc. Psychol.*, **3**, 124–128, 1960.
14. RUSSELL, W. A. & JENKINS, J. J., *The Complete Minnesota Norms for Responses to 100 Words from the Kent-Rosanoff Word Association Test*. Tech. Rep. No. 11, University of Minnesota, Contract N8 onr 66216, Office of Naval Research, 1954.
15. SPENCE, D. P., Conscious and pre-conscious influence on recall: another sample of the restricting effects of awareness. *J. abnorm. soc. Psychol.*, **68**, 92–99, 1964.

16. —— & HOLLAND, B., The restricting effects of awareness: a paradox and an explanation. *J. abnorm. soc. Psychol.*, **64,** 163–174, 1962.
17. THORNDIKE, E. L. & LORGE, I., *The Teacher's Word Book of 30,000 Words*. New York: Teachers Coll., Columbia University, Bur. of publ., 1944.
18. WORELL, L. & WORELL, J., An experimental and theoretical note on 'Conscious and preconscious influences on recall'. *J. Pers. soc. Psychol.*, **3,** 119–123, 1966.

61

Extraversion, Neuroticism and Paired-Associates Learning

R. J. MCLAUGHLIN & H. J. EYSENCK[1]

First published in
Journal of Experimental Research in Personality, **2**, 128–132, 1967

SUBJECTS were tested on the Eysenck Personality Inventory and put into four groups: neurotic-extraverts, stable-extraverts, neurotic-introverts and stable-introverts. Ss were tested on either an easy list (low stimulus-low response similarity) or a difficult list (low stimulus-high response similarity) of 7 pairs of nonsense syllables. It was predicted and confirmed that extraverts learned faster on both lists. Moderate anxiety, determined by the relationship of neuroticism and extraversion-introversion, was shown to facilitate learning the easy list, while low anxiety was superior for learning the difficult list. An ex planation of this finding was attempted in terms of higher cortical arousal in introverts, facilitating consolidation and interfering with integration of learned material. The observed list difficulty × personality interaction was interpreted in terms of the Yerkes-Dodson Law.

Eysenck argued that extraverts build up reactive inhibition more quickly than introverts; he deduced that extraverts should have higher reminiscence scores on pursuit rotor learning tasks (Ref. 2). The evidence has strongly supported the deduction (Ref. 3), but it was found that instead of having lower pre-rest scores extraverts differed from introverts by having higher post-rest scores (Ref. 6). In addition, it was found that many other facts were difficult to reconcile with an inhibition theory of reminiscence for pursuit rotor learning (Ref. 7) and Eysenck proposed a consolidation theory according to which performance sets up cortical events which, in order to become available to the organism, require rest for consolidation (Ref. 8). Eysenck also postulated that consolidation interferes with performance, along lines familiar from Walker's theory (Ref. 23). It follows from this theory that individuals in whom a strong process of consolidation takes place would suffer more interference

[1] We are indebted to the Maudsley and Bethlem Royal Research Fund for financial assistance.

during post-rest performance, thus having lower reminiscence scores. Now Walker (Ref. 23) has suggested that cortical arousal is related to strong consolidation and Eysenck has argued that introverts are characterized by higher states of arousal than extraverts (Refs. 3, 4 & 5); from this it would follow that introverts should show stronger consolidation and accordingly less reminiscence (provided the rest period is short enough to make post-rest practice begin before the consolidation process has run its course completely). Kleinsmith & Kaplan have provided evidence to show that the postulated interference of consolidation with recall does in fact take place in verbal learning (Refs. 18 & 19) and Walker & Tarte have also demonstrated the postulated relation between arousal and consolidation-interference (Ref. 24).

Walker's theory has also received additional support from a series of studies investigating the effects of delayed auditory feed-back on retention (Refs. 15, 16 & 17) and the effects of drugs on retention (Ref. 21).

Applying the same arguments to verbal learning which we have used to explain the greater reminiscence scores of extraverts in pursuit rotor learning, we would predict that extraverts would perform better in serial learning, P-A learning and digit repetition tasks when only a short interval elapsed between learning and reproduction, but that introverts would perform in a superior manner with a lengthy rest pause intervening. Jensen investigated serial learning and found that extraverts made fewer errors in reaching the learning criterion ($r = -0.31$) than introverts in both a slow paced (4sec rate) and a fast pace (2sec rate) condition (Ref. 12). Shangmugan & Santhanan tested personality differences in serial learning under conditions of no interference and when interference stimuli were presented at the marginal visual levels (Ref. 22). Under conditions of no interference, a correlation of 0.65 was obtained between extraversion and number of correct responses. When interference was produced by another series of words the correlation was 0.82 and when interference was produced by letters and numbers it was 0.58. Howarth investigating digit span found no significant differences between extraverts and introverts in size of the span, but ability to hold the information over a larger time period proved to be greater in the extraverts (Ref. 11). The extraverts had a mean score of 14.0 sec, compared with introverts whose mean score was 11.8 sec. Jensen found various significant correlations between extraversion and serial learning and digit span; he also carried out a factor analysis of learning tasks and personality variables. His conclusion was that:

'Extraverts perform better than introverts, especially in serial learning and extraversion had a substantial loading of 0·41 on the general learning ability factor. Extraversion seemed to correlate mainly with resistance to response competition' (Ref. 13, pp. 7–8).

These findings support the theory here offered, as far as short-term memory is concerned. The study to be reported is also concerned with short-term memory, but deals with P-A learning rather than with serial or digit span.

In addition to extraversion, the personality dimension of neuroticism (Ref. 2) was also measured; a good review of the theories and research relating neuroticism/anxiety to learning has been given by Jones (Ref. 14). If we regard this personality variable as analogous to a drive state, then the Yerkes-Dodson Law (Ref. 1) would suggest a curvilinear (inverse-U) relation between neuroticism-drive and performance, with intermediate levels of the former giving optimal performance. We would also expect the optimum level of neuroticism-drive to be lower for more complex, difficult tasks. In addition, Eysenck has suggested the importance of investigating the interaction of the two personality dimensions under investigation (Ref. 7). Neuroticism, which is conceived of as a predisposition to strong autonomic activation, also produces higher cortical arousal, both directly and through the reticular formation and under the conditions of the experiment to be described it does not seem far-fetched to argue that both high neuroticism and high introversion contribute to a state of high arousal. This would suggest that, under relatively easy task conditions, the stable extraverts groups would show suboptimal arousal, while the neurotic introvert group would show superoptimal arousal; both would perform at a lower level than the intermediate groups, between whom theory does not enable us to make a clear-cut choice as far as performance is concerned. When we now consider a more difficult task, the shape of the inverted-U would be expected to be changed, with the apex further to the low drive end of the abscissa; this would lead to a relative improvement in the performance of the stable extravert group, a relative decline in that of the neurotic introvert group, and an unpredictable change in the performance of the intermediate groups.

METHOD

Lists

The two lists which were employed are reproduced in Table 1. The lists were constructed to meet the requirements of having stimulus members of high meaningfulness, low similarity and response members of intermediate meaningfulness and either high similarity or low similarity. Meaningfulness was measured by Noble's 'm' scale (Ref. 20). Stimulus and response members of low similarity had a minimal number of letters in common, while the responses of high similarity all had the same vowel and one consonant in common. In all pairs similarity between stimuli and responses was minimized as much as possible.

TABLE 1

LISTS OF PAIRS OF CVCs REPRESENTING THE COMBINATION OF HIGH MEANINGFULNESS, LOW SIMILARITY STIMULUS MEMBERS WITH INTERMEDIATE MEANINGFULNESS, LOW SIMILARITY RESPONSE MEMBERS (EASY LIST) AND INTERMEDIATE MEANINGFULNESS, HIGH SIMILARITY RESPONSE MEMBERS (DIFFICULT LIST)

Easy List		Difficult List	
Stimulus Members High meaningfulness, low similarity	Response Members Intermediate meaningfulness, low similarity	Stimulus Members High meaningfulness, low similarity	Response Members Intermediate meaningfulness, low similarity
JET (4·01)*	SAH (2·19)	HIT (4·01)	WOD (2·33)
SIN (4·03)	GED (1·99)	LAW (4·25)	ZOW (2·26)
LOG (4·16)	BIM (2·46)	BUS (4·23)	YOW (2·42)
COW (4·00)	LIR (2·21)	RED (4·16)	WOT (2·06)
DAM (4·00)	CEY (2·14)	PEN (4·12)	WOB (2·42)
FUR (4·08)	TAQ (2·25)	JOB (4·25)	FOW (2·30)
TEL (4·12)	NIS (2·11)	VOL (3·82)	WOR (3·22)
Mean (4·11)	(2·19)	(4·12)	(2·43)

* Nobel M values are in parenthesis

The stimulus materials were presented by a memory drum to each S individually. The CVCs were typed in pica capitals and appeared in the window at a 2:2sec rate with a 6sec inter-trial interval. The 7 pairs were presented in two different orders to minimize serial learning of the responses.

A practice list of 3 pairs was constructed using intermediate meaningfulness and low similarity stimulus and response members.

Procedure

64 paid volunteers were tested on the Eysenck Personality Inventory (EPI) (Ref. 10) and the Mill Hill Vocabulary Scale (Part B). On the basis of the scores on the EPI Ss were put into four groups: Neurotic-

extraverts (NE); Stable-extraverts (SE); Neurotic-introverts (NI); and Stable-introverts (SI). Any S scoring either 11 or 12 on the Introversion-Extraversion scale and/or 9 or 10 on the Neuroticism scale was excluded. Testing was continued until 16 Ss were obtained for each of the four personality groups. These 64 Ss consisted of 47 males and 17 females and averaged 25·29 years of age (SD = 6·73). The Ss were randomly assigned to be tested on either of two lists. This randomization was made with the restriction that 8 Ss of each of the 4 personality groups were assigned to each of the two lists. Standard instructions for P-A learning, with anticipation spelling of the responses were given to all Ss. The testing continued until the S learned the list to a criterion of one errorless trial.

RESULTS

Learning was measured by the number of errors and trials to reach a criterion of one perfect anticipation of all seven responses. The summary statistics for both measures are given in Table 2.

TABLE 2

MEANS AND SDS OF TRIALS AND ERRORS TO CRITERION

| | Easy List | | | | Difficult List | | | |
| | Extravert | | Introvert | | Extravert | | Introvert | |
	H–N	L–N	H–N	L–N	H–N	L–N	H–N	L–N
Mean errors	28·62	83·25	85·12	53·50	139·00	82·00	148·13	167·25
SD	17·29	45·63	56·93	37·55	46·41	26·40	93·38	83·25
Mean trials	8·50	23·25	21·25	16·38	34·75	21·25	35·38	29·25
SD	4·55	9·72	9·63	10·54	11·51	5·60	15·70	10·73

The results of the analysis of variance on the number of errors to criterion is summarized in Table 3. Because of significant heterogeneity of variance, a square root transformation was made of these scores. List difficulty, Extraversion and the interaction of List Difficulty × Extraversion × Neuroticism yielded the only significant results.

The significance of the second-order interaction indicates that neurotic extraverts are superior to stable extraverts on the easy list, while the reverse is true on the difficult list and that neurotic introverts learn faster on the difficult task and slower on the easy task than stable introverts.

Number of trials, which correlated 0·95 with number of errors, yielded

TABLE 3

ANALYSIS OF VARIANCE OF NUMBER OF ERRORS TO CRITERION

Source	SS	df	MS	
List difficulty	237·78	1	237·78	32·22‡
Extraversion	29·76	1	29·76	4·03*
Neuroticism	0·03	1	0·03	
L.D. × E	4·33	1	4·33	
L.D. × N	11·83	1	11·83	1·60
E × N	4·01	1	4·01	
L.D. × E × N	83·77	1	83·77	11·96†
Within	413·28	56	7·38	
Total	784·89	63		

* $p < 0.05$
† $p < 0.01$
‡ $p < 0.001$

the same significant effects in a similar analysis of variance (again after a square root transformation). The intelligence quotient of the Mill Hill Vocabulary Scale, which correlated -0.08 with number of errors to criterion, was not significantly ($p < 0.05$) related to either number of errors or number of trials to criterion.

DISCUSSION

The results of the present experiment are consistent with the prediction that extraversion facilitates P-A acquisition as measured by number of errors, or number of trials to criterion.

The finding of the significance of the second-order interaction can be clarified by reference to Fig. 67. The four personality groups are plotted in relation to their achieved level of performance. What was predicted was that the stable-extraverts and the neurotic-introverts would be below and above, respectively, the optimum level for performance in learning the easy list. In learning the difficult list it was predicted that the optimum level for performance would shift toward the low drive group. Thus the stable-extraverts were found to be best and the neurotic-introverts significantly poorer. A reversal was found in achieved level for learning the difficult list with the stable-introverts making more errors than the neurotic-introverts. The difference between these two groups was not significant ($t = 0.40$, $p < 0.05$) and may have been due to chance. No prediction was made concerning the difference between the two inter-

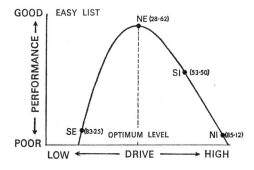

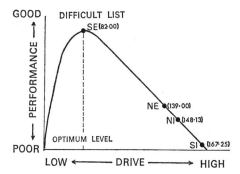

Figure 67. The relationship of number of errors to criterion and the hypothesized level of arousal for the easy and difficult lists.

mediate personality groups, i.e., neurotic-extraverts and stable-introverts; the neurotic-extraverts in both lists did not differ significantly from the stable-introverts.

It can be noted that the superiority of extraverts to introverts is much more marked in the difficult list, although the appropriate interaction effect is not significant. This may be regarded as partial support for Jensen's finding, mentioned in the introduction, that extraverts are particularly at an advantage when resistance to response competition is involved (Ref. 13).

Having obtained evidence that extraverts learn P-A lists faster than introverts, the remaining portion of the theory, i.e., that introverts are only at a disadvantage with immediate recall, but that when time is allowed for consolidation to occur, their performance should increase, remains as a crucial experiment which awaits further evidence.

REFERENCES

1. BROADHURST, P. L., The interaction of task difficulty and motivation: the Yerkes-Dodson Law revived. *Acta Psychol.*, **16,** 321–338, 1959.
2. EYSENCK, H. J., *The Dynamics of Anxiety and Hysteria*. London: Routledge & Kegan Paul, 1957.
3. ——, Reminiscence, drive and personality—revision and extension of a theory. *Brit. J. soc. clin. Psychol.*, **1,** 127–140, 1962.
4. ——, The biological basis of personality. *Nature*, **199,** 1031–1034, 1963.
5. ——, Biological factors in neurosis and crime. *Scientia*, Dec., 1–11, 1964.
6. ——, Personality and reminiscence—an experimental study of the 'Reactive Inhibition' and the 'Conditioned Inhibition' theories. *Life Sci.*, **3,** 189–198, 1964.
7. ——, A three-factor theory of reminiscence. *Brit. J. Psychol.*, **56,** 163–181, 1965.
8. ——, Personality and experimental psychology. *Bull. Brit. Psychol. Soc.*, **19,** 1–28, 1966.
9. ——, On the dual function of consolidation. *Percept. mot. Skills*, **22,** 273–274, 1966.
10. —— & EYSENCK, S. B. G., *Manual of the Eysenck Personality Inventory*. London: University of London Press, 1964.
11. HOWARTH, E., Some laboratory measures of extraversion-introversion. *Percept. mot. Skills*, **17,** 55–60, 1963.
12. JENSEN, A. R., Extraversion, neuroticism and serial learning. *Acta Psychol.*, **20,** 66–67, 1962.
13. ——, *Individual Differences in Learning: Interference Factor*. Co-operative Research Project No. 1867. Office of Education, U.S. Dept. of Health, Education and Welfare, 1964.
14. JONES, H. G., Learning and abnormal behaviour. In *Handbook of Abnormal Psychology* (ed. H. J. Eysenck). London: Pitman Medical, 1960.
15. KING, D. J., Immediate memory of connected meaningful material practiced under delayed auditory feedback. *Psychol. Rep.*, **13,** 91–96, 1963.
16. —— & DODGE, A. M., The influence of oral recall on immediate and delayed memory meaningful material practiced under delayed auditory feedback. *J. Psychol.*, **59,** 141–147, 1965.

17. —— & WOLF, S., The influence of delayed auditory feedback on immediate and delayed memory. *J. Psychol.*, **59**, 131–139, 1965.

18. KLEINSMITH, L. J. & KAPLAN, S., Paired-associate learning as a function of arousal and interpolated interval. *J. exp. Psychol.*, **65**, 190–193, 1963.

19. —— & ——, Interaction of arousal and recall interval in nonsense syllable paired-associate learning. *J. exp. Psychol.*, **67**, 124–126, 1964.

20. NOBLE, C. E., Measurements of association value (a) rated association (b) and scaled meaningfulness (m) for the 2100 CVC combinations of the English alphabet. *Psychol. Rep.*, **8**, 487–521, 1961.

21. PARÉ, W., The effect of caffeine and seconal on a visual discrimination task. *J. comp. physiol. Psychol.*, **54**, 506–509, 1961.

22. SHANGMUGAN, T. E. & SANTHANAN, M. L., Personality differences in serial learning when interference is presented at the marginal visual level. *J. Indian Acad. appl. Psychol.*, **1**, 25–28, 1964.

23. WALKER, E. L., Action decrement and its relation to learning. *Psychol. Rev.*, **65**, 129–142, 1958.

24. —— & TARTE, R. D., Memory storage as a function of arousal and time with homogeneous and heterogeneous lists. *Journal of Verbal Learning & Verbal Behaviour*, **2**, 113–119, 1963.

62

Extraversion, Reminiscence and Satiation Effects

R. LYNN

First published in *British Journal of Psychology*, **51**, 319–324, 1960

EYSENCK'S theory that extraverts accumulate reactive inhibition quickly and that it dissipates in them slowly and his application of this theory to aftereffects and reminiscence is made the basis of six predictions: using the spiral aftereffect, there should be (1) a negative correlation between extraversion and duration of the aftereffect; (2) a tendency for extraverts to see progressively less of the aftereffect with repeated massed trials; (3) a tendency for extraverts to recover more in their perception of the aftereffect after a period rest; (4) a negative correlation between the duration of the aftereffect and a measure of reminiscence using the inverted alphabet printing task; (5) a positive correlation between extraversion and reminiscence; (6) a tendency for extraverts to show more work decrement with massed practice on the inverted alphabet printing task. Using 40 male university students as subjects, predictions 1, 2, 4 and 5 are confirmed at a statistically significant level and predictions 3 and 6 show non-significant results in the predicted direction.

INTRODUCTION

In view of the recent criticisms of Eysenck's theory linking introversion-extraversion with reactive inhibition (Ref. 3), figural aftereffects and satiation effects, this paper presents the results of an independent investigation of some predictions from the theory. Essentially, the Eysenck theory postulates that extraverts accumulate reactive inhibition quickly and dissipate it slowly. This theory mediates a large number of predictions, e.g., that extraverts should show greater work decrement and more reminiscence, for which there is confirmatory evidence (Ref. 3). Eysenck has also postulated that figural aftereffects and satiation effects are affected by reactive inhibition and hence related to introversion-extraversion and evidence in support of this postulate has been published for the kinaesthetic aftereffect and the Archimedes spiral satiation effect (Ref. 3).

The experiment reported here concerns the relation between extraversion, reminiscence and the spiral satiation effect. Eysenck's theory of the spiral satiation effect is as follows: as the subject fixates the spiral reactive inhibition is generated and this interferes with the aftereffect according to its strength. Further, the processes underlying the reversal phenomenon must themselves generate satiation and therefore curtail the aftereffect. Both processes would tend to make extraverts experience the aftereffect less than introverts. Although little direct evidence is available, two additional hypotheses of Eysenck provide deductions about which there is evidence relevant to this theory. First, it is postulated that depressant drugs increase reactive inhibition and hence curtail the aftereffect, while stimulant drugs decrease inhibition and hence increase the duration of the aftereffect; this deduction has been partially confirmed by Eysenck, Holland & Trouton (Ref. 5). Secondly, it is postulated that brain injury increases the tendency to generate reactive inhibition and hence brain injured subjects should have smaller satiation effects. This deduction has been confirmed by Price & Deabler (Ref. 11), although some doubt has been thrown on this finding as a result of the findings of Spivack & Levine (Ref. 13) and what would appear to be the important question of the site of the injury remains uninvestigated. So far as reminiscence is concerned, Eysenck accepts Hull's theory that reminiscence is due to the dissipation of reactive inhibition; when Eysenck's own postulate that extraverts generate reactive inhibition quickly and dissipate it slowly is added to Hull's theory, the prediction is that extraverts should show greater reminiscence.

This theory has not been without its critics, notably Hamilton and Rechtschaffen, who maintain that there is insufficient evidence in its support (Refs. 6 & 14). Rechtschaffen presents evidence showing some positive association between extraversion, figural aftereffects and reminiscence using inverted alphabet printing, but the correlations were too low for statistical significance. However, since Rechtschaffen used an unusually short rest interval in his reminiscence test, it is arguable that his experiment cannot be regarded as an adequate test of the theory.

The present paper reports an investigation of six predictions from the Eysenck theory, namely: (1) under certain conditions of administration the inverted alphabet printing task should yield reminiscence scores which correlate positively with extraversion; (2) extraverts should show more work decrement in inverted alphabet printing under conditions of massed practice; (3) there should be a negative correlation between extraversion and duration of the spiral aftereffect; (4) with repeated presentation, extraverts should show a greater fall off in the spiral aftereffect as a result of their tendency to generate reactive inhibition more quickly; (5) after a period of rest extraverts should show a greater recovery in seeing the spiral aftereffect as a result of the dissipation of reactive inhibition; (6) the duration of the spiral aftereffect and reminiscence should be negatively correlated.

METHOD

Subjects

The sample consisted of 40 male university students living in a university hall of residence; volunteers for the experiment were asked for and the first 40 to volunteer were taken as the subjects. All subjects fell in the age range 18–23 with the exception of one who was slightly older. On the Maudsley Personality Inventory the mean score for extraversion was 23·5, S.D. 8·42, compared with the norm for the general population of 24·9, S.D. 9·71; and for neuroticism 27·6, S.D. 9·27, compared with the norm for the general population of 19·9, S.D. 11·02. It is evident therefore that the sample was representative of the normal population on the introversion-extraversion dimension but on neuroticism it scored somewhat more neurotic. However, it has been shown that English university students as a whole score more neurotic than the general population by something like ½ S.D. (Ref. 12) and it may therefore be concluded that the present sample was representative of English university students though not representative of the general population on the neuroticism dimension.

Procedure

The spiral used in this experiment was a 4-throw spiral of 180° similar to the one illustrated by Eysenck (Ref. 3) except that it was 10 inches in diameter; it rotated at 78 rpm and subjects were tested in daylight conditions. Subjects were seated 6 feet from the spiral and instructed to concentrate on the central point. The aftereffect was explained to the subjects and they were asked to report when the apparent movement ceased. Subjects were given a practice trial of 40 sec. They were then given 10 trials of 30 sec each in 'massed' conditions, i.e., the spiral was rotated as soon as the subject had made his judgment of the cessation of the aftereffect. Following this a 2 minute rest was allowed, after which subjects underwent one more trial. The reliability of this test, calculated by the split-half method, was 0·86.

Subjects were then asked to answer the Maudsley Personality Inventory which gives a measure of introversion-extraversion and neuroticism.

Finally, subjects were asked to do the inverted alphabet printing task. Subjects were instructed to print the alphabet upside down as fast as they could for 14 trials with massed practice. They were then given a 2 minute rest and asked to print the alphabet once more.

RESULTS

The variables about which predictions were made were scored in the following way: (1) reminiscence: a score was obtained by subtracting the speed on trial 15 of the inverted alphabet printing from the mean of the speeds on the trials 8–14; (2) work decrement: speed on trial 14 of alphabet printing; (3) duration of spiral aftereffect: the reported duration on the first trial; (4) decline of the spiral aftereffect; a score was obtained by subtracting the time of the aftereffect on trial 10 from that on trial 1; (5) recovery of the aftereffect with rest: duration of aftereffect on the 11th (post-rest) trial minus duration of the aftereffect on trial 10. The product-moment correlations between these variables and extraversion are shown in Table 1. To afford comparison with other studies, the product-moment correlations of neuroticism with some of these measures are also shown in Table 1.

TABLE 1

PRODUCT-MOMENT CORRELATIONS OF MEASURES OF
INHIBITION WITH EXTRAVERSION AND NEUROTICISM

Measure	E	N	Measure 3
1. Reminiscence	+0·42*	+0·29	−0·34*
2. Work decrement	+0·21	—	—
3. Duration of spiral aftereffect	−0·43*	−0·13	—
4. Decline of spiral aftereffect	+0·42*	—	—
5. Recovery of aftereffect after rest	+0·18	—	—
Speed of alphabet printing, trial 1	—	+0·29	—

* Significant at 0·05 probability level

Two extreme groups of 12 extraverts and 11 introverts were obtained by considering only the subjects whose scores fell 7 or more points away from the mean. Fig. 68 shows the mean scores for the two groups over the 11 trials on the spiral aftereffect and illustrates the greater decrement of the extraverts with repeated presentation. Fig. 69 shows the mean scores for the two groups on the inverted alphabet printing task and illustrates the tendency of extraverts to slow down and to show greater reminiscence. The means and S.D.s of these two extreme groups on the measures calculated are shown in Table 2.

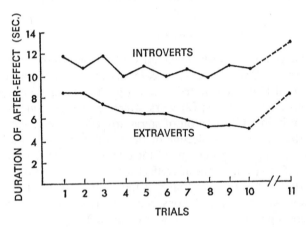

Figure 68. Duration of spiral after-effects of introverts and extraverts.

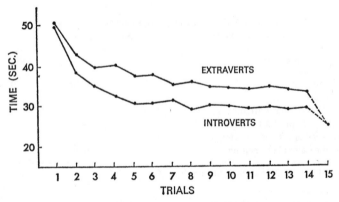

Figure 69. Mean times and reminiscence of introverts and extraverts on the inverted alphabet printing task.

TABLE 2

MEANS AND S.D.s OF INTROVERT AND EXTRAVERT
GROUPS ON MEASURES OF REACTIVE INHIBITION

	Introverts		Extraverts	
	Mean	S.D.	Mean	S.D.
Inverted alphabet printing				
1. Reminiscence	5·10	2·28	10·42	4·98
2. Speed on trial 14	29·18	6·32	33·00	6·00
Spiral aftereffect				
3. Duration on trial 1	12·09	8·50	7·52	5·31
4. Decline of aftereffect	1·18	5·33	3·65	4·36
5. Recovery of aftereffect	2·55	2·62	3·17	4·32

DISCUSSION

It is evident that the correlations tend to support Eysenck's theory. The two that do not reach statistical significance are in the predicted direction and the lowest, that of $+0.18$ between extraversion and recovery of the spiral, is probably reduced by the method of scoring, since the extraverts show a greater proportional post-rest increase in aftereffect which is to some extent masked by considering the absolute increase. On the other hand, it should be noted that the correlation between extraversion and the decline of the aftereffect might have been increased by the experimental procedure used, since extraverts experienced more 'massing' as a result of their shorter aftereffect.

The difference between the present results and those obtained by Rechtschaffen (Ref. 14) deserves some discussion. Rechtschaffen used Guilford's R scale for assessing extraversion and this correlates only about 0·5 with the extraversion scale of the M.P.I. (Ref. 4). But it is likely that the differences in methods of assessing reactive inhibition are also important. The method employed by Rechtschaffen was to give subjects 5 trials of distributed practice followed by 5 trials of massed practice and to obtain an estimate of reactive inhibition by subtracting the number of letters printed under massed practice from the number printed under distributed practice. Using this measure he obtained a correlation of $+0.18$ between extraversion and the amount of reactive inhibition accumulated. He also obtained a score of reminiscence by giving a 1 minute rest after the 5 massed trials, followed by 2 further trials. Reminiscence and extraversion correlated only $+0.08$. The difference between this finding and the present one might be due to at least two factors. First, Rechtschaffen's failure to get large reminiscence scores for his extraverts could be due to an insufficiently long rest pause; the rest given was only 1 minute which is considerably less than most investigators have used with the inverted alphabet printing task, e.g., Archer gave a 5 minute rest (Ref. 1) and Kimble a 10 minute rest (Ref. 8); and Eysenck obtained his correlation between extraversion and reminiscence with a 10 minute rest pause. It is likely that the 1-minute rest is insufficient for reactive inhibition to dissipate fully in extraverted subjects. Hence they would not show the full reminiscence effect obtained with a longer rest interval. Rechtschaffen argues that since it is postulated that extraverts generate reactive inhibition more quickly and dissipate it more slowly, conflicting predictions about reminiscence scores can be made from the Eysenck theory: either extraverts should dissipate more I_R because they have more and hence show more reminiscence; or because they dissipate I_R more slowly they should show less reminiscence; or the two effects might cancel each other out. This argument could easily explain Rechtschaffen's finding using his particular experimental conditions, but it cannot be accepted as a valid criticism of the Eysenck theory; for, once the time interval for reactive inhibition to dissipate in extraverts has been established by the standard method of plotting reminiscence scores with different rest intervals, the theory yields the quite unequivocal prediction that if this time interval is allowed extraverts will show more reminiscence.

A second factor which could explain Rechtschaffen's low correlation between extraversion and reminiscence arises from the part played by conditioned inhibition. Reminiscence scores are most satisfactorily obtained either very quickly, before sI_R has had time to develop, or after a number of trials, when sI_R has reached its asymptote. Rechtschaffen's choice of 10 trials may be unsatisfactory from this point of view. Since reactive inhibition develops more quickly in extraverts, it is possible that by the 11th trial they will have greater conditioned inhibition and this would obscure the recovery from reactive inhibition in the measurement of reminiscence. Since in the present study extraverts and introverts both work at the same speed on the 15th trial, it appears that sI_R has reached its asymptote and the greater reminiscence of extraverts emerges.

The small correlation of neuroticism with duration of the spiral aftereffect confirms previous reports that there is no association between the spiral aftereffect and affective states (Ref. 13). The correlation between neuroticism and time on trial 1 of the inverted alphabet printing task would be predicted on the basis of the Yerkes-Dodson Law, i.e., the task is one in which the dominant habits are incorrect and are made more dominant by high drive, with the result that high drive impairs performance. Although the correlation falls short of significance, it is in the predicted direction and may be regarded as giving some support to the findings of Taylor & Rechtschaffen of a significant correlation between anxiety and time on inverted alphabet printing (Ref. 14). On the other hand, the independence of neuroticism and reminiscence is inconsistent both with Eysenck's finding of a positive correlation between neuroticism and reminiscence on the pursuit rotor (Ref. 2) and Kimble's finding of a correlation between drive and reminiscence in inverted alphabet printing (Ref. 9). The discrepancy adds one more finding to the many reviewed by Jensen (Ref. 7) showing that experiments using questionnaire measure of drive give extremely conflicting results, probably determined in part by the degree to which drive is mobilized by the experimental situation.

ACKNOWLEDGEMENTS

The writer is indebted to Mr Ian Gordon of Exeter University for help in carrying out part of the experiment.

REFERENCES

1. ARCHER, E. J., Post-rest performance in motor learning as a function of pre-rest degree of distribution of practice. *J. exp. Psychol.*, **47**, 47–51, 1954.
2. EYSENCK, H. J., Reminiscence, drive and personality theory. *J. abnorm. soc. Psychol.*, **53**, 328–333, 1956.
3. ——, *The Dynamics of Anxiety and Hysteria.* London: Routledge & Kegan Paul, 1957.
4. ——, Comments on a test of the personality-satiation-inhibition theory. *Psychol. Rep.*, **5**, 395–396, 1959.
5. EYSENCK, H. J., HOLLAND, H. & TROUTON, D. S., Drugs and personality. 3. The effects of stimulant and depressant drugs on visual aftereffects. *J. ment. Sci.*, **103**, 650–5, 1957.
6. HAMILTON, V., Eysenck's theories of anxiety and hysteria—a methodological critique. *Brit. J. Psychol.*, **50**, 48–63, 1959.

7. JENSEN, A. R., Personality. *Ann. Rev. Psychol.*, **9,** 295–322, 1958.
8. KIMBLE, G. A., An experimental test of a two factor theory of inhibition. *J. exp. Psychol.*, **39,** 15–23, 1949.
9. ——, Evidence for the role of motivation in determining the amount of reminiscence in pursuit rotor learning. *J. exp. Psychol.*, **40,** 248–253, 1950.
10. LYNN, R., Two personality characteristics related to educational attainment. *Brit. J. educ. Psychol.*, **29,** 213–216, 1959.
11. PRICE, A. G. & DEABLER, H. L., Diagnosis of organicity by means of the spiral aftereffect. *J. consult. Psychol.*, **19,** 299–302, 1955.
12. RECHTSCHAFFEN, A., Neural satiation, reactive inhibition and introversion-extraversion. *J. abnorm. soc. Psychol.*, **57,** 283–291, 1958.
13. SPIVACK, G. & LEVINE, M., Spiral aftereffect and measures of satiation in brain injured and normal subjects. *J. Pers.*, **27,** 211–227, 1959.
14. TAYLOR, J. A. & RECHTSCHAFFEN, A., Manifest anxiety and reversed alphabet printing. *J. abnorm. soc. Psychol.*, **58,** 221–224, 1959.

63

Personality and Reminiscence—An Experimental Study of the 'Reactive Inhibition' and the 'Conditioned Inhibition' Theories

H. J. EYSENCK[1]

First published in *Life Sciences*, **3**, 189–198, 1964

INTRODUCTION

IN a previous article (Ref. 7) Eysenck has proposed a three-factor theory of reminiscence, involving reactive inhibition (temporary work decrement), conditioned inhibition (permanent work decrement) and consolidation (perseveration). It was also postulated that experimental tasks differed greatly among themselves with respect to the degree to which these factors were involved; thus pursuit rotor learning was suggested to give rise to reminiscence scores dependent almost purely on consolidation, while vigilance tasks depended far more on reactive inhibition and the dissipation of reactive inhibition. Fig. 70 is quoted from the above-mentioned article to show the precise difference between the inhibition and the consolidation theories. According to the former, point B is depressed by inhibition-produced performance decrement, the dissipation of which raises C above B after rest; according to the latter, consolidation takes place during the rest, thus raising C above B. Evidence was found in the article for the importance of the consolidation variable in pursuit rotor learning and also for the belief that pursuit rotor learning was situated at one extreme of the continuum extending to vigilance tasks of the other extreme (Ref. 7).

The postulation of a continuum of this kind throws some light on a very important correlate of reminiscence, namely the personality trait of extraversion-introversion. The writer has postulated that extraverts are characterized by strong inhibitory and weak excitatory potentials and has also proposed that this hypothesis could be tested by means of

[1] The writer is indebted to the Maudsley and Bethlem Royal Hospital Research Fund for the support of this investigation. He is also grateful to Mr C. Atwood for kindly allowing him to test apprentices at the Ford works at Dagenham.

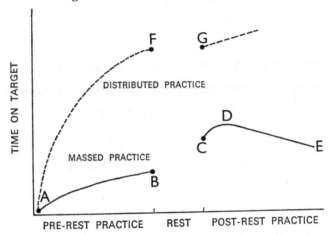

Figure 70. Shape of work curves under conditions of massed and distributed practice.

reminiscence experiments. This proposal was made on the basis of accepting the 'inhibition' theory of reminiscence, according to which reminiscence is a measure of the total amount of inhibition accumulated during pre-rest practice (Ref. 3). A survey of the available literature has disclosed that this prediction was in fact borne out, but that the correlations found were all disappointingly low (Ref. 4). It will be clear from our discussion above that pursuit rotor performance (which has been used in the great majority of these experiments) is far from being an ideal method for testing the personality theory in question, by virtue of the fact that reminiscence here is due almost entirely to consolidation and only to a very small degree to inhibition. Vigilance tests would appear to be far more suitable and indeed the evidence in this field is much more clear-cut and reliable than in the case of pursuit-rotor work. We thus derive from our consideration of the consolidation-inhibition continuum an important pointer regarding the choice of proper tests for the measurement of extraversion and for the testing of the general theory linking inhibition and extraversion.

It is interesting to consider why, precisely, investigations of reminiscence in pursuit rotor learning have usually discovered greater reminiscence in extraverted than in introverted subjects, in spite of the fact that we have shown reminiscence to be due to consolidation rather than to inhibition on this task. It could, of course, be postulated that extraverts learn better than do introverts and therefore improve more during the consolidation period; such an *ad hoc* postulate, however, would not link up with anything known about the experimental correlates of extraversion and introversion. It might also be thought that perhaps inhibition did play some part in the genesis of the reminiscence phenomenon, although rather less than did consolidation and that this small contribution was mirrored in the rather slight correlation usually found between reminiscence and extraversion. This hypothesis would demand that extraverts and introverts should differ in pre-rest performance at point B, but not at points A or C. Some support for such a view comes from the work of Ray (Ref. 11) and Bendig & Eigenbrode (Ref. 1).

An alternative theory is here presented which, while also accounting for the observed differences in reminiscence, would differ in certain testable ways from the theory just mentioned. According to the view defended in this article, we are dealing with a highly complex phenomenon in our work on reminiscence and the position of point C must be compared, not only with point B, but also with point G (Fig. 70) which shows the performance achieved by a group of subjects after an equivalent amount of practice *on a distributed practice schedule*. The fact that C falls short of G, in spite of the fact that maximum dissipation of inhibition has occurred (Ref. 10), or that maximum consolidation has taken place (Ref. 7), is due to the accumulation of conditioned inhibition (sI_R). This conditioned inhibition arises because of the reinforcing effect of the 'blocks' or involuntary rest pauses which are the result of reactive inhibition building up to the level of the drive (D) under which the individual subject is working. These I.R.P.s, which have good experimental support in relation to many tasks, may or may not depress the actual level of performance, depending on certain properties of the task; it is here assumed that they do not depress performance on the pursuit rotor. Now it has been shown that introverts condition more quickly and more strongly than do extraverts (Ref. 5) and it might be predicted that in consequence they should also accumulate more sI_R, which would depress their performance at point C. This would give rise to a difference in reminiscence between extraverts and introverts in the predicted direction, not because of poorer performance of extraverts at point B, but because of poorer performance of introverts at point C. Such an hypothesis is, of course, readily testable and an experiment along these lines will be reported presently.

Before doing so, however, we must deal with a theoretical objection to the scheme outlined above. According to our personality postulate, extraverts should have more I.R.P.s than introverts and Spielmann

v

(Ref. 12) and Eysenck (Ref. 8) have shown, in connection with a tapping task, that this is actually so. As level of conditioning is a function of number of reinforcements (in this case, I.R.P.s), we would, on these grounds, expect extraverts, rather than introverts, to develop greater conditioned inhibition. This is a serious objection and it is impossible to be certain that it is not fatal to our hypothesis. However, Eysenck has shown in a comparison of eye-blink conditioning records of extraverted and introverted subjects (Ref. 5), that 30 reinforcements for an extraverted group resulted in a level of performance roughly equal to that of an introverted group which had received only 3 or 4 reinforced trials. Even quite large differences in number of reinforcements may therefore be postulated to be incapable of overcoming the greater speed and strength of conditioning in introverted subjects, although it would, of course, require to be proved more directly that results obtained with eye-blink conditioning can indeed be taken over into a field of conditioning so very different in many ways.

A rather different objection might be raised on the grounds that at point B there is no differentiation between introverts and extraverts, although they are postulated to differ with respect to sI_R which is assumed to have a depressing effect; should not introverts be inferior in performance to extraverts at this point? The answer surely must be that according to the consolidation theory *all* habits require a rest pause after massed practice before learning can take place on any permanent basis; this must apply to sI_R just as much as to sH_R. Consequently the differential effects of the growth of sI_R will not become apparent until *after* consolidation has taken place during the rest pause.

Experiment

211 male applicants for an apprenticeship training scheme were administered the pursuit rotor under conditions of high drive (Ref. 6); they were also administered the Eysenck Personality Inventory (E.P.I.) (Ref. 9), a modified and improved form of the M.P.I. This instrument provides scores on the two personality dimensions of Extraversion and Neuroticism; in the present experiment only the E scale (Form A) has been used. Of the subjects who had filled in the E.P.I., 23 could not be matched by name with pursuit rotor records (names were illegibly written, or initials did not match). Of the remainder, 28 had E scores of 16 and above; these will be called the extraverted group. 23 subjects had scores of 9 or below; these will be called the introverted group. (The standardization group for this test had a mean of 12·08 and a S.D.

of 4·37.) Very roughly, therefore, our two groups are about one S.D. above and below the mean for E.

The apprentices were all aged between 15 and 17 years and took the pursuit rotor test as part of a selection battery, not knowing that scores would not in fact contribute to their acceptance or rejection. All Ss practised for 5 minutes, rested for 10 minutes and practised for another 5 minutes. The apparatus and procedure have been described in detail elsewhere (Ref. 6). Practice was massed, recording being switched every 10 sec from one of the two clocks to the other, to enable the score to be read and recorded. The first post-rest trial was preceded by 2 sec of rotary pursuit, so that Ss should not enter the first trial 'cold', but would have an equal chance on this as on succeeding trials of starting off 'on target'. Standard instructions were given to all Ss and verbal correction applied if they did not act according to instructions. Scores were recorded to the nearest 0·01 sec. The reminiscence measure used subtracted the mean of the last three pre-rest scores from the mean of the first three post-rest scores.

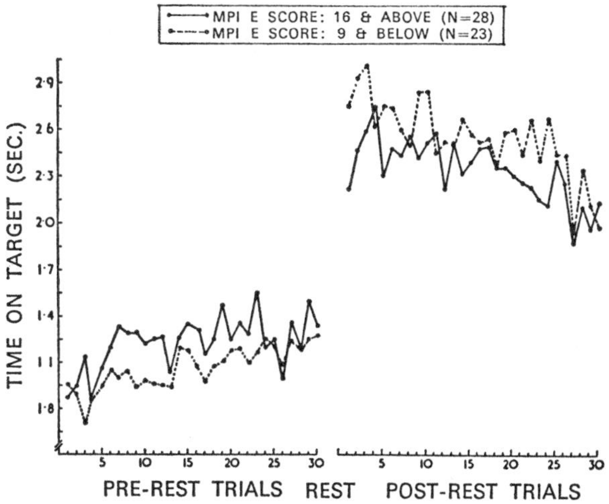

Figure 71. Pre-rest and post-rest performance of extraverted and introverted subjects on the pursuit rotor.

The performance of the two groups is plotted in Fig. 71 and it will be seen that as predicted the extraverts have a higher reminiscence score than do the introverts (1·67 as compared with 1·09). This difference is significant at the $p<0·05$ level, $t = 2·36$. It will also be seen that the two groups do not differ at all at point B (terminal pre-rest practice) but differ profoundly at point C (initial post-rest practice). These data are as predicted from the 'conditioned inhibition' hypothesis and contrary to the 'reactive inhibition' hypothesis. It will be remembered that these were 'high drive' apprentices and it might be thought that under conditions of low drive different results might be found. Star has produced a diagram (Ref. 13, Fig. 19) of the pursuit rotor performance of the 26 highest and lowest M.P.I. E scale scorers out of 100 low drive apprentices; the predicted differences in reminiscence are observed between phase 1 and phase 2 and it can be seen from the diagram that this is due entirely to post-rest performance superiority of the extraverted group, rather than to pre-rest superiority of the introverted group. (In fact, in his study the extraverted group shows a slight superiority in performance in their terminal pre-rest performance.)

Evidence from the literature, however, is by no means unanimous, although it is often impossible to decide because results are usually reported in terms of correlations between extraversion and reminiscence, thus obscuring the nature of the relationship. However, Eysenck's original data (Ref. 2) were still available for inspection; the extraverts show both a depressed pre-rest and an elevated post-rest performance, with the former contributing rather more to the total reminiscence score. The number of cases is, of course, too small to take this result too seriously (10 extraverts and 10 introverts), but in conjunction with the reported findings of Ray (Ref. 11) and Bendig & Eigenbrode (Ref. 1) the results do suggest that under certain as yet unspecified circumstances reactive inhibition may produce performance decrement on the pursuit rotor and thus contribute to the total reminiscence score. For the greater part, however, it may be suggested that reminiscence on this instrument is more likely to be due to greater conditioned inhibition on the part of introverted subjects, giving rise to lower post-rest performance.

DISCUSSION

The results of this experiment, while supporting the hypothesis that conditioned inhibition, rather than reactive inhibition, is responsible for reminiscence effects in pursuit rotor learning, do not of course directly support the particular hypothesis relating reminiscence to personality put forward in this article. It is entirely feasible to put forward alternative theories relating personality to learning, or to the consolidation process proper, rather than to the differential effects of conditioned inhibition. The only definite conclusion the experiment suggests in this connection is that the original hypothesis linking personality to reminiscence through individual differences in reactive inhibition (Ref. 2) is not tenable any longer and must be replaced by a theory taking into account the facts here discovered. It should not prove impossible to design adequate tests for the adequacy or otherwise of the alternative hypothesis here presented; enough is known about the shape of the acquisition of conditioning curve to suggest that the length of pre-rest practice should be an important parameter in linking personality and reminiscence. Short periods would be expected to show less relationship between these variables than longer periods and a comparison of the present results with those reported by Star shows that this is indeed so (Ref. 13). Star originally predicted that on the basis of the 'reactive inhibition' hypothesis shorter periods of pre-rest practice would give higher correlations between extraversion and reminiscence; his discovery of an opposite result could not be explained in terms of this hypothesis, but fits in well with the theory here outlined.

SUMMARY

28 extraverted Ss and 23 introverted Ss were administered the pursuit-rotor twice for 5 minutes, with a rest of 10 minutes intervening. Reminiscence scores were found to be significantly higher for the extraverted group. Plotting of the performance data showed that the observed differences were due to post-rest superiority in performance of the extraverts, as predicted by the 'conditioned inhibition' hypothesis and not to pre-rest inferiority of the extraverts, as predicted by the 'reactive inhibition' hypothesis. The results were interpreted in terms of the writer's three-factor theory of reminiscence.

REFERENCES

1. BENDIG, A. W. & EIGENBRODE, C. R., A factor analytic investigation of personality variables and reminiscence in motor learning. *J. abnorm. soc. Psychol.*, **62**, 698, 1961.

2. EYSENCK, H. J., Reminiscence, drive and personality theory. *J. abnorm. soc. Psychol.*, **53**, 328-333, 1956.

3. ——, *Dynamics of Anxiety and Hysteri* London: Routledge & Kegan Paul, 1957.

598   *Bearings on Basic Psychological Processes*

4. ——, Reminiscence, drive and personality—revision and extension of a theory. *Brit. J. soc. clin. Psychol.*, **1**, 127–140, 1962.
5. ——, Conditioning and personality. *Brit. J. Psychol.*, **53**, 299–305, 1962.
6. ——, (ed.) *Experiments in Motivation.* Oxford: Pergamon Press, 1964.
7. ——, An experimental test of the 'inhibition' and consolidation theories of reminiscence. *Life Sci.*, **3**, 175–188, 1964.
8. ——, Involuntary rest pauses in tapping as a function of drive and personality. *Percept. mot. Skills*, **18**, 173–174, 1964.
9. —— & EYSENCK, S., *Manual of the E.P.I.* London: University of London Press, 1964.
10. KIMBLE, G. A., An experimental test of a two-factor theory of inhibition. *J. exp. Psychol.*, **39**, 15–23, 1949.
11. RAY, O. S., Personality factors in motor learning and reminiscence. *J. abnorm. soc. Psychol.*, **59**, 199–202, 1959.
12. SPIELMANN, I., The Relation Between Personality and the Frequency and Duration of Involuntary Rest Pauses During Massed Practice. Unpublished Ph.D. thesis, University of London Library, 1963.
13. STAR, K. H., An Experimental Study of 'Reactive Inhibition' and its Relation to Certain Personality Traits. Unpublished Ph.D. thesis, University of London Library, 1957.

64

Reminiscence, Performance and Personality[1]

FRANK H. FARLEY

INTRODUCTION

A MAJOR source of interest in the study of pursuit-rotor performance and reminiscence has been the attempt to identify individual differences in these parameters along the personality dimension of extraversion-introversion. This interest arose from Eysenck's personality-behaviour theory in which individual differences in cortical excitation-inhibition were postulated as underlying the personality trait of extraversion-introversion, with extraverts being characterized as having greater inhibitory cortical potentials (Ref. 9). This theory is too well known to require detailed elaboration here and at any rate has been outlined in its main aspects in Farley (Ref. 23). One of the earliest tests of the theory derived from the inhibition theory of pursuit-rotor reminiscence (Ref. 8), by which it would be predicted that extraverts would demonstrate depressed terminal pre-rest performance and a larger reminiscence effect than introverts. Eysenck has reviewed some 20 studies relevant to this hypothesis and on the whole the results have tended to support the predicted relationship between reminiscence and extraversion, though the relationship when found has not tended to be a marked one (Ref. 13). In view of the almost overwhelming evidence in favour of a consolidation theory of pursuit-rotor reminiscence (Ref. 15), the question as to why previous studies have tended to find a positive relationship between pursuit-rotor reminiscence and extraversion requires examination. As mentioned above, on the inhibition theory of pursuit-rotor reminiscence, extraverts were expected to have a more depressed terminal pre-rest performance curve than introverts and were expected to demonstrate more reminiscence than introverts. Eysenck (Ref. 9) originally postulated that extraverts are characterized by strong, quickly developing and

[1] The author would like to express his great appreciation to Professor H. J. Eysenck for his interest and encouragement in this research, and to Mr M. J. Kirton and the Principal of the Hatfield College of Technology (Herts.) for their assistance in allowing this research to be undertaken in the College.

slowly dissipating inhibition, while introverts are characterized by weak, slowly developing and quickly dissipating inhibition. However, that part of the postulate referring to the 'strength' or amount of inhibition ran foul of the experimentally demonstrated positive relationship between drive level and reminiscence (Refs. 20, 21 & 46), as the assumption that extraverts accumulate a greater amount of inhibition than introverts therefore implied a higher level of drive in the extraverts, an implication without other theoretical or empirical support. This state of affairs led Eysenck to reformulate the extraversion-inhibition-reminiscence relationship by dropping the hypothesis relating to *amount* of inhibition and showing that the prediction of greater reminiscence in the extraverts could be derived from '. . . the two hypotheses that (a) inhibition develops more quickly and (b) dissipates less quickly in extraverts' (Ref. 13, p. 134). These two hypotheses would lead to the prediction that involuntary rest pauses (IRPs) during massed rotary-pursuit would be longer for extraverts than introverts (slow I_R dissipation in extraverts), work intervals between the IRPs would accordingly be shorter for extraverts and finally IRPs would occur earlier in massed practice for extraverts (more rapid growth of I_R). The main consequence of these events would be '. . . extraverts should show a higher degree of reminiscence, not because, as in the original version of the theory, they had accumulated more I_R than introverts, but because they were *on the average* more likely to be in a state of not working (IRP) during the pre-rest period, which in the determination of reminiscence is subtracted from the post-rest period . . .' (Ref. 13, p. 135). It should be noted that this reformulation still demanded a greater terminal pre-rest depression of performance in the extraverts, with this pre-rest depression accounting for the extraverts' greater reminiscence. On this revised hypothesis we would still expect overall differences between extraverts and introverts on reminiscence scores, but we would not expect these to be very large. Furthermore, in view of the chance character of the probability of finding any particular person in a state of not working (IRP) during the pre-rest period we would expect rather low reliabilities (re-test) for measures of reminiscence; the facts seem to bear out this deduction (Refs. 8 and 44).

As mentioned earlier, the question remains as to why, with the strong evidence now favouring a consolidation theory of pursuit-rotor reminiscence, extraverts should generally have demonstrated greater reminiscence than introverts. Is the reminiscence superiority of extraverts due to depressed terminal pre-rest practice? Such an eventuality would clearly be antithetical to the recently formulated three-factor theory of reminiscence (Ref. 15), at least where rotary-pursuit is concerned. Because of the failure of a traditional two-factor inhibition (I_R and sI_R) theory of reminiscence to account for enough of the facts of reminiscence, Eysenck has advanced a theory which includes the essential features of the two-factor inhibition theory and additionally the concept of consolidation (Ref. 15). That is I_R, sI_R and consolidation are all considered to be necessary constructs in the discussion of reminiscence and its associated phenomena. In this theory, reminiscence in learning tasks, such as rotary-pursuit, is due primarily to consolidation, that is, consolidation of the new learning during a rest interval. On the other hand, reminiscence in performance tasks, such as simple tapping or vigilance, is due primarily to reactive inhibition; there is, so to speak, no learning to consolidate. That pursuit-rotor reminiscence is brought about mainly by consolidation of pre-rest learning has been demonstrated by Farley (Ref. 24) and Rachman & Grassi (Ref. 39).

The neurophysiological evidence for a consolidation theory of memory is strong (Refs. 23 & 35). In human verbal learning and memory, the work of Kleinsmith & Kaplan (Ref. 35) and Walker & Tarte (Ref. 45) has provided evidence implicating consolidation in reminiscence and has provided valuable theoretical analysis.

Eysenck has accordingly taken the concepts of consolidation, I_R and sI_R and reconstructed '... the course of events during pursuit-rotor learning somewhat as follows: (i) During pre-rest practice, I_R builds up and finally enforces I.R.P.s; the point at which I.R.P.s begin to occur depends on the drive level under which the subject is working. No permanent memory traces are laid down and hence no learning takes place. (This statement may require qualification; I.R.P.s may provide occasion for laying down permanent memory traces, but the very short periods in question are not likely to influence our argument to any great extent.) I.R.P.s provide the reinforcement for the growth of sI_R, but this also, being a habit, fails to lay down permanent memory traces. (ii) A programmed rest pause allows consolidation of the pursuit-rotor habit to take place, following a negatively accelerated curve of acquisition; this provides the basis of the reminiscence phenomenon. The rest pause also allows sI_R to consolidate; this habit too follows a negatively accelerated curve of acquisition. The consolidation of sI_R provides the basis for the permanent work decrement. (iii) Resumption of work after the rest pause produces extinction of sI_R, due to non-reinforcement: sI_R begins to accumulate again once sufficient I_R has been built up to produce I.R.P.s. Working against the post-rest upswing produced by this extinction process is the still-continuing consolidation process; as our quotation from Walker & Tarte (Ref. 45) has made clear, we conceive of consolidation and work as mutually interfering processes. This interference produces post-rest downswing, which in turn ceases when consolidation is complete; at this point we may then return to the gentle upward-sloping course characteristic of massed practice without rest pause interference (Ref. 15, pp. 172–173). It should be noted that although pursuit-rotor reminiscence is considered to be a product of consolidation rather than reactive inhibition the position with respect to $_sI_R$ remains essentially unchanged; permanent work decrement is still assumed to be due to $_sI_R$.

A distinction between two aspects of consolidation, 'primary consolidation' and 'secondary consolidation', might be made. Eysenck has suggested that primary consolidation represents that function of consolidation which makes the '... neural changes which underlie learning available to the organism for future action'. The neural patterns, e.g., cell assemblies, set up during massed practice in rotary-pursuit are largely unavailable for immediate improved performance, but require the interpolation of a rest interval to ensure that they are '... transformed into learned action patterns which can be indexed in terms of improved performance after the rest (reminiscence)' (Ref. 16, p. 274). Studies of particular relevance to primary consolidation would be those on drug enhancement of consolidation discussed by Farley (Ref. 23) and the study of Rachman & Grassi (Ref. 39). Secondary consolidation, on the other hand, is not concerned with what one might call the *potentiation function* (primary function) of consolidation, but refers to the *protective function* of consolidation. This refers to the protection of the memory trace against disruption and retrograde amnesia. Most of the studies cited in Glickman's review of consolidation of the memory trace dealt with secondary consolidation (Ref. 29). They were concerned with the interruption of perseveration, with disruption of the trace. Most of the studies on consolidation reviewed by Farley and particularly the ECS experiments, have been concerned with this protective aspect of consolidation (Ref. 23). Eysenck notes that little or no work has been done on secondary consolidation in tracking tasks such as rotary-pursuit (Ref. 16). Reminiscence is considered to be a product of primary consolidation.

Where reminiscence as related to extraversion-introversion is concerned, it was mentioned earlier that the general finding of greater reminiscence in extraverts over introverts is difficult to interpret in the light of evidence for a consolidation theory of reminiscence. Is this reminiscence difference due to depressed terminal pre-rest performance in extraverts? Such a finding would not be in accord with a consolidation theory of pursuit-rotor reminiscence. As most studies have reported correlation coefficients only between extraversion and reminiscence, it has not been possible to establish with confidence whether the reminiscence-extraversion relationship is in fact due to depressed terminal pre-rest performance in the extraverts, or elevated initial post-rest performance, or both. Eysenck conducted a study specifically to investigate this point and reported that extraverts did not differ from introverts in terminal pre-rest performance, but demonstrated significantly greater reminiscence. No statistical analysis was performed on the data other than that involving the reminiscence measure. Eysenck concluded that the major contribution to the reminiscence difference between the groups lay in the immediate post-rest performance, not in the terminal pre-rest performance. He considered that the post-rest relative depression of the introverts was due to the consolidation of sI_R during the programmed rest. As introverts have been shown to have greater speed and strength of conditioning than extraverts (Refs. 13 & 17) they accordingly may be expected to develop greater conditioned inhibition during the pre-test massed practice period. Post-rest this greater sI_R would be expected to depress performance level. This hypothesis was chosen in place of one linking extraversion with better consolidation, as such an introversion-conditioning hypothesis has a great deal of independent supporting evidence, whereas a suggested extraversion-superior consolidation hypothesis would largely be unrelated to previous data. The finding of no terminal pre-rest performance difference between extraverts and introverts, but a significant reminiscence difference, is of importance to three-factor theory and requires replication and extension. The overall trend during pre-rest practice toward inferior performance on the part of the extraverts, being based on a relatively small sample (28 extraverts and 23 introverts), merits further examination with a full statistical analysis of performance trends based on large samples. This is particularly desirable in light of the fact that a few previous experiments employing massed rotary-pursuit have reported a pre-rest performance inferiority of extraverts (Refs. 2 & 41). On the other hand, Star found no performance difference between his extraverts and introverts (visual inspection of the data) (Ref. 44) and Costello, Feldman & Slater reported a non-significant tendency for extraversion to be associated with superior overall performance (Ref. 6). Most of these studies, however, did not statistically analyse for personality × trials interactions.

Besides the interest in pre-rest performance and reminiscence, a major concern in the present research is the detailed examination of post-rest performance over an extended duration of practice. Of particular relevance to three-factor theory is the post-rest downswing and research reported by Farley has shown that with sufficiently extended post-rest practice this downswing ceases and performance assumes a gently upward-sloping progression (Ref. 24). This finding at least holds true for the male adolescent (high and low drive) apprentices tested by Farley. No studies of the extended post-rest pursuit-rotor performance of extraverts and introverts have been reported. Most of the experiments covered in Eysenck's review (Ref. 13) have been exclusively concerned with reminiscence, with, as mentioned above, a very few studies additionally reporting analyses of pre-rest performance. The Eysenck study (Ref. 14) employed a design involving 5 minutes of massed practice followed after a 10-minute rest by a further 5 minute massed-practice period. The duration of the latter period was just sufficient to allow the downswing to be discernible, but with no hint of a reversal of this trend. No statistical comparison between the extraverts and introverts in this downswing trend was undertaken, although visual inspection suggests that the two groups are undifferentiated. There is, interestingly, a tendency for the extraverts to be slightly above the introverts throughout most of the 5 minutes of post-rest practice. This study represents the only pursuit-rotor experiment to date employing the improved version of the Maudsley Personality Inventory (MPI) (Ref. 10) entitled the Eysenck Personality Inventory (EPI) (Ref. 19). The experimental sample consisted of 28 extraverts and 23 introverts drawn from a sample of 188 (high drive) apprentices. An extension of this study (where post-rest practice is concerned) involving larger extreme groups would, of course, provide more replications within each personality group. The use of larger samples would also allow the separate role of neuroticism to be examined, as the groups could be reconstituted on the basis of EPI neuroticism scores. Employment of the EPI as the personality criterion, as well as a more heterogeneous sample were likewise indicated. The latter consideration was based on the fact that the apprentices used in the Eysenck study were highly homogeneous with respect to age (range 15–17 years) and to a large extent with respect to education, social class, etc. More importantly, however, the fact that these subjects were tested on both the pursuit-rotor and EPI when under the high-drive condition may have introduced unknown motivational interactions. The relationship of extraversion-introversion to pre-rest performance, reminiscence and extended post-rest performance would best be studied under conditions of normal motivation. On the basis of the theoretical and parametric considerations outlined above, the following study was undertaken.

METHOD

Subjects

An attempt was made to select the extraverts and introverts from the whole student body of a college of technology 30 miles north of London. This involved pre-testing on the EPI, so as to be able to construct extreme groups for pursuit-rotor testing. A total of 51 separate classes were tested (i.e., 51 EPI testing sessions), with the class sizes ranging from 2 to 28 students. The total number of subjects tested was 623. Many of the students were not in full-time attendance at the college, but rather were employed in industry and were attending the college for 'sandwich courses', 'day release', half-day courses, or other similar arrangements. This meant that class schedules were complicated and included evening lectures. Subjects were tested at all times that classes were available, which meant that testing was undertaken from 9 a.m. to 9 p.m. Only the EPI records of male subjects were used in forming the personality groups; there were but a handful of females enrolled in the college and their number is not included in the 623. Because of logistical difficulties in pre-testing with the EPI, it was not possible to conclude this phase quickly and accordingly the pursuit-rotor testing was begun before the EPI testing was fully completed. Therefore the extreme groups were not selected strictly on the basis of the distribution of EPI extraversion (E) scores in the population of 623, but were selected by using pre-determined cut-off points of 16 for extraversion and 9 for introversion. These values are those used by Eysenck (Ref. 14) and represent values of approximately one S.D. above and below the mean in the EPI standardization sample (Ref. 19). That the values of 16 and 9 chosen as the cut-off points do not differ markedly from those which would have been used if the extreme groups had been based on the distribution of the present 623 scores is indicated by the mean E score of 11·6850, S.D. = 4·0823, of the 623 subjects (EPI neuroticism (N) mean of 9·3926, S.D. = 4·4518). Choice of the 16 and 9 cut-off points slightly over-represented introverts in terms of the distribution of 623, that is, when using a criterion of one S.D. above and below the mean.

Besides the E and N scales, the EPI contains a lie (L) scale of 9 items; an attempt to control for response distortion on the other scales was made by eliminating extreme dissimulators as measured by this scale. The cutoff point for extreme L scores was set at 5 (a point suggested in personal communication by S. B. G. Eysenck) so that a total of 69 subjects with L scores of 5 or greater were excluded from the sample.

In the EPI testing sessions, the students were told that the questionnaire was part of a survey being conducted strictly as a research project having no practical connection with the college or industrial firms outside the college, that is, the results were being used solely for research purposes.

A total of 110 introverts and 90 extraverts were selected using the procedure outlined above and these subjects were tested in the experiment.

Apparatus and Testing Conditions

The pursuit-rotor was a Lafayette 60 rpm model.

A room in a relatively quiet section of the college was selected for testing. This room was located between two classrooms and was separated from a hallway serving the two classrooms by a small antechamber. Considerable reconstruction and soundproofing of the room was undertaken. Elimination of external noise was considered important in the light of Rachman's work demonstrating the significant effect on reminiscence of the brief presentation of a buzzer during pre-rest practice (Ref. 38). In the present case, the location of the antechamber between the testing room and the general hallway, coupled with the soundproofing undertaken inside the testing room, had the effect of all but eliminating any external sound. The walls were a homogenous white flat paint. There were no windows in the testing room. Lighting in the room was normally provided by (50 cps) fluorescent bulbs, but as flicker may have affected pursuit-rotor performance (Ref. 1), the room was rewired employing incandescent lighting. A 100w frosted light bulb was located $42\frac{1}{2}$ inches above the rotor, providing 0·867 log foot Lamberts illumination at the rotor surface. A second 100w frosted bulb was located in the centre of the testing room at a height of 84 inches above floor level and provided 1·685 log foot Lamberts illumination in the centre of the room, measured at eye level. The rotor surface was set at 34 inches above floor level. The experimenter and recording equipment were located to the left of the subject and were separated from him by a softboard partition. An observation hole out of the subject's line of vision permitted the experimenter to monitor the subject's adherence to experimental instructions. The testing room dimensions were 63 inches × 86 inches × 84 inches high.

Procedure

Subjects were given standard instructions for the pursuit-rotor. No subject was tested who had an injury to his working arm, or who usually wore glasses but was not doing so at the time of testing. The experimental paradigm involved 5 minutes of massed practice, followed after a 10-minute rest by a 15-minute continuous practice period. At the beginning of post-rest practice, the usual 2·5sec 'warm-up' period was given before actual recording of performance was undertaken. Subjects were not informed at the termination of pre-rest practice that a second practice session was to follow.

RESULTS

1. Extraversion-Introversion

Reminiscence

Where previous studies of extraversion and pursuit-rotor reminiscence have been concerned, the procedure in the measurement of reminiscence has not been agreed upon. Some studies have used 10-sec trials, some 20-sec trials and others yet longer periods. For the present purposes, reminiscence was measured as performance on the first of two 10-sec post-rest trials minus performance on the terminal two pre-rest 10-sec trials. The main reason for adopting this measure was to achieve greater reliability of score than that associated with single 10-sec trials and as the present data were not being compared directly with a large number of other studies that had employed a uniform choice of reminiscence measure, as was true of the drive experiment reported by Farley (Ref. 24), the present measure was preferred. The desire for a greater reliability of reminiscence score in the analysis of data derived from extreme groups of extraverts and introverts stems from the demonstrated lower stability and greater variability of performance of the extravert over the introvert in a number of tasks (Refs. 7, 31, 35, 40 & 43). The low reliability of 10-sec trials has been reported by Eysenck (Ref. 8) and Star (Ref. 44).

The mean reminiscence score for the extraverts was 3·4956 S.D. = 2·1868 and for the introverts 2·9173, S.D. = 2·1462. A t-test of the mean difference between groups yielded a t of 1·8706 (p<0·03, 198 df, one-tailed test). The result is in the predicted direction and significant but, as expected, it is not a very large effect. To check on the difference between the groups on the terminal pre-rest trials and again on the initial post-rest trials, total performance on the last two pre-rest trials was compared between the two groups and total performance on the first two post-rest trials was similarly compared. The mean pre-rest performance for the extraverts was 3·8511, S.D. = 2·4237, while that of the introverts was 3·6582, S.D. = 2·1764. The resultant t-ratio was 0·5895 (N.S., 198 df.). The mean post-rest performance for the extraverts was 7·3467, S.D. = 2·6753, while that of the introverts was 6·5755, S.D. = 2·7108. The t-ratio here was 2·0033 (p<0·025, one-tailed test, 198 df.). These results clearly support our predictions of no difference between the groups pre-rest, but a superiority of the extraverts in the immediate post-rest period. Given that the present groups were probably more carefully constructed where the criterion of extraversion was concerned, larger and tested under more adequately controlled conditions than most previous studies, the results must be interpreted as support for Eysenck's contention that extraverts demonstrate greater reminiscence than introverts following 5 minutes of massed rotary-pursuit and a 10-minute rest interval and that this difference is attributable to immediate post-rest superiority of the extraverts, rather than being brought about by terminal pre-rest inferiority of the extraverts (Ref. 14). In fact, the extraverts demonstrated slightly higher performance than the introverts at the termination of pre-rest practice.

Performance

The mean performance curves of the two groups are found in Fig. 72. Data in Fig. 72 are plotted in 20-sec trials in keeping with the reminiscence measure discussed above and in order to render the curves somewhat less variable. It is clear that the groups do not differ in pre-rest performance although there is a slight chance divergence of the groups on the last trial. The lack of a pre-rest performance difference is confirmed by the analysis of variance reported in Table 1. The only significant term is, as expected, that one referring to the between trials variance. (It should be noted here that as the pursuit-rotor trials cannot be considered to be independent of each other, it is improper to assign the large number of degrees of freedom associated with trials to the sources of variance. Geisser & Greenhouse have derived a 'conservative' F-test for such cases of correlated observations which effectively reduces

Reminiscence, Performance and Personality   609

the degrees of freedom, thus providing a more rigorous test of significance (Ref. 28). This conservative test is used in all the analyses of variance of pursuit-rotor performance data reported in the present paper. A further point regarding the analyses, as illustrated in Table 1, bears on the choice of error term. Two error terms are used. The between-group effect is not based on performance of the same subjects under different conditions, but is composed of separate groups of subjects, so that the appropriate error term is the variance between subjects within each group, summed across groups. The error term for the trials component and interaction term is the residual.

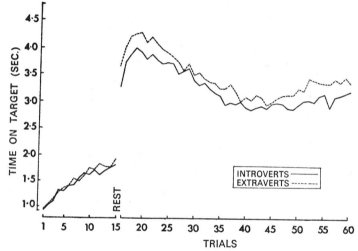

Figure 72. Performance curves of extraverts (N = 90) and introverts (N = 110).

TABLE 1

ANALYSIS OF VARIANCE OF THE PRE-REST PERFORMANCE OF THE EXTRAVERTED AND INTROVERTED GROUPS

Source	df	SS	MSV	VR	p
Between groups	1	2·62	2·6200	0·1114	N.S.
Between trials	29	463·16	15·9710	31·4699	0·001
Groups × trials	29	13·17	0·4541	0·8947	N.S.
Subjects within groups	198	4656·37	23·5170		
Residual	5742	2914·10	0·5075		
Total	5999	8049·42			

w

The lack of a significant between-groups term indicates a failure to repeat the finding of Bendig & Eigenbrode of a positive association between introversion and total performance over 5 minutes of massed pre-rest pursuit-rotor practice (Ref. 2). Although both the present study and that of Bendig & Eigenbrode employed large samples (200 and 160 respectively), the latter authors did not draw their subjects from a larger population on the basis of their extreme extraversion or introversion scores, but rather correlated personality scores with total pursuit-rotor performance in the group of 160 unselected with respect to extraversion-introversion. The studies differed in the measures of personality employed, with Bendig & Eigenbrode using the Guilford-Zimmerman Temperament Survey (GZTS) (Ref. 30) and identifying the Restraint and Thoughtfulness scales from the GZTS as measures of extraversion. Out of 21 correlations between the GZTS variables, total pursuit-rotor performance and a reminiscence measure, one correlation, that between Restraint and total performance, was significant ($r = 0.24$). This is certainly not a marked relationship and it might be suggested that one should expect one correlation out of 21 to be significant by chance. The Restraint scale was derived from the Rhathymia scale of Guilford's STDCR, which was early considered by Eysenck to be one of the best available measures of extraversion. However, it has since been superseded by the MPI and then the EPI, with the latter now considered to be the best available criterion measure of extraversion. It is possible that the relationship between total performance and introversion reported by Bendig & Eigenbrode did not involve so much the extraversion-introversion dimension as conceived by Eysenck, but one facet of extraversion, namely impulsivity (Ref. 22). In a factor analysis by Bendig & Eigenbrode of the matrix of intercorrelations of GZTS variables, total pursuit-rotor performance and reminiscence, the latter two variables loaded 0.33 and -0.25 respectively on a factor labelled extraversion-introversion. However, this factor was defined wholly by two scales of the GZTS—Restraint and Thoughtfulness—with quite negligible loadings of Sociability, Friendliness and Personal Relations. This suggests that the factor was more one of impulsiveness, rather than extraversion-introversion as such and given that the reminiscence and total performance scores had negligible loadings on a Social Activities factor and a Friendliness factor, it is suggested that further factoring of the four factors identified by Bendig & Eigenbrode (Emotionality, Social Activities, Extraversion-Introversion and Friendliness) would have revealed two higher-order factors, viz Extraversion-Introversion and Neuroticism or Emotionality, with theoretically negligible loadings of at least pursuit-rotor total performance. It would seem that, given the difficulties of interpretation mentioned, the Bendig & Eigenbrode study does not represent a clear-cut test of theoretical relationships between extraversion and pursuit-rotor variables. Greater weight must be placed on the present data, not only in respect of the personality criterion and sample selection, but also where the statistical analysis is concerned.

The lack of a significant interaction term in Table 1 indicates that the slopes of the two curves are not different; these data suggest that Ray's finding of a significant difference in the slope of the 5 minute pursuit-rotor pre-rest massed practice curve for extraverts and introverts (Ref. 41) is not replicable. Although Ray also employed a large sample (N = 240), it was not homogeneous with respect to sex (168 males, 72 females), nor was it as extreme with respect to personality score as the present sample. Ray pre-tested 515 students on the MPI and selected the top 30 per cent and bottom 30 per cent on the E scale to constitute his extraverted and introverted groups respectively. The present study employed a more stringent cut-off point in the selection of groups (approximately the top 16 per cent and bottom 16 per cent on the E scale out of 623 subjects), yet was quite unable to detect any pre-rest performance differences attributable to personality. An important factor may lie in Ray's report of a significant negative correlation between the E and N scales of the MPI and the fact that his extravert and introvert groups were significantly differentiated with respect to N. Although his analysis to some extent took this correlation into account, the fact that complete orthogonality of E and N has been achieved in the EPI (Refs. 19 & 25) (the E and N correlation based on the present 623 subjects was -0.31) indicates that the present analysis was based on a rather more pure criterion measure of extraversion. (In the present study the mean N score of the extraverts was 9·4778, S.D. = 4·3056, while the mean of the introverts was 10·2450, S.D. = 4·5451. A t-test of the difference between means yielded a non-significant t-ratio of 1·2107.)

The finding as reported in Table 1 of no pre-rest performance differences between the extravert and introvert groups are in line with the results of visual inspection of the pre-rest practice curves of 26 extraverts and 26 introverts reported by Star (Ref. 44), though Star did not perform a statistical analysis of these data.

Turning to the post-rest performance curves of the extraverts and introverts as presented in Fig. 72, it can be seen that here rather more dramatic effects emerge. The introverts are considerably inferior to the

TABLE 2

COMPARISON OF THE 15 MINUTE POST-REST PERFORMANCE
CURVES OF THE EXTRAVERTS AND INTROVERTS

Source	df	SS	MSV	VR	p
Between groups	1	226·7280	226·7280	1·6461	N.S.
Between trials	89	2377·6500			
G × T linear	1	0·3176	0·3176	0·0428	N.S.
G × T quadratic	1	14·0447	14·0447	4·4925	0·05
G × T cubic	1	3·0879	3·0879	1·0676	N.S.
G × T higher powers	86	72·6208	0·8444		
Subjects within groups	198	27271·7000	137·7360		
S × T linear	198	1468·0100	7·4142		
S × T quadratic	198	572·6630	2·8922		
S × T cubic	198	572·6630	2·8922		
S × T higher powers	17028	14701·9990	0·8634		
Total	17999				

extraverts during the first 5 minutes approximately, less inferior during the middle 5 minute period approximately and noticeably inferior again during the final 5 minutes of practice. The most notable feature, however, is that the introverts are consistently inferior throughout the 15 minute period. The analysis of the full 15 minute practice period is reported in Table 2, where it may be seen that the groups differ significantly on the quadratic component, but that the overall difference in

TABLE 3

COMPARISON OF THE POST-REST PERFORMANCE CURVES OF THE EXTRAVERTS AND
INTROVERTS OVER THE FIRST 5 MINUTES OF PRACTICE

Source	df	SS	MSV	VR	p
Between groups	1	80·1701	80·1701	1·3706	N.S.
Between trials	29	291·3460			
G × T linear	1	11·0565	11·0565	3·8935	0·05
G × T quadratic	1	1·0803	1·0803	0·5774	N.S.
G × T cubic	1	0·4693	0·4693	0·3349	N.S.
G × T higher powers	26	19·3261	0·7433		
Subjects within groups	198	11582·0000	58·4950		
S × T linear	198	562·2650	2·8397		
S × T quadratic	198	370·4390	1·8709		
S × T cubic	198	277·4310	1·4012		
S × T higher powers	5148	4038·9810	0·7846		
Total	5999				

level does not attain significance. It is difficult to interpret a difference of this type over such a lengthy and variable series of data points. The quadratic component indicates curvature in the difference between the two curves, which, although the component is not highly significant even though based on a large number of degrees of freedom, is suggestive that the difference between the curves tends to decrease then increase. In other words, there is some agreement here with visual inspection of the data which indicated a tendency for the groups to be apart early and late in practice. However, it was considered necessary to perform further analyses to establish more precisely where the differences lay. Accordingly, the post-rest performance curves were broken up into three sections—the first 5 minutes, middle 5 minutes and terminal 5 minutes and a separate analysis was performed on each one of these three sections. The analysis of the first 5-minute section is reported in Table 3,

TABLE 4

COMPARISON OF THE POST-REST PERFORMANCE CURVES OF THE EXTRAVERTS AND INTROVERTS OVER THE SECOND 5 MINUTES OF PRACTICE

Source	df	SS	MSV	VR	p
Between groups	1	40·0801	40·0801	0·9130	N.S.
Between trials	29	171·5360			
G × T linear	1	0·8150	0·8150	0·4747	N.S.
G × T quadratic	1	1·8104	1·8104	1·5486	N.S.
G × T cubic	1	0·3887	0·3887	0·4685	N.S.
G × T higher powers	26	16·3045	0·6271		
Subjects within groups	198	8692·5300	43·9017		
S × T linear	198	339·9320	1·7168		
S × T quadratic	198	231·4730	1·1691		
S × T cubic	198	164·2920	0·8298		
S × T higher powers	5148	3668·4670	0·7170		
Total	5999				

that of the second 5-minute section in Table 4 and in Table 5 is found the analysis of the third 5-minute section.

On the basis of these three analyses it appears that the groups differ significantly during the first 5 minutes, are undifferentiated during the middle 5 minutes and that the tendency toward late divergence of the curves has not achieved significance in the present analysis. The significant linear component obtained in the comparison of the groups over the first 5 minutes of post-rest practice indicates that the groups are

TABLE 5

COMPARISON OF THE POST-REST PERFORMANCE CURVES OF THE EXTRAVERTS AND INTROVERTS OVER THE THIRD 5 MINUTES OF PRACTICE

Source	df	SS	MSV	VR	p
Between groups	1	100·6590	100·6590	2·1969	N.S.
Between trials	29	72·1347			
G×T linear	1	0·7906	0·7906	0·3277	N.S.
G×T quadratic	1	4·7566	4·7566	3·3660	N.S.
G×T cubic	1	0·0479	0·0479	0·0354	N.S.
G×T higher powers	26	20·0932	0·7728		
Subjects within groups	198	9071·9200	45·8178		
S×T linear	198	477·6530	2·4124		
S×T quadratic	198	279·7960	1·4131		
S×T cubic	198	268·2540	1·3548		
S×T higher powers	5148	4808·8210	0·9341		
Total	5999				

converging. However, visual inspection again is important in the interpretation of this result. It is suggested that the two curves are converging up to Trial 60, with the implication that the introvert curve is flatter, the extravert curve more steep.

Although the pre-rest performance data have already been discussed at some length, consideration of the foregoing results will be deferred until the Discussion section.

2. Neuroticism

Because of the large size of the sample used in this study, it was possible to constitute two groups on the basis of extreme EPI neuroticism scores and compare their pursuit-rotor performance and reminiscence. Accordingly, a high-N and low-N group were formed from the total of 200 subjects tested on the pursuit-rotor. The basis of selection was the same as that used in originally selecting the 200 subjects, i.e., extreme scores on the basis of published norms rather than on the specific E and N distribution in the 623 subjects tested on the EPI, giving a cut-off point of 13 for high-N and 5 for low-N. This selection resulted in a high-N group of 51 subjects and a low-N group of 37 subjects. As these groups were small in relation to the extraversion-introversion groups, a few additional subjects were tested on the pursuit-rotor who were extreme on N but on the E scale would be classified as ambivert. It was possible to test 18 subjects in this category, these subjects being additional to the 200 in the main study. The final high-N group therefore consisted of 63 subjects and the low-N group 43 subjects. These groups did not differ with respect to extraversion, with the mean E score of the high-N group being 11·175, S.D. = 5·2328 and that of the low-N group being 12·581, S.D. = 5·4867. A t-test of the difference between the E scores of the two groups yielded a non-significant t-ratio of 1·3199 (105 df).

The evidence with respect to the relation of neuroticism to reminiscence has been reviewed by Eysenck, who noted that there has been no clear-cut trend in the available literature toward either a positive or negative relationship (Ref. 13). Eysenck reported a significant positive relationship between N and reminiscence (Ref. 8), Eysenck and Star have reported negative relationships (Refs. 11 & 44) and Eysenck found no significant relationships between N and pursuit-rotor reminiscence over four different rest intervals (Ref. 12). No studies have reported analyses of extended post-rest practice in high-N and low-N groups. Ray found no relation between neuroticism (MPI-N) and 5 minutes of (pre-rest) pursuit-rotor performance, nor any relationship between N and reminiscence (Ref. 41). Bendig & Eigenbrode in the factor-analytic study discussed earlier found no evidence of a significant relationship between pre-rest pursuit-rotor performance, reminiscence and a factor of emotionality (Ref. 2). However, their performance analysis was particularly insensitive to the extent that total pursuit-rotor performance was the basic datum, thus disallowing any analysis of practice × personality trends. Star found a relatively consistent trend for the pre- and post-rest performance of his low-N subjects to be superior to that of high-N subjects, but as his groups were small (26 top and bottom N scores from a distribution of 100) and no statistical analysis was performed, it cannot be said that N has been shown to account for any significant amount of the variance in pursuit-rotor performance (Ref. 44).

Reminiscence

The mean reminiscence scores of the high-N group in the present study was 1·281, S.D. = 1·262, while that of the low-N group was 1·361, S.D. = 1·170. A t-test of the difference between means yielded a t-ratio of 0·3249, which was non-significant by two-tailed test (105 df). This lack of a significant difference in reminiscence must be interpreted as fairly strong evidence against any significant relationship between questionnaire-defined neuroticism and pursuit-rotor reminiscence under the present experimental conditions. This conclusion is lent emphasis by the fact that the present N groups were larger, constituted on the basis of a superior criterion and probably tested under better controlled conditions than in most previous studies. However, it may be worth noting, parenthetically, that these results fit in with the trend of results of Eysenck's and Star's experiments (Refs. 11 & 44) and, taken in conjunction with Claridge's finding of superior reminiscence of normals when compared with (clinical) neurotics (Ref. 5), suggest that N may possibly bear a very slight negative relationship to pursuit-rotor reminiscence following a 10-minute rest interval preceded by 5 minutes of massed practice, but that the magnitude of any such relationship is too small to be of any further interest.

Eysenck has suggested that, 'As the originators of the Yerkes-Dodson Law (Ref. 3) were the first to point out, the relationship between drive and performance is curvilinear and also dependent on the difficulty level of the task; if we conceive of neuroticism-anxiety as a drive variable, then the contradictory data from measures of performance obtained on groups of Ss differing in their position on the neuroticism continuum cannot come as a surprise. Our argument is of course concerned with reminiscence rather than with performance as such, but as I_R is produced in the course of massed practice, interference in performance by drive-produced stimuli, as posited by Mandler & Sarason (Ref. 36) and Child (Ref. 4), must also affect reminiscence. Thus it is not impossible that in groups of individuals low in neuroticism a positive correlation of neuroticism with reminiscence may be observed, while in groups of individuals high in neuroticism, a negative correlation may be found' (Ref. 13, p. 133). As this suggestion was based on the reactive inhibition theory of reminiscence, it is of little relevance in the present context, but out of interest, the correlation between N and reminiscence in the present high-N group was computed, with the same analysis being repeated in the low-N group. The former correlation was -0.102 (N.S., 61 df) and the latter -0.031 (N.S., 41 df). It can be seen that neither correlation approaches significance.

Performance

Turning now to the pre- and post-rest performance data of the high-N and low-N groups, a plot of the mean performance curves for the two groups is presented in Fig. 73. Visual inspection suggests no obvious difference between the groups either pre- or post-rest, although there is a slight tendency for high-N to be superior to low-N toward

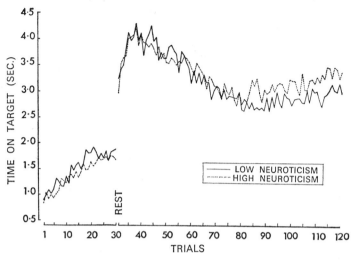

Figure 73. Performance curves of high-N (63 subjects) and low-N (43 subjects) groups.

the end of post-rest practice. The analysis of the pre-rest performance data is presented in Table 6.

TABLE 6

ANALYSIS OF VARIANCE OF THE PRE-REST PERFORMANCE OF THE HIGH-N AND LOW-N GROUPS

Source	df	SS	MSV	VR	p
Between groups	1	10·11	10·110	0·483	N.S.
Between trials	29	262·76	9·061	16·326	0·001
Groups × trials	29	14·42	0·497	0·895	N.S.
Subjects within groups	104	2176·76	20·930		
Residual	3016	1674·08	0·555		
Total	3179	4138·13			

It can be seen from Table 6 that the groups are quite undifferentiated both with respect to level of performance and slope. Turning to post-rest performance, in Table 7 is found the comparison between the high-N and low-N groups.

From Table 7 it is apparent that neither the main effect of neuroticism nor the interaction with trials is significant. As a further check on the significance of the slight superiority of the high-N subjects over the

w*

TABLE 7

COMPARISON OF THE POST-REST PERFORMANCE OF
THE HIGH-N AND LOW-N GROUPS

Source	df	SS	MSV	VR	p
Between groups	1	39·07	39·070	0·2138	N.S.
Between trials	89	1372·29	15·418	16·2981	0·001
Groups × trials	89	119·54	1·343	1·4197	N.S.
Subjects within groups	104	14135·93	135·913		
Residual	9256	8757·15	0·946		
Total	9539	24423·98			

low-N subjects during the final few minutes of practice, the total score for each subject during the final 5 minutes of practice was calculated and scores for the two groups were compared by t-test. The resultant t-ratio was 1·240, which with 104 df was clearly non-significant. It must be concluded from the foregoing analyses that neuroticism has borne no significant relationship either to pre-rest performance or post-rest performance, nor has it been significantly related to reminiscence.

DISCUSSION

The major findings of the experiment may be summarized as follows:
(1) Reminiscence is greater in extraverts than in introverts when measured following a 10-minute rest pause that has been preceded by 5 minutes of massed pursuit-rotor practice. The magnitude of this difference is small.
(2) Extraverts are quite undifferentiated from introverts during pre-rest massed practice, both with respect to level and slope of performance.
(3) During 15 minutes of post-rest massed practice, extraverts and introverts are not significantly differentiated with respect to overall level of performance. However, the introverts generally perform below the level of the extraverts throughout the 15-minute period. (4) Extraverts and introverts are significantly different during the first 5 minutes of post-rest practice; it is suggested that the mean performance curve of the introverts is relatively flatter following the termination of upswing than is that of the extraverts. (5) Extraverts and introverts both demonstrate post-rest reversal of downswing, but they are undifferentiated in this effect. (6) Neuroticism accounts for no significant amount of variance in reminiscence, pre-rest performance or post-rest performance.

The finding of no pre-rest performance differences between the extra-verts and introverts has already been discussed at some length. Such a result, coupled with the observed reminiscence difference, is in line with Eysenck's conditioned inhibition hypothesis (Ref. 14). One feature of the post-rest curve that is important in this interpretation is the consistent trend for the introverts to perform at a level *below* that of the extraverts throughout the 15 minutes of practice; this trend lends support to the hypothesized greater permanent work decrement of $_sI_R$ of the former subjects. It would be predicted that with a much longer period of pre-rest practice (e.g., 10–15 minutes) the post-rest overall difference between extraverts and introverts would be more marked due to the greater amount of $_sI_R$ developed by the introverts during such a long practice session.

Another feature of the post-rest curves that requires examination is the upswing and downswing portions. It may be seen from inspection of Fig. 72, that the introverts do not differ detectably from the extraverts in the extent or duration of the upswing or 'warm-up' section, even though it would have been expected that the greater $_sI_R$ of the introvert would have led in the immediate post-rest period to a longer upswing section because of the greater amount of $_sI_R$ undergoing extinction. However, in line with the interference hypothesis as discussed in the introduction to this report in which the *mutual interference* of consoli-dation and work was emphasized, it is suggested here that interference begins at approximately the same point for each group so that the intro-verts' upswing section is 'cut off' earlier than would have been expected strictly from an 'extinction of $_sI_R$' hypothesis. It is suggested that the peak of the upswing and subsequent start of the downswing come at approximately the same ordinal trial for the two groups because it is assumed that the still consolidating trace hypothesized to underly the interference effect has similar temporal characteristics between the personality groups. As the interference effect is conceived of as due to the *mutual interference* of consolidation and work, then the reason for the downswing of the extraverts from a relatively elevated level in com-parison to introverts to no more than a slight non-significant superiority over introverts is hypothesized to be the greater stimulus input of the extraverts due to their higher performance level which provides a larger amount of relevant input to degrade the still consolidating trace. This 'the higher they rise the farther they fall' hypothesis would lead one to expect that with normally motivated subjects who have practised on a distributed schedule to a high level of performance and then are switched to a massed schedule (e.g., 15 minutes massed practice), performance would downswing to the level of a no-rest continuous practice group. With high drive subjects, or very extended rests (e.g., 24-hour distribution schedule), secondary or protective consolidation would be completed, or nearly so and the downswing upon switching to massed practice would be greatly attenuated. In an unpublished study by Eysenck, Star & Willett employing low-drive subjects who had been assigned to pursuit-rotor practice periods of various durations ranging from 20 sec to 2 minutes with each practice period separated by 5 minutes rest and with the last practice period followed by a switch to a 15-minute massed practice schedule as used in the present study, it was found that in the 15-minute session performance of the various groups tended to converge, even though they had differed markedly under the distributed condition. The groups performing at the highest level in the distributed practice session showed the greatest decrement in the 15-minute session; convergence of the various groups in this fashion suggested a 'golden mean' of performance, that is, the performance level of a continuous practice group that would have practised the same length of time as the other groups. (Such a continuous practice group was not included in the Eysenck, Star & Willett study.) These results on the present interpretation would be attributed to incomplete secondary consolidation.

The major results of the present experiment where extraversion-introversion are concerned can be most parsimoniously accounted for at present by the conditioned inhibition hypothesis, with the additional emphasis on the importance of the amount of relevant stimulus input in the determination of the post-rest interference effect. However, one attractive, potentially powerful hypothesis that might avoid the logical and empirical problems associated with the $_sI_R$ concept (Ref. 33) is related to the hypothesized higher cortical arousal characteristic of introverts (Ref. 18) and the hypothesized relationship of arousal to consolidation (Ref. 45). The latter authors have theorized that: '(1) The occurrence of any psychological event sets up an active, perseverative trace process which persists for a considerable period of time. (2) The perseverative process has two important dynamic characteristics: (a) permanent memory is laid down during this active phase in a gradual fashion; (b) during the active period, there is a degree of temporary inhibition of recall, i.e., action decrement (this negative bias against repetition serves to protect the consolidating trace against disruption). (3) High arousal during the associative process will result in a more intensely active trace process. The more intense activity will result in greater ultimate memory but great temporary inhibition against recall' (Ref. 45, p. 113). The evidence relevant to the foregoing theory has been reviewed by Eysenck (Ref. 18) and Farley (Ref. 23) and is generally favourable. The third point in the Walker & Tarte formulation would lead one to suggest that introverts should demonstrate poorer short-term memory but superior long-term memory as compared to extraverts. Evidence using verbal materials that supports the latter hypothesis has been reported by Farley & Gaa (Ref. 26), Howarth & Eysenck (Ref. 32) and McLean (Ref. 37), although Farley & Gaa were able to obtain the hypothesized differences between extraverts and introverts only at short-term recall. As applied to the present pursuit-rotor data, the discussion above might suggest that the 10-minute rest interval represented a short-term retention period and the introverts would thus be expected to show less reminiscence than the extraverts, but that if a long-term retention period had been employed, e.g., 24 hours or 1 week, then the introverts would demonstrate *greater* reminiscence than the extraverts. The above formulation may be a useful one in approaching the present data, but suggests that necessary evidence relating extraversion-introversion to reminiscence and post-rest performance on the pursuit-rotor following short- and long-term rest intervals is required. Such an approach might provide a beginning for subsuming reminiscence data in verbal learning and pursuit-rotor learning under the same explanatory constructs.

The results with respect to neuroticism might be thought to be unusual in that if N contributes to a subject's drive state then a positive relationship between N and reminiscence should be obtained. As mentioned in the Results section, Eysenck in reviewing the work on reminiscence and N was unable to detect any obvious trend towards either a positive or negative relationship between the two variables (Ref. 13). Comparing the present results to those from the Maudsley drive studies (see Ref. 23) that have employed a comparable duration of pre-rest practice (i.e. 5 minutes, Ref. 27), it is apparent that drive level as manipulated in those studies has likewise had no significant effect on reminiscence, although it should be added that although the duration of pre-rest practice was 5 minutes, the duration of rest was 15 minutes (Ref. 27), i.e., 5 minutes longer than that employed in the present experiment. The most likely reason for the lack of effect of N on reminiscence in most pursuit-rotor studies is that the usual conditions of testing in these studies have probably not been threatening enough to elicit emotionality and a high drive state in high-N subjects. Eysenck (personal communication) considers N to be reactive emotionality, that is, it functions as a drive only in threatening situations, so that in the usual (non-threatening) pursuit-rotor experiment, no relationship between N and reminiscence would be expected.

REFERENCES

1. BACH, L. M. N., SPERRY, C. J. & RAY, J. T., Tulane studies on the effects of flickering light on human subjects. In *ERDL Tulane Symposium on Flicker* (ed. L. M. N. Bach). Tulane: Tulane University Press, 1957.
2. BENDIG, A. W. & EIGENBRODE, C. R., A factor analytic investigation of personality variables and reminiscence in motor learning. *J. abnorm. soc. Psychol.*, **62**, 698–700, 1961.
3. BROADHURST, P. L., The interaction of task difficulty and motivation: The Yerkes-Dodson Law revived. *Acta Psychol.*, **16**, 321–338, 1959.
4. CHILD, I. L., Personality. *Ann. Rev. Psychol.*, **5**, 149–170, 1954.
5. CLARIDGE, G., The excitation-inhibition balance in neurotics. In *Experiments in Personality* (ed. H. J. Eysenck). London: Routledge & Kegan Paul, 1960.
6. COSTELLO, C. G., FELDMAN, M. P. & SLATER, P. A., The effect of success and failure reports on pursuit rotor performance and reminiscence. In *Experiments in Motivation* (ed. H. J. Eysenck). Oxford: Pergamon Press, 1964.
7. EYSENCK, H. J., *Dimensions of Personality*. London: Routledge & Kegan Paul, 1947.
8. ——, Reminiscence, drive and personality theory. *J. abnorm. soc. Psychol.*, **53**, 328–333, 1956.
9. ——, *The Dynamics of Anxiety and Hysteria*. London: Routledge & Kegan Paul, 1957.
10. ——, *Manual of the Maudsley Personality Inventory*. London: University of London Press, 1959.
11. ——, Reminiscence as a function of rest, practice and personality. *Percept. mot. Skills*, **11**, 91–94, 1960.
12. ——, Reminiscence, extraversion and neuroticism. *Percept. mot. Skills*, **11**, 21–22, 1960.
13. ——, Reminiscence, drive and personality—revision and extension of a theory. *Brit. J. soc. clin. Psychol.*, **1**, 127–140, 1962.

14. ——, Personality and reminiscence—an experimental study of the 'reactive inhibition' and the 'conditioned inhibition' theories. *Life Sci.*, **3**, 189–198, 1964.
15. ——, A three-factor theory of reminiscence. *Brit. J. Psychol.*, **56**, 163–181, 1965.
16. ——, On the dual functions of consolidation. *Percept. mot. Skills*, **22**, 273–274, 1966.
17. ——, Conditioning, Introversion-Extraversion and the Strength of the Nervous System. Paper given at International Congress of Psychology, Moscow, 1966.
18. ——, *The Biological Basis of Personality*. Springfield, Illinois: Thomas, 1967.
19. —— & EYSENCK, S. B. G., *Manual of the Eysenck Personality Inventory*. London: University of London Press, 1964.
20. —— & MAXWELL, A. E., Reminiscence as a function of drive, *Brit. J. Psychol.*, **52**, 43–52, 1961.
21. —— & WILLETT, R. A., The measurement of motivation through the use of objective indices. *J. ment. Sci.*, **107**, 961–968, 1961.
22. EYSENCK, S. B. G. & EYSENCK, H. J., On the dual nature of extraversion. *Brit. J. soc. clin. Psychol.*, **2**, 46–55, 1963.
23. FARLEY, F. H., The Current Status of Reminiscence. Chapter in F. H. Farley, Unpublished Ph.D. thesis, University of London Library, 1966.
24. ——, Reminiscence and Post-Rest Performance as a Function of Level of Drive and Duration of Rest. Chapter in F. H. Farley, Unpublished Ph.D. thesis, University of London Library, 1966.
25. ——, On the independence of extraversion and neuroticism. *J. clin. Psychol.*, **23**, 154–156, 1967.
26. —— & GAA, J., Unpublished paper.
27. FELDMAN, M. P., Pursuit rotor performance and reminiscence as a function of drive level. In *Experiments in Motivation* (ed. H. J. Eysenck). Oxford: Pergamon Press, 1964.
28. GEISSER, S. & GREENHOUSE, S. W., An extension of Box's results on the use of the F distribution in multivariate analysis. *Ann. math. Statist.*, **29**, 885–891, 1958.
29. GLICKMAN, S. E., Perseverative neural processes and consolidation of the memory trace, *Psychol. Bull.*, **58**, 218–233, 1961.
30. GUILFORD, J. P. & ZIMMERMAN, W., *The Guilford-Zimmerman Temperament Survey*. Beverly Hills, California: Sheridan Supply Company, 1949.

31. HOWARTH, E., Some laboratory measures of extraversion-introversion. *Percept. mot. Skills*, **17**, 55–60, 1963.
32. —— & EYSENCK, H. J., Extraversion, arousal and paired-associates recall. *J. exper. Res. in Person.*, **3**, 109–116, 1968.
33. JENSEN, A. R., On the reformulation of inhibition in Hull's system. *Psychol. Bull.*, **58**, 274–298, 1961.
34. JOHN, E. R., *Mechanisms of Memory.* New York: Academic Press, 1967.
35. KLEINSMITH, L. J. & KAPLAN, S., Paired-associate learning as a function of arousal and interpolated interval. *J. exp. Psychol.*, **65**, 190–193, 1963.
36. MANDLER, G. & SARASON, S. B., A study of anxiety and learning. *J. abnorm. soc. Psychol.*, **74**, 166–173, 1952.
37. MCLEAN, P., Unpublished study, 1968.
38. RACHMAN, S., Disinhibition and the reminiscence effect in a motor learning task. *Brit. J. Psychol.*, **53**, 149–157, 1962.
39. —— & GRASSI, J., Reminiscence, inhibition and consolidation. *Brit. J. Psychol.*, **56**, 157–162, 1965.
40. RANKIN, E. F., JR., Reading test reliability and validity as function of introversion-extraversion. *J. developmental Reading*, **6**, 106–117, 1963.
41. RAY, O. S., Personality factors in motor learning and reminiscence. *J. abnorm. soc. Psychol.*, **59**, 199–203, 1959.
42. REED, G. F. & FRANCIS, T. R., Drive, personality and audiometric response consistency. *Percept. mot. Skills*, **15**, 681–682, 1962.
43. SPIELMANN, I., The Relation Between Personality and the Frequency and Duration of Involuntary Rest Pauses During Massed Practice. London: Unpublished Ph.D. thesis, University of London Library, 1963.
44. STAR, K. H., An Experimental Study of 'Reactive Inhibition' and its Relation to Certain Personality Traits. London: unpublished Ph.D. thesis, University of London Library, 1957.
45. WALKER, E. L. & TARTE, R. D., Memory storage as a function of arousal and time with homogeneous and heterogeneous lists. *Journal of Verbal Learning & Verbal Behaviour*, **2**, 113–119, 1963.
46. WILLETT, R. A. & EYSENCK, H. J., An experimental study of human motivation. *Life Sci.*, **4**, 119–127, 1962.

Editor's Epilogue

THE articles reprinted in this volume represent only a small portion of all that has been published on the concepts of extraversion and introversion, either theoretically or experimentally; it would be easy to fill another two or three volumes with articles of equal quality. What conclusions does this material suggest? It is easy in science to say that more evidence is needed, that more detailed studies are required, that no final conclusions can be drawn, that issues are still in doubt, that results are only suggestive, that possibly with different tests, or different populations, or different instructions, or different parameters, or different experimenters . . . the list is endless. But it applies equally in all areas where research is still going on—not only in psychology, but also in physics, astronomy, or chemistry. In spite of all qualifications, certain solid findings stand out and may with some advantage be highlighted.

In the first place, then, there seems little doubt that some such higher-order concept as extraversion-introversion is needed to describe the way in which large numbers of simple, first-order traits like sociability, impulsiveness, activity, rhathymia and responsiveness hang together. Descriptively, almost every single investigator who has covered a large enough area of personality in his studies has come up with a factor, type or continuum closely resembling E-I and when this resemblance is put on a statistical footing, as for instance in the comparative studies of Guilford's, Cattell's and Eysenck's factors (published in *The Structure and Measurement of Personality*), results show it to fall little short of unity. Such universal agreement is rare in psychology and deserves welcome and recognition.

In the second place, E-I seems to play an important part in many social areas, from psychiatry to criminology; the marked susceptibility of introverts to dysthymic types of neurotic breakdown and of extraverts to antisocial conduct, crime and psychopathy, has been amply documented. Many other areas, such as school and university attainment, leadership selection, industrial and vocational guidance, have been shown to be susceptible to E-I differences and it seems likely that more concentrated work will in the near future put the findings adumbrated on these pages on a more secure footing.

In the third place, there seems little doubt that the greatest part of the individual differences descriptively referred to E-I are constitutional in nature and due to heredity, acting upon and through environmental conditions. There is no suggestion of course that E-I, as measured and observed, is anything but *phenotypic*; we cannot by simple psychological tests reach the genotype. But by suitable experiments we can estimate the relative contribution of hereditary and environmental causes in a particular population, at a particular moment of history and results suggest that roughly two thirds to three quarters of the causes of individual differences are due to heredity, on the average. A detailed discussion of the evidence and of possible objections and criticisms, is given in *The Biological Basis of Personality*; there is no room in this book to substantiate these points fully.

In the fourth place, we now seem to have theories capable of bringing some degree of order into this field. These theories may with advantage be extended to include physiological notions of arousal and the ascending reticular activating system; the demonstration of hereditary causes almost compels us to seek for anatomical structures and physiological and neurological mediating concepts in order to bridge the gap between genes and conduct. Both direct (physiological) and indirect (experimental) methods of testing such theories exist and will no doubt be even more widely used in the future than in the past.

In the fifth place, personality theory in the form described above has linked up with experimental psychology in such a way as to suggest that future work in either field will have to pay more and more attention to progress in the other. Experimentalists have in the past been content to relegate individual differences to the limbo of the error term in their analyses of variance, until this term grew so large as to swallow up the greater part of the total variance! The demonstration that much of this error term could in fact be reduced to experimental control by introducing personality variables, such as E-I, should forever banish this habit of disregarding individual differences from the experimental scene; experimenters who wilfully disregard methods of control over relevant variables because of preconceived ideas are not acting as responsible scientists, but give vent rather to unscientific bias and prejudice.

The unattractive old thing with a caricature of a face I referred to in the Historical Introduction has received the proverbial kiss from the dashing young prince and has been turned into a ravishingly beautiful young maiden; a bright future seems to lie ahead. Just what this future will be like in detail is not given to scientists to foretell; theories come and go but the facts are likely to prove more durable. In the meantime, this book may serve to whet the appetite of young experimentalists to contribute to the future by well-conceived, well-controlled experiments, aimed to test established theories and to advance our knowledge along factual lines.

H.J.E.

NAME INDEX

628

SUBJECT INDEX

Age and the adult sleep-wakefulness pattern, 173–188

A.H.4 Intelligence Test, 132, 135

Alcoholics and conditioning 525–533

Anxiety and the spiral aftermovement, 255–267

Anxious children
and perceptual defence, 112–116
and psychogenic deafness, 112–116

Bernreuter Personality Inventory, 327–328

College Entrance Examination Board, 156

Conditioning and strength of nervous system, 499–511

Continuous Performance Test, 157–158

Cyclothymic personality and brain waves, 5

Depression factor and electrical vestibular stimulation, 82–88

Draw-a-person test, 309

Drive and involuntary rest pauses, 420–422

Dysthymics
and brain waves, 13–17
and conditioning, 470–484
and cortical inhibition, 209–230
and figural aftereffects, 209–230
and overactive behaviour under stress, 344–356
and paired associates learning, 573–579
and probability learning, 534–545
and sodium amytal, 35–44
speed and accuracy of, 409–417

Edwards Personnel Performance Schedule, 405, 406

Embedded Figures Test, 309

Emotionality
and brain waves, 6–12

and degrees of visual constancy, 195–199

Eysenck Personality Inventory, 61, 63, 65, 71, 73, 162, 163, 168, 280, 328, 334, 425, 576, 594, 604, 605, 610, 614

Extraversion-Introversion
and accuracy in judgements of vertical, 285–286
and the adult sleep-wakefulness pattern, 173–188
and aesthetic preferences, 316–318, 321–322
and alternation in choice behaviour, 425–428
and the arousel jag, 320–322
and auditory threshold, 71–80
and circadian rhythm of body temperature, 54–57
and conditionability, 24, 26–27, 30–31, 33, 470–484, 487–496, 513–522, 525–533
and conscious and preconscious influences on recall, 558–570
and cortical arousal levels, 3, 69–70
and cortical inhibition, 209–230
and degrees of visual constancy, 195–199, 200–207
and depersonalization under sensory deprivation and conditions, 109–110
and dogmatism, 548–556
and drive, 444–464
and effects of illumination on perceived intensity of acid tastes, 100–105
and effects of noise on critical flicker fusion performance, 165–171
and effects of noise in visual vigilance performance, 141–152
and effect of social isolation on performance, 46–52
and effect of time of day on performance, 46–52